Arctic Ocean

RUSSIA

FINLAND

Helsinki ■

■ Tallinn
EST.

Riga
■ LAT.

LITH.
Vilnius ■

■ Minsk

BELARUS

ND
aw ■

Moscow
■

OVAKIA
atislava
■ Budapest
NGARY

Kiev
■

UKRAINE

MOLDOVA
■ Chisinau

Dnieper R.

Don R.

KAZAKHSTAN

Volga R.

ROMANIA

Belgrade ■   ■ Bucharest

Black Sea

Caspian Sea

YUGO.

Sofia
Skopje ■
ane ■
■ F.Y.R.O.M.

BULGARIA

GEORGIA
Tbilisi ■

ALB.

ARM.
Yerevan ■   ■ Baku

AZER.

■ Ankara

GREECE

TURKEY

■ Athens

Crete

CYPRUS

Tigris R.

Euphrates

Tehran ■

rranean   Sea

LEB. SYRIA
Beirut ■ ■ Damascus

Baghdad
■

IRAN

ISR.
Jerusalem ■   ■ Amman

IRAQ

R.

JOR.

Cairo ■

Kuwait
■

YA

EGYPT

Nile

R.

SAUDI
ARABIA

KUWAIT

QATAR

THIRD EDITION

WESTERN CIVILIZATION

Volume C: Since 1789

THIRD EDITION

WESTERN CIVILIZATION

Volume C: Since 1789

JACKSON J. SPIELVOGEL

The Pennsylvania State University

WEST PUBLISHING COMPANY

MINNEAPOLIS/ST. PAUL

NEW YORK

LOS ANGELES

SAN FRANCISCO

Production Credits

COPYEDITING Patricia Lewis
DESIGN Diane Beasley
COMPOSITION Carlisle Communications
DUMMY ARTIST Techarts
ARTWORK Maryland Cartographics
INDEX Patricia Lewis
PERMISSIONS Lynn Reichel
COVER ILLUSTRATION Hippolyte Lecomte, *Battle of the rue de Rohan*, 1830. Musee de la Ville de Paris, Musee Carnavalet, Paris, France. Giraudon/Art Resource, NY

COPYRIGHT © 1991, 1994   By West Publishing Company
COPYRIGHT © 1997   By West Publishing Company
                          610 Opperman Drive
                          P.O. Box 64526
                          St. Paul, MN 55164-0526

Library of Congress Cataloging-in-Publication Data

Spielvogel, Jackson J., 1939–
    Western civilization / Jackson J. Spielvogel.—3rd ed.
       p.   cm.
    Includes bibliographical references and index.
    ISBN 0-314-09674-4 (comprehensive hbk.).—ISBN
0-314-20533-0
    (pbk. v. I : to 1715).—ISBN 0-314-20526-8 (pbk. v. II : since
1550).—ISBN 0-314-20523-3 (pbk. v. A : to 1550).—ISBN
0-314-20524-1 (pbk. v. B : 1300 to 1815).—ISBN
0-314-20525-X
    (pbk. v. C : since 1789).—ISBN 0-314-20527-6 (pbk. since
1300)
    1. Civilization, Western—History. I. Title.
CB245.S63   1997
909'.09812—dc20   96-30605
                                                          CIP

West's Commitment to the Environment

Photo Credits

FRONT MATTER ESSAY

xxiv (Left) © John and Anne Abbott, New York; (Right) *Archers of the Persian Guard,* Musee du Louvre, © Photo R. M. N.; **xxv** © Michael Holford, London; **xxvi** (Top left) Photo Vatican Museums; (Top right) Bibliotheque Nationale, Paris, Ms. Nouv. Acq. Fr. 1098; (Bottom right) *Statue of Charlemagne,* Musee du Louvre, © Photo R. M. N.; **xxvii** (Left) Bibliotheque Nationale, Paris; (Right) Giraudon/Art Resource, NY; **xxviii** (Top left) © Bibliotheque royale Albert ler (Ms IV 119, fol. 72 verso); (Bottom left) © Sylvain Grandadam/Photo Researchers, Inc.; (Top right) © Bibliotheque royale Albert ler, Bruxelles (Ms. 13076-77, f. 12v); (Bottom right) Scala/Art Resource, NY; **xxix** (Left) Cranach the Younger, *Martin Luther and the Wittenberg Reformers,* The Toledo Museum of Art, Toledo, Ohio: Gift of Edward Drummond Libbey; (Right) Francois Dubois D'Amiens, *The St. Bartholomew's Day Massacre,* Musee Cantonal des Beaux-Arts, Lausanne; **xxx** (Left) Hyacinthe Rigaud, *Louis XIV,* Musee du Louvre, © Photo R. M. N.; (Right) Giraudon/Art Resource, NY; **xxxi** Kunsthistorisches Museum, Vienna

CHAPTER 20

672 Anonymous, *Fall of the Bastille,* (Detail) Musee National des Chateau de Versailles, © Photo R.M.N.; **676** John Trumbull, *The Declaration of Independence, 4 July 1776,* Yale University Art Gallery, Trumbull Collection; **681** Giraudon/Art Resource, NY; **683** Anonymous, *Fall of the Bastille,* Musee National des Chateau de Versailles, © Photo R.M.N.; **685** Bibliotheque Nationale, Paris; **689** *Execution of Louis XVI, 21 January 1793,* Musee Carnavalet, Paris/Bridgeman Art Library; **691** Giraudon/Art Resource, NY; **695** Giraudon/Art Resource; NY; **696** Giraudon/Art Resource, NY; **697** Antoine Jean Gros, *Napoleon Crossing the Bridge at Arcola,* Musee du Louvre, © Photo R.M.N.; **700** Louis David, *Sacre de l'empereur* (detail), Musee du Louvre, © Photo R.M.N.

continued following index

About the Author

Jackson J. Spielvogel is associate professor of history at The Pennsylvania State University. He received his Ph.D. from The Ohio State University, where he specialized in Reformation history under Harold J. Grimm. His articles and reviews have appeared in such journals as Moreana, Journal of General Education, Catholic Historical Review, Archiv für Reformationsgeschichte, *and* American Historical Review. *He has also contributed chapters or articles to* The Social History of the Reformation, The Holy Roman Empire: A Dictionary Handbook, Simon Wiesenthal Center Annual of Holocaust Studies, *and* Utopian Studies. *His work has been supported by fellowships from the Fulbright Foundation and the Foundation for Reformation Research. At Penn State, he helped inaugurate the Western civilization courses as well as a popular course on Nazi Germany. His book* Hitler and Nazi Germany *was published in 1987 (third edition, 1996). He is the co-author (with William Duiker) of* World History, *published in January 1994. Professor Spielvogel has won three major university-wide teaching awards. During the year 1988–1989, he held the Penn State Teaching Fellowship, the university's most prestigious teaching award. In 1996, he won the Dean Arthur Ray Warnock Award for Outstanding Faculty Member.*

◆

To Diane,
whose love and support made it all possible

Contents

CHAPTER 20

A Revolution in Politics: The Era of the French Revolution and Napoleon   672

CHAPTER 21

The Industrial Revolution and Its Impact on European Society   706

CHAPTER 22

Reaction, Revolution, and Romanticism, 1815–1850   736

CHAPTER 23

An Age of Nationalism and Realism, 1850–1871   776

CHAPTER 24

Mass Society in an "Age of Progress," 1871–1894   812

CHAPTER 25

An Age of Modernity and Anxiety, 1894–1914   846

CHAPTER 26

The Beginning of the Twentieth-Century Crisis: War and Revolution   886

CHAPTER 27

The Futile Search for a New Stability: Europe Between the Wars, 1919–1939   922

CHAPTER 28

The Deepening of the European Crisis: World War II   960

CHAPTER *29*

✦✦✦✦✦✦✦✦✦✦✦

Cold War and a New Europe, 1945–1970   994

CHAPTER *30*

✦✦✦✦✦✦✦✦✦✦✦

The Contemporary Western World (since 1970)   1026

Documents

We are grateful to the authors and publishers acknowledged here for their permission to reprint copyrighted material. We have made every reasonable effort to identify copyright owners of materials in the boxed documents. If any information is found to be incomplete, we will gladly make whatever additional acknowledgements might be necessary.

Document credits continued following index

Maps

Chronologies

Preface

We are often reminded how important it is to understand today's world if we are to deal with our growing number of challenges. And yet that understanding will be incomplete if we in the Western world do not comprehend the meaning of Western civilization and the role Western civilization has played in the world. For all of our modern progress, we still greatly reflect our religious traditions, our political systems and theories, our economic and social structures, and our cultural heritage. I have written this history of Western civilization to assist a new generation of students in learning more about the past that has helped create them and the world in which they live.

As a teacher of Western civilization courses at a major university, I have become aware of the tendency of many textbooks to simplify the content of Western civilization courses by emphasizing an intellectual perspective or political perspective or, most recently, a social perspective, often at the expense of sufficient details in a chronological framework. This approach is confusing to students whose high school social studies programs have often neglected a systematic study of Western civilization. I have attempted to write a well-balanced work in which the political, economic, social, religious, intellectual, cultural, and military aspects of Western civilization have been integrated into a chronologically ordered synthesis. I have been especially aware of the need to integrate the latest research on social history and women's history into each chapter of the book rather than isolating it either in lengthy topical chapters, which confuse the student by interrupting the chronological narrative, or in separate sections that appear at periodic intervals between chapters. If the results of the new social and women's history are to be taken seriously, they must be fully integrated into the basic narrative itself.

Another purpose in writing this history of Western civilization has been to put the story back in history. That story is an exciting one; yet many textbooks, often the product of several authors with different writing styles, fail to capture the imagination of their readers. Narrative history effectively transmits the knowledge of the past and is the form that best aids remembrance. At the same time, I have not overlooked the need for the kind of historical analysis that makes students aware that historians often disagree in their interpretations of the past.

To enliven the past and let readers see for themselves the materials that historians use to create their pictures of the past, I have included in each chapter primary sources (boxed documents) they are keyed to the discussion in the text. The documents include examples of the religious, artistic, intellectual, social, economic, and political aspects of Western life. Such varied sources as a Roman banquet menu, a student fight song in twentieth-century Britain, letters exchanged between a husband on the battle front and his wife in World War I, the Declaration of the Rights of Woman and the Citizen in the French Revolution, and a debate in the Reformation era all reveal in a vivid fashion what Western civilization meant to the individual men and women who shaped it by their activities.

Each chapter has a lengthy introduction and conclusion to help maintain the continuity of the narrative and to provide a synthesis of important themes. For the third edition, I have added anecdotes to the introductions in order to convey more dramatically the major theme or themes of each chapter. Detailed chronologies reinforce the events discussed in the text while time-lines at the beginning of each chapter, new to the third edition, enable students to see at a glance the major developments of an era. An annotated bibliography at the end of each chapter reviews the most recent literature on each period and also gives references to some of the older, "classic" works in each field. Extensive maps and illustrations serve to deepen the reader's understanding of the text. To facilitate understanding of cultural movements, illustrations of artistic works discussed in the text are placed next to the discussions.

As preparation for the revision of *Western Civilization*, I reexamined the entire book and analyzed the comments and reviews of many colleagues who have found the book to be a useful instrument for introducing their students to the history of Western civilization. In making revisions for the third edition, I sought to build upon the strengths of the first and second editions and, above all, to maintain the balance, synthesis, and narrative qualities that characterized those editions. To keep up with the ever-growing body of historical scholarship, new or revised material has been added throughout the book on many topics, including, for example, early human beings in the Neolithic and Paleolithic eras; civilization in Mesopotamia and Egypt; early Greece; Sparta; women in the Hellenistic kingdoms; the Roman Republic; women and sexual attitudes in early Christianity; the world of Islam; medieval guilds; the crusades; the artistic Renaissance; the English Reformation; the age of expansion and discovery; women and witchcraft; art in the seventeenth century; the "Women's Question" in the Enlightenment; neoclassicism and David; women in the French Revolution and Napoleonic eras; the last years of Napoleon; public health in the nineteenth century; John Stuart Mill and liberalism; Imperial Russia; the emergence of Canada; the Dada movement; the Holocaust; the Korean War; the Cuban Missile Crisis; and Western politics, society, and culture since 1970. Throughout the revising process, I also worked to craft a book that I hope students will continue to find very readable. Headings and subheadings in every chapter were revised to give students a more vivid introduction to the content of the chapters.

To provide a more logical arrangement of the material, I also made organizational changes in Chapters 5, 6, 7, 8, 12, 13, 15, 16, 17, 18, 20, 22, 23, 27, and 30. Chapters 24 and 25 were reduced in length and completely reorganized on a chronological basis and are now entitled "Mass Society in an 'Age of Progress,' 1871–1894" and "An Age of Modernity and Anxiety, 1894–1914." Moreover, all "Suggestions for Further Reading" at the end of each chapter were updated, and new illustrations were added to every chapter.

The enthusiastic response to the primary sources (boxed documents) led me to evaluate the content of each document carefully and add a number of new documents throughout the text, including such subjects as "A New Autonomy for Women in Hellenistic Society," "The Achievements of Charlemagne," "Women in Medieval Thought," "The Letters of Isabella d'Este," "Hobbes and Locke: Two Views of Political Authority," "British Victory at Quebec," "A Victim of the Reign of Terror," "Bismarck and the Welfare of the Workers," and "Women in the Factories." For the third edition,

the maps have been revised where needed and, as in the second edition, are carefully keyed to all text references. New maps have also been added, including "Trading Routes and Products in the Roman Empire," "Pilgrimage Routes in the Middle Ages," and "The Death Camps of the Holocaust."

Because courses in Western civilization at American and Canadian colleges and universities follow different chronological divisions, a one-volume edition, two two-volume editions, and a three-volume edition of this text are being made available to fit the needs of instructors. Teaching and learning ancillaries include the following:

For Instructors: Instructor's Manual with Test Bank; map acetates and commentary; computerized test items; Western Civilization video library; videodiscs with maps, still images, video clips, and music; slide set with commentary, and color slides of all maps.

For Students: Study Guide, Document Exercise Workbook, Workbook, Primary Source Reader, Student Study Tips Booklet (shrink-wrapped free with the text at the request of instructors), and Computerized Study Guide.

For Both: CD-ROM and Web site.

Acknowledgments

I began to teach at age five in my family's grape arbor. By the age of ten, I wanted to know and understand everything in the world so I set out to memorize our entire set of encyclopedia volumes. At seventeen, as editor of the high school yearbook, I chose "Patterns" as its theme. With that as my early history, followed by twenty rich years of teaching, writing, and family nurturing, it seemed quite natural to accept the challenge of writing a history of Western civilization as I approached that period in life often described as the age of wisdom. Although I see this writing adventure as part of the natural unfolding of my life, I gratefully acknowledge that without the generosity of many others, it would not have been possible.

David Redles gave generously of his time and ideas, especially for Chapters 29 and 30. Chris Colin provided research on the history of music, while Laurie Batitto, Alex Spencer, Stephen Maloney, Shaun Mason, Peter Angelos, and Fred Schooley offered valuable editorial assistance. I deeply appreciate the valuable technical assistance provided by Dayton Coles. I am also thankful to the thousands of students whose questions and responses have caused me to see many aspects of Western civilization in new ways.

My ability to undertake a project of this magnitude was in part due to the outstanding European history teachers that I had as both an undergraduate and a graduate student. These included Kent Forster (modern Europe) and Robert W. Green (early modern Europe) at The Pennsylvania State University; and Franklin Pegues (medieval), Andreas Dorpalen (modern Germany), William MacDonald (ancient), and Harold J. Grimm (Renaissance and Reformation) at The Ohio State University. These teachers provided me with profound insights into Western civilization and also taught me by their examples that learning only becomes true understanding when it is accompanied by compassion, humility, and open-mindedness.

Thanks to West Publishing Company's comprehensive review process, many historians were asked to evaluate my manuscript and review the first and second editions. I am grateful to the following for the innumerable suggestions that have greatly improved my work:

Gerald Anderson
North Dakota State University

Letizia Argenteri
University of San Diego

Roy A. Austensen
Illinois State University

James A. Baer
Northern Virginia Community College—Alexandria

James T. Baker
Western Kentucky University

Patrick Bass
Morningside College

John F. Battick
University of Maine

Frederic J. Baumgartner
Virginia Polytechnic Institute

Phillip N. Bebb
Ohio University

Anthony Bedford
Modesto Junior College

F. E. Beemon
Middle Tennessee State University

Leonard R. Berlanstein
University of Virginia

Douglas T. Bisson
Belmont University

Stephen H. Blumm
Montgomery County Community College

Hugh S. Bonar
California State University

Werner Braatz
University of Wisconsin—Oshkosh

Alfred S. Bradford
University of Missouri

Maryann E. Brink
College of William & Mary

Blaine T. Browne
Broward Community College

J. Holden Camp, Jr.,
Hillyer College, University of Hartford

Elizabeth Carney
Clemson University

Eric H. Cline
Xavier University

Robert Cole
Utah State University

William J. Connell
Rutgers University

Nancy Conradt
College of DuPage

Marc Cooper
Southwest Missouri State

Richard A. Cosgrove
University of Arizona

David A. Crain
South Dakota State University

Michael F. Doyle
Ocean County College

James W. Ermatinger
University of Nebraska—Kearney

Porter Ewing
Los Angeles City College

Carla Falkner
Northeast Mississippi Community College

Steven Fanning
University of Illinois—Chicago

Ellsworth Faris
California State University—Chico

Gary B. Ferngren
Oregon State University

Mary Helen Finnerty
Westchester Community College

A. Z. Freeman
Robinson College

Frank J. Frost
University of California—Santa Barbara

Frank Garosi
California State University—Sacramento

Richard M. Golden
University of North Texas

Manuel G. Gonzales
Diablo Valley College

Amy G. Gordon
Denison University

Richard J. Grace
Providence College

Hanns Gross
Loyola University

John F. Guilmartin
Ohio State University

Jeffrey S. Hamilton
Gustavus Adolphus College

J. Drew Harrington
Western Kentucky University

James Harrison
Siena College

A. J. Heisserer
University of Oklahoma

Shirley Hickson
North Greenville College

Martha L. Hildreth
University of Nevada

Boyd H. Hill, Jr.
University of Colorado—Boulder

Michael Hofstetter
Bethany College

Donald C. Holsinger
Seattle Pacific University

Frank L. Holt
University of Houston

Paul Hughes
Sussex County Community College

Richard A. Jackson
University of Houston

Fred Jewell
Harding University

Jenny M. Jochens
Towson State University

William M. Johnston
University of Massachusetts

Jeffrey A. Kaufmann
Muscatine Community College

David O. Kieft
University of Minnesota

Patricia Killen
Pacific Lutheran University

William E. Kinsella, Jr.
Northern Virginia Community College—Annandale

James M. Kittelson
Ohio State University

Cynthia Kosso
Northern Arizona University

Harold Marcuse
University of California—Santa Barbara

Mavis Mate
University of Oregon

T. Ronald Melton
Brewton Parker College

Jack Allen Meyer
University of South Carolina

Eugene W. Miller, Jr.
The Pennsylvania State University—Hazleton

Thomas M. Mulhern
University of North Dakota

Pierce Mullen
Montana State University

Frederick I. Murphy
Western Kentucky University

William M. Murray
University of South Florida

Otto M. Nelson
Texas Tech University

Sam Nelson
Willmar Community College

John A. Nichols
Slippery Rock University

Lisa Nofzinger
Albuquerque Technical Vocational Institute

Donald Ostrowski
Harvard University

James O. Overfield
University of Vermont

Matthew L. Panczyk
Bergen Community College

Kathleen Parrow
Black Hills State University

Carla Rahn Phillips
University of Minnesota

Keith Pickus
Wichita State University

Linda J. Piper
University of Georgia

Janet Polasky
University of New Hampshire

Charles A. Povlovich
California State University—Fullerton

Nancy Rachels
Hillsborough Community College

Jerome V. Reel, Jr.
Clemson University

Joseph Robertson
Gadsden State Community College

Jonathan Roth
San Jose State University

Constance M. Rousseau
Providence College

Julius R. Ruff
Marquette University

Richard Saller
University of Chicago

Magdalena Sanchez
Texas Christian University

Jack Schanfield
Suffolk County Community College

Roger Schlesinger
Washington State University

Joanne Schneider
Rhode Island College

Thomas C. Schunk
University of Wisconsin—Oshkosh

Kyle C. Sessions
Illinois State University

Linda Simmons
Northern Virginia Community College—Manassas

Donald V. Sippel
Rhode Island College

John W. Steinberg
Georgia Southern University

Paul W. Strait
Florida State University

James E. Straukamp
California State University—Sacramento

Brian E. Strayer
Andrews University

Fred Suppe
Ball State University

Roger Tate
Somerset Community College

Tom Taylor
Seattle University

Jack W. Thacker
Western Kentucky University

Thomas Turley
Santa Clara University

John G. Tuthill
University of Guam

Maarten Ultee
University of Alabama

Donna L. Van Raaphorst
Cuyahoga Community College

Allen M. Ward
University of Connecticut

Richard D. Weigel
Western Kentucky University

Michael Weiss
Linn-Benton Community College

Arthur H. Williamson
*California State University—
Sacramento*

Judith T. Wozniak
Cleveland State University

Walter J. Wussow
University of Wisconsin—Eau Claire

Edwin M. Yamauchi
Miami University

The editors at West Publishing Company have been both helpful and congenial at all times. Their flexible policies allowed the creative freedom that a writer cherishes. I especially wish to thank Clark Baxter, whose faith in my ability to do this project was inspiring. His clever wit, good insight, and friendship have added much depth to our working relationship. Linda Poirier and Patricia MacDonald were always helpful with their insightful analyses and organization of many practical details. Members of the the West production team—Kara ZumBahlen, Amy Gabriel, and Peter Krall—were as cooperative as they were competent. John Och's artful cover designs greatly enhanced the appearance of the book. Pat Lewis, an outstanding copy editor, taught me

much about the fine points of the English language. Lynn Reichel provided valuable assistance in obtaining permissions for the boxed documents. I appreciate the professional and personal relationships that I have shared with the West "family."

Above all, I thank my family for their support. The gifts of love, laughter, and patience from my daughters, Jennifer and Kathryn, my sons Eric and Christian, and my daughters-in-law, Liz and Michele were invaluable. My wife and best friend, Diane, provided me with editorial assistance, wise counsel, and the loving support that made it possible for me to complete a project of this magnitude. I could not have written the book without her.

Introduction to Students of Western Civilization

Civilization, as historians define it, first emerged between 5,000 and 6,000 years ago when people began to live in organized communities with distinct political, military, economic, and social structures. Religious, intellectual, and artistic activities also assumed important roles in these early societies. The focus of this book is on Western civilization, a civilization that for most of its history has been identified with the continent of Europe. Its origins, however, go back to the Mediterranean basin, including lands in North Africa, and the Near East as well as Europe itself. Moreover, the spread of Europeans abroad led to the development of offshoots of Western civilization in other parts of the world.

Because civilized life includes all the deeds and experiences of people organized in communities, the history of a civilization must encompass a series of studies. An examination of Western civilization requires us to study the political, economic, social, military, cultural, intellectual, and religious aspects that make up the life of that civilization and show how they are interrelated. In so doing, we need also at times to focus on some of the unique features of Western civilization. Certainly, science played a crucial role in the development of modern Western civilization. Although such societies as those of the Greeks, the Romans, and medieval Europeans were based largely on a belief in the existence of a spiritual order, Western civilization experienced a dramatic departure to a natural or material view of the universe in the seventeenth-century Scientific Revolution. Science and technology have been important in the growth of a modern and largely secular Western civilization, although antecedents to scientific development also existed in Greek, Islamic, and medieval thought and practice.

Many historians have also viewed the concept of political liberty, the fundamental value of every individual, and the creation of a rational outlook, based on a system of logical, analytical thought, as unique aspects of Western civilization. Of course, Western civilization has also witnessed the frightening negation of liberty, individualism, and reason. Racism, violence, world wars,

totalitarianism—these, too, must form part of the story. Finally, regardless of our concentration on Western civilization and its characteristics, we need to take into account that other civilizations have influenced Western civilization and it, in turn, has affected the development of other civilizations.

In our examination of Western civilization, we need also to be aware of the dating of time. In recording the past, historians try to determine the exact time when events occurred. World War II in Europe, for example, began on September 1, 1939, when Hitler sent German troops into Poland, and ended on May 7, 1945, when Germany surrendered. By using dates, historians can place events in order and try to determine the development of patterns over periods of time.

If someone asked you when you were born, you would reply with a number, such as 1978. In the United States, we would all accept that number without question because it is part of the dating system followed in the Western world (Europe and the Western Hemisphere). In this system, events are dated by counting backward or forward from the birth of Christ (assumed to be the year 1). An event that took place 400 years before the birth of Christ would be dated 400 B.C. (before Christ). Dates after the birth of Christ are labeled A.D. These letters stand for the Latin words *anno Domini*, which mean "in the year of the lord." Thus, an event that took place 250 years after the birth of Christ is written A.D. 250, or in the year of the lord 250. It can also be written as 250, just as you would not give your birth year as A.D. 1978, but simply 1978.

Historians also make use of other terms to refer to time. A decade is 10 years; a century is 100 years; and a millennium is 1,000 years. The phrase fourth century B.C. refers to the fourth period of 100 years counting backward from 1, the assumed date of the birth of Christ. Since the first century B.C. would be the years 100 B.C. to 1 B.C., the fourth century B.C. would be the years 400 B.C. to 301 B.C. We could say, then, that an event in 350 B.C. took place in the fourth century B.C.

The phrase fourth century A.D. refers to the fourth period of 100 years after the birth of Christ. Since the first period of 100 years would be the years 1 to 100, the fourth period or fourth century would be the years 301 to 400. We could say, then, for example, that an event in 350 took place in the fourth century. Likewise, the first millennium B.C. refers to the years 1000 B.C. to 1 B.C.; the second millennium A.D. refers to the years 1001 to 2000.

Some historians now prefer to use the abbreviations B.C.E. ("before the common era") and C.E. ("common era") instead of B.C. and A.D. This is especially true of world historians who prefer to use symbols that are not so Western or Christian oriented. The dates, of course, remain the same. Thus, 1950 B.C.E. and 1950 B.C. would be the same year. In keeping with current usage by many historians of Western civilization, this book will use the terms B.C. and A.D.

The dating of events can also vary from people to people. Most people in the Western world use the Western calendar, also known as the Gregorian calendar after Pope Gregory XIII who refined it in 1582. The Hebrew calendar, on the other hand, uses a different system in which the year 1 is the equivalent of the Western year 3760 B.C., considered by Jews to be the date of the creation of the world. Thus, the Western year 2000 will be the year 5760 on the Jewish calendar. The Islamic calendar begins year 1 on the day Muhammad fled Mecca, which is the year 622 on the Western calendar.

Western Civilization to 1789

*T*he beginnings of Western civilization can be traced back to the ancient Near East, where people in Mesopotamia and Egypt developed organized societies and created the ideas and institutions that we associate with civilization. The later Greeks and Romans, who played such a crucial role in the development of Western civilization, were themselves nourished and influenced by these older societies in the Near East. Around 3000 B.C., people in Mesopotamia and Egypt began to develop cities and wrestle with the problems of organized states. They developed writing to keep records and created

literature. They constructed monumental architecture to please their gods, symbolize their power, and preserve their culture for all time. They developed new political, military, social, and religious structures to deal with the basic problems of human existence and organization. These first literate civilizations left detailed records that allow us to view how they grappled with three of the fundamental problems that humans have pondered: the nature of human relationships, the nature of the universe, and the role of divine forces in that cosmos. Although later peoples in Western civilization would provide different answers from those of the Mesopotamians and Egyptians, it was they who first posed the questions, gave answers, and wrote them down. Human memory begins with these two civilizations.

By 1500 B.C., much of the creative impulse of the Mesopotamian and Egyptian civilizations was beginning to wane. The entry of new peoples known as Indo-Europeans who moved into Asia Minor and Anatolia (modern Turkey) led to the creation of a Hittite kingdom that entered into conflict with the Egyptians. The invasion of the Sea Peoples around 1200 B.C., however, destroyed the Hittites, severely weakened the Egyptians, and created a power vacuum that allowed a patchwork

of petty kingdoms and city-states to emerge, especially in the area of Syria and Palestine. These small states did not last, however. Ever since the first city-states had arisen in the Near East around 3000 B.C., there had been an ongoing movement toward the creation of larger territorial states with more sophisticated systems of control. This process reached a high point in the first millennium B.C. with the appearance of empires that embraced the entire Near East. Between 1000 and 500 B.C., the Assyrians, Chaldeans, and Persians all created empires that encompassed either large areas or all of the ancient Near East. The Assyrian Empire was the first to unite almost all of the ancient Near East. Even larger, however, was the empire of the Great Kings of Persia.

Although it owed much to the administrative organization created by the Assyrians, the Persian Empire had its own peculiar strengths. Persian rule was tolerant as well as efficient. Conquered peoples were allowed to keep their own religions, customs, and methods of doing business. The many years of peace that the

Persian Empire brought to the Near East facilitated trade and the general well-being of its peoples. It is no wonder that many Near Eastern peoples expressed their gratitude for being subjects of the Great Kings of Persia.

The Hebrews were one of these peoples. They created no empire and were dominated by the Assyrians, Chaldeans, and Persians in turn. Nevertheless, they left a spiritual legacy that influenced much of the later development of Western civilization. The evolution of Hebrew monotheism (belief in a single god) created in Judaism one of the world's greatest religions; it influenced the development of both Christianity and Islam. When we speak of the Judaeo-Christian heritage of Western civilization, we refer not only to the concept of monotheism, but also to ideas of law, morality, and social justice that have become important parts of Western culture.

On the western fringes of the Persian Empire, another relatively small group of people, the Greeks, were creating cultural and political ideals that would also have an important impact on Western civilization. The first Greek civilization, known as Mycenaean civilization, took shape around 1600 B.C. and fell to new Greek-speaking invaders around 1100 B.C. The ensuing so-called Dark Age (c. 1100–c. 750 B.C.) did witness the creation of a system of writing and the work of Homer, whose ideals formed the basis of Greek education for hundreds of years. By the eighth century B.C., the *polis* or city-state had become the chief focus of Greek life. Loyalty to the *polis* created a close-knit community, but also divided Greece into a host of independent states. Two of them, Sparta and Athens, became the most important. They were very different, however. Sparta created a closed, highly disciplined society while Athens moved toward an open, democratic civilization.

The classical age in Greece (c. 500–338 B.C.) began with a mighty confrontation between the Greeks and the Persian Empire. After their victory over the Persians, the Greeks began to divide into two large alliances, one headed by Sparta and the other by Athens. Athens created a naval empire and flourished during the age of Pericles, but fear of Athens led to the Great Peloponnesian War between Sparta and Athens and their allies. For all of their brilliant accomplishments, the Greeks were unable to rise above the divisions and rivalries that caused them to fight each other and undermine their own civilization.

The accomplishments of the Greeks formed the fountainhead of Western culture. Socrates, Plato, and Aristotle established the foundations of Western philosophy. Herodotus and Thucydides created the discipline of history. Our literary forms are largely derived from Greek poetry and drama. Greek notions of harmony, proportion, and beauty have remained the touchstones for all subsequent Western art. A rational method of inquiry, so important to modern science, was conceived in ancient Greece. Many of our political terms are Greek in origin, and so too are our concepts of the rights and duties of citizenship, especially as they were conceived in Athens, the first great democracy the world had seen. Especially during their classical period, the Greeks raised and debated the fundamental questions about the purpose of human existence, the structure of human society, and the nature of the universe that have concerned Western thinkers ever since.

While the Greek city-states were continuing to fight each other, to their north a new and powerful kingdom—Macedonia—emerged in its own right. Under King Philip II, the Macedonians defeated a Greek allied army in 338 B.C. and then consolidated their control over the Greek peninsula. Although the independent Greek city-states lost their freedom when they were conquered by the Macedonians, Greek culture did not die. Under the leadership of Alexander the Great, son of Philip II, both Macedonians and Greeks invaded and conquered the Persian Empire. In the conquered lands, Greeks and non-Greeks established a series of kingdoms (known as the Hellenistic kingdoms) and inaugurated the Hellenistic era.

The Hellenistic period was, in its own way, a vibrant one. New cities arose and flourished. New philosophical ideas captured the minds of many. Significant achievements occurred in art, literature, and science. Greek culture spread throughout the Near East and made an impact wherever it was carried. In some areas of the Hellenistic world, queens played an active role in political life, and many upper-class women found new avenues for expressing themselves.

But serious problems remained. Hellenistic kings continued to engage in inconclusive wars. The gulf between rich and poor was indeed great. Much of the formal culture was the special preserve of the Greek conquerors whose attitude of superiority kept them largely separated from the native masses of the Hellenistic kingdoms. Although the Hellenistic world achieved a degree of political stability, by the late third century B.C., signs of decline were beginning to multiply. Some of the more farsighted perhaps realized the danger presented to the Hellenistic world by the growing power of Rome.

Sometime in the eighth century B.C., a group of Latin-speaking people built a small community called Rome on the Tiber River in Italy. Between 509 and 264 B.C., this city expanded and united almost all of Italy under its control. Even more dramatically, between 264 and 133 B.C., Rome expanded to the west and east and became master of the Mediterranean Sea.

After 133 B.C., however, Rome's republican institutions proved inadequate for the task of ruling an empire. In the breakdown that ensued, ambitious individuals saw opportunities for power unparalleled in Roman history and succumbed to the temptations. After a series of bloody civil wars, peace was finally achieved when Octavian defeated Antony and Cleopatra. Octavian's

real task was at hand: to create a new system of government that seemed to preserve the Republic while establishing the basis for a new system that would rule the empire in an orderly fashion. Octavian, who came to be known by the title of Augustus, proved equal to the task.

After a century of internal upheaval, Augustus established a new order that began the Roman Empire, which experienced a lengthy period of peace and prosperity between 14 and 180. During this era, trade flourished and the provinces were governed efficiently. In the course of the third century, however, the Roman Empire came near to collapse due to invasions, civil wars, and economic decline. Although the emperors Diocletian and Constantine brought new life to the so-called Late Empire at the beginning of the fourth century, their efforts only shored up the empire temporarily. In the course of the fifth century, the empire divided into western and eastern parts, and in 476, the Roman Empire in the west came to an end with the ouster of Emperor Romulus Augustulus.

The Roman Empire was the largest empire in antiquity. Using their practical skills, the Romans made achievements in language, law, engineering, and government that were bequeathed to the future. The Romance languages of today (French, Italian, Spanish, Portuguese, and Romanian) are based on Latin. Western practices of impartial justice and trial by jury owe much to Roman law. As great builders, the Romans left monuments to their skills throughout Europe, some of which, such as aqueducts and roads, are still in use today. Aspects of Roman administrative practices survived in the Western world for centuries. The Romans also preserved the intellectual heritage of the ancient world.

During its last two hundred years, a slow transformation of the Roman world took place with the spread of Christianity. The rise of Christianity marked an important break with the dominant values of the Roman world. Christianity began as a small Jewish sect, but under the guidance of Paul of Tarsus it became a world religion that appealed to both Jews and non-Jews. Despite persecution by Roman authorities, Christianity grew and became widely accepted by the fourth century. At the end of that century, it was made the official state religion of the Roman Empire.

The period that saw the disintegration of the western part of the Roman Empire also witnessed the emergence of a new European civilization in the Early Middle Ages. The early medieval civilization that arose out of the collapse of the Western Roman Empire was formed by the coalescence of three major elements: the Germanic peoples who moved into the western part of the empire and established new kingdoms;

the continuing attraction of the Greco-Roman cultural legacy; and the Christian church. Politically, a new series of Germanic kingdoms emerged in western Europe. Each fused Roman and Germanic elements to create a new society. The Christian church (or Roman Catholic church as it came to be called in the west) played a crucial role in the growth of the new European civilization. The church developed an organized government under the leadership of the pope. It also assimilated the classical tradition and through its clergy brought Christianized civilization to the Germanic tribes. Especially important were the monks and nuns who led the way in converting the Germanic peoples in Europe to Christianity.

At the end of the eighth century, a new kingdom— the Carolingian Empire—came to control much of western and central Europe, especially during the reign of Charlemagne. The pope's coronation of Charlemagne, descendant of a Germanic tribe that had converted to Christianity, as Roman emperor in 800 symbolized the fusion of the three chief components of the new European civilization: the German tribes, the classical tradition, and Christianity. In the long run, the creation of a western empire fostered the idea of a distinct European identity and marked the shift of power from the south to the north. Italy and the Mediterranean had been the center of the Roman Empire. The lands north of the Alps now became the political center of Europe, and increasingly, Europe emerged as the focus and center of Western civilization.

Building upon a fusion of Germanic, classical, and Christian elements, the medieval European world first became visible in the Carolingian Empire of Charlemagne. His empire was well governed, but was ultimately held together by personal loyalty to a strong king. The economy of the eighth and ninth centuries was based almost entirely on farming, however, and this

proved inadequate to maintain a large monarchical system. As a result, a new political and military order—known as feudalism—subsequently evolved to become an integral part of the political world of the Middle Ages. The feudal system was characterized by a decentralization of political power, in which lords exercised legal, administrative, and military power. The practice of feudalism transferred public power into many private hands and seemed to provide the security sorely lacking in a time of weak central government.

European civilization began on a shaky and uncertain foundation, however. In the ninth century, Vikings, Magyars, and Muslims posed threats that could easily have stifled the new society, but the new European civilization managed to meet these challenges. The Vikings and Magyars were assimilated, and recovery slowly began to set in. By 1000, European civilization was ready to embark upon a period of dazzling vitality and expansion.

The new European civilization that had emerged in the ninth and tenth centuries began to come into its own in the eleventh and twelfth centuries as Europeans established new patterns that reached their high point in the thirteenth century. The High Middle Ages (1000–1300) was a period of recovery and growth for Western civilization, characterized by a greater sense of security and a burst of energy and enthusiasm. Climatic improvements that produced better growing conditions, an expansion of cultivated land, and technological changes combined to enable Europe's food supply to increase significantly after 1000. This increase in agricultural production helped sustain a dramatic rise in population that was physically apparent in the expansion of towns and cities.

The development of trade and the rise of cities added a dynamic new element to the civilization of the High Middle Ages. Trading activities flourished first in northern Italy and Flanders and then spread outward from these centers. In the late tenth and eleventh centuries, this renewal of commercial life led to a revival of cities. Old Roman sites came back to life while new towns arose at major crossroads or natural harbors favorable to trading activities. By the twelfth and thirteenth centuries, both the urban centers and the urban population of Europe were experiencing a dramatic expansion. The revival of trade, the expansion of towns and cities, and the

development of a money economy did not mean the end of a predominantly rural European society, but they did open the door to new ways to make a living and new opportunities for people to expand and enrich their lives. Eventually, they created the foundations for the development of a predominantly urban industrial society. Commerce, cities, and a money economy also helped to undermine feudal institutions while strengthening monarchical authority.

During the High Middle Ages, European society was dominated by a landed aristocracy whose primary function was to fight. These nobles built innumerable castles that gave a distinctive look to the countryside. Although lords and vassals seemed forever mired in endless petty conflicts, over time medieval kings began to exert a centralizing authority and inaugurated the process of developing new kinds of monarchical states. By the thirteenth century, European monarchs were solidifying their governmental institutions in pursuit of greater power. The nobles, whose warlike attitudes were rationalized by labeling them the defenders of Christian society, continued to dominate the medieval world politically, economically, and socially. But quietly and surely, within this world of castles and private power, kings gradually began to extend their public powers and developed the machinery of government that would enable them to become the centers of political authority in Europe. Although they could not know it

then, the actions of these medieval monarchs laid the foundation for the European kingdoms that in one form or another have dominated the European political scene ever since.

During the High Middle Ages, the power of both nobles and kings was often overshadowed by the authority of the Catholic church, perhaps the dominant institution of the High Middle Ages. In the Early Middle Ages, the Catholic church had shared in the challenge of new growth by reforming itself and striking out on a path toward greater papal power, both within the church and over European society. The High Middle Ages witnessed a spiritual renewal that led to numerous and even divergent paths: revived papal leadership, the development of centralized administrative machinery that buttressed papal authority, and new dimensions to the religious life of the clergy and laity. A wave of religious enthusiasm in the twelfth and thirteenth cen-

turies led to the formation of new religious orders that worked to provide for the needs of the people, especially their concern for achieving salvation.

The economic, political, and religious growth of the High Middle Ages also gave European society a new confidence that enabled it to look beyond its borders to the lands and empires of the east. Only a confident Europe could have undertaken the crusades, the military effort to recover the Holy Land of the Near East from the Muslims. The crusades gave the revived papacy of the High Middle Ages yet another opportunity to demonstrate its influence over European society.

Western assurance and energy, so crucial to the crusades, were also evident in a burst of intellectual and artistic activity. New educational institutions known as universities came into being in the twelfth century. New literature, written in the vernacular language, appealed to the growing number of people in cities or at courts

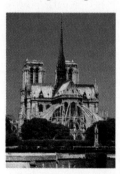

who could read. The study of theology, "queen of the sciences," reached a high point in the work of Thomas Aquinas. At the same time, a religious building spree—especially evident in the great Romanesque and Gothic cathedrals of the age—left the landscape bedecked with churches that were the visible symbols of Christian Europe's vitality.

Growth and optimism seemed to characterize the High Middle Ages, but underneath the calm exterior lay seeds of discontent and change. Dissent from church teaching and practices grew in the thirteenth century, leading to a climate of fear and intolerance as the church responded with inquisitorial instruments to enforce conformity to its teachings. Minorities of all kinds suffered intolerance and, worse still, persecution at the hands of people who worked to maintain the image of an ideal Christian society. The breakdown of the old agricultural system and the creation of new relationships between lords and peasants led to local peasant uprisings in the late thirteenth century. The crusades ended ignominiously with the fall of the last crusading foothold in the east in 1291. By that time, more and more signs of ominous troubles were appearing. The fourteenth century would prove to be a time of crisis for European civilization.

In the High Middle Ages, European civilization had developed many of its fundamental features. Monarchical states, capitalist trade and industry, banks, cities, and vernacular literature were all products of that fertile period. During the same time, the Catholic church under the direction of the papacy reached its apogee. Fourteenth-century European society, however, was challenged by an overwhelming number of crises that led to the disintegration of medieval civiliza-

tion. At mid-century, one of the most destructive natural disasters in history erupted—the Black Death, a devastating plague that wiped out at least one-third of the European population. Economic crises and social upheavals, including a decline in trade and industry, bank failures, and peasant revolts pitting lower classes against the upper classes, followed in the wake of the Black Death. The Hundred Years' War, a long, drawn-out conflict between the English and French, undermined political stability. The Catholic church, too, experienced a crisis with the absence of the popes from Rome and even the spectacle of two popes condemning each other as the anti-Christ. Not surprisingly, much of the art of the period depicted the Four Horsemen of the Apocalypse described in the New Testament book of Revelation: Death, Famine, Pestilence, and War. No doubt, to some people the last days of the world appeared to be at hand.

The new European society proved remarkably resilient, however. Periods of disintegration are often fertile grounds for change and new developments. Out of the dissolution of medieval civilization came a rebirth of culture that many historians have labeled the Renaissance. It was a period of transition that witnessed a continuation of the economic, political, and social trends that had begun in the High Middle Ages. It was also a movement in which intellectuals and artists proclaimed a new vision of humankind and raised fundamental questions about the value and importance of the individual. The humanists or intellectuals of the age called their period (from the mid-fourteenth to the mid-sixteenth century) an age of rebirth, believing that they had restored arts and letters to new glory after they had been "neglected" or "dead" for centuries.

The humanists' view of their age as a rebirth of the classical civilization of the Greeks and Romans ultimately led historians to use the word *Renaissance* to identify this age. Of course, intellectuals and artists wrote and painted for the upper classes, and the brilliant intellectual, cultural, and artistic accomplishments of the Renaissance were really products of and for the elite. The ideas of the Renaissance did not have a broad base among the masses of the people.

The Renaissance did, however, raise new questions about medieval traditions. In advocating a return to the early sources of Christianity and criticizing current religious practices, the humanists raised fundamental issues about the Catholic church, which was still an important institution. In the sixteenth century, the intellectual revolution of the fifteenth century gave way to a religious renaissance that touched the lives of people, including the masses, in new and profound ways.

When the monk Martin Luther entered the public scene with an attack on the sale of indulgences, few people in Europe, or Germany for that matter, suspected that he would eventually produce a division of Europe

along religious lines. But the yearning for reform of the church and meaningful religious experience caused a seemingly simple dispute to escalate into a powerful movement. Clearly, the papacy and other elements in the Catholic church underestimated the strength of Martin Luther and the desire for religious change.

Although Luther felt that this revival of Christianity based on his interpretation of the Bible should be acceptable to all, others soon appeared who also read the Bible but interpreted it in different ways. Protestantism split into different sects, which, though united in their dislike of Catholicism, were themselves divided over the interpretation of religious beliefs and practices. As reform ideas spread, religion and politics became ever more intertwined. Political support played a crucial role in the spread of the Reformation.

Although Lutheranism was legally acknowledged in the Holy Roman Empire by the Peace of Augsburg in 1555, it had lost much of its momentum and outside Scandinavia had scant ability to attract new supporters. Its energy was largely replaced by the new Protestant form of Calvinism, which had clarity of doctrine and a fervor that made it attractive to a whole new generation of Europeans. But while Calvinism's militancy enabled it to expand across Europe, Catholicism was also experi-

encing its own revival and emerged as a militant faith, prepared to do combat for the souls of the faithful. An age of religious passion would tragically be followed by an age of religious warfare.

By the middle of the sixteenth century, it was apparent that the religious passions of the Reformation era had brought an end to the religious unity of medieval Europe. The religious division (Catholics versus Protestants) was instrumental in beginning a series of wars that dominated much of European history between 1560 and 1650. The wars, in turn, worsened the economic and social crises that were besetting Europe. Wars, rebellions and constitutional crises, economic depression, social disintegration, a witchcraft craze, and a population crisis all afflicted Europe and have led some historians to speak of the ninety years between 1560 and 1650 as an age of crisis in European life. It took almost one hundred years of religious warfare complicated by serious political, economic, and social issues—the worst series of wars and civil wars since the collapse of the Roman Empire in the west—before Europeans finally

admitted that they would have to tolerate different ways of worshiping God. That men who were disciples of the Apostle of Peace would kill each other—often in brutal and painful fashion—aroused skepticism about Christianity itself.

Periods of crisis, however, are frequently ages of opportunities, nowhere more apparent than in the geographical discoveries that made this an era of European expansion into new worlds. The discovery of new trade routes to the Far East and the "accidental" discovery of the Americas led Europeans to plunge outside the medieval world in which they had been enclosed for virtually a thousand years. The conquest of the Americas brought out the worst and some of the best of European civilization. The greedy plundering of resources and the brutal repression, enslavement, and virtual annihilation of millions of Indians were hardly balanced by attempts to create new institutions, convert the natives to Christianity, and foster the rights of the indigenous peoples.

To many historians, the seventeenth century has assumed extraordinary proportions. The concept of a united Christendom, held as an ideal since the Middle Ages, had been irrevocably destroyed by the religious wars, making possible the emergence of a system of nation-states in which power politics took on an increasing significance. The growth of political thought focusing on the secular origins of state power reflected the changes that were going on in seventeenth-century society. Within those states, there slowly emerged some of the machinery that made possible a growing centralization of power. In those states called absolutist, strong monarchs with the assistance of their aristocracies took the lead in creating greater centralization. The best example of absolute monarchy was the France of Louis XIV. In England, where the landed aristocracy gained power at the expense of the monarchs, the foundations were laid, not for absolutism, but for a constitutional government in which Parliament provided the focus for the institutions of centralized power. In all the major

European states, a growing concern for power and dynastic expansion led to larger armies and greater conflict. The growth of international law represented an attempt to create a rational system for this conflict, but it did nothing to achieve a peaceful solution to human problems. War remained a basic feature of Western civilization.

At the same time, though it would be misleading to assert that Europe had become a secular world, we would have to say that religious preoccupations and values were losing ground to secular considerations. The seventeenth century was a transitional period to a more secular spirit that has characterized modern Western civilization until the present time. No stronger foundation for this spirit could be found than in the new view of the universe that was created by the Scientific Revolution of the seventeenth century.

The Scientific Revolution represents a major turning point in modern Western civilization. In the Scientific Revolution, the Western world overthrew the medieval, Ptolemaic-Aristotelian worldview (earth was at the center of the universe) and arrived at a new conception of the universe: the sun at the center, the planets as material bodies revolving around the sun in elliptical orbits, and an infinite rather than finite world. With the changes in the conception of "heaven" came changes in the conception of "earth." The work of Bacon and Descartes left Europeans with the separation of mind and matter and the belief that by using only reason they could, in fact, understand and dominate the world of nature. The development of a scientific method furthered the work of scientists while the creation of scientific societies and learned journals spread its results.

Although traditional churches stubbornly resisted the new ideas and a few intellectuals pointed to some inherent flaws, nothing was able to halt the replacement of the traditional ways of thinking by new ways of thinking that created a more fundamental break with the past than that represented by the breakup of Christian unity in the Reformation.

The Scientific Revolution forced Europeans to change their conception of themselves. At first, some were appalled and even frightened by its implications. Formerly, humans on earth had been at the center of the universe. Now the earth was only a tiny planet revolving around a sun that was itself only a speck in a boundless universe. Most people remained optimistic despite the apparent blow to human dignity. After all, had Newton not demonstrated that the universe was a great machine governed by natural laws? Newton had found one—the universal law of gravitation. Could others not find other laws?

Were there not natural laws governing every aspect of human endeavor that could be found by the new scientific method? Thus, the Scientific Revolution leads us logically to the age of the Enlightenment of the eighteenth century.

In the eighteenth century, a group of intellectuals known as the philosophes popularized the ideas of the Scientific Revolution and used them to undertake a dramatic reexamination of all aspects of life. Highly influenced by the new worldview created by the Scientific Revolution, the philosophes hoped that they could make progress toward creating a new society by using reason to discover the natural laws that governed it. They believed that education could produce better human beings and a better human society. By attacking traditional religion as the enemy and creating the new "sciences of man" in economics, politics, justice, and education, the philosophes laid the foundation for a modern worldview based on rationalism and secularism. The ideas of the philosophes had such a widespread impact on their society that historians ever since have called the eighteenth century an age of Enlightenment.

But the eighteenth century was also an age of tradition. Everywhere in Europe at the beginning of the eighteenth century, the old order remained strong. Nobles, clerics, towns, and provinces all had privileges, some medieval in origin, others the result of the attempt of monarchies in the sixteenth and seventeenth centu-

ries to gain financial support from their subjects. Everywhere in the eighteenth century, monarchs sought to enlarge their bureaucracies to raise taxes to support the new large standing armies that they needed to compete militarily with the other European states. The existence of these armies made wars more likely. Within the European state system, the nations that would dominate Europe until World War I—Britain, France, Austria, Prussia, and Russia—emerged as the five great powers of Europe. The existence of five great powers, with two of them (France and Britain) in conflict in the Far East and the New World, initiated a new scale of conflict; the Seven Years' War could legitimately be viewed as the first world war. The wars altered some boundaries on the European continent, but were perhaps most significant for the British victories that marked the emergence of Great Britain as the world's greatest naval and colonial power. Everywhere in Europe, increased demands for taxes to support these conflicts led to attacks on the privileged orders and a desire for change not met by the ruling monarchs.

At the same time, sustained population growth, dramatic changes in finance, trade, and industry, and the growth of poverty created tensions that undermined the traditional foundations of European society. The inability of the old order to deal meaningfully with these changes led to a revolutionary outburst at the end of the eighteenth century that brought the beginning of the end for that old order and the emergence of a modern new order.

CHAPTER
20

A Revolution in Politics: The Era of the French Revolution and Napoleon

On the morning of July 14, 1789, a Parisian mob of some 8,000 people in search of weapons streamed toward the Bastille, a royal armory filled with arms and ammunition. The Bastille was also a state prison, and, although it now contained only seven prisoners, in the eyes of these angry Parisians it was a glaring symbol of the government's despotic policies. The armory was defended by the Marquis de Launay and a small garrison of 114 men. The attack began in earnest in the early afternoon, and, after three hours of fighting, de Launay and the garrison surrendered. Angered by the loss of ninety-eight of their members, the victorious mob beat de Launay to death, cut off his head, and carried it aloft in triumph through the streets of Paris. When King Louis XVI was told the news of the fall of the Bastille by the duc de La Rochefoucauld-Liancourt, he exclaimed, "Why, this is a revolt." "No, Sire," replied the duc, "It is a revolution."

Historians have long assumed that the modern history of Europe began with two major transformations—the French Revolution and the Industrial Revolution (on the latter, see Chapter 21). Accordingly, the French Revolution has been portrayed as the major turning point in European political and social history when the institutions of the "old regime" were destroyed and a new order was created based on individual rights, representative institutions, and a concept of loyalty to the nation rather than the monarch. This perspective does have certain limitations, however.

France was only one of a number of areas in the Western world where the assumptions of the old order were challenged. Although some historians have used the phrase "democratic revolution" to refer to the upheavals of the late eighteenth and early nineteenth centuries, it is probably more appropriate to speak not of a "democratic movement," but of a liberal movement to extend political rights and power to the bourgeoisie "possessing capital," namely, those besides the aristocracy who were literate and had become wealthy

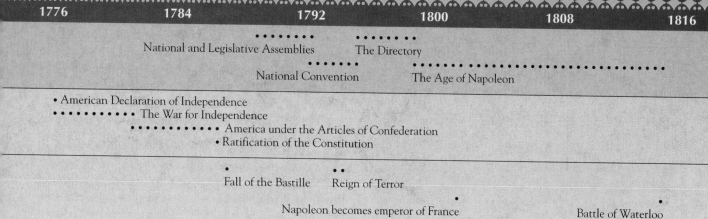

National and Legislative Assemblies   The Directory

National Convention   The Age of Napoleon

• American Declaration of Independence
• • • • • • • • • • • The War for Independence
• • • • • • • • • • • • America under the Articles of Confederation
• Ratification of the Constitution

Fall of the Bastille   Reign of Terror

Napoleon becomes emperor of France   Battle of Waterloo

through capitalist enterprises in trade, industry, and finance. The years preceding and accompanying the French Revolution included attempts at reform and revolt in the North American colonies, Britain, the Dutch Republic, some Swiss cities, and the Austrian Netherlands. The success of the American and French Revolutions makes them the center of attention for this chapter.

Not all of the decadent privileges that characterized the old European regime were destroyed in 1789, however. The revolutionary upheaval of the era, especially in France, did create new liberal and national political ideals, summarized in the French revolutionary slogan, "Liberty, Equality, and Fraternity," that transformed France and were then spread to other European countries through the conquests of Napoleon. After Napoleon's defeat, however, the forces of reaction did their best to restore the old order and resist pressures for reform.

The Beginnings of the Revolutionary Era: The American Revolution

The revolutionary era began in North America when the thirteen British colonies along the eastern seaboard revolted against their mother country. Despite their differences, the colonists found ways to create a new government based on liberal principles that made an impact on the "old world" European states.

Reorganization, Resistance, and Rebellion

The immediate causes of the American Revolution stemmed from Britain's response to its victory over France in the Seven Years' War (1756–1763), known as the French and Indian War in America. British imperial policies toward the American colonies changed dramatically after 1763. The western lands of the Ohio and Mississippi valleys, surrendered to the British by the French, appeared to land-hungry Americans as an ideal territory for expansion. The British, however, feared conflict with the numerous Indian tribes settled there and forbade purchases of land west of the Appalachians. Furthermore, they decided to enforce this policy and, at the same time, to guard against any French attempt to recover Canada by sending a standing army of 10,000 men to the colonies, a totally unprecedented peacetime act in the eyes of the colonists. Nor were the colonists pleased when British policymakers asked them to contribute new revenues to pay the expenses the British army incurred in defending the colonies. In 1765, the British Parliament enacted the Stamp Act, which attempted to levy new taxes on the colonies, but riots quickly led to the statute's repeal.

The immediate crisis had ended, but the fundamental cause of the dispute had not been resolved. In the course of the eighteenth century, significant differences had arisen between the American and British political worlds. The property requirement for voting—voters had to possess property that could be rented for at least forty shillings a year—was the same in both areas, but the number of voters differed markedly. In Britain fewer than one in five adult males had the right to vote. In the colonies, where a radically different economic structure led to an enormous group of independent farmers, the property requirement allowed over 50 percent of adult males to vote.

While both the British and Americans had representative governments, different systems had evolved. Representation in Britain was indirect; the members of Parliament did not speak for local interests but for the entire kingdom. In the colonies representation was direct; representatives were expected not only to reside in and own property in the communities electing them, but also to represent the interests of those local districts.

This divergence in political systems was paralleled by conflicting conceptions of the British Empire. The British envisioned the empire as a single unit with Parliament as the supreme authority throughout. All the people in the empire, including the American colonists, were represented indirectly by members of Parliament, whether they were from the colonies or not. Colonial assemblies in the British perspective were only committees that made "temporary by-laws"; the real authority to make laws for the empire resided in London.

The Americans had developed their own peculiar view of the British Empire. To them, the empire was composed of self-regulating parts. While they conceded that as British subjects they owed allegiance to the king and that Parliament had the right to make laws for the peace and prosperity of the whole realm, they argued, nevertheless, that neither king nor Parliament had any right to interfere in the internal affairs of the colonies since they had their own representative assemblies. American colonists were especially defensive about property and believed strongly that no tax could be levied without the consent of an assembly whose members actually represented the people.

By the 1760s, the American colonists had developed a sense of a common identity. It was not unusual for American travelers to Britain in the eighteenth century to see British society as old and decadent in sharp contrast to the youthfulness and vitality of their own. This sense of superiority made Americans resentful of British actions that seemed to treat them like children. Resentment eventually led to a desire for independence.

Crisis followed crisis in the early 1770s. The Tea Act of 1773, which was an attempt by Parliament to help the financially hard-pressed East India Company by allowing it to bypass American wholesalers and sell its tea directly to distributors, was roundly denounced by Americans as an attempt to ruin colonial businesses. In Boston, protest took a destructive turn when 150 Americans dressed as Indians dumped the East India Company's tea into Boston harbor. Parliament responded vigorously with the Coercive Acts, which closed the port of Boston until compensation for the destroyed tea was paid, restricted town meetings, and strengthened the power of the royal governor of Massachusetts. Designed to punish radical Massachusetts as an example to the other colonies, the Coercive Acts backfired. Colonial assemblies everywhere denounced the British action, and the colonies' desire to take collective action led to the First Continental Congress, which met at Philadelphia in September 1774. The more militant members refused to compromise and urged the colonists to "take up arms and organize militias." When the British army under General Gage attempted to stop rebel mobilization in Massachusetts, fighting erupted at Lexington and Concord between colonists and redcoats in April 1775.

The War for Independence

Despite the outbreak of hostilities, the colonists did not rush headlong into rebellion and war. More than a year passed after Lexington and Concord before the colonists decided to declare their independence from the British Empire. An important factor in mobilizing public pressure for that decision was *Common Sense*, a pamphlet published in January 1776 by Thomas Paine, a recently arrived English political radical. Within three months, it had sold 120,000 copies. Paine's pamphlet argued that it was ridiculous for "a continent to be perpetually gov-

≥ *The Argument for Independence* ≤

On July 2, 1776, the Second Continental Congress adopted a resolution declaring the independence of the American colonies. Two days later the delegates approved the Declaration of Independence, which gave the reasons for their action. Its principal author was Thomas Jefferson who basically restated John Locke's theory of revolution (see Chapter 16).

The Declaration of Independence

When in the course of human events it becomes necessary for one people to dissolve the political bands which have connected them with another, and to assume among the Powers of the earth, the separate and equal station to which the Laws of Nature and of Nature's God entitle them, a decent respect to the opinions of mankind requires that they should declare the causes which impel them to the separation.

We hold these truths to be self-evident, that all men are created equal, that they are endowed by their Creator with certain unalienable Rights, that among these are Life, Liberty and the pursuit of Happiness. That to secure these rights, Governments are instituted among Men, deriving their just powers from the consent of the governed, That whenever any Form of Government becomes destructive of these ends, it is the Right of the People to alter or to abolish it and to institute new Government, laying its foundation on such principles and organizing its powers in such form, as to them shall seem most likely to effect their Safety and Happiness. Prudence, indeed, will dictate that Governments long established should not be changed for light and transient causes; and accordingly all experience has shown, that mankind are more disposed to suffer, while evils are sufferable, than to right themselves by abolishing the forms to which they are accustomed. But when a long train of abuses and usurpations, pursuing invariably the same Object evinces a design to reduce them under absolute Despotism, it is their right, it is their duty, to throw off such Government, and to provide new Guards for their future security.—Such has been the patient sufferance of these Colonies; and such is now the necessity which constrains them to alter their former Systems of government. The history of the present King of Great Britain is a history of repeated injuries and usurpations, all having in direct object the establishment of an absolute Tyranny over these States.

---

erned by an island." On July 4, 1776, the Second Continental Congress approved a Declaration of Independence written by Thomas Jefferson (see the box above). A stirring political document, the Declaration of Independence affirmed the Enlightenment's natural rights of "life, liberty, and the pursuit of happiness" and declared the colonies to be "free and independent states absolved from all allegiance to the British crown." The war for American independence had formally begun.

The war against Great Britain was a great gamble. Britain was a strong European military power with enormous financial resources; by 1778 Britain had sent 50,000 regular British troops and 30,000 German mercenaries to America. The Second Continental Congress had authorized the formation of a Continental Army under George Washington as commander-in-chief. Washington, who had had political experience in Virginia and military experience in the French and Indian War, was a good choice for the job. As a southerner, he brought balance to an effort that up to now had been led by New Englanders. Nevertheless, compared to the British forces, the Continental Army consisted of undisciplined amateurs whose terms of service were usually very brief. The colonies also had militia units, but they likewise tended to be unreliable. Although 400,000 men served in the Continental Army and the militias during the course of the war, Washington never had more than 20,000 troops available for any single battle.

Of great importance to the colonies' cause was the assistance provided by foreign countries who were eager to gain revenge for their defeats in earlier wars at the hands of the British. The French were particularly generous in supplying arms and money to the rebels from the beginning of the war. French officers also served in Washington's army. Uncertain of the military outcome, however, France was at first unwilling to recognize the new republic. The defeat of the British at Saratoga in October 1777 finally led the French to grant diplomatic recognition to the American state. When Spain and the Dutch Republic entered the war against Great Britain in 1779 and 1780, respectively, and Russia formed the League of Armed Neutrality in 1780 to protect neutral shipping from British attacks, the British were faced with war against much of Europe as well as the Americans. Despite having won most of the battles, the British were in danger of losing the war. When the army of General Cornwallis was forced to surrender to a combined American and French army and French fleet under Washington at Yorktown in 1781, the British decided to call it quits. After extensive negotiations, complicated by French and Spanish aims that often conflicted with American desires, the Treaty of Paris was signed in 1783. It recognized the independence of the American colonies and granted the Americans control of the western territory from the Appalachians to the Mississippi River. By playing off the mutual fears of the European powers, the Americans had cleverly gained a peace settlement that stunned the Europeans. The Americans were off to a good start but soon showed signs of political disintegration.

Toward a New Nation

Although the thirteen American colonies agreed to "hang together" to gain their independence from the British, a fear of concentrated power and concern for their own interests caused them to have little enthusiasm for establishing a united nation with a strong central government. The Articles of Confederation, proposed in 1777 but not completely ratified until 1781, did little to provide for a strong central government. A series of economic, political, and international problems soon led to a movement for a different form of national government. In the summer of 1787, fifty-five delegates attended a convention in Philadelphia that was authorized by the Confederation Congress "for the sole and express purpose of revising the Articles of Confederation." The convention's delegates—wealthy, politically experienced, well educated and nationalistically inclined—rejected revision and decided to devise a new constitution.

The proposed Constitution created a central government distinct from and superior to the governments of the individual states. The national government was given the power to levy taxes, raise a national army, regulate domestic and foreign trade, and establish a national currency. While states were not eliminated, their powers were noticeably diminished. Following Montesquieu's principle of a "separation of powers" to provide a system of "checks and balances," the central or federal government was divided into three branches, each with some power to check the functioning of the

◆ **The Declaration of Independence.** John Trumbull's famous painting, *The Signing of the Declaration*, shows members of the committee responsible for the Declaration of Independence (from left to right, John Adams, Roger Sherman, Robert Livingston, Thomas Jefferson, and Benjamin Franklin) standing before John Hancock, president of the Second Continental Congress.

others. A president, elected by the indirect system of an Electoral College, would serve as the chief executive with the power to execute laws, veto the legislature's acts, make judicial and executive appointments, supervise foreign affairs, and direct military forces. Legislative power was vested in the second branch of government, a bicameral legislature composed of a Senate elected by the state legislatures and a House of Representatives elected directly by the people. The federal judiciary, embodied in a Supreme Court and other courts "as deemed necessary" by Congress, provided the third branch of government. With judges nominated by the executive and approved by the legislative branch, the federal judiciary would enforce the Constitution as the "supreme law of the land."

The Constitutional Convention had stipulated that the new Constitution would have to be ratified by popularly chosen conventions in nine of the thirteen states before it would take effect. The process of ratification led to fierce debates between the Federalists, who favored the new Constitution, and the Antifederalists, who believed that the Constitution would create another tyranny by destroying the power of the states. The well-organized Federalists won the debate but certainly not because of a massive outpouring of public support. The public remained largely passive; only one-fourth of the eligible voters bothered to choose the delegates to the state conventions.

The margin of victory for the Federalists had been quite slim. Important to their success had been a

Map 20.1 North America, 1700–1803.

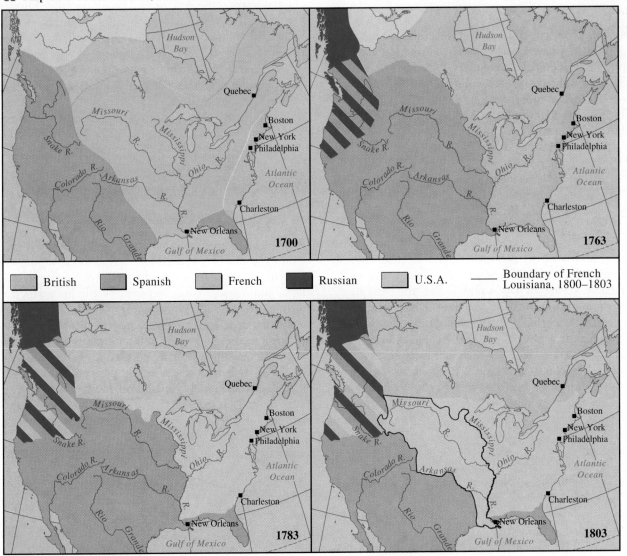

promise to add a Bill of Rights to the Constitution as the new government's first piece of business. Accordingly, in March of 1789, the new Congress enacted the first ten amendments to the Constitution, ever since known as the Bill of Rights. These guaranteed freedom of religion, speech, press, petition, and assembly, as well as the right to bear arms, protection against unreasonable searches and arrests, trial by jury, due process of law, and the protection of property rights. Although many of these guarantees had their origins in English law, others were derived from the natural rights philosophy of the eighteenth-century philosophes and American experience. Is it any wonder that many European intellectuals saw the American Revolution as the embodiment of the Enlightenment's political dreams?

The Impact of the American Revolution on Europe

The year 1789 witnessed two far-reaching events, the beginning of a new United States of America and the eruption of the French Revolution. Was there a connection between the two great revolutions of the last half of the eighteenth century?

There is no doubt that the American Revolution had an important impact on Europeans. Books, newspapers, and magazines provided a newly developing reading public with numerous accounts of American events. To many in Europe, it seemed to portend an era of significant changes, including new arrangements in international politics. The Venetian ambassador to Paris astutely observed in 1783 that "if only the union of the [American] provinces is preserved, it is reasonable to expect that, with the favorable effects of time, and of European arts and sciences, it will become the most formidable power in the world."[1] But the American Revolution also meant far more than that. It proved to many Europeans that the liberal political ideas of the Enlightenment were not merely the vapid utterances of intellectuals. The rights of man, ideas of liberty and equality, popular sovereignty, freedom of religion, thought, and press, and the separation of powers were not merely utopian ideals. The Americans had created a new social contract, embodied it in a written constitution, and made concepts of liberty and representative government a reality. The premises of the Enlightenment seemed confirmed; a new age and a better world could be achieved. As a Swiss philosophe expressed it, "I am tempted to believe that North America is the country where reason and humanity will develop more rapidly than anywhere else."[2]

Europeans obtained much of their information about America from returning soldiers, especially the hundreds of French officers who had served in the American war. One of them, the aristocratic marquis de Lafayette, had volunteered for service in America in order to "strike a blow against England," France's old enemy. Closely associated with Washington, Lafayette returned to France with ideas of individual liberties and notions of republicanism and popular sovereignty. He became a member of the Society of Thirty, a club composed of people from the Paris salons. These "lovers of liberty" were influential in the early stages of the French Revolution. The Declaration of the Rights of Man and the Citizen (see The Destruction of the Old Regime later in this chapter) showed unmistakable signs of the influence of the American Declaration of Independence as well as the American state constitutions. Yet, for all of its obvious impact, the American Revolution proved in the long run to be far less important to Europe than the French Revolution. The French Revolution was more complex, more violent, and far more radical with its attempt to reconstruct both a new political order and a new social order. The French Revolution provided a model of revolution for Europe and much of the rest of the world; to many it has remained the political movement that truly inaugurated the modern political world.

The French Revolution

Although we associate events like the French Revolution with sudden changes, the causes of such events involve long-range problems as well as immediate, precipitating forces. Revolutions, as has been repeatedly shown, are not necessarily the result of economic collapse and masses of impoverished people hungering for change. In fact, in the fifty years before 1789, France had experienced a period of economic growth due to an expansion of foreign trade and an increase in industrial production, although many people, especially peasants, no doubt failed to share in the prosperity. Thus, the causes of the French Revolution must be found in a multifaceted examination of French society and its problems in the late eighteenth century.

Background to the French Revolution

Although France experienced an increase in economic growth in the eighteenth century, the wealth was not evenly distributed. The long-range or indirect causes of the French Revolution must first be sought in the condition of French society. Before the Revolution, French society was grounded in the inequality of rights or the idea of privilege. The population of 27 million was divided, as it had been since the Middle Ages, into legal categories known as the three orders or estates.

The first estate consisted of the clergy and numbered about 130,000 people. The church owned approximately 10 percent of the land. Clergy were exempt from the *taille*, France's chief tax, although the church had agreed to pay a "voluntary" contribution every five years to the state. Clergy were also radically divided, since the higher clergy, stemming from aristocratic families, shared the interests of the nobility while the parish priests were often poor commoners.

The second estate was the nobility, composed of no more than 350,000 people who nevertheless owned about 25 to 30 percent of the land. Under Louis XV and Louis XVI, the nobility had continued to play an important and even crucial role in French society, holding many of the leading positions in the government, the military, the law courts, and the higher church offices. Much heavy industry in France was controlled by nobles, either through investment or by ownership of mining and metallurgical enterprises. The French nobility was also divided. The nobility of the robe derived their status from officeholding, a pathway that had often enabled commoners to attain noble rank. These nobles now dominated the royal law courts and important administrative offices. The nobility of the sword claimed to be descendants of the original medieval nobility. As a group, the nobles sought to expand their privileges at the expense of the monarchy—to defend liberty by resisting the arbitrary actions of monarchy, as some nobles asserted—and to maintain their monopolistic control over positions in the military, church, and government. In 1781, in reaction to the ambitions of aristocrats newly arrived from the bourgeoisie, the Ségur Law attempted to limit the sale of military officerships to fourth-generation nobles, thus excluding newly enrolled members of the nobility.

Although there were many poor nobles, on the whole the fortunes of the wealthy aristocrats outstripped those of most others in French society. Generally, the nobles tended to marry within their own ranks making the nobility a fairly closed group. Although their privileges varied from region to region, the very possession of privileges remained a hallmark of the nobility. Common to all were tax exemptions, especially from the *taille*.

The third estate, or the commoners of society, constituted the overwhelming majority of the French population. They were divided by vast differences in occupation, level of education, and wealth. The peasants who alone constituted 75 to 80 percent of the total population were by far the largest segment of the third estate. They owned about 35 to 40 percent of the land, although their landholdings varied from area to area and over half had no or little land on which to survive. Serfdom no longer existed on any large scale in France, but French peasants still owed seigneurial obligations to their local landlords. These "relics of feudalism," survivals from an earlier age, had continued and even been reaffirmed in the eighteenth century as a result of aristocratic strength. These obligations included the payment of fees for the use of village facilities, such as the flour mill, community oven, and winepress, as well as tithes to the clergy. The nobility also maintained the right to hunt on peasants' land. Peasants resented these obligations as well as the attempt of noble landowners in the eighteenth century to enclose open fields and divide village common lands since enclosure eliminated the open pastures where poor peasants grazed their livestock.

Another part of the third estate consisted of skilled artisans, shopkeepers, and other wage earners in the cities. Although the eighteenth century had been a period of rapid urban growth, 90 percent of French towns had fewer than 10,000 inhabitants while only nine cities had more than 50,000. In the eighteenth century, consumer prices rose faster than wages, with the result that these urban groups experienced a noticeable decline in purchasing power. In Paris, for example, income lagged behind food prices and especially behind a 140 percent rise in rents for working people in skilled and unskilled trades. The economic discontent of this segment of the third estate—and often simply their struggle for survival—led them to play an important role in the Revolution, especially in the city of Paris. Insubordination, one observer noted, "has been visible among the people for some years now and above all among craftsmen." One historian has charted the ups and downs of revolutionary riots in Paris by showing their correlation to changes in bread prices. Sudden increases in the price of bread, which constituted three-fourths of an ordinary person's diet and cost one-third to one-half of his or her income, immediately affected public order. People expected bread prices to be controlled. They grew desperate when prices rose, and their only recourse was mob action to try to change the situation. The towns and cities were also home to large groups of unskilled workers. One magistrate complained that "misery . . . has thrown into the towns people who overburden them with their uselessness, and who find nothing to do, because there is not enough for the people who live there."[3]

About 8 percent or 2.3 million people constituted the bourgeoisie or middle class who owned about 20 to 25 percent of the land. This group included merchants, industrialists, and bankers who controlled the resources of trade, manufacturing, and finance and benefited from the economic prosperity after 1730. The bourgeoisie also included professional people—lawyers, holders of public offices, doctors, and writers. Many members of the bourgeoisie sought security and status through the purchase of land. They had their own set of grievances because they were often excluded from the social and political privileges monopolized by the nobles. These resentments of the middle class were for a long time assumed to be a major cause of the French Revolution. But although these tensions existed, the situation was not a simple case of a unified bourgeoisie against a unified noble class. As is evident, neither group was monolithic. Nobles were separated by vast differences in wealth and importance. A similar gulf separated wealthy financiers from local lawyers in French provincial towns.

Remarkable similarities existed at the upper levels of society between the wealthier bourgeoisie and the nobility. It was still possible for wealthy middle-class individuals to enter the ranks of the nobility by obtaining public offices and entering the nobility of the robe. In fact, between 1774 and 1789, the not insignificant number of 2,500 wealthy bourgeoisie entered the ranks of the nobility. Over the century as a whole, 6,500 new noble families were created. In addition, as we saw in Chapter 19, the aristocrats were also participating in capitalist activities on their landed estates, such as mining, metallurgy, and glassmaking, and were even investing in foreign trade. Viewed in terms of economic function, many members of the bourgeoisie and nobility formed a single class. Finally, the new and critical ideas of the Enlightenment proved attractive to both aristocrats and bourgeoisie. Members of both groups shared a common world of liberal political thought. The old view that the French Revolution was the result of the conflict between two rigid orders, the bourgeoisie and nobility, has been enlarged and revised. Both aristocratic and bourgeois elites, long accustomed to a new socioeconomic reality based on wealth and economic achievement, were increasingly frustrated by a monarchical system resting on privileges and on an old and rigid social order based on the concept of estates. The opposition of these elites to the old order ultimately led them to take drastic action against the monarchical regime, although they soon split over the question of how far to proceed in eliminating traditional privileges. In a real sense, the Revolution had its origins in political grievances.

While the long-range causes of the French Revolution, then, can be found in part in the growing frustration at the monarchy's inability to deal with new social realities and problems, other factors were also present. The failure of the French monarchy was exacerbated by specific problems in the 1780s. Although the country had enjoyed fifty years of growth overall, periodic economic crises still occurred. Bad harvests in 1787 and 1788 and the beginnings of a manufacturing depression resulted in food shortages, rising prices for food and other necessities, and unemployment in the cities. The number of poor, estimated by some at almost one-third of the population, reached crisis proportions on the eve of the Revolution. An English traveler noted the misery of the poor in the countryside: "All the country girls and women are without shoes or stockings; and the ploughmen at their work have neither sabots nor stockings to their feet. This is a poverty that strikes at the root of national prosperity."[4]

Increased criticism of existing privileges as well as social and political institutions also characterized the eighteenth century. Although the philosophes did not advocate revolution, their ideas were widely circulated among the literate bourgeois and noble elites of France. The actual influence of the ideas of the philosophes is difficult to prove, but once the Revolution began, the revolutionary leaders frequently quoted Enlightenment writers, especially Rousseau.

The French Parlements often frustrated efforts at reform. Responsible for registering royal decrees, these thirteen law courts could block royal edicts by not registering them. Although Louis XIV had forced them into submission, the Parlements had gained new strength in the eighteenth century as they and their noble judges assumed the role of defenders of "liberty" against the arbitrary power of the monarchy. As noble defenders, however, they often pushed their own interests as well, especially by blocking new taxes. This last point reminds us that one of the fundamental problems facing the monarchy was financial.

The immediate cause of the French Revolution was the near collapse of government finances. French governmental expenditures continued to grow due to costly wars and royal extravagance. Since the government responded by borrowing, by 1788 the interest on the debt alone constituted half of the government's spending. The king's finance ministry wrestled with the problem but met with resistance. In 1786, Charles de Calonne, the controller-general of finance, proposed a complete revamping of the fiscal and administrative system of the state. To gain support, Calonne convened an Assembly of Notables early in 1787. This gathering of nobles, prelates, and magistrates refused to cooperate, and the government's attempt to go it alone brought further disaster. On the verge of a complete financial collapse, the government was finally forced to call a meeting of the Estates-General, the French parliamentary body that had not met since 1614. By calling the Estates-General, the government was virtually admitting that the consent of the nation was required to raise taxes.

The Estates-General consisted of representatives from the three orders of French society. In the elections for the Estates-General, the government had ruled that the Third Estate should get double representation (it did, after all, constitute 97 percent of the population). Consequently, while both the First Estate (the clergy) and the Second (the nobility) had about 300 delegates each, the commoners had almost 600 representatives. Two-thirds of the latter were people with legal training while three-fourths were from towns with over 2,000 inhabitants, giving the Third Estate a particularly strong legal and urban representation. Of the 282 representatives of the nobility, about 90 were liberal minded, urban oriented, and interested in the enlightened ideas of the century; half of them were under forty years of age. The activists of the Third Estate and reform-minded individuals among the First and Second Estates had common ties in their youth, urban background, and hostility to privilege. The *cahiers de doléances* or statements of local grievances, which were drafted throughout France during the elections to the Estates-General, advocated a regular constitutional government that would abolish the fiscal privileges of the church and nobility as the major way to regenerate the country.

The Estates-General opened at Versailles on May 5, 1789. It was divided from the start over the question of whether voting should be by order or by head (each delegate having one vote). The Parlement of Paris, consisting of nobles of the robe, had advocated voting by order according to the form used in 1614. Each order would vote separately; each would have veto power over the other two, thus guaranteeing aristocratic control over reforms. But opposition to the Parlement of Paris's proposal had arisen from a group calling themselves the patriots or "lovers of liberty." Although they claimed to be the nation, they consisted primarily of bourgeoisie and nobles. One group of patriots known as the Society of Thirty drew most of its members from the salons of Paris. Some of this largely noble group had been directly influenced by the American Revolution, but all had been affected by the ideas of the Enlightenment and favored reforms made in the light of reason and utility.

The failure of the government to assume the leadership at the opening of the Estates-General created an opportunity for the Third Estate to push its demands for voting by head. Since it had double representation, with the assistance of liberal nobles and clerics, it could turn the three estates into a single-chamber legislature that would reform France in its own way. One representative, the Abbé Sieyès, issued a pamphlet in which he asked, "What is the third estate? Everything. What has it been thus far in the political order? Nothing. What does it demand? To become something." Sieyès's sentiment,

✦ The Tennis Court Oath.
Finding themselves locked out of their regular meeting place on June 20, 1789, the deputies of the Third Estate met instead in the nearby tennis courts of the Jeu de Paume and committed themselves to continue to meet until they established a new constitution for France. In this painting, the neoclassicist Jacques-Louis David presents a dramatic rendering of the Tennis Court Oath.

The Fall of the Bastille

On July 14, 1789, Parisian crowds in search of weapons attacked and captured the royal armory known as the Bastille. It had also been a state prison, and its fall marked the triumph of "liberty" over despotism. This intervention of the Parisian populace saved the Third Estate from Louis XVI's attempted counterrevolution.

A Parisian Newspaper Account of the Fall of the Bastille

First, the people tried to enter this fortress by the Rue St.—Antoine, this fortress, which no one has ever penetrated against the wishes of this frightful despotism and where the monster still resided. The treacherous governor had put out a flag of peace. So a confident advance was made; a detachment of French Guards, with perhaps five to six thousand armed bourgeois, penetrated the Bastille's outer courtyards, but as soon as some six hundred persons had passed over the first drawbridge, the bridge was raised and artillery fire mowed down several French Guards and some soldiers; the cannon fired on the town, and the people took fright; a large number of individuals were killed or wounded; but then they rallied and took shelter from the fire . . . meanwhile, they tried to locate some cannon; they attacked from the water's edge through the gardens of the arsenal, and from there made an orderly siege; they advanced from various directions, beneath a ceaseless round of fire. It was a terrible scene. . . . The fighting grew steadily more intense; the citizens had become hardened to the fire; from all directions they clambered onto the roofs or broke into the rooms; as soon as an enemy appeared among the turrets on the tower, he was fixed in the sights of a hundred guns and mown down in an instant; meanwhile cannon fire was hurriedly directed against the second drawbridge, which it pierced, breaking the chains; in vain did the cannon on the tower reply, for most people were sheltered from it; the fury was at its height; people bravely faced death and every danger; women, in their eagerness, helped us to the utmost; even the children, after the discharge of fire from the fortress, ran here and there picking up the bullets and shot; [and so the Bastille fell and the governor, De Launey, was captured]. . . . Serene and blessed liberty, for the first time, has at last been introduced into this abode of horrors, this frightful refuge of monstrous despotism and its crimes.

Meanwhile, they get ready to march; they leave amidst an enormous crowd; the applause, the outbursts of joy, the insults, the oaths hurled at the treacherous prisoners of war; everything is confused; cries of vengeance and of pleasure issue from every heart; the conquerors, glorious and covered in honor, carry their arms and the spoils of the conquered, the flags of victory, the militia mingling with the soldiers of the fatherland, the victory laurels offered them from every side, all this created a frightening and splendid spectacle. On arriving at the square, the people, anxious to avenge themselves, allowed neither De Launey nor the other officers to reach the place of trial; they seized them from the hands of their conquerors, and trampled them underfoot one after the other. De Launey was struck by a thousand blows, his head was cut off and hoisted on the end of a pike with blood streaming down all sides. . . This glorious day must amaze our enemies, and finally usher in for us the triumph of justice and liberty. In the evening, there were celebrations.

---

however, was not representative of the general feeling in 1789. Most delegates still wanted to make changes within a framework of respect for the authority of the king; revival or reform did not mean the overthrow of traditional institutions. When the First Estate declared in favor of voting by order, the Third Estate felt compelled to respond in a significant fashion. On June 17, 1789, the Third Estate voted to constitute itself a "National Assembly" and decided to draw up a constitution. Three days later, on June 20, the deputies of the Third Estate arrived at their meeting place, only to find the doors locked; thereupon they moved to a nearby indoor tennis court and swore (hence, the Tennis Court Oath) that they would continue to meet until they had produced a French constitution. These actions of June 17 and June 20 constitute the first step in the French Revolution since the Third Estate had no legal right to act as the National Assembly. This revolution, largely the work of the lawyers of the Third Estate, was soon in jeopardy, however, as the king sided with the First Estate and threatened to dissolve the Estates-General. Louis XVI now prepared to use force. The revolution of the lawyers appeared doomed.

The intervention of the common people, however, in a series of urban and rural uprisings in July and August of 1789 saved the Third Estate from the king's attempt to stop the revolution. From now on, the common people would be mobilized by both revolutionary and counterrevolutionary politicians and used to support their interests. The common people had their own interests as well and would use the name of the Third Estate to wage a war on the rich, claiming that the aristocrats were plotting to destroy the Estates-General and retain its privileges. This war was not what the deputies of the Third Estate had planned.

The most famous of the urban risings was the fall of the Bastille (see the box on p. 682). The king's attempt to take defensive measures by increasing the number of troops at the arsenals in Paris and along the roads to Versailles served not to intimidate but rather to inflame public opinion. Increased mob activity in Paris led

Parisian leaders to form a Permanent Committee to keep order. Needing arms, they organized a popular force to capture the Invalides, a royal armory, and on July 14 attacked the Bastille, another royal armory. But the Bastille had also been a state prison, and though it now contained only seven prisoners (five forgers and two insane people), its fall quickly became a popular symbol of triumph over despotism. Paris was abandoned to the insurgents, and Louis XVI was soon informed that the royal troops were unreliable. Louis's acceptance of that reality signaled the collapse of royal authority; the king could no longer enforce his will. Louis then confirmed the appointment of the marquis de Lafayette as com-

◆ **Storming of the Bastille.** Louis XVI planned to use force to dissolve the Estates-General, but a number of rural and urban uprisings by the common people prevented this action.

The fall of the Bastille, pictured here in an anonymous painting, is perhaps the most famous of the urban risings.

mander of a newly created citizens' militia known as the National Guard. The fall of the Bastille had saved the National Assembly.

At the same time, independently of what was going on in Paris, popular revolutions broke out in numerous cities. In Nantes, Permanent Committees and National Guards were created to maintain order after crowds had seized the chief citadels. This collapse of royal authority in the cities was paralleled by peasant revolutions in the countryside.

A growing resentment of the entire seigneurial system with its fees and obligations, greatly exacerbated by the economic and fiscal activities of the great estate holders—whether noble or bourgeois—in the difficult decade of the 1780s, created the conditions for a popular uprising. The fall of the Bastille and the king's apparent capitulation to the demands of the Third Estate now encouraged peasants to take matters into their own hands. From July 19 to August 3, peasant rebellions occurred in five major areas of France. Patterns varied. In some places, peasants simply forced their lay and ecclesiastical lords to renounce dues and tithes; elsewhere they burned charters listing their obligations. The peasants were not acting in blind fury; they knew what they were doing. Many also believed that the king supported their actions. As a contemporary chronicler wrote: "For several weeks, news went from village to village. They announced that the Estates-General was going to abolish tithes, quitrents and dues, that the King agreed but that the peasants had to support the public authorities by going themselves to demand the destruction of titles."[5]

The agrarian revolts served as a backdrop to the Great Fear, a vast panic that spread like wildfire through France between July 20 and August 6. Fear of invasion by foreign troops, aided by a supposed aristocratic plot, encouraged the formation of more citizens' militias and permanent committees. The greatest impact of the agrarian revolts and Great Fear was on the National Assembly meeting in Versailles. We will now examine its attempt to reform France.

The Destruction of the Old Regime

One of the first acts of the National Assembly, which was also called the Constituent Assembly because from 1789 to 1791 it was writing a new constitution, was to destroy the relics of feudalism or aristocratic privileges. To some deputies, this measure was necessary to calm the peasants and restore order in the countryside, although many urban bourgeoisie were willing to abolish feudalism as a matter of principle. On the night of August 4, 1789, the National Assembly in an astonishing session voted to abolish seigneurial rights as well as the fiscal privileges of nobles, clergy, towns, and provinces.

On August 26, the assembly provided the ideological foundation for its actions and an educational device for the nation by adopting the Declaration of the Rights of Man and the Citizen (see the box on p. 686). This charter of basic liberties reflected the ideas of the major philosophes of the French Enlightenment and also owed much to the American Declaration of Independence and American state constitutions. The declaration began with a ringing affirmation of "the natural and imprescriptible rights of man" to "liberty, property, security and resistance to oppression." It went on to affirm the destruction of aristocratic privileges by proclaiming an end to exemptions from taxation, freedom and equal rights for all men, and access to public office based on talent. The monarchy was restricted, and all citizens were to have the right to take part in the legislative process. Freedom of speech and press were coupled with the outlawing of arbitrary arrests.

The Declaration also raised another important issue. Did the proclamation's ideal of equal rights for all men also include women? Many deputies insisted that it did, at least in terms of civil liberties, provided that, as one said, "women do not aspire to exercise political rights and functions." Olympe de Gouges, a playwright and pamphleteer, refused to accept this exclusion of women from political rights. Echoing the words of the official declaration, she penned a Declaration of the Rights of Woman and the Female Citizen, in which she insisted that women should have all the same rights as men (see the box on p. 687). The National Assembly ignored her demands.

In the meantime, Louis XVI had remained inactive at Versailles. He did refuse, however, to promulgate the decrees on the abolition of feudalism and the Declaration of Rights, but an unexpected turn of events soon forced the king to change his mind. On October 5, after marching to the Hôtel de Ville, the city hall, to demand bread, crowds of Parisian women numbering in the thousands set off for Versailles, twelve miles away, to confront the king and the National Assembly. One eyewitness was amazed at the sight of "detachments of women coming up from every direction, armed with broomsticks, lances, pitchforks, swords, pistols and muskets." After meeting with a delegation of these women, who tearfully described how their children were starving from a lack of bread, Louis XVI promised them grain supplies for Paris, thinking that this would end the protest. But the women's action had forced the Parisian National Guard under Lafayette to follow their lead and march to Versailles. The crowd now insisted that the royal family return to Paris. On October 6, the king complied. As a goodwill gesture, he brought along wagonloads of flour from the palace stores. All were escorted by women armed with pikes (some of which held the severed heads of the king's guards) singing, "We are bringing back the baker, the baker's wife, and the baker's boy" (the king, queen, and their son). The king now accepted the National Assembly's decrees; it was neither the first nor the last occasion when Parisian crowds would affect national politics. The king was virtually a prisoner in Paris, and the National Assembly, now meeting in Paris, would also feel the influence of Parisian insurrectionary politics.

The Catholic church was viewed as an important pillar of the old order, and it soon also felt the impact of reform. Because of the need for money, most of the lands of the church were confiscated, and assignats, a form of

paper money, were issued based on the collateral of the newly nationalized church property. The church was also secularized. In July 1790, a new Civil Constitution of the Clergy was put into effect. Both bishops and priests of the Catholic church were to be elected by the people and paid by the state. All clergy were also required to swear an oath of allegiance to the Civil Constitution. Since the pope forbade it, only 54 percent of the French parish clergy took the oath while the majority of bishops refused. This was a critical development because the Catholic church, still an important institution in the life of the French people, now became an enemy of the Revolution. This has often been viewed as a serious tactical blunder on the part of the National Assembly for it gave counterrevolution a popular base from which to operate.

By 1791, the National Assembly had finally completed a new constitution that established a limited, constitutional monarchy. There was still a monarch (now called king of the French), but he enjoyed few

◆ **Session of August 4, 1789.** During its session of August 4, 1789, the National Assembly voted to abolish not only the fiscal privileges of the nobility, clergy, towns, and provinces, but seigneurial rights as well. As seen in this contemporary rendering of the event, the Third Estate applauded as members of the First and Second Estates offered to give up their privileges.

⇒ *Declaration of the Rights of Man and the Citizen* ⇐

One of the important documents of the French Revolution, the Declaration of the Rights of Man and the Citizen, was adopted in August 1789 by the National Assembly. The declaration affirmed that "Men are born and remain free and equal in rights," that governments must protect these natural rights, and that political power is derived from the people.

Declaration of the Rights of Man and the Citizen

The representatives of the French people, organized as a national assembly, considering that ignorance, neglect, and scorn of the rights of man are the sole causes of public misfortunes and of corruption of governments, have resolved to display in a solemn declaration the natural, inalienable, and sacred rights of man, so that this declaration, constantly in the presence of all members of society, will continually remind them of their rights and their duties. . . . Consequently, the National Assembly recognizes and declares, in the presence and under the auspices of the Supreme Being, the following rights of man and citizen:

1. Men are born and remain free and equal in rights; social distinctions can be established only for the common benefit.
2. The aim of every political association is the conservation of the natural and imprescriptible rights of man; these rights are liberty, property, security, and resistance to oppression.
3. The source of all sovereignty is located in essence in the nation; no body, no individual can exercise authority which does not emanate from it expressly.
4. Liberty consists in being able to do anything that does not harm another person. . . .
6. The law is the expression of the general will; all citizens have the right to concur personally or through their representatives in its formation; it must be the same for all, whether it protects or punishes. All citizens being equal in its eyes are equally admissible to all honors, positions, and public employments, according to their capabilities and without other distinctions than those of their virtues and talents.
7. No man can be accused, arrested, or detained except in cases determined by the law, and according to the forms which it has prescribed. . . .
10. No one may be disturbed because of his opinions, even religious, provided that their public demonstration does not disturb the public order established by law.
11. The free communication of thoughts and opinions is one of the most precious rights of man: every citizen can therefore freely speak, write, and print. . . .
12. The guaranteeing of the rights of man and citizen necessitates a public force; this force is therefore instituted for the advantage of all, and not for the private use of those to whom it is entrusted. . . .
14. Citizens have the right to determine for themselves or through their representatives the need for taxation of the public, to consent to it freely, to investigate its use, and to determine its rate, basis, collection, and duration.
15. Society has the right to demand an accounting of his administration from every public agent.
16. Any society in which guarantees of rights are not assured nor the separation of powers determined has no constitution.
17. Property being an inviolable and sacred right, no one may be deprived of it unless public necessity, legally determined, clearly requires such action, and then only on condition of a just and prior indemnity.

powers not subject to review by the new Legislative Assembly. The Legislative Assembly, in which sovereign power was vested, was to sit for two years and consist of 745 representatives chosen by an indirect system of election that preserved power in the hands of the more affluent members of society. A distinction was drawn between active and passive citizens. While all had the same civil rights, only active citizens (those men over the age of twenty-five paying taxes equivalent in value to three days' unskilled labor) could vote. The active citizens probably numbered 4.3 million in 1790. These citizens did not elect the members of the Legislative Assembly directly, but voted for electors (those men paying taxes equal in value to ten days' labor). This relatively small group of 50,000 electors chose the deputies. To qualify as a deputy, one had to pay at least

❧ *Declaration of the Rights of Woman and the Female Citizen* ❧

O lympe de Gouges (a pen name for Marie Gouze) was a butcher's daughter who wrote plays and pamphlets. She argued that the Declaration of the Rights of Man and the Citizen did not apply to women and composed her own Declaration of the Rights of Woman in 1791.

...Declaration of the Rights of Woman and the Female Citizen

. . . .Mothers, daughters, sisters and representatives of the nation demand to be constituted into a national assembly. Believing that ignorance, omission, or scorn for the rights of woman are the only causes of public misfortunes and of the corruption of governments, the women have resolved to set forth in a solemn declaration the natural, inalienable, and sacred rights of woman in order that this declaration, constantly exposed before all the members of the society, will ceaselessly remind them of their rights and duties. . . .

Consequently, the sex that is as superior in beauty as it is in courage during the sufferings of maternity recognizes and declares in the presence and under the auspices of the Supreme Being, the following Rights of Woman and of Female Citizens.

1. Woman is born free and lives equal to man in her rights. Social distinctions can be based only on the common utility.
2. The purpose of any political association is the conservation of the natural and imprescriptible rights of woman and man; these rights are liberty, property, security, and especially resistance to oppression.
3. The principle of all sovereignty rests essentially with the nation, which is nothing but the union of woman and man; no body and no individual can exercise any authority which does not come expressly from it [the nation].
4. Liberty and justice consist of restoring all that belongs to others; thus, the only limits on the exercise of the natural rights of woman are perpetual male tyranny; these limits are to be reformed by the laws of nature and reason.
6. The law must be the expression of the general will; all female and male citizens must contribute either personally or through their representatives to its formation; it must be the same for all: male and female citizens, being equal in the eyes of the law, must be equally admitted to all honors, positions, and public employment according to their capacity and without other distinctions besides those of their virtues and talents.
7. No woman is an exception; she is accused, arrested, and detained in cases determined by law. Women, like men, obey this rigorous law.
10. No one is to be disquieted for his very basic opinions; woman has the right to mount the scaffold; she must equally have the right to mount the rostrum, provided that her demonstrations do not disturb the legally established public order.
11. The free communication of thoughts and opinions is one of the most precious rights of woman, since that liberty assured the recognition of children by their fathers. . . .
12. The guarantee of the rights of woman and the female citizen implies a major benefit; this guarantee must be instituted for the advantage of all, and not for the particular benefit of those to whom it is entrusted.
14. Female and male citizens have the right to verify, either by themselves or through their representatives, the necessity of the public contribution. This can only apply to women if they are granted an equal share, not only of wealth, but also of public administration, and in the determination of the proportion, the base, the collection, and the duration of the tax.
15. The collectivity of women, joined for tax purposes to the aggregate of men, has the right to demand an accounting of his administration from any public agent.
16. No society has a constitution without the guarantee of rights and the separation of powers; the constitution is null if the majority of individuals comprising the nation have not cooperated in drafting it.
17. Property belongs to both sexes whether united or separate; for each it is an inviolable and sacred right; no one can be deprived of it, since it is the true patrimony of nature, unless the legally determined public need obviously dictates it, and then only with a just and prior indemnity. . . .

a "silver mark" in taxes, an amount equivalent to fifty-four days' labor.

The National Assembly also undertook an administrative restructuring of France. In 1789, it abolished all the old local and provincial divisions and divided France into eighty-three departments, roughly equal in size and population. In turn, departments were divided into districts and communes, all supervised by elected councils and officials who oversaw financial, administrative, judicial, and ecclesiastical institutions within their domains. Although both bourgeoisie and aristocrats were eligible for offices based on property qualifications, few nobles were elected, leaving local and departmental governments in the hands of the bourgeoisie, especially lawyers of various types.

By 1791, France had moved into a revolutionary reordering of the old regime that had been achieved by a revolutionary consensus that was largely the work of the wealthier bourgeoisie. By mid-1791, however, this consensus faced growing opposition from clerics angered by the Civil Constitution of the Clergy, lower classes hurt by the rise in the cost of living resulting from the inflation of the assignats, peasants who remained opposed to dues that had still not been abandoned, and political clubs offering more radical solutions to the nation's problems. The most famous were the Jacobins, who first emerged as a gathering of more radical deputies at the beginning of the Revolution, especially during the events of the night of August 4, 1789. After October 1789, they occupied the former Jacobin convent in Paris. Jacobin clubs also formed in the provinces where they served primarily as discussion groups. Eventually, they joined together in an extensive correspondence network and, by spring 1790, were seeking affiliation with the Parisian club. One year later, there were 900 Jacobin clubs in France associated with the Parisian center. Members were usually the elite of their local societies, but they also included artisans and tradesmen.

In addition, by mid-1791, the government was still facing severe financial difficulties due to massive tax evasion. Despite all of their problems, however, the bourgeois politicians in charge remained relatively unified on the basis of their trust in the king. But Louis XVI disastrously undercut them. Quite upset with the whole turn of revolutionary events, he sought to flee France in June 1791 and almost succeeded before being recognized, captured at Varennes, and brought back to Paris. While radicals called for the king to be deposed, the members of the National Assembly, fearful of the popular forces in Paris calling for a republic, chose to ignore the king's flight and pretended that he had been kidnapped. In this unsettled situation, with a discredited and seemingly disloyal monarch, the new Legislative Assembly held its first session in October 1791.

Because the National Assembly had passed a "self-denying ordinance" that prohibited the reelection of its members, the composition of the Legislative Assembly tended to be quite different from that of the National Assembly. The clerics and nobles were largely gone. Most of the representatives were men of property; many were lawyers. Although lacking national reputations, most had gained experience in the new revolutionary politics and prominence in their local areas through the National Guard, the Jacobin clubs, and the many elective offices spawned by the administrative reordering of France. The king made what seemed to be a genuine effort to work with the new Legislative Assembly, but France's relations with the rest of Europe soon led to Louis's downfall.

Over a period of time, some European countries had become concerned about the French example and feared that revolution would spread to their countries. On August 27, 1791, Emperor Leopold II of Austria and King Frederick William II of Prussia issued the Declaration of Pillnitz, which invited other European monarchs to take "the most effectual means . . . to put the king of France in a state to strengthen, in the most perfect liberty, the bases of a monarchical government equally becoming to the rights of sovereigns and to the wellbeing of the French Nation."[6] But European monarchs were too suspicious of each other to undertake such a plan, and in any case French enthusiasm for war led the Legislative Assembly to declare war on Austria on April 20, 1792. But why take such a step in view of its obvious dangers? Many people in France wanted war. Reactionaries hoped that a preoccupation with war would cool off the Revolution; French defeat, which seemed likely in view of the army's disintegration, might even lead to the restoration of the old regime. Leftists hoped that war would consolidate the Revolution at home and spread it to all of Europe.

The French fared badly in the initial fighting, and loud recriminations were soon heard in Paris. A frantic search for scapegoats began; as one observer noted, "Everywhere you hear the cry that the king is betraying us, the generals are betraying us, that nobody is to be trusted; . . . that Paris will be taken in six weeks by the Austrians . . . we are on a volcano ready to spout flames."[7] Defeats in war coupled with economic shortages in the spring reinvigorated popular groups that had been dormant since the previous summer and led to renewed political demonstrations, especially against the king. Radical Parisian political groups, declaring themselves an insurrectionary commune, organized a mob attack on the royal palace and Legislative Assembly in August 1792, took the king captive, and forced the Legislative Assembly to suspend the monarchy and call for a National Convention, chosen on the basis of universal male suffrage, to decide on the future form of government. The French Revolution was about to enter a more radical stage as power passed from the assembly to the new Paris Commune, composed of many who proudly called themselves the sans-culottes, ordinary patriots without fine clothes. Although it has become customary to equate the more radical sans-culottes with working people or the poor, many were merchants and better-off artisans who were often the elite of their neighborhoods and trades.

The Radical Revolution

Before the National Convention met, the Paris Commune dominated the political scene. Led by the newly appointed minister of justice, Georges Danton, the sans-culottes sought revenge on those who had aided the king and resisted the popular will. Thousands of presumed traitors were arrested and then massacred as ordinary Parisian tradesmen and artisans solved the problem of overcrowded prisons by mass executions of their inmates. In September 1792, the newly elected National Convention began its sessions. Although it was called to draft a new constitution, it also acted as the sovereign ruling body of France.

Socially, the composition of the National Convention was similar to its predecessors. Dominated by lawyers, professionals, and property owners, it also included for the first time a handful of artisans. Two-thirds of the deputies were under forty-five, and almost all had had political experience as a result of the Revolution. Almost all were also intensely distrustful of the king and his activities. It was therefore no surprise that the convention's first major step on September 21 was to abolish the monarchy and establish a republic. But that was about as far as members of the convention could agree, and the National Convention soon split into factions over the fate of the king. The two most important were the Girondins and the Mountain. Both were members of the Jacobin club.

Representing primarily the provinces, the Girondins came to fear the radical mobs in Paris and were disposed to keep the king alive as a hedge against future eventualities. The Mountain, on the other hand, represented the interests of the city of Paris and owed much of its strength to the radical and popular elements in the city, although the members of the Mountain themselves were middle class. The Mountain won out at the beginning of

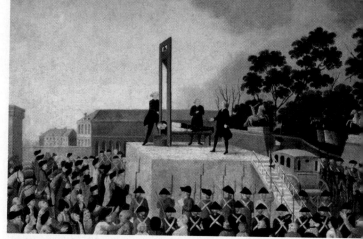

✦ **Execution of the King.** At the beginning of 1793, the National Convention decreed the death of the king, and on January 21 of that year, Louis XVI was executed. As seen in this painting, the execution of the king was accomplished by the new revolutionary device of the guillotine.

1793 when they passed a decree condemning Louis XVI to death, although by a very narrow margin. On January 21, 1793, the king was executed and the destruction of the old regime was complete. Now there could be no turning back. But the execution of the king produced new challenges by creating new enemies for the Revolution both at home and abroad while strengthening those who were already its enemies.

Factional disputes between Girondins and the Mountain were only one aspect of France's domestic crisis in 1792 and 1793. Within Paris the local government was controlled by the Commune, which drew a number of its leaders from the city's artisans and shopkeepers. The Commune favored radical change and put constant pressure on the National Convention, pushing it to ever more radical positions. As one man warned his fellow deputies, "Never forget that you were sent here by the sansculottes."[8] At the end of May and the beginning of June 1793, the Commune organized a demonstration, invaded the National Convention, and forced the arrest and execution of the leading Girondins, thus leaving the Mountain in control of the convention. The National Convention itself still did not rule all France. The authority of the convention was repudiated in western France, particularly in the department of the Vendée, by peasants who revolted against the new military draft (see A Nation in Arms later in this chapter). The Vendéan rebellion soon escalated into a full-blown counterrevolutionary appeal: "Long live the king and our good priests. We want our king, our priests and the old regime." Some of France's major provincial cities, including Lyons and Marseilles, also began to break away from central authority. Arguing as Marseilles did that "it is time for the anarchy of a few men of blood to stop,"[9] these cities favored a decentralized republic to free themselves from the ascendancy of Paris. In no way did they favor breaking up the "indivisible Republic."

Domestic turmoil was paralleled by a foreign crisis. By the beginning of 1793, after the king had been executed, much of Europe—an informal coalition of Austria, Prussia, Spain, Portugal, Britain, and the Dutch Republic—was pitted against France. Carried away by initial successes and their own rhetoric, the French welcomed the struggle. Danton exclaimed to the convention: "They threaten you with kings! You have thrown down your gauntlet to them, and this gauntlet is a king's head, the signal of their coming death."[10] Grossly overextended, the French armies began to experience reverses, and by late spring some members of the anti-French coalition were poised for an invasion of France. If successful, both the Revolution and the revolutionaries would be destroyed and the old regime reestablished. The Revolution had reached a decisive moment.

To meet these crises, the program of the National Convention became one of curbing anarchy and counterrevolution at home while attempting to win the war by a great national mobilization. To administer the government, the convention gave broad powers to an executive committee known as the Committee of Public Safety, which was dominated initially by Danton. Maximilien Robespierre eventually became one of its most important members. For a twelve-month period, from 1793 to 1794, virtually the same twelve members were reelected and gave the country the leadership it needed to weather the domestic and foreign crises of 1793.

A NATION IN ARMS

To meet the foreign crisis and save the Republic from its foreign enemies, the Committee of Public Safety decreed a universal mobilization of the nation on August 23, 1793:

> Young men will fight, young men are called to conquer. Married men will forge arms, transport military baggage and guns and will prepare food supplies. Women, who at long last are to take their rightful place in the revolution and follow their true destiny, will forget their futile tasks: their delicate hands will work at making clothes for soldiers; they will make tents and they will extend their tender care to shelters where the defenders of the Patrie will receive the help that their wounds require. Children will make lint of old cloth. It is for them that we are fighting: children, those beings destined to gather all the fruits of the revolution, will raise their pure hands toward the skies. And old men, performing their missions again, as of yore, will be guided to the public squares of the cities where they will kindle the courage of young warriors and preach the doctrines of hate for kings and the unity of the Republic.[11]

In less than a year, the French revolutionary government had raised an army of 650,000; by September 1794, it numbered 1,169,000. The Republic's army was the largest ever seen in European history. It now pushed the allies back across the Rhine and even conquered the Austrian Netherlands. By May 1795, the anti-French coalition of 1793 was breaking up.

Historians have focused on the importance of the French revolutionary army in the creation of modern nationalism. Previously, wars had been fought between governments or ruling dynasties by relatively small armies of professional soldiers. The new French army, however, was the creation of a "people's" government; its wars were now "people's" wars. The entire nation was to be involved in the war. But when dynastic wars became people's wars, warfare increased in ferocity and lack of restraint. Although innocent civilians had suffered in the earlier struggles, now the carnage became appalling at times. The wars of the French revolutionary era opened the door to the total war of the modern world.

THE COMMITTEE OF PUBLIC SAFETY AND THE REIGN OF TERROR

To meet the domestic crisis, the National Convention and the Committee of Public Safety established the "Reign of Terror." Revolutionary courts were organized to protect the revolutionary Republic from its internal enemies, those "who either by their conduct, their contacts, their words or their writings, showed themselves to be supporters of tyranny or enemies of liberty," or those "who have not constantly manifested their attachment to the revolution."[12] Victims of the Terror ranged from royalists, such as Queen Marie Antoinette, to former revolutionary Girondins, including Olympe de Gouges, the chief advocate for political rights for women, and even included thousands of peasants. Many victims were persons who had opposed the radical activities of the sans-culottes (see the box on p. 692). In the course of nine months, 16,000 people were officially killed under the blade of the guillotine, the latter a revolutionary device for the quick and efficient separation of heads from bodies. But the true number of the Terror's victims was probably closer to 50,000. The bulk of the Terror's executions took place in the Vendée and in cities such as Lyons and Marseilles, places that had been in open rebellion against the authority of the National Convention.

Military force in the form of Revolutionary Armies was used to bring recalcitrant cities and districts back under the control of the National Convention. Marseilles fell to a Revolutionary Army in August. Starving Lyons surrendered early in October after two months of bombardment and resistance. Since Lyons was France's second city after Paris and had defied the National Convention during a time when the Republic was in peril, the Committee of Public Safety decided to

◆ **Citizens Enlist in the New French Army.** To save the Republic from its foreign enemies, the National Convention created a new revolutionary army of unprecedented size. In this painting, citizens joyfully hasten to sign up at the recruitment tables set up in the streets. On this occasion, officials are distributing coins to those who have enrolled.

make an example of it. By April 1794, 1,880 citizens of Lyons had been executed. When guillotining proved too slow, cannon fire and grape shot were used to blow condemned men into open graves. A German observed:

> . . . whole ranges of houses, always the most handsome, burnt. The churches, convents, and all the dwellings of the former patricians were in ruins. When I came to the guillotine, the blood of those who had been executed a few hours beforehand was still running in the street . . . I said to a group of sansculottes that it would be decent to clear away all this human blood. Why should it be cleared? one of them said to me. It's the blood of aristocrats and rebels. The dogs should lick it up.[13]

In the Vendée, Revolutionary Armies were also brutal in defeating the rebel armies. After destroying one army on December 12, the commander of the Revolutionary Army ordered that no quarter be given: "The road to Laval is strewn with corpses. Women, priests, monks, children, all have been put to death. I have spared nobody." The Terror was at its most destructive in the Vendée. Forty-two percent of the death sentences during the Terror were passed in territories affected by the Vendée rebellion. Perhaps the most notorious act of violence occurred in Nantes where victims were executed by sinking them in barges in the Loire River.

Contrary to popular opinion, the Terror demonstrated no class prejudice. Estimates are that the nobles constituted 8 percent of its victims, the middle classes,

A Victim of the Reign of Terror

The Reign of Terror created a repressive environment in which even quite innocent people could be accused of crimes against the Republic. As seen in this letter by Anne-Félicité Guinée, wife of a wig maker, merely insulting an official could lead to arrest and imprisonment.

Letter of Anne-Félicité Guinée

Citizen Anne-Félicité Guinée, twenty-four years old . . . informs you that she was arrested at the Place des Droits de l'Homme, where I had gone to get butter. I point out to you that for a long time I have had to feed the members in my household on bread and cheese and that, tired of complaints from my husband and my boys, I was compelled to go wait in line to get something to eat. For three days I had been going to the same market without being able to get anything, despite the fact that I had waited from 7 or 8 A.M. until 5 or 6 P.M. After the distribution of butter on the twenty-second, . . . a citizen came over to me and said that I was in very delicate condition. To that I answered, "You can't be delicate and be on your legs for so long. I wouldn't have come if there were any other food." He replied that I needed to drink milk. I answered that I had men in my house who worked and that I couldn't nourish them with milk, that I was convinced that if he, the speaker, was sensitive to the difficulty of obtaining food, he would not vex me so, and that he was an imbecile and wanted to play despot, and no one had that right. Here, on the spot, I was arrested and brought to the guard house. I wanted to explain myself. I was silenced and dragged off to prison. . . .

About 7 P.M., I was led to the Revolutionary Committee [of the section], where I was called a counterrevolutionary and was told I was asking for the guillotine because I told them I preferred death to being treated ignominiously the way he was treating me. . . . I was asked if I knew whom I had called a despot. I answered, "I didn't know him," and I was told that he was the commander of the post. I said that he was more [a commander] beneath his own roof than anyone, given that he was there to maintain order and not to provoke bad feelings. . . . I was told that I had done three times more than was needed to get the guillotine and that I would be explaining myself before the Revolutionary Tribunal. The next day, I was taken to the Revolutionary Committee, which, without waiting to hear me, had me taken to the Mairie, where I stayed for nine days without a bed or a chair with vermin and with women addicted to all sorts of crimes. . . .

On the ninth day I was transferred to the prison of La Force. . . . In the end I can give you only the very slightest idea of all the horrors that are committed in these terrible prisons. . . . I was thrown together not with women but with monsters who gloried in all their crimes and who gave themselves over to all the most horrible excesses. One day, two of them fought each other with knives. Day and night I lived in mortal fear. The food that was sent in to me was grabbed away immediately. That was my cruel situation for seventeen days. My whole body was swollen from . . . the poor treatment I had endured. . . . [Anne-Félicité Guinée was discharged provisionally after the authorities realized that she was pregnant.]

25, the clergy, 6, and the peasant and laboring classes, 60. To the Committee of Public Safety, this bloodletting was only a temporary expedient. Once the war and domestic emergency were over, "the republic of virtue" would ensue, and the Declaration of the Rights of Man and the Citizen would be fully established. Although theoretically a republic, the French government during the Terror was led by a group of twelve men who ordered the execution of people as enemies of the Republic. But how did they justify this? Saint-Just, one of the younger members of the Committee of Public Safety explained their rationalization in a speech to the convention: "Since the French people has manifested its will, everything opposed to it is outside the sovereign. Whatever is outside the sovereign is an enemy."[14] Clearly, Saint-Just

was referring to Rousseau's concept of the general will, but it is equally apparent that these twelve men, in the name of the Republic, had taken to themselves the right to ascertain the sovereign will of the French people (see the box on p. 694) and to kill their enemies as "outside the sovereign."

THE "REPUBLIC OF VIRTUE"

Along with the Terror, the Committee of Public Safety took other steps both to control France and to create a new republican order and new republican citizens. By spring 1793, they were sending "representatives on mission" as agents of the central government to all departments to explain the war emergency measures and to implement the laws dealing with the wartime emergency.

The committee also attempted to provide some economic controls, especially since members of the more radical working class were advocating them. They established a system of requisitioning food supplies for the cities enforced by the forays of Revolutionary Armies into the countryside. The Law of the General Maximum established price controls on goods declared of first necessity ranging from food and drink to fuel and clothing. The controls failed to work very well since the government lacked the machinery to enforce them.

Women continued to play an active role in this radical phase of the French Revolution. As spectators at sessions of revolutionary clubs and the National Con-

vention, women made the members and deputies aware of their demands. When on Sunday, February 25, 1793, a group of women appealed formally to the National Convention for lower bread prices, the convention reacted by adjourning until Tuesday. The women responded bitterly by accosting the deputies: "We are adjourned until Tuesday; but as for us, we adjourn ourselves until Monday. When our children ask us for milk, we don't adjourn them until the day after tomorrow."[15] In 1793, two women—an actress and a chocolate manufacturer—founded the Society for Revolutionary Republican Women. Composed largely of working-class women, this Parisian group viewed themselves as a "family of sisters" and vowed "to rush to the defense of the Fatherland."

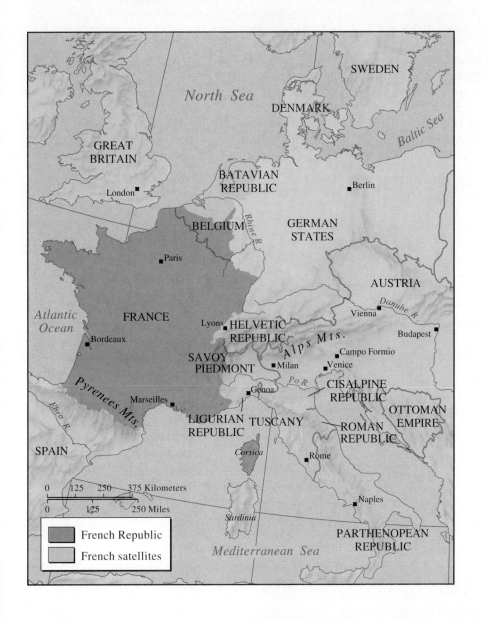

Map 20.2 French Conquests during the Revolutionary Wars.

Robespierre and Revolutionary Government

In its time of troubles, the National Convention, under the direction of the Committee of Public Safety, instituted a Reign of Terror to preserve the Revolution from its internal enemies. In this selection, Maximilien Robespierre, one of the committee's leading members, tries to justify the violence to which these believers in republican liberty resorted.

Robespierre, Speech on Revolutionary Government

The theory of revolutionary government is as new as the Revolution that created it. It is as pointless to seek its origins in the books of the political theorists, who failed to foresee this revolution, as in the laws of the tyrants, who are happy enough to abuse their exercise of authority without seeking out its legal justification. And so this phrase is for the aristocracy a mere subject of terror or a term of slander, for tyrants an outrage and for many an enigma. It behooves us to explain it to all in order that we may rally good citizens, at least, in support of the principles governing the public interest.

It is the function of government to guide the moral and physical energies of the nation toward the purposes for which it was established.

The object of constitutional government is to preserve the Republic; the object of revolutionary government is to establish it.

Revolution is the war waged by liberty against its enemies; a constitution is that which crowns the edifice of freedom once victory has been won and the nation is at peace.

The revolutionary government has to summon extraordinary activity to its aid precisely because it is at war. It is subjected to less binding and less uniform regulations, because the circumstances in which it finds itself are tempestuous and shifting above all because it is compelled to deploy, swiftly and incessantly, new resources to meet new and pressing dangers.

The principal concern of constitutional government is civil liberty; that of revolutionary government, public liberty. Under a constitutional government little more is required than to protect the individual against abuses by the state, whereas revolutionary government is obliged to defend the state itself against the factions that assail it from every quarter.

To good citizens revolutionary government owes the full protection of the state; to the enemies of the people it owes only death.

Despite the importance of women to the revolutionary cause, male revolutionaries reacted disdainfully to female participation in political activity. In the radical phase of the Revolution, the Paris Commune outlawed women's clubs and forbade women to be present at its meetings. One of its members explained why:

> It is horrible, it is contrary to all laws of nature for a woman to want to make herself a man. The Council must recall that some time ago these denatured women, these viragos, wandered through the markets with the red cap to sully that badge of liberty and wanted to force all women to take off the modest headdress that is appropriate for them [the bonnet]. . . . Is it the place of women to propose motions? Is it the place of women to place themselves at the head of our armies?[16]

Most men—whether radical or conservative—agreed that a woman's place was in the home and not in military or political affairs. As one man asked, "Since when is it considered normal for a woman to abandon the pious care of her home, the cradle of her children, to listen to speeches in the public forum?"[17]

In its attempt to create a new order, the National Convention also pursued a policy of dechristianization. The word "saint" was removed from street names, churches were pillaged and closed by Revolutionary Armies, and priests were encouraged to marry. In Paris, the cathedral of Notre Dame was designated a Temple of Reason. In November 1793, a public ceremony dedicated to the worship of reason was held in the former cathedral; patriotic maidens adorned in white dresses paraded before a temple of reason where the high altar once stood. At the end of the ceremony, a female figure personifying Liberty rose out of the temple. As Robespierre came to realize, dechristianization backfired because France was still overwhelmingly Catholic. In fact, dechristianization created more enemies than friends.

Yet another manifestation of dechristianization was the adoption of a new republican calendar on October 5, 1793. Years would would no longer be numbered from the birth of Christ but from September 22, 1792, the day the French Republic was proclaimed. Thus, at the time the calendar was adopted, the French were already living in year two. The calendar contained twelve months; each month consisted of three ten-day weeks (*décades*) with the tenth day of each week a rest-day (*décadi*). This eliminated Sundays and Sunday worship services and put an end to the ordering of French lives by a Christian calendar that emphasized Sundays, saints' days, and church holidays and festivals. The latter were to be replaced by revolutionary festivals. Especially important were the five days (six in leap years) left over in the calendar at the end of the year. These days were to form a half-week of festivals to celebrate the revolutionary virtues—Virtue, Intelligence, Labor, Opinion, and Rewards. The sixth extra day in a leap year would be a special festival day when Frenchmen would "come from all parts of the Republic to celebrate liberty and equality, to cement by their embraces the national fraternity." Of course, ending church holidays also reduced the number of nonworking holidays from fifty-six to thirty-two, a goal long recommended by eighteenth-century economic theorists.

The anti-Christian purpose of the calendar was reinforced in the naming of the months of the year. The months were given names that were supposed to evoke the seasons, the temperature, or the state of the vegetation: Vendémiaire (harvest—the first month of thirty days beginning September 22), Brumaire (mist), Frimaire (frost), Nivôse (snow), Pluviôse (rain), Ventôse (wind), Germinal (seeding), Floréal (flowering), Prairial (meadows), Messidor (wheat harvest), Thermidor (heat), and Fructidor (ripening).

The new calendar faced intense popular opposition, and the revolutionary government relied primarily on coercion to win its acceptance. Journalists, for example, were commanded to use republican dates in their newspaper articles. But many people refused to give up the old calendar, as one official reported:

> Sundays and Catholic holidays, even if there are ten in a row, have for some time been celebrated with as much pomp and splendor as before. The same cannot be said of *décadi*, which is observed by only a small handful of citizens. The first to disobey the law are the wives of public officials, who dress up on the holidays of the old calendar and abstain from work more religiously than anyone else.[18]

The government could hardly expect peasants to follow the new calendar when government officials were ignoring it. Napoleon later perceived that the revolutionary calendar was politically unpopular, and he simply abandoned it on January 1, 1806.

In addition to its anti-Christian function, the revolutionary calendar had also served to mark the Revolution as a new historical beginning, a radical break in time.

Revolutionary upheavals often project millenarian expectations, the hope that a new age is dawning. The revolutionary dream of a new order presupposed the creation of a new human being freed from the old order and its symbols, a new citizen surrounded by a framework of new habits. Restructuring time itself offered the opportunity to forge new habits and create a lasting new order.

But maintaining the revolutionary ideals was not easy. By the Law of 14 Frimaire (passed on December 4, 1793), the Committee of Public Safety sought to centralize the administration of France more effectively and to exercise greater control in order to check the excesses of the Reign of Terror. The activities of both the representatives on mission and the Revolutionary Armies were scrutinized more carefully, and the campaign against Christianity was also dampened. Finally, in 1794, the Committee of Public Safety turned against its radical Parisian supporters, executed the leaders of the revolutionary Paris Commune, and turned it into a docile tool. This might have been a good idea for the sake of order, but in suppressing the people who had been its chief supporters, the National Convention alienated an important group. At the same time, the French had been successful against their foreign foes. The military successes meant that the Terror no longer served much purpose. But the Terror continued because Robespierre, now its dominant figure, had become obsessed with purifying the body politic of all the corrupt. Only then could the Republic of Virtue follow. Many deputies in the National Convention feared, however,

✦ **Women Patriots.** Women played a variety of roles in the events of the French Revolution. This picture shows a women's patriotic club discussing the decrees of the National Convention, an indication that some women had become highly politicized by the upheavals of the Revolution.

that they were not safe while Robespierre was free to act. An anti-Robespierre coalition in the National Convention, eager now to destroy Robespierre before he destroyed them, gathered enough votes to condemn him. Robespierre was guillotined on July 28, 1794, beginning a reaction that brought an end to this radical stage of the French Revolution.

The National Convention and its Committee of Public Safety had accomplished a great deal. By creating a nation-in-arms, they preserved the French Revolution and prevented it from being destroyed by its foreign enemies, who, if they had been successful, would have reestablished the old monarchical order. Domestically, the Revolution had also been saved from the forces of counterrevolution. The committee's tactics, however, provided an example for the use of violence in domestic politics that has continued to bedevil the Western world until this day.

Reaction and the Directory

After the death of Robespierre on July 28, 1794, revolutionary fervor began to give way to the Thermidorean Reaction, named after the month of Thermidor. The

◆ **Robespierre.** Maximilien Robespierre eventually came to exercise much control over the Committee of Public Safety. Robespierre and the committee worked to centralize the administration of France and curb the excesses of the Reign of Terror. However, fear of Robespierre led many in the National Convention to condemn him, and on July 28, 1794, he was executed.

Terror began to abate. The National Convention curtailed the power of the Committee of Public Safety, shut down the Jacobin club, and attempted to provide better protection for its deputies against the Parisian mobs. Churches were allowed to reopen for public worship while a decree of February 21, 1795, gave freedom of worship to all cults. Economic regulation was dropped in favor of laissez-faire policies, another clear indication that moderate forces were again gaining control of the Revolution. In addition, a new constitution was created in August 1795 that reflected this more conservative republicanism or a desire for a stability that did not sacrifice the ideals of 1789.

To avoid the dangers of another single legislative assembly, the Constitution of 1795 established a national legislative assembly consisting of two chambers: a lower house, known as the Council of 500, whose function was to initiate legislation, and an upper house of 250 members, the Council of Elders, composed of married or widowed members over forty, which accepted or rejected the proposed laws. The 750 members of the two legislative bodies were chosen by electors who had to be owners or renters of property worth between 100 and 200 days' labor, a requirement that limited their number to 30,000, an even smaller base than the Constitution of 1791 had provided. The electors were chosen by the active citizens, now defined as all male taxpayers over twenty-one. The Council of Elders elected five directors from a list presented by the Council of 500 to act as the executive authority or Directory. To ensure some continuity from the old order to the new, the members of the National Convention ruled that two-thirds of the new members of the National Assembly must be chosen from their ranks. This produced disturbances in Paris and an insurrection at the beginning of October that was dispersed after fierce combat by an army contingent under the artillery general Napoleon Bonaparte. This would be the last time in the great French Revolution that the city of Paris would attempt to impose its wishes on the central government. Even more significant and ominous was this use of the army, which made it clear that the Directory from the beginning had to rely upon the military for survival.

The period of the Directory was an era of stagnation, corruption, and graft, a materialistic reaction to the sufferings and sacrifices that had been demanded in the Reign of Terror and the Republic of Virtue. Speculators made fortunes in property by taking advantage of the government's severe monetary problems. Elaborate fashions, which had gone out of style because of their identification with the nobility, were worn again. Gambling and roulette became popular once more.

The government of the Directory was faced with political enemies from both the left and the right of the political spectrum. On the right, royalists who dreamed of restoring the monarchy continued their agitation; some still toyed with violent means. On the left, Jacobin hopes of power were revived by continuing economic problems, especially the total collapse in the value of the assignats. Some radicals even went beyond earlier goals, especially Gracchus Babeuf who raised the question "What is the French Revolution? An open war between patricians and plebeians, between rich and poor." Babeuf, who was appalled at the misery of the common people, wanted to abolish private property and eliminate private enterprise. His Conspiracy of Equals was crushed in 1796, and he was executed in 1797.

New elections in 1797 created even more uncertainty and instability. Battered by the left and right, unable to find a definitive solution to the country's economic problems, and still carrying on the wars left from the Committee of Public Safety, the Directory increasingly relied on the military to maintain its power. This led to a coup d'etat in 1799 in which the successful and popular general Napoleon Bonaparte was able to seize power.

The Age of Napoleon

Napoleon dominated both French and European history from 1799 to 1815. The coup d'etat that brought him to power occurred exactly ten years after the outbreak of the French Revolution. In a sense, Napoleon brought the Revolution to an end in 1799, but Napoleon was also a child of the Revolution; he called himself the son of the Revolution. The French Revolution had made possible his rise first in the military and then to supreme power in France. Even beyond this, Napoleon had once said, "I am the revolution," and he never ceased to remind the French that they owed to him the preservation of all that was beneficial in the revolutionary program.

The Rise of Napoleon

Napoleon was born in Corsica in 1769, only a few months after France had annexed the island. The son of a lawyer whose family stemmed from the Florentine nobility, the young Napoleon obtained a royal scholarship to study at a military school in France. His educa-

◆ **Napoleon as a Young Officer.** Napoleon had risen quickly through the military ranks, being promoted to the rank of brigadier general at the age of twenty-five. This painting of Napoleon by the Romantic painter Baron Gros presents an idealized, heroic image of the young Napoleon.

tion in French military schools led to his commission in 1785 as a lieutenant, although he was not well liked by his fellow officers because he was short, spoke with an Italian accent, and had little money. For the next seven years, Napoleon spent much of his time reading the works of the philosophes and educating himself in military matters by studying the campaigns of great military leaders from the past. The French Revolution and the European war that followed broadened his sights and presented him with new opportunities.

Napoleon rose quickly through the ranks. In 1792, he became a captain and in the following year performed so well as an artillery commander that he was promoted to the rank of brigadier general in 1794, when he was only twenty-five. In October 1795, he saved the National Convention from the Parisian mob and in 1796 was made commander of the French army in Italy (see the box on p. 698). There he turned a group of ill-disciplined soldiers into an effective fighting force and, in a series of stunning victories, defeated the Austrians and dictated peace to them in 1797. Throughout his

Napoleon and Psychological Warfare

In 1796, at the age of twenty-seven, Napoleon Bonaparte was given command of the French army in Italy where he won a series of stunning victories. His use of speed, deception, and surprise to overwhelm his opponents is well known. In this selection from a proclamation to his troops in Italy, Napoleon also appears as a master of psychological warfare.

Napoleon Bonaparte, Proclamation to the French Troops in Italy (April 26, 1796)

Soldiers:

In a fortnight you have won six victories, taken twenty-one standards, fifty-five pieces of artillery, several strong positions, and conquered the richest part of Piedmont [in northern Italy]; you have captured 15,000 prisoners and killed or wounded more than 10,000 men. . . . You have won battles without cannon, crossed rivers without bridges, made forced marches without shoes, camped without brandy and often without bread. Soldiers of liberty, only republican troops could have endured what you have endured. Soldiers, you have our thanks! The grateful Patrie [nation] will owe its prosperity to you. . . .

The two armies which but recently attacked you with audacity are fleeing before you in terror; the wicked men who laughed at your misery and rejoiced at the thought of the triumphs of your enemies are confounded and trembling.

But, soldiers, as yet you have done nothing compared with what remains to be done. . . . Undoubtedly the greatest obstacles have been overcome; but you still have battles to fight, cities to capture, rivers to cross. Is there one among you whose courage is abating? No. . . . All of you are consumed with a desire to extend the glory of the French people; all of you long to humiliate those arrogant kings who dare to contemplate placing us in fetters; all of you desire to dictate a glorious peace, one which will indemnify the Patrie for the immense sacrifices it has made; all of you wish to be able to say with pride as you return to your villages, "I was with the victorious army of Italy!"

Italian campaigns, Napoleon won the confidence of his men by his energy, charm, and ability to comprehend complex issues quickly and make decisions rapidly. These qualities, combined with his keen intelligence, ease with words, and supreme confidence in himself, enabled him throughout the rest of his life to influence people and win their firm support (see the box on p. 699).

In 1797, Napoleon returned to France as a conquering hero and was given command of an army in training to invade England. Believing that the French were unready for such an invasion, he proposed instead to strike indirectly at Britain by taking Egypt and threatening India, a major source of British wealth. But the British controlled the seas and, by 1799, had cut off supplies from Napoleon's army in Egypt. Seeing no future in certain defeat, Napoleon did not hesitate to abandon his army and return to Paris where he participated in the coup d'etat that ultimately led to his virtual dictatorship of France. He was only thirty years old at the time.

With the coup d'etat of 1799, a new form of the Republic was proclaimed with a constitution that established a bicameral legislative assembly elected indirectly to reduce the role of elections. Executive power in the new government was vested in the hands of three consuls although as Article 42 of the constitution said, "The decision of the First Consul shall suffice." As first consul, Napoleon directly controlled the entire executive authority of government. He had overwhelming influence over the legislature, appointed members of the bureaucracy, controlled the army, and conducted foreign affairs. In 1802, Napoleon was made consul for life and in 1804 returned France to monarchy when he crowned himself as Emperor Napoleon I. This step undoubtedly satisfied his enormous ego but also stabilized the regime and provided a permanency not possible in the consulate. The revolutionary era that had begun with an attempt to limit arbitrary government had ended with a government far more autocratic than the monarchy of the old regime. As his reign progressed and the demands of war increased, Napoleon's regime became ever more dictatorial.

The Domestic Policies of Emperor Napoleon

Napoleon often claimed that he had preserved the gains of the Revolution for the French people. The ideal of republican liberty had, of course, been destroyed by Napoleon's thinly disguised autocracy. But were revolu-

The Man of Destiny

Napoleon possessed an overwhelming sense of his own importance. Among the images he fostered, especially as his successes multiplied and his megalomaniacal tendencies intensified, were those of the man of destiny and the great man who masters luck.

Selections from Napoleon

When a deplorable weakness and ceaseless vacillations become manifest in supreme councils; when, yielding in turn to the influences of opposing parties, making shift from day to day, and marching with uncertain pace, a government has proved the full measure of its impotence; when even the most moderate citizens are forced to admit that the State is no longer governed; when, in fine, the administration adds to its nullity at home the gravest guilt it can acquire in the eyes of a proud nation—I mean its humiliation abroad—then a vague unrest spreads through the social body, the instinct of self-preservation is stirred, and the nation casts a sweeping eye over itself, as if to seek a man who can save it.

This guardian angel a great nation harbors in its bosom at all times; yet sometimes he is late in making his appearance. Indeed, it is not enough for him to exist: he also must be known. He must know himself. Until then, all endeavors are in vain, all schemes collapse. The inertia of the masses protects the nominal government, and despite its ineptitude and weakness the efforts of its enemies fail. But let that impatiently awaited savior give a sudden sign of his existence, and the people's instinct will divine him and call upon him. The obstacles are smoothed before his steps, and a whole great nation, flying to see him pass, will seem to be saying: "Here is the man!"

. . . A consecutive series of great actions never is the result of chance and luck; it always is the product of planning and genius. Great men are rarely known to fail in their most perilous enterprises. . . . Is it because they are lucky that they become great? No, but being great, they have been able to master luck.

tionary ideals maintained in other ways? An examination of his domestic policies will enable us to judge the truth or falsehood of Napoleon's assertion.

In 1801, Napoleon established peace with the oldest and most implacable enemy of the Revolution, the Catholic church. Napoleon himself was devoid of any personal faith; he was an eighteenth-century rationalist who regarded religion at most as a convenience. In Egypt, he called himself a Muslim; in France, a Catholic. But Napoleon saw the necessity to come to terms with the Catholic church in order to stabilize his regime. In 1800, he had declared to the clergy of Milan: "It is my firm intention that the Christian, Catholic, and Roman religion shall be preserved in its entirety. . . . No society can exist without morality; there is no good morality without religion. It is religion alone, therefore, that gives to the State a firm and durable support."[19] Soon after making this statement, Napoleon opened negotiations with Pope Pius VII to reestablish the Catholic church in France.

Both sides gained from the Concordat that Napoleon arranged with the pope in 1801. Although the pope gained the right to depose French bishops, this gave him little real control over the French Catholic church since the state retained the right to nominate bishops. The

Catholic church was also permitted to hold processions again and reopen the seminaries. But Napoleon gained more than the pope. Just by signing the Concordat, the pope acknowledged the accomplishments of the Revolution. Moreover, the pope agreed not to raise the question of the church lands confiscated during the Revolution. Contrary to the pope's wishes, Catholicism was not reestablished as the state religion; Napoleon was only willing to recognize Catholicism as the religion of a majority of the French people. The clergy would be paid by the state, but to avoid the appearance of a state church, Protestant ministers were also put on the state payroll. As a result of the Concordat, the Catholic church was no longer an enemy of the French government. At the same time, the agreement reassured those who had acquired church lands during the Revolution that they would not be stripped of them, an assurance that obviously made them supporters of the Napoleonic regime.

Before the Revolution, France did not have a single set of laws, but rather virtually 300 different legal systems. During the Revolution, efforts were made to prepare a codification of laws for the entire nation, but it remained for Napoleon to bring the work to completion in seven codes of law, of which the most important was the Civil Code (or Code Napoléon). This preserved most of the revolutionary gains by recognizing the principle of the equality of all citizens before the law, the right of the individual to choose his profession, religious toleration, and the abolition of serfdom and feudalism. Property rights continued to be carefully protected while the interests of employers were safeguarded by outlawing trade unions and strikes. The Civil Code clearly reflected the revolutionary aspirations for a uniform legal system, legal equality, and protection of property and individuals.

But the rights of some people were strictly curtailed by the Civil Code. During the radical phase of the French Revolution, new laws had made divorce an easy process for both husbands and wives, restricted the rights of fathers over their children (they could no longer have their children put in prison arbitrarily), and allowed all children (including daughters) to inherit property equally. Napoleon's Civil Code undid most of this legislation. The control of fathers over their families was restored. Divorce was still allowed, but made more difficult for women to obtain. A wife caught in adultery, for example, could be divorced by her husband and even imprisoned. A husband, on the other hand, could only be accused of adultery if he moved his mistress into his home. Women were now "less equal than men" in other ways as well. When they married, their property was brought under the control of their husbands. In lawsuits they were treated as minors, and their testimony was regarded as less reliable than that of men.

Napoleon also worked on rationalizing the bureaucratic structure of France by developing a powerful, centralized administrative machine. During the Revolution, the National Assembly had divided France into eighty-three departments and replaced the provincial estates, nobles, and intendants with self-governing assemblies. Napoleon kept the departments but eliminated the locally elected assemblies and instituted new officials, the most important of which were the prefects. As the central government's agents, appointed by the first consul (Napoleon), the prefects were responsible for supervising all aspects of local government. Yet they were not local men and their careers depended on the central government.

As part of Napoleon's overhaul of the administrative system, tax collection became systematic and efficient (which it had never been under the old regime). Taxes were now collected by professional collectors employed by the state who dealt directly with each individual taxpayer. No tax exemptions due to birth, status, or special arrangement were granted. In principle these changes had been introduced in 1789, but not until Napoleon did they actually work. In 1802, the first consul proclaimed a balanced budget.

◆ **The Coronation of Napoleon.** In 1804, Napoleon restored monarchy to France when he had himself crowned as emperor. In the coronation scene painted by Jacques-Louis David, Napoleon is shown crowning the empress Josephine while the pope looks on. Shown seated in the box in the background is Napoleon's mother, even though she was not at the ceremony.

Administrative centralization required a bureaucracy of capable officials, and Napoleon worked hard to develop one. Early on, the regime showed its preference for experts and cared little whether that expertise had been acquired in royal or revolutionary bureaucracies. Promotion, whether in civil or military offices, was to be based not on rank or birth but only on demonstrated abilities. This was, of course, what many bourgeoisie had wanted before the Revolution. Napoleon, however, also created a new aristocracy based on merit in the state service. Napoleon created 3,263 nobles between 1808 and 1814; nearly 60 percent were military officers while the remainder came from the upper ranks of the civil service and other state and local officials. Socially, only 22 percent of Napoleon's aristocracy came from the nobility of the old regime; almost 60 percent were bourgeois in origin.

In his domestic policies, then, Napoleon both destroyed and preserved aspects of the Revolution. Liberty had been replaced by an initially benevolent despotism that grew increasingly arbitrary as the demands of war overwhelmed Napoleon and the French. While equality was preserved in the law code and the opening of careers to talent, the creation of a new aristocracy, the strong protection accorded to property rights, and the practices associated with conscription make it clear that a loss of equality accompanied the loss of liberty.

Napoleon's Empire and the European Response

When Napoleon became consul in 1799, France was at war with a second European coalition of Russia, Great Britain, and Austria. Napoleon realized the need for a pause. He remarked to a Prussian diplomat "that the French Revolution is not finished so long as the scourge of war lasts ... I want peace, as much to settle the present French government, as to save the world from chaos."[20] The peace he sought was achieved at Amiens in March 1802 and left France with new frontiers and a number of client territories from the North Sea to the Adriatic. But the peace did not last because the British and French both regarded it as temporary and had little intention of adhering to its terms. War was renewed in 1803 with Britain, who was soon joined by Austria, Russia, and Prussia in the Third Coalition. In a series of battles at Ulm, Austerlitz, Jena, and Eylau from 1805 to 1807, Napoleon's Grand Army defeated the continental members of the coalition, giving him the opportunity to create a new European order. The Grand Empire was composed of three major parts: the French empire, a series of dependent states, and allied states. The French empire, the inner core of the Grand Empire, consisted of

an enlarged France extending to the Rhine in the east and including the western half of Italy north of Rome. Dependent states included Spain, Holland, the kingdom of Italy, the Swiss Republic, the Grand Duchy of Warsaw, and the Confederation of the Rhine, the latter a union of all German states except Austria and Prussia. Allied states were those defeated by Napoleon and forced to join his struggle against Britain; they included Prussia, Austria, and Russia. Although the internal structure of the Grand Empire varied outside its inner core, Napoleon considered himself leader of the whole: "Europe cannot be at rest except under a single head who will have kings for his officers, who will distribute his kingdom to his lieutenants."

Within his empire, Napoleon demanded obedience, in part because he needed a common front against the British and in part because his growing egotism required obedience to his will. But as a child of the Enlightenment and Revolution, Napoleon also sought acceptance everywhere of certain revolutionary principles, including legal equality, religious toleration, and economic freedom. As he explained to his brother Jerome after he had made him king of the new German state of Westphalia:

> What the peoples of Germany desire most impatiently is that talented commoners should have the same right to your esteem and to public employments as the nobles, that any trace of serfdom and of an intermediate hierarchy between the sovereign and the lowest class of the people should be completely abolished. The benefits of the Code Napoléon, the publicity of judicial procedure, the creation of juries must be so many distinguishing marks of your monarchy. . . . What nation would wish to return under the arbitrary Prussian government once it had tasted the benefits of a wise and liberal administration? The peoples of Germany, the peoples of France, of Italy, of Spain all desire equality and liberal ideas. I have guided the affairs of Europe for many years now, and I have had occasion to convince myself that the buzzing of the privileged classes is contrary to the general opinion. Be a constitutional king.[21]

In the inner core and dependent states of his Grand Empire, Napoleon tried to destroy the old order. Nobility and clergy everywhere in these states lost their special privileges. He decreed equality of opportunity with offices open to talent, equality before the law, and religious toleration. This spread of French revolutionary principles was an important factor in the development of liberal traditions in these countries. These reforms have led some historians to view Napoleon as the last of the enlightened absolutists.

Like Hitler one hundred and thirty years later, Napoleon hoped that his Grand Empire would last for centuries; like Hitler's empire, it collapsed almost as rapidly as it had been formed. Two major reasons help to explain this, the survival of Great Britain and the force of nationalism. Britain's survival was primarily due to its seapower. As long as Britain ruled the waves, it was almost invulnerable to military attack. Although Napoleon contemplated an invasion of England and even collected ships for it, he could not overcome the British navy's decisive defeat of a combined French-Spanish fleet at Trafalgar in 1805. Napoleon then turned to his Continental System to defeat Britain. Put into effect between 1806 and 1807, it attempted to prevent British goods from reaching the European continent in order to weaken Britain economically and destroy its capacity to wage war. But the Continental System failed. Allied states resented the ever-tightening French economic hegemony; some began to cheat and others to resist, thereby opening the door to British collaboration. New markets in the Levant and in Latin America also provided compensation for the British. Indeed, by 1809–1810 British overseas exports were at near-record highs.

A second important factor in the defeat of Napoleon was nationalism. This political creed had arisen during the French Revolution in the French people's emphasis on brotherhood (*fraternité*) and solidarity against other peoples. Nationalism involved the unique cultural identity of a people based on common language, religion, and national symbols. The spirit of French nationalism had made possible the mass armies of the revolutionary

Map 20.3 Napoleon's Grand Empire.

and Napoleonic eras. But Napoleon's spread of the principles of the French Revolution beyond France inadvertently brought a spread of nationalism as well. The French aroused nationalism in two ways: by making themselves hated oppressors and thus arousing the patriotism of others in opposition to French nationalism, and by showing the people of Europe what nationalism was and what a nation in arms could do. The lesson was not lost on other peoples and rulers. A Spanish uprising against Napoleon's rule, aided by British support, kept a French force of 200,000 pinned down for years.

The beginning of Napoleon's downfall came in 1812 with his invasion of Russia. The latter's defection from the Continental System left Napoleon with little choice. Although aware of the risks in invading such a large country, he also knew that if the Russians were allowed to challenge the Continental System unopposed, others would soon follow suit. In June 1812, a Grand Army of more than 600,000 men entered Russia. Napoleon's hopes for victory depended on quickly meeting and defeating the Russian armies, but the Russian forces refused to give battle and retreated for hundreds of miles while torching their own villages and countryside to prevent Napoleon's army from finding food and forage. When the Russians did stop to fight at Borodino, Napoleon's forces won an indecisive and costly victory. When the remaining troops of the Grand Army arrived in Moscow, they found the city ablaze. Lacking food and supplies, Napoleon abandoned Moscow late in October and made the "Great Retreat" across Russia in terrible winter conditions. Only 40,000 out of the original army managed to straggle back to Poland in January 1813. This military disaster then led to a war of liberation all over Europe, culminating in Napoleon's defeat in April 1814.

The defeated emperor of the French was allowed to play ruler on the island of Elba, off the cost of Tuscany, while the Bourbon monarchy was restored to France in the person of Louis XVIII, brother of the executed king. But the new king had little support, and Napoleon, bored on the island of Elba, slipped back into France. The troops sent to capture him went over to his side, and Napoleon entered Paris in triumph on March 20, 1815. The powers who had defeated him pledged once more to fight this person they called the "Enemy and Disturber of the Tranquility of the World." Having decided to strike first at his enemies, Napoleon raised yet another army and moved to attack the nearest allied forces stationed in Belgium. At Waterloo on June 18, Napoleon met a combined British and Prussian army under the duke of Wellington and suffered a bloody defeat. This time the victorious Allies exiled him to St.

Helena, a small and forsaken island in the south Atlantic. Only Napoleon's memory would continue to haunt French political life.

Conclusion

The revolutionary era of the late eighteenth century witnessed a dramatic political transformation. Revolutionary upheavals, beginning in North America and continuing in France, produced movements for political liberty and equality. The documents created by these revolutions, the Declaration of Independence and the Declaration of the Rights of Man and the Citizen, embodied the fundamental ideas of the Enlightenment and set forth a liberal political agenda based on a belief in popular sovereignty—the people are the source of political power—and the principles of liberty and equality. Liberty, frequently limited in practice, meant, in theory, freedom from arbitrary power as well as the freedom to think, write, and worship as one chose. Equality meant equality in rights and equality of opportunity based on talent rather than birth. In practice, equality remained limited; those who owned property had greater opportunities for voting and officeholding while there was certainly no equality between men and women.

The leaders of France's liberal revolution, achieved between 1789 and 1791, were men of property, both bourgeois and noble, but they were assisted by commoners, both sans-culottes and peasants. Yet the liberal revolution, despite the hopes of the men of property, was not the end of the Revolution. The decision of the revolutionaries to go to war "revolutionized the Revolution," opening the door to a more radical, democratic, and violent stage. The excesses of the Reign of Terror, however, led to a reaction, first under the Directory and then under Napoleon, when men of property were willing to give up liberty in exchange for order, security, and economic opportunity. Napoleon, while diminishing freedom by establishing order and centralizing the government, shrewdly preserved equality of rights and the opening of careers to talent and integrated the bourgeoisie and old nobility into a new elite of property owners. For despite the anti-aristocratic revolutionary rhetoric and the loss of their privileges, nobles remained important landowners. Though the nobles lost some of their lands during the Revolution, they were still the largest proprietors in the early 1800s. The great gainers from the redistribution of clerical and noble property, however, had been the bourgeoisie, who also gained dramatically when important government and military positions were opened to men of talent. After 1800, an elite group of property owners, both noble and middle class, dominated French society.

The French Revolution created a modern revolutionary concept. No one had foreseen or consciously planned the upheaval that began in 1789, but after 1789 "revolutionaries" knew that the proper use of mass uprisings could succeed in overthrowing unwanted governments. The French Revolution became the classical political and social model for revolution. At the same time, the liberal and national political ideals created by the Revolution and spread through Europe by Napoleon's conquests dominated the political landscape of the nineteenth and early twentieth centuries. A new European era had begun and Europe would never again be the same.

NOTES

1. Quoted in R. R. Palmer, *The Age of the Democratic Revolutions* (Princeton, N.J., 1959), 1:239.
2. Quoted in ibid., p. 242.
3. Quoted in O. J. Hufton, "Towards an Understanding of the Poor of Eighteenth Century France," in J. F. Bosher, ed., *French Government and Society: 1500–1850* (London, 1973), p. 152.
4. Arthur Young, *Travels in France during the Years 1787, 1788 and 1789* (Cambridge, 1929), p. 23.
5. Quoted in D. M. G. Sutherland, *France 1789–1815: Revolution and Counter-Revolution* (New York, 1986), p. 74.
6. Quoted in William Doyle, *The Oxford History of the French Revolution* (Oxford, 1989), p. 156.
7. Quoted in ibid., p. 184.
8. Quoted in J. Hardman, ed., *French Revolution Documents* (Oxford, 1973), 2:23.
9. Quoted in W. Scott, *Terror and Repression in Revolutionary Marseilles* (London, 1973), p. 84.
10. Quoted in H. Morse Stephens, *The Principal Speeches of the Statesmen and Orators of the French Revolution* (Oxford, 1892), 2:189.
11. Quoted in Leo Gershoy, *The Era of the French Revolution* (Princeton, N.J., 1957), p. 157.
12. Quoted in J. M. Thompson, *French Revolution Documents* (Oxford, 1933), pp. 258–59.
13. Quoted in Doyle, *The Oxford History of the French Revolution*, p. 254.
14. Quoted in R. R. Palmer, *Twelve Who Ruled* (New York, 1965), p. 75.
15. Quoted in Darline Gay Levy, Harriet Branson Applewhite, and Mary Durham Johnson, eds., *Women in Revolutionary Paris, 1789–1795* (Urbana, Ill., 1979), p. 132.
16. Ibid., pp. 219–20.
17. Quoted in Elizabeth G. Sledziewski, "The French Revolution as the Turning Point," in Geneviève Fraisse and Michelle Perrot, eds., *A History of Women in the West* (Cambridge, 1993), 4:39.
18. Quoted in François Furet and Mona Ozouf, *A Critical Dictionary of the French Revolution*, trans. Arthur Goldhammer (Cambridge, Mass., 1989), p. 545.
19. Quoted in Felix Markham, *Napoleon* (New York, 1963), pp. 92–93.
20. Quoted in Doyle, *The Oxford History of the French Revolution*, p. 381.
21. Quoted in J. Christopher Herold, ed., *The Mind of Napoleon* (New York, 1955), pp. 74–75.

SUGGESTIONS FOR FURTHER READING

A well-written, up-to-date introduction to the French Revolution can be found in W. Doyle, *The Oxford History of the French Revolution* (Oxford, 1989). For the entire revolutionary and Napoleonic eras, see O. Connelly, *The French Revolution and Napoleonic Era*, 2d ed. (Fort Worth, 1991); and D. M. G. Sutherland, *France 1789–1815: Revolution and Counter-Revolution* (New York, 1986). Although controversial, the massive and beautifully written work by S. Schama, *Citizens* (New York, 1989), makes exciting reading. A different approach to the French Revolution can be found in E. Kennedy, *A Cultural History of the French Revolution* (New Haven, Conn., 1989). Three comprehensive reference works are S. F. Scott and B. Rothaus, eds., *Historical Dictionary of the French Revolution*, 2 vols. (Westport, Conn., 1985); F. Furet and M. Ozouf, *A Critical Dictionary of the French Revolution*, trans. A. Goldhammer (Cambridge, Mass., 1989); and O. Connelly, et al., *Historical Dictionary of Napoleonic France, 1799–1815* (Westport, Conn., 1985).

The origins of the French Revolution are examined in the classic work by G. Lefebvre, *The Coming of the French Revolution* (Princeton, N.J., 1947), although his interpretive framework has been superseded by new work. On the latter, see especially W. Doyle, *Origins of the French Revolution* (Oxford, 1988). See also R. Chartier, *The Cultural Origins of the French Revolution* (Durham, N.C., 1991). On the early years of the Revolution, see M. Kennedy, *The Jacobin Clubs in the French Revolution: The First Years* (Princeton, N.J., 1982); and N. Hampson, *Prelude to Terror* (Oxford, 1988). Important works on the radical stage of the French Revolution include N. Hampson, *The Terror in the French Revolution* (London, 1981); A. Soboul, *The Sans-Culottes* (New York, 1972); R. R. Palmer, *Twelve Who Ruled* (New York, 1965); D. Jordan, *The King's Trial* (Berkeley, 1979); and R. Cobb, *The People's Armies* (London, 1987). For a biography of Robespierre, one of the leading figures of this period, see N. Hampson, *The Life and Opinions of Maximilien Robespierre* (London, 1974). The importance of the revolutionary wars in the radical stage of the Revolution is underscored in T. C. W. Blanning, *The Origins of the French Revolutionary Wars* (London, 1986). The importance of the popular revolutionary crowds is examined in the classic work by G. Rudé, *The Crowd in the French Revolution* (Oxford, 1959); and D. Roche, *The People of Paris: An Essay in Popular Culture* (Berkeley, 1987). On the Directory, see M. Lyons, *France under the Directory* (Cambridge, 1975); and R. B. Rose, *Gracchus Babeuf* (Stanford, 1978).

The religious history of the French Revolution is covered in J. McManners, *The French Revolution and the Church* (London, 1969). The relationship between religion and counterrevolution is examined in C. Tilly, *The Vendée* (Cambridge, Mass., 1964); and D. M. G. Sutherland, *The Chouans* (Oxford, 1982). On the Great Fear, there is the classic work by G. Lefebvre, *The Great Fear of 1789: Rural Panic in Revolutionary France* (London, 1973). Two recent works that take rather different approaches to the French Revolution are W. H. Sewell, *Work and Revolution in France* (Cambridge, 1980); and P. Higonnet, *Class, Ideology and the Rights of Nobles during the French Revolution* (Oxford, 1981). See also L. Hunt, *Politics, Culture and Class in the French Revolution* (Berkeley, 1984). On the role of women in revolutionary Paris, there is much to be found in the collection of documents edited by D. G. Levy, H. B. Applewhite, and M. D. Johnson, *Women in Revolutionary Paris, 1789–1795* (Urbana, Ill., 1979); and the essays in G. Fraisse and M. Perrot, eds., *A History of Women in the West*, vol. 4 (Cambridge, Mass., 1993).

The best, brief biography of Napoleon is F. Markham, *Napoleon* (New York, 1963). Also valuable are J. M. Thompson, *Napoleon Bonaparte* (Oxford, 1963); and P. Geyl, *Napoleon, For and Against* (New Haven, Conn., 1963), a study of biographical writings on the French leader. A good, recent treatment is L. Bergeron, *France under Napoleon* (Princeton, N.J., 1981). On Napoleon's military campaigns, see D. Chandler, *The Campaigns of Napoleon* (London, 1966).

A good, brief survey of the revolutionary era in America can be found in the relevant chapters of S. Thernstrom, *A History of the American People*, 2d ed. (San Diego, 1989); and E. S. Morgan, *Birth of the Republic, 1763–1789*, rev. ed. (New York, 1977). The importance of ideology is treated in G. Wood, *The Radicalism of the American Revolution* (New York, 1992). A comparative study that puts the American Revolution into a larger context is R. R. Palmer, *The Age of the Democratic Revolutions: A Political History of Europe and America, 1760–1800*, 2 vols. (Princeton, N.J., 1959–64). A more recent comparative study is the stimulating work by P. Higonnet, *Sister Republics: Origins of the French and American Revolutions* (Cambridge, Mass., 1988).

CHAPTER

21

The Industrial Revolution and Its Impact on European Society

The French Revolution dramatically and quickly altered the political structure of France while the Napoleonic conquests spread many of the revolutionary principles in an equally rapid and stunning fashion to other parts of Europe. During the late eighteenth and early nineteenth centuries, another revolution—an industrial one—was transforming the economic and social structure of Europe, although in a less dramatic and rapid fashion.

The period of the Industrial Revolution witnessed a quantum leap in industrial production. New sources of energy and power, especially coal and steam, replaced wind and water to create labor-saving machines that dramatically decreased the use of human and animal labor and, at the same time, increased the level of productivity. In turn, power machinery called for new ways of organizing human labor to maximize the benefits and profits from the new machines; factories replaced shop and home workrooms. Many early factories were dreadful places with difficult working conditions. Reformers, appalled at these conditions, were especially critical of the treatment of married women. One reported: "We have repeatedly seen married females, in the last stage of pregnancy, slaving from morning to night beside these never-tiring machines, and when . . . they were obliged to sit down to take a moment's ease, and being seen by the manager, were fined for the offense." But there were also examples of well-run factories. William Cobbett described one in Manchester in 1830: "In this room, which is lighted in the most convenient and beautiful manner, there were five hundred pairs of looms at work, and five hundred persons attending those looms; and, owing to the goodness of the masters, the whole looking healthy and well-dressed."

During the Industrial Revolution, Europe experienced a shift from a traditional, labor-intensive economy based on farming and handicrafts to a more capital-intensive economy based on manufacturing by machines, specialized labor, and industrial factories. Although the Industrial Revolution took decades to

Watt's steam engine

Stephenson's *Rocket*

Cartwright's power loom

Great Exhibition in Britain

First textile factory in the United States

Factory Act

People's Charter

Chadwick's Report on Cities

Luddites

Formation of Owen's
Grand National
Trades Union

List's *National
System of Political
Economy*

Great Famine
in Ireland

spread, it was truly revolutionary in the way it funda-mentally changed Europeans, their society, and their relationship to other peoples. The development of large factories encouraged mass movements of people from the countryside to urban areas where impersonal coexistence replaced the traditional intimacy of rural life. Higher levels of productivity led to a search for new sources of raw materials, new consumption patterns, and a revolution in transportation that allowed raw materials and finished products to be moved quickly around the world. The creation of a wealthy industrial middle class and a huge industrial working class (or proletariat) substantially transformed traditional social relationships.

The Industrial Revolution in Great Britain

Although the Industrial Revolution evolved out of antecedents that occurred over a long period of time, historians generally agree that it had its beginnings in Britain in the second half of the eighteenth century. By 1850, the Industrial Revolution had made Great Britain the wealthiest country in the world; by that time it had also spread to the European continent and the New World. By the end of the nineteenth century, both Germany and the United States would surpass Britain in industrial production.

Origins

A number of factors or conditions coalesced in Britain to produce the first Industrial Revolution. One of these was the agricultural revolution of the eighteenth century. The changes in the methods of farming and stock breeding that characterized this agricultural transformation led to a significant increase in food production. British agriculture could now feed more people at lower prices with less labor. Unlike the rest of Europe, even ordinary British families did not have to use most of their income to buy food, giving them the potential to purchase manufactured goods. At the same time, a rapid growth of population in the second half of the eighteenth century provided a pool of surplus labor for the new factories of the emerging British industry. Rural workers in cottage industries also provided a potential labor force for industrial enterprises.

Britain had a ready supply of capital for investment in the new industrial machines and the factories that were needed to house them. In addition to profits from trade and cottage industry, Britain possessed an effective central bank and well-developed, flexible credit facilities. Nowhere in Europe were people so accustomed to using paper instruments to facilitate capital transactions. Many early factory owners were merchants and entrepreneurs who had profited from eighteenth-century cottage industry. Of 110 cotton spinning mills in operation in the area known as the Midlands between 1769 and 1800, 62 were established by hosiers, drapers, mercers, and others involved in some fashion in the cottage textile industry. But capital alone is only part of the story. Britain had a fair number of individuals who were interested in making profits if the opportunity presented

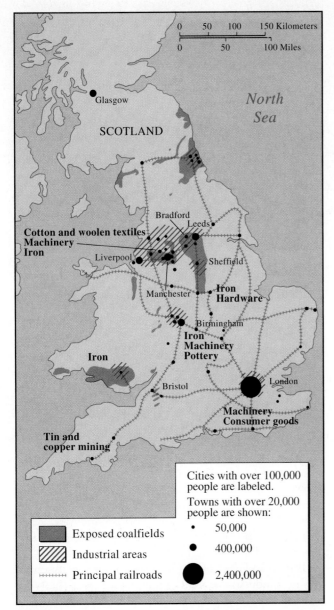

threw out his partners: "As they could neither of them be of any further use, I released them from the firm and took the whole upon myself."[1]

Britain was richly supplied with important mineral resources, such as coal and iron ore, needed in the manufacturing process. Britain was also a small country, and the relatively short distances made transportation readily accessible. In addition to nature's provision of abundant rivers, from the mid-seventeenth century onward, both private and public investment poured into the construction of new roads, bridges, and, beginning in the 1750s and 1760s, canals. By 1780, roads, rivers, and canals linked the major industrial centers of the North, the Midlands, London, and the Atlantic. Unlike the continental countries, Britain had no internal customs barriers to hinder domestic trade.

Britain's government also played a significant role in the process of industrialization. Parliament contributed to the favorable business climate by providing a stable government and passing laws that protected private property. Moreover, Britain was remarkable for the freedom it provided for private enterprise. It placed fewer restrictions on private entrepreneurs than any other European state.

Finally, a supply of markets gave British industrialists a ready outlet for their manufactured goods. British exports quadrupled from 1660 to 1760. In the course of its eighteenth-century wars and conquests, Great Britain had developed a vast colonial empire at the expense of its leading continental rivals, the Dutch Republic and France. Britain also possessed a well-developed merchant marine that was able to transport goods to any place in the world. A crucial factor in Britain's successful industrialization was the ability to produce cheaply those articles most in demand abroad. And the best markets abroad were not in Europe, where countries protected their own incipient industries, but in the Americas, Africa, and the Far East, where people wanted sturdy, inexpensive clothes rather than costly, highly finished, luxury items. Britain's machine-produced textiles fulfilled that demand. Nor should we overlook the British domestic market. Britain had the highest standard of living in Europe and a rapidly growing population. As Daniel Defoe noted already in 1728:

For the rest, we see their Houses and Lodgings tolerably furnished, at least stuff'd well with useful and necessary household Goods: Even those we call poor People, Journey-men, working and Pains-staking People do thus; they lye warm, live in Plenty, work hard, and [need] know

Map 21.1 Britain in the Industrial Revolution.

itself (see the box on p. 709). The British were a people, as one historian has said, "fascinated by wealth and commerce, collectively and individually." These early industrial entrepreneurs faced considerable financial hazards, however. Fortunes were made quickly and lost just as quickly. The structure of early firms was open and fluid. An individual or family proprietorship was the usual mode of operation, but entrepreneurs also brought in friends to help them. They just as easily jettisoned them. John Marshall, who made money in flax spinning,

The Traits of the British Industrial Entrepreneur

Richard Arkwright (1732–1792), inventor of a spinning frame and founder of cotton factories, was a good example of the successful entrepreneur in the early Industrial Revolution in Britain. In this selection, Edward Baines, who wrote The History of the Cotton Manufacture in Great Britain *in 1835, discusses the traits that explain the success of Arkwright and presumably other British entrepreneurs.*

Edward Baines, *The History of the Cotton Manufacture in Great Britain*

Richard Arkwright rose by the force of his natural talents from a very humble condition in society. He was born at Preston on the 23rd of December, 1732, of poor parents: being the youngest of thirteen children, his parents could only afford to give him an education of the humblest kind, and he was scarcely able to write. He was brought up to the trade of a barber at Kirkham and Preston, and established himself in that business at Bolton in the year 1760. Having become possessed of a chemical process for dyeing human hair, which in that day (when wigs were universal) was of considerable value, he travelled about collecting hair, and again disposing of it when dyed. In 1761, he married a wife from Leigh, and the connexions he thus formed in that town are supposed to have afterwards brought him acquainted with Highs's experiments in making spinning machines. He himself manifested a strong bent for experiments in mathematics, which he is stated to have followed with so much devotedness as to have neglected his business and injured his circumstances. His natural disposition was ardent, enterprising, and stubbornly persevering: his mind was as coarse as it was bold and active, and his manners were rough and unpleasing. . . .

The most marked traits in the character of Arkwright were his wonderful ardour, energy, and perseverance. He commonly laboured in his multifarious concerns from five o'clock in the morning till nine at night; and when considerably more than fifty years of age,—feeling that the defects of his education placed him under great difficulty and inconvenience in conducting his correspondence, and in the general management of his business,—he encroached upon his sleep, in order to gain an hour each day to learn English grammar, and another hour to improve his writing and orthography [spelling]! He was impatient of whatever interfered with his favorite pursuits; and the fact is too strikingly characteristic not to be mentioned, that he separated from his wife not many years after their marriage, because she, convinced that he would starve his family [because of the impractical nature of his schemes], broke some of his experimental models of machinery. Arkwright was a severe economist of time; and, that he might not waste a moment, he generally travelled with four horses, and at a very rapid speed. His concerns in Derbyshire, Lancashire, and Scotland were so extensive and numerous, as to [show] at once his astonishing power of transacting business and his all grasping spirit. In many of these he had partners, but he generally managed in such a way, that, whoever lost, he himself was a gainer.

---

no Want. These are the People that carry off the Gross of your Consumption; 'tis for these your Markets are kept open late on Saturday nights; because they usually receive their Week's Wages late . . . in a Word, these are the Life of our whole Commerce, and all by their Multitude: Their Numbers are not Hundreds or Thousands, or Hundreds of Thousands, but Millions; . . . by their Wages they are able to live plentifully, and it is by their expensive, generous, free way of living, that the Home Consumption is rais'd to such a Bulk, as well of our own, as of foreign Production.[2]

This demand from both domestic and foreign markets and the inability of the old system to fulfill it led entrepreneurs to seek and adopt the new methods of manufacturing that a series of inventions provided. In so doing, these individuals produced the Industrial Revolution.

Technological Changes and New Forms of Industrial Organization

In the 1770s and 1780s, the cotton textile industry took the first major step toward the Industrial Revolution with the creation of the modern factory.

THE COTTON INDUSTRY

Already in the eighteenth century, Great Britain had surged ahead in the production of cheap cotton goods using the traditional methods of cottage industry. The development of the flying shuttle had sped the process of weaving on a loom and enabled weavers to double their output. This created shortages of yarn, however, until James Hargreaves's spinning jenny, perfected by 1768, enabled spinners to produce yarn in greater quantities. Richard Arkwright's water frame spinning machine, powered by water or horse, and Samuel Crompton's so-called mule, which combined aspects of the water frame and spinning jenny, increased yarn production even more. Edmund Cartwright's power loom, invented in 1787, allowed the weaving of cloth to catch up with the spinning of yarn. Even then, early power looms were grossly inefficient, enabling cottage, hand-loom weavers to continue to prosper, at least until the mid-1820s. After that they were gradually replaced by the new machines. In 1813, there were 2,400 power looms in operation in Great Britain; they numbered 14,150 in 1820, 100,000 in 1833, and 250,000 by 1850. In the 1820s, there were still 250,000 hand-loom weavers in Britain; by 1860, only 3,000 were left.

The water frame, Crompton's mule, and power looms presented new opportunities to entrepreneurs. It was much more efficient to bring workers to the machines and organize their labor collectively in factories located next to rivers and streams, the sources of power for many of these early machines, than to leave the workers dispersed in their cottages. The concentration of labor in the new factories also brought the laborers and their families to live in the new towns that rapidly grew up around the factories.

The early devices used to speed up the processes of spinning and weaving were the products of weavers and spinners, in effect, of craftsmen tinkerers. But the subsequent expansion of the cotton industry and the ongoing demand for even more cotton goods created additional pressure for new and more complicated technology. The invention that pushed the cotton industry to even greater heights of productivity was the steam engine.

THE STEAM ENGINE

The invention of the steam engine played a major role in the Industrial Revolution. It revolutionized the production of cotton goods and caused the factory system to spread to other areas of production, thereby creating whole new industries. The steam engine secured the triumph of the Industrial Revolution.

As in much of the Industrial Revolution, one kind of change forced other changes. In many ways the steam engine was the result of the need for more efficient pumps to eliminate water seepage from deep mines. Deep coal mines were in turn the result of Britain's need and desire to find new sources of energy to replace wood. By the early eighteenth century, the British were acutely aware of a growing shortage of timber, which was used in heating, to build homes and ships, and in enormous quantities to produce the charcoal utilized in smelting iron ore to make pig iron. At the beginning of the eighteenth century, the discovery of new processes for smelting iron ore with coal and coke (see the next section) led to deeper and deeper mines for more intensive mining of coal. But as mines were dug below the water table, they filled with water. An early solution to the problem was the use of mechanical pumps powered by horses walking in circles. In one coal mine in Warwickshire, for example, 500 horses were used to lift the water from the mine, bucket by bucket. The need for more efficient pumps led Thomas Newcomen to develop a steam pump or, as it was called, an "atmospheric engine" that was first used in 1712. Though better than horses, it was still inefficient.

In the 1760s, a Scottish engineer, James Watt (1736–1819), was asked to repair a Newcomen engine. Instead he added a separate condenser and steam pump and transformed Newcomen's machine into a genuine steam engine. Power was derived not from air pressure as in Newcomen's atmospheric engine, but from steam itself. Much more efficient than a Newcomen engine, Watt's engine could pump water three times as quickly. Initially, it possessed one major liability, however; as a contemporary noted in 1778: "the vast consumption of fuel in these engines is an immense drawback on the profit of our mines, for every fire-engine of magnitude consumes £3000 worth of coals per annum. This heavy tax amounts almost to a prohibition."[3] As steam engines were made more efficient, however, they also became cheaper to use.

In 1782, James Watt enlarged the possibilities of the steam engine when he developed a rotary engine that could turn a shaft and thus drive machinery. Steam power could now be applied to spinning and weaving cotton, and before long cotton mills using steam engines were multiplying across Britain. By 1850, seven-eighths of the power available to the entire British cotton industry came from steam. Since steam engines were fired by coal, they did not need to be located near rivers; entrepreneurs now had greater flexibility in their choice of location.

The new boost given to cotton textile production by technological changes became readily apparent. In 1760, Britain had imported 2.5 million pounds of raw cotton, which was farmed out to cottage industries. All work was done by hand either in workers' homes or in the small shops of master weavers. In 1787, the British imported 22 million pounds of cotton; most of it was spun on machines, some powered by water in large mills. By 1840, 366 million pounds of cotton were imported annually, much of it from the American South where it was grown by slaves. By this time, cotton cloth was Britain's most important product by value and was produced mainly in factories, although some hand-loom weavers still worked in their cottages. The price of yarn was but one-twentieth of what it had been. The cheapest labor in India could not compete in quality or quantity with Britain. British cotton goods sold everywhere in the world. And in Britain itself, cheap cotton cloth made it possible for millions of poor people to wear undergarments, long a preserve of the rich who alone could afford underwear made with expensive linen cloth. New work clothing that was tough, comfortable to the skin, and yet cheap and easily washable became common. Even the rich liked the colorful patterns of cotton prints and their light weight for summer use.

The steam engine proved invaluable to Britain's Industrial Revolution. In 1800, engines were generating 10,000 horsepower; by 1850, 500,000 horsepower were being generated by stationary engines and 790,000 by mobile engines, the last largely in locomotives (see A Revolution in Transportation later in this chapter). Unlike horses, the steam engine was a tireless source of power and depended for fuel on a substance—namely, coal—that seemed then to be unlimited in quantity. The popular saying that "Steam is an Englishman" had real significance by 1850. The steam engine also replaced waterpower in such places as flour and sugar mills. Just as the need for more coal had helped lead to the steam engine, so the success of the steam engine increased the demand for coal and led to an expansion in coal production; between 1815 and 1850, the output of coal quadrupled. In turn, new processes using coal furthered the development of an iron industry.

THE IRON INDUSTRY

The British iron industry was radically transformed during the Industrial Revolution. Britain had large resources of iron ore, but at the beginning of the eighteenth century, the basic process of producing iron had altered little since the Middle Ages and still depended heavily on charcoal. In the early eighteenth century, new methods of smelting iron ore to produce cast iron were devised based on the use of coke derived

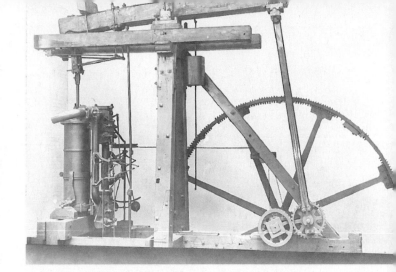

◆ **A Boulton and Watt Steam Engine.** Encouraged by his business partner, Matthew Boulton, James Watt developed the first genuine steam engine. Pictured here is a typical Boulton and Watt engine. Steam pressure in the cylinder on the left drives the beam upward and sets the flywheel in motion.

from coal. Still, a better quality of iron was not possible until the 1780s when Henry Cort developed a system called puddling, in which coke was used to burn away impurities in pig iron to produce an iron of high quality. A boom then ensued in the British iron industry. In 1740, Britain produced 17,000 tons of iron; in the 1780s, almost 70,000 tons; by the 1840s, over 2 million tons; and by 1852, almost 3 million tons, more than the rest of the world combined.

The development of the iron industry was in many ways a response to the demand for the new machines. The high-quality wrought iron produced by the Cort process made it the most widely used metal until the production of cheaper steel in the 1860s. The growing supply of less costly metal encouraged the use of machinery in other industries, most noticeably in new means of transportation.

A REVOLUTION IN TRANSPORTATION

The eighteenth century had witnessed an expansion of transportation facilities in Britain as entrepreneurs realized the need for more efficient means of moving resources and goods. Turnpike trusts constructed new roads, and between 1760 and 1830 a network of canals was built. But both roads and canals were soon overtaken by a new form of transportation that dazzled people with its promise. To many economic historians, railroads were the "most important single factor in promoting European economic progress in the 1830s and 1840s." Again, Britain was the leader in the revolution.

✦ **An Early Ironworks.** This picture shows the coke-fired ironworks of Abraham Darby at Coalbrookdale in Shropshire. Darby's ironworks produced more and better iron than any other establishment in Europe and made the iron shells used in James Watt's rotary steam engine.

The beginnings of railways can be found in mining operations in Germany as early as 1500 and in British coal mines after 1600 where small handcarts filled with coal were pushed along parallel wooden rails. The rails reduced friction, enabling horses to haul more substantial loads. By 1700, some entrepreneurs began to replace wooden rails with cast-iron rails, and by the early nineteenth century, railways—still dependent on horsepower—were common in British mining and industrial districts. The development of the steam engine brought a radical transformation to the railways.

In 1804, Richard Trevithick pioneered the first steam-powered locomotive on an industrial rail-line in south Wales. It pulled ten tons of ore and seventy people at five miles per hour. Better locomotives soon followed. The engines built by George Stephenson and his son proved superior, and it was in their workshops in Newcastle upon Tyne that the locomotives for the first modern railways in Britain were built. George Stephenson's *Rocket* was used on the first public railway line, which opened in 1830, extending thirty-two miles from Liverpool to Manchester. *Rocket* sped along at sixteen miles per hour. Within twenty years, locomotives had reached fifty miles per hour, an incredible speed to contemporary passengers. During the same period, new companies were formed to build additional railroads as the infant industry proved to be not only technically but financially successful. In 1840, Britain had almost 2,000 miles of railroads; by 1850, 6,000 miles of railroad track crisscrossed much of the country.

The railroad contributed significantly to the success and maturing of the Industrial Revolution. The railroad's demands for coal and iron furthered the growth of those industries. British supremacy in civil and mechanical engineering, so evident after 1840, was in large part based upon the skills acquired in railway building. The huge capital demands necessary for railway construction encouraged a whole new group of middle-class investors to invest their money in joint-stock companies (see Limitations to Industrialization later in this chapter). Railway construction created new job opportunities, especially for farm laborers and peasants who had

✦ **Railroad Line from Liverpool to Manchester.** The railroad line from Liverpool to Manchester, first opened in 1830, relied on steam locomotives. As is evident in this illustration, carrying passengers was the railroad's main business. First-class passengers rode in covered cars; second- and third-class passengers in open cars.

long been accustomed to finding work outside their local villages. Perhaps most importantly, a cheaper and faster means of transportation had a rippling effect on the growth of an industrial economy. By reducing the price of goods, larger markets were created; increased sales necessitated more factories and more machinery, thereby reinforcing the self-sustaining nature of the Industrial Revolution, which marked a fundamental break with the traditional European economy. The great productivity of the Industrial Revolution enabled entrepreneurs to reinvest their profits in new capital equipment, further expanding the productive capacity of the economy. Continuous, even rapid, self-sustaining economic growth came to be seen as a fundamental characteristic of the new industrial economy.

The railroad was the perfect symbol of this aspect of the Industrial Revolution. The ability to transport goods and people at dramatic speeds also provided visible confirmation of a new sense of power. When railway engineers pierced mountains with tunnels and spanned chasms with breathtaking bridges, contemporaries experienced a sense of power over nature not felt before in Western civilization.

THE INDUSTRIAL FACTORY

Initially the product of the new cotton industry, the factory became the chief means of organizing labor for the new machines. As the workplace shifted from the artisan's shop and the peasant's cottage to the factory, the latter was not viewed as just a larger work unit. Employers hired workers who no longer owned the

✦ **Inside an Early Cotton Factory.** The development of the factory changed the relationship between workers and employers as workers were encouraged to adjust to a new system of discipline that forced them to work regular hours and in shifts. This engraving depicts the inside of an early textile factory.

means of production but were simply paid wages to run the machines

From its beginning, the factory system demanded a new type of discipline from its employees. Factory owners could not afford to let their expensive machinery stand idle. Workers were forced to work regular hours and in shifts to keep the machines producing at a steady pace for maximum output. This represented a massive adjustment for early factory laborers.

✦ **Opening of the Royal Albert Bridge.** This painting by Thomas Roberts shows the ceremonies attending the official opening of the Royal Albert Bridge. I. K. Brunel, one of Britain's great engineers, designed this bridge, which carried a railroad line across the Tamar River into Cornwall. As is evident in the picture, the bridge was high enough to allow shipping to pass underneath.

Discipline in the New Factories

Workers in the new factories of the Industrial Revolution had been accustomed to a lifestyle free of overseers. Unlike the cottages, where workers spun thread and wove cloth in their own rhythm and time, the factories demanded a new, rigorous discipline geared to the requirements of the machines. This selection is taken from a set of rules for a factory in Berlin in 1844. They were typical of company rules everywhere the factory system had been established.

The Foundry and Engineering Works of the Royal Overseas Trading Company, Factory Rules

In every large works, and in the co-ordination of any large number of workmen, good order and harmony must be looked upon as the fundamentals of success, and therefore the following rules shall be strictly observed.

1. The normal working day begins at all seasons at 6 A.M. precisely and ends, after the usual break of half an hour for breakfast, an hour for dinner and half an hour for tea, at 7 P.M., and it shall be strictly observed. . . .

   Workers arriving 2 minutes late shall lose half an hour's wages; whoever is more than 2 minutes late may not start work until after the next break; or at least shall lose his wages until then. Any disputes about the correct time shall be settled by the clock mounted above the gatekeeper's lodge. . . .

3. No workman, whether employed by time or piece, may leave before the end of the working day, without having first received permission from the overseer and having given his name to the gatekeeper. Omission of these two actions shall lead to a fine of ten silver groschen [pennies] payable to the sick fund.

4. Repeated irregular arrival at work shall lead to dismissal. This shall also apply to those who are found idling by an official or overseer, and refused to obey their order to resume work. . . .

6. No worker may leave his place of work otherwise than for reasons connected with his work.

7. All conversation with fellow-workers is prohibited; if any worker requires information about his work, he must turn to the overseer, or to the particular fellow-worker designated for the purpose.

8. Smoking in the workshops or in the yard is prohibited during working hours; anyone caught smoking shall be fined five silver groschen for the sick fund for every such offense. . . .

10. Natural functions must be performed at the appropriate places, and whoever is found soiling walls, fences, squares, etc., and similarly, whoever is found washing his face and hands in the workshop and not in the places assigned for the purpose, shall be fined five silver groschen for the sick fund. . . .

12. It goes without saying that all overseers and officials of the firm shall be obeyed without question, and shall be treated with due deference. Disobedience will be punished by dismissal.

13. Immediate dismissal shall also be the fate of anyone found drunk in any of the workshops. . . .

14. Every workman is obliged to report to his superiors any acts of dishonesty or embezzlement on the part of his fellow workmen. If he omits to do so, and it is shown after subsequent discovery of a misdemeanor that he knew about it at the time, he shall be liable to be taken to court as an accessory after the fact and the wage due to him shall be retained as punishment.

Preindustrial workers were not accustomed to a "timed" format. Agricultural laborers had always kept irregular hours; hectic work at harvest time might be followed by periods of inactivity. Even in the burgeoning cottage industry of the eighteenth century, weavers and spinners who worked at home might fulfill their weekly quotas by working around the clock for two or three days, followed by a leisurely pace until the next week's demands forced another work spurt.

Factory owners, therefore, faced a formidable task. They had to create a system of time-work discipline in which employees became accustomed to working regular, unvarying hours during which they performed a set number of tasks over and over again as efficiently as possible. One early industrialist said that his aim was "to make such machines of the men as cannot err." Such work, of course, tended to be repetitive and boring, and factory owners resorted to tough methods to accomplish their goals. Factory regulations were minute and detailed (see the box on p. 714). Adult workers were fined for a wide variety of minor infractions, such as being a few minutes late for work, and dismissed for more serious misdoings, especially drunkenness. The latter was viewed as particularly offensive because it set a bad example for younger workers and also courted disaster in the midst of dangerous machinery. Employers found that dismissals and fines worked well for adult employees; in a time when great population growth had produced large numbers of unskilled workers, dismissal could be disastrous. Children were less likely to understand the implications of dismissal so they were sometimes disciplined more directly—frequently by beating.

The efforts of factory owners in the early Industrial Revolution to impose a new set of values were frequently reinforced by the new evangelical churches. Methodism, in particular, emphasized that people reborn in Christ must forgo immoderation and follow a disciplined path. Laziness and wasteful habits were sinful. The acceptance of hardship in this life paved the way for the joys of the next. Evangelical values paralleled the efforts of the new factory owners to instill laborers with their own middle-class values of hard work, discipline, and thrift. In one crucial sense, the early industrialists proved successful. As the nineteenth century progressed, the second and third generations of workers came to view a regular working week as a natural way of life. It was, of course, an attitude that made possible Britain's incredible economic growth in that century.

The Great Exhibition: Britain in 1851

In 1851, the British organized the world's first industrial fair. It was housed at Kensington in London in the Crystal Palace, an enormous structure made entirely of glass and iron, a tribute to British engineering skills. Covering nineteen acres, the Crystal Palace contained 100,000 exhibits that showed the wide variety of products created by the Industrial Revolution. Six million people visited the fair in six months. While most of them were Britons, who had traveled to London by train, foreign visitors were also prominent. The Great Exhibition displayed Britain's wealth to the world; it was a gigantic symbol of British success. Even trees were brought inside the Crystal Palace as a visible symbol of how the Industrial Revolution had achieved human domination over nature. Prince Albert, Queen Victoria's husband, expressed the sentiments of the age when he described the exhibition as a sign that "man is approaching a more complete fulfillment of that great and sacred mission which he has to perform in this world . . . to conquer nature to his use." Not content with that, he also linked British success to divine will: "In promoting [the progress of the human race], we are accomplishing the will of the great and blessed God."[4]

By the year of the Great Exhibition, Great Britain had become the world's first and richest industrial nation. Britain was the "workshop, banker, and trader of the world." It produced one-half of the world's coal and manufactured goods; its cotton industry alone in 1851

✦ **The Crystal Palace.** The Great Exhibition, organized in 1851, was a symbol of the success of Great Britain, which had become the world's first and richest industrial nation. Over 100,000 exhibits were housed in the Crystal Palace, a giant structure of cast iron and glass. This illustration shows the front of the palace and some of its numerous visitors.

was equal in size to the industries of all other European countries combined. The quantity of goods produced was growing at three times the growth rate in 1780. No doubt, Britain's certainty about its mission in the world in the nineteenth century was grounded in its incredible material success story.

The Spread of Industrialization

Beginning first in Great Britain, industrialization spread to the continental countries of Europe and the United States at different times and speeds during the nineteenth century. First to be industrialized on the Continent were Belgium, France, and the German states and in North America, the new nation of the United States. Not until after 1850 did the Industrial Revolution spread to the rest of Europe and other parts of the world.

Limitations to Industrialization

In 1815, Belgium, France, and the German states were still largely agrarian. During the eighteenth century, some of the continental countries had experienced developments similar to those of Britain. They, too, had achieved population growth, made agricultural improvements, expanded their cottage industries, and witnessed growth in foreign trade. But while Britain's economy began to move in new industrial directions in the 1770s and 1780s, continental countries lagged behind because they did not share some of the advantages that had made Britain's Industrial Revolution possible. Lack of good roads and problems with river transit made transportation difficult. Toll stations on important rivers and customs barriers along state boundaries increased the costs and prices of goods. Guild restrictions were also more prevalent, creating restrictions that pioneer industrialists in Britain did not have to face. Finally, continental entrepreneurs were generally less enterprising than their British counterparts and tended to adhere to traditional business attitudes, such as a dislike of competition, a high regard for family security coupled with an unwillingness to take risks in investment, and an excessive worship of thriftiness.

One additional factor also affected most of the Continent between 1790 and 1812: the upheavals associated with the wars of the French revolutionary and Napoleonic eras. Disruption of regular communications between Britain and the Continent made it difficult for continental countries to keep up with the new British technology. Moreover, the wars wreaked havoc with trade, caused much physical destruction and loss of manpower, weakened currencies, and led to political and social instability. Napoleon's Continental System helped to ruin a number of hitherto prosperous ports. The elimination of European markets for British textiles did temporarily revive the woolen industry in France and Belgium and stimulated textile manufacturing along the Rhine and in Silesia. After 1815, however, when cheap British goods again flooded European markets, the European textile industry suffered.

In the long run, the revolutionary and Napoleonic wars created an additional obstacle to rapid industrialization by widening the gap between British and continental industrial machinery. By 1815, after Napoleon had finally been defeated and normal communication between Britain and the Continent had been restored, British industrial equipment had grown larger and become more expensive. As a result, self-financed family enterprises were either unable or unwilling to raise the amount of capital necessary to modernize by investing in the latest equipment. Instead, most entrepreneurs in France, Belgium, and Germany initially chose to invest in used machines and less productive mills. Consequently, industrialization on the Continent faced numerous hurdles, and as it proceeded in earnest after 1815, it did so along lines that were somewhat different from Britain's.

Lack of technical knowledge was initially a major obstacle to industrialization. But the continental countries possessed an advantage here; they could simply borrow British techniques and practices. Of course, the British tried to prevent that. Until 1825, British artisans were prohibited from leaving the country; until 1842, the export of important machinery and machine parts, especially for textile production, was forbidden. Nevertheless, the British were not able to control this situation by legislation. Already by 1825, there were at least 2,000 skilled British mechanics on the Continent, and British equipment was also being sold abroad, whether legally or illegally.

Although many Britons who went abroad to sell their skills were simply skilled mechanics, a number of them were accomplished entrepreneurs who had managerial as well as technical skills. John Cockerill, for example, was an aggressive businessman who established a highly profitable industrial plant at Seraing near Liège in southern Belgium in 1817. Encouraged by the Belgian government, Cockerill thought nothing of pirating the

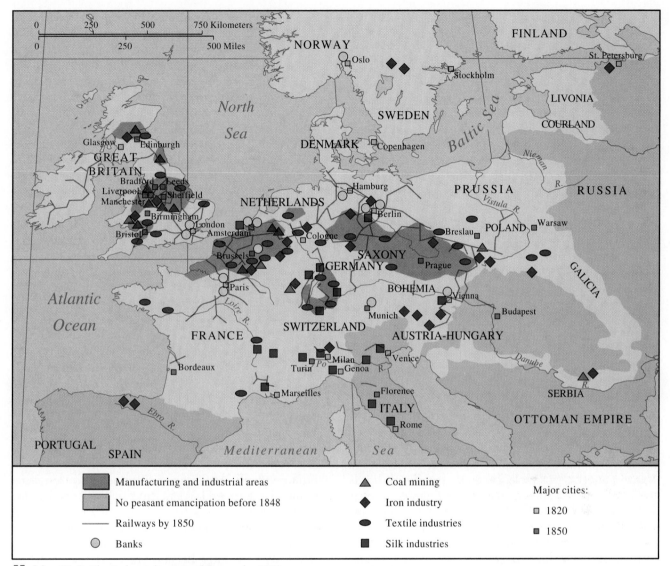

Map 21.2 The Industrialization of Europe by 1850.

Legend:
- Manufacturing and industrial areas
- No peasant emancipation before 1848
- Railways by 1850
- Banks
- Coal mining
- Iron industry
- Textile industries
- Silk industries
- Major cities: 1820, 1850

innovations of other British industrialists to further his own factories. Aware of their importance, British technicians abroad were often contentious and arrogant, arousing the anger of continental industrialists. Fritz Harkort, who initiated the engineering industry in Germany, once exclaimed that he could scarcely wait for Germans to be trained "so that the Englishmen could all be whipped out: we must even now tread softly with them, for they're only too quick to speak of quitting if one does so little as not look at them in a friendly fashion."[5]

Gradually, the Continent achieved technological independence as local people learned all the skills their British teachers had to offer. By the 1840s, a new generation of skilled mechanics from Belgium and France was spreading their knowledge east and south, playing the same role that the British had earlier. More importantly, however, continental countries, especially France and the German states, began to establish a wide range of technical schools to train engineers and mechanics.

That government played an important role in this regard brings us to a second difference between British and continental industrialization. Governments in most of the continental countries were accustomed to playing a significant role in economic affairs. Furthering the development of industrialization was a logical extension of that attitude. Hence, governments provided for the costs of technical education; awarded grants to inventors and foreign entrepreneurs; exempted foreign industrial equipment from import duties; and, in some places, even financed factories. Of equal, if not greater importance in the long run, governments actively bore much of the cost of building roads and canals, deepening and widening river channels, and constructing railroads. By 1850, a network of iron rails had spread across Europe, although only Germany and Belgium had completed major parts of their systems by that time. Although European markets did not feel the real impact of the railroad until after 1850, railroad construction itself in the 1830s and 1840s gave great impetus to the metalworking and engineering industries.

Governments on the Continent also used tariffs to further industrialization. After 1815, cheap British goods flooded continental markets. The French responded with high tariffs to protect their fledgling industries. The most systematic exposition for the use of tariffs, however, was made by a German writer, Friedrich List (1789–1846), who emigrated to America and returned to Germany as a United States consul. In his *National System of Political Economy*, written in 1844, List advocated a rapid and large-scale program of industrialization as the surest path to develop a nation's strength. To assure that path to industrialization, he felt that a nation must use protective tariffs. If countries followed the British policy of free trade, then cheaper British goods would inundate national markets and destroy infant industries before they had a chance to grow. Germany, he insisted, could not compete with Britain without protective tariffs.

A third significant difference between British and continental industrialization was the role of the joint-stock investment bank on the Continent. Such banks mobilized the savings of thousands of small and large investors, creating a supply of capital that could then be plowed back into industry. Previously, continental banks had been mostly merchant or private banks, but in the 1830s two Belgian banks, the Société Générale and the Banque de Belgique, took a new approach. By accepting savings from many depositors, they developed large capital resources that they invested on a large scale in railroads, mining, and heavy industry. These investments were especially important to the Belgian coal industry, which became the largest on the Continent in the 1840s. Shareholders in these joint-stock corporations had limited liability; they could only be held responsible for the amount of their investment.

Similar institutions emerged in France and German-speaking lands as well in the 1850s with the establishment of the Crédit Mobilier in France, the Darmstadt Bank in Germany, and the Kreditanstalt in Austria. They, too, took in savings of small investors and bought shares in the new industries. The French consul in Leipzig noted their significance: "every town and state [in Germany]," he pointed out, "however small it may be, wants its bank and its Crédit Mobilier." These investments proved invaluable to continental industrialization. By starting with less expensive machines, the British had been able to industrialize largely through the private capital of successful individuals who reinvested their profits. On the Continent advanced industrial machines necessitated large amounts of capital; joint-stock industrial banks provided it.

Centers of Continental Industrialization

The Industrial Revolution on the Continent occurred in three major centers between 1815 and 1850—Belgium, France, and the German states. Here, too, cotton played an important role, although it was not as significant as heavy industry. France was the continental leader in the manufacture of cotton goods but still lagged far behind Great Britain. In 1849, France used 64,000 tons of raw cotton, Belgium, 11,000, and Germany, 20,000, while Britain utilized 286,000 tons. Continental cotton factories were older, used less efficient machines, and had less productive labor. In general, continental technology in the cotton industry was a generation behind Great Britain. But that is not the whole story. With its cheap coal and scarce water, Belgium gravitated toward the use of the steam engine as the major source of power and invested in the new machines. By the mid-1840s, Belgium had the most modern cotton-manufacturing system on the Continent.

The development of cotton manufacturing on the Continent and in Britain differed in two significant ways. Unlike Britain, where cotton manufacturing was mostly centered in Lancashire (in northwestern England) and the Glasgow area, cotton mills in France, Germany, and, to a lesser degree, Belgium were dispersed through many regions. Noticeable, too, was the mixture of old and new. The old techniques of the cottage system, such as the use of hand looms, held on much longer. In the French district of Normandy, for example, in 1849 eighty-three mills were still driven by hand or animal power.

As traditional methods persisted alongside the new methods in cotton manufacturing, the new steam engine came to be used primarily in mining and metallurgy on the Continent rather than in textile manufacturing. At first, almost all of the steam engines on the Continent came from Britain; not until the 1820s was a domestic machine industry developed.

In Britain, the Industrial Revolution had been built upon the cotton industry; on the Continent, the iron and coal of heavy industry led the way. As in textiles, however, heavy industry on the Continent before 1850 was a mixture of old and new. The adoption of new techniques, such as coke-smelted iron and puddling furnaces, coincided with the expansion of old-type charcoal blast furnaces. Before 1850, Germany lagged significantly behind both Belgium and France in heavy industry, and most German iron manufacturing remained based on old techniques. Not until the 1840s was coke-blast iron produced in the Rhineland. At that time, no one had yet realized the treasure of coal buried in the Ruhr valley. A German official wrote in 1852, "It is clearly not to be expected that Germany will ever be able to reach the level of production of coal and iron currently attained in England. This is implicit in our far more limited resource endowment." Little did he realize that although the industrial development of continental Europe was about a generation behind Britain at mid-century, after 1850 an incredibly rapid growth in continental industry would demonstrate that Britain was not, after all, destined to remain the world's greatest industrial nation.

The Industrial Revolution in the United States

In 1800, the United States was an agrarian society. There were no cities over 100,000, and six out of every seven American workers were farmers. By 1860, however, the population had grown from 5 to 30 million people, larger than Great Britain. Almost half of them lived west of the Appalachian Mountains. The number of states had more than doubled, from sixteen to thirty-four, and nine American cities had over 100,000 in population. Only 50 percent of American workers were farmers. From 1800 to the eve of the Civil War, the United States had experienced an industrial revolution and the urbanization that accompanied it.

The initial application of machinery to production was accomplished—as in continental Europe—by bor-

rowing from Great Britain. A British immigrant, Samuel Slater, established the first textile factory using water-powered spinning machines in Rhode Island in 1790. By 1813, factories with power looms copied from British versions were being established. Soon thereafter, however, Americans began to equal or surpass British technical inventions. The Harpers Ferry arsenal, for example, built muskets with interchangeable parts. Because all the individual parts of a musket were identical (e.g., all triggers were the same), the final product could be put together quickly and easily; this enabled Americans to avoid the more costly system in which skilled craftsmen fitted together individual parts made separately. The so-called American system reduced costs and revolutionized production by saving labor, important to a society that had few skilled artisans.

Unlike Britain, the United States was a large country. The lack of a good system of internal transportation seemed to limit American economic development by making the transport of goods prohibitively expensive. This was gradually remedied, however. Thousands of miles of roads and canals were built linking east and west. The steamboat facilitated transportation on the Great Lakes, Atlantic coastal waters, and rivers. It was especially important to the Mississippi valley; by 1860, a thousand steamboats plied that river (see the box on p. 720). Most important of all in the development of an American transportation system was the railroad. Beginning with 100 miles in 1830, by 1860 there were over 27,000 miles of railroad track covering the United States. This transportation revolution turned the United States into a single massive market for the manufactured goods of the Northeast, the early center of American industrialization.

Labor for the growing number of factories in this area came primarily from rural New England. The United States did not possess a large number of craftsmen, but it did have a rapidly expanding farm population; its size in the Northeast soon outstripped the available farmland. While some of this excess population, especially men, went west, others, mostly women, found work in the new textile and shoe factories of New England. Indeed, women made up more than 80 percent of the laboring force in the large textile factories. In Massachusetts mill towns, company boarding houses provided rooms for large numbers of young women who worked for several years before marriage. Outside Massachusetts, factory owners sought entire families including children to work in their mills; one mill owner ran this advertisement in a newspaper in Utica, New York: "Wanted: A few sober and industrious families of at least five children each,

"S–t–e–a–m–boat a–coming!"

Steamboats and railroads were crucial elements in a transportation revolution that enabled industrialists to expand markets by shipping goods cheaply and efficiently. At the same time, these marvels of technology aroused a sense of power and excitement that was an important aspect of the triumph of industrialization. The American novelist Mark Twain captured this sense of excitement in this selection from Life on the Mississippi.

Mark Twain, *Life on the Mississippi*

After all these years I can picture that old time to myself now, just as it was then: the white town drowsing in the sunshine of a summer's morning; the streets empty, or pretty nearly so; one or two clerks sitting in front of the Water street stores, with their splint-bottomed chairs tilted back against the walls, chins on breasts, hats slouched over their faces, asleep; . . . two or three lonely little freight piles scattered about the "levee"; a pile of "skids" on the slope of the stone-paved wharf, and the fragrant town drunkard asleep in the shadow of them; . . . the great Mississippi, the majestic, the magnificent Mississippi, rolling its mile- wide along, shining in the sun; the dense forest away on the other side; the "point" above the town, and the "point" below, bounding the river glimpse and turning it into a sort of sea, and withal a very still and brilliant and lonely one. Presently a film of dark smoke appears above on those remote "points"; instantly a negro drayman, famous for his quick eye and prodigious voice, lifts up to cry, "S–t–e–a–m–boat a–coming'!" and the scene changes! The town drunkard stirs, the clerks wake up, a furious clatter of drays follows, every house and store pours out a human contribution, and all in a twinkling the dead town [Hannibal, Missouri] is alive and moving. Drays, carts, men, boys, all go hurrying from many quarters to a common center, the wharf. Assembled there, the people fasten their eyes upon the coming boat as upon a wonder they are seeing for the first time. And the boat is rather a handsome sight, too. She is long and sharp and trim and pretty; she has two tall, fancy-topped chimneys, with a gilded device of some kind swung between them; a fanciful pilot-house, all glass and "ginger bread," perched on top of the "texas" deck behind them; the paddle-boxes are gorgeous with a picture or with gilded rays above the boat's name; the boiler deck, the hurricane deck, and the texas deck are fenced and ornamented with clean white railings; there is a flag gallantly flying from the jack-staff; the furnace doors are open and the fires glaring bravely; the upper decks are black with passengers; the captain stands by the big bell, calm, imposing, the envy of all; great volumes of the blackest smoke are rolling and tumbling out of the chimneys—a husbanded grandeur created with a bit of pitch pine just before arriving at a town; the crew are grouped on the forecastle; the broad stage is run far out over the port bow, and an envied deck-hand stands picturesquely on the end of it with a coil of rope in his hand; the pent steam is screaming through the gauge-cocks; the captain lifts his hand, a bell rings, the wheels stop; then they turn back, churning the water to foam, and the steam is at rest. Then such a scramble as there is to get aboard, and to get ashore, and to take in freight and to discharge freight, all at one and the same time; and such a yelling and cursing as the mates facilitate it all with! Ten minutes later the steamer is under way again, with no flag on the jack-staff and no black smoke issuing from the chimneys. After ten more minutes the town is dead again, and the town drunkard asleep by the skids once more.

over the age of eight years, are wanted at the Cotton Factory in Whitestown. Widows with large families would do well to attend this notice." When a decline in rural births threatened to dry up this labor pool in the 1830s and 1840s, European immigrants, especially poor and unskilled Irish, English, Scottish, and Welsh, appeared in large numbers to replace American women and children in the factories.

Women, children, and these immigrants had one thing in common as employees; they were largely unskilled laborers. Unskilled labor pushed American industrialization into a capital-intensive pattern. Factory owners invested heavily in machines that could produce in quantity at the hands of untrained workers. In Britain, the pace of mechanization was never as rapid because Britain's supply of skilled craftsmen made it more profitable to pursue a labor-intensive economy.

By 1860, the United States was well on its way to being an industrial nation. In the Northeast, the most industrialized section of the country, per capita income was 40 percent higher than the national average. Diets, it has been argued, were better and more varied;

machine-made clothing was more abundant. Industrialization did not necessarily lessen economic disparities, however. Despite a growing belief in a myth of social mobility based upon equality of economic opportunity, the reality was that the richest 10 percent of the population in the cities held 70 to 80 percent of the wealth compared to 50 percent in 1800. Nevertheless, American historians generally argue that while the rich got richer, the poor, as a result of experiencing an increase in their purchasing power, did not get poorer.

The Social Impact of the Industrial Revolution

Eventually, the Industrial Revolution revolutionized the social life of Europe and the world. Although much of Europe remained bound by its traditional ways, already in the first half of the nineteenth century, the social impact of the Industrial Revolution was being felt, and future avenues of growth were becoming apparent. Vast changes in the number of people and where they lived were already dramatically evident.

Population Growth

Population increases had already begun in the eighteenth century, but they became dramatic in the nineteenth century. They were also easier to discern because record keeping became more accurate. In the nineteenth century, governments began to take periodic censuses and systematically collect precise data on births, deaths, and marriages. In Britain, for example, the first census was taken in 1801, and a systematic registration of births, deaths, and marriages was begun in 1836. In 1750, the total European population stood at an estimated 140 million; by 1800, it had increased to 187 million and by 1850 to 266 million, almost twice its 1750 level.

This population explosion cannot be explained by a higher birthrate for birthrates were declining after 1790. Between 1790 and 1850, Germany's birthrate dropped from 40 per thousand to 36.1; Great Britain's from 35.4 to 32.6, and France's from 32.5 to 26.7. The key to the expansion of population was the decline in death rates evident throughout Europe. Historians now believe that two major causes explain this decline. There was a drop in the number of deaths from famines, epidemics, and war. Major epidemic diseases, in particular, such as plague and smallpox declined noticeably, although

small-scale epidemics continued. The ordinary death rate also declined as a general increase in the food supply, already evident in the agricultural revolution of Britain in the late eighteenth century, spread to more areas. More food enabled a greater number of people to be better fed and therefore more resistant to disease. Famine largely disappeared from western Europe, although there were dramatic exceptions in isolated areas, Ireland being the most significant.

Although industrialization itself did not cause population growth, industrialized areas did experience a change in the composition of the population. By 1850, the proportion of the active population involved in manufacturing, mining, or building had risen to 48 percent in Britain, 37 percent in Belgium, and 27 percent in France. But the actual areas of industrialization in 1850 were minimal, being concentrated in northern and central England, northern France, Belgium, and sections of western and eastern Germany. As one author has commented, "they were islands in an agricultural sea."

This minimal industrialization, in light of the growing population, meant severe congestion in the countryside where a growing population divided the same amount of land into ever-smaller plots and also created an ever-larger mass of landless peasants. Overpopulation, especially noticeable in parts of France, northern Spain, southern Germany, Sweden, and Ireland, magnified the already existing problem of rural poverty. In Ireland, it produced the century's greatest catastrophe.

Ireland was one of the most oppressed areas in western Europe. The predominantly Catholic peasant population rented land from mostly absentee British Protestant landlords whose primary concern was collecting their rents. Irish peasants lived in mud hovels in desperate poverty. The cultivation of the potato, a nutritious and relatively easy food to grow that produced three times as much food per acre as grain, gave Irish peasants a basic staple that enabled them to survive and even expand in numbers. As only an acre or two of potatoes was sufficient to feed a family, Irish men and women married earlier than elsewhere and started having children earlier as well. This led to significant growth in the population. Between 1781 and 1845, the Irish population doubled from 4 to 8 million. Probably half of this population depended on the potato for survival. In the summer of 1845, the potato crop in Ireland was struck by blight due to a fungus that turned the potatoes black. Between 1845 and 1851, the Great Famine decimated the Irish population (see the box on p. 722). Over 1 million died of starvation and disease

The Great Irish Famine

The Great Irish Famine was one of the nineteenth century's worst natural catastrophes. Overly dependent on a single crop, the Irish were decimated by the potato blight. In this selection, an Irish nationalist reported what he had witnessed in Galway in 1847.

John Mitchel, *The Last Conquest of Ireland*

In the depth of winter we travelled to Galway, through the very centre of that fertile island, and saw sights that will never wholly leave the eyes that beheld them—cowering wretches, almost naked in the savage weather, prowling in turnip-fields, and endeavouring to grub up roots which had been left, but running to hide as the mail-coach rolled by;—very large fields where small farms had been "consolidated," showing dark bars of fresh mould running through them where the ditches had been levelled;—groups and families, sitting or wandering on the high-road, with failing steps and dim patient eyes, gazing hopelessly into infinite darkness; before them, around them, above them, nothing but darkness and despair—parties of tall brawny men, once the flower of Meath and Galway, stalking by with a fierce but vacant scowl; as if they knew that all this ought not to be, but knew not whom to blame, saw none whom they could rend in their wrath; . . . . Around those farmhouses which were still inhabited were to be seen hardly any stacks of grain; the poor-rate collector, the rent agent, the county-cess collector had carried it off; and sometimes I could see in front of the cottages little children leaning against a fence when the sun shone out—for they could not stand—their limbs fleshless, their bodies half naked, their faces bloated yet wrinkled, and of a pale greenish hue,—children who would never, it was too plain, grow up to be men and women.

while almost 2 million emigrated to the United States and Britain. Of all the European nations, only Ireland had a declining population in the nineteenth century. But other countries, too, faced problems of dire poverty and declining standards of living as their populations exploded.

The flight of so many Irish to America reminds us that the traditional safety valve for overpopulation has always been emigration. Between 1821 and 1850, the number of emigrants from Europe averaged about 110,000 a year. Most of these emigrants came from places like Ireland and southern Germany, where peasant life had been reduced to marginal existence. Times of agrarian crisis resulted in great waves of emigration. Bad harvests in Europe in 1846–1847 (such as the catastrophe in Ireland) produced massive numbers of emigrants. In addition to the estimated 1.6 million from Ireland, for example, 935,000 people left Germany between 1847 and 1854. More often than emigrating, however, the rural masses sought a solution to their poverty by moving to towns and cities within their own countries to find work. It should not astonish us then that the first half of the nineteenth century was a period of rapid urbanization.

The Growth of Cities

Although the Western world would not become a predominantly urban society until the twentieth century, cities and towns had already grown dramatically in the first half of the nineteenth century, a phenomenon related to industrialization. Cities had traditionally been centers for princely courts, government and military offices, churches, and commerce. By 1850, especially in Great Britain and Belgium, they were rapidly becoming places for manufacturing and industry. With the steam engine, entrepreneurs could locate their manufacturing plants in urban centers where they had ready access to transportation facilities and unemployed people from the country looking for work.

In 1800, Great Britain had one major city, London, with a population of 1 million, and six cities between 50,000 and 100,000. Fifty years later, London's population had swelled to 2,363,000 while there were nine cities over 100,000 and eighteen cities with populations between 50,000 and 100,000. All together, these twenty-eight cities accounted for 5.7 million or one-fifth of the total British population. When the populations of cities under 50,000 are added to this total, we realize that more than 50 percent of the British population lived in towns and cities by 1850. Britain was forced to become a food importer rather than an exporter as the number of people involved in agriculture declined to 20 percent of the population.

Urban populations also grew on the Continent, but less dramatically. Paris had 547,000 inhabitants in 1800, but only two other French cities had populations of 100,000: Lyons and Marseilles. In 1851, Paris had grown to 1 million while Lyons and Marseilles were still under 200,000. German and Austrian lands had only three cities with over 100,000 inhabitants (Vienna had 247,000) in 1800; fifty years later, there were only five while Vienna had grown to 440,000. As these figures show, urbanization did not proceed as rapidly here as in Britain; of course, neither had industrialization. Even in Belgium, the most heavily industrialized country on the Continent, almost 50 percent of the male workforce was still engaged in agriculture by midcentury.

URBAN LIVING CONDITIONS IN THE EARLY INDUSTRIAL REVOLUTION

The dramatic growth of cities in the first half of the nineteenth century produced miserable living conditions for many of the inhabitants. Of course, this had been true for centuries in European cities, but the rapid urbanization associated with the Industrial Revolution intensified the problems in the first half of the nineteenth century and made these wretched conditions all the more apparent. City authorities of whatever kind either felt little responsibility for these conditions or more frequently did not have the skills to cope with the complex, new problems associated with such rapidly growing populations. City authorities might also often be factory owners who possessed little or no tradition of public service or public responsibility.

Wealthy, middle-class inhabitants, as usual, insulated themselves as best they could, often living in suburbs or the outer ring of the city where they could have individual houses and gardens. In the inner ring of the city stood the small row houses, some with gardens, of the artisans and lower middle class. Finally, located in the center of most industrial towns were the row houses of the industrial workers. This report on working-class housing in the British city of Birmingham in 1843 gives an idea of the general conditions they faced:

> The courts [of working-class row houses] are extremely numerous; . . . a very large portion of the poorer classes of the inhabitants reside in them. . . . The courts vary in the number of the houses which they contain, from four to twenty, and most of these houses are three stories high, and built, as it is termed, back to back. There is a wash-house, an ash-pit, and a privy at the end, or on one side of the court, and not unfrequently one or more pigsties and heaps of manure. Generally speaking, the privies in the old courts are in a most filthy condition. Many which we have inspected were in a state which renders it impossible for us to conceive how they could be used; they were without doors and overflowing with filth.

The people who lived in such houses were actually the fortunate; the truly unfortunate were those forced to live in cellars. As one reformer asked, "how can a hole underground of from 12 to 15 feet square admit of ventilation so as to fit it for a human habitation?" Rooms were not large and were frequently overcrowded, as this government report of 1838 revealed: "I entered several of the tenements. In one of them, on the ground floor, I found six persons occupying a very small room, two in bed, ill with fever. In the room above this were two more persons in one bed ill with fever." Another report said: "There were 63 families where there were at least five persons to one bed; and there were some in which even six were packed in one bed, lying at the top and bottom—children and adults."[6]

Sanitary conditions in these towns were appalling. Due to the lack of municipal direction, city streets were often used as sewers and open drains: "In the centre of this street is a gutter, into which potato parings, the refuse of animal and vegetable matters of all kinds, the dirty water from the washing of clothes and of the houses, are all poured, and there they stagnate and putrefy."[7] Unable to deal with human excrement, cities in the new industrial era smelled horrible and were extraordinarily unhealthy. Towns and cities were fundamentally death traps. As deaths outnumbered births in most large cities in the first half of the nineteenth century, only a constant influx of people from the country kept them alive and growing.

◆ **A New Industrial Town.** Cities and towns grew dramatically in Britain in the first half of the nineteenth century, largely as a result of industrialization. Pictured here is Saltaire, a model textile factory and town founded near Bradford by Titus Salt in 1851. To facilitate the transportation of goods, the town was built on the Leeds and Liverpool canals.

Adding to the deterioration of urban life was the adulteration of food. Consumers were defrauded in a variety of ways: alum was added to make bread look white and hence more expensive; beer and milk were watered down; and red lead despite its poisonous qualities was substituted for pepper. The government refused to intervene; a parliamentary committee stated that "more benefit is likely to result from the effects of a free competition . . . than can be expected to result from any regulations." It was not until 1875 that an effective Food and Drugs Act was passed in Britain.

Our knowledge of the pathetic conditions in the early industrial cities is largely derived from an abundance of social investigations. Such investigations began in France in the 1820s. In Britain the Poor Law Commissioners produced detailed reports. The investigators were often struck by the physically and morally debilitating effects of urban industrial life on the poor. They observed, for example, that young working-class men were considerably shorter and scrawnier than the sons of middle-class families and much more subject to disease. They were especially alarmed by what they considered the moral consequences of such living conditions: prostitution, crime, and sexual immoralities, all of which they saw as the effect of such squalid lives.

To many of the well-to-do middle classes, this situation presented a clear danger to society. Were not these masses of workers, sunk in crime, disease, and immorality, a potential threat to their own well-being? Might not the masses be organized and used by unscrupulous demagogues to overthrow the established order? One of the most eloquent British reformers of the 1830s and 1840s, James Kay-Shuttleworth, described them as "volcanic elements, by whose explosive violence the structure of society may be destroyed." Another observer spoke more contemptuously in 1850:

> They live precisely like brutes, to gratify . . . the appetites of their uncultivated bodies, and then die, to go they have never thought, cared, or wondered whither. . . . Brought up in the darkness of barbarism, they have no idea that it is possible for them to attain any higher condition; they are not even sentient enough to desire to change their situation. . . . they eat, drink, breed, work and die; and . . . the richer and more intelligent classes are obliged to guard them with police.[8]

Some observers were less arrogant, however, and wondered if the workers could be held responsible for their fate.

One of the best of a new breed of urban reformers was Edwin Chadwick (1800–1890). With a background in law, Chadwick became obsessed with eliminating the poverty and squalor of the metropolitan areas. He became a civil servant and was soon appointed to a number of government investigatory commissions. As secretary of the Poor Law Commission, he initiated a passionate search for detailed facts about the living

◆ **Slums of Industrial London.** Industrialization and rapid urban growth produced dreadful living conditions in many nineteenth-century cities. Filled with garbage and human waste, cities often smelled terrible and were extremely unhealthy. This drawing by Gustave Doré shows a London slum district overshadowed by rail viaducts.

conditions of the working classes. After three years of investigation, Chadwick summarized the results in his *Report on the Condition of the Labouring Population of Great Britain*, published in 1842. In it he concluded that "the various forms of epidemic, endemic, and other disease" were directly caused by the "atmospheric impurities produced by decomposing animal and vegetable substances, by damp and filth, and close overcrowded dwellings [prevailing] amongst the population in every part of the kingdom." Such conditions, he argued, could be eliminated. As to the means: "The primary and most important measures, and at the same time the most practicable, and within the recognized province of public administration, are drainage, the removal of all refuse of habitations, streets, and roads, and the improvement of the supplies of water."[9] In other words, Chadwick was advocating a system of modern sanitary reforms consisting of efficient sewers and a supply of piped water. Six years after his report and largely due to his efforts, Britain's first Public Health Act created a National Board of Health empowered to form local boards that would establish modern sanitary systems.

Many middle-class citizens were quite willing to support the public health reforms of men like Chadwick because of their fear of cholera. Outbreaks of this deadly disease had ravaged Europe in the early 1830s and late 1840s and were especially rampant in the overcrowded cities. As city authorities and wealthier residents became convinced that filthy conditions helped to spread the disease, they began to support the call for new public health measures.

New Social Classes: The Industrial Middle Class

The rise of industrial capitalism produced a new middle-class group. The bourgeois or middle class was not new; it had existed since the emergence of cities in the Middle Ages. Originally, the bourgeois was the burgher or town dweller, whether active as a merchant, official, artisan, lawyer, or man of letters, who enjoyed a special set of rights from the charter of his town. As wealthy townspeople bought land, the original meaning of the word *bourgeois* became lost, and the term came to include people involved in commerce, industry, and banking as well as professionals, such as lawyers, teachers, physicians, and government officials at various levels. At the lower end of the economic scale were master craftsmen and shopkeepers.

Lest we make the industrial middle class too much of an abstraction, we need to look at who the new industrial entrepreneurs actually were. These were the people who constructed the factories, purchased the machines, and figured out where the markets were. Their qualities included resourcefulness, single-mindedness, resolution, initiative, vision, ambition, and often, of course, greed. As Jedediah Strutt, the cotton manufacturer said, "Getting of money . . . is the main business of the life of men."

But this was not an easy task. The early industrial entrepreneurs were called upon to superintend an enormous array of functions that are handled today by teams of managers; they raised capital, determined markets, set company objectives, organized the factory and its labor, and trained supervisors who could act for them. The opportunities for making money were great, but the risks were also tremendous. The cotton trade, for example, which was so important to the early Industrial Revolution, was intensely competitive. Only through constant expansion could one feel secure, so early entrepreneurs reinvested most of their initial profits. Fear of bankruptcy was constant, especially among small firms. Furthermore, most early industrial enterprises were small. Even by the 1840s, only 10 percent of British industrial firms employed more than 5,000 workers; 43 percent had fewer than 100 workers. As entrepreneurs went bankrupt, new people could enter the race for profits, especially since the initial outlay required was not gigantic. In 1816, only one mill in five in the important industrial city of Manchester was in the hands of its original owners.

The social origins of industrial entrepreneurs were incredibly diverse. Many of the most successful came from a mercantile background. Three London merchants, for example, founded a successful ironworks in Wales that owned eight steam engines and employed 5,000 men. In Britain, land and domestic industry were often interdependent. Joshua Fielden, for example, acquired sufficient capital to establish a factory by running a family sheep farm while working looms in the farmhouse. Intelligent, clever, and ambitious apprentices who had learned their trades well could also strike it rich. William Radcliffe's family engaged in agriculture and spinning and weaving at home; he learned quickly how to succeed:

> Availing myself of the improvements that came out while I was in my teens . . . with my little savings and a practical knowledge of every process from the cotton bag to the piece of cloth . . . I was ready to commence business for myself and by the year 1789 I was well established and employed many hands both in spinning and weaving as a master manufacturer.[10]

By 1801, Radcliffe was operating a factory employing 1,000 workers.

Members of dissenting religious minorities were often prominent among the early industrial leaders of Britain. The Darbys and Lloyds who were iron manufacturers, the Barclays and Lloyds who were bankers, and the Trumans and Perkins who were brewers were all Quakers. These were expensive trades and depended upon the financial support that co-religionists in religious minorities provided for each other. Most historians believe that a major reason members of these religious minorities were so prominent in business was that they lacked other opportunities. Legally excluded from many public offices, they directed their ambitions into the new industrial capitalism.

It is interesting to note that in Britain in particular aristocrats also became entrepreneurs. The Lambtons in Northumberland, the Curwens in Cumberland, the Norfolks in Yorkshire, and the Dudleys in Staffordshire all invested in mining enterprises. This close relationship between land and industry helped Britain to assume the leadership role in the early Industrial Revolution.

By 1850, in Britain at least, the kind of traditional entrepreneurship that had created the Industrial Revolution was declining and was being replaced by a new business aristocracy. This new generation of entrepreneurs stemmed from the professional and industrial middle classes, especially as sons inherited the successful businesses established by their fathers. It must not be forgotten, however, that even after 1850 a large number of small businesses existed in Britain and some were still founded by people from humble backgrounds. Indeed, the age of large-scale corporate capitalism did not begin until the 1890s (see Chapter 24).

Increasingly, the new industrial entrepreneurs—the bankers and owners of factories and mines—came to amass much wealth and play an important role alongside the traditional landed elites of their societies. The Industrial Revolution began at a time when the pre-industrial agrarian world was still largely dominated by landed elites. As the new bourgeoisie bought great estates and acquired social respectability, they also sought political power, and in the course of the nineteenth century, their wealthiest members would merge with those old elites.

New Social Classes: Workers in the Industrial Age

At the same time the members of the industrial middle class were seeking to reduce the barriers between themselves and the landed elite, they also were trying to separate themselves from the laboring classes below them. The working class was actually a mixture of different groups in the first half of the nineteenth century. In the course of the nineteenth century, factory workers would form an industrial proletariat, but in the first half of that century, they by no means constituted a majority of the working class in any major city, even in Britain. According to the 1851 census in Britain, while there were 1.8 million agricultural laborers and 1 million domestic servants, there were only 811,000 workers in the cotton and woolen industries. Even one-third of these were still working in small workshops or in their own homes.

Within the cities, artisans or craftsmen remained the largest group of urban workers during the first half of the nineteenth century. They worked in numerous small industries, such as shoemaking, glovemaking, bookbinding, printing, and bricklaying. Some craftsmen formed a kind of aristocracy of labor, especially those employed in such luxury trades as coachbuilding and clockmaking who earned higher wages than others. Artisans were not factory workers; they were traditionally organized in guilds where they passed on their skills to apprentices. But guilds were increasingly losing their power, especially in industrialized countries. Fearful of losing out to the new factories that could produce goods more cheaply, artisans tended to support movements against industrialization. Industrialists welcomed the decline of skilled craftsmen, as one perceptive old tailor realized in telling his life story:

It is upwards of 30 years since I first went to work at the tailoring trade in London. . . . I continued working for the honourable trade and belonging to the Society [for tailors] for about 15 years. My weekly earnings then averaged £1 16s. a week while I was at work, and for several years I was seldom out of work . . . no one could have been happier than I was. . . . But then, with my sight defective . . . I could get no employment at the honourable trade, and that was the ruin of me entirely; for working there, of course, I got "scratched" from the trade society, and so lost all hope of being provided for by them in my helplessness. The workshop . . . was about seven feet square, and so low, that as you [sat] on the floor you could touch the ceiling with the tip of your finger. In this place seven of us worked. [The master] paid little more than half the regular wages, and employed such men as myself—only those who couldn't get anything better to do. . . . I don't think my wages there averaged above 12s a week. . . . I am convinced I lost my eyesight by working in that cheap shop. . . . It is by the ruin of such men as me that these masters are enabled to undersell the better shops. . . . That's the way, sir, the cheap clothes is produced, by making blind beggars of the workmen, like myself, and throwing us on the parish in our old age.[11]

Servants also formed another large group of urban workers, especially in major cities like London and Paris. Many were women from the countryside who became utterly dependent upon their upper- and middle-class employers.

WORKING CONDITIONS FOR THE INDUSTRIAL WORKING CLASS

Workers in the new industrial factories also faced wretched working conditions. We have already observed the psychological traumas workers experienced from their employers' efforts to break old preindustrial work patterns and create a well-disciplined labor force. But what were the physical conditions of the factories?

Unquestionably, in the early decades of the Industrial Revolution, "places of work," as early factories were called, were dreadful. Work hours ranged from twelve to sixteen hours a day, six days a week, with a half hour for lunch and dinner. There was no security of employment and no minimum wage. The worst conditions were in the cotton mills where temperatures were especially debilitating. One report noted that "in the cotton-spinning work, these creatures are kept, fourteen hours in each day, locked up, summer and winter, in a heat of from eighty to eighty-four degrees." Mills were also dirty, dusty, and unhealthy:

Not only is there not a breath of sweet air in these truly infernal scenes, but . . . there is the abominable and pernicious stink of the gas to assist in the murderous effects of the heat. In addition to the noxious effluvia of the gas, mixed with the steam, there are the dust, and what is called cotton-flyings or fuz, which the unfortunate creatures have to inhale; and . . . the notorious fact is that well constitutioned men are rendered old and past labour at forty years of age, and that children are rendered decrepit and deformed, and thousands upon thousands of them slaughtered by consumptions, before they arrive at the age of sixteen.[12]

Thus ran a report on working conditions in the cotton industry in 1824.

Conditions in the coal mines were also harsh. The introduction of steam power meant only that steam-powered engines mechanically lifted coal to the top. Inside the mines, men still bore the burden of digging the coal out while horses, mules, women, and children hauled coal carts on rails to the lift. Dangers abounded in coal mines; cave-ins, explosions, and gas fumes (called "bad air") were a way of life. The cramped conditions—tunnels often did not exceed three or four feet in height—and constant dampness in the mines resulted in deformed bodies and ruined lungs.

Both children and women were employed in large numbers in early factories and mines. Children had been an important part of the family economy in preindustrial times, working in the fields or carding and spinning wool at home with the growth of cottage industry. In the Industrial Revolution, however, child labor was exploited more than ever and in a considerably more systematic fashion (see the boxes on pp. 728–729). The owners of cotton factories appreciated certain features of child labor. Children had an especially delicate touch as spinners of cotton. Their smaller size made it easier for them to crawl under machines to gather loose cotton. Moreover, children were more

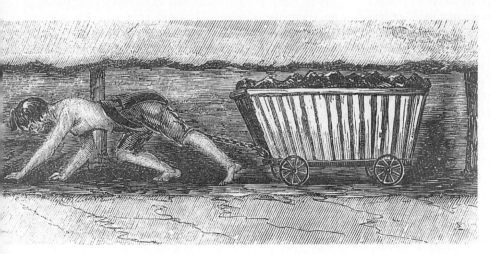

✦ **Women in the Mines.** Both women and children were often employed in the early factories and mines of the nineteenth century. As is evident in this illustration of a woman dragging a cart loaded with coal behind her, they often worked under very trying conditions.

Child Labor: Discipline in the Textile Mills

Child labor was certainly not new, but in the early Industrial Revolution it was exploited more systematically. These selections are taken from the Report of Sadler's Committee, which was commissioned in 1832 to inquire into the condition of child factory workers.

How They Kept the Children Awake

It is a very frequent thing at Mr. Marshall's [at Shrewsbury] where the least children were employed (for there were plenty working at six years of age), for Mr. Horseman to start the mill earlier in the morning than he formerly did; and provided a child should be drowsy, the overlooker walks round the room with a stick in his hand, and he touches that child on the shoulder, and says, "Come here." In a corner of the room there is an iron cistern; it is filled with water; he takes this boy, and takes him up by the legs, and dips him over head in the cistern, and sends him to work for the remainder of the day. . . .

What means were taken to keep the children to their work?—Sometimes they would tap them over the head, or nip them over the nose, or give them a pinch of snuff, or throw water in their faces, or pull them off where they were, and job them about to keep them waking.

The Sadistic Overlooker

Samuel Downe, age 29, factory worker living near Leeds; at the age of about ten began work at Mr. Marshall's mills at Shrewsbury, where the customary hours when work was brisk were generally 5 A.M. to 8 P.M., sometimes from 5:30 A.M. to 8 or 9:

What means were taken to keep the children awake and vigilant, especially at the termination of such a day's labour as you have described?—There was generally a blow or a box, or a tap with a strap, or sometimes the hand.

Have you yourself been strapped?—Yes, most severely, till I could not bear to sit upon a chair without having pillows, and through that I left. I was strapped both on my own legs, and then I was put upon a man's back, and then strapped and buckled with two straps to an iron pillar, and flogged, and all by one overlooker; after that he took a piece of tow, and twisted it in the shape of a cord, and put it in my mouth, and tied it behind my head.

He gagged you?—Yes; and then he ordered me to run round a part of the machinery where he was overlooker, and he stood at one end, and every time I came there he struck me with a stick, which I believe was an ash plant, and which he generally carried in his hand, and sometimes he hit me, and sometimes he did not; and one of the men in the room came and begged me off, and that he let me go, and not beat me any more, and consequently he did.

You have been beaten with extraordinary severity?—Yes, I was beaten so that I had not power to cry at all, or hardly speak at one time. What age were you at that time?—Between 10 and 11.

easily broken to factory work. Above all, children represented a cheap supply of labor. In 1821, 49 percent of the British people were under twenty years of age. Hence, children made up a particularly abundant supply of labor, and they were paid only about one-sixth or one-third of what a man was paid. In the cotton factories in 1838, children under eighteen made up 29 percent of the total workforce; children as young as seven worked twelve to fifteen hours per day six days a week in cotton mills.

Especially terrible in the early Industrial Revolution was the use of so-called pauper apprentices. These were orphans or children abandoned by their parents who had wound up in the care of local parishes. To save on their upkeep, parish officials found it convenient to apprentice them to factory owners looking for a cheap source of labor. These children worked long hours under strict discipline and received inadequate food and recreation; many became deformed from being kept too long in unusual positions. Although economic liberals and some industrialists were against all state intervention in economic matters, Parliament eventually remedied some of the worst ills of child abuse in factories and mines (see Efforts at Change: Reformers and Government later in this chapter). The legislation of the 1830s and 1840s, however, primarily affected child labor in textile factories and mines. It did not touch the use of children in small workshops or the nonfactory trades that were not protected. As these trades were in competition with the new factories, conditions there were often even worse. Pottery works, for example, were not investigated until the 1860s when it was found that 17 percent of the workers were under eleven years of age. One investigator reported what he found:

Child Labor: The Mines

After examining conditions in British coal mines, a government official commented that "the hardest labour in the worst room in the worst-conducted factory is less hard, less cruel, and less demoralizing than the labour in the best of coal-mines." Yet it was not until 1842 that legislation was passed eliminating the labor of boys under ten from the mines. This selection is taken from a government report on the mines in Lancashire.

The Black Holes of Worsley

Examination of Thomas Gibson and George Bryan, witnesses from the coal mines at Worsley:

Have you worked from a boy in a coal mine?—(Both) Yes.

What had you to do then?—Thrutching the basket and drawing. It is done by little boys; one draws the basket and the other pushes it behind. Is that hard labour?—Yes, very hard labour.

For how many hours a day did you work?—Nearly nine hours regularly; sometimes twelve; I have worked about thirteen. We used to go in at six in the morning, and took a bit of bread and cheese in our pocket, and stopped two or three minutes; and some days nothing at all to eat.

How was it that sometimes you had nothing to eat?—We were over-burdened. I had only a mother, and she had nothing to give me. I was sometimes half starved. . . .

Do they work in the same way now exactly?—Yes, they do; they have nothing more than a bit of bread and cheese in their pocket, and sometimes can't eat it all, owing to the dust and damp and badness of air; and sometimes it is as hot as an oven; sometimes I have seen it so hot as to melt a candle.

What are the usual wages of a boy of eight?—They used to get 3d or 4d a day. Now a man's wages is divided into eight eighths; and when a boy is eight years old he gets one of those eighths; at eleven, two eighths; at thirteen, three eighths; at fifteen, four eighths; at twenty, man's wages.

What are the wages of a man?—About 15s if he is in full employment, but often not more than 10s, and out of that he has to get his tools and candles. He consumes about four candles in nine hours' work, in some places six; 6d per pound, and twenty-four candles to the pound.

Were you ever beaten as a child?—Yes, many a score of times; both kicks and thumps.

Are many girls employed in the pits?—Yes, a vast of those. They do the same kind of work as the boys till they get about 14 years of age, when they get the wages of half a man, and never get more, and continue at the same work for many years.

Did they ever fight together?—Yes, many days together. Both boys and girls; sometimes they are very loving with one another.

The boys were kept in constant motion throughout the day, each carrying from thirty to fifty dozen of moulds into the stoves, and remaining . . . long enough to take the dried earthenware away. The distance thus run by a boy in the course of a day . . . was estimated at seven miles. From the very nature of this exhausting occupation children were rendered pale, weak and unhealthy. In the depth of winter, with the thermometer in the open air sometimes below zero, boys, with little clothing but rags, might be seen running to and fro on errands or to their dinners with the perspiration on their foreheads, "after labouring for hours like little slaves." The inevitable result of such transitions of temperature were consumption, asthma, and acute inflammation.[13]

Little wonder that child labor legislation enacted in 1864 included pottery works.

By 1830, women and children made up two-thirds of the cotton industry's labor. However, as the number of children employed declined under the Factory Act of 1833, their places were taken by women, who came to dominate the labor forces of the early factories. Women made up 50 percent of the labor force in textile (cotton and woolen) factories before 1870. They were mostly unskilled labor and were paid half or less of what men received. Excessive working hours for women were outlawed in 1844, but only in textile factories and mines; not until 1867 were they outlawed in craft workshops.

The employment of children and women in large part represents a continuation of a preindustrial kinship pattern. Cottage industry had always involved the efforts of the entire family, and it seemed perfectly natural to continue this pattern. Men migrating from the countryside to industrial towns and cities took their wives and children with them into the factory or into the mines. Of 136 employees in Robert Peel's factory at Bury in 1801, 95 belonged to twenty-six families. The impetus for this family work often came from the family itself. The factory owner Jedediah Strutt was opposed to child labor under ten but was forced by parents to take children as young as seven.

The employment of large numbers of women in factories did not produce a significant transformation in female working patterns, as was once assumed. Studies of urban households in France and Britain, for example, have revealed that throughout the nineteenth century traditional types of female labor still predominated in women's work world. In 1851, fully 40 percent of the female workforce in Britain consisted of domestic servants. In France, the largest group of female workers, 40 percent, worked in agriculture. In addition, only 20 percent of female workers in Britain labored in factories, while only 10 percent did so in France. Regional and local studies have also found that most of the workers were single women. Few married women worked outside their homes.

The Factory Acts that limited the work hours of children and women also began to break up the traditional kinship pattern of work and led to a new pattern based on a separation of work and home. Men came to be regarded as responsible for the primary work obligations while women assumed daily control of the family and performed low-paying jobs such as laundry work that could be done in the home. Domestic industry made it possible for women to continue their contributions to family survival.

Historians have also reminded us that if the treatment of children in the mines and factories seems particularly cruel and harsh, contemporary treatment of children in general was often brutal. Beatings, for example, had long been regarded, even by dedicated churchmen and churchwomen, as the best way to discipline children.

Standards of Living

One of the most heated debates on the Industrial Revolution concerns the standard of living. Most historians assume that in the long run the Industrial Revolution increased living standards dramatically in the form of higher per capita incomes and greater consumer choices. But did the first generation of industrial workers experience a decline in their living standards and suffer unnecessarily? Some historians have argued that early industrialization required huge profits to be reinvested in new and ever more expensive equipment; thus, to make the requisite profits, industrialists had to keep wages low. Others have questioned that argument, pointing out that initial investments in early machinery were not necessarily large nor did they need to be. What certainly did occur in the first half of the nineteenth century was a widening gap between rich and poor. One estimate, based on income tax returns in Britain, is that the wealthiest 1 percent of the population increased its share of the national product from 25 percent in 1801 to 35 percent in 1848.

Wages, prices, and consumption patterns are some of the criteria used for measuring the standard of living. Between 1780 and 1850, as far as we can determine from the available evidence, both wages and prices fluctuated widely. Most historians believe that during the Napoleonic wars the increase in prices outstripped wages. Between 1815 and 1830, a price fall was accompanied by a slight increase in wages. But from 1830 to the late 1840s, real wages seem to have improved although regional variations make generalizations dangerous.

When we look at consumption patterns, we find that in Britain in 1850 tea, sugar, and coffee were still semiluxuries consumed primarily by the upper and middle classes and better-off artisans. Meat consumption per capita was less in 1840 than in 1780. On the other hand, a mass market had developed in the cheap cotton goods so important to the Industrial Revolution. As a final note on the question of the standard of living, some historians who take a positive view of the early Industrial Revolution have questioned what would have happened to Britain's growing population without the Industrial Revolution. Would it have gone the way of Ireland's in the Great Hunger of the mid-nineteenth century? No one really knows.

No doubt the periodic crises of overproduction that haunted industrialization from its beginnings caused even further economic hardship. Short-term economic depressions brought high unemployment and increased social tensions. Unemployment figures could be astronomical. During one of these economic depressions in 1842, for example, 60 percent of the factory employees in Bolton were laid off. Cyclical depressions were particularly devastating in towns whose prosperity rested on one industry.

Overall we can say that some evidence exists for an increase in real wages for the working classes between

1790 and 1850, especially in the 1840s. But standards of living be assessed only in terms of prices, wages, and consumption patterns? No doubt those meant little to people who faced dreadful housing, adulterated food, public health hazards, and the psychological traumas associated with a complete change in work habits and way of life. The real gainers in the early Industrial Revolution were members of the middle class—and some skilled workers whose jobs were not eliminated by the new machines. But industrial workers themselves would have to wait until the second half of the nineteenth century to reap the benefits of industrialization.

Efforts at Change: The Workers

Before long, workers looked to the formation of labor organizations to gain decent wages and working conditions. The British government, reacting against the radicalism of the French revolutionary working classes, had passed a series of Combination Acts in 1799 and 1800 outlawing associations of workers. The legislation failed to prevent the formation of trade unions, however. Similar to the craft societies of earlier times, these new associations were formed by skilled workers in a number of new industries, including the cotton spinners, ironworkers, coal miners, and shipwrights. These unions served two purposes. One was to preserve their own workers' position by limiting entry into their trade; another was to gain benefits from the employers. These early trade unions had limited goals. They favored a working-class struggle against employers, but only to win improvements for the members of their own trades.

Some trade unions were even willing to strike to gain their goals. Bitter strikes were carried out by hand-loom weavers in Glasgow in 1813, cotton spinners in Manchester in 1818, and miners in Northumberland and Durham in 1810. Such blatant illegal activity caused Parliament to repeal the Combination Acts in 1824, accepting the argument of some members that the acts themselves had so alienated workers that they had formed unions. Unions were now tolerated, but other legislation enabled authorities to keep close watch over their activities.

In the 1820s and 1830s, the union movement began to focus on the creation of national unions. One of the leaders in this effort was a well-known cotton magnate and social reformer, Robert Owen (1771–1858). Owen came to believe in the creation of voluntary associations that would demonstrate to others the benefits of cooperative rather than competitive living (see Chapter 22 on the utopian socialists). Although Owen's program was not directed specifically to trade unionists, his ideas had great appeal to some of their leaders. Under Owen's direction, plans emerged for a Grand National Consolidated Trades Union, which was formed in February 1834. As a national federation of trade unions, its primary purpose was to coordinate a general strike for the eight-hour working day. Rhetoric, however, soon outpaced reality, and by the summer of the same year, the lack of real working-class support led to its total

✦ **A Trade Union Membership Card.** Skilled workers in a number of new industries formed trade unions in an attempt to gain higher wages, better working conditions, and special benefits. The scenes at the bottom of this membership card for the Associated Shipwright's Society illustrate some of the medical and social benefits for its members.

collapse. Afterward, the union movement reverted to trade unions for individual crafts. The largest and most successful was the Amalgamated Society of Engineers, formed in 1850. Its provision of generous unemployment benefits in return for a small weekly payment was precisely the kind of practical gains these trade unions sought. Larger goals would have to wait.

Trade unionism was not the only type of collective action by workers in the early decades of the Industrial Revolution. The Luddites were skilled craftsmen in the Midlands and northern England who in 1812 attacked the machines that they believed threatened their livelihoods. These attacks failed to stop the industrial mechanization of Britain and have been viewed as utterly naive. Some historians, however, have also seen them as an intense eruption of feeling against unrestrained industrial capitalism. The inability of 12,000 troops to find the culprits provides stunning evidence of the local support they received in their areas.

A much more meaningful expression of the attempts of British workers to improve their condition developed in the movement known as Chartism. It was the first "important political movement of working men organized during the nineteenth century." Its aim was to achieve political democracy. A People's Charter drawn up in 1838 demanded universal male suffrage, payment for members of Parliament, and annual sessions of Parliament (see the box on p. 733). Two national petitions incorporating these points, affixed with millions of signatures, were presented to Parliament in 1839 and 1842. Both were rejected by the members of Parliament who were not at all ready for political democracy. As one member said, universal suffrage would be "fatal to all the purposes for which government exists" and was "utterly incompatible with the very existence of civilization." After 1843, Chartism as a movement had largely played itself out. It had never really posed a serious threat to the British establishment, but it had not been a total failure either. Its true significance stemmed from its ability to arouse and organize millions of working-class men and women, to give them a sense of working-class consciousness that they had not really possessed before. This political education of working people was important to the ultimate acceptance of all the points of the People's Charter in the future.

Efforts at Change: Reformers and Government

Efforts to improve the worst conditions of the industrial factory system also came from outside the ranks of the working classes. From its beginning, the Industrial Revolution had drawn much criticism. Romantic poets like William Wordsworth (see Chapter 22) decried the destruction of the natural world:

> I grieve, when on the darker side
> Of this great change I look; and there behold
> Such outrage done to nature as compels
> The indignant power to justify herself.

Reform-minded individuals, be they factory owners who felt twinges of conscience or social reformers in Parliament, campaigned against the evils of the industrial factory, especially condemning the abuse of children. One hoped for the day "that these little ones should once more see the rising and setting of the sun."

As it became apparent that the increase in wealth generated by the Industrial Revolution was accompanied by ever-increasing numbers of poor people, more and more efforts were made to document and deal with the problems. As reports from civic-minded citizens and parliamentary commissions intensified and demonstrated the extent of poverty, degradation, and suffering, the reform efforts began to succeed.

Their first success was a series of Factory Acts passed between 1802 and 1819 that limited labor for children between the ages of nine and sixteen to twelve hours a day; the employment of children under nine years old was forbidden. Moreover, the laws stipulated that children were to receive instruction in reading and arithmetic during working hours. But these acts applied only to cotton mills, not to factories or mines where some of the worst abuses were taking place. Just as important, no provision was made for enforcing the acts through a system of inspection.

In the reform-minded decades of the 1830s and 1840s, new legislation was passed. The Factory Act of 1833 strengthened earlier labor legislation. All textile factories were now included. Children between nine and thirteen could work only eight hours a day; those between thirteen and eighteen, twelve hours. Factory inspectors were appointed with the power to fine those who broke the law. Another piece of legislation in 1833 required that children between nine and thirteen have at least two hours of elementary education during the working day. In 1847, the Ten Hours Act reduced the work day for children between thirteen and eighteen to ten hours. Women were also now included in the ten-hour limitation. In 1842, a Coal Mines Act eliminated the employment of boys under ten and women in mines. Eventually, men too would benefit from the move to restrict factory hours.

The Political Demands of the Chartist Movement

In the late 1830s and early 1840s, working-class protest centered on achieving a clear set of political goals, particularly universal male suffrage, as the means to achieve economic and social improvements. This selection is taken from one of the national petitions presented to Parliament by the Chartist movement. Although the petition failed, Chartism helped to arouse and organize millions of workers.

National Petition (1839)

To the Honourable the Commons of the United Kingdom of Great Britain and Ireland, in Parliament assembled, the Petition of the undersigned, their suffering countrymen, HUMBLY SHOWS,—

The energies of a mighty kingdom have been wasted in building up the power of selfish and ignorant men, and its resources squandered for their aggrandisement. The good of a part has been advanced at the sacrifice of the good of the nation. The few have governed for the interest of the few, while the interests of the many have been sottishly neglected, or insolently. . . trampled upon. . . . We come before your honourable house to tell you, with all humility, that this state of things must not be permitted to continue. That it cannot long continue, without very seriously endangering the stability of the throne, and the peace of the kingdom, and that if, by God's help, and all lawful and constitutional appliances, an end can be put to it, we are fully resolved that it shall speedily come to an end. . . . Required, as we are universally, to support and obey the laws, nature and reason entitle us to demand that in the making of the laws the universal voice shall be implicitly listened to. We perform the duties of freemen; we must have the privileges of freemen. Therefore, we demand universal suffrage.

The suffrage, to be exempt from the corruption of the wealthy and the violence of the powerful, must be secret. . . . To public safety, as well as public confidence, frequent elections are essential. Therefore, we demand annual parliaments. With power to choose, and freedom in choosing, the range of our choice must be unrestricted. We are compelled, by the existing laws, to take for our representatives men who are incapable of appreciating our difficulties, or have little sympathy with them; merchants who have retired from trade and no longer feel its harassings; proprietors of land who are alike ignorant of its evils and its cure; lawyers by whom the notoriety of the senate is courted only as a means of obtaining notice in the courts. . . . We demand that in the future election of members of your . . . house, the approbation of the constituency shall be the sole qualification, and that to every representative so chosen, shall be assigned out of the public taxes, a fair and adequate remuneration for the time which he is called upon to devote to the public service. . . . Universal suffrage will, and it alone can, bring true and lasting peace to the nation; we firmly believe that it will also bring prosperity. May it therefore please your honourable house, to take this our petition into your most serious consideration, and to use your utmost endeavours, by all constitutional means, to have a law passed, granting to every male of lawful age, sane mind, and unconvicted of crime, the right of voting for members of parliament, and directing all future elections of members of parliament to be in the way of secret ballot, and ordaining that the duration of parliament, so chosen, shall in no case exceed one year, and abolishing all property qualifications in the members, and providing for their due remuneration while in attendance on their parliamentary duties.

Conclusion

The Industrial Revolution became one of the major forces of change in the nineteenth century as it led Western civilization into the industrial era that has characterized the modern world. Beginning in Britain, its spread to the Continent and the new American nation ensured its growth and domination of the Western world.

The Industrial Revolution seemed to prove to Europeans the underlying assumption of the Scientific Revolution of the seventeenth century—that human beings were capable of dominating nature. By rationally manipulating the material environment for human benefit, people could create new levels of material prosperity and produce machines not dreamed of in their wildest imaginings. Lost in the excitement of the Industrial Revolution were the voices that pointed to the dehumanization of the workforce and the alienation from one's work, one's associates, one's self, and the natural world.

The Industrial Revolution also transformed the social world of Europe. The creation of an industrial proletariat produced a whole new force for change. The development of a wealthy industrial middle class presented a challenge to the long-term hegemony of landed wealth. While that wealth had been threatened by the fortunes of commerce, it had never been overturned. But the new bourgeoisie was more demanding. How, in some places, this new industrial bourgeoisie came to play a larger role in the affairs of state will become evident in the next chapter.

NOTES

1. Quoted in W. Gorden Rimmer, *Marshall's of Leeds, Flax-Spinners 1788–1886* (Cambridge, 1960), p. 40.
2. Daniel Defoe, *A Plan of the English Commerce* (Oxford, 1928), pp. 76–77.
3. Quoted in David Landes, *The Unbound Prometheus: Technological Change and Industrial Development in Western Europe from 1750 to the Present* (Cambridge, 1969), pp. 99–100.
4. Quoted in Albert Tucker, *A History of English Civilization* (New York, 1972), p. 583.
5. Quoted in Landes, *The Unbound Prometheus,* pp. 149–50.
6. Quotations can be found in E. Royston Pike, *Human Documents of the Industrial Revolution in Britain* (London, 1966), pp. (in order of quotations) 320, 313, 314, 343.

7. Ibid., p. 315.
8. Quoted in A. J. Donajgrodzi, ed., *Social Control in Nineteenth Century Britain* (London, 1977), p. 141.
9. Quoted in Pike, *Human Documents of the Industrial Revolution in Britain*, pp. 343–44.
10. Quoted in Eric J. Evans, *The Forging of the Modern State: Early Industrial Britain, 1783–1870* (London, 1983), p. 113.
11. Henry Mayhew, *London Labour and the London Poor* (London, 1851), 1:342–43.
12. Quoted in Pike, *Human Documents of the Industrial Revolution in Britain*, pp. 60–61.
13. Quoted in Evans, *The Forging of the Modern State,* p. 124.

SUGGESTIONS FOR FURTHER READING

The well-written work by D. Landes, *The Unbound Prometheus: Technological Change and Industrial Development in Western Europe from 1750 to the Present* (Cambridge, 1969) is still the best introduction to the Industrial Revolution. Although more technical, also of value are C. Trebilcock, *The Industrialization of the Continental Powers, 1780–1914* (London, 1981); and S. Pollard, *Peaceful Conquest: The Industrialization of Europe, 1760–1970* (Oxford, 1981). There is a good collection of essays in P. Mathias and J. A. Davis, eds., *The First Industrial Revolutions* (Oxford, 1989). A volume in the Fontana Economic History of Europe edited by C. M. Cipolla, *The Industrial Revolution* (London, 1973) is also valuable. Although older and dated, T. S. Ashton, *The Industrial Revolution, 1760–1830* (New York, 1948) still provides an interesting introduction to the Industrial Revolution in Britain. Much better, however, are P. Mathias, *The First Industrial Nation: An Economic History of Britain, 1700–1914*, 2d ed. (New York, 1983); and R. Brown, *Society and Economy in Modern Britain, 1700–1850* (London, 1991). On the spread of industrialization to the Continent, see A. Milward and S. B. Saul, *The Development of the Economies of Continental Europe* (Oxford, 1977).

Given the importance of Great Britain in the Industrial Revolution, a number of books are available that place the Industrial Revolution in Britain into a broader context. See E. J. Evans, *The Forging of the Modern State: Early Industrial Britain, 1783–1870* (London, 1983); S. Checkland, *British Public Policy, 1776–1939: An Eco-*

nomic, Social and Political Perspective (Cambridge, 1983); and E. J. Hobsbawm, *Industry and Empire* (London, 1968).

The early industrialization of the United States is examined in P. Temin, *Causal Factors in American Economic Growth in the Nineteenth Century* (London, 1975); and D. C. North, *The Economic Growth of the United States, 1790–1860* (New York, 1961). G. R. Taylor, *The Transportation Revolution, 1815–60* (New York, 1951) examines the importance of transportation in American industrialization. On the economic ties between Great Britain and the United States, see D. Jeremy, *Transatlantic Industrial Revolution: The Diffusion of Textile Technology between Britain and America, 1790–1830* (Cambridge, Mass., 1981).

A general discussion of population growth in Europe can be found in T. McKeown, *The Modern Rise of Population* (London, 1976), although it has been criticized for its emphasis on nutrition and hygiene as the two major causes of that growth. For an examination of urban growth, see the older but classic work of A. F. Weber, *The Growth of Cities in the Nineteenth Century: A Study in Statistics* (Ithaca, N.Y., 1963); and the more recent work by A. R. Sutcliffe, *Towards the Planned City: Germany, Britain, the United States and France, 1780–1914* (Oxford, 1981). C. Woodham Smith, *The Great Hunger* (New York, 1962) is a well-written account of the great Irish tragedy. Many of the works cited above have much information on the social impact of the Industrial Revolution, but additional material is available in C. Morazé, *The Triumph of the Middle Classes* (London, 1966); F. Crouzet, *The First Industrialists: The Problems of Origins* (Cambridge, 1985), on British entrepreneurs; E. P. Thompson, *The Making of the English Working Class* (New York, 1964); and E. Gauldie, *Cruel Habitations, A History of Working-Class Housing, 1790–1918* (London, 1974). G. Himmelfarb, *The Idea of Poverty: England in the Early Industrial Age* (New York, 1984) traces the concepts of poverty and poor from the mid-eighteenth century to the mid-nineteenth century. A valuable work on female labor patterns is L. A. Tilly and J. W. Scott, *Women, Work, and Family* (New York, 1978).

CHAPTER

22

Reaction, Revolution, and Romanticism, 1815–1850

In September 1814, hundreds of foreigners began to converge on Vienna, the capital city of the Austrian Empire. Many were members of European royalty— kings, archdukes, princes, and their wives— accompanied by their diplomatic advisers and scores of servants. Their congenial host was the Austrian emperor Francis I, who never tired of providing Vienna's guests with concerts, glittering balls, sumptuous feasts, and an endless array of hunting parties. One participant remembered, "Eating, fireworks, public illuminations. For eight or ten days, I haven't been able to work at all. What a life!" Of course, not every waking hour was spent in pleasure during this gathering of notables, known to history as the Congress of Vienna. These people were also representatives of all the states that had fought Napoleon, and their real business was to arrange a final peace settlement after almost a decade of war. On June 8, 1815, they finally completed their task.

The forces of upheaval unleashed during the French revolutionary and Napoleonic wars were temporarily quieted in 1815 as rulers sought to restore stability by reestablishing much of the old order to a Europe ravaged by war. Kings, landed aristocrats, and bureaucratic elites regained their control over domestic governments while internationally the forces of conservatism tried to maintain the new status quo; some states even used military force to intervene in the internal affairs of other countries in their desire to crush revolutions.

But the European world had been changed, and it would not readily go back to the old system. New ideologies of change, especially liberalism and nationalism, both products of the revolutionary upheaval initiated in France, had become too powerful to be contained. Not content with the status quo, the forces of change gave rise first to the revolts and revolutions that periodically shook Europe in the 1820s and 1830s and then to the widespread revolutions of 1848. Some of the revolutions and revolutionaries were successful; most were not. Although the old

Congress of Vienna

Revolutions in Belgium, Poland, and Italian states

July Revolution in France •

Revolutions in France, German and Italian states, and Austrian Empire

Revolutions in Latin America

London police

Reform Act in Britain

Frankfurt Assembly

Shelley, *Prometheus Unbound*   Beethoven's Ninth Symphony

Friedrich, *Man and Woman Gazing at the Moon*   Tristan, *Worker's Union*

order usually appeared to have prevailed, by 1850, it was apparent that its days were numbered. This perception was reinforced by the changes wrought by the Industrial Revolution. Together the forces unleashed by the dual revolutions—the French Revolution and the Industrial Revolution—made it impossible to return to prerevolutionary Europe. Nevertheless, although these two revolutions initiated what historians like to call the modern European world, it will also be apparent that much of the old still remained in the midst of the new.

The Conservative Order, 1815–1830

The immediate response to the defeat of Napoleon was the desire to contain revolution and the revolutionary forces by restoring much of the old order. But the triumphant rulers were not naive and realized that they could not return to 1789.

The Peace Settlement

In March 1814, even before Napoleon had been defeated, his four major enemies—Great Britain, Austria, Prussia, and Russia—had agreed to remain united, not only to defeat France but to ensure peace after the war. After Napoleon's defeat, this Quadruple Alliance restored the Bourbon monarchy to France in the person of Louis XVIII and concluded the first Treaty of Paris with the conquered nation. It was a lenient treaty. The Bourbons had not been responsible for France's revolu-

tionary upheaval, and the four allies saw little need to burden the government of Louis XVIII unnecessarily. Not only were the French allowed to keep the territories they had acquired by 1792 (some parts of Germany and the Austrian Netherlands), but they paid no indemnity as well. Since the Treaty of Paris did not deal with the problems created by Napoleon's rearrangement of the map of Europe, the great powers agreed to meet at a congress in Vienna in September 1814 to arrange a final peace settlement.

Although all the powers were invited to attend the congress, important decisions were closely guarded by the representatives of the four great powers. The victorious British, who had no desire for territorial gains on the Continent but did wish to secure their control of the seas, were ably represented at the conference by Viscount Castlereagh (1769–1822), a shy but determined man. The skillful maneuvering of the French representative, the clever Prince Talleyrand, enabled the defeated power, France, to participate in some of the decisions. Above all, however, the congress was dominated by the Austrian foreign minister, Prince Klemens von Metternich (1773–1859). An experienced diplomat who was also conceited and self-assured, Metternich described himself in his memoirs in 1819: "There is a wide sweep about my mind. I am always above and beyond the preoccupation of most public men; I cover a ground much vaster than they can see. I cannot keep myself from saying about twenty times a day: 'How right I am, and how wrong they are.'"[1]

Metternich claimed that he was guided at Vienna by the principle of legitimacy. To reestablish peace and stability in Europe, he considered it necessary to restore the legitimate monarchs who would preserve traditional

✦ Metternich. Prince Klemens von Metternich, the foreign minister of Austria, played a major role at the Congress of Vienna as the chief exponent of the principle of legitimacy. To maintain the new conservative order after 1815, Metternich espoused the principle of intervention, by which he meant that the great powers had the right to intervene militarily in other countries in order to crush revolutionary movements against legitimate rulers.

institutions. This had already been done in the restoration of the Bourbons in France and Spain, as well as in the return of a number of rulers to their thrones in the Italian states. Elsewhere, however, the principle of legitimacy was largely ignored and completely overshadowed by more practical considerations of power. The congress's treatment of Poland, to which Russia, Austria, and Prussia all had claims, illustrates this approach. Prussia and Austria were allowed to keep some Polish territory. A new, nominally independent Polish kingdom, about three-quarters of the size of the duchy of Warsaw, was established with the Romanov dynasty of Russia as its hereditary monarchs. Although the Russian tsar Alexander I (1801–1825) voluntarily granted the new kingdom a constitution guaranteeing its independence, Poland's foreign policy (and Poland) remained under Russian control. Prussia was compensated for its loss of Polish lands by receiving two-fifths of Saxony, the Napoleonic German kingdom of Westphalia, and the left bank of the Rhine. Austria in turn was compensated for its loss of the Austrian Netherlands by being given control of two northern Italian provinces, Lombardy and Venetia.

In making these territorial rearrangements, the powers at Vienna believed they were following the familiar eighteenth-century practice of maintaining a balance of power or equilibrium among the great powers. Essentially, this meant a balance of political and military forces that guaranteed the independence of the great powers by ensuring that no one country could dominate Europe. To balance Russian gains, Prussia and Austria had been strengthened. According to Metternich, this arrangement had clearly avoided a great danger: "Prussia and Austria are completing their systems of defense; united, the two monarchies form an unconquerable barrier against the enterprises of any conquering prince who might perhaps once again occupy the throne of France or that of Russia."[2]

Considerations of the balance of power also dictated the allied treatment of France. France had not been overly weakened so that it could remain a great power. Nevertheless, the fear that France might again upset the European peace remained strong enough that the great powers attempted to establish major defensive barriers against possible French expansion. To the north of France, they created a new enlarged kingdom of the Netherlands composed of the former Dutch Republic and the Austrian Netherlands (Belgium) under a new ruler, King William I of the House of Orange. To the southeast, Piedmont (officially styled the kingdom of Sardinia) was enlarged. On France's eastern frontier, Prussia was strengthened by giving it control of the territory along the east bank of the Rhine. The British at least expected Prussia to be the major bulwark against French expansion in central Europe, but the Congress of Vienna also created a new league of German states, the Germanic Confederation, to replace the Napoleonic Confederation of the Rhine.

Napoleon's escape from Elba and his One Hundred Days in the midst of the Congress of Vienna delayed the negotiations but did not significantly alter the overall agreement. It was decided, however, to punish the French people for their enthusiastic response to Napoleon's return. By the second Treaty of Paris, France's borders were returned to those of 1790, and it was forced to pay an indemnity and accept an army of occupation for five years.

The Vienna peace settlement of 1815 has sometimes been criticized for its failure to recognize the liberal and national forces unleashed by the French revolutionary and Napoleonic eras. Containing these revolutionary forces was precisely what the diplomats at Vienna hoped to achieve. Their transfers of territories and peoples to the victors to create a new balance of power, with little or no regard for the wishes of the peoples themselves, was in accord with long-standing traditions of European diplomacy. One could hardly expect Metternich, foreign minister of the Austrian Empire, a dynastic state composed of many different peoples, to espouse a principle of self-determination for European nationalities. Whatever its weaknesses, the Congress of Vienna has received credit for establishing a European order that managed to avoid a general European conflict for almost a century.

The Ideology of Conservatism

The peace arrangements of 1815 were but the beginning of a conservative reaction determined to contain the liberal and nationalist forces unleashed by the French Revolution. Metternich and his kind were representatives of the ideology known as conservatism (see the box on p. 740). As a modern political philosophy, conservatism dates from 1790 when Edmund Burke wrote his *Reflections on the Revolution in France* in reaction to the French Revolution, especially its radical republican and democratic ideas. Those people labeled conservatives, however, did not always agree on all principles.

Edmund Burke (1729–1797) enunciated the principles of an evolutionary conservatism. In his *Reflections on the Revolution in France*, Burke maintained that society was a contract, but "the state ought not to be considered as nothing better than a partnership agreement in a trade of pepper and coffee, to be taken up for a temporary interest and to be dissolved by the fancy of the parties." The state was a partnership but one "not only between those who are living, but between those who are living, those who are dead and those who are to be born." No one generation therefore has the right to destroy this partnership; instead, each generation has the duty to preserve and transmit it to the next. Indeed, "changing the state as often as there are floating fancies, . . . no one generation could link with the other." Burke advised against the violent overthrow of a government by revolution, but he did not reject the possibility of change. Sudden change was unacceptable, but that did not eliminate gradual or evolutionary improvements. As Burke said, "a disposition to preserve and an ability to improve, taken together, would be my standard of a statesman."[3]

Burke's conservatism, however, was not the only kind. The Frenchman Joseph de Maistre (1753–1821) was the most influential spokesman for a counterrevolutionary and authoritarian conservatism. De Maistre unequivocally espoused the restoration of hereditary monarchy. He went beyond Burke's pragmatic justification for monarchy as a necessary foundation to keep society together to a defense of monarchy as a divinely sanctioned institution. Only absolute monarchy could guarantee "order in society" and avoid the chaos generated by movements like the French Revolution.

Despite their differences, most conservatives held to a general body of beliefs. They favored obedience to

Map 22.1 Europe after the Congress of Vienna.

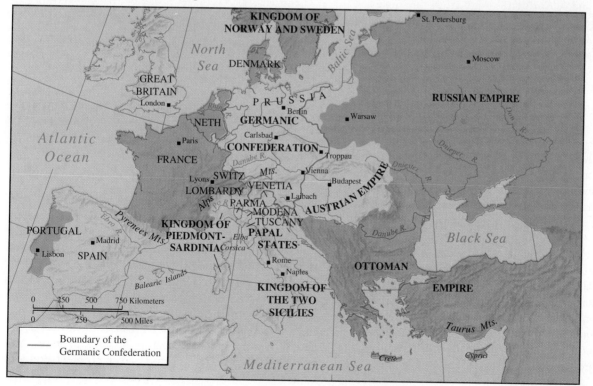

The Voice of Conservatism: Metternich of Austria

There was no greater symbol of conservatism in the first half of the nineteenth century than Prince Klemens von Metternich of Austria. Metternich played a crucial role at the Congress of Vienna and worked tirelessly for thirty years to repress the "revolutionary seed," as he called it, that had been spread to Europe by the "military despotism of Bonaparte."

Klemens von Metternich, *Memoirs*

We are convinced that society can no longer be saved without strong and vigorous resolutions on the part of the Governments still free in their opinions and actions.

We are also convinced that this may be, if the Governments face the truth, if they free themselves from all illusion, if they join their ranks and take their stand on a line of correct, unambiguous, and frankly announced principles.

By this course the monarchs will fulfill the duties imposed upon them by Him who, by entrusting them with power, has charged them to watch over the maintenance of justice, and the rights of all, to avoid the paths of error, and tread firmly in the way of truth. . . .

If the same elements of destruction which are now throwing society into convulsions have existed in all ages—for every age has seen immoral and ambitious men, hypocrites, men of heated imaginations, wrong motives, and wild projects—yet ours, by the single fact of the liberty of the press, possesses more than any preceding age the means of contact, seduction, and attraction whereby to act on these different classes of men.

We are certainly not alone in questioning if society can exist with the liberty of the press, a scourge unknown to the world before the latter half of the seventeenth century, and restrained until the end of the eighteenth, with scarcely any expectations but England—a part of Europe separated from the continent by the sea, as well as by her language and by her peculiar manners.

The first principle to be followed by the monarchs, united as they are by the coincidence of their desires and opinions, should be that of maintaining the stability of political institutions against the disorganized excitement which has taken possession of men's minds; the immutability of principles against the madness of their interpretation; and respect for laws actually in force against a desire for their destruction. . . .

The first and greatest concern for the immense majority of every nation is the stability of the laws, and their uninterrupted action—never their change. Therefore, let the Governments govern, let them maintain the groundwork of their institutions, both ancient and modern; for if it is at all times dangerous to touch them, it certainly would not now, in the general confusion, be wise to do so. . . .

Let them maintain religious principles in all their purity, and not allow the faith to be attacked and morality interpreted according to the social contract or the visions of foolish sectarians.

Let them suppress Secret Societies, that gangrene of society. . . .

To every great State determined to survive the storm there still remain many chances of salvation, and a strong union between the States on the principles we have announced will overcome the storm itself.

political authority, believed that organized religion was crucial to social order, hated revolutionary upheavals, and were unwilling to accept either the liberal demands for civil liberties and representative governments or the nationalistic aspirations generated by the French revolutionary era. The community took precedence over individual rights; society must be organized and ordered, and tradition remained the best guide for order. After 1815, the political philosophy of conservatism was supported by hereditary monarchs, government bureaucracies, landowning aristocracies, and revived churches, be they Protestant or Catholic. Although not unopposed, both internationally and domestically the conservative forces appeared dominant after 1815.

The Conservative Domination: The Concert of Europe

The conservative order that European diplomats were constructing at Vienna must have seemed fragile when the French people greeted Napoleon enthusiastically after his escape from Elba. The great powers' fear of revolution and war led them to develop the Concert of Europe as a means to maintain the new status quo they had constructed. This Concert of Europe grew out of the reaffirmation of the Quadruple Alliance in November 1815. Great Britain, Russia, Prussia, and Austria renewed their commitment against any attempted restoration of Bonapartist power and agreed to meet periodically in conferences to discuss their common interests and examine measures that "will be judged most salutary for the repose and prosperity of peoples, and for the maintenance of peace in Europe."

In accordance with the agreement for periodic meetings, four congresses were held between 1818 and 1822. The first congress, held in 1818 at Aix-la-Chapelle, was by far the most congenial. "Never have I known a prettier little congress," said Metternich. The four great powers agreed to withdraw their army of occupation from France and to add France to the Concert of Europe. The Quadruple Alliance became a Quintuple Alliance.

The next congress proved far less pleasant and produced the first fissure in the ranks of the allies. This session at Troppau was called in the autumn of 1820 to deal with the outbreak of revolution in Spain and Italy. The revolt in Spain was directed against Ferdinand VII, the Bourbon king who had been restored to the throne in 1814. In southern Italy, the restoration of another Bourbon, Ferdinand I, as king of Naples and Sicily was accompanied by the return of the nobility and clergy to their privileged positions. Army officers and businessmen led a rebellion that soon spread to the northern Italian kingdom of Piedmont.

Metternich was especially disturbed by the revolts in Italy since he saw them as a threat to Austria's domination of the peninsula. At Troppau, he proposed a protocol that established the principle of intervention. It read:

> States which have undergone a change of Government due to revolution, the results of which threaten other states, *ipso facto* cease to be members of the European Alliance, and remain excluded from it until their situation gives guarantees for legal order and stability. If, owing to such situations, immediate danger threatens other states, the Powers bind themselves, by peaceful means, or if need be by arms, to bring back the guilty state into the bosom of the Great Alliance.[4]

The principle of intervention meant the great powers had the right to send armies into countries where there were revolutions to restore legitimate monarchs to their thrones. Britain refused to agree to the principle, arguing that it had never been the intention of the Quadruple Alliance to interfere in the internal affairs of other states, except in France. In Britain's eyes, only revolutionary outbursts threatening the peace of Europe necessitated armed intervention. Ignoring the British response, Austria, Prussia, and Russia met in a third congress at Laibach in January 1821 and authorized the

sending of Austrian troops to Naples. These forces crushed the revolt, restored Ferdinand I to the throne, and then moved north to suppress the rebels in Sardinia. At the fourth postwar conference, held at Verona in October 1822, the same three powers authorized France to invade Spain to crush the revolt against Ferdinand VII. In the spring of 1823, French forces restored the Bourbon monarch. By this time, the split between Britain and the more conservative powers of central and eastern Europe had become irreversible.

The policy of intervention had succeeded in defeating revolutionary movements in Spain and Italy and in restoring legitimate (and conservative) monarchs to their thrones. It had been done at a price, however. The Concert of Europe had broken down when the British rejected Metternich's principle of intervention. And although the British had failed to thwart allied intervention in Spain and Italy, they were successful in keeping the continental powers from interfering with the revolutions in Latin America.

THE REVOLT OF LATIN AMERICA

While much of North America had been freed of European domination in the eighteenth century by the American Revolution, Latin America remained in the hands of the Spanish and Portuguese. Napoleon's continental wars at the beginning of the nineteenth century, however, soon had repercussions in Latin America. When the Bourbon monarchy of Spain was toppled by Bonaparte, Spanish authority in its colonial empire was weakened. By 1810, the disintegration of royal power in Argentina had led to that nation's independence. In Venezuela a bitter struggle for independence was led by Simón Bolivar, hailed as the Liberator. His forces freed Colombia in 1819 and Venezuela in 1821. A second liberator was José de San Martin who liberated Chile in 1817 and then, in 1821, moved on to Lima, Peru, the center of Spanish authority. He was soon joined by Bolivar who assumed the task of crushing the last significant Spanish army in 1824. Mexico and the Central American provinces also achieved their freedom, and by 1825, after Portugal had recognized the independence of Brazil, almost all of Latin America had been freed of colonial domination.

In the early 1820s, only one major threat to the newly independent Latin American states remained. Flushed by their success in crushing rebellions in Spain and Italy, the victorious continental powers favored the use of troops to restore Spanish control in Latin America. This time British opposition to intervention prevailed. Eager to gain access to an entire continent for investment and trade, the British proposed joint action with the United States against European interference in Latin America. Distrustful of British motives, President James Monroe acted alone in 1823, guaranteeing the independence of the new Latin American nations and warning against any further European intervention in the New World in the famous Monroe Doctrine. Actually, British ships were more important to Latin American independence than American words. Britain's navy stood between Latin America and any European invasion force, and the continental powers were extremely reluctant to challenge British naval power.

THE GREEK REVOLT, 1821–1832

The principle of intervention proved to be a double-edged sword. Designed to prevent revolution, it could also be used to support revolution if the great powers found it in their interest to do so. Despite their differences in the congresses, Great Britain, France, and Russia found cause for cooperation.

In 1821, the Greeks revolted against their Turkish masters. Although subject to Muslim control for four hundred years, the Greeks had been allowed to maintain their language and their Greek Orthodox faith. A revival of Greek national sentiment at the beginning of

Map 22.2 Latin America in the First Half of the Nineteenth Century.

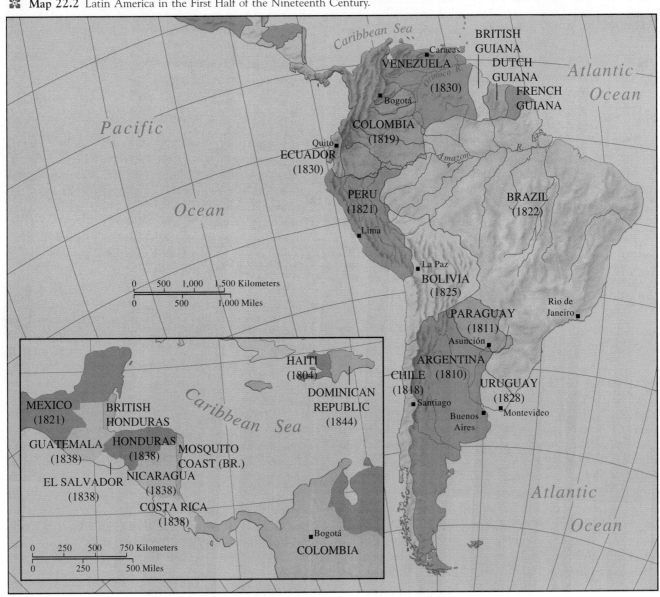

the nineteenth century added to the growing desire for "the liberation of the fatherland from the terrible yoke of Turkish oppression." Initial reaction to the Greek revolt by the European powers was negative since this appeared to be simply another revolt against established authority that should be crushed. But the Greek revolt was soon transformed into a noble cause by an outpouring of European sentiment for the Greeks' struggle. Liberals rallied to the cause of Greek freedom, arguing that Greek democracy was being reborn. Romantic poets and artists (see Romanticism later in this chapter) also publicized the cause of Greek independence.

Despite the public groundswell, mutual fears and other interests kept the European powers from intervening until 1827 when a combined British and French fleet went to Greece and defeated a large Turkish fleet. In 1828, Russia declared war on Turkey and invaded its European provinces of Moldavia and Wallachia. By the Treaty of Adrianople in 1829, which ended the Russian-Turkish war, the Russians received a protectorate over the two provinces. By the same treaty, the Turks agreed to allow Russia, France, and Britain to decide the fate of Greece. In 1830, the three powers declared Greece an independent kingdom, and two years later a new royal dynasty was established in the hands of a son of the Bavarian king.

The Greek revolt made a deep impression on Europeans. It was the first successful revolt against the status quo and represented a victory for both the liberal and the national forces that the great powers were trying so hard to repress. But to keep this in perspective, we need to remember that the European powers did not quite see it that way. They had given the Greeks a German king, and the revolution had been successful only because the great powers themselves supported it. Until 1830 the Greek revolt had been the only successful one in Europe; the conservative domination was still largely intact.

The Conservative Domination: The European States

Between 1815 and 1830, the conservative domination of Europe evident in the Concert of Europe was also apparent in domestic affairs.

GREAT BRITAIN: RULE OF THE TORIES

In 1815, Great Britain was governed by the aristocratic landowning classes that dominated both houses of Parliament. Suffrage for elections to the House of Commons, controlled by the landed gentry, was restricted

◆ **The Greek Struggle for Freedom: Eugène Delacroix,** *Greece Expiring on the Ruins of Missolonghi.* The Greek revolt against the Ottoman Empire brought a massive outpouring of European sentiment for the Greeks. Romantic artists and poets were especially eager to publicize the struggle of the Greeks for independence. In this painting, the French painter Delacroix personified Greece as a majestic, defenseless woman appealing for aid against the victorious Turk seen in the background. Delacroix's painting was done soon after the fall of the Greek fortress of Missolonghi to the Turks.

and unequal, especially in light of the changing distribution of the British population due to the Industrial Revolution. Large, new industrial cities such as Birmingham and Manchester, for example, had no representatives while landowners used pocket and rotten boroughs (see Chapter 19) to control seats in the House of Commons. Although the monarchy was not yet powerless, in practice the power of the crown was largely in the hands of the ruling party in Parliament.

Within Parliament there were two political factions, the Tories and Whigs. Although both of them were still dominated by members of the landed classes, the Whigs

CHRONOLOGY

The Conservative Domination: The Concert of Europe

Congress of Vienna	1814–1815
Reaffirmation of the Quadruple Alliance	1815
Congress of Aix-la-Chapelle	1818
Revolutions in Latin America	1819–1824
Congress of Troppau	1820
Congress of Laibach	1821
Crushing of revolt in southern Italy	1821
Greek revolt against the Turks	1821
Congress of Verona	1822
Crushing of revolt in Spain	1823
Monroe Doctrine	1823
Treaty of Adrianople	1829
Greek independence	1830

were beginning to receive support from the new moneyed interests generated by industrialization. Tory ministers largely dominated the government until 1830 and had little desire to change the existing political and electoral system. Tory leadership during the Napoleonic wars made them wary of radicalism and reform movements, an attitude that governed their activities after 1815.

Popular discontent grew apace after 1815 because of severe economic difficulties. The Tory government's response to falling agricultural prices was the Corn Law of 1815, a measure that placed extraordinarily high tariffs on foreign grain. Though beneficial to the landowners, subsequent high prices for bread made conditions for the working classes more difficult. Mass protest meetings took a nasty turn when a squadron of cavalry attacked a crowd of 60,000 demonstrators at St. Peter's Fields in Manchester in 1819. The death of eleven people, called the Peterloo Massacre by government detractors, led Parliament to take even more repressive measures. The government restricted large public meetings and the dissemination of pamphlets among the poor. Before further repression could lead to greater violence, the Tory ministry was broadened by the addition of men who believed that some concessions to change rather than sheer repression might best avoid revolution. By making minor reforms in the 1820s, the Tories managed to avoid meeting the demands for

electoral reforms—at least until 1830 (see Reform in Great Britain later in this chapter).

RESTORATION IN FRANCE

In 1814, the Bourbon family was restored to the throne of France in the person of Louis XVIII (1814–1824). Louis was clever enough to realize that the restored monarchy had to accept the constructive work of the revolutionary and Napoleonic eras or face disaster. Consequently, the constitutional Charter of 1814 maintained Napoleon's Concordat with the pope and accepted Napoleon's Civil Code with its recognition of the principle of equality before the law (see Chapter 20). The property rights of those who had purchased confiscated lands during the Revolution were preserved. The Charter of 1814 also established a bicameral (two-house) legislature with a Chamber of Peers chosen by the king and a Chamber of Deputies chosen by an electorate restricted to slightly less than 100,000 wealthy people.

Louis's grudging moderation, however, was opposed by liberals anxious to extend the revolutionary reforms and by a group of ultraroyalists who criticized the king's willingness to compromise and retain so many features of the Napoleonic era. The ultras hoped to return to a monarchical system dominated by a privileged landed aristocracy and to restore the Catholic church to its former position of influence.

The initiative passed to the ultraroyalists in 1824 when Louis XVIII died and was succeeded by his brother, the count of Artois, who became Charles X (1824–1830). Charles had been the leader of the ultraroyalists and was determined to restore the old regime as far as possible. In 1825, he granted an indemnity to aristocrats whose lands had been confiscated during the Revolution. Moreover, the king pursued a religious policy that encouraged the church to reestablish control over the French educational system. Public outrage, fed by liberal newspapers, forced the king to compromise in 1827 and even to accept the principle of ministerial responsibility—that the ministers of the king were responsible to the legislature. But in 1829 he violated his commitment. A protest by the deputies led the king to dissolve the legislature in 1830 and call for new elections. France was on the brink of another revolution.

INTERVENTION IN THE ITALIAN STATES AND SPAIN

In 1815, many of the inhabitants of the Italian peninsula were poverty-stricken, illiterate peasants who cared little that Italy had shifted from French to Austrian control in 1815. A small, educated middle class in the cities of northern Italy, however, who had benefited from Napoleon's changes, objected to the restoration of despotic governments controlled by Austria. The peninsula was still divided into a number of states; as Metternich contemptuously noted, Italy was only a "geographical expression." The Congress of Vienna had established nine states, including Piedmont (officially Sardinia) in the north ruled by the house of Savoy; the kingdom of the Two Sicilies (Naples and Sicily); the Papal States; a handful of small duchies ruled by relatives of the Austrian emperor; and the important northern provinces of Lombardy and Venetia that were now part of the Austrian Empire.

Much of Italy was under Austrian domination while all the states had extremely reactionary governments eager to smother any liberal or nationalist sentiment. The crushing of attempts at revolt in the kingdom of the Two Sicilies and Piedmont in 1821 discouraged opposition, although secret societies motivated by nationalistic dreams and known as the Carbonari—the charcoal burners—continued to conspire and plan for revolution.

In Spain, another Bourbon dynasty had been restored in the person of Ferdinand VII in 1814. Ferdinand (1814–1833) had agreed to observe the liberal constitution of 1812, which allowed for the functioning of an elected parliamentary assembly known as the Cortes. But the king soon reneged on his promises, tore up the constitution, dissolved the Cortes, and persecuted its members. Economic crisis and government despotism, inefficiency, and corruption soon led a combined group of army officers, upper-middle-class merchants, and liberal intellectuals to revolt. The king capitulated in March 1820 and promised once again to restore the constitution and the Cortes.

Metternich's policy of intervention came to Ferdinand's rescue. In April 1823, a French army moved into Spain and forced the revolutionary government to flee Madrid. By August of that year, the king had been restored to his throne. Ignoring French advice to adopt moderate policies, Ferdinand VII tortured to death, imprisoned, or exiled the supporters of a constitutional system. Intervention had succeeded.

REPRESSION IN CENTRAL EUROPE

After 1815, the forces of reaction were particularly successful in central Europe. The Habsburg empire and its chief agent, Prince Klemens von Metternich, played an important role. Metternich boasted: "You see in me the chief Minister of Police in Europe. I keep an eye on everything. My contacts are such that nothing escapes

me."[5] Metternich's spies were everywhere, searching for evidence of liberal or nationalist plots. Metternich worried too much in 1815. Although both liberalism and nationalism emerged in the German states and the Austrian Empire, they were initially weak as central Europe tended to remain under the domination of aristocratic landowning classes and autocratic, centralized monarchies. Real opposition to the conservative order came from a relatively small group of army officers, merchants, students, teachers, and liberal nobles. Since the Industrial Revolution did not have much impact in this area until the 1830s and 1840s, there was no substantial industrial middle class to take on the liberal cause (see Liberalism later in this chapter).

The Vienna settlement in 1815 recognized the existence of thirty-eight sovereign states in what had once been the Holy Roman Empire. Austria and Prussia were the two great powers although their non-German territory was not included in the confederation. The other states varied considerably in size from the large south German kingdom of Bavaria to the small principality of Schaumburg-Lippe. Together these states formed the Germanic Confederation, but the confederation had little real power. It had no real executive, and its only central organ was the federal diet, which needed the consent of all member states to take action, making it virtually powerless. The purpose of the Germanic Confederation was not to govern the German states but to provide a common defense against France or Russia. However, it also came to serve as Metternich's instrument to repress revolutionary movements within the German states.

Initially, Germans who favored liberal principles and German unity looked to Prussia for leadership. During the Napoleonic era, King Frederick William III (1797–1840), following the advice of his two chief ministers, Baron Heinrich von Stein and Baron Karl von Hardenberg, instituted political and institutional reforms in response to Prussia's defeat at the hands of Napoleon. Hardenberg told the king in 1806: "Your Majesty! We must do from above what the French have done from below." The reforms included the abolition of serfdom, the removal of some of the restrictions on the nobles' ability to go into trade, municipal self-government through town councils, the expansion of primary and secondary schools, and universal military conscription to form a national army. The reforms, however, did not include the creation of a legislative assembly or representative government as Stein and Hardenberg wished. After 1815 Frederick William grew more reactionary and was content to follow Metternich's lead. Though reforms had made Prussia strong, it remained largely an absolutist state with little interest in German unity.

⇒ University Students and German Unity ⇐

In the early nineteenth century, university students and professors were the chief supporters of German nationalism. Especially important were the Burschenschaften, student societies that espoused the cause of German unity. In this selection, the liberal Heinrich von Gagern explains the purpose of the Burschenschaften to his father.

Heinrich von Gagern, Letter to His Father

It is very hard to explain the spirit of the student movement to you, but I shall try, even though I can only give you a few characteristics. . . . It speaks to the better youth, the man of heart and spirit and love for all this good, and gives him nourishment and being. For the average student of the past, the university years were a time to enjoy life, and to make a sharp break with his own background in defiance of the philistine world, which seemed to him somehow to foreshadow the tomb. Their pleasures, their organizations, and their talk were determined by their *status* as students, and their university obligation was only to avoid failing the examination and scraping by adequately—bread-and-butter learning. They were satisfied with themselves if they thought they could pass the examination. There are still many of those nowadays, indeed the majority over-all. But at several universities, and especially here, another group—in my eyes a better one—has managed to get the upper hand in the sense that it sets the mood. I prefer really not to call it a mood; rather, it is something that presses hard and tried to spread its ideas. . . .

Those who share in this spirit have then quite another tendency in their student life, Love of Fatherland is their guiding principle. Their purpose is to make a better future for the Fatherland, each as best he can, to spread national consciousness, or to use the much ridiculed and maligned Germanic expression, more folkishness, and to work for better constitutions. . . .

We want more sense of community among the several states of Germany, greater unity in their policies and in their principles of government; no separate policy for each state, but the nearest possible relations with one another; above all, we want Germany to be considered *one* land and the German people *one* people. In the forms of our student comradeship we show how we want to approach this as nearly as possible in the real world. Regional fraternities are forbidden, and we live in a German comradeship, one people in spirit, as we want it for all Germany in reality. We give our selves the freest of constitutions, just as we should like Germany to have the freest possible one, insofar as that is suitable for the German people. We want a constitution for the people that fits in with the spirit of the times and with the people's own level of enlightenment, rather than what each prince gives his people according to what he likes and what serves his private interest. Above all, we want the princes to understand and to follow the principle that they exist for the country and not the country for them. In fact, the prevailing view is that the constitution should not come from the individual states at all. The main principles of the German constitution should apply to all states in common, and should be expressed by the German federal assembly. This constitution should deal not only with the absolute necessities, like fiscal administration and justice, general administration and church and military affairs and so on; this constitution ought to be extended to the education of the young, at least at the upper age levels, and to many other such things.

⇒⇒⇒⇒⇒⇒⇒⇒⇒⇒⇒⇒⇒⇒⇒⇒⇒⇒⇒⇒ ⇐⇐⇐⇐⇐⇐⇐⇐⇐⇐⇐⇐⇐⇐⇐⇐⇐⇐⇐⇐⇐

Liberal and national movements in the German states seemed largely limited to university professors and students. The latter began to organize *Burschenschaften* or student societies dedicated to fostering the goal of a free, united Germany (see the box above). Their ideas and their motto, "Honor, Liberty, Fatherland," were in part inspired by Friedrich Ludwig Jahn, who had organized gymnastic societies during the Napoleonic wars to promote the regeneration of German youth. Jahn was a noisy nationalist who encouraged Germans to pursue their Germanic heritage and urged his followers to disrupt the lectures of professors whose views were not nationalistic.

From 1817 to 1819, the *Burschenschaften* pursued a variety of activities that alarmed German governments. An aide wrote to Metternich that "of all the evils affecting Germany today, even including the licentiousness of the press, this student nuisance is the greatest, the most urgent and the most threatening."[6] At an assembly held at the Wartburg Castle in 1817, marking the three-hundredth anniversary of Luther's Ninety-Five Theses, the crowd burned books written by conservative authors. When a deranged student assassinated a reactionary playwright, Metternich had the diet of the Germanic Confederation draw up the Karlsbad Decrees of 1819. These closed the *Burschenschaften*, provided for censorship of the press, and placed the universities under close supervision and control. Thereafter, except for a minor flurry of activity from 1830 to 1832, Metternich and the cooperative German rulers maintained the conservative status quo.

The Austrian Empire was a multinational state, a collection of different peoples under the Habsburg emperor who provided a common bond. Eleven peoples of different national origin constituted the empire, including Germans, Czechs, Magyars (Hungarians), Slovaks, Romanians, Slovenes, Poles, Serbians, and Italians. The Germans, though only a quarter of the population, were economically the most advanced and played a leading role in governing Austria. Since Austria was predominantly agricultural, the landed nobility continued to be the most important class and held most of the important positions as army officers, diplomats, ministers, and civil servants. Essentially, the Austrian Empire was held together by the dynasty, the imperial civil service, the imperial army, and the Catholic church. But its national groups, especially the Hungarians, with their increasing desire for autonomy acted as forces to break the Austrian Empire apart.

Still Metternich managed to hold it all together after 1815. His antipathy to liberalism and nationalism was understandably grounded in the realization that these forces threatened to tear the empire apart. The growing liberal belief that each national group had the right to its own system of government could only mean disaster for the multinational Austrian Empire. Metternich, however, realized the need for some change and hoped to establish a central parliament with deputies from the different nationalities making up the empire. But he was never permitted to do so by Emperor Francis II (1806–1835) who resisted all change. Thus, the Austrian Empire largely stagnated while the forces of liberalism and nationalism grew. Metternich had not prevented an explosion in Austria; he only postponed it until 1848.

RUSSIA: AUTOCRACY OF THE TSARS

At the beginning of the nineteenth century, Russia was overwhelmingly rural, agricultural, and autocratic. The Russian tsar was still regarded as a divine-right monarch with unlimited power although the extent of the Russian empire made the claim impractical. Most of the Russian land remained in the control of a class of noble landlords who monopolized the civil service and army officer corps. The land was tilled by serfs, the most exploited lower class in Europe.

In 1801, Alexander I (1801–1825) came to the Russian throne after a group of aristocrats assassinated his detested father, Tsar Paul I (1796–1801). Alexander had been raised in the tradition and ideas of the Enlightenment and gave every appearance of being liberal minded. But his liberalism was always conditioned by the autocratic tradition of the tsars. As one adviser said, "He would have willingly agreed that every man should be free, on the condition that he should voluntarily do only what the Emperor wished."

Initially, however, Alexander seemed willing to make reforms. With the aid of his liberal adviser, Michael Speransky, he relaxed censorship, freed political prisoners, and reformed the educational system. Substantial changes, however, such as the granting of a constitution and the freeing of the serfs never materialized in the face of opposition from the nobility. Then, too, Alexander himself gradually moved away from his reforming tendencies. No doubt, the struggle against Napoleon contributed to his abandonment of liberal reforms, but after the defeat of Napoleon, Alexander's reactionary tendencies blossomed as he became engrossed in religious mysticism. Now the government reverted to strict and arbitrary censorship. Soon opposition to Alexander arose from a group of secret societies.

One of these societies, known as the Northern Union, was composed of young aristocrats who had served in the Napoleonic wars and had become aware of the world outside Russia as well as intellectuals alienated by the censorship and lack of academic freedom in Russian universities. The Northern Union favored the establishment of a constitutional monarchy and the abolition of serfdom. The sudden death of Alexander in 1825 offered them their opportunity.

Although Alexander's brother Constantine was the legal heir to the throne, he had renounced his claims in favor of his brother Nicholas. Constantine's abdication had not been made public, however, and during the ensuing confusion in December 1825, the military leaders of the Northern Union rebelled against the accession of Nicholas. This so-called Decembrist Revolt was soon crushed by troops loyal to Nicholas and its leaders executed.

The revolt transformed Nicholas I (1825–1855) from a conservative into a reactionary determined to avoid another rebellion. Under Nicholas both the bureaucracy and the secret police were strengthened. Constituting the Third Section of the tsar's chancellery, the political police were given sweeping powers over much of Russian life. They deported suspicious or dangerous persons, maintained close surveillance of foreigners in Russia, and reported regularly to the tsar on public opinion.

Matching Nicholas's fear of revolution at home was his fear of revolution abroad. There would be no revo-

◆ **Portrait of Nicholas I.** Tsar Nicholas I was a reactionary ruler who sought to prevent rebellion in Russia by strengthening the government bureaucracy, increasing censorship, and suppressing individual freedom by the use of political police. One of his enemies remarked about his facial characteristics: "The sharply retreating forehead and the lower jaw were expressive of iron will and feeble intelligence."

lution in Russia during the rest of his reign; if he could help it, there would be none in Europe either. Contemporaries called him the Policeman of Europe because of his willingness to use Russian troops to crush revolutions.

The Ideologies of Change

Although the conservative forces were in the ascendancy from 1815 to 1830, powerful movements for change were also at work. These depended on ideas embodied in a series of political philosophies or ideologies that came into their own in the first half of the nineteenth century. They continue to affect the entire world.

Liberalism

One of the most prominent ideologies of the nineteenth century was liberalism, which owed much to the Enlightenment of the eighteenth century and to the

American and French Revolutions at the end of that century. In addition, liberalism became even more significant as the Industrial Revolution made rapid strides, since the developing industrial middle class largely adopted the doctrine as its own. There were divergences of opinion among people classified as liberals, but all began with a common denominator, the belief that people should be as free from restraint as possible. This idea is evident in both economic and political liberalism.

Also called classical economics, economic liberalism has as its primary tenet the concept of laissez-faire, whose principal exponent had been Adam Smith, author of the *Wealth of Nations* (see Chapter 18). Laissez-faire meant that the state should not interrupt the free play of natural economic forces, especially supply and demand. According to Smith, government should not interfere with the economic liberty of the individual and should restrict itself to only three primary functions: defense of the country, police protection of individuals, and the construction and maintenance of public works too expensive for individuals to undertake. In Smith's view, if individuals were allowed economic liberty, ultimately they would bring about the maximum good for the maximum number and benefit the general welfare of society.

The case against government interference in economic matters was greatly enhanced by Thomas Malthus (1766–1834). In his major work, *Essay on the Principles of Population*, Malthus argued that population, when unchecked, increases in a geometric ratio while the food supply correspondingly increases only in an arithmetic ratio. The result will be severe overpopulation and ultimately starvation for the human race if this growth is not held in check. According to Malthus, nature imposes a major restraint: "unwholesome occupations, severe labor and exposure to the seasons, extreme poverty, bad nursing of children, great towns, excesses of all kinds, the whole train of common disease, and epidemics, wars, plague and famine." Malthus's ideas justified the policies of many industrialists who could not fail to notice his arguments. Misery and poverty were simply the inevitable result of the law of nature; no government or individual should interfere with its operation.

The ideas of Thomas Malthus were further developed by David Ricardo (1772–1823). In his *Principles of Political Economy*, written in 1817, Ricardo developed his famous "iron law of wages." Following Malthus, Ricardo argued that an increase in population means more workers; more workers in turn cause wages to fall below the subsistence level. The result is misery and starvation, which then reduce the population. Consequently, the number of workers declines, and wages rise above the subsistence level again, which in turn encourages workers to have larger families as the cycle is repeated. According to Ricardo, raising wages arbitrarily would be pointless since it would accomplish little but this vicious cycle. Nature is harsh, but attempting to change the laws of nature through the charity of employers or legislation by the state would merely make the situation worse.

Like economic liberalism, political liberalism stressed that people should be free from restraint. One French liberal proclaimed "The liberty of the individual is the object of all human associations. This liberty is the peaceful enjoyment of private independence, the right to pursue our own ends unimpeded, so long as they do not interfere with the equally legitimate activities of others."

The emphasis on liberty was directly connected to liberal ideas on power. Since power was seen as the ability by people to control the behavior of others, there needed to be limits on the exercise of power so that humans could be free. Politically, liberals came to hold a common set of beliefs. Chief among them was the protection of civil liberties or the basic rights of all people, which included equality before the law, freedom of assembly, speech, and press, and freedom from arbitrary arrest. All of these freedoms should be guaranteed by a written document, such as the American Bill of Rights or the French Declaration of the Rights of Man and the Citizen. In addition to religious toleration for all, most liberals advocated separation of church and state. The right of peaceful opposition to the government in and out of parliament and the making of laws by a representative assembly (legislature) elected by qualified voters constituted two other liberal demands. Many liberals believed, then, in a constitutional monarchy or constitutional state with limits on the powers of government in order to prevent despotism, and in written constitutions that would also help to guarantee these rights.

Many liberals also advocated ministerial responsibility or a system in which ministers of the king were responsible to the legislature rather than to the king, giving the legislative branch a check upon the power of the executive. Liberals in the first half of the nineteenth century also believed in a limited suffrage. While all people were entitled to equal civil rights, they should not have equal political rights. The right to vote and hold office would be open only to men who met certain property qualifications. As a political philosophy, liberalism was tied to middle-class men, especially industrial, middle-class men who favored the extension of voting

rights so that they could share power with the landowning classes. They had little desire to let the lower classes share that power. Liberals were not democrats.

One of the most prominent advocates of liberalism in the nineteenth century was the English philosopher John Stuart Mill (1806–1873). *On Liberty*, his most famous work published in 1859, has long been regarded as a classic statement on the liberty of the individual (see the box on p. 750). Mill argued for an "absolute freedom of opinion and sentiment on all subjects" that needed to be protected from both government censorship and the tyranny of the majority.

Mill was also instrumental in expanding the meaning of liberalism by becoming an enthusiastic supporter of women's rights. When his attempt to include women in the voting reform bill of 1867 failed, Mill published an essay entitled *On the Subjection of Women*, which he had written earlier with his wife, Harriet Taylor. He argued that "the legal subordination of one sex to the other" was wrong. Differences between women and men, he claimed, were due not to different natures but simply to social practices. With equal education, women could achieve as much as men. *On the Subjection of Women* would become an important work in the nineteenth-century movement for women's rights.

Nationalism

Nationalism can be defined as a state of mind rising out of an awareness of being part of a community that has common institutions, traditions, language, and customs. This community is called a "nation," and it, rather than a dynasty, city-state, or other political unit, becomes the focus of the individual's primary political loyalty. Nationalism did not become a popular force for change until the French Revolution, and even then nationalism was not so much political as cultural with its emphasis upon the uniqueness of a particular nationality. People began to undertake the study of their language, history, literature, art, and folklore to understand the spirit of their nation.

This cultural idea of nationality normally preceded the longing for political unity; cultural nationalism evolved into political nationalism. The latter advocated that governments should coincide with nationalities. Thus, a divided people such as the Germans wanted national unity in a German nation-state with one central government. Subject peoples, such as the Hungarians, wanted national self-determination or the right to establish their own autonomy rather than be subject to a German minority in a multinational empire.

≋ *The Voice of Liberalism: John Stuart Mill on Liberty* ≋

John Stuart Mill (1806–1873) was one of Britain's most famous philosophers of liberalism. Mill's On Liberty is viewed as a classic statement of the liberal belief in the unfettered freedom of the individual. In this excerpt, Mill defends freedom of opinion from both government and the coercion of the majority.

John Stuart Mill, *On Liberty*

The object of this Essay is to assert one very simple principle, as entitled to govern absolutely the dealings of society with the individual in the way of compulsion and control, whether the means used by physical force in the form of legal penalties, or the moral coercion of public opinion. That principle is, that the sole end for which mankind are warranted, individually or collectively, interfering with the liberty of action of any of their number, is self-protection. That the only purpose for which power can be rightfully exercised over any member of a civilized community, against his will, is to prevent harm to others. His own good, either physical or moral, is not a sufficient warrant. . . . These are good reasons for remonstrating with him, or reasoning with him, or persuading him, or entreating him, but not for compelling him, or visiting him with any evil in case he do otherwise. To justify that, the conduct from which it is desired to deter him, must be calculated to produce evil to some one else. The only part of the conduct of any one, for which he is amenable to society, is that which concerns others. In the part which merely concerns himself, his independence is, of right, absolute. Over himself, over his own body and mind, the individual is sovereign. . . .

Society can and does execute its own mandates: and if it issues wrong mandates instead of right, or any mandates at all in things with which it ought not to meddle, it practices a social tyranny more formidable than many kinds of political oppression, since, though not usually upheld by such extreme penalties, it leaves fewer means of escape, penetrating more deeply into the details of life, and enslaving the soul itself. Protection, there-fore, against the tyranny of the magistrate is not enough: there needs protection also against the tyranny of prevailing opinion and feeling, against the tendency of society to impose, by other means than civil penalties, its own ideas and practices as rules of conduct on those who dissent from them. . . .

But there is a sphere of action in which society, as distinguished from the individual has, if any, only an indirect interest; comprehending all that portion of a person's life and conduct which affects only himself, or if it also affects others, only with their free, voluntary and undeceived consent and participation. . . . This then is the appropriate region of human liberty. It comprises, first, the inward domain of consciousness; demanding liberty of conscience in the most comprehensive sense; liberty of thought and feeling; absolute freedom of opinion and sentiment on all subjects, practical or speculative, scientific, moral, or theological. . . .

Let us suppose, therefore, that the government is entirely at one with the people, and never thinks of exerting any power of coercion unless in agreement with what it conceives to be their voice. But I deny the right of the people to exercise such coercion, either by themselves or by their government. The power itself is illegitimate. The best government has no more title to it than the worst. It is as noxious, or more noxious, when exerted in accordance with public opinion, than when in opposition to it. If all mankind minus one were of one opinion, and only one person were of the contrary opinion, mankind would be no more justified in silencing that one person, than he, if he had the power, would be justified in silencing mankind. . . . The peculiar evil of silencing the expression of an opinion is, that it is robbing the human race; posterity as well as the existing generation; those who dissent from the opinion, still more than those who hold it. If the opinion is right, they are deprived of the opportunity of exchanging error for truth: if wrong, they lose, what is almost as great a benefit, the clearer perception and livelier impression of truth, produced by its collision with error.

Nationalism was fundamentally radical in that it threatened to upset the existing political order, both internationally and nationally. A united Germany or united Italy would upset the balance of power established in 1815. By the same token, an independent Hungarian state would mean the breakup of the Austrian Empire. The conservatives tried so hard to repress nationalism because they were acutely aware of its potential to bring about such dramatic change.

At the same time, in the first half of the nineteenth century, nationalism and liberalism became strong allies. Most liberals believed that liberty could only be realized by peoples who ruled themselves. One British liberal said, "it is in general a necessary condition of free institutions that the boundaries of governments should coincide in the main with those of nationalities." The combination of liberalism with nationalism also gave a cosmopolitan dimension to nationalism. Many nationalists believed that once each people obtained their own state, all nations could be linked together into a broader community of all humanity.

In its German expression, nationalism took a turn that was hardly cosmopolitan and foreshadowed an aggressive kind of nationalism that was popular in the second half of the nineteenth century. An important

contribution to German nationalism came from the famous philosopher, Georg Wilhelm Friedrich Hegel (1770–1831). Aspects of Hegel's philosophy of history eventually made their way into German nationalistic thought.

One of these was his emphasis on the nation, which he envisioned as the direct manifestation of the "world-spirit" or "divine idea" operating in history. Since Hegel believed that this spirit of history was progressing toward an ideal of freedom, he implied that individuals could only find their true freedom or meaning by identifying

Map 22.3 Nationalism in Europe in the Nineteenth Century.

fully with the nation. Moreover, Hegel stressed that the Germanic nation would play a special role as the final "world historical people" in the realization of freedom or the spiritual liberation of humanity. As a philosopher, Hegel did not derive a specific political program from his philosophical system. But others did, and what they stressed was the role of the state and a belief in the peculiar historical destiny of Germany; both became an integral part of German nationalism in the second half of the nineteenth century.

Early Socialism

In the first half of the nineteenth century, the pitiful conditions found in the slums, mines, and factories of the Industrial Revolution gave rise to another ideology for change known as socialism. The term eventually became associated with a Marxist analysis of human society (see Chapter 23), but early socialism was largely the product of political theorists or intellectuals who wanted to introduce equality into social conditions and believed that human cooperation was superior to the competition that characterized early industrial capitalism. To later Marxists, such ideas were impractical dreams, and they contemptuously labeled the theorists utopian socialists. The term has endured to this day.

The early socialists accepted the Enlightenment belief that people are not evil by nature and will be virtuous if they live in a suitable environment. The economic system of their day, which they believed had brought wealth to some and misery to others, was incapable of providing this environment. The utopian socialists were against private property and the competitive spirit of early industrial capitalism. By eliminating them and creating new systems of social organization, they thought that a better environment for humanity could be achieved. Early socialists proposed a variety of ways to accomplish that task.

One approach, set out in the teachings of the Frenchman Henri de Saint-Simon (1760–1825), was the organization of all society into a cooperative community. Two elites, the intellectual leaders and the industrial managers, would use industrial and scientific technology to coordinate society for the benefit of all. In the process, government would vanish, as it would no longer be needed in the new society.

Another group of early socialists rejected Saint-Simon's collectivist approach in favor of creating voluntary associations that would demonstrate the advantages of cooperative living. Charles Fourier (1772–1838) offered a concrete scheme for this kind of approach. To Fourier, the competitive industrial system was failing to satisfy human passions and actually repressed them. He proposed instead the creation of small model communities called phalansteries. These were self-contained cooperatives, each consisting ideally of 1,620 people. Communally housed, the inhabitants of the phalanstery would live and work together for their mutual benefit. Work assignments would be rotated frequently to relieve workers of undesirable tasks. Unable to gain financial backing for his phalansteries, Fourier's plan remained untested, although his followers did set up a number of communities in the United States.

Robert Owen (1771–1858), the British cotton manufacturer, also believed that humans would reveal their true natural goodness if they lived in a cooperative environment. At New Lanark in Scotland, he was successful in transforming a squalid factory town into a flourishing, healthy community. But when he attempted to create a self-contained cooperative community at New Harmony, Indiana, in the United States in the 1820s, internal bickering within the community eventually destroyed his dream.

The Frenchman Louis Blanc (1813–1882) offered yet another early socialist approach to a better society, based on the idea that government had a responsibility

✦ **Children at New Lanark.** Robert Owen created an early experiment in utopian socialism by establishing a model industrial community at New Lanark, Scotland. In this illustration, the children of factory workers are shown dancing the quadrille.

for the welfare of its citizens. In *The Organization of Work,* he maintained that social problems could be solved by government assistance. Denouncing competition as the main cause of the economic evils of his day, he called for the establishment of workshops that would manufacture goods for public sale. The state would finance these workshops, but the workers would own and operate them. Blanc believed that the gradual spread of these workshops would provide a cooperative rather than competitive foundation for the entire economic life of the nation.

In their plans for the reconstruction of society, utopian socialists included schemes to change the roles of women and the relations between men and women. Saint-Simon's cooperative society included a recognition of equality between men and women, and his movement attracted a group of women who published a newspaper dedicated to the emancipation of women. Fourier's cooperative model communities were supposed to provide the same educational and job opportunities for men and women. Collective living would also entail both male and female responsibilities for child care and housecleaning.

One female utopian socialist, Flora Tristan (1803–1844), even attempted to foster a "utopian synthesis of socialism and feminism." She traveled through France preaching the need for the liberation of women. Her *Worker's Union,* published in 1843, advocated the application of Fourier's ideas to reconstruct both family and work:

> Workers, be sure of it. If you have enough equity and justice to inscribe into your Charter the few points I have just outlined, this declaration of the rights of women will soon pass into custom, from custom into law, and before twenty-five years pass you will then see inscribed in front of the book of laws which will govern French society: THE ABSOLUTE EQUALITY of man and woman. Then, my brothers, and only then, will human unity be constituted.[7]

She envisioned this absolute equality as the only hope to free the working class and transform civilization.

Flora Tristan, like the other utopian socialists, was largely ignored by her contemporaries. Although criticized for their impracticality, the utopian socialists at least laid the groundwork for later attacks on capitalism that would have a far-reaching result. But further industrialization would have to occur before those changes could be realized. In the first half of the nineteenth century, socialism remained merely a fringe movement compared to liberalism and nationalism.

Revolution and Reform, 1830–1850

Beginning in 1830, the forces of change began to break through the conservative domination of Europe, more successfully in some places than in others. Finally, in 1848 a wave of revolutionary fervor moved through Europe, causing liberals and nationalists everywhere to think that they were on the verge of creating a new order.

Another French Revolution

The new elections Charles X had called in 1830 produced another victory for the French liberals; at this point the king decided to seize the initiative. He believed that concessions had brought the downfall of Louis XVI during the first French Revolution. He was determined not to go in that direction. On July 26, 1830, Charles issued a set of edicts (July Ordinances) that imposed a rigid censorship on the press, dissolved the legislative assembly, and reduced the electorate in preparation for new elections. This unilateral revocation of the Charter of 1814 produced an immediate rebellion—the July Revolution. Barricades went up in Paris as a provisional government led by a group of moderate, propertied liberals was hastily formed and appealed to Louis-Philippe, the duke of Orléans, a cousin of Charles X, to become the constitutional king of France. Charles X fled to Britain; a new monarchy had been born.

Louis-Philippe (1830–1848) was soon called the bourgeois monarch because political support for his rule came from the upper middle class. Louis-Philippe even dressed like a member of the middle class in business suits and hats. Constitutional changes that favored the interests of the upper bourgeoisie were instituted. The Charter of 1814 was reinstated. Financial qualifications for voting were reduced, yet remained sufficiently high that the number of voters only increased from 100,000 to barely 200,000, guaranteeing that only the wealthiest people would vote.

To the upper middle class, the bourgeois monarchy represented the stopping place for political progress. To the lesser bourgeoisie and the Parisian working class, who had helped to overthrow Charles X in 1830, it was a severe disappointment because they had been completely excluded from political power. The rapid expansion of French industry in the 1830s and 1840s gave rise to an industrial working class concentrated in certain urban areas. Terrible working and living conditions and the periodic economic crises that created high levels of unemployment led to worker unrest and sporadic outbursts of violence. In 1831 and 1834, government troops were used to crush working-class disturbances in Lyons, center of the silk industry. These insurrections witnessed an emerging alliance between workers and radical advocates of a republic. The government's response—repression and strict censorship of the press—worked temporarily to curb further overt resistance.

Even in the legislature—the Chamber of Deputies—there were differences of opinion about the bourgeois monarchy and the direction in which it should grow. Two groups rapidly emerged, although both were composed of upper-middle-class representatives. The Party of Movement, which was led by Adolphe Thiers, favored ministerial responsibility and the pursuit of an active foreign poicy. They also favored limited expansion of the franchise, but Thiers was by no means a democrat. The Party of Resistance was led by François Guizot who believed that France had finally reached the "perfect form" of government and needed no further institutional changes. After 1840, the Party of Resistance dominated the Chamber of Deputies. Guizot cooperated with Louis-Philippe in suppressing ministerial responsibility and pursuing a policy favoring the interests of the wealthier manufacturers and tradesmen. The government's unwillingness to allow any reform of the electoral system or to deal with either republican demands for greater political representation or working-class demands for improved social conditions led to growing frustration and revolutionary stirrings. They finally erupted in 1848.

Revolutionary Outbursts in Belgium, Poland, and Italy

Supporters of liberalism played a primary role in the July Revolution in France, but nationalism was the crucial force in three other revolutionary outbursts in 1830. Rebels in all three states, however, were motivated by the success of the French revolutionaries. Nationalism was the key factor in a revolt that took place in the Netherlands. In an effort to create a stronger, larger state on France's northern border, the Congress of Vienna had added the area once known as the Austrian Netherlands to the Dutch Republic. The combination of two states with different languages, traditions, and religions was never really acceptable to the Belgians, nor did they appreciate the absolutist rule of the Dutch king, William of Orange. In 1830, the Belgians rose up against the Dutch and succeeded in convincing the major European powers to accept an independent, neutral Belgium. Leopold of Saxe-Coburg, a minor German prince, was designated to be the new king while a Belgian national congress established a constitutional monarchy for the new state.

The revolutionary scenarios in Italy and Poland were much less successful. Metternich sent Austrian troops to crush revolts in three Italian states. Poland, too, had a nationalist uprising in 1830 when revolutionaries tried to end Russian control of their country. But the Polish insurgents failed to get hoped-for support from France and Britain, and by September 1831 the Russians had crushed the revolt and established an oppressive military dictatorship over Poland.

✦ **The July Revolution in Paris.** In 1830, the forces of change began to undo the conservative domination of Europe. In France, the reactionary Charles X was overthrown. In this painting, students, former soldiers of the Empire, and middle-class citizens are seen joining the rebels who are marching on city hall to demand a republic. The forces of Charles X, seen firing from a building above, failed to halt the rebels.

The Voice of Reform: Macaulay on the Reform Bill of 1832

Thomas Babington Macaulay (1800–1859) was a historian and Whig member of Parliament. This selection is an excerpt from his speech given in Parliament in support of the Reform Bill of 1832, which extended the right to vote to the industrial middle classes of Britain. His argument was very simple: it is better to reform than to have a political revolution.

Thomas Babington Macaulay, Speech of March 2, 1831

My hon. friend the member of the University of Oxford tells us that, if we pass this law, England will soon be a Republic. The reformed House of Commons will, according to him, before it has sat ten years, depose the King, and expel the Lords from their House. Sir, if my hon. friend could prove this, he would have succeeded in bringing an argument for democracy infinitely stronger than any that is to be found in the works of Paine. His proposition is, in fact, this—that our monarchical and aristocratical institutions have no hold on the public mind of England; that these institutions are regarded with aversion by a decided majority of the middle class. . . . Now, sir, if I were convinced that the great body of the middle class in England look with aversion on monarchy and aristocracy, I should be forced, much against my will, to come to this conclusion, that monarchical and aristocratical institutions are unsuited to this country. Monarchy and aristocracy, valuable and useful as I think them, are still valuable and useful as means, and not as ends. The end of government is the happiness of the people; and I do not conceive that, in a country like this, the happiness of the people can be promoted by a form of government in which the middle classes place no confidence, and which exists only because the middle classes have no organ by which to make their sentiments known. But, sir, I am fully convinced that the middle classes sincerely wish to uphold the royal prerogatives, and the constitutional rights of the Peers. . . .

But let us know our interest and our duty better. Turn where we may—within, around—the voice of great events is proclaiming to us, "Reform, that you may preserve." Now, therefore, while everything at home and abroad forebodes ruin to those who persist in a hopeless struggle against the spirit of the age; now, while the crash of the proudest throne of the Continent is still resounding in our ears; . . . now, while the heart of England is still sound; now, while the old feelings and the old associations retain a power and a charm which may too soon pass away; now, in this your accepted time; now, in this your day of salvation, take counsel, not of prejudice, not of party spirit, not of the ignominious pride of a fatal consistency, but of history, of reason, of the ages which are past, of the signs of this most portentous time. Pronounce in a manner worthy of the expectation with which this great debate has been anticipated, and of the long remembrance which it will leave behind. Renew the youth of the State. Save property divided against itself. Save the multitude, endangered by their own ungovernable passions. Save the aristocracy, endangered by its own unpopular power. Save the greatest, and fairest, and most highly civilized community that ever existed, from calamities which may in a few days sweep away all the rich heritage of so many ages of wisdom and glory. The danger is terrible. The time is short. If this Bill should be rejected, I pray to God that none of those who concur in rejecting it may ever remember their votes with unavailing regret, amidst the wreck of laws, the confusion of ranks, the spoliation of property, and the dissolution of social order.

Reform in Great Britain

In 1830, new parliamentary elections brought the Whigs to power in Britain. At the same time, the successful July Revolution in France served to catalyze change in Britain. The Industrial Revolution had led to an expanding group of industrial leaders who objected to the corrupt British electoral system, which excluded them from political power. The Whigs, though also members of the landed classes, realized that concessions to reform were superior to revolution; the demands of the wealthy industrial middle class could no longer be ignored. In 1830, the Whigs introduced an election reform bill that was enacted in 1832 after an intense struggle (see the box above).

The Reform Bill gave explicit recognition to the changes wrought in British life by the Industrial Revolution. It disfranchised fifty-six rotten boroughs and enfranchised forty-two new towns and cities and reapportioned others. This gave the new industrial urban communities some voice in government. A property qualification (of £10 annual rent) for voting was retained, however, so the number of voters only increased from 478,000 to 814,000, a figure that still meant that only one in every thirty people was represented in Parliament. Thus, the Reform Bill of 1832 primarily benefited the upper middle class; the lower middle class, artisans, and industrial workers still had no vote. Moreover, the change did not significantly alter the composition of the House of Commons. One political leader noted that the Commons chosen in the first election after the Reform Bill seemed "to be very much like every other parliament." Nevertheless, a significant step had been taken. The "monied, manufacturing, and educated elite" had been "hitched" to the landed interests in ruling Britain. At the same time, the Reform Bill established a precedent for electoral reform bills in the second half of the nineteenth century that would extend the right to vote to significantly larger numbers of Britons.

The 1830s and 1840s witnessed considerable reform legislation. The aristocratic landowning class was usually (but not always) the driving force for legislation that halted some of the worst abuses in the industrial system by instituting government regulation of working conditions in the factories and mines. The industrialists and manufacturers now in Parliament opposed such legislation and were usually (but not always) the driving forces behind legislation that favored the principles of economic liberalism. The Poor Law of 1834 was based on the theory that giving aid to the poor and unemployed only encouraged laziness and increased the number of paupers. The Poor Law of 1834 tried to remedy this by making paupers so wretched they would choose to work. Those unable to support themselves were crowded together in workhouses where living and working conditions were intentionally miserable so that people would be encouraged to find profitable employment.

Another piece of liberal legislation involved the repeal of the Corn Laws. This was primarily the work of the manufacturers Richard Cobden and John Bright who formed the Anti-Corn Law League in 1838 to help workers by lowering bread prices. But this also aided the industrial middle classes who, as economic liberals, favored the principles of free trade. Repeal came in 1846

✖ **Map 22.4** European Revolts in the 1820s and 1830s.

when Robert Peel (1788–1850), leader of the Tories, persuaded some of his associates to support free trade principles and abandon the Corn Laws.

The year 1848, which witnessed revolutions in most of Europe, ended without a major crisis in Britain. On the Continent, middle-class liberals and nationalists were at the forefront of the revolutionary forces. In Britain, however, the middle class had been largely satisfied by the Reform Act of 1832 and the repeal of the Corn Laws in 1846. The British working classes were discontented, but they would have to wait until the second half of the nineteenth century to begin to achieve their goals.

The Growth of the United States

The American Constitution, ratified in 1789, committed the United States to two of the major forces of the first half of the nineteenth century, liberalism and nationalism. Initially, this constitutional commitment to national unity was challenged by divisions over the power of the federal government vis-à-vis the individual states. Bitter conflict erupted between the Federalists and the Republicans. Led by Alexander Hamilton (1757–1804), the Federalists favored a financial program that would establish a strong central government. The Republicans, guided by Thomas Jefferson (1743–1826) and James Madison (1751–1836), feared centralization and its consequences for popular liberties. These divisions were intensified by European rivalries as the Federalists were pro-British and the Republicans pro-French. The successful conclusion of the War of 1812 brought an end to the Federalists, who had opposed the war, while the surge of national feeling generated by the war served to heal the nation's divisions.

Another strong force for national unity came from the Supreme Court where John Marshall (1755–1835) was chief justice from 1801 to 1835. Marshall made the Supreme Court into an important national institution by asserting the right of the Court to overrule an act of Congress if the Court found it to be in violation of the Constitution. Under Marshall, the Supreme Court contributed further to establishing the supremacy of the national government by curbing the actions of state courts and legislatures.

The election of Andrew Jackson (1767–1845) as president in 1828 opened a new era in American politics. Jacksonian democracy introduced a mass democratic politics. The electorate was expanded by dropping traditional property qualifications; by the 1830s suffrage had been extended to almost all adult white males.

During the period from 1815 to 1850, the traditional liberal belief in the improvement of human beings was also given concrete expression. Americans developed detention schools for juvenile delinquents and new penal institutions, both motivated by the liberal belief that the right kind of environment would rehabilitate those in need of it. The abolitionist or national antislavery movement that developed in the 1830s also stemmed from liberal convictions. The American Anti-Slavery Society, established by William Lloyd Garrison (1805–1879) in 1833, already had 250,000 members by 1838.

By 1850, Europeans had become well aware of the growth of the American republic. Between 1830 and 1850, a wide variety of European political writers visited and examined the United States. The general thrust of their collective wisdom was that the United States was emerging as a world power. The French critic Sainte-Beuve wrote in 1847 that "Russia is still barbarous, but she is great. . . . The other youthful people is America . . . the future of the world is there, between these two great worlds." Sainte-Beuve had the right idea even if he was somewhat premature.

The Revolutions of 1848

Europe had experienced two waves of revolution, one in the early 1820s and another in 1830–1831. And yet, despite successes in France, Belgium, and Greece, the conservative order continued to dominate much of Europe. Revolutions in Spain, the Italian states, the German states, Russia, and Poland had all failed. Oftentimes liberal forces depended almost exclusively on junior army officers, liberal nobles, writers, university students, professors, and adventurers. But the forces of liberalism and nationalism, first generated by the French Revolution, continued to grow as the second great revolution—the Industrial Revolution—expanded and brought new groups of people who wanted change. In 1848, these forces of change erupted once more. As usual, revolution in France provided the spark for other countries, and soon most of central and southern Europe was ablaze with revolutionary fires. Tsar Nicholas I of Russia lamented to Queen Victoria in April 1848, "What remains standing in Europe? Great Britain and Russia."

YET ANOTHER FRENCH REVOLUTION

Numerous signs of trouble preceded the revolution. A severe industrial and agricultural depression beginning in 1846 brought untold hardship to the lower middle class, workers, and peasants. One-third of the workers in Paris were unemployed by the end of 1847. Scandals, graft, and corruption were rife while the government's persistent refusal to extend the suffrage angered the disfranchised members of the middle class. Even members of the upper middle class were discontented with the colorless reign of Louis-Philippe.

As Louis-Philippe's government continued to refuse to make changes, opposition grew. Radical republicans and socialists, joined by the upper middle class under the leadership of Adolphe Thiers, agitated for the dismissal of Guizot. Since they were forbidden by law to stage political rallies, they used the political banquet to call for reforms. Almost seventy such banquets were held in France during the winter of 1847–1848; a grand, culminating banquet was planned for Paris on February 22. When the government forbade it, people came anyway; students and workers threw up barricades in Paris. Although Louis-Philippe called out the National Guard, many of its bourgeois members joined the opposition. The king now proposed reform, but unable to form another ministry, he abdicated on February 24 and fled to Britain. A provisional government was established by a group of moderate and radical republicans; the latter even included the socialist Louis Blanc. The provisional government ordered that representatives for a Constituent Assembly to draw up a new constitution be elected by universal manhood suffrage.

The provisional government also established national workshops under the influence of Louis Blanc. As Blanc envisioned them, the workshops were to be cooperative factories run by the workers. In fact, the workshops became unemployment compensation units or public works, except that they provided little work beyond leaf raking and ditch digging. The cost of the program became increasingly burdensome to the government.

The result was a growing split between the moderate republicans, who had the support of most of France, and the radical republicans, whose main support came from the Parisian working class. In the elections for the National Assembly, 500 seats went to moderate republicans and 300 to avowed monarchists while the radicals gained only 100. From March to June, the number of unemployed enrolled in the national workshops rose from 10,000 to almost 120,000, emptying the treasury and frightening the moderates who responded by closing the workshops on June 21. The workers refused to accept this decision and poured into the streets. Four days of bitter and bloody fighting by government forces crushed the working-class revolt, described by some as a "class struggle." Thousands were killed, and 11,000

prisoners were deported to the French colony of Algeria in North Africa. These "June days" produced a legacy of hate. They had aspects of class warfare as the propertied classes became convinced that they had barely averted an attempt by the working class to destroy the social order. To many Europeans, the "June days" appeared to be a struggle of the bourgeoisie against the working class.

The new constitution, ratified on November 4, 1848, established a republic (Second Republic) with a unicameral (one-house) legislature of 750 elected by universal male suffrage for three years and a president, also elected by universal male suffrage, for four years. In the elections for the presidency held in December 1848, four republicans who had been associated with the early months of the Second Republic were resoundingly defeated by Charles Louis Napoleon Bonaparte, the nephew of Napoleon Bonaparte.

How could a virtual unknown who had been arrested twice and sent into exile once be chosen president by a landslide? The name of Bonaparte had obviously worked its magic. The Napoleonic revival had been going on for years as romanticists glorified his legend. One old veteran said: "Why shouldn't I vote for this gentleman. I, whose nose was frozen near Moscow." Perhaps just as important, the French were tired of revolution, and Louis Napoleon had posed as a defender of order. Members of the rural and urban masses who voted for Napoleon in large numbers saw him as a man of the people. Since they had been excluded from political life since 1815, what better choice did they have? Within four years President Napoleon would become Emperor Napoleon (see Chapter 23). The French had once again made a journey from republican chaos to authoritarian order, a pattern that was becoming all too common in French history.

REVOLUTION IN CENTRAL EUROPE

Like France, central Europe experienced rural and urban tensions due to an agricultural depression beginning in 1845. But the upheaval here seems to have been set off by news of the revolution in Paris in February 1848 (see the box on p. 759). By early March 1848, handicraft workers in many German states were destroying the machines and factories that they blamed for depriving them of their jobs; peasants looted and burned the manor houses of the nobility. Many German rulers promised constitutions, a free press, jury trials, and other liberal reforms. In Prussia concessions were also made to appease the revolutionaries. King Frederick William IV (1840–1861) agreed to abolish censorship, establish a

Revolutionary Excitement: Carl Schurz and the Revolution of 1848 in Germany

The excitement with which German liberals and nationalists received the news of the February Revolution in France and their own expectations for Germany are well captured in this selection from the Reminiscences *of Carl Schurz (1829–1906). Schurz made his way to America after the failure of the German revolution and eventually became a United States senator.*

Carl Schurz, Reminiscences

One morning, toward the end of February, 1848, I sat quietly in my attic-chamber, working hard at my tragedy of "Ulrich von Hutten," [a sixteenth-century German knight] when suddenly a friend rushed breathlessly into the room, exclaiming: "What, you sitting here! Do you not know what has happened?"

"No; what?"

"The French have driven away Louis Philippe and proclaimed the republic."

I threw down by pen—and that was the end of "Ulrich von Hutten." I never touched the manuscript again. We tore down the stairs, into the street, to the market-square, the accustomed meeting-place for all the student societies after their midday dinner. Although it was still forenoon, the market was already crowded with young men talking excitedly. There was no shouting, no noise, only agitated conversation. What did we want there? This probably no one knew. But since the French had driven away Louis Philippe and proclaimed the republic, something of course must happen here, too. . . . We were dominated by a vague feeling as if a great outbreak of elemental forces had begun, as if an earthquake was impending of which we had felt the first shock, and we instinctively crowded together. . . .

The next morning there were the usual lectures to be attended. But how profitless! The voice of the professor sounded like a monotonous drone coming from far away. What he had to say did not seem to concern us. The pen that should have taken notes remained idle. At last we closed with a sigh the notebook and went away, impelled by a feeling that now we had something more important to do—to devote ourselves to the affairs of the fatherland. And this we did by seeking as quickly as possible again the company of our friends, in order to discuss what had happened and what was to come. In these conversations, excited as they were, certain ideas and catchwords worked themselves to the surface, which expressed more or less the feelings of the people. Now had arrived in Germany the day for the establishment of "German Unity," and the founding of a great, powerful national German Empire. In the first line the convocation of a national parliament. Then the demands for civil rights and liberties, free speech, free press, the right of free assembly, equality before the law, a freely elected representation of the people with legislative power, responsibility of ministers, self-government of the communes, the right of the people to carry arms, the formation of a civic guard with elective officers, and so on—in short, that which was called a "constitutional form of government on a broad democratic basis." Republican ideas were at first only sparingly expressed. But the word democracy was soon on all tongues, and many, too, though it a matter of course that if the princes should try to withhold from the people the rights and liberties demanded, force would take the place of mere petition. Of course the regeneration of the fatherland must, if possible, be accomplished by peaceable means. . . . Like many of my friends, I was dominated by the feeling that at last the great opportunity had arrived for giving to the German people the liberty which was their birthright and to the German fatherland its unity and greatness, and that it was now the first duty of every German to do and to sacrifice everything for this sacred object.

new constitution, and work for a united Germany. The latter promise had its counterpart throughout all the German states as governments allowed elections by universal male suffrage for deputies to an all-German parliament. Its purpose was to fulfill a liberal dream—the preparation of a constitution for a new united Germany.

This Frankfurt Assembly was dominated by well-educated, articulate, middle-class delegates. When it came to nationalism, many were ahead of the times and certainly ahead of the governments of their respective states. From the beginning, the assembly aroused controversy by claiming to be the government for all of Germany. Then, it became embroiled in a sticky debate over the composition of the new German state. Supporters of a *Grossdeutsch* ("Big German") solution wanted to include the German province of Austria while proponents of a *Kleindeutsch* ("Small German") solution favored excluding Austria and making the Prussian king the emperor of the new German state. The problem was solved when the Austrians withdrew, leaving the field to the supporters of the *Kleindeutsch* solution. Their victory was short-lived, however, as Frederick William IV gruffly refused the assembly's offer of the title of "emperor of the Germans" and ordered the Prussian delegates home.

The Frankfurt Assembly soon disbanded. Although some members spoke of using force, they had no real means of compelling the German rulers to accept the constitution they had drawn up. The attempt of the German liberals at Frankfurt to create a German state had failed, and leadership for unification would now pass to the Prussian military monarchy.

The Austrian Empire also had its social, political, and nationalist grievances and needed only the news of the revolution in Paris to encourage it to erupt in flames in March 1848. The Hungarian liberal gentry under Louis Kossuth agitated for "commonwealth" status; they were willing to keep the Habsburg monarch, but wanted their own legislature. In March, demonstrations in Budapest, Prague, and Vienna led to Metternich's dismissal. The arch-symbol of the conservative order fled abroad. In Vienna, revolutionary forces, carefully guided by the educated and propertied classes, took control of the capital and insisted that a constituent assembly be summoned to draw up a liberal constitution. Hungary was granted its wish for its own legislature, a separate national army, and control over its foreign policy and budget. Allegiance to the Habsburg dynasty was now Hungary's only tie to the Austrian Empire. In Bohemia, the Czechs began to demand their own government as well.

Although Emperor Ferdinand I and Austrian officials had made concessions to appease the revolutionaries, they awaited an opportunity to reestablish their firm control. As in the German states, the conservatives were increasingly encouraged by the divisions between radical and moderate revolutionaries and played upon the middle-class fear of a working-class social revolution. Their first success came in June 1848 when a military force under General Alfred Windischgrätz ruthlessly suppressed the Czech rebels in Prague. In October the death of the minister for war at the hands of a Viennese mob gave Windischgrätz the pretext for an attack on Vienna. By the end of the month, radical rebels there had been crushed. In December the feebleminded Ferdinand I agreed to abdicate in favor of his nephew, Francis Joseph I (1848–1916), who worked vigorously to restore the imperial government in Hungary. The Austrian armies, however, were unable to defeat Kossuth's forces, and it was only through the intervention of Nicholas I, who sent a Russian army of 140,000 men to aid the Austrians, that the Hungarian revolution was finally crushed in 1849. The revolutions in Austria had also failed. Autocratic government was restored; emperor and propertied classes remained in control while the numerous nationalities were still subject to the Austrian government.

REVOLTS IN THE ITALIAN STATES

The failure of the revolutionary uprisings in Italy in 1830–1831 had served to discredit the secret societies that had fomented them and encouraged the Italian

◆ **Austrian Students in the Revolutionary Civil Guard.** In 1848, revolutionary fervor swept through Europe and toppled governments in France, central Europe, and Italy. In the Austrian Empire, students joined the revolutionary civil guard in taking control of Vienna and forcing the Austrian emperor to call a constituent assembly to draft a liberal constitution.

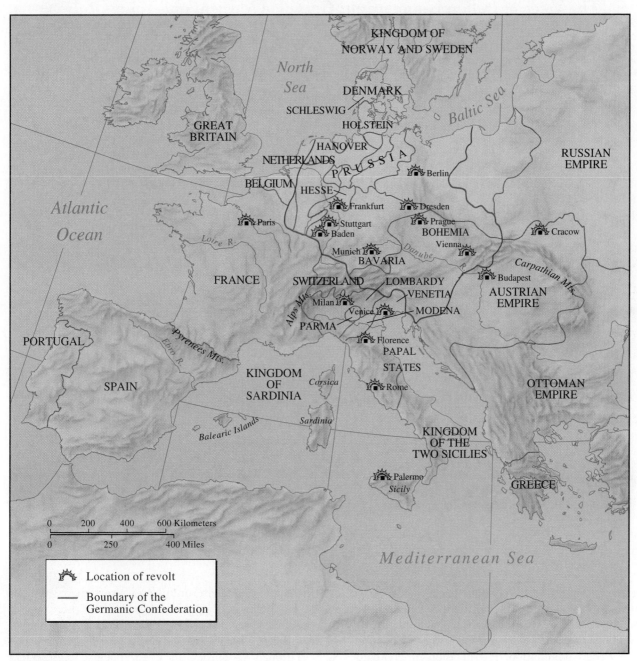

Map 22.5 The Revolutions of 1848–1849.

movement for unification to take a new direction. The leadership of Italy's *risorgimento* ("Resurgence") passed into the hands of Giuseppe Mazzini (1805–1872), a dedicated Italian nationalist who founded an organization known as Young Italy in 1831 (see the box on p. 762). This group set as its goal the creation of a united Italian republic. In his work *The Duties of Man*, Mazzini urged Italians to dedicate their lives to the Italian nation: "O my Brother! love your Country. Our

Country is our home." And yet to Mazzini love of country represented but one step toward the higher responsibility of loving humanity: "You are men before you are either citizens or fathers."

Mazzini's dreams seemed on the verge of fulfillment when a number of Italian states rose in revolt in 1848. Beginning in Sicily, rebellions spread northward as ruler after ruler granted a constitution to his people. Citizens in Lombardy and Venetia also rebelled against their

The Voice of Italian Nationalism: Giuseppe Mazzini and Young Italy

After the failure of the uprisings in Italy in 1830–1831, Giuseppe Mazzini emerged as the leader of the Italian risorgimento—the movement for Italian nationhood. In 1831, he founded an organization known as Young Italy whose goal was the creation of a united Italian republic. This selection is excerpted from the oath that the members of Young Italy were required to take.

Giuseppe Mazzini, The Young Italy Oath

Young Italy is a brotherhood of Italians who believe in a law of Progress and Duty, and are convinced that Italy is destined to become one nation,—convinced also that she possesses sufficient strength within herself to become one, and that the ill success of her former efforts is to be attributed not to the weakness, but to the misdirection of the revolutionary elements within her,—that the secret of force lies in constancy and unity of effort. They join this association in the firm intent of consecrating both thought and action to the great aim of reconstituting Italy as one independent sovereign nation of free men and equals. . . .

Each member will, upon his initiation into the association of Young Italy, pronounce the following form of oath, in the presence of the initiator:

In the name of God and of Italy;

In the name of all the martyrs of the holy Italian cause who have fallen beneath foreign and domestic tyranny;

By the duties which bind me to the land wherein God has placed me, and to the brothers whom God has given me;

By the love—innate in all men—I bear to the country that gave my mother birth, and will be the home of my children. . . .

By the sufferings of the millions,—

I, . . . believing in the mission intrusted by God to Italy, and the duty of every Italian to strive to attempt its fulfillment; convinced that where God has ordained that a nation shall be, He has given the requisite power to create it; that the people are the depositaries of that power, and that in its right direction for the people, and by the people, lies the secret of victory; convinced that virtue consists in action and sacrifice, and strength in union and constancy of purpose: I give my name to Young Italy, an association of men holding the same faith, and swear:

To dedicate myself wholly and forever to the endeavor with them to constitute Italy one free, independent, republican nation; to promote by every means in my power—whether by written or spoken word, or by action—the education of my Italian brothers toward the aim of Young Italy; toward association, the sole means of its accomplishment, and to virtue, which alone can render the conquest lasting; to abstain from enrolling myself in any other association from this time forth; to obey all the instructions, in conformity with the spirit of Young Italy, given me by those who represent with me the union of my Italian brothers; and to keep the secret of these instructions, even at the cost of my life; to assist my brothers of the association both by action and counsel—NOW AND FOREVER.

Austrian overlords. The Venetians declared a republic in Venice. The king of the northern Italian state of Piedmont, Charles Albert (1831–1849), took up the call and assumed the leadership for a war of liberation from Austrian domination. His invasion of Lombardy proved unsuccessful, however, and by 1849 the Austrians had reestablished complete control over Lombardy and Venetia.

Counterrevolutionary forces also prevailed throughout Italy. French forces helped Pope Pius IX regain control of Rome. Elsewhere Italian rulers managed to recover power on their own. Only Piedmont was able to keep its liberal constitution. Despite the lack of success, revolutionaries in Italy had learned two valuable lessons. Only Piedmont could be relied upon for leadership in the cause of Italian unity, and even then, without foreign help, Italy could not succeed in throwing off Austrian domination. Both lessons later proved helpful in achieving Italian unification.

Throughout Europe in 1848, popular revolts had initiated revolutionary upheavals that had led to the formation of liberal constitutions and liberal governments. But how could so many immediate successes in 1848 be followed by so many disasters only months later? Two reasons stand out. The unity of the revolutionaries had made the revolutions possible, but divisions soon shattered their ranks. Except in France, moderate liberals from the propertied classes failed to extend suffrage to the working classes who had helped to achieve the revolutions. But as radicals pushed for

Reaction, Reform, and Revolution: The European States, 1815–1850

Great Britain	
Corn Law	1815
Peterloo Massacre	1819
Reform Act	1832
Poor Law	1834
Formation of Anti-Corn Law League	1838
Repeal of Corn Laws	1846
France	
Louis XVIII	1814–1824
Constitutional Charter	1814
Charles X	1824–1830
July Revolution	1830
Louis-Philippe	1830–1848
Abdication of Louis-Philippe; formation of provisional government	1848 (February 22–24)
Formation of national workshops	1848 (February 26)
June days: workers' revolt in Paris	1848 (June)
Establishment of Second Republic	1848 (November)
Election of Louis Napoleon as French president	1848 (December)
Low Countries	
Union of Netherlands and Belgium	1815
Belgian revolt	1830
The German States	
Frederick William III of Prussia	1797–1840
Germanic Confederation established	1815
Burschenschaften at the Wartburg	1817
Karlsbad Decrees	1819
Frederick William IV of Prussia	1840–1861

Revolution in Germany	1848
Frankfurt Assembly	1848–1849
The Austrian Empire	
Emperor Francis II	1806–1835
Emperor Ferdinand I	1835–1848
Revolt in Austrian Empire; Metternich dismissed	1848 (March)
Austrian forces under General Windischgrätz crush Czech rebels	1848 (June)
Viennese rebels crushed	1848 (October)
Abdication of Ferdinand I	1848 (December)
Francis Joseph I	1848–1916
Defeat of Hungarians with help of Russian troops	1849
The Italian States	
Revolts in southern Italy and Sardinia crushed	1821
Aborted revolutions in Modena, Parma, and Papal States	1830
King Charles Albert of Piedmont	1831–1849
Revolutions in Italy	1848
Charles Albert attacks Austrians	1848
Austrians reestablish control in Lombardy and Venetia	1849
Russia	
Tsar Paul I	1796–1801
Tsar Alexander I	1801–1825
Decembrist Revolt	1825
Tsar Nicholas I	1825–1855
Polish uprising	1830
Suppression of Polish revolt	1831

universal male suffrage, liberals everywhere pulled back. Concerned about their property and security, they rallied to the old ruling classes for the sake of order and out of fear of social revolution by the working classes. All too soon, established governments were back in power.

In 1848, nationalities everywhere had also revolted in pursuit of self-government. But here too, frightfully little was achieved as divisions among nationalities proved utterly disastrous. Though the Hungarians demanded autonomy from the Austrians, at the same time they refused the same to their minorities—the Slovenes, Croats, and Serbs. Instead of joining together against the old empire, minorities fought each other. No wonder that one Czech could remark in April 1848: "If the Austrian state had not already existed for so long, it would have been in the interests of Europe, indeed of humanity itself, to endeavor to create it as soon as possible."[8] The Austrians' efforts to recover the Hungarian provinces met with little success until they began to play off Hungary's rebellious minority nationalities against the Hungarians.

The Emergence of an Ordered Society

Everywhere in Europe, the revolutionary upheavals of the late eighteenth and early nineteenth centuries made the ruling elite nervous about social disorder and the potential dangers to their lives and property. At the same time, the influx of large numbers of people from the countryside into rapidly growing cities had led to horrible living conditions, poverty, unemployment, and great social dissatisfaction. The first half of the nineteenth century witnessed a significant increase in crime rates, especially against property, in Britain, France, and Germany. The rise in incidences of pickpocketing, burglary, shoplifting, and embezzlement may in part have reflected the increased desperation of the poor, but it also provoked a severe reaction against crimes of property by middle-class urban inhabitants who feared the threat the urban poor posed to their security and possessions. New police forces soon appeared to defend the propertied classes from criminals and social misfits.

◆ **The London Police.** One response to the revolutionary upheavals of the late eighteenth and early nineteenth centuries was the development of civilian police forces that would be responsible for preserving property, arresting criminals, and maintaining domestic order. This early photograph shows a group of London policemen who came to be known as bobbies after Sir Robert Peel, the man who was responsible for introducing the legislation that initiated the London police force.

The Development of New Police Forces

The first major contribution of the nineteenth century to the development of a disciplined or ordered society in Europe was a regular system of police. A number of European states established civilian police forces—a group of well-trained law enforcement officers who were to preserve property and lives, maintain domestic order, investigate crime, and arrest offenders. It was hoped that their very presence would prevent crime. The new police forces were not readily welcomed, especially in countries where the memory of oppressive acts carried out by political and secret police still lingered. The function of the new police—to protect citizens—eventually made them acceptable, and by the end of the nineteenth century, many Europeans viewed them approvingly.

This new approach to policing made its first appearance in France in 1828 when Louis-Maurice Debelleyme, the prefect of Paris, proclaimed as his goal: "The essential object of our municipal police is the safety of the inhabitants of Paris. Safety by day and night, free traffic movement, clean streets, the supervision of and precaution against accidents, the maintenance of order in public places, the seeking out of offenses and their perpetrators."[9] In March 1829, the new policemen, known as *serjents*, became visible on Paris streets. They were dressed in blue uniforms to make them easily recognizable by all citizens. They were also lightly armed with a white cane during the day and a saber at night, underscoring the fact that they made up a civilian, not a military, body. Initially, there were not many of the new policemen. Paris had 85 by August of 1829 and only 500 in 1850. Before the end of the century, their number had increased to 4,000.

The British, fearful of the powers exercised by military or secret police in authoritarian continental European states, had long resisted the creation of a professional police force. Instead, Britain depended upon a system of unpaid constables recruited by local authorities. Often these local constables were incapable of keeping order, preventing crimes, or apprehending criminals. Such jobs could also be dangerous and involve incidents like the one reported by a man passing by a local pub in 1827:

> I saw Thomas Franklin [constable of the village of Leighton Buzzard] coming out backwards. John Brandon . . . was opposite and close to the constable. I saw the said John Brandon strike the said constable twice "bang full in the face" the blows knocked the constable down on his

back. John Brandon fell down with him. Sarah Adams
... got on top of the constable and jostled his head
against the ground.... The constable appeared very
much hurt and his face was all over blood.[10]

The failure of the local constables led to a new approach. Between September 1829 and May 1830, 3,000
uniformed policemen appeared on the streets of London.
They came to be known as bobbies after Sir Robert Peel,
who had introduced the legislation that created the
force. The Municipal Corporations Act of 1835 spread
the new police into provincial boroughs while counties
were permitted to establish police forces in 1839. By
1856, the new police had become obligatory for all local
authorities.

As is evident from the first instruction book for the
new British police, their primary goal was to prevent
crime: "Officers and police constables should endeavour
to distinguish themselves by such vigilance and activity
as may render it impossible for any one to commit a
crime within that portion of the town under their
charge."[11] The municipal authorities soon found, however, that the police were also useful for imposing order
on working-class urban inhabitants. On Sundays they
were called upon to clean up after Saturday night's
drinking bouts. As demands for better pay and treatment
led to improved working conditions, British policemen
began to develop a sense of professionalism (see the box
on p. 766).

Police systems were reorganized throughout the
Western world during the nineteenth century. Reformers followed first the French and then the British model,
but local traditions were often important in shaping a
nation's system. After the revolutions of 1848 in Germany, a state-financed police force called the *Schutzmannschaft*, modeled after the London police, was established for the city of Berlin. The *Schutzmannschaft* began
as a civilian body, but already by 1851 the force had
become organized more along military lines and was
used for political purposes. In addition to performing
welfare services, which helped make them acceptable to
the city's residents, the Berlin police exercised considerably more power than their British counterparts. Their
military nature was reinforced by their weaponry, which
included swords, pistols, and brass knuckles. One observer noted that "A German policeman on patrol is
armed as if for war."[12]

While the new policemen alleviated some of the fears
about the increase in crime, contemporary reformers
approached the problem in other ways. Some of them
believed that the increase in crime was related to the

dramatic increase in poverty. As one commented in
1816: "Poverty, misery are the parents of crime." Relief
for the poverty-stricken became a major concern.
Strongly influenced by the middle-class belief that unemployment was the result of sheer laziness, European
states passed poor laws that attempted to force paupers
to find work on their own or enter workhouses designed
to make people so utterly uncomfortable they would
choose to reenter the labor market.

Meanwhile, another group of reformers was arguing
that poor laws failed to address the real problem, which
was that poverty was a result of the moral degeneracy of
the lower classes, increasingly labeled the "dangerous
classes" because of the threat they posed to middle-class
society. This belief led one group of secular reformers to
form institutes to instruct the working classes in the
applied sciences in order to make them more productive
members of society. The London Mechanics' Institute,
established in Britain, and the Society for the Diffusion
of Useful Knowledge in the Field of Natural Sciences,
Technical Science, and Political Economy, founded in
Germany, are but two examples of this approach to the
"dangerous classes."

Organized religion took a different approach. British
evangelicals set up Sunday Schools to improve the
morals of working children while in Germany evangelical Protestants established nurseries for orphans and
homeless children, women's societies to care for the sick
and poor, and prison societies that prepared women to
work in prisons. The Catholic church attempted the
same kind of work through a revival of its religious
orders; dedicated priests and nuns used spiritual instruction and recreation to turn young male workers away
from the moral vices of gambling and drinking and
female workers from lives of prostitution.

The Reform of Prisons

The increase in crime led to a rise in arrests. By the
1820s, in most countries the indiscriminate use of
capital punishment, even for crimes against property,
was increasingly being viewed as ineffective and was
replaced by imprisonment. Although the British had
shipped people convicted of serious offenses to their
colonial territory of Australia, that practice began to
slow down in the late 1830s when the colonists loudly
objected. Incarceration, then, was the only alternative.
Prisons served to isolate criminals from society, but a
growing number of reformers questioned their purpose
and effectiveness, especially when prisoners were subjected to harsh and even humiliating work as punish-

The New British Police: "We Are Not Treated as Men"

The new British police forces, organized first in London in 1829, were generally well established throughout a good part of Britain by the 1840s. As professionalism arose in the ranks of the forces, so too did demands for better pay and treatment. In these two selections, police constables make clear their demands and complaints.

Petition for Higher Pay by a Group of Third-Class Constables (1848)

Men joining the Police service as 3rd Class Constables and having a wife and 3 children to support on joining, are not able properly to do so on the pay of 16/8d. Most of the married men on joining are somewhat in debt, and are unable to extricate themselves on account of rent to pay and articles to buy which are necessary for support of wife and children. We beg leave to state that a married man having a wife and 2 children to support on joining, that it is as much as he can do upon 16/8d per week, and having to remain upon that sum for the first 12 to 18 months.

Complaints from Constables of D Division of the London Metropolitan Police

We are not treated as men but as slaves we englishmen do not like to be terrorized by a set of Irish sergeants who are only lenient to their own countrymen we the D division of Paddington are nearly all ruled by these Irish Sergeants after we have done our night-Duty may we not have the privilege of going to Church or staying at home to Suit our own inclination when we are ordered by the Superintendent to go to church in our uniform on wednesday we do not object to the going to church we like to go but we do not like to be ordered there and when we go on Sunday nights we are asked like so many schoolboys have we been to church should we say no let reason be what it may it does not matter we are forthwith ordered from Paddington to Marylebone lane the next night—about 2 hours before we go to Duty that is 2 miles from many of our homes being tired with our walk there and back we must either loiter about the streets or in some public house and there we do not want to go for we cannot spare our trifling wages to spend them there but there is no other choice left—for us to make our time out to go on Duty at proper time on Day we are ordered there for that offence another Man may faultlessly commit—the crime of sitting 4 minutes during the night—then we must be ordered there another to Shew his old clothes before they are given in even we must go to the expense of having them put in repair we have indeed for all these frightful crimes to walk 3 or 4 miles and then be wasting our time that makes our night 3 hours longer than they ought to be another thing we want to know who has the money that is deducted out of our wages for fines and many of us will be obliged to give up the duty unless we can have fair play as to the stationing of us on our beats why cannot we follow round that may all and each of us go over every beat and not for the Sergeants to put their favourites on the good beats and the others kept back their favourites are not the best policemen but those that will spend the most with them at the public house there are a great many of these things to try our temper.

---

ment. By the 1830s, European governments were seeking ways to reform their penal systems. Motivated by the desire not just to punish, but to rehabilitate and transform criminals into new persons, the British and French sent missions to the United States in the early 1830s to examine how the two different systems then used in American prisons accomplished this goal. At the Auburn Prison in New York, for example, prisoners were separated at night but worked together in the same workshop during the day. At Walnut Street Prison in Philadelphia, prisoners were separated into individual cells.

After examining the American prisons, both the French and British constructed prisons on the Walnut Street model with separate cells that isolated prisoners from one another. At Petite Roquette in France and Pentonville in Britain, prisoners wore leather masks while they exercised and sat in separate stalls when in chapel. Solitary confinement, it was believed, forced prisoners back on their own consciences, led to greater remorse, and increased the possibility that they would change their evil ways. One supporter of the separate-cell system noted how:

> a few months in the solitary cell renders a prisoner strangely impressible. The chaplain can then make the brawny navvy cry like a child; he can work on his feelings in almost any way he pleases; he can, so to speak, photograph his thoughts, wishes and opinions on his patient's mind, and fill his mouth with his own phrases and language.[13]

As prison populations increased, however, solitary confinement proved expensive and less feasible. The French even returned to their custom of sending prisoners to French Guiana to handle the overload.

Prison reform and police forces were geared toward one primary end, the creation of a more disciplined society. Disturbed by the upheavals associated with revolutions and the social discontent wrought by industrialization and urbanization, the ruling elites sought to impose some order upon society. Even many radical working-class activists, who were often the object of police activity, welcomed the domestication and discipline that the new system imposed.

Culture in an Age of Reaction and Revolution: The Mood of Romanticism

At the end of the eighteenth century, a new intellectual movement was developing to challenge the ideas of the Enlightenment. Although some historians have argued that Romanticism was more a "mood" than a movement, it revolutionized painting, literature, and music in the first half of the nineteenth century. Romanticism was a reaction against the Enlightenment's preoccupation with reason in discovering truth. While the Romantics, especially the early Romantics, by no means disparaged reason, they tried to balance its use by stressing the importance of intuition, feeling, emotion, and imagination as sources of knowing. As one German Romantic put it, "It was my heart that counseled me to do it, and my heart cannot err." Romanticism manifested itself in a remarkable variety of ways, evident in a survey of its major characteristics and some of its major figures.

The Characteristics of Romanticism

Romanticism had its beginnings in Germany when a group of German poets began to emphasize emotion, sentiment, and the importance of inner feelings in their works. An important model for Romantics was the tragic figure in *The Sorrows of the Young Werther*, a novel by the great German writer, Johann Wolfgang von Goethe (1749–1832), who later rejected Romanticism in favor of classicism. Werther was a Romantic figure who sought freedom in order to fulfill himself. Misunderstood and rejected by society, he continued to believe in his own worth through his inner feelings, but his deep love for a girl who did not love him finally led him to commit suicide. After Goethe's *Sorrows of the Young*

Werther, numerous novels and plays appeared whose plots revolved around young maidens tragically carried off at an early age (twenty-three was most common) by disease (usually tuberculosis, at that time a protracted disease that was usually fatal) to the sorrow and sadness of their male lovers.

Another important characteristic of Romanticism was individualism or an interest in the unique traits of each person. The Romantics' desire to follow their inner drives led them to rebel against middle-class conventions. Long hair, beards, and outrageous clothes served to reinforce the individualism that young Romantics were trying to express. Many Romantic novels focused on the theme of the individual's conflict with society. This conflict could take other directions as well. In his novel *Lucinde*, the German writer and critic, Friedrich Schlegel (1772–1829), presented a portrait of a free and "innocent" girl who followed the demands of her heart by advocating the so-called "natural" practice of free love.

Sentiment and individualism came together in the Romantics' stress on the heroic. The Romantic hero was a solitary genius who was ready to defy the world and sacrifice his life for a great cause. In the hands of the British writer, Thomas Carlyle (1795–1881), however, the Romantic hero did not destroy himself in ineffective protests against society, but transformed society instead. In his historical works, Carlyle stressed that historical events were largely determined by the deeds of such heroes.

Many Romantics believed that states and societies, like individual organisms, evolved through time, and that each people had a *Geist* or spirit that made that people unique. This perspective inspired Romantics to study history because they saw it as a way to understand how a nationality came to be what it was. They singled out one period of history—the Middle Ages—for special attention because the European states had first emerged during that time. The medieval period was also seen as an age of faith and religious emotion rather than reason. No doubt, the Romantic reverence for history contributed to the nineteenth century's fascination with nationalism.

This historical mindedness was manifested in many ways. In Germany, the Grimm brothers collected and published local fairy tales, as did Hans Christian Andersen in Denmark. The revival of medieval Gothic architecture left European countrysides adorned with pseudo-medieval castles and cities bedecked with grandiose neo-Gothic cathedrals, city halls, parliamentary buildings, and even railway stations.

◆ **Neo-Gothic Revival (British Houses of Parliament).**
The Romantic movement of the first half of the nineteenth century led, among other things, to a revival of medieval Gothic architecture that left European cities bedecked with neo-Gothic buildings. After the Houses of Parliament in London burned down in 1834, they were replaced with the new buildings of neo-Gothic design seen in this photograph.

Literature, too, reflected this historical consciousness. The novels of Walter Scott (1771–1832) became European best-sellers in the first half of the nineteenth century. Scott had a background in law but was raised on old tales of Scottish history. He first made his mark as a writer of verse romances, but his historical novels brought him even greater attention. *Ivanhoe*, in which he tried to evoke the clash between Saxon and Norman knights in medieval England, became one of his most popular works. On the Continent, Alexandre Dumas (1802–1870) likewise gained fame for his historical evocations. Most famous was *The Three Musketeers* with its vivid portrayal of swashbuckling adventurers in seventeenth-century France.

To the historical mindedness of the Romantics could be added an attraction to the bizarre and unusual. In an exaggerated form, this preoccupation gave rise to so-called Gothic literature (see the box on p. 769), chillingly evident in the short stories of horror by the American Edgar Allan Poe (1808–1849) and in *Frankenstein* by Mary Shelley (1797–1851). Her novel was the story of a mad scientist who brings into being a humanlike monster who goes berserk. Some Romantics even sought the unusual in their own lives by pursuing extraordinary states of experience in dreams, nightmares, frenzies, and suicidal depression or by experimenting with cocaine, opium, and hashish to produce drug-induced, altered states of consciousness.

Romantic Poets and the Love of Nature

To the Romantics, poetry ranked above all other literary forms because they believed it was the direct expression of one's soul. The Romantic poets were viewed as seers who could reveal the invisible world to others. Their incredible sense of drama made some of them the most colorful figures of their era, living intense but short lives. Percy Bysshe Shelley (1792–1822), expelled from school for advocating atheism, set out to reform the world. His *Prometheus Unbound*, completed in 1820, is a portrait of the revolt of human beings against the laws and customs that oppress them. He drowned in a storm in the Mediterranean. Lord Byron (1788–1824) dramatized himself as the melancholy Romantic hero that he had described in his work, *Childe Harold's Pilgrimage*. He participated in the movement for Greek independence and died in Greece fighting the Turks.

Romantic poetry gave full expression to one of the most important characteristics of Romanticism: love of nature, especially evident in William Wordsworth (1770–1850). He spent days wandering through British forests, often hiking as much as forty miles a day. Like other Romantics, he was fascinated by the different moods of nature:

> From Nature doth emotion come, and moods
> Of calmness equally are Nature's gift:
> This is her glory; these two attributes
> Are sister horns that constitute her strength.[14]

But Wordsworth's admiration of nature went beyond a simple observation of streams and trees. His experience of nature was almost mystical as he claimed to receive "authentic tidings of invisible things":

> One impulse from a vernal wood
> May teach you more of man,
> Of Moral Evil and of good,
> Than all the sages can.[15]

To Wordsworth, nature contained a mysterious force that the poet could perceive and learn from. Nature served as a mirror into which humans could look to learn about themselves. Nature was, in fact, alive and sacred:

> To every natural form, rock, fruit or flower,
> Even the loose stones that cover the high-way,
> I gave a moral life, I saw them feel,
> Or link'd them to some feeling: the great mass
> Lay bedded in a quickening soul, and all
> That I beheld, respired with inward meaning.[16]

⮑ Gothic Literature: Edgar Allan Poe ⮐

American writers and poets made significant contributions to the movement of Romanticism. Although Edgar Allan Poe (1809–1849) was influenced by the German Romantic school of mystery and horror, many literary historians give him the credit for pioneering the modern short story. This selection from the conclusion of "The Fall of the House of Usher" gives a sense of the nature of so-called Gothic literature.

Edgar Allan Poe, "The Fall of the House of Usher"
No sooner had these syllables passed my lips, than—as if a shield of brass had indeed, at the moment, fallen heavily upon a floor of silver—I became aware of a distinct, hollow, metallic, and clangorous, yet apparently muffled, reverberation. Complete unnerved, I leaped to my feet; but the measured rocking movement of Usher was undisturbed. I rushed to the chair in which he sat. His eyes were bent fixedly before him, and throughout his whole countenance there reigned a stony rigidity. But, as I placed my hand upon his shoulder, there came a strong shudder over his whole person; a sickly smile quivered about his lips and I saw that he spoke in a low, hurried, and gibbering murmur, as if unconscious of my presence. Bending closely over him, I at length drank in the hideous import of his words.

"Not hear it?—yes, I hear it, and *have* heard it. Long-long-long-many minutes, many hours, many days, have I heard it—yet I dared not—oh, pity me, miserable wretch that I am!—I dared not—I *dared* not speak! *We have put her living in the tomb!* Said I not that my senses were acute? I *now* tell you that I heard her first feeble movements in the hollow coffin. I heard them—many, many days ago—yet I dared not—I *dared not speak!* And now—to-night—. . . the rending of her coffin, and the grating of the iron hinges of her prison, and her struggles within the coppered archway of the vault! Oh wither shall I fly? Will she not be here anon? Is she not hurrying to upbraid me for my haste? Have I not heard her footstep on the stair? Do I not distinguish that heavy and horrible beating of her heart? MADMAN!"—here he sprang furiously to his feet, and shrieked out his syllables, as if in the effort he were giving up his soul—"MADMAN! I TELL YOU THAT SHE NOW STANDS WITHOUT THE DOOR!"

As if in the superhuman energy of his utterance there had been found the potency of a spell, the huge antique panels to which the speaker pointed threw slowly back, upon the instant, their ponderous and ebony jaws. It was the work of the rushing gust—but then without those doors there DID stand the lofty and enshrouded figure of the lady Madeline of Usher. There was blood upon her white robes, and the evidence of some bitter struggle upon every portion of her emaciated frame. For a moment she remained trembling and reeling to and fro upon the threshold, then, with a low moaning cry, fell heavily inward upon the person of her brother, and in her violent and now final death-agonies, bore him to the floor a corpse, and a victim to the terrors he had anticipated.

Other Romantics carried this worship of nature further into pantheism by identifying the great force in nature with God. The Romantics would have nothing to do with the deist God of the Enlightenment, the remote creator of the world-machine. As the German Romantic poet Friedrich Novalis said, "Anyone seeking God will find him anywhere."

The worship of nature also led Wordsworth and other Romantic poets to a critique of the mechanistic materialism of eighteenth-century science, which, they believed, had reduced nature to a cold object of study (see the box on p. 770). Against that view of the natural world, Wordsworth offered his own vivid and concrete experience. To him the scientists' dry, mathematical approach left no room for the imagination or for the human soul. The poet who left to the world "one single moral precept, one single affecting sentiment," Wordsworth said, did more for the world than scientists who were soon forgotten. The monster created by Frankenstein in Mary Shelley's Gothic novel symbolized well the danger of science when it tries to conquer nature. Many Romantics were convinced that the emerging industrialization would cause people to become alienated from their inner selves and the natural world around them.

Romanticism in Art and Music

Like the literary arts, the visual arts were also deeply affected by Romanticism. Although their works varied widely, Romantic artists shared at least two fundamental characteristics. All artistic expression to them was a reflection of the artist's inner feelings; a painting should mirror the artist's vision of the world and be the

William Blake and the Romantic Attack on Science

William Blake (1757–1827) was a British poet, painter, and graphic artist who combined all of these vocations to produce visually stunning books. He was a religious mystic, and much of his poetic and artistic work was an attempt to give visible form to his profound visionary experiences. In this selection from his poem Milton, he expressed his deep distrust of "the Reasoning Power in Man" and materialistic science.

William Blake, Milton

The Negation is the Spectre; the Reasoning Power in
   Man
This is a false body: an Incrustation over my Immortal
Spirit; a Selfhood, which must be put off and annihilated
   away
To cleanse the Face of my Spirit by Self-examination.
To bathe in the Waters of Life; to wash off the Not
   Human
I come in Self-annihilation and the grandeur of
   Inspiration
To cast off Rational Demonstration by Faith in the
   Saviour
To cast off the rotten rags of Memory by Inspiration
To cast off Bacon, Locke and Newton [three English
   forerunners of science] from Albion's [usually ancient
   name of Britain] covering
To take off his filthy garments, & clothe him with
   Imagination
To cast aside from Poetry, all that is not Inspiration
That it no longer shall dare to mock with the aspersion of
   Madness
Cast on the Inspired, by the tame high finisher of paltry
   Blots,

Indefinite, or paltry Rhymes; or paltry Harmonies,
Who creeps into State Government like a catterpiller to
   destroy
To cast off the idiot Questioner who is always
   questioning,
But never capable of answering; who sits with a sly grin
Silently plotting when to question, like a thief in a cave;
Who publishes doubt & calls it knowledge; whose Science
   is Despair,
Whose pretence to knowledge is Envy, whose whole
   Science is
To destroy the wisdom of ages to gratify ravenous Envy
That rages round him like a Wolf day & night without
   rest
He smiles with condescension; he talks of Benevolence &
   Virtue
And those who act with Benevolence & Virtue, they
   murder time on time
These are the destroyers of Jerusalem, these are the
   murderers
Of Jesus, who deny the Faith & mock at Eternal Life:
Who pretend to Poetry that they may destroy
   Imagination;
By imitation of Nature's Images drawn from
   Remembrance
These are the Sexual Garments, the Abomination of
   Desolation
Hiding the Human Lineaments as with an Ark &
   Curtains
Which Jesus rent: & now shall wholly purge away with
   Fire
Till Generation is swallowed up in Regeneration.

instrument of his own imagination. Moreover, Romantic artists deliberately rejected the principles of classicism. Beauty was not a timeless thing; its expression depended on one's culture and one's age. The Romantics abandoned classical restraint for warmth, emotion, and movement. Through an examination of three painters, we can see how Romanticism influenced the visual arts.

The early life experiences of Caspar David Friedrich (1774–1840) left him with a lifelong preoccupation with God and nature. Friedrich painted many landscapes but with an interest that transcended the mere presentation of natural details. His portrayal of mountains shrouded in mist, gnarled trees bathed in moon-

light, and the stark ruins of monasteries surrounded by withered trees all conveyed a feeling of mystery and mysticism. For Friedrich, nature was a manifestation of divine life. As in Man and Woman Gazing at the Moon, he liked to depict one or two solitary figures gazing upon the grandeur of a natural scene with their backs to the viewer. Not only were his human figures dwarfed by the overwhelming presence of nature, but they expressed the human yearning for infinity, the desire to lose oneself in the universe. To Friedrich, the artistic process depended upon the use of an unrestricted imagination that could only be achieved through inner vision. He advised artists: "Shut your physical eye and look first at your picture with your spiritual eye, then bring to the light of day what you have seen in the darkness."

Another artist who dwelled on nature and made landscape his major subject was the Englishman Joseph Malford William Turner (1775–1851). Turner was an incredibly prolific artist who produced over 20,000 paintings, drawings, and watercolors. Turner's concern with nature manifested itself in innumerable landscapes and seascapes, sunrises and sunsets. He did not idealize nature or reproduce it with realistic accuracy, however. He sought instead to convey its moods by using a skilled interplay of light and color to suggest natural effects. In allowing his objects to melt into their surroundings, he anticipated the Impressionist painters of the last half of the nineteenth century (see Chapter 25). John Constable, a contemporary English Romantic painter, described Turner's paintings as "airy visions, painted with tinted steam."

Eugène Delacroix (1798–1863) was the most famous French Romantic artist. Largely self-taught, he was fascinated by the exotic and had a passion for color. Both characteristics are visible in his *Women of Algiers*. Significant for its use of light and its patches of interrelated color, this portrayal of the world of harem concubines in exotic North Africa was actually somewhat scandalous to the early nineteenth century. In Delacroix, theatricality and movement combined with a daring use of color. Many of his works reflect his own belief that "a painting should be a feast to the eye."

To many Romantics, music was the most Romantic of the arts since it enabled the composer to probe deeply into human emotions. One Romantic writer noted: "It has been rightly said that the object of music is the awakening of emotion. No other art can so sublimely arouse human sentiments in the innermost heart of man."[17] Although music historians have called the eighteenth century an age of classicism and the nineteenth the era of Romanticism, there was much carryover of classical forms from one century to the next. One of the greatest composers of all time, Ludwig van Beethoven, served as a bridge between classicism and Romanticism.

Beethoven (1770–1827) is one of the few composers who was able singlehandedly to transform the art of music. Beethoven was a child of the Enlightenment, and the new notions of liberty and human rights voiced by the philosophes echo sharply in his music. Set ablaze by the events in France, a revolutionary mood burned brightly across Europe, and Beethoven, like other creative personalities, yearned to communicate his cherished beliefs. He said, "I *must* write, for what weighs on my heart, I *must* express." For Beethoven, music had to reflect his deepest inner feelings.

Born in Bonn, Beethoven came from a family of musicians who worked for the electors of Cologne and became assistant organist at the court by the age of thirteen. He soon made his way to Vienna, then the musical capital of Europe, where he studied briefly under

✦ **Caspar David Friedrich,** *Man and Woman Gazing at the Moon.* The German artist Caspar David Friedrich sought to express in painting his own mystical view of nature. "The divine is everywhere," he once wrote, "even in a grain of sand." In this painting, two solitary wanderers are shown from the back gazing at the moon. Overwhelmed by the all-pervasive presence of nature, the two figures express the human longing for infinity.

Haydn. Beginning in 1792, this city became his permanent residence although his unruly manner and offensive appearance made him barely tolerable to Viennese society.

During his first major period of composing, which extended from 1792 to 1800, his work was still largely within the classical framework of the eighteenth century, and the influences of Haydn and Mozart are paramount. During the next period of his creative life, which began in 1800, Beethoven declared, "I am making a fresh start." With the composition of the Third Symphony (1804), also called the *Eroica*, which was originally intended for Napoleon, Beethoven broke through to the elements of Romanticism in his use of uncontrolled rhythms to create dramatic struggle and uplifted resolutions. E. T. A. Hoffman, a contemporary composer and writer, said, "Beethoven's music opens the flood gates of fear, of terror, of horror, of pain, and arouses that longing for the eternal which is the essence of Romanticism. He is thus a pure Romantic composer."[18] Beethoven went on to write a vast quantity of works including symphonies, piano and violin sonatas, concerti, masses, an opera, and a cycle of songs. In the midst of this productivity and growing fame, Beethoven was more and more burdened by his growing deafness, which intensified noticeably after 1800. One of the most moving pieces of music of all time, the chorale finale of his Ninth Symphony, was composed when Beethoven was totally deaf.

Beethoven served as a bridge from the classical era to Romanticism; after him came a number of musical geniuses who composed in the Romantic style. The Frenchman Hector Berlioz (1803–1869) was one of the most outstanding. His father, a doctor in Grenoble, intended that his son should also study medicine. The young Berlioz eventually rebelled, however, maintaining to his father's disgust that he would be "no doctor or apothecary but a great composer." Berlioz managed to fulfill his own expectations, achieving fame in Germany, Russia, and Britain, although the originality of his work kept him from receiving any real recognition in his native France. To earn a living while studying music composition in Paris, and even later while composing, Berlioz worked as a music critic for literary journals.

Berlioz was one of the founders of program music, which was an attempt to use the moods and sound effects of instrumental music to depict the actions and emotions inherent in a story, event, or even a personal experience. This development of program music was evident in his concert overtures to Shakespeare's plays and, above all, in his most famous piece, the first complete program symphony known as the *Symphonie*

◆ **J. M. W. Turner, *Rain, Steam, and Speed—The Great Western Railway*.** Although Turner began his artistic career by painting accurate representations of the natural world, he increasingly sought to depict an atmosphere by a skillful use of light and color. In this painting, Turner eliminates specific details and uses general fields of color to portray the image of a locomotive rushing toward the spectator.

fantastique. In this work, Berlioz used music to evoke the passionate emotions of a tortured love affair, including a fifth movement in which he musically creates an opium-induced nightmare of a witches' gathering.

The Revival of Religion in the Age of Romanticism

After 1815, Catholicism experienced a revival. In the eighteenth century, Catholicism had lost its attraction for many of the educated elite as even the European nobility flirted with the ideas of the Enlightenment. The restoration of the nobility brought a new appreciation for the Catholic faith as a force for order in society. This appreciation was greatly reinforced by the Romantic movement. The attraction of Romantics to the Middle Ages and their emphasis on emotion led them to their own widespread revival of Christianity.

Catholicism, in particular, benefited from this Romantic enthusiasm for religion. Especially among German Romantics, there were many conversions to the Catholic faith. One of the most popular expressions of this Romantic revival of Catholicism was found in the work of the Frenchman François-René de Chateaubriand (1768–1848). His book, _Genius of Christianity_, published in 1802, was soon labeled the "Bible of Romanticism." His defense of Catholicism was based not upon historical, theological, or even rational grounds, but largely upon Romantic sentiment. As a faith, Catholicism echoed the harmony of all things. Its liturgy contained the divine mysteries that mirrored the universe. Its cathedrals brought one into the very presence of God; according to Chateaubriand: "You could not enter a Gothic church without feeling a kind of awe and a vague sentiment of the Divinity . . . every thing in a Gothic church reminds you of the labyrinths of a wood; every thing excites a feeling of religious awe, of mystery, and of the Divinity."[19]

Protestantism also experienced a revival. That revival or Awakening as it was called had already begun in the eighteenth century with the enthusiastic emotional experiences of Methodism in Britain and Pietism in Germany (see Chapter 18). Methodist missionaries from England and Scotland carried their messages of sin and redemption to liberal Protestant churches in France and Switzerland, winning converts to their strongly evangelical message. Germany, too, witnessed a Protestant Awakening as enthusiastic evangelical preachers found that their messages of hellfire and their methods of

✦ **Eugène Delacroix, _Women of Algiers_.** Also characteristic of Romanticism was its love of the exotic and unfamiliar. In his _Women of Algiers_, Delacroix reflected this fascination with the exotic in his portrayal of harem concubines from Morocco. At the same time, Delacroix's painting reflects his preoccupation with light and color.

emotional conversion evoked a ready response among people alienated by the highly educated establishment clergy of the state churches.

Conclusion

In 1815, a conservative order was reestablished throughout Europe, and the cooperation of the great powers, embodied in the Concert of Europe, tried to ensure its durability. But the revolutionary waves of the early 1820s and the early 1830s made it clear that the ideologies of liberalism and nationalism, unleashed by the French Revolution and now reinforced by the spread of the Industrial Revolution, were still alive and active. They faced enormous difficulties, however, as failed revolutions in Poland, Russia, Italy, and Germany all testify. At the same time, reform legislation in Britain and successful revolutions in Greece, France, and Belgium demonstrated the continuing strength of these forces of change. In 1848, they erupted once more all across Europe. And once more they failed. But not all was lost. Both liberalism and nationalism would succeed in the second half of the nineteenth century but in ways not foreseen by the idealistic liberals and nationalists who were utterly convinced that their time had come when they manned the barricades in 1848.

NOTES

1. Quoted in Charles Breunig, *The Age of Revolution and Reaction, 1789–1850* (New York, 1970), p. 119.
2. Quoted in M. S. Anderson, *The Ascendancy of Europe, 1815–1914*, 2d ed. (London, 1985), p. 1.
3. Quotations from Burke can be found in Peter Viereck, *Conservatism* (Princeton, N.J., 1956), pp. 27, 114.
4. Quoted in René Albrecht-Carrié, *The Concert of Europe* (New York, 1968), p. 48.
5. Quoted in G. de Berthier de Sauvigny, *Metternich and His Times* (London, 1962), p. 105.
6. Quoted in Donald E. Emerson, *Metternich and the Political Police* (The Hague, 1968), p. 110.
7. Quoted in S. Joan Moon, "Feminism and Socialism: The Utopian Synthesis of Flora Tristan," in Marilyn J. Boxer and Jean H. Quataert, eds., *Socialist Women* (New York, 1978), p. 38.
8. Quoted in Stanley Z. Pech, *The Czech Revolution of 1848* (Chapel Hill, N.C., 1969), p. 82.
9. Quoted in Clive Emsley, *Policing and Its Context, 1750–1870* (New York, 1984), p. 58.
10. Quoted in Clive Emsley, *Crime and Society in England, 1750–1900* (London, 1987), p. 173.
11. Quoted in Emsley, *Policing and Its Context, 1750–1870*, p. 66.
12. Quoted in ibid., p. 102.
13. Quoted in Emsley, *Crime and Society in England, 1750–1900*, p. 226.
14. William Wordsworth, *The Prelude* (Harmondsworth, 1971), p. 489.
15. William Wordsworth, "The Tables Turned," *Poems of Wordsworth*, ed. Matthew Arnold (London, 1963), p. 138.
16. Wordsworth, *The Prelude*, p. 109.
17. Quoted in H. G. Schenk, *The Mind of the European Romantics* (Garden City, N.Y., 1969), p. 205.
18. Quoted in Siegbert Prawer, ed., *The Romantic Period in Germany* (London, 1970), p. 285.
19. Quoted in John B. Halsted, ed., *Romanticism* (New York, 1969), p. 156.

SUGGESTIONS FOR FURTHER READING

For a good survey of the entire nineteenth century, see R. Gildea, *Barricades and Borders: Europe 1800–1914* (Oxford, 1987) in the Short Oxford History of the Modern World series. Also valuable is M. S. Anderson, *The Ascendancy of Europe, 1815–1914*, 2d ed. (London, 1985). For surveys of the period covered in this chapter, see C. Breunig, *The Age of Revolution and Reaction, 1789–1850*, 2d ed. (New York, 1979); and J. Droz, *Europe between Revolutions, 1815–1848* (London, 1967). There are also some useful books on individual countries that cover more than the subject of this chapter. These include R. Magraw, *France, 1815–1914: The Bourgeois Century* (London, 1983); H. Seton-Watson, *The Russian Empire, 1801–1917* (Oxford, 1967); H. Holborn, *A History of Modern Germany*, vol. 2, *1648–1840* (New York, 1964); C. A. Macartney, *The Habsburg Empire, 1790–1918* (London, 1971); S. J. Woolf, *A History of Italy, 1700–1860* (London, 1979);

and N. Gash, *Aristocracy and People: Britain 1815–1865* (London, 1979).

On the peace settlement of 1814–1815, there is the older work by H. Nicolson, *The Congress of Vienna, 1814–15* (New York, 1946). A concise summary of the international events of the entire nineteenth century can be found in R. Bullen and F. R. Bridge, *The Great Powers and the European States System, 1815–1914* (London, 1980). For the period covered in this chapter, see A. Sked, ed., *Europe's Balance of Power, 1815–1848* (London, 1979). On the man whose conservative policies dominated this era, see the brief but good biography by A. Palmer, *Metternich* (New York, 1972). On the revolutions in Europe in 1830, see C. Church, *Europe in 1830: Revolution and Political Change* (Chapel Hill, N.C., 1983). The standard work on the revolution of 1830 in France is D. Pinkney, *The French Revolution of 1830* (Princeton, N.J., 1972). On Great Britain's reform legislation, see M. Brock, *Great Reform Act* (London, 1973); and D. C. Moore, *The Politics of Deference: A Study of the Mid-Nineteenth Century English Political System* (New York, 1976). The Greek revolt is examined in detail in D. Dakin, *The Greek Struggle for Independence, 1821–33* (Berkeley, 1973).

The best introduction to the revolutions of 1848 is P. Stearns, *1848: The Revolutionary Tide in Europe* (New York, 1974). Good accounts of the revolutions in individual countries include G. Duveau, *1848: The Making of a Revolution* (New York, 1967); R. J. Rath, *The Viennese Revolution of 1848* (Austin, Tex., 1957); I. Déak, *The Lawful Revolution: Louis Kossuth and the Hungarians, 1848–49* (New York, 1979); P. Brock, *The Slovak National Awakening* (Toronto, 1976); R. Stadelmann, *Social and Political History of the German 1848 Revolution* (Athens, Ohio, 1975); and P. Ginsborg, *Daniele Manin and the Venetian Revolution of 1848–9* (New York, 1979). An important book on France's relations to the European revolutions of 1848 is L. C. Jennings, *France and Europe in 1848: A Study of French Foreign Affairs in Time of Crisis* (Oxford, 1973).

Good introductions to the major ideologies of the first half of the nineteenth century including both analysis and readings from the major figures can be found in H. Kohn, *Nationalism* (Princeton, N.J., 1955); J. S. Schapiro, *Liberalism: Its Meaning and History* (Princeton, N.J., 1958); and P. Viereck, *Conservatism* (Princeton, N.J., 1956). For a general survey, see R. Stromberg, *An Intellectual History of Modern Europe*, 5th ed. (Engle-

wood Cliffs, N.J., 1990). An excellent work on French utopian socialism is F. Manuel, *The Prophets of Paris* (New York, 1962).

On changes in the treatment of crime and punishment, see M. Foucault, *Discipline and Punish: The Birth of the Prison* (New York, 1977). The new policemen are examined in C. Emsley, *Policing and Its Context, 1750–1870* (New York, 1984). Also useful on crime, policemen, and prisons are M. Ignatieff, *A Just Measure of Pain: The Penitentiary in the Industrial Revolution, 1750–1850* (New York, 1978); and C. Emsley, *Crime and Society in England, 1750–1900* (London, 1987).

G. L. Mosse, *The Culture of Western Europe: The Nineteenth and Twentieth Centuries* (Chicago, 1961), remains a good introduction to the cultural history of Europe. On the ideas of the Romantics, see H. G. Schenk, *The Mind of the European Romantics* (Garden City, N.Y., 1969); and M. Cranston, *The Romantic Movement* (Oxford, 1994). There is an excellent collection of writings by Romantics in J. B. Halsted, ed., *Romanticism* (New York, 1969). On Wordsworth and English Romanticism, see J. Wordsworth, *William Wordsworth and the Age of English Romanticism* (New Brunswick, N.J., 1987). A beautifully illustrated introduction to the arts can be found in H. Honour, *Romanticism* (New York, 1979). Briefer surveys (with illustrations) can be found in D. M. Reynolds, *Cambridge Introduction to the History of Art: The Nineteenth Century* (Cambridge, 1985); and B. Cole and A. Gealt, *Art of the Western World* (New York, 1989).

CHAPTER
23

An Age of Nationalism and Realism, 1850–1871

Across the Continent, the revolutions of 1848 had failed. The forces of liberalism and nationalism appeared to have been decisively defeated as authoritarian governments reestablished their control almost everywhere in Europe by 1850. And yet within twenty-five years, many of the goals sought by the liberals and nationalists during the first half of the nineteenth century seemed to have been achieved. National unity became a reality in Italy and Germany while many European states were governed by constitutional monarchies, even though the constitutional-parliamentary features were frequently facades.

All the same, these goals were not achieved by liberal and nationalist leaders but by a new generation of conservative leaders who were proud of being practitioners of Realpolitik, the "politics of reality." One reaction to the failure of the revolutions of 1848 had been a new toughness of mind in which people prided themselves on being realistic in their handling of power. The new conservative leaders used armies and power politics to achieve their foreign policy goals. And they did not hesitate to manipulate liberal means to achieve conservative ends at home. Nationalism had failed as a revolutionary movement in 1848–1849, but between 1850 and 1871, these new leaders found a variety of ways to pursue nation building. One of the most successful was the Prussian Otto von Bismarck who used both astute diplomacy and war to achieve the unification of Germany. On January 18, 1871, Bismarck and six hundred German princes, nobles, and generals filled the Hall of Mirrors in the palace of Versailles, twelve miles outside Paris. The Prussian army had defeated the French, and the assembled notables were gathered for the proclamation of the Prussian king as the new emperor of a united German state. When the words, "Long live His Imperial Majesty, the Emperor William!" rang out, the assembled guests took up the cry. One participant wrote, "A thundering cheer, repeated at least six times, thrilled through the room while the flags and

Louis Napoleon becomes emperor · · · · · · · · · · · · · · · · · Creation of Austro-Hungarian dual monarchy

• •

Unification of Italy · Unification of Germany

• Emancipation of the Russian serfs

• • • • • • • • • • • • • American Civil War

• British Reform Act

• Creation of Canada as a nation

Marx and Engels, *The Communist Manifesto* · · · · · · · · Flaubert, *Madame Bovary*

Darwin, *On the Origin of Species* · · · · · · · · Pasteur and pasteurization

---

standards waved over the head of the new emperor of Germany." European rulers who feared the power of the new German state were not so cheerful. "The balance of power has been entirely destroyed," declared the British prime minister.

The France of Napoleon III

After 1850 a new generation of conservative leaders came to power in Europe. Foremost among them was Napoleon III (1852–1870) of France who taught his contemporaries how authoritarian governments could use liberal and nationalistic forces to bolster their own power. It was a lesson others quickly learned.

Louis Napoleon: Toward the Second Empire

Even after his election as the president of the French Republic, many of his contemporaries dismissed Napoleon "the Small" as a nonentity whose success was due only to his name. But physical appearances can be deceiving. Louis Napoleon was a clever politician who was especially astute at understanding the popular forces of his day. Some historians think that as a Bonaparte, Louis Napoleon believed he was destined to govern France. Indeed, as he told a friend shortly after the election, the presidency of the Republic was only the beginning: "We are not at the summit yet. This is only a stop on the way, a terrace where we may rest a moment to gaze at the horizon."

Louis Napoleon was a patient man. For three years he persevered in winning the support of the French people

while using governmental favors to gain the loyalty of the army and the Catholic church. He faced considerable opposition from the National Assembly, which had a conservative-monarchist majority after elections in May of 1849. When the assembly voted to deprive three million men of the right to vote, Louis Napoleon achieved even more popular favor by posing as the savior of universal male suffrage. When the assembly rejected his proposal to revise the constitution and allow him to stand for reelection, Louis resorted to a coup d'etat. On December 1, 1851, troops loyal to the president seized the major administrative buildings and arrested opposition leaders. After restoring universal male suffrage, Louis Napoleon asked the French people to restructure the government by electing him president for ten years (see the box on p. 778). By an overwhelming majority, 7.5 million "yes" votes to 640,000 "no" votes, they agreed. A year later, on November 21, 1852, Louis Napoleon returned to the people to ask for the restoration of the Empire. This time 97 percent responded affirmatively, and on December 2, 1852, Louis Napoleon assumed the title of Napoleon III (the first Napoleon had abdicated in favor of his son, Napoleon II, on April 6, 1814). The Second Empire had begun.

The Second Napoleonic Empire

The government of Napoleon III was clearly authoritarian in a Bonapartist sense. Louis Napoleon had asked, "Since France has carried on for fifty years only by virtue of the administrative, military, judicial, religious and financial organization of the Consulate and Empire, why should she not also adopt the political institutions of that period?"[1] As chief of state, Napoleon III controlled

➤ Louis Napoleon Appeals to the People ◆

After his coup d'etat on December 1, 1851, Louis Napoleon asked the French people to approve his actions. By making this appeal, the clever politician was demonstrating how universal male suffrage, considered a democratic and hence revolutionary device, could be used to bolster a basically authoritarian regime. It was a lesson eagerly learned by other conservative rulers in the second half of the nineteenth century. This selection is from Louis Napoleon's proclamation to the French people in 1851.

Louis Napoleon, Proclamation to the People (1851)

Frenchmen! The present situation cannot last much longer. Each passing day increases the danger to the country. The [National] Assembly, which ought to be the firmest supporter of order, has become a center of conspiracies . . . it attacks the authority that I hold directly from the people; it encourages all evil passions; it jeopardizes the peace of France: I have dissolved it and I make the whole people judge between it and me. . . .

I therefore make a loyal appeal to the whole nation, and I say to you: If you wish to continue this state of uneasiness which degrades us and makes our future uncertain, choose another in my place, for I no longer wish an authority which is powerless to do good, makes me responsible for acts I cannot prevent, and chains me to the helm when I see the vessel speeding toward the abyss.

If, on the contrary, you still have confidence in me, give me the means to accomplish the great mission that I hold from you. This mission consists in bringing to a close the era of revolutions by satisfying the legitimate wants of the people and by protecting them against subversive passions. It consists, especially, in creating institutions that may survive men and that may be at length foundations on which something durable can be established.

Persuaded that the instability of authority and the preponderance of a single Assembly are permanent causes of trouble and discord, I submit to you the following fundamental bases of a constitution which the Assemblies will develop later.

1. A responsible chief elected for ten years.
2. Ministers dependent upon the executive power alone.
3. A Council of State composed of the most distinguished men to prepare the laws and discuss them before the legislative body.
4. A legislative body to discuss and vote the laws, elected by universal [male] suffrage. . . .

This system, created by the First Consul [Napoleon I] at the beginning of the century, has already given France calm and prosperity; it will guarantee them to her again.

Such is my profound conviction. If you share it, declare that fact by your votes. If, on the contrary, you prefer a government without force, monarchical or republican, borrowed from I know not what past or from which chimerical future, reply in the negative. . . .

If I do not obtain a majority of your votes, I shall then convoke a new assembly, and I shall resign to it the mandate that I received from you. But if you believe that the cause of which my name is the symbol, that is, France regenerated by the revolution of 1789 and organized by the Emperor, is forever yours, proclaim it by sanctioning the powers that I ask from you. Then France and Europe will be saved from anarchy, obstacles will be removed, rivalries will disappear, for all will respect the decree of Providence in the decision of the people.

---

the armed forces, police, and civil service. Only he could introduce legislation and declare war. His ministers had no collective responsibility and were answerable only to the emperor. The Legislative Corps gave an appearance of representative government since its members were elected by universal male suffrage for six-year terms. But they could neither initiate legislation nor affect the budget. Moreover, only government candidates were allowed to campaign freely. Candidates were supposedly selected from "men enjoying public esteem,

concerned more with the interests of the country than with the strife of parties, sympathetic towards the suffering of the laboring classes."[2]

The first five years of Napoleon III's reign were a spectacular success as he reaped the benefits of worldwide economic prosperity as well as of some of his own economic policies. In light of the loss of political freedom, Napoleon realized the importance of diverting "the attention of the French from politics to economics." He believed in using the resources of government to stimulate the national economy and took many steps to encourage industrial growth. He promoted the expansion of credit by backing the formation of new investment banks, which provided long-term loans for industrial, commercial, and agricultural expansion. Government subsidies were used to foster the rapid construction of railroads as well as harbors, roads, and canals. The major French railway lines were completed during Napoleon's reign while industrial expansion was evident in the tripling of iron production. In his concern to reduce tensions and improve the social welfare of the nation, Napoleon provided hospitals and free medicine for the workers, and advocated better housing for the working class.

In the midst of this economic expansion, Napoleon III undertook a vast reconstruction of the city of Paris. Under the direction of Baron Haussmann, the medieval Paris of narrow streets and old city walls was destroyed and replaced by a modern Paris of broad boulevards, spacious buildings, circular plazas, public squares, an underground sewage system, a new public water supply, and gaslights. The new Paris served a military as well as an aesthetic purpose. Broad streets made it more difficult for would-be insurrectionists to throw up barricades and easier for troops to move rapidly through the city in the event of revolts.

Napoleon III took a great interest in public opinion. Freedom of speech was, of course, not permitted in the authoritarian empire. Freedom of assembly was limited and newspapers were regularly censored. Nevertheless, Napoleon's desire to know the mood of his people led him to request regular reports on public opinion from his subordinates. In the 1860s, as opposition to some of Napoleon's policies began to mount, his sensitivity to the change in the public mood led him to undertake new policies liberalizing his regime. As a result, historians speak of the "liberal empire" for the latter part of the 1860s.

Opposition to Napoleon came from a variety of sources. His attempt to move toward free trade by lowering tariffs on foreign goods, especially those of the British, angered French manufacturers. Then, too, the financial crash of 1857, a silkworm disease, and the devastation of French vineyards by plant lice caused severe damage to the French economy. Retrenchment in government spending proved unpopular as well. To shore up his regime, Napoleon III reached out to the working class by legalizing trade unions and granting them the right to strike. He also began to liberalize the political process.

The Legislative Corps had been closely controlled during the 1850s. In the 1860s, opposition candidates

✦ **Emperor Napoleon III.** On December 2, 1852, Louis Napoleon took the title of Napoleon III and then proceeded to create an authoritarian monarchy. As opposition to his policies intensified in the 1860s, Napoleon III began to liberalize his government. However, a disastrous military defeat at the hands of Prussia in 1870–1871 brought the collapse of his regime.

were allowed greater freedom to campaign, and the Legislative Corps was permitted more say in affairs of state, including debate over the budget. Historians do not agree about the ultimate aim and potential of Napoleon's liberalization, although it did initially strengthen the hands of the government. In another plebiscite in May 1870, on whether to accept a new constitution that might have inaugurated a parliamentary regime, the French people gave Napoleon another resounding victory. This triumph was short-lived, however. Foreign policy failures led to growing criticism, and war with Prussia in 1870 turned out to be the death blow for Napoleon III's regime (see The Franco-Prussian War, 1870–1871 later in this chapter).

Foreign Policy: The Crimean War

As heir to the Napoleonic Empire, Napoleon III was motivated by the desire to free France from the restrictions of the peace settlements of 1814–1815 and to make France the chief arbiter of Europe. Although his foreign policy ultimately led to disaster and his own undoing, Napoleon had an initial success in the Crimean War (1854–1856).

The Crimean War was another chapter in the story of the Eastern Question, or who would be the chief beneficiaries of the disintegration of the Turkish or Ottoman Empire. The Ottoman Empire had long been in control of much of southeastern Europe, but by the beginning of the nineteenth century, it had begun to decline. As Turkish authority over the outlying territories in southeastern Europe waned, European governments began to take an active interest in the empire's apparent demise. Russia's proximity to the Ottoman Empire and the religious bonds between the Russians and the Greek Orthodox Christians in Turkish-dominated southeastern Europe naturally gave it special opportunities to enlarge its sphere of influence. Other European powers not only feared Russian ambitions but had ambitions of their own in the area. Austria craved more land in the Balkans, a desire that inevitably meant conflict with Russia, while France and Britain were interested in commercial opportunities and naval bases in the eastern Mediterranean.

War erupted between the Russians and Turks in 1853 when the Russians demanded the right to protect Christian shrines in Palestine, a privilege that had already been extended to the French. When the Turks refused, the Russians invaded Turkish Moldavia and Walachia. Failure to resolve the dispute by negotiations led the Turks to declare war on Russia on October 4, 1853. In the following year, on March 28, Great Britain and France declared war on Russia.

Why did Britain and France take such a step? Concern over the prospect of an upset in the balance of power was clearly one reason. The British in particular feared that an aggressive Russia would try to profit from the obvious weakness of the Ottoman government by seizing Turkish territory or the long-coveted Dardanelles. Such a move would make Russia the major power in eastern Europe and would enable the Russians to challenge British naval control of the eastern Mediterranean. Napoleon III believed the Russians had insulted France, first at the Congress of Vienna and now by their insistence on replacing the French as the protectors of Christians living in the Ottoman Empire. The Russians assumed that they could count on support from the Austrians (since Russian troops had saved the Austrian government in 1849). However, the Austrian prime minister blithely explained, "We will astonish the world by our ingratitude," and Austria remained neutral. Since the Austrians had perceived that it was not in their best interest to intervene, Russia had to fight alone.

The Crimean War was poorly planned and poorly fought. Britain and France decided to attack Russia's Crimean peninsula in the Black Sea. After a long siege and at a terrible cost in manpower for both sides, the main Russian fortress of Sevastopol fell in September 1855, six months after the death of Tsar Nicholas I. His successor, Alexander II, soon sued for peace. By the Treaty of Paris, signed in March 1856, Russia was forced to give up Bessarabia at the mouth of the Danube and accept the neutrality of the Black Sea. In addition, the Danubian principalities of Moldavia and Walachia were placed under the protection of all the great powers.

The Crimean War broke up long-standing European power relationships and effectively destroyed the Concert of Europe. Austria and Russia, the two chief powers maintaining the status quo in the first half of the nineteenth century, were now enemies because of Austria's unwillingness to support Russia in the war. Russia, defeated, humiliated, and weakened by the obvious failure of its serf-armies, withdrew from European affairs for the next two decades to set its house in order and await a better opportunity to undo the Treaty of Paris. Great Britain, disillusioned by its role in the war, also pulled back from continental affairs. Austria, paying the price for its neutrality, was now without friends among the great powers. Not until the 1870s were new combinations formed to replace those that had disappeared, and in the meantime the European international situation remained fluid. Those willing to pursue the "politics of reality" found themselves in a situation rife with opportunity. It was this new international situation that made possible the unification of Italy and Germany.

Only Louis Napoleon seemed to have gained in prestige from the Crimean War. His experiences in the war had taught him that he was not the military genius his uncle had been, but he became well aware of the explosive power of the forces of nationalism and determined to pursue a foreign policy that would champion national movements. Some historians have argued that

Napoleon believed ardently in the cause of national liberation. Be that as it may, as the liberator of national peoples, Napoleon III envisioned France as the natural leader of free European states. His policy proved to be a disaster as we can observe by examining the movements for unification in Italy and Germany.

National Unification: Italy and Germany

The breakdown of the Concert of Europe opened the way for the Italians and the Germans to establish national states. Their successful unifications transformed the power structure of the Continent. Well into the twentieth century, Europe would still be dealing with the consequences.

The Unification of Italy

The Italians were the first people to benefit from the breakdown of the Concert of Europe. In 1850, Austria was still the dominant power on the Italian peninsula. Austria controlled Lombardy and Venetia while Modena and Tuscany were ruled by members of Austria's house of Habsburg. Moreover, the Papal States governed by the pope, the other petty Italian states, and even the Bourbon Kingdom of the Two Sicilies looked to the Austrians to maintain the status quo.

Although a minority, Italian liberals and nationalists had tried earnestly to achieve unification in the first half of the nineteenth century. Some had favored the *risorgimento* movement led by Giuseppe Mazzini, which favored a republican Italy; others looked to a confederation of Italian states under the direction of the pope. Neither of those alternatives was feasible after the defeats of 1849. A growing number of advocates of Italian unification now focused on the northern Italian state of Piedmont as their best hope to achieve their goal. As one observed, "To defeat cannons and soldiers, cannons and soldiers are needed. Arms are needed, and not Mazzinian pratings. Piedmont has soldiers and cannons. Therefore I am Piedmontese. By ancient custom, inclination and duty, Piedmont these days is a monarchy. Therefore I am not a republican."[3]

The royal house of Savoy ruled the kingdom of Piedmont, which also included the island of Sardinia. Although soundly defeated by the Austrians in 1848–1849, Piedmont under King Charles Albert had made a valiant effort; it seemed reasonable that Piedmont would now assume the leading role in the cause of national unity. The little state seemed unlikely to supply the needed leadership, however, until the new king, Victor Emmanuel II (1849–1878), named Count Camillo di Cavour (1810–1861) as his prime minister in 1852.

Cavour was a liberal-minded nobleman who had made a fortune in agriculture and went on to make even more money in banking, railroads, and shipping. He admired the British, especially their parliamentary system, industrial techniques, and economic liberalism. Cavour was a moderate who favored constitutional government. While he might have wanted Italian unification, he had no preconceived notions about how to obtain it. He was a consummate politician with the ability to persuade others of the rightness of his own convictions. After becoming prime minister in 1852, he pursued a policy of economic expansion, encouraging the building of roads, canals, and railroads and fostering business enterprise by expanding credit and stimulating investment in new industries. The growth in the Piedmontese economy and the subsequent increase in government revenues enabled Cavour to pour money into equipping a large army.

Cavour had no illusions about Piedmont's military strength and was only too well aware that he could not challenge Austria directly. He would need the French. In 1858, Cavour came to an agreement with Napoleon III. The emperor agreed to ally with Piedmont in driving the Austrians out of Italy provided that the war could be justified "in the eyes of the public opinion of France and Europe." Once the Austrians were driven out, Italy would be reorganized. Piedmont would be extended into the kingdom of Upper Italy by adding Lombardy, Venetia, Parma, Modena, and part of the Papal States to its territory. In compensation for its efforts, France would receive the Piedmontese provinces of Nice and Savoy. A kingdom of Central Italy would be created for Napoleon III's cousin, Prince Napoleon, who would be married to the younger daughter of King Victor Emmanuel. This agreement between Napoleon and Cavour seemed to assure the French ruler of the opportunity to control Italy. Confident that the plan would work, Cavour provoked the Austrians into invading Piedmont in April 1859, thus fulfilling Napoleon's demand that the war be justified "in the eyes of the public opinion of France and Europe."

In the initial stages of fighting, it was the French who were largely responsible for defeating the Austrians in two major battles at Magenta and Solferino. It was also the French who made peace with Austria on July 11, 1859, without informing their Italian ally. Why did Napoleon withdraw so hastily? For one thing, he realized that, despite two losses, the Austrian army had not yet been defeated; the struggle might be longer and more costly than he had anticipated. Moreover, the Prussians were mobilizing in support of Austria, and Napoleon III had no desire to take on two enemies at once. As a result of Napoleon's peace with Austria, Piedmont received only Lombardy; Venetia remained under Austrian control. Cavour was furious at the French perfidy, but events in northern Italy now turned in his favor. Soon after the war with Austria had begun, some northern Italian states, namely, Parma, Modena, Tuscany, and part of the Papal States, had been taken over by nationalists. In plebiscites held in 1860, these states agreed to join Piedmont. Napoleon, in return for Nice and Savoy, agreed to the annexations.

Italian unification might have stopped here since there is little indication that Cavour envisioned uniting all of Italy in the spring of 1860. But the forces of romantic republican nationalism forced Cavour to act. Giuseppe Garibaldi (1807–1882) was a dedicated Italian patriot who had supported Mazzini and the republi-

can cause of Young Italy. While in exile in Latin America, he had gained much experience in guerrilla warfare, which he put to good use in the Italian revolutionary struggles of 1848–1849. In 1859, he became involved in the fighting against Austria. Cavour regarded Garibaldi as a nuisance and encouraged him to move on to southern Italy where a revolt had broken out against the Bourbon king of the Two Sicilies. With his thousand Red Shirts, as his volunteers were called because of their distinctive dress, Garibaldi landed in Sicily on May 11, 1860.

Although greatly outnumbered, Garibaldi's daring tactics won the day (see the box on p. 784). By the end of July 1860, most of Sicily had been pacified under Garibaldi's control. In August Garibaldi and his forces crossed over to the mainland and began a victorious march up the Italian peninsula. Naples and the Kingdom of the Two Sicilies fell in early September. At this point Cavour reentered the scene. Aware that Garibaldi planned to march on Rome, Cavour feared that such a move would bring war with France as the defender of

Map 23.1 The Unification of Italy.

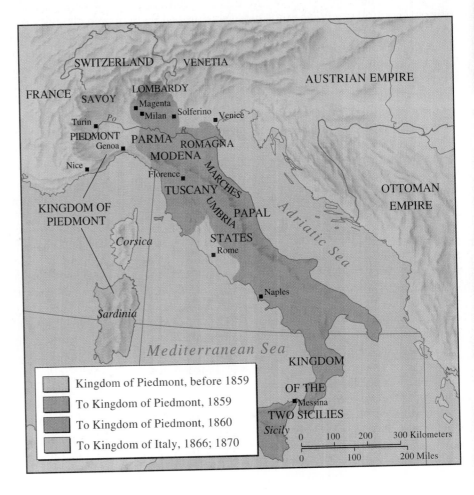

The Unification of Germany

After the failure of the Frankfurt Assembly to achieve German unification in 1848–1849, German nationalists focused on Austria and Prussia as the only two states powerful enough to dominate German affairs. Austria had long controlled the existing Germanic Confederation, but Prussian power had grown, strongly reinforced by economic expansion in the 1850s. Prussia had formed the *Zollverein,* a German customs union, in 1834. By eliminating tolls on rivers and roads among member states, the *Zollverein* had stimulated trade and added to the prosperity of its member states. By 1853, all the German states except Austria had joined the Prussian-dominated customs union. A number of middle-class liberals now began to see Prussia in a new light; some even looked openly to Prussia to bring about the unification of Germany.

◆ **Garibaldi Arrives in Sicily.** The dream of Italian nationalists for a united Italian state finally became a reality by 1870. An important figure in the cause of unification was Giuseppe Garibaldi, a determined Italian patriot. Garibaldi is shown here arriving in Sicily on May 11, 1860, with his band of Red Shirts.

papal interests. Moreover, Garibaldi and his men favored a democratic republicanism; Cavour did not and acted quickly to preempt Garibaldi. The Piedmontese army invaded the Papal States and, bypassing Rome, moved into the kingdom of Naples. Ever the patriot, Garibaldi chose to yield to Cavour's fait accompli rather than provoke a civil war so he retired to his farm. Plebiscites in the Papal States and the Kingdom of the Two Sicilies resulted in overwhelming support for union with Piedmont. On March 17, 1861, a new kingdom of Italy was proclaimed under a centralized government subordinated to the control of Piedmont and King Victor Emmanuel II (1861–1878) of the house of Savoy. Worn out by his efforts, Cavour died three months later.

Despite the proclamation of a new kingdom, the task of unification was not yet complete since Venetia in the north was still held by Austria and Rome was under papal control, supported by French troops. To attack either one meant war with a major European state, which the Italian army was not prepared to handle. It was the Prussian army that indirectly completed the task of Italian unification. In the Austro-Prussian War of 1866 (see The Austro-Prussian War, 1866 later in this chapter), the new Italian state became an ally of Prussia. Although the Italian army was defeated by the Austrians, Prussia's victory left the Italians with Venetia. In 1870, the Franco-Prussian War (see The Franco-Prussian War, 1870–1871 later in this chapter) resulted in the withdrawal of French troops from Rome. The Italian army then annexed the city on September 20, 1870, and Rome became the new capital of the united Italian state.

Garibaldi and Romantic Nationalism

Giuseppe Garibaldi was one of the more colorful figures involved in the unification of Italy. Accompanied by only a thousand of his famous "Red Shirts," the Italian soldier of fortune left Genoa on the night of May 5, 1860, for an invasion of the Kingdom of the Two Sicilies. The ragged band entered Palermo, the chief city on the island of Sicily, on May 31. This selection is taken from an account by a correspondent for The Times *of London, the Hungarian-born Nandor Eber.*

The Times, June 13, 1860

Palermo, May 31—Anyone in search of violent emotions cannot do better than set off at once for Palermo. However blasé he may be, or however milk-and-water his blood, I promise it will be stirred up. He will be carried away by the tide of popular feeling. . . .

In the afternoon Garibaldi made a tour of inspection round the town. I was there, but find it really impossible to give you a faint idea of the manner in which he was received everywhere. It was one of those triumphs which seem to be almost too much for a man. . . . The popular idol, Garibaldi, in his red flannel shirt, with a loose colored handkerchief around his neck, and his worn "wide-awake," [a soft-brimmed felt hat] was walking on foot among those cheering, laughing, crying, mad thousands; and all his few followers could do was to prevent him from being bodily carried off the ground. The people threw themselves forward to kiss his hands, or, at least, to touch the hem of his garment, as if it contained the panacea for all their past and perhaps coming suffering. Children were brought up, and mothers asked on their knees for his blessing; and all this while

the object of this idolatry was calm and smiling as when in the deadliest fire, taking up the children and kissing them, trying to quiet the crowd, stopping at every moment to hear a long complaint of houses burned and property sacked by the retreating soldiers, giving good advice, comforting, and promising that all damages should be paid for. . . .

One might write volumes of horrors on the vandalism already committed, for every one of the hundred ruins has its story of brutality and inhumanity. . . . In these small houses a dense population is crowded together even in ordinary times. A shell falling on one, and crushing and burying the inmates, was sufficient to make people abandon the neighboring one and take refuge a little further on, shutting themselves up in the cellars. When the Royalists retired they set fire to those of the houses which had escaped the shells, and numbers were thus burned alive in their hiding places. . . .

If you can stand the exhalation, try and go inside the ruins, for it is only there that you will see what the thing means and you will not have to search long before you stumble over the remains of a human body, a leg sticking out here, an arm there, a black face staring at you a little further on. You are startled by a rustle. You look round and see half a dozen gorged rats scampering off in all directions, or you see a dog trying to make his escape over the ruins. . . . I only wonder that the sight of these scenes does not convert every man in the town into a tiger and every woman into a fury. But these people have been so long ground down and demoralized that their nature seems to have lost the power of reaction.

In 1848, Prussia had framed a constitution that at least had the appearance of constitutional monarchy in that it had established a bicameral legislature with the lower house elected by universal male suffrage. However, the voting population was divided into three classes determined by the amount of taxes they paid, a system that allowed the biggest taxpayers to gain the most seats. Unintentionally, by 1859 this system had allowed control of the lower house to fall largely into the hands of the rising middle classes, whose numbers were growing as a result of continuing industrialization. Their desire was to have a real parliamentary system, but the king's

executive power remained too strong; royal ministers answered for their actions only to the king, not the parliament. Nevertheless, the parliament had been granted important legislative and taxation powers upon which it could build.

In 1861, King Frederick William IV died and was succeeded by his brother. King William I (1861–1888) had definite ideas about the Prussian army because of his own military training. He and his advisers believed that the army was in dire need of change if Prussia was to remain a great power. Working closely with Albrecht von Roon as minister for war and Helmuth von Moltke as chief of the army general staff, the king planned to double the size of the army, diminish the role of the *Landwehr*, the popular militia reserves that had first been formed to fight Napoleon in 1806, and institute three years of compulsory military service for all young men.

Middle-class liberals in the parliament, while willing to have reform, feared compulsory military service because they believed the government would use it to inculcate obedience to the monarchy and strengthen the influence of the conservative-military clique in Prussia. The liberals were powerful enough to reject the new military budget submitted to parliament in March 1862. Though frustrated, William I was unwilling to use the army to seize control and instead appointed a new prime minister, Count Otto von Bismarck (1815– 1898). Bismarck, regarded even by the king as too conservative, came to determine the course of modern German history. Until 1890, he dominated both German and European politics.

Otto von Bismarck was born into the Junker class, the traditional, landowning aristocracy of Prussia, and remained loyal to it throughout his life. "I was born and raised as an aristocrat," he once said. As a university student, Bismarck indulged heartily in wine, women, and song, yet managed to read widely in German history. After earning a law degree, he embarked upon a career in the Prussian civil service but soon tired of bureaucratic, administrative routine and retired to manage his country estates. Comparing the civil servant to a musician in an orchestra, he responded, "But I want to play the tune the way it sounds good to me or not at all. . . . My pride bids me command rather than obey."[4] In 1847, desirous of more excitement and power than he could find in the country, he reentered public life. Four years later, he began to build a base of diplomatic experience as the Prussian delegate to the diet (parliament) of the Germanic Confederation. This, combined with his experience as Prussian ambassador to Russia and later to France, gave him opportunities to acquire a wide knowledge of European affairs and to learn how to assess the character of rulers.

Because Bismarck succeeded in guiding Prussia's unification of Germany, it is often assumed that he had determined upon a course of action that led precisely to that goal. That is hardly the case. Bismarck was a consummate politician and opportunist. He had a clear idea of his goals, but was willing to show great flexibility in how he reached them. He was not a political gambler, but a moderate who waged war only when all other diplomatic alternatives had been exhausted and when he was reasonably sure that all the military and diplo-

matic advantages were on his side. Nor was he doctrinaire. Although loyal to the Junkers, the Prussian king, and Lutheranism, he was capable of transcending them all in favor of a broader perspective, although there is no doubt that he came to see the German empire, which he had helped to create, as the primary focus of his efforts. Bismarck has often been portrayed as the ultimate realist, the foremost nineteenth-century practitioner of *Realpolitik*—the "politics of reality." His ability to manipulate people and power makes that claim justified, but Bismarck also recognized the limitations of power. When he perceived that the advantages to be won from war "no longer justified the risks involved," he could become an ardent defender of peace.

In 1862, the immediate problem facing Bismarck was domestic Prussian politics. Bismarck resubmitted the army appropriations bill to parliament along with a passionate appeal to his liberal opponents: "Germany does not look to Prussia's liberalism but to her power. . . . Not by speeches and majorities will the great questions of the day be decided—that was the mistake of 1848– 1849—but by iron and blood."[5] His opponents were not impressed and rejected the bill once again. Bismarck went ahead, collected the taxes, and reorganized the army anyway, blaming the liberals for causing the breakdown of constitutional government. From 1862 to 1866, Bismarck governed Prussia by largely ignoring parliament. Unwilling to revolt, parliament did nothing. In the meantime, opposition to his domestic policy determined Bismarck upon an active foreign policy, which in 1864 led to his first war.

THE DANISH WAR, 1864

In the three wars that he waged, Bismarck's victories were as much diplomatic and political as they were military. Before war was declared, Bismarck always saw to it that Prussia would be fighting only one power and that that opponent was isolated diplomatically. He knew enough Prussian history to realize that Frederick the Great had almost been crushed by a mighty coalition in the eighteenth century (see Chapter 19).

The Danish War arose over the duchies of Schleswig and Holstein. In 1863, contrary to international treaty, the Danish government moved to incorporate the two duchies into Denmark. German nationalists were outraged since both duchies had large German populations and were regarded as German states. The diet of the Germanic Confederation urged its member states to send troops against Denmark, but Bismarck did not care to subject Prussian policy to the Austrian-dominated

German diet. Instead, he persuaded the Austrians to join Prussia in declaring war on Denmark on February 1, 1864. The Danes were quickly defeated and surrendered Schleswig and Holstein to the victors. Austria and Prussia then agreed to divide the administration of the two duchies; Prussia took Schleswig while Austria administered Holstein. The plan was Bismarck's. By this time Bismarck had come to the realization that for Prussia to expand its power by dominating the northern, largely Protestant part of the Germanic Confederation, Austria would have to be excluded from German affairs or, less likely, be willing to accept Prussian domination of Germany. The joint administration of the two duchies offered plenty of opportunities to create friction with Austria and provide a reason for war if it came to that. While he pursued negotiations with Austria, he also laid the foundations for the isolation of Austria.

THE AUSTRO-PRUSSIAN WAR, 1866

Bismarck had no problem gaining Russia's agreement to remain neutral in the event of an Austro-Prussian war because Prussia had been the only great power to support Russia's repression of a Polish revolt in 1863. Napoleon III was a thornier problem, but Bismarck was able to buy his neutrality with vague promises of territory in the Rhineland. Finally, Bismarck made an alliance with the new Italian state and promised it Venetia in the event of Austrian defeat.

With the Austrians isolated, Bismarck used the joint occupation of Schleswig-Holstein to goad the Austrians

Map 23.2 The Unification of Germany.

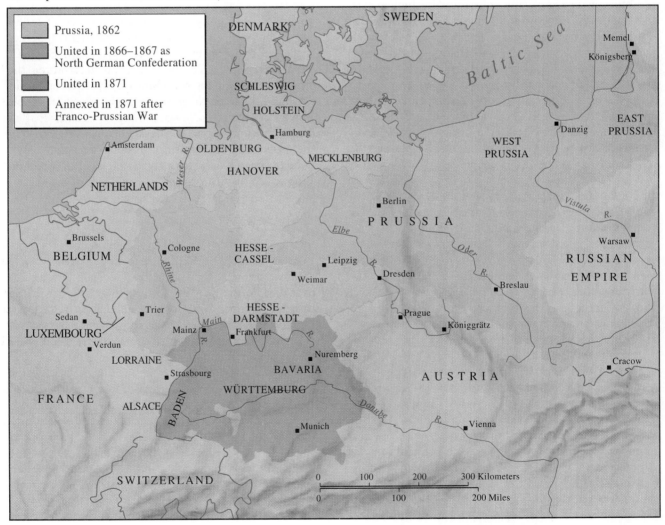

into a war on June 14, 1866. Many Europeans, including Napoleon III, expected a quick Austrian victory, but they overlooked the effectiveness of the Prussian military reforms of the 1860s. The Prussian breech-loading needle gun had a much faster rate of fire than the Austrian muzzle-loader, and a superior network of railroads enabled the Prussians to mass troops quickly. At Königgrätz (or Sadowa) on July 3, the Austrian army was decisively defeated. Looking ahead, Bismarck refused to create a hostile enemy by burdening Austria with a harsh peace as the Prussian king wanted. Austria lost no territory except Venetia to Italy but was excluded from German affairs. The German states north of the Main River were organized into a North German Confederation controlled by Prussia. The south German states, largely Catholic, remained independent but were coerced into signing military agreements with Prussia. In addition to Schleswig and Holstein, Prussia annexed Hanover, Hesse-Cassel, and the free city of Frankfurt because they had openly sided with Austria.

The Austrian War was a rather decisive turning point in Prussian domestic affairs. After the war, Bismarck asked the Prussian parliament to pass a bill of indemnity, retroactively legalizing the taxes he had collected illegally since 1862. Even most of the liberals voted in favor of the bill because they had been won over by Bismarck's successful use of military power. With his victory over Austria and the creation of the North German Confederation, Bismarck had proved Napoleon III's dictum that nationalism and authoritarian government could be combined. In using nationalism to win support from liberals and prevent governmental reform, Bismarck showed that liberalism and nationalism, the two major forces of change in the early nineteenth century, could be separated.

He showed the same flexibility in the creation of a new constitution for the North German Confederation. Each German state kept its own local government, but the king of Prussia was head of the confederation while the chancellor (Bismarck) was responsible directly to the king. Both the army and foreign policy remained in the hands of the king and his chancellor. Parliament consisted of two bodies: a Bundesrat, or federal council composed of delegates nominated by the states, and a lower house, the Reichstag, elected by universal male suffrage. Like Napoleon, Bismarck believed that the peasants and artisans who made up most of the population were conservative at heart and could be used to overcome the advantages of the liberals. He had not counted on the industrial proletariat whose growth in the years ahead would provide him with some of his most vehement opposition (see Chapter 24).

THE FRANCO-PRUSSIAN WAR, 1870–1871

Bismarck and William I had achieved a major goal by 1866. Prussia now dominated all of northern Germany, and Austria had been excluded from any significant role in German affairs. Nevertheless, unsettled business led to new international complications and further change. Bismarck realized that France would never be content with a strong German state to its east because of the potential threat to French security. At the same time, after a series of setbacks, Napoleon III needed a diplomatic triumph to offset his serious domestic problems. The French were not happy with the turn of events in Germany and looked for opportunities to humiliate the Prussians.

After a successful revolution had deposed Queen Isabella II, the throne of Spain was offered to Prince Leopold of Hohenzollern-Sigmaringen, a distant relative of the Hohenzollern king of Prussia. Bismarck welcomed this possibility for the same reason that the French objected to it. If Leopold were placed on the throne of Spain, France would be virtually encircled by members of the Hohenzollern dynasty. French objections caused King William I to force his relative to withdraw his candidacy. Bismarck was disappointed with the king's actions, but at this point the French overreached themselves. Not content with their diplomatic victory, they pushed William I to make a formal apology to France and promise never to allow Leopold to be a candidate again. When Bismarck received a telegraph from the king informing him of the French request, Bismarck edited it to make it appear even more insulting to the French, knowing that the French would be angry and declare war (see the box on p. 788). Through diplomacy,

Bismarck "Goads" France into War

After his meeting with the French ambassador at Ems, King William I of Prussia sent a telegraph to Bismarck with a report of their discussions. By editing the telegraph from King William I before he released it to the press, Bismarck made it sound as if the Prussian king had treated the ambassador in a demeaning fashion. Six days later, France declared war on Prussia.

The Abeken [Privy Councillor] Text, Ems, July 13, 1870

To the Federal Chancellor, Count Bismarck. His Majesty the King writes to me:

"M. Benedetti intercepted me on the Promenade in order to demand of me most insistently that I should authorize him to telegraph immediately to Paris that I shall obligate myself for all future time never again to give my approval to the candidacy of the Hohenzollerns should it be renewed. I refused to agree to this, the last time somewhat severely, informing him that one dare not and cannot assume such obligations *à tout jamais* [forever]. Naturally, I informed him that I had received no news as yet, and since he had been informed earlier than I by way of Paris and Madrid, he could easily understand why my government was once again out of the matter."

Since then His Majesty has received a dispatch from the Prince [father of the Hohenzollern candidate for the Spanish throne]. As His Majesty has informed Count Benedetti that he was expecting news from the Prince, His Majesty himself, in view of the above-mentioned demand and in consonance with the advice of Count Eulenburg and myself, decided not to receive the French envoy again but to inform him through an adjutant that His Majesty had now received from the Prince confirmation of the news which Benedetti had already received from Paris, and that he had nothing further to say to the Ambassador. His Majesty leaves it to the judgment of Your Excellency whether or not to communicate at once the new demand by Benedetti and its rejection to our ambassadors and to the press.

Bismarck's Edited Version

After the reports of the renunciation by the hereditary Prince of Hohenzollern had been officially transmitted by the Royal Government of Spain to the Imperial Government of France, the French Ambassador presented to His Majesty the King at Ems the demand to authorize him to telegraph to Paris that His Majesty the King would obligate himself for all future time never again to give his approval to the candidacy of the Hohenzollerns should it be renewed.

His Majesty the King thereupon refused to receive the French envoy again and informed him through an adjutant that His Majesty had nothing further to say to the Ambassador.

Bismarck had already made it virtually certain that no other European power would interfere in a war between France and Prussia. The French reacted as Bismarck expected they would and declared war on Prussia on July 15, 1870. The French prime minister remarked, "We go to war with a light heart."

Unfortunately for the French, a "light heart" was not enough. They had barely started their military reorganization and proved no match for the better led and organized Prussian forces. The south German states honored their military alliances with Prussia and joined the war effort against the French. The Prussian armies advanced into France, and at Sedan, on September 2, 1870, an entire French army and Napoleon III himself were captured. Although the Second French Empire collapsed, the war was not yet over. After four months of bitter resistance, Paris finally capitulated on January 28, 1871, and an official peace treaty was signed in May.

France had to pay an indemnity of five billion francs (about one billion dollars) which Bismarck thought would cripple the French for years and keep them out of European affairs. The French responded by paying it off in three years. Even worse, however, the French had to give up the provinces of Alsace and Lorraine to the new German state, a loss that angered the French and left them burning for revenge.

Even before the war had ended, the south German states had agreed to enter the North German Confederation. On January 18, 1871, in the Hall of Mirrors in Louis XIV's palace at Versailles, William I was proclaimed kaiser or emperor of the Second German Empire (the first was the medieval Holy Roman Empire). German unity had been achieved by the Prussian monarchy and the Prussian army. In a real sense, Germany had been merged into Prussia, not Prussia into Germany. German liberals also rejoiced. They had dreamed of unity and freedom, but the achievement of unity now seemed much more important. One old liberal proclaimed:

> I cannot shake off the impression of this hour. I am no devotee of Mars; I feel more attached to the goddess of beauty and the mother of graces than to the powerful god of war, but the trophies of war exercise a magic charm even upon the child of peace. One's view is involuntarily chained and one's spirit goes along with the boundless row of men who acclaim the god of the moment—success.[6]

The Prussian leadership of German unification meant the triumph of authoritarian, militaristic values over liberal, constitutional sentiments in the development of the new German state. With its industrial resources and military might, the new state had become the strongest power on the Continent. A new European balance of power was at hand.

Nation Building and Reform: The National State in Mid-Century

While European affairs were dominated by the unification of Italy and Germany, other states were also undergoing transformations. War, civil war, and changing political alignments served as catalysts for domestic reforms.

The Austrian Empire: Toward a Dual Monarchy

After the Habsburgs had crushed the revolutions of 1848–1849, they restored centralized, autocratic government to the empire. What seemed to be the only lasting result of the revolution of 1848 was the act of emancipation of September 7, 1848, that freed the serfs and eliminated all compulsory labor services. Nevertheless, the development of industrialization after 1850, especially in Vienna and the provinces of Bohemia and Galicia, served to bring some economic and social change to the empire in the form of an urban proletariat, labor unrest, and a new industrial middle class.

In 1851, the revolutionary constitutions were abolished, and a system of centralized autocracy was imposed on the empire. Under the leadership of Alexander von Bach (1813–1893), local privileges were subordinated to a unified system of administration, law, and taxation implemented by German-speaking officials. Hungary was subjected to the rule of military officers while the

✦ **The Unification of Germany.** Under Prussian leadership, a new German empire was proclaimed on January 18, 1871, in the Hall of Mirrors in the palace at Versailles. King William of Prussia became Emperor William I of the Second German Empire. In this painting by Anton von Werner, Otto von Bismarck, the man who had been so instrumental in creating the new German state, is shown, resplendently attired in his white uniform, standing at the foot of the throne.

Catholic church was declared the state church and given control of education. The Bach regime, according to one critic, was composed of "a standing army of soldiers, a sitting army of officials, a kneeling army of priests, and a creeping army of denunciators." Economic troubles and war soon brought change. Failure in war usually had severe internal consequences for European states after 1789, and Austria was no exception. After Austria's defeat in the Italian war in 1859, the Emperor Francis Joseph (1848–1916) attempted to establish an imperial parliament (*Reichsrat*) with a nominated upper house and an elected lower house of representatives. Although the system was supposed to provide representation for the nationalities of the empire, the complicated formula used for elections ensured the election of a German-speaking majority, serving once again to alienate the ethnic minorities, particularly the Hungarians.

Only when military disaster struck again did the Austrians deal with the fiercely nationalistic Hungarians. The result was the negotiated *Ausgleich*, or Compromise, of 1867, which created the dual monarchy of Austria-Hungary. Each part of the empire now had its constitution, its own bicameral legislature, its own governmental machinery for domestic affairs, and its own capital (Vienna for Austria and Budapest for Hungary). Holding the two states together were a single monarch (Francis Joseph was emperor of Austria and king of Hungary) and a common army, foreign policy, and system of finances. In domestic affairs, the Hungarians had become an independent nation. The *Ausgleich* did not, however, satisfy the other nationalities that made up the multinational Austro-Hungarian Empire. The dual monarchy simply enabled the German-speaking Austrians and Hungarian Magyars to dominate the minorities, especially the Slavic peoples (Poles, Croats, Czechs, Serbs, Slovaks Slovenes, Little Russians), in their respective states. As the Hungarian nationalist Louis Kossuth remarked, "Dualism is the alliance of the conservative, reactionary and any apparently liberal elements in Hungary with those of the Austrian Germans who despise liberty, for the oppression of the other nationalities and races."[7] The nationalities problem persisted until the demise of the empire at the end of World War I.

Imperial Russia

The Russian imperial autocracy, based on soldiers, secret police, repression, and censorship, had withstood the revolutionary fervor of 1848 and even served as the "arsenal of autocracy" in crushing revolutions elsewhere in Europe. The defeat in the Crimean War at the hands of the British and French revealed the blatant deficiencies behind the facade of absolute power and made it

Map 23.3 Ethnic Groups in the Dual Monarchy, 1867.

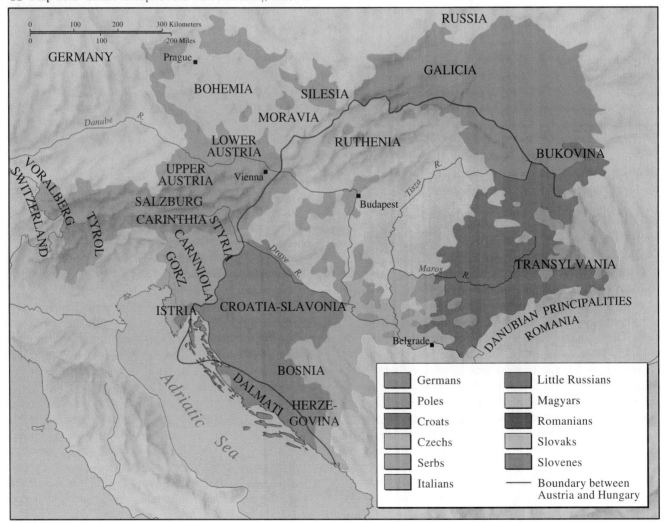

clear even to staunch conservatives that Russia was falling hopelessly behind the western European powers. Tsar Alexander II (1855–1881), who came to power in the midst of the Crimean War, turned his energies to a serious overhaul of the Russian system. Though called the Liberator because of his great reforms, Alexander II was no liberal but a thoughtful realist who knew reforms could not be postponed. Following the autocratic procedures of his predecessors, he attempted to impose those reforms upon the Russian people.

Serfdom was the most burdensome problem in tsarist Russia. The continuing subjugation of millions of peasants to the land and their landlords was an obviously corrupt and failing system. Reduced to antiquated methods of production based on serf labor, Russian landowners were economically pressed and unable to compete with foreign agriculture. The serfs, who formed the backbone of the Russian infantry, were uneducated and consequently increasingly unable to deal with the more complex machines and weapons of war. It was, after all, the failure of the serf-armies in the Crimean War that created the need for change in the first place. Then, too, peasant dissatisfaction still led to local peasant revolts that disrupted the countryside. Alexander II seemed to recognize the inevitable: "The existing order of serfdom," he told a group of Moscow nobles, "cannot remain unchanged. It is better to abolish serfdom from above than to wait until it is abolished from below."

On March 3, 1861, Alexander issued his emancipation edict (see the box on p. 792). Peasants could now own property, marry as they chose, and bring suits in the law courts. Nevertheless, the benefits of emancipation were limited. The government provided land for the peasants by purchasing it from the landlords, but the landowners often chose to keep the best lands. The Russian peasants soon found that they had inadequate amounts of good arable land to support themselves, a situation that worsened as the peasant population increased rapidly in the second half of the nineteenth century.

Nor were the peasants completely free. The state compensated the landowners for the land given to the peasants, but the peasants, in turn, were expected to repay the state in long-term installments. To ensure that the payments were made, peasants were subjected to the authority of their *mir* or village commune, which was collectively responsible for the land payments to the government. In a very real sense, then, the village commune, not the individual peasants, owned the land the peasants were purchasing. And since the village communes were responsible for the payments, they were

reluctant to allow peasants to leave their land. Emancipation, then, led not to a free, landowning peasantry along the Western model, but to an unhappy, land-

Emancipation: Serfs and Slaves

Although overall their histories have been quite different, Russia and the United States shared a common feature in the 1860s. They were the only states in the Western world that still had large enslaved populations (the Russian serfs were virtually slaves). The leaders of both countries issued emancipation proclamations within two years of each other. The first excerpt is taken from the Imperial Decree of March 3, 1861, which freed the Russian serfs. The second excerpt is from Abraham Lincoln's Emancipation Proclamation, issued on January 1, 1863.

The Imperial Decree, March 3, 1861

By the grace of God, we, Alexander II, Emperor and Autocrat of all the Russias, King of Poland, Grand Duke of Finland, etc., to all our faithful subjects, make known:

Called by Divine Providence and by the sacred right of inheritance to the throne of our ancestors, we took a vow in our innermost heart to respond to the mission which is intrusted to us as to surround with our affection and our Imperial solicitude all our faithful subjects of every rank and of every condition, from the warrior, who nobly bears arms for the defense of the country to the humble artisan devoted to the works of industry; from the official in the career of the high offices of the State to the laborer whose plough furrows the soil. . . .

We thus came to the conviction that the work of a serious improvement of the condition of the peasants was a sacred inheritance bequeathed to us by our ancestors, a mission which, in the course of events, Divine providence called upon us to fulfill. . . .

In virtue of the new dispositions above mentioned, the peasants attached to the soil will be in-vested within a term fixed by the law with all the rights of free cultivators. . . .

At the same time, they are granted the right of purchasing their close, and, with the consent of the proprietors, they may acquire in full property the arable lands and other appurtenances which are allotted to them as a permanent holding. By the acquisition in full property of the quantity of land fixed, the peasants are free from their obligations toward the proprietors for land thus purchased, and they enter definitely into the condition of free peasants—landholders.

The Emancipation Proclamation, January 1, 1863

Now therefore, I, Abraham Lincoln, President of the United States, by virtue of the power in me vested as Commander-in-Chief of the Army and Navy of the United States in time of actual armed rebellion against the authority and government of the United States, and as a fit and necessary war measure for suppressing such rebellion, do, on this 1st day of January, A.D. 1863, and in accordance with my purpose to do so, . . . order and designate as the States and parts of States wherein the people thereof, respectively, are this day in rebellion against the United States the following, to wit:

Arkansas, Texas, Louisiana, . . . Mississippi, Alabama, Florida, Georgia, South Carolina, North Carolina, and Virginia . . .

And by virtue of the power for the purpose aforesaid, I do order and declare that all persons held as slaves within said designated States and parts of States are, and henceforward shall be free; and that the Executive Government of the United States, including the military and naval authorities thereof, will recognize and maintain the freedom of said persons.

starved peasantry that largely followed the old ways of farming. Comprehensive reforms that would have freed the peasants completely and given them access to their own land were unfortunately left until the early twentieth century.

Alexander II also attempted other reforms. In 1864, he instituted a system of zemstvos, or local assemblies, that provided a moderate degree of self-government. Representatives to the zemstvos were to be elected from the noble landowners, townspeople, and peasants, but the property-based system of voting gave a distinct advantage to the nobles. Zemstvos were given a limited power to provide public services, such as education, famine relief, and road and bridge maintenance. They could levy taxes to pay for these services, but their efforts were frequently disrupted by bureaucrats who feared any hint of self-government. As one official noted, "In Russia reform can be carried out only by authority. We have too much disturbance and too much divergence of interests to expect anything good from the representation of those interests."[8] The hope of liberal nobles and other social reformers that the zemstvos would be expanded into a national parliament remained unfulfilled. The legal reforms of 1864, which created a regular system of local and provincial courts and a judicial code that accepted the principle of equality before the law, proved successful, however.

Even the autocratic tsar was unable to control the forces he unleashed by his reform program. Reformers wanted more and rapid change; conservatives opposed what they perceived as the tsar's attempts to undermine the basic institutions of Russian society. By 1870, Russia was witnessing an increasing number of reform movements. One of the most popular stemmed from the radical writings of Alexander Herzen (1812–1870), a Russian exile living in London, whose slogan of "land and freedom" epitomized his belief that the Russian peasant must be the chief instrument for social reform. Herzen believed that the peasant village commune could serve as an independent, self-governing body that would form the basis of a new Russia. Russian students and intellectuals who followed Herzen's ideas formed a movement called populism, whose aim was to create a new society through the revolutionary acts of the peasants. The peasants' lack of interest in these revolutionary ideas, however, led some of the populists to resort to violent means to overthrow tsarist autocracy. One such group of radicals, known as the People's Will, succeeded in assassinating Alexander II in 1881. His son and successor, Alexander III (1881–1894), turned against reform and returned to the traditional methods of repression.

Great Britain: The Victorian Age

Like Russia, Britain was not troubled by revolutionary disturbances during 1848, although for quite different reasons. The Reform Act of 1832 had opened the door to political representation for the industrial middle class, and in the 1860s Britain's liberal parliamentary system demonstrated once more its ability to make both social and political reforms that enabled the country to remain stable and prosperous.

One of the reasons for Britain's stability was its continuing economic growth. The British had flaunted their wealth and satisfaction with their achievements to the world in the great Industrial Exhibition in 1851. Now middle-class prosperity was at last coupled with some improvements for the working classes as well. Real wages for laborers increased over 25 percent between 1850 and 1870. The British sense of national pride was well reflected in Queen Victoria (1837–1901), whose self-contentment and sense of moral respectability mirrored the attitudes of her age. The Victorian Age, as Britain during the reign of Queen Victoria has ever since been known, was characterized by a pious complacency.

✦ **Russian Peasants.** Although Tsar Alexander II legally freed the serfs on March 3, 1861, Russian peasants remained economically bound to the land, and the end of serfdom brought few real improvements for them. This 1870 photograph shows a peasant family living in one room, with one person sleeping on the stove.

Politically, this was an era of uneasy stability as the aristocratic and upper-middle-class representatives who dominated Parliament blurred party lines by their internal strife and shifting positions. One political figure who stood out was Henry John Temple, Lord Palmerston (1784–1865), who was prime minister for most of the period from 1855 to 1865. Although a Whig, Palmerston was without strong party loyalty and found it easy to make political compromises. His primary interest was foreign policy, and his chauvinistic defense of British interests worldwide made him a popular figure with his countrymen. He was not a reformer, however, and opposed expanding the franchise. By extending representation from one class to another, he said, "We should by such an arrangement increase the number of Bribeable Electors and overpower Intelligence and Property by Ignorance and Poverty."

After Palmerston's death in 1865, the movement for the extension of the franchise only intensified. One mass meeting even led to a riot in London's Hyde Park. Although the Whigs (now called the Liberals), who had been responsible for the Reform Act of 1832, talked about passing additional reform legislation, it was actually the Tories (now called the Conservatives) who

✖ **Map 23.4** Europe in 1871.

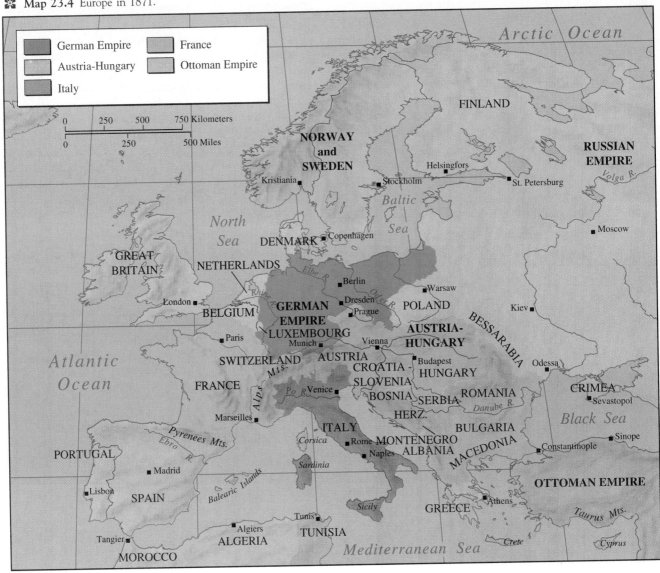

carried it through. The Tory leader in Parliament, Benjamin Disraeli (1804–1881), was apparently motivated by the desire to win over the newly enfranchised groups to the Conservative Party. He believed that the uneducated classes would defer to their social superiors when they voted. He knew that the Liberals, viewed as the party of reform, would not dare to oppose the reform bill. The Reform Act of 1867 was an important step toward the democratization of Britain. By lowering the monetary requirements for voting (taxes paid or income earned), it by and large enfranchised many male urban workers. The number of voters increased from about one million to slightly over two million. Although Disraeli believed this would benefit the Conservatives, industrial workers helped to produce a huge Liberal victory in 1868.

The extension of the right to vote had an important by-product as it forced the Liberal and Conservative Parties to organize carefully in order to manipulate the electorate. Party discipline intensified, and the rivalry between two well-established political parties, the Liberals and Conservatives, became a regular feature of parliamentary life. In large part this was due to the personal and political opposition of the two leaders of these parties, William Gladstone (1809–1898) and Disraeli.

The first Liberal administration of William Gladstone from 1868 to 1874 was responsible for a series of impressive reforms. In fact, historians have called the first Gladstone ministry the apex of "classical British liberalism." Legislation and government orders opened civil service positions to competitive exams rather than patronage, dropped religious requirements for degrees at Oxford and Cambridge, introduced the secret ballot for voting, and abolished the practice of purchasing military commissions. The Education Act of 1870 attempted to make elementary schools available for all children (see Chapter 25). These reforms were typically liberal. By eliminating abuses and enabling people with talent to compete fairly, they sought to strengthen the nation and its institutions.

The United States: Civil War and Reunion

While the Germans and Italians were fighting Austria and France to achieve national unity, some Americans were hoping to dissolve theirs. During its early existence, the young republic had shown a remarkable ability to resolve peacefully many issues that might have disrupted national unity. Slavery, however, proved to be an issue beyond compromise.

Like the North, the South had experienced dramatic population growth during the first half of the nineteenth century. But its development was quite different. Its cotton economy and social structure were based on the exploitation of enslaved black Africans and their descendants. The importance of cotton is evident from

✦ **Queen Victoria and Her Family.** Queen Victoria, who ruled Britain from 1837 to 1901, married Prince Albert of Saxe-Coburg and Gotha in 1840 and subsequently gave birth to four sons and five daughters, who were married into a number of European royal families. Queen Victoria is seated at the center of this 1881 photograph, surrounded by members of her family.

production figures. In 1810, the South produced a raw cotton crop of 178,000 bales worth $10 million. By 1860, it was generating 4.5 million bales of cotton with a value of $249 million. Ninety-three percent of southern cotton in 1850 was produced by a slave population that had grown dramatically in fifty years. Although new slave imports had been barred in 1808, there were 4 million Afro-American slaves in the South by 1860 compared to 1 million in 1800. The cotton economy and a plantation-based slavery were intimately related, and the attempt to maintain them in the course of the first half of the nineteenth century led the South to become increasingly defensive, monolithic, and isolated. At the same time, the rise of an abolitionist movement in the North challenged the southern order and created an "emotional chain reaction" that led to civil war.

The issue arose in the 1810s when the westward movement began to produce new states west of the Appalachians. A balance between slave states and free states was carefully maintained until Missouri applied for admission to the Union in 1819 as a slave state and there was no free state to maintain the balance. The ensuing crisis was settled with the Missouri Compromise of 1820, which separated Maine from Massachusetts in order to maintain the balance. To prevent future crises, the remainder of the territory acquired by the Louisiana Purchase was to be divided at the latitude 36°30′. States formed south of the line would be slave states, and states formed north of the line would be free.

Unfortunately, the line drawn by the Missouri Compromise did not legally extend to the vast new territories acquired by the United States during the 1840s. The Mexican Cession acquired at the close of the Mexican War posed a particular problem because some of its lands were south of 36°30′. By 1850, the country was again facing a crisis over the balance of slave states and free

Map 23.5 The United States: The West and Civil War.

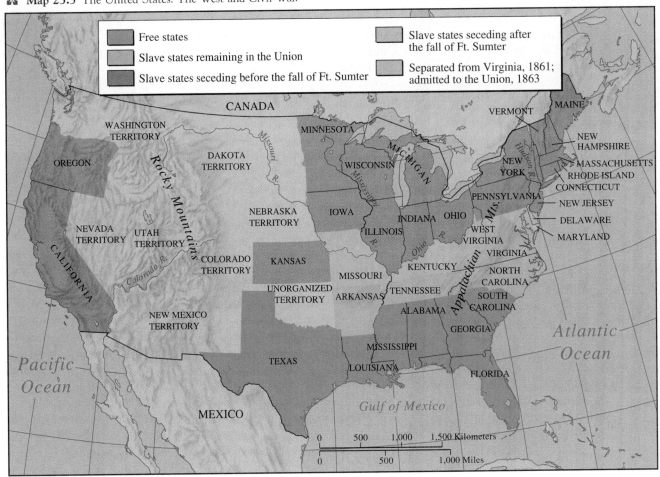

states. This time the problem was caused by California's application for admission as a free state.

The Compromise of 1850, which admitted California as a free state, was really an armistice, not a compromise. It had not solved this divisive issue, but merely postponed it. By the 1850s, the slavery question had caused the Whig Party to become defunct while the Democrats were splitting along North-South lines. The Kansas-Nebraska Act of 1854, which effectively repealed the Missouri Compromise by allowing slavery in the Kansas-Nebraska territories to be determined by popular sovereignty, created a firestorm in the North and led to the creation of a new sectional party. The Republicans were united by antislavery principles and were especially driven by the fear that the "slave power" of the South would attempt to spread the slave system throughout the country.

As polarization over the issue of slavery intensified, compromise became less feasible. When Abraham Lincoln, the man who had said in a speech in Illinois in 1858 that "this government cannot endure permanently half slave and half free," was elected president in November 1860, the die was cast. Lincoln carried only 2 of the 1,109 counties in the South; the Republicans were not even on the ballot in ten southern states. On December 20, 1860, a South Carolina convention voted to repeal the state's ratification of the Constitution of the United States. In February 1861, six more southern states did the same, and a rival nation—the Confederate States of America—was formed. In April fighting erupted between North and South.

The American Civil War (1861–1865) was an extraordinarily bloody struggle, a clear foretaste of the total war to come in the twentieth century. More than 360,000 soldiers died, either in battle or from deadly infectious diseases spawned by filthy camp conditions. Over a period of four years, the Union states mobilized their superior assets and gradually wore down the South. As the war dragged on, it had the effect of radicalizing public opinion in the North. What began as a war to save the Union became a war against slavery. On January 1, 1863, Lincoln's Emancipation Proclamation made most of the nation's slaves "forever free" (see the box on p. 792). The increasingly effective Union blockade of the South combined with a shortage of fighting men made the Confederate cause desperate by the end of 1864. The final push of Union troops under General Ulysses S. Grant forced General Robert E. Lee's army to surrender on April 9, 1865. Although the problems of reconstruction were ahead, the Union victory confirmed that the United States would be "one nation, indivisible."

The Emergence of a Canadian Nation

To the north of the United States, the process of nation building was also making progress. By the Treaty of Paris in 1763, Canada—or New France as it was called—passed into the hands of the British. By 1800, most Canadians favored more autonomy, although the colonists disagreed on the form this autonomy should take. Upper Canada (now Ontario) was predominantly English-speaking while Lower Canada (now Quebec) was dominated by French Canadians. Increased immigration to Canada after 1815 also fueled the desire for self-government.

Fearful of American designs on Canada during the American Civil War, the British government finally capitulated to Canadian demands, and in 1867, Parliament established a Canadian nation—the Dominion of Canada—with its own constitution. Canada now possessed a parliamentary system and ruled itself, although foreign affairs still remained under the control of the British government.

*I*ndustrialization and the Marxist Response

Between 1850 and 1871, continental industrialization came of age. The innovations of the British Industrial Revolution—mechanized factory production, the use of coal, the steam engine, and the transportation revolution—all became regular features of economic expansion. Although marred periodically by economic depression (1857–1858) or recession (1866–1867), this was an age of considerable economic prosperity, particularly evident in the growth of domestic and foreign markets.

Industrialization on the Continent

The transformation of textile production from hand looms to power looms had largely been completed in Britain by the 1850s (for cotton) and 1860s (for wool). On the Continent, the period from 1850 to 1870 witnessed increased mechanization of the cotton and textile industries, although continental countries still remained behind Britain. By 1870, hand looms had virtually disappeared in Britain whereas in France there were still 200,000 of them compared to 80,000 power looms. However, this period of industrial expansion on

◆ **Opening of the Suez Canal.** Between 1850 and 1871, continental Europeans built railways, bridges, and canals as part of the ever-spreading process of industrialization. A French diplomat, Ferdinand de Lesseps, was the guiding force behind the construction of the Suez Canal, which provided a link between the Mediterranean and Red Seas. Work on the canal began in 1859 and was completed ten years later. As seen here, an elaborate ceremony marked the opening of the canal. A French vessel led the first convoy of ships through the canal.

the Continent was fueled not so much by textiles as by the growth of railroads. Between 1850 and 1870, European railroad track mileage increased from 14,500 to almost 70,000. The railroads, in turn, stimulated growth in both the iron and coal industries.

Between 1850 and 1870, continental iron industries made the transition from charcoal iron smelting to coke-blast smelting. In Prussia, for example, the portion of the iron output produced with charcoal declined from 82 percent in 1842 to 60 percent in 1852, and to only 12.3 percent by 1862. Despite the dramatic increases in the production of pig iron, the continental countries had not yet come close to surpassing British iron production. In 1870, the British iron industry produced one-half of the world's pig iron, four times as much as Germany and five times as much as France. In the middle decades of the nineteenth century, the textile, mining, and metallurgical industries on the Continent also rapidly converted to the use of the steam engine.

Although policies varied from country to country, continental governments took a more or less active role in passing laws and initiating actions that were favorable to the expansion of industry and commerce. While some countries exercised direct control over nationalized industries, such as Prussia's development of coal mines in

the Saar region, others provided financial assistance to private companies to develop mines, ironworks, dockyards, and railways.

An important factor in the expansion of markets was the elimination of barriers to international trade. Essential international waterways were opened up by the elimination of restrictive tolls. The Danube River in 1857 and the Rhine in 1861, for example, were declared freeways for all ships. The negotiation of trade treaties in the 1860s reduced or eliminated protective tariffs throughout much of western Europe.

Governments also played a role in first allowing and then encouraging the formation of joint-stock investment banks (see Chapter 21). These banks were crucial to continental industrial development since they mobilized enormous capital resources for investment. In the 1850s and 1860s, they were very important in the promotion of railway construction, although they were not always a safe investment. During a trip to Spain to examine possibilities for railroad construction, the locomotive manufacturer George Stephenson reported: "I have been a month in the country, but have not seen during the whole of that time enough people of the right sort to fill a single train."[9] His misgivings proved to be well-founded. In 1864, the Spanish banking system, which depended largely on investments in railway shares, collapsed.

During this ongoing process of industrialization between 1850 and 1870, capitalist factory owners remained largely free to hire labor on their own terms based on market forces. Increased mechanization of industry meant further displacement of skilled artisans by semiskilled workers. The working classes needed organizations that would fight for improved working conditions and reasonable wages, but the liberal bourgeoisie condemned such associations as criminal agencies that threatened private property through the use of strikes and pickets. This did not stop the gradual organization of trade unions in the 1860s, however, as conservative regimes sanctioned the formation of trade unions in order to gain popular support against liberals. Bismarck did so in Prussia in 1863, and Napoleon III did likewise in France in 1864. Even where they did form, however, trade unions tended to represent only a small part of the industrial working class, usually such select groups as engineers, shipbuilders, miners, and printers. Real change for the industrial proletariat would only come with the development of socialist parties and socialist trade unions. These emerged after 1870, but the theory that made them possible had already been developed by mid-century in the work of Karl Marx.

Marx and Marxism

The beginnings of Marxism can be found in 1848 with the publication of a short treatise entitled *The Communist Manifesto*, written by two Germans, Karl Marx (1818–1883) and Friedrich Engels (1820–1895). Karl Marx was born into a relatively prosperous middle-class family in Trier in western Germany. He descended from a long line of Jewish rabbis although his father, a lawyer, had become a Protestant to keep his job. Marx enrolled at the University of Bonn in 1835, but a year later his carefree student ways led his father to send him to the more serious-minded University of Berlin, where he encountered the ideas of Georg Wilhelm Friedrich Hegel (see Chapter 22). After receiving a Ph.D. in philosophy, he planned to teach at a university. Unable to obtain a position because of his professed atheism, Marx decided upon a career in journalism and eventually became the editor of a liberal bourgeois newspaper in Cologne in 1842. After the newspaper was suppressed because of his radical views, Marx moved to Paris. There he met Friedrich Engels, who became his lifelong friend and financial patron.

Engels, the son of a wealthy German cotton manufacturer, had worked in Britain at one of his father's factories in Manchester. There he had acquired a first-hand knowledge of what he came to call the "wage slavery" of the British working classes, which he detailed in a damning indictment of industrial life entitled *The Conditions of the Working Class in England*, written in 1844. Engels would contribute his knowledge of actual working conditions as well as monetary assistance to the financially strapped Marx.

In 1847, Marx and Engels joined a tiny group of primarily German socialist revolutionaries known as the Communist League. By this time, both Marx and Engels were enthusiastic advocates of the radical working-class movement and agreed to draft a statement of their ideas for the league. The resulting *Communist Manifesto*, published in German in January 1848, appeared on the eve of the revolutions of 1848. One would think from its opening lines that the pamphlet alone had caused this revolutionary upheaval: "A spectre is haunting Europe—the spectre of Communism. All the Powers of Old Europe have entered into a holy alliance to exorcize this spectre: Pope and Czar, Metternich and Guizot, French Radicals and German police spies."[10] In fact, *The Communist Manifesto* was known to only a few of Marx's friends. Although its closing words—"The proletarians have nothing to lose but their chains. They have a world to win. WORKING MEN OF ALL COUN-

TRIES, UNITE!"—were clearly intended to rouse the working classes to action, they passed unnoticed in 1848. The work, however, became one of the most influential political treatises in modern European history.

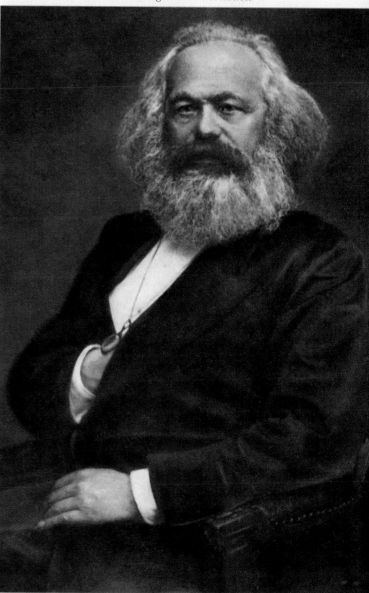

◆ **Karl Marx.** Karl Marx was a radical journalist who joined with Friedrich Engels to write *The Communist Manifesto*, which proclaimed the ideas of a revolutionary socialism. After the failure of the 1848 revolution in Germany, Marx fled to Britain, where he continued to write and became involved in the work of the first International Working Men's Association.

According to Engels, Marx's ideas were a synthesis of British, French, and German thought. He said that Marx derived his doctrine of surplus value from British classical economists who argued that the value of a product depended on the amount of labor that went into its production. Marx maintained that the difference between a product's real value and the wages of the worker who produced it was "surplus value." By pocketing this surplus value, mill owners were retarding economic growth, causing depressions, and setting the stage for revolution. The French provided Marx with ample documentation for his assertion that a revolution could totally restructure society. They also provided him with several examples of socialism. From the German idealistic philosophers such as Hegel, Marx took the idea of dialectic: everything evolves, and all change in history is the result of clashes between antagonistic elements. Marx was particularly impressed by Hegel, but he disagreed with Hegel's belief that history is determined by ideas manifesting themselves in historical forces. Instead, said Marx, the course of history is determined by material forces.

Marx and Engels began the *Manifesto* with the statement, "the history of all hitherto existing society is the history of class struggles." Throughout history, oppressed and oppressor have "stood in constant opposition to one another." In an earlier struggle, the feudal classes of the Middle Ages were forced to accede to the emerging middle class or bourgeoisie. As the bourgeoisie took control in turn, their ideas became the dominant views of the era, and government became their instrument. Marx and Engels declared: "The executive of the modern State is but a committee for managing the common affairs of the whole bourgeoisie."[11] In other words, the government of the state reflected and defended the interests of the industrial middle class and its allies.

Although bourgeois society had emerged victorious out of the ruins of feudal society, Marx and Engels insisted that it had not triumphed completely. Now once again the bourgeoisie were antagonists in an emerging class struggle, but this time they faced the proletariat, or the industrial working class. The struggle would be fierce; in fact, Marx and Engels predicted that the workers would eventually overthrow their bourgeois masters. After their victory, the proletariat would form a dictatorship to reorganize the means of production. Then, a classless society would emerge, and the state—itself an instrument of the bourgeoisie—would wither away since it no longer represented the interests of a particular class. Class struggles would then be over (see the box on p. 801). Marx believed that the emergence of a classless society would lead to progress in science,

technology, and industry and to greater wealth for all.

After the outbreak of revolution in 1848, Marx returned to Germany where he edited a new newspaper in Cologne, optimistic that the ideas of *The Communist Manifesto* were beginning to be fulfilled in a "colossal eruption of the revolutionary crater." The counterrevolution ended his hopes, and in August 1849, Marx was forced to return to Britain, where he spent the rest of his life in exile. At first life was not easy for Marx, whose income from Engels and newspaper articles was never sufficient for him and his family. After 1869, however, Engels provided an annuity that made Marx's later years quite comfortable. Marx continued his writing on political economy, especially his famous work, *Das Kapital (Capital)*. He only completed one volume. After his death, the remaining volumes were edited by his friend Engels.

One of the reasons *Capital* was not finished was Marx's own preoccupation with organizing the working-class movement. In *The Communist Manifesto*, Marx had defined the communists as "the most advanced and resolute section of the working-class parties of every country." Their advantage was their ability to understand "the line of march, the conditions, and the ultimate general results of the proletarian movement." Marx saw his role in this light and participated enthusiastically in the activities of the International Working Men's Association. Formed in 1864 by British and French trade unionists, this "First International" served as an umbrella organization for working-class interests. Marx was the dominant personality on the organization's General Council and devoted much time to its activities. He wrote in 1865: "Compared with my work on the book [*Capital*] the International Association takes up an enormous amount of time, because I am in fact in charge of the whole business."[12] Internal dissension within the ranks soon damaged the organization. In 1871, Marx supported the Paris Commune as a genuine proletarian uprising (see Chapter 24), but British trade unionists did not want to be identified with the crimes of the Parisians. In 1872, Marx essentially ended the association by moving its headquarters to the United States. The First International had failed. Although it would be revived in 1889, the fate of socialism by that time was in the hands of national socialist parties.

Science and Culture in an Age of Realism

Between 1850 and 1870, two major intellectual developments are evident: the growth of scientific knowledge

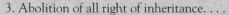

In The Communist Manifesto, *Karl Marx and Friedrich Engels projected the creation of a classless society as the final end product of the struggle between the bourgeoisie and the proletariat. In this selection, they discuss the steps by which that classless society would be reached. Although Marx had criticized the utopian socialists for their failure to approach the labor problem scientifically, his solution sounds equally utopian.*

Karl Marx and Friedrich Engels,
The Communist Manifesto

We have seen above, that the first step in the revolution by the working class, is to raise the proletariat to the position of ruling class. . . . The proletariat will use its political supremacy to wrest, by degrees, all capital from the bourgeoisie, to centralize all instruments of production in the hands of the State, i.e., of the proletariat organized as the ruling class; and to increase the total of productive forces as rapidly as possible.

Of course, in the beginning, this cannot be effected except by means of despotic inroads on the rights of property, and on the conditions of bourgeois production; by means of measures, therefore, which appear economically insufficient and untenable, but which, in the course of the movement, outstrip themselves, necessitate further inroads upon the old social order, and are unavoidable as a means of entirely revolutionizing the mode of production.

These measures will of course be different in different countries.

Nevertheless, in the most advanced countries, the following will be pretty generally applicable:

1. Abolition of property in land and application of all rents of land to public purposes.
2. A heavy progressive or graduated income tax.
3. Abolition of all right of inheritance. . . .
5. Centralization of credit in the hands of the State, by means of a national bank with State capital and an exclusive monopoly.
6. Centralization of the means of communication and transport in the hands of the State.
7. Extension of factories and instruments of production owned by the State. . . .
8. Equal liability of all to labor. Establishment of industrial armies, especially for agriculture.
9. Combination of agriculture with manufacturing industries; gradual abolition of the distinction between town and country, by a more equable distribution of the population over the country.
10. Free education for all children in public schools. Abolition of children's factory labor in its present form. . . .

When, in the course of development, class distinctions have disappeared, and all production has been concentrated in the whole nation, the public power will lose its political character. Political power, properly so called, is merely the organized power of one class for oppressing another. If the proletariat during its contest with the bourgeoisie is compelled, by the force of circumstances, to organize itself as a class, if, by means of a revolution, it makes itself the ruling class, and, as such, sweeps away by force the old conditions of production, then it will, along with these conditions, have swept away the conditions for the existence of class antagonisms and of classes generally, and will thereby have abolished its own supremacy as a class.

In place of the old bourgeois society, with its classes and class antagonisms, we shall have an association, in which the free development of each is the condition for the free development of all.

with its rapidly increasing impact on the Western worldview; and the shift from Romanticism with its emphasis on the inner world of reality to Realism with its focus on the outer, material world.

A New Age of Science

By the mid-nineteenth century, science was having a greater and greater impact on European life. The Scientific Revolution of the sixteenth and seventeenth centuries had fundamentally transformed the Western worldview and created a modern, rational approach to the study of the natural world. Even in the eighteenth century, however, these intellectual developments had remained the preserve of an educated elite and resulted in few practical benefits. Moreover, the technical advances of the early Industrial Revolution had depended little on pure science and much more on the practical experiments of technologically oriented amateur inventors. Advances in industrial technology, however, fed an interest in basic scientific research, which, in turn, in the 1830s and afterward resulted in a rash of basic scientific discoveries that were soon converted into technological improvements that affected everybody.

The development of the steam engine was important in encouraging scientists to work out its theoretical foundations, a preoccupation that led to thermodynamics, the science of the relationship between heat and mechanical energy. The laws of thermodynamics were at the core of nineteenth-century physics. In biology, the Frenchman Louis Pasteur formulated the germ theory of disease, which had enormous practical applications in the development of modern, scientific medical practices (see A Revolution in Health Care later in this chapter). In chemistry, in the 1860s the Russian Dmitri Mendeleyev classified all the material elements then known on the basis of their atomic weights and provided the systematic foundation for the periodic law. The Englishman Michael Faraday discovered the phenomenon of electromagnetic induction and put together a primitive generator that laid the foundation for the use of electricity, although economically efficient generators were not built until the 1870s.

The steadily increasing and often dramatic material gains generated by science and technology led to a growing faith in the benefits of science. Even ordinary people who did not understand the theoretical concepts of science were impressed by its accomplishments. The popularity of scientific and technological achievement led to the widespread acceptance of the scientific method, based on observation, experiment, and logical analysis, as the only path to objective truth and objective reality. This, in turn, undermined the faith of many people in religious revelation and truth. It is no accident that the nineteenth century was an age of increasing secularization, particularly evident in the growth of materialism or the belief that everything mental, spiritual, or ideal was simply an outgrowth of physical forces. Truth was to be found in the concrete material existence of human beings, not as Romanticists imagined in revelations gained by feeling or intuitive flashes. The importance of materialism was strikingly evident in the most important scientific event of the nineteenth century, the development of the theory of organic evolution according to natural selection. On the theories of Charles Darwin could be built a picture of humans as material beings that were simply part of the natural world.

Charles Darwin and the Theory of Organic Evolution

The concept of evolution was not new when Darwin first postulated his theory in 1859. Until the early nineteenth century, most European intellectuals still believed that a divine power had created the world and its species. Humans, of course, occupied a special superior position because the Book of Genesis in the Bible stated: "Let us make man in our image and likeness and let him have dominion over all other things." By the beginning of the nineteenth century, however, people were questioning the biblical account; some had already posited an evolutionary theory. In 1809, the Frenchman Jean-Baptiste Lamarck had presented a theory of evolution that argued that various types of plants and animals exist because of their efforts to adjust to different environments. His assumption that they subsequently passed on their acquired characteristics was later rejected. Geologists had also been busy demonstrating that the earth underwent constant change and was far older than had been believed. They argued that it had evolved slowly over millions of years rather than the thousands of years postulated by theological analysis of the biblical account of creation. Despite the growth in evolutionary ideas, however, even by the mid-nineteenth century there was no widely accepted theory of evolution that explained things satisfactorily.

Charles Darwin (1809–1882), like many of the great scientists of the nineteenth century, was a scientific amateur. Born into an upper-middle-class family, he studied theology at Cambridge University while pursuing an intense side interest in geology and biology. In 1831, at the age of twenty-two, his hobby became his vocation when he accepted an appointment as a naturalist to study animals and plants on an official Royal Navy scientific expedition aboard the H.M.S. *Beagle*. Its purpose was to survey and study the landmasses of South America and the South Pacific. Darwin's specific job was to study the structure of various forms of plant and animal life. He was able to observe animals on islands virtually untouched by external influence and compare them to animals on the mainland. As a result, Darwin came to discard the notion of a special creation and to believe that animals evolved over time and in response to their environment. When he returned to Britain, he eventually formulated an explanation for evolution in the principle of natural selection, a theory that he presented in 1859 in his celebrated book, *On the Origin of Species by Means of Natural Selection*.

The basic idea of this book was that all plants and animals had evolved over a long period of time from earlier and simpler forms of life, a principle known as organic evolution. Darwin was important in explaining how this natural process worked. He took the first step from Thomas Malthus's theory of population: in every species, "many more individuals of each species are born than can possibly survive." This results in a "struggle for existence." Darwin believed that "as more individuals are produced than can possibly survive, there must in every case be a struggle for existence, either one individual with another of the same species, or with the individuals of distinct species, or with the physical conditions of life." Those who succeeded in this struggle for existence had adapted better to their environment, a process made possible by the appearance of "variants." Chance variations that occurred in the process of inheritance enabled some organisms to be more adaptable to the environment than others, a process that Darwin called natural selection:

> Owing to this struggle [for existence], variations, however slight..., if they be in any degree profitable to the individuals of a species, in their infinitely complex relations to other organic beings and to their physical conditions of life, will tend to the preservation of such individuals, and will generally be inherited by the offspring.[13]

Those that were naturally selected for survival ("survival of the fit") survived. The unfit did not and became extinct. The fit who survived, in turn, propagated and passed on the variations that enabled them to survive until, from Darwin's point of view, a new separate species emerged. Darwin was not able to explain how variants first occurred and did not arrive at the modern explanation of mutations.

In *On the Origin of Species*, Darwin discussed plant and animal species only. He was not concerned with humans themselves and only later applied his theory of natural selection to humans. In *The Descent of Man*, published in 1871, he argued for the animal origins of human beings: "man is the co-descendant with other mammals of a common progenitor." Humans were not an exception to the rule governing other species (see the box on p. 804).

Although Darwin's ideas were eventually accepted, initially they were highly controversial. Some people objected to what they considered Darwin's debasement of humans; his theory, they claimed, made human beings ordinary products of nature rather than unique beings. The acceptance of Darwinism, one professor of geology at Cambridge declared, would "sink the human race into a lower grade of degradation than any into which it has fallen since its written records tell of its history." Others were disturbed by the implications of life as a struggle for survival, of "nature red in tooth and claw." Was there a place in the Darwinian world for moral values? For those

who believed in a rational order in the world, Darwin's theory seemed to eliminate purpose and design from the universe. Gradually, however, Darwin's theory was accepted by scientists and other intellectuals although Darwin was somewhat overly optimistic when he wrote in 1872 that "almost every scientist admits the principle of evolution." In the process of accepting Darwin's ideas, some people even tried to apply them to society, yet another example of science's increasing prestige.

A Revolution in Health Care

The application of natural science to the field of medicine in the nineteenth century led to revolutionary breakthroughs in health care. The first steps toward a more scientific basis for medicine were taken in Paris hospitals during the first half of the nineteenth century. Clinical observation, consisting of an active physical examination of patients, was combined with the knowledge gained from detailed autopsies to create a new clinical medicine. Nevertheless, the major breakthrough toward a scientific medicine occurred with the discovery of microorganisms, or germs, as the agents causing disease. The germ theory of disease was largely the work of Louis Pasteur (1822–1895). Pasteur was not a doctor but a chemist who approached medical problems in a scientific fashion. In 1857, Pasteur went to Paris as director of scientific studies at the École Normale. Through his experiments on fermentations, he soon proved that various microorganisms were responsible for the process of fermentation, thus launching the science of bacteriology.

Government and private industry soon perceived the inherent practical value of Pasteur's work. His examination of a disease threatening the wine industry led to the development in 1863 of a process—subsequently known as pasteurization—for heating a product to destroy the organisms causing spoilage. In 1877, Pasteur turned his attention to human diseases. His desire to do more than simply identify disease-producing organisms led him in 1885 to a preventive vaccination against rabies. In the 1890s, the principle of vaccination was extended to diphtheria, typhoid fever, cholera, and plague, creating a modern immunological science.

The work of Pasteur and the many others who followed him in isolating the specific bacteriological causes of numerous diseases had a far-reaching impact. By providing a rational means of treating and preventing infectious diseases, they transformed the medical world. Both the practice of surgery and public health experienced a renaissance.

❧ Darwin and the Descent of Man ❧

Although Darwin published his theory of organic evolution in 1859, his book, The Descent of Man, did not appear until 1871. In it, Darwin argued that human beings have also evolved from lower forms of life. The theory encountered a firestorm of criticism, especially from clergymen. One described Darwin's theory as a "brutal philosophy—to wit, there is no God, and the ape is our Adam."

Charles Darwin, *The Descent of Man*

The main conclusion here arrived at, and now held by many naturalists, who are well competent to form a sound judgment, is that man is descended from some less highly organized form. The grounds upon which this conclusion rests will never be shaken, for the close similarity between man and the lower animals in embryonic development, as well as in innumerable points of structure and constitution, both of high and of the most trifling importance,—the rudiments which he retains, and the abnormal reversions to which he is occasionally liable,—are facts which cannot be disputed. They have long been known, but until recently they told us nothing with respect to the origin of man. Now when viewed by the light of our knowledge of the whole organic world, their meaning is unmistakable. The great principle of evolution stands up clear and firm, when these groups of facts are considered in connection with others, such as the mutual affinities of the members of the same group, their geographical distribution in past and present times, and their geological succession. It is incredible that all these facts should speak falsely. He who is not content to look, like a savage, at the phenomena of nature as disconnected, cannot any longer believe that man is the work of a separate act of creation. He will be forced to admit that the close resemblance of the embryo of man to that, for instance, of a dog—the construction of his skull, limbs and whole frame on the same plan with that of other mammals, independently of the uses to which the parts may be put—the occasional reappearance of various structures, for instance of several muscles, which man does not normally possess . . .—and a crowd of analogous facts—all point in the plainest manner to the conclusion that man is the co-descendant with other mammals of a common progenitor. . . .

Man may be excused for feeling some pride at having risen, though not through his own exertions, to the very summit of the organic scale; and the fact of his having thus risen, instead of having been aboriginally placed there, may give him hope for a still higher destiny in the distant future. But we are not here concerned with hopes or fears, only with the truth as far as our reason permits us to discover it; and I have given the evidence to the best of my ability. We must, however, acknowledge, as it seems to me, that man with all his noble qualities, with sympathy which feels for the most debased, with benevolence which extends not only to other men but to the humblest living creature, with his god-like intellect which has penetrated into the movements and constitution of the solar system—with all these exalted powers—Man still bears in his bodily frame the indelible stamp of his lowly origin.

Surgeons had already experienced a new professionalism by the end of the eighteenth century (see Chapter 18), but the discovery of germs and the introduction of anesthesia created a new environment for surgical operations. Traditionally, surgeons had mainly set broken bones, treated wounds, and amputated limbs, usually shattered in war. One major obstacle to more successful surgery was the inevitable postoperative infection, which was especially rampant in hospitals.

Joseph Lister (1827–1912), who developed the antiseptic principle, was one of the first people to deal with this problem. Following the work of Pasteur, Lister perceived that bacteria might enter a wound and cause infection. His use of carbolic acid, a newly discovered disinfectant, proved remarkably effective in eliminating infections during surgery. Lister's discoveries dramatically transformed surgery wards as patients no longer succumbed regularly to what was called "hospital gangrene."

The second great barrier to large-scale surgery stemmed from the inability to lessen the pain of the patient. Alcohol and opiates had been used for centuries during surgical operations, but even their use did not allow unhurried operative maneuvers. After experiments with numerous agents, sulfuric ether was first used successfully in an operation at the Massachusetts General Hospital in 1846 (see the box on p. 805). Within a year chloroform began to rival ether as an anesthetic agent.

Although the great discoveries of bacteriology came after the emergence of the first public health movement, they significantly furthered its development. Based on the principle of preventive, rather than curative, medicine, the urban public health movement of the 1840s

⇒ Anesthesia and Modern Surgery ⇐

Modern scientific medicine became established in the nineteenth century. Important to the emergence of modern surgery was the development of anesthetic agents that would block the patient's pain and enable surgeons to complete their surgery without the haste that had characterized earlier operations. This document is an eyewitness account of the first successful use of ether anesthesia, which took place at the Massachusetts General Hospital in 1846.

The First Public Demonstration of Ether Anesthesia, October 16, 1846

The day arrived; the time appointed was noted on the dial, when the patient was led into the operating-room, and Dr. Warren and a board of the most eminent surgeons in the State were gathered around the sufferer. "All is ready—the stillness oppressive." It had been announced "that a test of some preparation was to be made for which the astonishing claim had been made that it would render the person operated upon free from pain." These are the words of Dr. Warren that broke the stillness.

Those present were incredulous, and, as Dr. Morton had not arrived at the time appointed and fifteen minutes had passed, Dr. Warren said, with significant meaning, "I presume he is otherwise engaged." This was followed with a "derisive laugh," and Dr. Warren grasped his knife and was about to proceed with the operation. At that moment Dr. Morton entered a side door, when Dr. Warren turned to him and in a strong voice said, "Well, sir, your patient is ready." In a few minutes he was ready for the surgeon's knife, when Dr. Morton said, "Your patient is ready, sir."

Here the most sublime scene ever witnessed in the operating-room was presented, when the patient placed himself voluntarily upon the table, which was to become the altar of future fame. Not that he did so for the purpose of advancing the science of medicine, nor for the good of his fellow-men, for the act itself was purely a personal and selfish one. He was about to assist in solving a new and important problem of therapeutics, whose benefits were to be given to the whole civilized world, yet wholly unconscious of the sublimity of the occasion or the art he was taking.

That was a supreme moment for a most wonderful discovery, and, had the patient died upon the operation, science would have waited long to discover the hypnotic effects of some other remedy of equal potency and safety, and it may be properly questioned whether chloroform would have come into use as it has at the present time.

The heroic bravery of the man who voluntarily placed himself upon the table, a subject for the surgeon's knife, should be recorded and his name enrolled upon parchment, which should be hung upon the walls of the surgical amphitheater in which the operation was performed. His name was Gilbert Abbott.

The operation was for a congenital tumor on the left side of the neck, extending along the jaw to the maxillary gland and into the mouth, embracing a margin of the tongue. The operation was successful; and when the patient recovered he declared he had suffered no pain.

Dr. Warren turned to those present and said, "Gentlemen, this is no humbug."

---

and 1850s was largely a response to the cholera epidemic (see Chapter 24). One medical man, in fact, called cholera "our best ally" in furthering public hygiene. The prebacteriological hygiene movement focused on providing clean water, adequate sewage disposal, and less crowded housing conditions. Bacterial discoveries, however, led to greater emphasis on preventive measures, such as the pasteurization of milk, greater purification of water supplies, immunization against disease, and control of waterborne diseases. The public health movement also resulted in the government hiring medical doctors not just to treat people but to deal with issues of public health.

The new scientific developments also had an important impact on the training of doctors for professional careers in health care. Although there were a few medical schools at the beginning of the nineteenth century, most medical instruction was still done by a system of apprenticeship. In the course of the nineteenth century, virtually every Western country founded new medical schools, but attempts to impose uniform standards on them through certifying bodies met considerable resistance. Entrance requirements were virtually nonexistent, and degrees were granted after several months of lectures. Professional organizations founded around the mid-century, such as the British Medical Association in 1832, the American Medical Association in 1847, and the German Doctors' Society in 1872, attempted to elevate professional standards but achieved little until the end of the century. The establishment of the Johns Hopkins University School of Medicine in 1893, with its four-year graded curriculum, clinical training for advanced students, and use of laboratories for teaching purposes, provided a new model for medical

✦ **Thomas Eakins, *The Gross Clinic*.** This painting, completed in 1875, shows Dr. Samuel Gross, one of America's foremost surgeons, scapel in hand, pausing midway in surgery on a young man's leg to discuss the operation with his students in the amphitheater of the Jefferson Medical College. Assistant doctors perform various tasks, including the anesthetist who holds his cloth over the youth's face. Eakins's painting is a realistic portrayal of the new medical science at work.

training that finally became standard practice in the twentieth century.

During most of the nineteenth century, medical schools in Europe and America were closed to female students. When Harriet Hunt applied to Harvard Medical School, the male students drew up resolutions that prevented her admission:

> Resolved, that no woman of true delicacy would be willing in the presence of men to listen to the discussion of subjects that necessarily come under consideration of the students of medicine.
>
> Resolved, that we object to having the company of any female forced upon us, who is disposed to unsex herself, and to sacrifice her modesty by appearing with men in the lecture room.[14]

Elizabeth Blackwell (1821–1910) achieved the first major breakthrough for women in medicine. Although she had been admitted to the Geneva College of Medicine in New York by a mistake, Blackwell's perseverance and intelligence won her the respect of her fellow male students. She received her M.D. degree in 1849 and eventually established a clinic in New York City.

European women experienced difficulties similar to those of Elizabeth Blackwell. In Britain, Elizabeth Garret and Sophia Jex-Blake had to struggle for years before they were finally admitted to the practice of medicine. The unwillingness of medical schools to open their doors to women led to the formation of separate medical schools for women. The Female Medical College of Pennsylvania, established in 1850, was the first in the United States while the London School of Medicine for women was founded in 1874. But even after graduation from such institutions, women faced obstacles when they tried to practice as doctors. Many were denied licenses and hospitals often closed their doors to them. In Britain, Parliament finally capitulated to pressure and passed a bill in 1876 allowing women the right to take qualifying examinations. Soon women were entering medical schools in ever-larger numbers. By the 1890s, universities in Great Britain, Sweden, Denmark, Norway, Finland, Russia, and Belgium were admitting women to medical training and practice. Germany and Austria did not do so until after 1900. Even then, medical associations refused to accept women as equals in the medical profession. Women were not given full membership in the American Medical Association until 1915.

Science and the Study of Society

The importance of science in the nineteenth century perhaps made it inevitable that a scientific approach would be applied to the realm of human activity. Marx himself presented his view of history as a class struggle grounded in the material conditions of life as a "scientific" work of analysis. The attempt to apply the methods of science systematically to the study of society was perhaps most evident in the work of the Frenchman Auguste Comte (1798–1857). His major work, entitled *System of Positive Philosophy*, was published between 1837 and 1842, but had its real impact after 1850.

Comte created a system of "positive knowledge based upon a hierarchy of all the sciences. Mathematics was the foundation on which the physical sciences, earth sciences, and biological sciences were built. At the top was sociology, the science of human society, which for Comte incorporated economics, anthropology, history, and social psychology. Comte saw sociology's task as a difficult one. The discovery of the general laws of society would have to be based upon the collection and analysis of data on humans and their social environment. Although his schemes were often complex and dense, Comte played an important role in making science and materialism so popular in the mid-nineteenth century.

Realism in Literature and Art

The belief that the world should be viewed realistically, frequently expressed after 1850, was closely related to the materialistic outlook. Evident in the "politics of reality" of a Bismarck or Cavour, Realism became a movement in the literary and visual arts as well. The word *Realism* was first employed in 1850 to describe a new style of painting and soon spread to literature.

THE REALISTIC NOVEL

Realism has been more or less a component of literature throughout time, although the literary Realists of the mid-nineteenth century were distinguished by their deliberate rejection of Romanticism. The literary Realists wanted to deal with ordinary characters from actual life rather than Romantic heroes in unusual settings. They also sought to avoid flowery and sentimental language by using careful observation and accurate description, an approach that led them to eschew poetry in favor of prose and the novel. Realists often combined their interest in everyday life with a searching examination of social questions. Even then they tried not to preach but to allow their characters to speak for themselves. Although the French were preeminent in literary Realism, it proved to be international in scope.

The leading novelist of the 1850s and 1860s, the Frenchman Gustave Flaubert (1821–1880), perfected the Realist novel. His *Madame Bovary* (1857) was a straightforward description of barren and sordid provincial life in France. Emma Bovary, a woman of some vitality, is trapped in a marriage to a drab provincial doctor. Impelled by the images of romantic love she has read about in novels, she seeks the same thing for herself in adulterous love affairs. Unfulfilled, she is ultimately driven to suicide, unrepentant to the end for her lifestyle. Flaubert's hatred of bourgeois society was evident in his portrayal of middle-class hypocrisy and smugness. *Madame Bovary* so offended French middle-class sensibilities that the author was prosecuted—unsuccessfully—for public obscenity.

William Thackeray (1811–1863) wrote the opening manifesto of the Realist novel in Britain with his *Vanity Fair* in 1848. Subtitled *A Novel without a Hero*, Thackeray deliberately flaunted the Romantic conventions. A novel, Thackeray said, should "convey as strongly as possible the sentiment of reality as opposed to a tragedy or poem, which may be heroical." Perhaps the greatest of the Victorian novelists was Charles Dickens (1812–1870), whose realistic novels focusing on the lower and middle classes in Britain's early industrial age became extraordinarily successful. His descriptions of the urban poor and the brutalization of human life were vividly realistic (see the box on p. 808).

✦ **Gustave Courbet, *The Stonebreakers*.** Realism, largely developed by French painters, aimed at a lifelike portrayal of the daily activities of ordinary people. Gustave Courbet was the most famous of the Realist artists. As is evident in *The Stonebreakers*, he sought to portray things as they really appear. He shows an old road builder and his young assistant in their tattered clothes, engrossed in their dreary work of breaking stones to construct a road.

Realism: Charles Dickens and an Image of Hell on Earth

Charles Dickens was one of Britain's greatest novelists. While he realistically portrayed the material, social, and psychological milieu of his time, an element of Romanticism still pervaded his novels. This is evident in this selection from The Old Curiosity Shop *in which his description of the English mill town of Birmingham takes on the imagery of Dante's Hell.*

Charles Dickens, *The Old Curiosity Shop*

A long suburb of red brick houses,—some with patches of garden ground, where coal-dust and factory smoke darkened the shrinking leaves, and coarse rank flowers; and where the struggling vegetation sickened and sank under the hot breath of kiln and furnace, making them by its presence seem yet more blighting and unwholesome than in the town itself,—a long, flat, straggling suburb passed, they came by slow degrees upon a cheerless region, where not a blade of grass was seen to grow; where not a bud put forth its promise in the spring; where nothing green could live but on the surface of the stagnant pools, which here and there lay idly sweltering by the black roadside.

Advancing more and more into the shadow of this mournful place, its dark depressing influence stole upon their spirits, and filled them with a dismal gloom. On every side, and as far as they eye could see into the heavy distance, tall chimneys, crowding on each other, and presenting that endless repetition of the same dull, ugly form, which is the horror of oppressive dreams, poured out their plague of smoke, obscured the light, and made foul the melancholy air. On mounds of ashes by the wayside, sheltered only by a few rough boards, or rotten pent-house roofs, strange engines spun and writhed like tortured creatures; clanking their iron chains, shrieking in their rapid whirl from time to time as though in torment unendurable, and making the ground tremble with their agonies. Dismantled houses here and there appeared, tottering to the earth, propped up by fragments of others that had fallen down, unroofed, windowless, blackened, desolate, but yet inhabited. Men, women, children, wan in their looks and ragged in attire, tended the engines, fed their tributary fires, begged upon the road, or scowled half-naked from the doorless houses. Then came more of the wrathful monsters, whose like they almost seemed to be in their wildness and their untamed air, screeching and turning to the right and left, with the same interminable perspective of brick towers, never ceasing in their black vomit, blasting all things living or inanimate, shutting out the face of day, and closing in on all these horrors with a dense dark cloud.

But night-time in this dreadful spot!—night, when the smoke was changed to fire; when every chimney spurted up its flame; and places, that had been dark vaults all day, now shone red-hot, with figures moving to and fro within their blazing jaws, and calling to one another with hoarse cries—night, when the noise of every strange machine was aggravated by the darkness; when the people near them looked wilder and more savage; when bands of unemployed labourers paraded in the roads, or clustered by torchlight round their leaders, who told them in stern language of their wrongs, and urged them on by frightful cries and threats; when maddened men, armed with sword and firebrand, spurning the tears and prayers of women who would restrain them, rushed forth on errands of terror and destruction, to work no ruin half so surely as their own—night, when carts came rumbling by, filled with rude coffins (for contagious disease and death had been busy with the living crops); or when orphans cried, and distracted women shrieked and followed in their wake—night, when some called for bread, and some for drink to drown their cares; and some with tears, and some with staggering feet, and so with bloodshot eyes, went brooding home—night, which, unlike the night that Heaven sends on earth, brought with it no peace, nor quiet, nor signs of blessed sleep—who shall tell the terrors of the night to that young wandering child!

REALISM IN ART

In the first half of the nineteenth century, Romanticism in art had been paralleled by the classical school of painting, but both were superseded by the new mood of the mid-nineteenth century. In art, too, Realism became dominant after 1850, although Romanticism was by no means dead. Among the most important characteristics of Realism are a desire to depict the everyday life of ordinary people, whether peasants, workers, or prostitutes; an attempt at photographic realism; and an interest in the natural environment. The French became leaders in Realist painting.

Gustave Courbet (1819–1877) was the most famous artist of the Realist school. In fact, the word *Realism* was first coined in 1850 to describe one of his paintings. Courbet reveled in a realistic portrayal of everyday life. His subjects were factory workers, peasants, and the wives of saloon keepers. "I have never seen either angels or goddesses, so I am not interested in painting them," he exclaimed. One of his famous works, *The Stonebreakers*, painted in 1849, shows two road workers engaged in the deadening work of breaking stones to build a road. This representation of human misery was a scandal to those who objected to his "cult of ugliness." To Courbet, no subject was too ordinary, too harsh, or too ugly to interest him.

Jean-François Millet (1814–1875) was preoccupied with scenes from rural life, especially peasants laboring in the fields, although his Realism still contained an element of romantic sentimentality. In *The Sower*, a peasant, energetically scattering seeds in a field, becomes a symbol of new life and the symbiotic relationship between humans and nature. Millet made landscape and country life an important subject matter for French artists, but he, too, was criticized by his contemporaries for crude subject matter and unorthodox technique.

Music: The Twilight of Romanticism

The mid-nineteenth century witnessed the development of a new group of musicians known as the New German School. It emphasized emotional content rather than abstract form and championed new methods of using music to express literary or pictorial ideas.

The Hungarian-born composer Franz Liszt (1811–1886) best exemplifies the achievements of the New German School. A child prodigy, he established himself as an outstanding concert artist by the age of twelve. Between 1824 and 1827, Liszt embarked on a series of concert tours throughout France, England, and Switzerland before settling in Paris, where he became an idolized figure of the salons. Liszt's performances and his dazzling personality made him the most highly esteemed virtuoso of his age. He has been called the greatest pianist of all time and has been credited with introducing the concept of the modern piano recital.

Liszt's compositions consist mainly of piano pieces, although he composed in other genres as well, including sacred music. He invented the term "symphonic poem" to refer to his orchestral works, which did not strictly obey traditional forms and were generally based on a literary or pictorial idea. Under the guidance of Liszt and the New German School, Romantic music reached its peak.

Although Liszt was an influential mentor to a number of young composers, he was most closely associated with

◆ **Jean-François Millet, *The Sower*.** Jean-François Millet, another prominent French Realist painter, took a special interest in the daily activities of French peasants, although he tended to transform his peasants into heroic figures who dominated their environment. In *The Sower*, for example, despite his rough clothes, the peasant scattering seed into the newly plowed fields appears as a powerful figure, symbolizing the union of humans with the earth.

his eventual son-in-law Richard Wagner (1813–1883). Building on the advances made by Liszt and the New German School, Wagner ultimately realized the German desire for a truly national opera. Wagner was not only a composer, but also a propagandist and writer in support of his unique conception of dramatic music. Called both the culmination of the Romantic era and the beginning of the avant-garde, Wagner's music may certainly be described as a monumental development in classical music.

Believing that opera is the best form of artistic expression, Wagner transformed opera into "music drama" through his *Gesamtkunstwerk* ("total art work"), a musical composition for the theater in which music, acting, dance, poetry, and scenic design are synthesized into a harmonious whole. He abandoned the traditional divisions of opera, which interrupted the dramatic line of the work, and instead used a device called a leitmotiv, a recurring musical theme in which the human voice combined with the line of the orchestra instead of rising above it. His operas incorporate literally hundreds of leitmotivs in order to convey the story. For his themes, Wagner looked to myth and epic tales from the past. His most ambitious work was the *Ring of the Nibelung*, a series of four operas dealing with the mythical gods of the ancient German epic.

Conclusion

Between 1850 and 1871, the national state became the focus of people's loyalty. Wars, both foreign and civil, were fought to create unified nation-states. Political nationalism had emerged during the French revolutionary era and had become a powerful force of change during the first half of the nineteenth century, but its triumph came only after 1850. Tied initially to middle-class liberals, by the end of the nineteenth century it would have great appeal to the broad masses as well. In 1871, however, the political transformations stimulated by the force of nationalism were by no means complete. Significantly large minorities, especially in the polyglot empires controlled by the Austrians, Turks, and Russians, had not achieved the goal of their own national states. Moreover, the nationalism that had triumphed by 1871 was no longer the nationalism that had been closely identified with liberalism. Liberal nationalists had believed that unified nation-states would preserve individual rights and lead to a greater community of European peoples. Rather than unifying people, however, the new, loud and chauvinistic nationalism of the late nineteenth century divided them as the new national states became embroiled in bitter competition after 1871.

Europeans, however, were hardly aware of nationalism's dangers in 1871. The spread of industrialization and the wealth of scientific and technological achievements were sources of optimism, not pessimism. After the revolutionary and military upheavals of the mid-century decades, many Europeans undoubtedly believed that they stood on the verge of a new age of progress.

NOTES

1. Quoted in Robert Gildea, *Barricades and Borders: Europe 1800–1914* (Oxford, 1987), p. 176.
2. Quoted in Maurice Agulhon, *The Republican Experiment, 1848–1852* (Cambridge, 1983), p. 177.
3. Quoted in Raymond Grew, *A Sterner Plan for Italian Unity: The Italian National Society in the Risorgimento* (Princeton, N.J., 1963), p. 10.
4. Quoted in Otto Pflanze, *Bismarck and the Development of Germany: The Period of Unification, 1815–1871* (Princeton, N.J., 1963), p. 60.
5. Louis L. Snyder, ed., *Documents of German History* (New Brunswick, N.J., 1958), p. 202.
6. Quoted in Pflanze, *Bismarck and the Development of Germany*, p. 327.
7. Quoted in György Szabad, *Hungarian Political Trends between the Revolution and the Compromise, 1849–1867* (Budapest, 1977), p. 163.
8. Quoted in George L. Yaney, *The Systematization of Russian Government, 1711–1905* (Champaign, Ill., 1973), p. 241.
9. Quoted in Rondo Cameron, "Crédit Mobilier and the Economic Development of Europe," *Journal of Political Economy* 61 (1953): 470.
10. Karl Marx and Friedrich Engels, *The Communist Manifesto* (Harmondsworth, 1967), p. 79.
11. Ibid., pp. (in order of quotations), 79, 81, 82.
12. Quoted in David McLellan, *Karl Marx* (New York, 1975), p. 14.
13. Charles Darwin, *On the Origin of Species* (New York, 1872), 1:77, 79.
14. Quoted in Albert Lyons and R. Joseph Petrucelli, *Medicine: An Illustrated History* (New York, 1978), p. 569.

SUGGESTIONS FOR FURTHER READING

Three general surveys of the mid-century decades are N. Rich, *The Age of Nationalism and Reform, 1850–1890*, 2d ed. (New York, 1979); E. Hobsbawm, *The Age of Capital, 1845–1875* (London, 1975); and J. A. S. Grenville, *Europe Reshaped, 1848–1878* (London, 1976). In addition to the books listed for individual countries in Chapter 22 that also cover the material of this chapter, see H. Holborn, *A History of Modern Germany*, vol. 3, *1840–1945* (New York, 1969); G. Craig, *Germany, 1866–1945* (Oxford, 1981); the two detailed volumes of T. Zeldin, *France, 1848–1945* (Oxford, 1973–77); A. J. May, *The Habsburg Monarchy, 1867–1914* (Cambridge, Mass., 1951); and D. Read, *England, 1868–1914* (London, 1979).

For a good introduction to the French Second Empire, see A. Plessis, *The Rise and Fall of the Second Empire, 1852–1871*, trans. J. Mandelbaum (New York, 1985). Napoleon's role can be examined in W. H. C. Smith, *Napoleon III* (New York, 1972). On life in France during the reign of Napoleon III, see R. L. Williams, *Gaslight and Shadow: The World of Napoleon III* (New York, 1957). The Crimean War and its impact are examined in P. W. Schroeder, *Austria, Great Britain and the Crimean War: The Destruction of the European Concert* (Ithaca, N.Y., 1972).

The unification of Italy can best be examined in the works of D. M. Smith, *Victor Emmanuel, Cavour and the Risorgimento* (London, 1971); and *Cavour* (London, 1985). The unification of Germany can be pursued first in two good biographies of Bismarck, E. Crankshaw, *Bismarck* (New York, 1981); and G. O. Kent, *Bismarck and His Times* (Carbondale, Ill., 1978). T. S. Hamerow, *The Social Foundations of German Unification, 1858–1871* (Princeton, N.J., 1969) is good on the political implications of social changes in Germany. Also valuable is O. Pflanze, *Bismarck and the Development of Germany: The Period of Unification, 1815–1871* (Princeton, N.J., 1963). A classic on the role of the Prussian military is G. Craig, *The Politics of the Prussian Army* (New York, 1955). On the position of liberals in the unification of Germany, see J. J. Sheehan, *German Liberalism in the Nineteenth Century* (Chicago, 1978).

On the emancipation of the Russian serfs, see D. Field, *The End of Serfdom: Nobility and Bureaucracy in Russia, 1855–1861* (Cambridge, 1976); and T. Emmons, ed., *Emancipation of the Russian Serfs* (New York, 1970). On the 1867 Reform Act in Britain, see M. Cowling, *1867: Disraeli, Gladstone and Revolution* (London, 1967), while the evolution of British political parties in mid-century is examined in H. J. Hanham, *Elections and Party Management: Politics in the Time of Disraeli and Gladstone*, 2d ed. (London, 1978). On the background to the American Civil War, see D. Potter, *The Impending Crisis, 1845–1861* (New York, 1976); and M. Holt, *The Political Crisis of the 1850's* (New York, 1978). A good, brief biography of Lincoln is O. and L. Handlin, *Abraham Lincoln and the Union* (Boston, 1980). A good one-volume survey of the Civil War can be found in P. J. Parish, *The American Civil War* (New York, 1975).

In addition to the general works on economic development listed in Chapters 21 and 23, some specialized works on this period are worthwhile. These include P. O'Brien, *The New Economic History of the Railways* (New York, 1977); W. O. Henderson, *The Rise of German Industrial Power, 1834–1914* (Berkeley, 1975); and F. Crouzet, *The Victorian Economy* (London, 1982). On Marx there is the standard work by D. McLellan, *Karl Marx: His Life and Thought* (New York, 1974), but it can be supplemented by the interesting and comprehensive work by L. Kolakowski, *Main Currents of Marxism*, 3 vols. (Oxford, 1978).

For an introduction to the intellectual changes of the nineteenth century, see O. Chadwick, *The Secularization of the European Mind in the Nineteenth Century* (Cambridge, 1975). A detailed biography of Darwin can be found in R. W. Clark, *The Survival of Charles Darwin* (New York, 1984). On the popularization of Darwinism, see A. Kelly, *The Descent of Darwin* (Chapel Hill, N.C., 1981). For an introduction to the transformation of medical practices in the nineteenth century, see the appropriate chapters in E. H. Ackerknecht, *A Short History of Medicine*, rev. ed. (Baltimore, 1982); and A. S. Lyons and R. J. Petrucelli, *Medicine: An Illustrated History* (New York, 1978). On Realism, L. Nochlin, *Realism* (Harmondsworth, 1971) is a good introduction.

CHAPTER

24

Mass Society in an "Age of Progress," 1871–1894

In the late nineteenth century, Europe witnessed a dynamic age of material prosperity. With new industries, new sources of energy, and new goods, a Second Industrial Revolution transformed the human environment, dazzled Europeans, and led them to believe that their material progress meant human progress. Scientific and technological achievements, many naively believed, would improve humanity's condition and solve all human problems. The doctrine of progress became an article of great faith.

The new urban and industrial world created by the rapid economic changes of the nineteenth century led to the emergence of a mass society by the late nineteenth century. A mass society meant improvements for the lower classes who benefited from the extension of voting rights, a better standard of living, and mass education. It also brought mass leisure. New work patterns established the "weekend" as a distinct time of recreation and fun while new forms of mass transportation—railroads and streetcars—enabled even workers to make brief excursions to amusement parks. Coney Island was only eight miles from central New York City; Blackpool in England was a short train ride from nearby industrial towns. With their Ferris wheels and other daring rides that threw young men and women together, amusement parks offered a whole new world of entertainment. Thanks to the railroad, seaside resorts, once the preserve of the wealthy, also became accessible to more people for weekend visits, much to the disgust of one upper-class regular who complained about the new "day-trippers": "They swarm upon the beach, wandering listlessly about with apparently no other aim than to get a mouthful of fresh air." Enterprising entrepreneurs in resorts like Blackpool welcomed the masses of new visitors, however, and built piers laden with food, drink, and entertainment to serve them.

The coming of mass society also created new roles for the governments of European nation-states, which now fostered national loyalty, created mass armies by conscription, and took more responsibility for public

Formation of German Social Democratic Party   Britain's first public power station

First birth control clinic   Germany's social welfare legislation

Bell's invention of the telephone   First streetcar in Berlin

Emergence of mass newspapers   Compulsory primary education in France

The Paris Commune   Second ministry of Gladstone   Bismarck as German chancellor

Reign of Tsar Alexander III

health and housing measures in their cities. By 1871, the national state had become the focus of Europeans' lives. Within many of these nation-states, the growth of the middle class had led to the triumph of liberal practices: constitutional governments, parliaments, and principles of equality. The period after 1871 also witnessed the growth of political democracy as the right to vote was extended to all adult males; women, though, would still have to fight for the same political rights. With political democracy came a new mass politics and a new mass press. Both would become regular features of the twentieth century.

The Growth of Industrial Prosperity

At the heart of Europeans' belief in progress after 1871 was the stunning material growth produced by what historians have called the Second Industrial Revolution. The first Industrial Revolution had given rise to textiles, railroads, iron, and coal. In the second revolution, steel, chemicals, electricity, and petroleum led the way to new industrial frontiers.

New Products and New Markets

The first major change in industrial development after 1870 was the substitution of steel for iron. New methods of rolling and shaping steel made it useful in the construction of lighter, smaller, and faster machines and engines, as well as railways, ships, and armaments. In 1860, Great Britain, France, Germany, and Belgium

together produced 125,000 tons of steel; by 1913, the total was 32 million tons. Whereas in the early 1870s Britain had produced twice as much steel as Germany, by 1910, German production was double that of Great Britain. Both had been surpassed by the United States in 1890.

Great Britain also fell behind in the new chemical industry. A change in the method of making soda enabled France and Germany to take the lead in producing the alkalies used in the textile, soap, and paper industries. German laboratories soon overtook the British in the development of new organic chemical compounds, such as artificial dyes. By 1900, German firms had cornered 90 percent of the market for dye stuffs and also led in the development of photographic plates and film.

Electricity was a major new form of energy that proved to be of great value since it could be easily converted into other forms of energy, such as heat, light, and motion, and moved relatively effortlessly through space by means of transmitting wires. In the 1870s, the first commercially practical generators of electrical current were developed. By 1881, Britain had its first public power station. By 1910, hydroelectric power stations and coal-fired steam-generating plants enabled entire districts to be tied into a single power distribution system that provided a common source of power for homes, shops, and industrial enterprises.

Electricity spawned a whole new series of inventions. The invention of the lightbulb by the American Thomas Edison and the Briton Joseph Swan opened homes and cities to illumination by electric lights. A revolution in communications was fostered when Alexander Graham Bell invented the telephone in 1876 and

◆ **An Age of Progress.** Between 1871 and 1914, a Second Industrial Revolution led many Europeans to believe that they were living in an age of progress when most human problems would be solved by scientific achievements. This illustration is taken from a special issue of *The Illustrated London News* celebrating the Diamond Jubilee of Queen Victoria in 1897. On the left are scenes from 1837, when Victoria came to the British throne; on the right are scenes from 1897. The vivid contrast underscored the magazine's conclusion: "The most striking . . . evidence of progress during the reign is the ever increasing speed which the discoveries of physical science have forced into everyday life. Steam and electricity have conquered time and space to a greater extent during the last sixty years than all the preceding six hundred years witnessed."

Guglielmo Marconi sent the first radio waves across the Atlantic in 1901. Although most electricity was initially used for lighting, it was eventually put to use in transportation. The first electric railway was installed in Berlin in 1879. By the 1880s, streetcars and subways had appeared in major European cities and had begun to replace horse-drawn buses. Electricity also transformed the factory. Conveyor belts, cranes, machines, and machine tools could all be powered by electricity and located anywhere. In the first Industrial Revolution, coal had been the major source of energy. Countries without adequate coal supplies lagged behind in industrialization. Thanks to electricity, they could now enter the industrial age.

The development of the internal combustion engine had a similar effect. The first internal combustion engine, fired by gas and air, was produced in 1878. It proved unsuitable for widespread use as a source of power in transportation until the development of liquid fuels, namely, petroleum and its distilled derivatives. An oil-fired engine was made in 1897, and by 1902, the Hamburg-Amerika Line had switched from coal to oil on its new ocean liners. By the end of the nineteenth century, some naval fleets had been converted to oil burners as well.

The development of the internal combustion engine gave rise to the automobile and airplane. Gottlieb Daimler's invention of a light engine in 1886 was the key to the development of the automobile. In 1900, world production stood at 9,000 cars; by 1906, Americans had overtaken the initial lead of the French. It was an American, Henry Ford, who revolutionized the car industry with the mass production of the Model T. By 1916, Ford's factories were producing 735,000 cars a year. In the meantime an age of air transportation began with the Zeppelin airship in 1900. In 1903, at Kitty Hawk, North Carolina, the Wright brothers made the first flight in a fixed-wing plane powered by a gasoline engine. It took World War I to stimulate the aircraft industry, however, and the first regular passenger air service was not established until 1919.

The growth of industrial production depended upon the development of markets for the sale of manufactured goods. After 1870, the best foreign markets were already heavily saturated, forcing Europeans to take a renewed look at their domestic markets. As Europeans were the richest consumers in the world, those markets offered abundant possibilities. The dramatic population increases after 1870 (see Population Growth later in this chapter) were accompanied by a steady rise in national incomes. The leading industrialized nations, Britain and Germany, doubled or tripled their national incomes. Between 1850 and 1900, real wages increased by two-thirds in Britain and by one-third in Germany. As the prices of both food and manufactured goods declined due to lower transportation costs, Europeans could spend more on consumer products. Businesses soon perceived the value of using new techniques of mass

The Department Store and the Beginnings of Mass Consumerism

Domestic markets were especially important for the sale of the goods being turned out by Europe's increasing number of industrial plants. New techniques of mass marketing arose to encourage people to purchase the new consumer goods. The Parisians pioneered in the development of the department store, and this selection is taken from a contemporary's account of the growth of these stores in the French capital city.

E. Lavasseur, On Parisian Department Stores, 1907

It was in the reign of Louis-Philippe that department stores for fashion goods and dresses, extending to material and other clothing began to be distinguished. The type was already one of the notable developments of the Second Empire; it became one of the most important ones of the Third Republic. These stores have increased in number and several of them have become extremely large. Combining in their different departments all articles of clothing, toilet articles, furniture and many other ranges of goods, it is their special object so to combine all commodities as to attract and satisfy customers who will find conveniently together an assortment of a mass of articles corresponding to all their various needs. They attract customers by permanent display, by free entry into the shops, by periodic exhibitions, by special sales, by fixed prices, and by their ability to deliver the goods purchased to customers' homes, in Paris and to the provinces. Turning themselves into direct intermediaries between the producer and the consumer, even producing sometimes some of their articles in their own workshops, buying at lowest prices because of their large orders and because they are in a position to profit from bargains, working with large sums, and selling to most of their customers for cash only, they can transmit these benefits in lowered selling prices. They can even de-cide to sell at a loss, as an advertisement or to get rid of out-of-date fashions. Taking 5–6 percent on 100 million brings them in more than 20 percent would bring to a firm doing a turnover of 50,000 francs.

The success of these department stores is only possible thanks to the volume of their business and this volume needs considerable capital and a very large turnover. Now capital, having become abundant, is freely combined nowadays in large enterprises, although French capital has the reputation of being more wary of the risks of industry than of State or railway securities. On the other hand, the large urban agglomerations, the ease with which goods can be transported by the railways, the diffusion of some comforts to strata below the middle classes, have all favored these developments.

As example we may cite some figures relating to these stores, since they were brought to the notice of the public in the *Revue des Deux-Mondes*. . . .

Le Louvre, dating to the time of the extension of the rue de Rivoli under the Second Empire, did in 1893 a business of 120 million at a profit of 6.4 percent. *Le Bon-Marché*, which was a small shop when Mr. Boucicaut entered it in 1852, already did a business of 20 million at the end of the Empire. During the republic its new buildings were erected; Mme. Boucicaut turned it by her will into a kind of cooperative society, with shares and an ingenious organization; turnover reached 150 million in 1893, leaving a profit of 5 percent. . . .

According to the tax records of 1891, these stores in Paris, numbering 12, employed 1,708 persons and were rated on their site values at 2,159,000 francs; the largest had then 542 employees. These same stores had, in 1901, 9,784 employees; one of them over 2,000 and another over 1,600; their site value has doubled (4,089,000 francs).

marketing to sell the consumer goods made possible by the development of the steel and electrical industries. By bringing together a vast array of new products in one place, they created the department store (see the box above). The desire to own sewing machines, clocks, bicycles, electric lights, and typewriters rapidly created a new consumer ethic that became a crucial part of the modern economy.

Meanwhile, increased competition for foreign markets and the growing importance of domestic demand led to a reaction against free trade. To many industrial and political leaders, protective tariffs guaranteed domestic markets for the products of their own industries. Thus, after a decade of experimentation with free trade in the 1860s, Europeans returned to tariff protection. The Austro-Hungarian Empire was the first in 1874, followed by Russia in 1877, Germany in 1879, Italy in 1887, the United States in 1890, and France in 1892. Only Britain, Denmark, and the Netherlands refused to follow suit.

During this same period, cartels were being formed to decrease competition internally. In a cartel, independent enterprises worked together to control prices and fix production quotas, thereby restraining the kind of competition that led to reduced prices. Cartels were especially strong in Germany, where banks moved to protect their investments by eliminating the "anarchy of competition." German businessmen established cartels in potash, coal, steel, and chemicals. Founded in 1893, the Rhenish-Westphalian Coal Syndicate controlled 98 percent of Germany's coal production by 1904.

The formation of cartels was paralleled by a move toward ever-larger manufacturing plants, especially in the iron and steel, machinery, heavy electrical equipment, and chemical industries. Although evident in Britain, France, and Belgium, the trend was most pronounced in Germany. Between 1882 and 1907, the number of people working in German factories with over 1,000 employees rose from 205,000 to 879,000. This growth in the size of industrial plants led to pressure for greater efficiency in factory production at the same time that competition led to demands for greater economy. The result was a desire to streamline or rationalize production as much as possible. One way to accomplish this was by cutting labor costs through the mechanization of transport within plants, such as using electric cranes to move materials. More importantly, the development of precision tools enabled manufacturers to produce interchangeable parts, which, in turn, led to the creation of the assembly line for production. First used in the United States for small arms and clocks, the assembly line had moved to Europe by 1850. In the last half of the nineteenth century, it was primarily used in manufacturing nonmilitary goods, such as sewing machines, typewriters, bicycles, and finally the automobile. Principles of scientific management were also introduced by 1900 to maximize workers' efficiency.

The emergence of protective tariffs and cartels was clearly a response to the growth of the multinational industrial system. Economic competition intensified the political rivalries of the age. The growth of the national state, which had seemed to be the answer to old problems in the mid-nineteenth century, now seemed to be creating new ones.

New Patterns in an Industrial Economy

The Second Industrial Revolution played a role in the emergence of basic economic patterns that have characterized much of modern European economic life. Al-

though we have described the period after 1871 as an age of material prosperity, recessions and crises were still very much a part of economic life. Although some historians have questioned the appropriateness of the title Great Depression for the period from 1873 to 1895, Europeans did experience a series of economic crises during those years. Prices, especially those of agricultural products, fell dramatically. Slumps in the business cycle reduced profits although economic recession occurred at different times in different countries. France and Britain, for example, sank into depression in the 1880s while Germany and the United States were recovering from their depression of the 1870s. After 1895, however, until World War I, Europe overall experienced an economic boom and achieved a level of prosperity that encouraged people later to look back to that era as *la belle époque*—a golden age in European civilization.

After 1870, Germany replaced Great Britain as the industrial leader of Europe. Already in the 1890s, Germany's superiority was evident in new areas of manufacturing, such as organic chemicals and electrical equipment, and increasingly apparent in its ever-greater share of worldwide trade. Why had industrial leadership passed from Britain to Germany?

Britain's early lead in industrialization gave it an established industrial plant and made it more difficult to shift to the new techniques of the Second Industrial Revolution. As later entrants to the industrial age, the Germans could build the latest and most efficient industrial plant. British entrepreneurs made the situation worse by their tendency to be suspicious of innovations and their reluctance to invest in new plants and industries. As one manufacturer remarked: "One wants to be thoroughly convinced of the superiority of a new method before condemning as useless a large plant that has hitherto done good service."[1] German managers, on the other hand, were accustomed to change, and the formation of large cartels encouraged German banks to provide enormous sums for investment. Then, too, unlike the Germans, the British were not willing to encourage formal scientific and technical education.

After 1870, the relationship of science and technology grew closer. Newer fields of industrial activity, such as organic chemistry and electrical engineering, required more scientific knowledge than the commonsense tinkering once employed by amateur inventors. Companies began to invest capital in laboratory equipment for their own research or hired scientific consultants for advice. Nowhere was the relationship between science and technology more apparent than in Germany. In 1899, German technical schools were allowed to award doctorate degrees, and by 1900, they were turning out 3,000 to 4,000 graduates a year. Many of these graduates made their way into industrial firms.

The struggle for economic (and political) supremacy between Great Britain and Germany should not cause us to overlook the other great polarization of the age. By 1900, Europe was divided into two economic zones. Great Britain, Belgium, France, the Netherlands, Germany, the western part of the Austro-Hungarian Empire, and northern Italy constituted an advanced industrial-ized core that had a high standard of living, decent systems of transportation, and relatively healthy and educated peoples. Another part of Europe, the backward and little industrialized area to the south and east, consisting of southern Italy, most of Austria-Hungary, Spain, Portugal, the Balkan kingdoms, and Russia, was still largely agricultural and relegated by the industrial countries to the function of providing food and raw materials. The presence of Romanian oil, Greek olive oil, and Serbian pigs and prunes in western Europe

Map 24.1 The Industrial Regions of Europe by 1914.

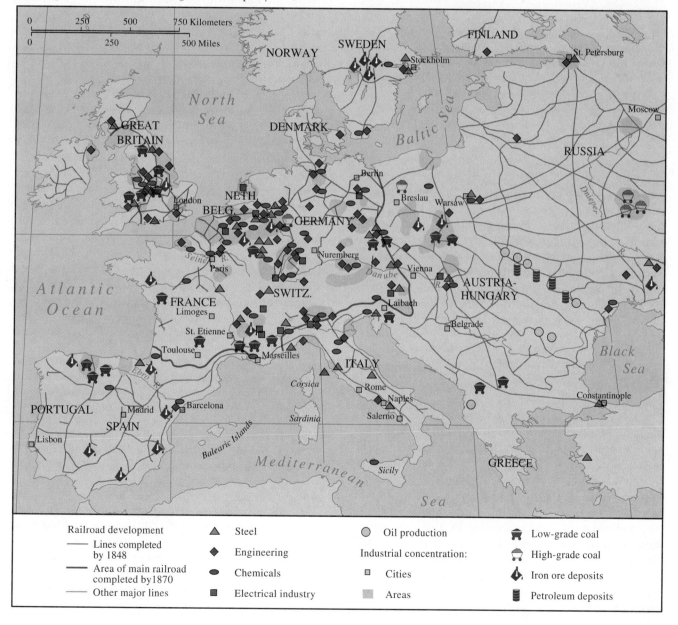

Railroad development		Steel		Oil production		Low-grade coal
— Lines completed by 1848		Engineering				High-grade coal
— Area of main railroad completed by 1870		Chemicals	Industrial concentration:	Cities		Iron ore deposits
— Other major lines		Electrical industry		Areas		Petroleum deposits

◆ **New Jobs for Women: The Telephone Exchange.** The invention of the telephone in 1876 soon led to its widespread use. As is evident from this illustration of a telephone exchange in Paris in 1904, most of the telephone operators were women. This was but one of a number of new job opportunities for women created by the Second Industrial Revolution.

served as reminders of an economic division of Europe that continued well into the twentieth century.

The growth of an industrial economy also led to new patterns for European agriculture. An abundance of grain and lower transportation costs caused the prices of farm commodities to plummet. Some countries responded with tariff barriers against lower priced foodstuffs. Where agricultural labor was scarce and hence expensive, as in Britain and Germany, landowners introduced machines for threshing and harvesting. The slump in grain prices also led some countries to specialize in other food products. Denmark, for example, exported eggs, butter, and cheese while sugar beets predominated in Bohemia and northern France, fruit in Mediterranean countries, and wine in Spain and Italy. This age also witnessed the introduction of chemical fertilizers. While large estates could make these adjustments easily, individual small farmers could not afford them and formed farm cooperatives that provided capital for making improvements and purchasing equipment and fertilizer.

The economic developments of the late nineteenth century, combined with the transportation revolution that saw the growth of marine transport and railroads, also fostered a true world economy. By 1900, Europeans were importing beef and wool from Argentina and Australia, coffee from Brazil, nitrates from Chile, iron ore from Algeria, and sugar from Java. European capital was also invested abroad to develop railways, mines, electrical power plants, and banks. High rates of return,

such as 11.3 percent on Latin American banking shares that were floated in London, provided plenty of incentive. Of course, foreign countries also provided markets for the surplus manufactured goods of Europe. With its capital, industries, and military might, Europe dominated the world economy by the end of the nineteenth century.

Women and Work: New Job Opportunities

The Second Industrial Revolution had an enormous impact on the position of women in the labor market. During the course of the nineteenth century, considerable controversy erupted over a woman's "right to work." Working-class organizations tended to reinforce the underlying ideology of domesticity; women should remain at home to bear and nurture children and should not be allowed in the industrial workforce. Working-class men argued that keeping women out of industrial work would ensure the moral and physical well-being of families. In reality, keeping women out of the industrial workforce simply made it easier to exploit them when they needed income to supplement their husbands' wages or to support their families when their husbands were unemployed. The desperate need to work at times forced women to do marginal work at home or labor as pieceworkers in sweatshops. "Sweating" referred to the subcontracting of piecework usually, but not exclusively, in the tailoring trades; it was done at home since it required few skills or equipment. Pieceworkers were poorly paid and worked long hours. The poorest paid jobs for the cheapest goods were called "slop work." In this description of the room of a London slopper, we see how precarious her position was:

> I then directed my steps to the neighborhood of Drury-lane, to see a poor woman who lived in an attic on one of the closest courts in that quarter. On the table was a quarter of an ounce of tea. Observing my eye to rest upon it, she told me it was all she took. "Sugar," she said, "I broke myself of long ago; I couldn't afford it. A cup of tea, a piece of bread, and an onion is generally all I have for my dinner, and sometimes I haven't even an onion, and then I sops my bread."[2]

Often excluded from factories and in need of income, many women had no choice but to work for the pitiful wages of the sweated industries.

After 1870, however, new job opportunities for women became available. Although the growth of heavy industry in the mining, metallurgy, engineering, chemicals, and electrical sectors meant fewer jobs for women in manufacturing, the development of larger industrial plants and the expansion of government services created a large number of service or white-collar jobs. The increased demand for white-collar workers at relatively low wages coupled with a shortage of male workers led employers to hire women. Big businesses and retail shops needed clerks, typists, secretaries, file clerks, and sales clerks. The expansion of government services created opportunities for women to be secretaries and telephone operators and to take jobs in health and social services. Compulsory education necessitated more teachers while the development of modern hospital services opened the way for an increase in nurses.

Many of the new white-collar jobs were by no means exciting. Their work was routine and, except for teaching and nursing, required few skills beyond basic literacy. Although there was little hope for advancement, these jobs had distinct advantages for the daughters of the middle classes and especially the upward-aspiring working classes. For some middle-class women, the new jobs offered freedom from the domestic patterns expected of them. Most of the jobs, however, were filled by working-class females who saw them as an opportunity to escape from the "dirty" work of the lower-class world. Studies in France and Britain indicate that the increase in white-collar jobs did not lead to a rise in the size of the female labor force, but only to a shift from industrial jobs to the white-collar sector of the economy.

Despite the new job opportunities, many lower-class women were forced to become prostitutes to survive. The rural, working-class girls who flocked into the cities in search of new opportunities often were highly vulnerable. Employment was unstable and wages were low. No longer protected by family or village community and church, some girls faced only one grim alternative—prostitution. In Paris, London, and many other large cities with transient populations, thousands of prostitutes plied their trade. One journalist estimated that there were 60,000 prostitutes in London in 1885. Most prostitutes were active for a short time, usually from late teens through early twenties. Many eventually rejoined the regular workforce or married when they could.

In most European countries, prostitution was licensed and regulated by government and municipal authorities. Although the British government provided minimal regulation of prostitution, it did attempt to enforce the Contagious Diseases Acts in the 1870s and 1880s by giving authorities the right to examine prostitutes for venereal disease. Prostitutes with the disease were confined for some time to special institutions called lock hospitals, where they were given moral instruction.

Opposition to the Contagious Diseases Acts by middle-class female reformers, who objected to laws that punished women and not men who suffered from venereal disease, led to the repeal of the acts in 1886.

Organizing the Working Classes

The desire to improve their working and living conditions led many industrial workers to form political parties and labor unions. One of the most important of the working-class or socialist parties was formed in Germany in 1875. Under the direction of its two Marxist leaders, Wilhelm Liebknecht and August Bebel, the German Social Democratic Party (SPD) espoused revolutionary Marxist rhetoric while organizing itself as a mass political party competing in elections for the Reichstag (the German parliament). Once in the Reichstag, SPD delegates worked to enact legislation to improve the condition of the working class. As August Bebel explained, "Pure negation would not be accepted by the voters. The masses demand that something should be done for today irrespective of what will happen on the morrow."[3] Despite government efforts to destroy it (see Central and Eastern Europe: Persistence of the Old Order later in this chapter), the German Social Democratic Party continued to grow. In 1890, it received 1.5 million votes and thirty-five seats in the Reichstag. When it received 4 million votes in the 1912 elections, it became the largest single party in Germany.

Socialist parties also emerged in other European states, although none proved as successful as the German Social Democrats. France had a variety of socialist parties, including a Marxist one. The leader of French socialism, Jean Jaurès (1859–1914), was an independent socialist who looked to the French revolutionary tradition rather than Marxism to justify revolutionary socialism. In 1905, the French socialist parties succeeded in unifying themselves into a single mostly Marxist-oriented socialist party. Social Democratic Parties on the German model were founded in Belgium, Austria, Hungary, Bulgaria, Poland, Romania, and the Netherlands before 1900. A Marxist Social Democratic Labor Party had also been organized in Russia by 1898.

As the socialist parties grew, agitation for an international organization that would strengthen their position against international capitalism also grew. In 1889, leaders of the various socialist parties formed the Second International, which was organized as a loose association of national groups. While the Second International took some coordinated actions—May Day (May 1), for example, was made an international labor day to be marked by strikes and mass labor demonstrations—differences often wreaked havoc at the congresses of the organization. Two issues proved particularly divisive: revisionism and nationalism.

Some Marxists believed in a pure Marxism that accepted the imminent collapse of capitalism and the need for socialist ownership of the means of production. The guiding light of the German Social Democrats, August Bebel, confided to another socialist that "Every night I go to sleep with the thought that the last hour of bourgeois society strikes soon." Earlier, Bebel had said, "I am convinced that the fulfillment of our aims is so close, that there are few in this hall who will not live to see the day."[4] But a severe challenge to this orthodox Marxist position arose in the form of revisionism.

✦ **"Proletarians of the World, Unite."** To improve their working and living conditions, many industrial workers, inspired by the ideas of Karl Marx, joined working-class or socialist parties. Pictured here is a socialist-sponsored poster that proclaims in German the closing words of *The Communist Manifesto:* "Proletarians of the World, Unite!"

Most prominent among the revisionists was Eduard Bernstein (1850–1932), a member of the German Social Democratic Party who had spent years in exile in Britain where he had been influenced by moderate English socialism and the British parliamentary system. In 1899, Bernstein challenged Marxist orthodoxy with a book entitled *Evolutionary Socialism* in which he argued that some of Marx's ideas had turned out to be quite wrong (see the box on p. 821). The capitalist system had not broken down, said Bernstein, nor did its demise seem near. Contrary to Marx's assertion, the middle class was actually expanding, not declining. At the same time, the proletariat was not sinking further down; instead, its position was improving as workers experienced a higher standard of living. In the face of this reality, Bernstein discarded Marx's emphasis on class struggle and revolution. The workers, he asserted, must continue to organize in mass political parties and even work together with the other advanced elements in a nation to bring about change. With the extension of the right to vote, workers were in a better position than ever to achieve their aims by democratic channels. Evolution by democratic means, not revolution, would achieve the desired goal of socialism. German and French socialist leaders, as well as the Second International, condemned revisionism as heresy and opportunism. But many socialist parties, including the German Social Democrats, while spouting revolutionary slogans, continued to practice Bernstein's revisionist, gradualist approach.

A second divisive issue for international socialism was nationalism. Marx and Engels had said that "the working men have no country" and that "national differences and antagonisms between peoples are daily more and more vanishing, owing to the development of the bourgeoisie."[5] They proved drastically wrong. Congresses of the Second International passed resolutions in 1907 and 1910 advocating joint action by workers of different countries to avert war, but provided no real machinery to implement the resolutions. In truth, socialist parties varied from country to country and remained tied to national concerns and issues. Socialist leaders always worried that in the end national loyalties might outweigh class loyalties among the masses. When World War I came in 1914, not only the working-class masses, but even many of their socialist party leaders, supported the war efforts of their national governments. Nationalism had proved a much more powerful force than socialism.

Workers also formed trade unions to improve their working conditions. Attempts to organize the workers did not come until the last two decades of the nine-

The Voice of Evolutionary Socialism: Eduard Bernstein

The German Marxist Eduard Bernstein was regarded as the foremost late nineteenth-century theorist of Marxist revisionism. In his book, Evolutionary Socialism, *Bernstein argued that Marx had made some fundamental mistakes and that socialists needed to stress cooperation and evolution rather than class conflict and revolution.*

Eduard Bernstein, *Evolutionary Socialism*

It has been maintained in a certain quarter that the practical deductions from my treatises would be the abandonment of the conquest of political power by the proletariat organized politically and economically. That is quite an arbitrary deduction, the accuracy of which I altogether deny.

I set myself against the notion that we have to expect shortly a collapse of the bourgeois economy, and that social democracy should be induced by the prospect of such an imminent, great, social catastrophe to adapt its tactics to that assumption. That I maintain most emphatically.

The adherents of this theory of a catastrophe, base it especially on the conclusions of the *Communist Manifesto*. This is a mistake in every respect.

The theory which the *Communist Manifesto* sets forth of the evolution of modern society was correct as far as it characterized the general tendencies of that evolution. But it was mistaken in several special deductions, above all in the estimate of the time the evolution would take. . . . But it is evident that if social evolution takes a much greater period of time than was assumed, it must also take upon itself forms and lead to forms that were not foreseen and could not be foreseen then.

Social conditions have not developed to such an acute opposition of things and classes as is depicted in the *Manifesto*. It is not only useless, it is the greatest folly to attempt to conceal this from ourselves. The number of members of the possessing classes is today not smaller but larger. The enormous increase of social wealth is not accompanied by a decreasing number of large capitalists but by an increasing number of capitalists of all degrees. The middle classes change their character but they do not disappear from the social scale. . . .

In all advanced countries we see the privileges of the capitalist bourgeoisie yielding step by step to democratic organizations. Under the influence of this, and driven by the movement of the working classes which is daily becoming stronger, a social reaction has set in against the exploiting tendencies of capital, a counteraction which, although it still proceeds timidly and feebly, yet does exist, and is always drawing more departments of economic life under its influence. Factory legislation, the democratizing of local government, and the extension of its area of work, the freeing of trade unions and systems of cooperative trading from legal restrictions, the consideration of standard conditions of labor in the work undertaken by public authorities—all these characterize this phase of the evolution.

But the more the political organizations of modern nations are democratized the more the needs and opportunities of great political catastrophes are diminished. . . . But is the conquest of political power by the proletariat simply to be by a political catastrophe? Is it to be the appropriation and utilization of the power of the State by the proletariat exclusively against the whole non-proletarian world? . . .

No one has questioned the necessity for the working classes to gain the control of government. The point at issue is between the theory of a social cataclysm and the question whether, with the given social development in Germany and the present advanced state of its working classes in the towns and the country, a sudden catastrophe would be desirable in the interest of the social democracy. I have denied it and deny it again, because in my judgment a greater security for lasting success lies in a steady advance than in the possibilities offered by a catastrophic crash.

---

teenth century after unions had won the right to strike in the 1870s. Strikes proved necessary to achieve the workers' goals. A walkout by female workers in the match industry in 1888 and by dock workers in London the following year led to the establishment of trade union organizations for both groups. By 1900, two million workers were enrolled in British trade unions, and by the outbreak of World War I, this number had risen to between three and four million, although this was still less than one-fifth of the total workforce.

Trade unions failed to develop as quickly on the Continent as they had in Britain. In France, the trade union movement was from the beginning closely tied to the socialist ideology. As there were a number of French socialist parties, the socialist trade unions remained badly splintered. Not until 1895 did French unions create a national organization called the General Confederation of Labor. Its decentralization and failure to include some of the more important individual unions, however, left it a weak and ineffective movement.

German trade unions, also closely attached to political parties, were first formed in the 1860s. Although there were liberal trade unions comprised of skilled craftsmen and Catholic or Christian trade unions, the largest German trade unions were those of the socialists. By 1899, even the latter had accepted the practice of collective bargaining with employers. As strikes and collective bargaining achieved successes, German workers were increasingly inclined to forgo revolution for gradual improvements. By 1914, its three million members made the German trade union movement the second largest in Europe after Great Britain's. Almost 85 percent of these three million belonged to socialist unions. Trade unions in the rest of Europe had varying degrees of success, but by the beginning of World War I, they had made considerable progress in bettering both the living and the working conditions of the laboring classes.

THE ANARCHIST ALTERNATIVE

Despite the revolutionary rhetoric, socialist parties and trade unions gradually became less radical in pursuing their goals. Indeed, this lack of revolutionary fervor drove some people from Marxian socialism into anarchism, a movement that was especially prominent in less industrialized and less democratic countries. The growth of universal male suffrage in Great Britain, France, and Germany had led workers there to believe that they could acquire tangible benefits by elections, not by revolution. These democratic channels were not open in other countries where revolutionary violence seemed the only alternative.

Initially, anarchism was not a violent movement. Early anarchists believed that people were inherently good but had been corrupted by the state and society. True freedom could only be achieved by abolishing the state and all existing social institutions. In the second half of the nineteenth century, however, anarchists in Spain, Portugal, Italy, and Russia began to advocate using radical means to accomplish this goal. The Russian Michael Bakunin, for example, believed that small groups of well-trained, fanatical revolutionaries could perpetrate so much violence that the state and all its institutions would disintegrate. To revolutionary anarchists, that would usher in the anarchist Golden Age. The Russian anarchist Lev Aleshker wrote shortly before his execution:

Slavery, poverty, weakness, and ignorance—the external fetters of man—will be broken. Man will be at the center of nature. The earth and its products will serve everyone dutifully. Weapons will cease to be a measure of strength and gold a measure of wealth; the strong will be those who are bold and daring in the conquest of nature, and riches will be the things that are useful. Such a world is called "Anarchy." It will have no castles, no place for masters and slaves. Life will be open to all. Everyone will take what he needs—this is the anarchist ideal. And when it comes about, men will live wisely and well. The masses must take part in the construction of this paradise on earth.[6]

After Bakunin's death in 1876, anarchist revolutionaries used assassinations as their primary instrument of terror. The list of victims of anarchist assassins at the turn of the century included a Russian tsar (1881), a president of the French Republic (1894), the king of Italy (1900), and a president of the United States (1901). Despite anarchist hopes, these states did not collapse.

The Emergence of Mass Society

The new patterns of industrial production, mass consumption, and working-class organization that we identify with the Second Industrial Revolution were only one aspect of the new mass society that emerged in Europe after 1870. A larger and vastly improved urban environment, new patterns of social structure, gender issues, mass education, and mass leisure were also important features of Europe's mass society.

Population Growth

The European population increased dramatically between 1850 and 1910, rising from 270 million to over 460 million by 1910 (see Table 24.1). Between 1850 and 1880, the main cause of the population increase was a rising birthrate, in least in western Europe, but after 1880, a noticeable decline in death rates largely explains the increase in population. Although the causes of this decline have been debated, two major factors—medical discoveries and environmental conditions—stand out. Some historians have stressed the importance of developments in medical science. Smallpox vaccinations, for example, were compulsory in many European countries by the mid-1850s. More important were improvements in the urban environment in the last half of the nineteenth century that greatly decreased fatalities from such infectious diseases as diarrhea, dysentery, typhoid fever, and cholera, which had been spread through contaminated water supplies and improper elimination of sewage. Improved nutrition also made a significant difference in the health of the population. The increase in agricultural productivity combined with improvements in transportation facilitated the shipment of food supplies from areas of surplus to regions with poor harvests. Better nutrition and food hygiene were especially instrumental in the decline in infant mortality by 1900. The pasteurization of milk reduced intestinal disorders that had been a major cause of infant deaths. Although growing agricultural and industrial prosperity supported an increase in European population, it could not do so indefinitely, especially in areas that had little industrialization and a severe problem of rural overpopulation. Some of the excess labor from underdeveloped areas migrated to the industrial regions of Europe. By 1913, more than 400,000 Poles were working in the heavily industrialized Ruhr region of western Germany while thousands of Italian laborers had migrated to France. The industrialized regions of Europe, however, were not able to absorb the entire surplus population of heavily agricultural regions like southern Italy, Spain, Hungary, and Romania, where the land could not support the growing numbers of people. A booming American economy after 1898 and cheap shipping fares after 1900 led to mass emigration from southern and eastern Europe to America at the beginning of the twentieth century. In 1880, about 500,000 people left Europe each year on average; between 1906 and 1910, annual departures increased to 1,300,000, many of them from southern and eastern Europe. Altogether, between 1846 and 1932, probably 60 million Europeans left Europe, half of them bound for the United States and most of the rest for Canada or Latin America (see Table 24.2).

It was not only economic motives that caused people to leave eastern Europe. Migrants from Austria and Hungary, for example, were not the dominant nationalities, the Germans and Magyars, but mostly their oppressed minorities, such as Poles, Slovaks, Serbs, Croats, Romanians, and Jews. Between 1880 and 1914, 3,500,000 Poles from Russia, Austria, and Germany went to the United States. Jews, who were severely persecuted, constituted 40 percent of the Russian emigrants to the United States between 1900 and 1913 and almost 12 percent of all emigrants to the United States during the first five years of the twentieth century.

Transformation of the Urban Environment

One of the most important consequences of industrialization and the population explosion of the nineteenth

❖ Table 24.1   European Populations, 1851–1911

	1851	1881	1911
England and Wales	17,928,000	25,974,000	36,070,000
Scotland	2,889,000	3,736,000	4,761,000
Ireland	6,552,000	5,175,000	4,390,000
France	35,783,000	37,406,000	39,192,000
Germany	33,413,000	45,234,000	64,926,000
Belgium	4,530,000	5,520,000	7,424,000
Netherlands	3,309,000	4,013,000	5,858,000
Denmark	1,415,000	1,969,000	2,757,000
Norway	1,490,000	1,819,000	2,392,000
Sweden	3,471,000	4,169,000	5,522,000
Spain	15,455,000	16,622,000	19,927,000
Portugal	3,844,000	4,551,000	5,958,000
Italy	24,351,000	28,460,000	34,671,000
Switzerland	2,393,000	2,846,000	3,753,000
Austria	17,535,000	22,144,000	28,572,000
Hungary	18,192,000	15,739,000	20,886,000
Russia	68,500,000	97,700,000	160,700,000
Romania		4,600,000	7,000,000
Bulgaria		2,800,000	4,338,000
Greece		1,679,000	2,632,000
Serbia		1,700,000	2,912,000

Source: B. R. Mitchell, *European Historical Statistics, 1750–1970* (1975).

century was urbanization. In the course of the nineteenth century, urban dwellers came to make up an ever-increasing percentage of the European population. In 1800, they constituted 40 percent of the population in Britain, 25 percent in France and Germany, and only 10 percent in eastern Europe. By 1914, urban inhabitants had increased to 80 percent of the population in Britain, 45 percent in France, 60 percent in Germany, and 30 percent in eastern Europe. The size of cities also expanded dramatically, especially in industrialized countries. In 1800, there were 21 European cities with populations over 100,000; by 1900, there were 147. Between 1800 and 1900, London's population grew from 960,000 to 6,500,000 and Berlin's from 172,000 to 2,700,000.

Urban populations grew faster than the general population primarily because of the vast migration from rural areas to cities. People were driven from the countryside to the cities by sheer economic necessity—unemployment, land hunger, and physical want. Urban centers offered something positive as well, usually mass employment in factories and later in service trades and professions. But cities also grew faster in the second half of the nineteenth century because health and living conditions in them were improving.

❖ **Table 24.2** European Emigration, 1876–1910 (Average Annual Emigration to Non-European Countries per 100,000 Population)

	1876–80	1881–85	1886–90	1891–95	1896–1900	1901–5	1906–10
Europe	94	196	213	185	147	271	322
Ireland	650	1,422	1,322	988	759	743	662
Great Britain	102	174	162	119	88	127	172
Denmark	157	380	401	338	117	292	275
Norway	432	1,105	819	597	312	903	746
Sweden	301	705	759	587	249	496	347
Germany	108	379	207	163	47	50	44
Belgium			86	50	23	57	69
Netherlands	32	136	111	76	25	45	58
France	8	14	49	14	13	12	12
Spain		280	437	434	446	391	758
Portugal	258	356	423	609	417	464	694
Italy	396	542	754	842	974	1,706	1,938
Austria	48	90	114	182	182	355	469
Hungary		92	156	134	205	437	616
Russia	6	13	42	47	32	63	67

Source: Robert Gildea, *Barricades and Borders: Europe, 1800–1914* (Oxford, 1987), p. 283.

In the 1840s, a number of urban reformers, such as Edwin Chadwick in England (see Chapter 21) and Rudolf Virchow and Solomon Neumann in Germany, had pointed to filthy living conditions as the primary cause of epidemic disease and urged sanitary reforms to correct the problem. Soon, legislative acts created boards of health that brought governmental action to bear on public heath issues. Urban medical officers and building inspectors were authorized to inspect dwellings for public health hazards. New building regulations made it more difficult for private contractors to build shoddy housing. The Public Health Act of 1875 in Britain, for example, prohibited the construction of new buildings without running water and an internal drainage system. For the first time in Western history, the role of municipal governments had been expanded to include detailed regulations for the improvement of the living conditions of urban dwellers.

Essential to the public health of the modern European city was the ability to bring clean water into the city and to expel sewage from it. The accomplishment of those two tasks was a major engineering feat in the last half of the nineteenth century. The problem of fresh water was solved by a system of dams and reservoirs that stored the water and aqueducts and tunnels that carried it from the countryside to the city and into individual dwellings. By the second half of the nineteenth century, regular private baths became accessible to more people as gas heaters in the 1860s and later electric heaters made hot baths possible. Even the shower had appeared by the 1880s. The treatment of sewage was also improved by building mammoth underground pipes that carried raw sewage far from the city for disposal. In the late 1860s, a number of German cities began to construct sewer systems. Frankfurt began its program after a lengthy public campaign enlivened by the slogan "from the toilet to the river in half an hour." London devised a system of five enormous sewers that discharged their loads twelve miles from the city where the waste was chemically treated. Unfortunately, in many places new underground sewers simply continued to discharge their raw sewage into what soon became highly polluted lakes and rivers. Nevertheless, the development of pure water and sewerage systems dramatically improved the public health of European cities by 1914.

Middle-class reformers who denounced the unsanitary living conditions of the working class also focused on their housing needs. Overcrowded, disease-ridden slums were viewed as dangerous not only to physical health, but to the political and moral health of the entire nation. V. A. Huber, the foremost early German housing reformer, wrote in 1861: "Certainly it would not be too much to say that the home is the communal embodiment of family life. Thus the purity of the

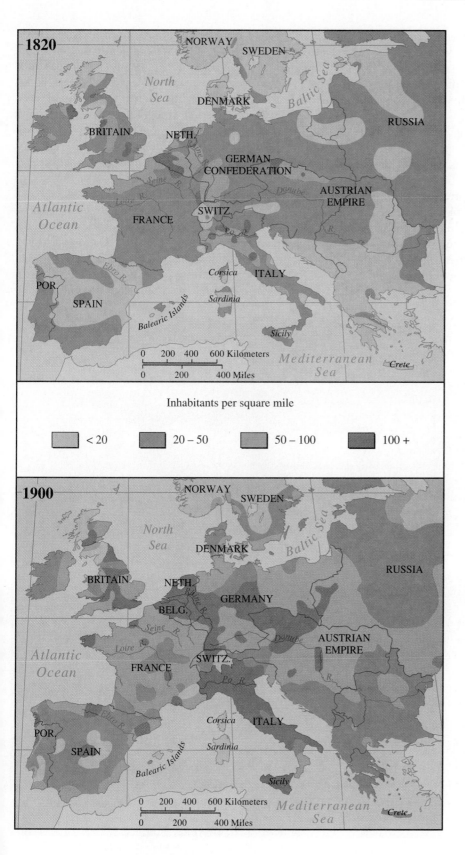

dwelling is almost as important for the family as is the cleanliness of the body for the individual."[7] To Huber, good housing was a prerequisite for stable family life, and without stable family life one of the "stabilizing elements of society" would be dissolved, much to society's detriment.

Early efforts to attack the housing problem emphasized the middle-class, liberal belief in the efficacy of private enterprise. Reformers such as Huber believed that the construction of model dwellings renting at a reasonable price would force other private landlords to elevate their housing standards. A fine example of this approach was the work of Octavia Hill, granddaughter of a celebrated social reformer (see the box on p. 827). With the financial assistance of a friend, she rehabilitated some old dwellings and constructed new ones to create housing for 3,500 tenants.

Other wealthy reformer-philanthropists took a different approach to the housing problem. In 1887, Lord Leverhulme began construction of a model village called Port Sunlight outside Liverpool for the workers at his soap factory. Port Sunlight offered pleasant living conditions in the belief that good housing would ensure a healthy and happy workforce. Yet another approach was the garden city. At the end of the nineteenth century, Ebenezer Howard founded the British garden city movement, which advocated the construction of new towns separated from each other by open country that would provide the recreational areas, fresh air, and sense of community that would encourage healthy family life. Letchward Garden City, started in 1903, was the first concrete result of Howard's theory.

As the number and size of cities continued to mushroom, governments by the 1880s came to the conclu-

♦ **The City at Night.** Industrialization and the population explosion of the nineteenth century fostered the growth of cities. At the same time, technological innovations dramatically improved living conditions in European cities. Gas lighting and later electricity also transformed the nighttime environment of Europe's cities, as is evident in this painting of Liverpool.

The Housing Venture of Octavia Hill

Octavia Hill was a practical-minded British housing reformer who believed that workers and their families were entitled to happy homes. At the same time, she was convinced that the poor needed guidance and encouragement, not charity. In this selection, she describes her housing venture.

Octavia Hill, *Homes of the London Poor*

About four years ago I was put in possession of three houses in one of the worst courts of Marylebone. Six other houses were bought subsequently. All were crowded with inmates.

The first thing to be done was to put them in decent tenantable order. The set last purchased was a row of cottages facing a bit of desolate ground, occupied with wretched, dilapidated cow-sheds, manure heaps, old timber, and rubbish of every description. The houses were in a most deplorable condition—the plaster was dropping from the walls; on one staircase a pail was placed to catch the rain that fell through the roof. All the staircases were perfectly dark; the banisters were gone, having been burnt as firewood by tenants. The grates, with large holes in them, were falling forward into the rooms. The washhouse, full of lumber belonging to the landlord, was locked up; thus the inhabitants had to wash clothes, as well as to cook, eat and sleep in their small rooms. The dustbin, standing in the front part of the houses, was accessible to the whole neighbourhood, and boys often dragged from it quantities of unseemly objects and spread them over the court. The state of the drainage was in keeping with everything else. The pavement of the backyard was all broken up, and great puddles stood in it, so that the damp crept up the outer walls. . . .

As soon as I entered into possession, each family had an opportunity of doing better: those who would

not pay, or who led clearly immoral lives, were ejected. The rooms they vacated were cleansed; the tenants who showed signs of improvement moved into them, and thus, in turn, an opportunity was obtained for having each room distempered and papered. The drains were put in order, a large slate cistern was fixed, the washhouse was cleared of its lumber, and thrown open on stated days to each tenant in turn. The roof, the plaster, the woodwork were repaired; the staircase walls were distempered; new grates were fixed; the layers of paper and rag (black with age) were torn from the windows, and glass put in; out of 192 panes only eight were found unbroken. The yard and footpath were paved.

The room, as a rule, were re-let at the same prices at which they had been let before; but tenants with large families were counselled to take two rooms, and for these much less was charged than if let singly: this plan I continue to pursue. In-coming tenants are not allowed to take a decidedly insufficient quantity of room, and no sub-letting is permitted. . . .

The pecuniary result has been very satisfactory. Five percent has been paid on all the capital invested. A fund for the repayment of capital is accumulating. A liberal allowance has been made for repairs. . . .

My tenants are mostly of a class far below that of mechanics. They are, indeed, of the very poor. And yet, although the gifts they have received have been next to nothing, none of the families who have passed under my care during the whole four years have continued in what is called "distress," except such as have been unwilling to exert themselves. Those who will not exert the necessary self-control cannot avail themselves of the means of livelihood held out to them. But, for those who are willing, some small assistance in the form of work has, from time to time, been provided—not much, but sufficient to keep them from want or despair.

sion—although reluctantly—that private enterprise could not solve the housing crisis. In 1890, a British Housing Act empowered local town councils to collect new taxes and construct cheap housing for the working classes. London and Liverpool were the first communities to take advantage of their new powers. Similar activity had been set in motion in Germany by 1900. In 1894, the French government took a lesser step by providing easy credit for private contractors to build working-class housing. Everywhere, however, these lukewarm measures failed to do much to meet the real housing needs of the working classes. In Britain, for example, only 5 percent of all dwellings erected between 1890 and 1914 were constructed by municipalities under the Housing Act of 1890. Nevertheless, by the start of World War I, the need for planning had been recognized, and after the war municipal governments moved into housing construction on a large scale. In housing, as in so many other areas of life in the late nineteenth century, the liberal principle that the government that governs least governs best had simply proved untrue. More and more, governments were stepping into areas of activity that they would never have touched earlier.

Housing was but one area of urban reconstruction after 1870. As urban populations expanded in the nineteenth century, the older layout in which the city was confined to a compact area enclosed by defensive walls seemed restrictive and utterly useless. In the second half of the nineteenth century, many of the old defensive walls—worthless anyway from a military standpoint—were pulled down, and the areas converted into parks and boulevards. In Vienna, for example, the great boulevards of the Ringstrasse replaced the old medieval walls. While the broad streets served a military purpose—the rapid deployment of troops to crush civil disturbances—they also offered magnificent views of the city hall, the university, and the parliament building, all powerful symbols of middle-class social values.

Like Vienna, many European urban centers were redesigned during the second half of the nineteenth century. The reconstruction of Paris after 1850 by Emperor Napoleon III was perhaps the most famous project and provided a model for other urban centers. The old residential districts in the central city, many of them working-class slums, were pulled down and replaced with town halls, government office buildings, retail stores, including the new department stores, museums, cafes, and theaters, all of which provided for the shopping and recreational pleasures of the middle classes.

As cities expanded and entire groups of people were displaced from urban centers by reconstruction, city populations spilled over into the neighboring villages and countrysides, which were soon incorporated into the cities. The construction of streetcars and commuter trains by the turn of the century enabled both working-class and middle-class populations to live in their own suburban neighborhoods far removed from their places of work. Cheap, modern transportation essentially separated home and work for many Europeans.

The Social Structure of Mass Society

Historians generally agree that after 1871 the average person enjoyed an improving standard of living. The real wages of British workers, for example, probably doubled between 1871 and 1910. We should not allow this increase in the standard of living to mislead us, however. Great poverty did remain in Western society, and the gap between rich and poor was enormous. In the western and central European countries most affected by

industrialization, the richest 20 percent of the populations received between 50 and 60 percent of the national income. This meant that while the upper and middle classes received almost three-fifths of the wealth, the remaining 80 percent of the population received only two-fifths. It would, however, be equally misleading to portray European society as split simply into rich and poor. Between the small group of the elite at the top and the large number of very poor at the bottom, there were many different groups of varying wealth.

THE ELITE

At the top of European society stood a wealthy elite, constituting only 5 percent of the population but controlling between 30 and 40 percent of its wealth. This nineteenth-century elite was an amalgamation of the traditional landed aristocracy that had dominated European society for centuries and the wealthy upper middle class. In the course of the nineteenth century, aristocrats coalesced with the most successful industrialists, bankers, and merchants to form a new elite. The growth of big business had created this group of wealthy plutocrats while aristocrats, whose income from landed estates declined, invested in railway shares, public utilities, government bonds, and even businesses, sometimes on their own estates. Gradually, the greatest fortunes shifted into the hands of the upper middle class. In Great Britain, for example, landed aristocrats constituted 73 percent of the country's millionaires in mid-century while the commercial and financial magnates made up 14 percent. By the period 1900–1914, landowners had declined to 27 percent. The wealthiest person in Germany was not an aristocrat, but Bertha Krupp, granddaughter of Alfred Krupp and heiress to the business dynasty left by her father Friedrich, who committed suicide in 1902 over a homosexual scandal.

Increasingly, aristocrats and plutocrats fused as the wealthy upper middle class purchased landed estates to join the aristocrats in the pleasures of country living while the aristocrats bought lavish town houses for part-time urban life. Common bonds were also forged when the sons of wealthy middle-class families were admitted to the elite schools dominated by the children of the aristocracy. At Oxford, the landed upper class made up 40 percent of the student body in 1870, but only 15 percent in 1910, while undergraduates from business families went from 7 to 21 percent during the same period. This educated elite, whether aristocratic or middle class in background, assumed leadership roles in government bureaucracies and military hierarchies.

Marriage also served to unite the two groups. Daughters of tycoons acquired titles while aristocratic heirs gained new sources of cash. Wealthy American heiresses were in special demand. When Consuelo Vanderbilt married the duke of Marlborough, the new duchess brought £2 million (approximately $10 million) to her husband.

It would be misleading, however, to assume that the alliance of the wealthy business elite and traditional aristocrats was always harmonious. In Germany class lines were sometimes well drawn, especially if they were complicated by anti-Semitism. Albert Ballin, the wealthy director of the Hamburg-Amerika luxury liners, may have been close to Emperor William II, who entertained him on a regular basis, but the Prussian aristocracy snubbed Ballin because of his Jewish origins. Although the upper middle class was allowed into the bureaucracy of the German empire, the diplomatic corps remained an aristocratic preserve.

THE MIDDLE CLASSES

The middle classes consisted of a variety of groups. Below the upper middle class was a middle level that included such traditional groups as professionals in law, medicine, and the civil service as well as moderately well-to-do industrialists and merchants. The industrial expansion of the nineteenth century also added new groups to this segment of the middle class. These included business managers and new professionals, such as the engineers, architects, accountants, and chemists who formed professional associations as the symbols of their newfound importance. A lower middle class of small shopkeepers, traders, manufacturers, and prosperous peasants provided goods and services for the classes above them.

Standing between the lower middle class and the lower classes were new groups of white-collar workers who were the product of the Second Industrial Revolution. They were the traveling salesmen, bookkeepers, bank tellers, telephone operators, department store salespeople, and secretaries. Although largely property-less and often little better paid than skilled laborers, these white-collar workers were often committed to middle-class ideals and optimistic about improving their status. Some even achieved professional standing and middle-class status.

The moderately prosperous and successful middle classes shared a common lifestyle, one whose values tended to dominate much of nineteenth-century society. The members of the middle class were especially active in preaching their worldview to their children and to the upper and lower classes of their society. This was especially evident in Victorian Britain, often considered a model of middle-class society. It was the European middle classes who accepted and promulgated the importance of progress and science. They believed in hard work, which they viewed as the primary human good, open to everyone and guaranteed to have positive results. Knowledge was important as an instrument for personal gain. They were also regular churchgoers who believed in the good conduct associated with traditional Christian morality. The middle class was concerned with propriety, the right way of doing things, which gave rise to an incessant number of books aimed at the middle-class market with such titles as *The Habits of Good Society* or *Don't: A Manual of Mistakes and Improprieties More or Less Prevalent in Conduct and Speech.*

THE LOWER CLASSES

The lower classes of European society constituted almost 80 percent of the European population. Many of them were landholding peasants, agricultural laborers, and sharecroppers, especially in eastern Europe. This was less true, however, in western and central Europe. About 10 percent of the British population worked in agriculture, while in Germany the figure was 25 percent. Many prosperous, landowning peasants shared the values of the middle class. Military conscription brought peasants into contact with the other groups of mass society while state-run elementary schools forced the children of peasants to speak the national dialect and accept national loyalties.

There was no such thing as a single urban working class. The elite of the working class included, first of all, skilled artisans in such traditional handicraft trades as cabinetmaking, printing, and jewelry making. As the production of more items was mechanized in the course of the nineteenth century, these highly skilled workers found their economic security threatened. Printers, for example, were replaced by automatic typesetting machines operated by semiskilled workers. The Second Industrial Revolution, however, also brought new entrants into the group of highly skilled workers, such as machine-tool specialists, shipbuilders, and metal workers. Many of the skilled workers attempted to pattern themselves after the middle class by seeking good housing and educating their children.

Semiskilled laborers, who included such people as carpenters, bricklayers, and many factory workers, earned wages that were about two-thirds of those of highly skilled workers. At the bottom of the working-class hierarchy stood the largest group of workers, the unskilled laborers. They included day laborers, who worked irregularly for very low wages, and large numbers of domestic servants. One out of every seven employed persons in Great Britain in 1900 was a domestic servant. Most of them were women.

Urban workers did experience a real improvement in the material conditions of their lives after 1871. For one thing, urban improvements meant better living conditions. A rise in real wages, accompanied by a decline in many consumer costs, especially in the 1880s and 1890s, made it possible for workers to buy more than just food and housing. French workers in 1900, for example, spent 60 percent of their income on food, down from 75 percent in 1870. Workers' budgets now provided money for more clothes and even leisure at the same time that strikes and labor agitation were providing ten-hour days and Saturday afternoons off.

The "Woman Question": The Role of Women

The "woman question" was the term used to identify the debate over the role of women in society. In the nineteenth century, women remained legally inferior, economically dependent, and largely defined by family and household roles. Many women still aspired to the ideal of femininity popularized by writers and poets. Alfred Lord Tennyson's *The Princess* expressed it well:

> Man for the field and woman for the hearth:
> Man for the sword and for the needle she:
> Man with the head and woman with the heart:
> Man to command and woman to obey;
> All else confusion.

Historians have pointed out that this traditional characterization of the sexes, based on gender-defined social roles, was virtually elevated to the status of universal male and female attributes in the nineteenth century, largely due to the impact of the Industrial Revolution on the family. As the chief family wage earners, men worked outside the home while women were left with the care of the family for which they were paid nothing. Of course, the ideal did not always match reality, especially for the lower classes, where the need for supplemental income drove women to do "sweated" work.

Throughout most of the nineteenth century, marriage was viewed as the only honorable and available career for most women. While the middle class glorified the ideal of domesticity (see the box on p. 831), for most women marriage was a matter of economic necessity. The lack of meaningful work and the lower wages paid to women made it difficult for single women to earn a living. Since retiring to convents as in the past was no longer an option, many spinsters, who could not find sufficiently remunerative work, entered domestic service as live-in servants. Most women chose instead to marry,

✦ **Working-Class Housing in London.** Although urban workers experienced some improvements in the material conditions of their lives after 1871, working-class housing remained drab and depressing. This 1912 photograph of working-class housing in the East End of London shows rows of similar-looking buildings on treeless streets. Most often, these buildings had no gardens or green areas.

Advice to Women: Be Dependent

Industrialization had a strong impact on middle-class women as gender-based social roles became the norm. Men worked outside the home to support the family while women provided for the needs of their children and husband at home. In this selection, one woman gives advice to middle-class women on their proper role and behavior.

Elizabeth Poole Sanford, *Woman in Her Social and Domestic Character*

The changes wrought by Time are many. It influences the opinions of men as familiarity does their feelings; it has a tendency to do away with superstition, and to reduce every thing to its real worth.

It is thus that the sentiment for woman has undergone a change. The romantic passion which once almost deified her is on the decline; and it is by intrinsic qualities that she must now inspire respect. She is no longer the queen of song and the star of chivalry. But if there is less of enthusiasm entertained for her, the sentiment is more rational, and, perhaps, equally sincere; for it is in relation to happiness that she is chiefly appreciated.

And in this respect it is, we must confess, that she is most useful and most important. Domestic life is the chief source of her influence; and the greatest debt society can owe to her is domestic comfort; for happiness is almost an element of virtue; and nothing conduces more to improve the character of men than domestic peace. A woman may make a man's home delightful, and may thus increase his motives for virtuous exertion. She may refine and tranquilize his mind,—may turn away his anger or allay his grief. Her smile may be the happy influence to gladden his heart, and to disperse the cloud that gathers on his brow. And in proportion to her endeavors to make those around her happy, she will be esteemed and loved. She will secure by her excellence that interest and that regard which she might formerly claim as the privilege of her sex, and will really merit the deference which was then conceded to her as a matter of course. . . .

Perhaps one of the first secrets of her influence is adaptation to the tastes, and sympathy in the feelings, of those around her. This holds true in lesser as well as in graver points. It is in the former, indeed, that the absence of interest in a companion is frequently most disappointing. Where want of congeniality impairs domestic comfort, the fault is generally chargeable on the female side. It is for woman, not for man, to make the sacrifice, especially in indifferent matters. She must, in a certain degree, be plastic herself if she would mould others. . . .

Nothing is so likely to conciliate the affections of the other sex as a feeling that woman looks to them for support and guidance. In proportion as men are themselves superior, they are accessible to this appeal. On the contrary, they never feel interested in one who seems disposed rather to offer than to ask assistance. There is, indeed, something unfeminine in independence. It is contrary to nature, and therefore it offends. We do not like to see a woman affecting tremors, but still less do we like to see her acting the amazon. A really sensible woman feels her dependence. She does what she can; but she is conscious of inferiority, and therefore grateful for support. She knows that she is the weaker vessel, and that as such she should receive honor. In this view, her weakness is an attraction, not a blemish.

In every thing, therefore, that women attempt, they should show their consciousness of dependence. If they are learners, let them evince a teachable spirit; if they give an opinion, let them do it in an unassuming manner. There is something so unpleasant in female self-sufficiency that it not unfrequently deters instead of persuading, and prevents the adoption of advice which the judgment even approves.

which was reflected in an increase in marriage rates and a decline in illegitimacy rates in the course of the nineteenth century.

Birthrates also dropped significantly at this time. A very important factor in the evolution of the modern family was the decline in the number of offspring born to the average woman. The change was not necessarily due to new technological products. Although the invention of vulcanized rubber in the 1840s made possible the production of condoms and diaphragms, they were not widely used as effective contraceptive devices until the era of World War I. Some historians maintain that the change in attitude that led parents to deliberately limit the number of offspring was more important than the method used. While some historians attribute increased birth control to more widespread use of coitus interruptus, or male withdrawal before ejaculation, others have emphasized the ability of women to restrict family size through abortion and even infanticide or abandonment. That a change in attitude occurred was apparent in the emergence of a movement to increase awareness of birth control methods. Authorities prosecuted those who spread information about contraception for "depraving public morals," but were unable to stop them. In 1882 in Amsterdam, Dr. Aletta Jacob founded Europe's first birth control clinic. Initially, "family planning" was the suggestion of reformers who thought that the problem of poverty could be solved by reducing the number of children among the lower classes. In fact, the practice spread quickly among the properted classes, rather than among the impoverished, a good reminder that considerable differences still remained between middle-class and working-class families.

THE MIDDLE-CLASS FAMILY

The family was the central institution of middle-class life. Men provided the family income while women focused on household and child care. The use of domestic servants in many middle-class homes, made possible by an abundant supply of cheap labor, reduced the amount of time middle-class women had to spend on household work. At the same time, by reducing the number of children in the family, mothers could devote more time to child care and domestic leisure. The idea that leisure should be used for constructive purposes supported and encouraged the cult of middle-class domesticity.

The middle-class family fostered an ideal of togetherness. The Victorians created the family Christmas with its yule log, Christmas tree, songs, and exchange of gifts. In the United States, Fourth of July celebrations changed from drunken revels to family picnics by the 1850s. The education of middle-class females in domestic crafts, singing, and piano playing prepared them for their function of providing a proper environment for home recreation.

The new domestic ideal had an impact on child raising and children's play. Late eighteenth-century thought, beginning with Rousseau, had encouraged a new view of children as unique beings, not small adults, which had carried over into the nineteenth century. They were entitled to a long childhood involved in activities with other children their own age. The early environment in which they were raised, it was thought, would determine how they turned out. And mothers were seen as the most important force in protecting children from the harmful influences of the adult world. New children's games and toys, including mass-produced dolls for girls, appeared in middle-class homes. The middle-class emphasis on the functional value of knowledge was also evident in these games. One advice manual maintained that young children should learn checkers because it "calls forth the resources of the mind in the most gentle, as well as the most successful manner."

Since the sons of the middle-class family were expected to follow careers like their father's, they were

♦ **A Middle-Class Family.** Nineteenth-century middle-class moralists considered the family the fundamental pillar of a healthy society. The family was a crucial institution in middle-class life, and togetherness constituted one of the important ideals of the middle-class family. This painting by William P. Frith, entitled *Many Happy Returns of the Day*, shows a family birthday celebration for a little girl in which grandparents, parents, and children take part. The servant at the left holds the presents for the little girl.

sent to schools where they were kept separate from the rest of society until the age of sixteen or seventeen. Sport was used in the schools to "toughen" boys up while their leisure activities centered around both national military concerns and character building. This combination was especially evident in the establishment of the Boy Scouts in Britain in 1908. Boy Scouts provided organized recreation for boys between twelve and eighteen; adventure was combined with the discipline of earning merit badges and ranks in such a way as to instill ideals of patriotism and self-sacrifice. Many men viewed such activities as a corrective to the possible dangers that female domination of the home posed for male development. As one scout leader wrote, "The REAL Boy Scout is not a sissy. [He] adores his mother [but] is not hitched to [her] apron strings." There was little organized recreational activity of this type for girls, although Robert Baden-Powell, the founder of the Boy Scouts, did encourage his sister to establish a girls' division as an afterthought. Its goal is evident from Agnes Baden-Powell's comment that "you do not want to make tomboys of refined girls, yet you want to attract, and thus raise, the slum girl from the gutter. The main object is to give them all the ability to be better mothers and Guides to the next generation."[8] Despite her comment, most organizations of this kind were for middle-class children, although some reformers tried to establish boys' clubs for working-class youths to reform them.

The new ideal of the middle-class woman as nurturing mother and wife who "determined the atmosphere of the household" through her character, not her work, frequently did not correspond to reality. Recent research indicates that in France, Germany, and even mid-Victorian Britain, relatively few families could actually afford to hire a host of servants. More often, middle-class families had one servant, usually a young working-class or country girl not used to middle-class lifestyles. Women, then, were often forced to work quite hard to maintain the expected appearance of the well-ordered household. A German housekeeping manual makes this evident:

> It often happens that even high-ranking ladies help at home with housework, and particularly with kitchen chores, scrubbing, etc., so that, above all the hands have good cause to become very rough, hard, and calloused. When these ladies appear in society, they are extremely upset at having such rough-looking hands. In order to perform the hardest and most ordinary chores . . . and, at the same time, to keep a soft hand like those fine ladies who have no heavier work to do than embroidering and sewing, always keep a piece of fresh bacon, rub your hands

with it just before bedtime, and you will fully achieve your goal. You will, as a result, have the inconvenience of having to sleep with gloves on, in order not to soil the bed.[9]

Many middle-class wives, then, were caught in a no-win situation. Often for the sake of the advancement of her husband's career, she was expected to maintain in public the image of the "idle" wife, freed from demeaning physical labor and able to pass her days in ornamental pursuits. In truth, it was frequently the middle-class woman who paid the price for this facade in a life of unpaid work, carefully managing the family budget and participating in housework that could never be done by simply one servant girl. As one historian has argued, the reality of many middle-class women's lives was that "what appears at first glance to be idleness is revealed, on closer examination, to be difficult and tiresome work."

THE WORKING-CLASS FAMILY

Hard work was, of course, standard fare for women in working-class families. Daughters in working-class families were expected to work until they married; even after marriage, they often did piecework at home to help support the family. For the children of the working classes, childhood was over by the age of nine or ten when they became apprentices or were employed in odd jobs.

Between 1890 and 1914, however, family patterns among the working class began to change. High-paying jobs in heavy industry and improvements in the standard of living made it possible for working-class families to depend on the income of husbands and the wages of grown children. By the early twentieth century, some working-class mothers could afford to stay at home, following the pattern of middle-class women. At the same time, new consumer products, such as sewing machines, clocks, bicycles, and cast-iron stoves, created a new mass consumer society whose focus was on higher levels of consumption.

These working-class families also followed the middle classes in limiting the size of their families. Children began to be viewed as dependents rather than wage earners as child labor laws and compulsory education took children out of the workforce and into schools. Improvements in public health as well as advances in medicine and a better diet resulted in a decline in infant mortality rates for the lower classes, especially noticeable in the cities after 1890, and made it easier for working-class families to choose to have fewer children.

At the same time, strikes and labor agitation led to laws that reduced work hours to ten per day by 1900 and eliminated work on Saturday afternoons, which enabled working-class parents to devote more attention to their children and develop more emotional ties with them. Even working-class fathers became involved in their children's lives. One observer in the French town of Belleville in the 1890s noted that "the workingman's love for his children borders on being an obsession."[10] Interest in educating children as a way to improve their future also grew.

Education and Leisure in an Age of Mass Society

Mass education was a product of the mass society of the late nineteenth century. Being "educated" in the early nineteenth century meant attending a secondary school or possibly even a university. Secondary schools, such as the *Gymnasien* in Germany and the public schools (which were really private boarding schools) in Britain, mostly emphasized a classical education based on the study of Greek and Latin. Secondary and university education were primarily for the elite, the sons of government officials, nobles, or wealthier middle-class families. After 1850, secondary education was expanded as more middle-class families sought employment in public service and the professions or entry into elite scientific and technical schools. Existing secondary schools also placed more emphasis on practical and scientific education by adding foreign languages and natural sciences to their curriculum.

At the beginning of the nineteenth century, European states showed little interest in primary education. Only in the German states was there a state-run system of elementary education. In 1833, the French government created a system of state-run, secular schools by instructing local government to establish an elementary school for both boys and girls. None of these primary schools required attendance, however, and it tended to be irregular at best. In rural society, children were still expected to work in the fields. In industrializing countries like Britain and France, both employers and parents were eager to maintain the practice of child labor.

In the decades after 1870, the functions of the state were extended to include the development of mass education in state-run systems. Between 1870 and 1914, most Western governments began to offer at least primary education to both boys and girls between the ages of six and twelve. In most countries it was not optional. Austria had established free, compulsory elementary education in 1869. In France, a law of March 29, 1882, made primary education compulsory for all children between six and thirteen. In 1880, elementary education was made compulsory in Britain, but it was not until 1902 that an act of Parliament brought all elementary schools under county and town control. States also assumed responsibility for the quality of teachers by establishing teacher-training schools. By 1900, many European states, especially in northern and western Europe, were providing state-financed primary schools, salaried and trained teachers, and free, compulsory mass elementary education.

Why did European states make this commitment to mass education? Liberals believed that education was important to personal and social improvement and also sought, as in France, to supplant Catholic education with moral and civic training based on secular values. Even conservatives were attracted to mass education as a means of improving the quality of military recruits and training people in social discipline. In 1875, a German military journal stated: "We in Germany consider education to be one of the principal ways of promoting the strength of the nation and above all military strength."[11]

Another incentive for mass education came from industrialization. In the early Industrial Revolution, unskilled labor was sufficient to meet factory needs, but the new firms of the Second Industrial Revolution demanded skilled labor. Both boys and girls with an elementary education had new possibilities of jobs beyond their villages or small towns, including white-collar jobs in railways, new metro stations, post offices, banking and shipping firms, teaching, and nursing. To industrialists, then, mass education furnished the trained workers they needed.

Nevertheless, the chief motive for mass education was political. On the one hand, the expansion of voting rights necessitated a more educated electorate. Even more important, however, mass compulsory education instilled patriotism and nationalized the masses, providing an opportunity for even greater national integration. As people lost their ties to local regions and even to religion, nationalism supplied a new faith. The use of a single national language created greater national unity than did loyalty to a ruler.

A nation's motives for universal elementary education largely determined what was taught in the elementary schools. Obviously, indoctrination in national values took on great importance. At the core of the academic curriculum were reading, writing, arithmetic, national history, especially geared to a patriotic view, geography, literature, and some singing and drawing. The education of boys and girls varied, however. Where possible, the sexes were separated. Girls did less math and no science but concentrated on such domestic skills as sewing, washing, ironing, and cooking, all prerequisites for providing a good home for husband and children. Boys were taught some practical skills, such as carpentry, and even some military drill. Most of the elementary schools also inculcated the middle-class virtues of hard work, thrift, sobriety, cleanliness, and respect for the family. For most students, elementary education led to apprenticeship and a job.

The development of compulsory elementary education created a demand for teachers, and most of them were female. In the United States, for example, women constituted two-thirds of all teachers by the 1880s. Many men viewed the teaching of children as an extension of women's "natural role" as nurturers of children. Moreover, females were paid lower salaries, in itself a considerable incentive for governments to encourage the establishment of teacher-training institutes for women. The first female colleges were really teacher-training schools. In Britain, the women's colleges of Queen's and Bedford were established in the 1840s to provide teacher training for middle-class spinsters who needed to work. A pioneer in the development of female education was Barbara Bodichon (1827-1891), who established her own school where girls were trained for economic independence as well as domesticity. It was not until the beginning of the twentieth century that women were permitted to enter the male-dominated universities. In France, 3 percent of university students in 1902 were women; by 1914, their number had increased to 10 percent of the total.

The most immediate result of mass education was an increase in literacy. Compulsory elementary education and the growth of literacy were directly related. In Germany, Great Britain, France, and the Scandinavian countries, adult illiteracy was virtually eliminated by 1900. Where there was less schooling, the story is very different. Adult illiteracy rates were 79 percent in Serbia, 78 percent in Romania, 72 percent in Bulgaria, and 79 percent in Russia. All of these countries had made only a minimal investment in compulsory mass education.

With the dramatic increase in literacy after 1871 came the rise of mass newspapers, such as the *Evening News* (1881) and *Daily Mail* (1896) in London, which sold millions of copies a day. Known as the "yellow press" in the United States, these newspapers shared some common characteristics. They were written in an easily understood style and tended to be extremely sensational. Unlike eighteenth-century newspapers, which were full of serious editorials and lengthy political

♦ **A Women's College.** Women were largely excluded from male-dominated universities before 1900. Consequently, the demand of women for higher education led to the foundation of women's colleges, most of which were primarily teacher-training schools. This photograph shows a group of women in an astronomy class at Vassar College in the United States in 1878. Maria Mitchell, a famous female astronomer, was head of the department.

analysis, these tabloids provided lurid details of crimes, jingoistic diatribes, gossip, and sports news. There were other forms of cheap literature as well. Specialty magazines, such as the *Family Herald* for the entire family, and women's magazines began in the 1860s. Pulp fiction for adults included the extremely popular westerns with their innumerable variations on conflicts between cowboys and Indians. Literature for the masses was but one feature of a new mass culture; another was the emergence of new forms of mass leisure.

MASS LEISURE

In the preindustrial centuries, play or leisure activities had been closely connected to work patterns based on the seasonal or daily cycles typical of the life of peasants and artisans. The process of industrialization in the nineteenth century had an enormous impact upon those traditional patterns. The factory imposed new work patterns that were determined by the rhythms of machines and clocks and removed work time completely from the family environment of farms and workshops. Work and leisure became opposites as leisure came to be viewed as what people do for fun after work. In fact, the new leisure hours created by the industrial system—evening hours after work, weekends, and later a week or two in the summer—largely determined the contours of the new mass leisure.

At the same time, the influx of rural people into industrial towns eventually caused the demise of traditional village culture, especially the fairs and festivals that had formed such an important part of that culture. Industrial progress, of course, demanded that such traditional celebrations as Whitsuntide, which had occasioned thirteen days of games and drinking, be eliminated or reduced. In fact, by the 1870s Whitsuntide had been reduced to a single one-day holiday.

New technology and business practices also determined the forms of the new mass leisure. The new technology created novel experiences for leisure, such as the Ferris wheel at amusement parks, while the mechanized urban transportation systems of the 1880s meant that even the working classes were no longer dependent on neighborhood bars, but could make their way to athletic events, amusement parks, and dance halls. Likewise, railroads could take people to the bleachers on weekends.

Music and dance halls appeared in the last half of the nineteenth century. The first music hall in London was constructed in 1849 for a lower-class audience. As is evident from one Londoner's observation, the music hall was primarily for males:

> [It was a] popular place of Saturday night resort with working men, as at them they can combine the drinking of the Saturday night glass and smoking of the Saturday night pipe, with the seeing and hearing of a variety of entertainments, ranging from magnificent ballets and marvelous scenic illusions to inferior tumbling, and from well-given operatic selections to the most idiotic of the so-called comic songs of the Jolly Dogs Class.[12]

By the 1880s, there were five hundred music halls in London. Promoters gradually made them more respectable and broadened their fare to entice both women and children to attend the programs. The new dance halls, which were all the rage by 1900, were more strictly oriented toward adults. Contemporaries were often shocked by the sight of young people engaged in sexually suggestive dancing.

The upper and middle classes had created the first market for tourism, but as wages increased and workers were given paid vacations, tourism, too, became another form of mass leisure. Thomas Cook (1808–1892) was a British pioneer of mass tourism. Secretary to a British temperance group, Cook had been responsible for organizing a railroad trip to temperance gatherings in 1841. This experience led him to offer trips on a regular basis after he found that he could make substantial profits by renting special trains, lowering prices, and increasing the number of passengers. In 1867, he offered tours to Paris and by the 1880s to Switzerland. Of course, overseas tours were for the industrial and commercial middle classes, but through their savings clubs even British factory workers were able to take weekend excursions by the turn of the century.

By the late nineteenth century, team sports had also developed into yet another form of mass leisure. Sports were by no means a new activity. Unlike the old rural games, however, they were no longer chaotic and spontaneous activities, but became strictly organized with sets of rules and officials to enforce them. These rules were the products of organized athletic groups, such as the English Football Association (1863) and the American Bowling Congress (1895).

The new sports were not just for leisure or fun, but like other forms of middle-class recreation, they were intended to provide excellent training for people, especially youth. Not only could the participants develop individual skills, but they could also acquire a sense of teamwork useful for military service. These characteris-

◆ **Middle Classes at the Beach.** By the beginning of the twentieth century, changing work and leisure patterns had created a new mass leisure. The upper and middle classes created the first market for tourism, although it too became another form of mass leisure as wages increased and workers received paid vacations. This photograph shows middle-class Britons enjoying a beach at the beginning of the twentieth century.

The Fight Song: Sports in the English Public School

In the second half of the nineteenth century, organized sports were often placed at the center of the curriculum in English public schools. These sports were not just for leisure but were intended to instill character, strength, and teamwork. This "fight song" was written by H. B. Tristam for the soccer team at Loretto School.

H. B. Tristam, Going Strong

Sing Football the grandest of sports in the world,
And you know it yourself if your pluck's never curled,
If you've gritted your teeth and gone hard to the last,
And sworn that you'll never let anyone past.

Chorus
Keeping close upon the ball—we drive it through them all,

And again we go rushing along, along, along;
O the tackle and the run, and the matches we have won,
From the start to the finish going strong, strong, strong, going strong!

If you live to be a hundred you'll never forget
How they hacked in the scrum, how you payed back the debt;
The joy of the swing when you tackled your man,
The lust of the fray when the battle began.

Long hence when you look with a quivering eye
On the little white tassel you value so high;
You'll think of the matches you've played in and won,
And you'll long for the days that are over and done.

tics were already evident in the British public schools in the 1850s and 1860s when such schools as Harrow, Uppingham, and Loretto placed organized sports at the center of the curriculum (see the box above). At Loretto, for example, education was supposed to instill "First—Character. Second—Physique. Third—Intelligence. Fourth—Manners. Fifth—Information."

The new team sports rapidly became professionalized. In Britain, soccer had its Football Association in 1863 and rugby its Rugby Football Union in 1871. In the United States, the first National Association to recognize professional baseball players was formed in 1863. By 1900, the National League and American League had a complete monopoly over professional baseball. The development of urban transportation systems made possible the construction of stadiums where thousands could attend, making mass spectator sports a big business. In 1872, 2,000 people watched the British Soccer Cup finals. By 1885, the crowd had increased to 10,000 and by 1901 to 100,000. Professional teams became objects of mass adulation by crowds of urbanites who compensated for their lost sense of identity in mass urban areas by developing these new loyalties. Spectator sports even reflected class differences. Upper-class soccer teams in Britain viewed working-class teams as vicious and prone to "money-grubbing, tricks, sensational displays, and utter rottenness."

The sports cult of the late nineteenth century was mostly male oriented. Many men believed that females were not particularly suited for "vigorous physical activity," although it was permissible for middle-class women to indulge in such easy sports as croquet and lawn tennis. Eventually, some athletics crept into women's colleges and girls' public schools in England.

The new forms of popular leisure were standardized forms of amusement that drew mass audiences. Although some argued that the new amusements were important for improving people, in truth, they mostly served to provide entertainment and distract people from the realities of their work lives. Much of mass leisure was secular. Churches found that they had to compete with popular amusements for people's attention on Sundays. The new mass leisure also represented a significant change from earlier forms of popular culture. Festivals and fairs had been based on an ethos of active community participation, whereas the new forms of mass leisure were standardized for largely passive mass audiences. Amusement parks and professional sports teams were, after all, big businesses organized to make profits.

The National State

Within the major European states, considerable progress was made in achieving liberal practices (constitutions, parliaments, and individual liberties) and reforms that encouraged the expansion of political democracy through voting rights for men and the creation of mass political parties. At the same time, however, these developments were strongly resisted in parts of Europe where the old political forces remained strong.

Western Europe: The Growth of Political Democracy

In general, parliamentary government was most firmly rooted in the western European states. The growth of political democracy was one of the preoccupations of British politics after 1871, and its cause was pushed along by the expansion of suffrage. Much advanced by the Reform Act of 1867 (see Chapter 23), the right to vote was further extended during the second ministry of William Gladstone (1880–1885) with the passage of

✦ **William Gladstone in His Later Years.** The first Liberal ministry of William Gladstone had been responsible for a series of significant liberal reforms. During his second ministry, Gladstone and the Liberals expanded the right to vote by enfranchising agricultural workers.

the Reform Act of 1884. It gave the vote to all men who paid regular rents or taxes, thus largely enfranchising the agricultural workers, a group previously excluded. The following year, a Redistribution Act eliminated historic boroughs and counties and established constituencies with approximately equal populations and one representative each. The payment of salaries to members of the House of Commons beginning in 1911 further democratized that institution by at least opening the door to people other than the wealthy. The British system of gradual reform through parliamentary institutions had become the way of British political life.

Gradual reform failed to solve the problem of Ireland, however. The Irish had long been subject to British rule, and an Act of Union in 1801 had united the English and Irish parliaments. Like other unfree ethnic groups in Europe, the Irish developed a sense of national self-consciousness. They detested the absentee British landlords and their burdensome rents.

In 1870, William Gladstone attempted to alleviate Irish discontent by enacting limited land reform, but as Irish tenants continued to be evicted in the 1870s, the Irish peasants responded with terrorist acts. When the government reacted in turn with more force, Irish Catholics began to demand independence. Although the Liberals introduced home rule bills that would have given Ireland self-government in 1886 and 1893, the bills failed to win a majority vote. When the Liberals finally enacted a Home Rule Act in 1914, an explosive situation in Ireland itself created more problems. Irish Protestants in northern Ireland, especially in the province of Ulster, wanted no part of an Irish Catholic state. The outbreak of World War I enabled the British government to sidestep the potentially explosive issue and to suspend Irish home rule for the duration of the war.

The defeat of France by the Prussian army in 1870 brought the downfall of Louis Napoleon's Second Empire. French republicans initially set up a provisional government, but the victorious Otto von Bismarck intervened and forced the French to choose a government by universal male suffrage. The French people rejected the republicans and overwhelmingly favored the monarchists, who won 400 of the 630 seats in the new National Assembly. In response, on March 26, 1871, radical republicans formed an independent republican government in Paris known as the Commune (see the box on p. 839).

But the National Assembly refused to give up its power and decided to crush the revolutionary Commune. Vicious fighting in April and May finally ended

Parisian Violence

In March 1871, an insurrection erupted in Paris when the National Assembly attempted to disarm the Parisian National Guard. When troops were sent to seize guns that had been moved earlier to the hills of Montmartre, fighting broke out. Georges Clemenceau, the mayor of Montmartre, wrote a description of the day's events. Two generals had been taken prisoner by the National Guard and shot before Clemenceau could arrive to prevent it. This excerpt describes what happened next. Eight days after the events described here, the Parisians established the Commune.

Georges Clemenceau, How the Uprising Began, March 18, 1871

We had hardly turned the corner of the wall when a man ran up and said that the Generals had just been shot. We did not stop to answer him but ran even faster. He did not seem very sure of his facts, anyhow, and seemed to be repeating a rumor rather than something he had seen for himself.

The *Buttes* [hills of Montmartre] were covered with armed National Guards. We made our way into this crowd. My sash called everybody's attention to me, and I at once became the object of the most hostile demonstrations. They reproached me for having conspired with the Government to have the guns taken away, they accused me of betraying the National Guard, they insulted me.

Keeping between Mayer and Sabourdy, who were both fairly well-known in the *arrondissement* [district] and were my only safeguard, I continued on my way without answering.

As we went on, I heard people saying, "It's all over! Justice has been done! The traitors are punished! If anybody doesn't like it, we'll do the same to him! It's too late!" . . . It was no longer possible to doubt the assassination of the Generals, for everyone was repeating the news with somber enthusiasm. . . .

Suddenly there was a great noise, and the mob which filled the courtyard of no. 6 burst into the street, in the grip of a kind of frenzy.

There were chasseurs, soldiers of the line, National Guards, women and children. They were all shrieking like wild beasts, without realizing what they were doing. I observed then that pathological phenomenon which could be called blood lust. A breath of madness seemed to have passed over this mob. From the top of a wall children were waving indescribable trophies, women with streaming hair and all disheveled twisted their bare arms and uttered raucous cries, bereft of any sense. I saw some of them weeping and shouting louder than the others. Men were dancing about and jostling one another in a kind of frenzied fury. It was one of those nervous phenomena so frequent in the Middle Ages, and occasionally occurring still among masses of human beings under the stress of some powerful emotion.

Suddenly a piece of artillery, drawn by four horses, arrived in front of the house. The confusion increased, if that was possible. Men clad in ill-matched uniforms, riding on the horses, swore and shouted. I saw one woman jump onto one of the horses. She was waving her bonnet and yelling, "Down with the traitors!"—a cry the crowd repeated and repeated.

The situation was becoming more and more dangerous for me. The mob looked at me in crazed defiance, shouting its cry of "Down with the traitors!" Several fists were raised.

I could do nothing more in this place. I had not been able to prevent the crime. It remained for me to look after the fate of the prisoners whom I had just seen go by, and to stop any misfortune befalling my prisoners at the Mairie, against whom there was very great hostility.

in a government victory when government troops massacred thousands of the Commune's defenders in the last week of May. Estimates are that 20,000 were shot; another 10,000 were shipped overseas to the French penal colony of New Caledonia. The brutal repression of the Commune bequeathed a legacy of hatred that continued to plague French politics for decades. The split between the middle and working classes, begun in the revolutionary hostilities of 1848–1849, had widened immensely.

Although a majority of the members of the monarchist-dominated National Assembly wished to restore a monarchy to France, inability to agree on who should be king caused the monarchists to miss their opportunity and led in 1875 to an improvised constitution that established a republican form of government as the least divisive compromise. This constitution established a bicameral legislature with an upper house or Senate elected indirectly and a lower house or Chamber of Deputies chosen by universal male suffrage; a president,

CHRONOLOGY

◆◆◆◆◆◆◆◆◆◆◆◆◆◆◆◆◆◆◆◆◆◆◆◆◆

The National States, 1871–1894

Great Britain	
Second ministry of William Gladstone	1880–1885
Reform Act	1884
Redistribution Act	1885
France	
Surrender of French provisional government to Germany	1871 (January 28)
Paris Commune	1871 (March-May)
Republican constitution (Third Republic)	1875
Boulanger is discredited	1889
Spain	
King Alfonso XII	1874–1885
New constitution	1875
Defeat in Spanish-American War	1898
Germany	
Bismarck as chancellor	1871–1890
Antisocialist law	1878
Social welfare legislation	1883–1889
Austria-Hungary	
Emperor Francis Joseph	1848–1916
Count Edward von Taaffe as prime minster	1879–1893
Imperial Russia	
Tsar Alexander III	1881–1894

selected by the legislature for a term of seven years, served as executive of the government. The Constitution of 1875, intended only as a stopgap measure, solidified the republic—the Third Republic—which lasted sixty-five years. New elections in 1876 and 1877 strengthened the hands of the republicans who managed by 1879 to institute ministerial responsibility and establish the power of the Chamber of Deputies. The prime minister or premier and his ministers were now responsible not to the president, but to the Chamber of Deputies.

Although the government's moderation gradually encouraged more and more middle-class and peasant sup-port, the position of the Third Republic remained precarious because monarchists, Catholic clergy, and professional army officers were still its enemies.

A major crisis in the 1880s, however, actually served to strengthen the republican government. General Georges Boulanger (1837–1891) was a popular military officer who attracted the public attention of all those discontented with the Third Republic: the monarchists, Bonapartists, aristocrats, and nationalists who favored a war of revenge against Germany. Boulanger appeared as the strong man on horseback, the savior of France. By 1889, just when his strength had grown to the point where many expected a coup d'etat, he lost his nerve and fled France, a completely discredited man. In the long run, the Boulanger crisis served to rally support for the resilient republic.

In Spain, a new constitution, created in 1875 under King Alfonso XII (1874–1885), established a parliamentary government dominated by two political groups, the Conservatives and Liberals, whose members stemmed from the same small social group of great landowners allied with a few wealthy industrialists. Because suffrage was limited to the propertied classes, Liberals and Conservatives alternated in power but followed basically the same conservative policies. Spain's defeat in the Spanish-American War in 1898 and the loss of Cuba and the Philippines to the United States increased the discontent with the status quo. When a group of young intellectuals known as the Generation of 1898 called for political and social reforms, both Liberals and Conservatives attempted to enlarge the electorate and win the masses' support for their policies. The attempted reforms did little to allay the unrest, however, while the growth of industrialization in some areas resulted in more workers being attracted to the radical solutions of socialism and anarchism. When violence erupted in Barcelona in July 1909, the military forces brutally suppressed the rebels. The revolt and its repression made clear that reform would not be easily accomplished because the Catholic church, large landowners, and the army remained tied to a conservative social order.

By 1870, Italy had emerged as a geographically united state with pretensions to great power status. Its internal weaknesses, however, gave that claim a particularly hollow ring. Sectional differences— a poverty-stricken south and an industrializing north—weakened any sense of community. Chronic turmoil between workers and industrialists undermined the social fabric. The Italian government was unable to deal effectively with these problems because of the extensive corruption among government officials and the lack of stability created by ever-changing government coalitions. The granting of universal male suffrage in 1912 did little to correct the extensive corruption and weak government. Even Italy's pretensions to great power status proved hollow when Italy became the first European power to lose to an African state—Ethiopia.

Central and Eastern Europe: Persistence of the Old Order

Germany, Austria-Hungary, and Russia pursued political policies that were quite different from those of the western European nations. The central European states (Germany and Austria-Hungary) had the trappings of parliamentary government including legislative bodies and elections by universal male suffrage, but authoritarian forces, especially powerful monarchies and conservative social groups, remained strong. In eastern Europe, especially Russia, the old system of autocracy was barely touched by the winds of change.

Despite unification, important divisions remained in German society that could not simply be papered over by the force of nationalism. These divisions were already evident in the new German constitution that provided for a federal system with a bicameral legislature. The Bundesrat or upper house represented the twenty-five states that made up Germany. Individual states, such as Bavaria and Prussia, kept their own kings, their own post offices, and even their own armies in peacetime. The lower house of the German parliament, known as the Reichstag, was elected on the basis of universal male suffrage, but it did not have ministerial responsibility. Ministers of government, the most important of which was the chancellor, were responsible not to the parliament, but to the emperor. The emperor also commanded the armed forces and controlled foreign policy and internal administration. While the creation of a parliament elected by universal male suffrage presented opportunities for the growth of a real political democracy, it failed to develop in Germany before World War I. The army and Bismarck were two major reasons why it did not.

The German (largely Prussian) army viewed itself as the defender of monarchy and aristocracy and sought to escape any control by the Reichstag by operating under a general staff responsible only to the emperor. Prussian military tradition was strong, and military officers took steps to ensure the loyalty of their subordinates to the emperor, which was easy as long as Junker landowners were officers. As the growth of the army made it necessary to turn to the middle class for officers, extreme care was taken to choose only sons "of honorable

bourgeois families in whom the love for King and Fatherland, a warm heart for the soldier's calling, and Christian morality are planted and nurtured."

The policies of Bismarck, who served as chancellor of the new German state until 1890, often served to prevent the growth of more democratic institutions. At first, Bismarck worked with the liberals to achieve greater centralization of Germany through common codes of criminal and commercial law. The liberals also joined Bismarck in his attack on the Catholic church, the so-called *Kulturkampf* or "struggle for civilization." Like Bismarck, middle-class liberals distrusted Catholic loyalty to the new Germany. Bismarck's strong-arm tactics against Catholic clergy and Catholic institutions proved counterproductive, however, and Bismarck welcomed an opportunity in 1878 to abandon the attack on Catholicism by making an abrupt shift in policy.

In 1878, Bismarck abandoned the liberals and began to persecute the socialists. When the Social Democratic Party elected twelve deputies to the Reichstag in 1877, Bismarck grew alarmed. He genuinely believed that the socialists' antinationalistic, anticapitalistic, and anti-

◆ **Bismarck and William II.** In 1890, Bismarck sought to undertake new repressive measures against the Social Democrats. Disagreeing with this policy, Emperor William II forced him to resign. This political cartoon shows William II reclining on a throne made of artillery and cannonballs and holding a doll labeled "socialism." Bismarck bids farewell while Germany, personified as a woman, looks on with grave concern.

⇒ Bismarck and the Welfare of the Workers ⇐

In his attempt to win workers away from socialism, Bismarck favored an extensive program of social welfare benefits, including old age pensions as well as compensation for absence from work due to sickness, accident, and disability. This selection is taken from Bismarck's address to the Reichstag on March 10, 1884, in which he explained his motives for social welfare legislation.

Bismarck, Address to the Reichstag

The positive efforts began really only in the year . . . 1881 . . . with the imperial message . . . in which His Majesty William I said: "Already in February of this year, we have expressed our conviction that the healing of social ills is not to be sought exclusively by means of repression of Social Democratic excesses, but equally in the positive promotion of the welfare of the workers."

In consequence of this, first of all the insurance law against accidents was submitted. . . . And it reads . . . "But those who have, through age or disability, become incapable of working have a confirmed claim on all for a higher degree of state care than could have been their share heretofore. . . ."

The workers' real sore point is the insecurity of his existence. He is not always sure he will always have work. He is not sure he will always be healthy, and he foresees some day he will be old and incapable of work. But also if he falls into poverty as a result of long illness, he is completely helpless with his own powers, and society hitherto does not recognize relief, even when he has worked ever so faithfully and diligently before. But ordinary poor relief leaves much to be desired, especially in the great cities where it is extraordinarily much worse than in the country. . . . We read in Berlin newspapers of suicide because of difficulty in making both ends meet, of people who died from direct hunger and have hanged themselves because they have nothing to eat, of people who announce in the paper they were tossed out homeless and have no income . . . For the worker it is always a fact that falling into poverty and onto poor relief in a great city is synonymous with misery, and this insecurity makes him hostile and mistrustful of society. That is humanly not unnatural, and as long as the state does not meet him halfway, just as long will this trust in the state's honesty be taken from him by accusations against the government, which he will find where he wills; always running back again to the socialist quacks . . . and, without great reflection, letting himself be promised things, which will not be fulfilled. On this account, I believe that accident insurance, with which we show the way, . . . will still work on the anxieties and ill-feeling of the working class.

---

monarchical stance represented a danger to the empire. In 1878, Bismarck got parliament to pass a stringent antisocialist law that outlawed the Social Democratic Party and limited socialist meetings and publications, although socialist candidates were still permitted to run for the Reichstag. In addition to repressive measures, Bismarck also attempted to woo workers away from socialism by enacting social welfare legislation (see the box above). Between 1883 and 1889, the Reichstag passed laws that created sickness, accident, and disability benefits as well as old age pensions financed by compulsory contributions from workers, employers, and the state. Bismarck's social security system was the most progressive the world had yet seen, although even his system left much to be desired as the Social Democrats pointed out. A full pension, for example, was payable only at age seventy after forty-eight years of contributions. In the event of a male worker's death, no benefits were paid to his widow or children.

Both the repressive and the social welfare measures failed to stop the growth of socialism, however. The Social Democratic Party continued to grow. In his frustration, Bismarck planned still more repressive measures in 1890, but before he could carry them out, the new emperor, William II (1888–1918), eager to pursue his own policies, cashiered the aged chancellor.

After the creation of the dual monarchy of Austria-Hungary in 1867, the Austrian part received a constitution that established a parliamentary system with the principle of ministerial responsibility. But Emperor Francis Joseph largely ignored ministerial responsibility and proceeded to personally appoint and dismiss his ministers and rule by decree when parliament was not in session.

The problem of the minorities continued to trouble the empire. The ethnic Germans, who made up only one-third of Austria's population, governed Austria but felt increasingly threatened by the Czechs, Poles, and other Slavic groups within the empire. The difficulties in dealing with this problem were especially evident from 1879 to 1893 when Count Edward von Taaffe served as prime minister. Taaffe attempted to "muddle through" by relying on a coalition of German conservatives, Czechs, and Poles to maintain a majority in parliament. But his concessions to national minorities, such as allowing the Slavic languages as well as German to be used in education and administration, served to antagonize the German-speaking Austrian bureaucracy and aristocracy, two of the basic pillars of the empire. Opposition to Taaffe's policies brought his downfall in 1893, but did not solve the nationalities problem. While the dissatisfied non-German groups demanded concessions, the ruling Austrian Germans resisted change. The granting of universal male suffrage in 1907 served only to make the problem worse as nationalities that had played no role in the government now agitated in the parliament for autonomy. This led prime ministers after 1900 to ignore the parliament and rely increasingly on imperial emergency decrees to govern.

Unlike Austria, Hungary had a working parliamentary system, but one controlled by the great Magyar landowners who dominated both the Hungarian peasantry and the other ethnic groups in Hungary. The Hungarians attempted to solve their nationalities problem by systematic Magyarization. The Magyar language was imposed upon all schools and was the only language that could be used by government and military officials.

In Russia, the government made no concession whatever to liberal and democratic reforms. The assassination of Alexander II in 1881 convinced his son and successor, Alexander III (1881–1894), that reform had been a mistake, and he quickly instituted what he said were "exceptional measures." The powers of the secret police were expanded. Advocates of constitutional monarchy and social reform, along with revolutionary groups, were persecuted. Entire districts of Russia were placed under martial law if the government suspected the inhabitants of treason. The powers of the zemstvos, created by the reforms of Alexander II, were sharply curtailed. When Alexander III died, his weak son and successor, Nicholas II (1894–1917), began his rule with his father's conviction that the absolute power of the tsars should be preserved: "I shall maintain the principle of autocracy just as firmly and unflinchingly as did my unforgettable father."[13] But conditions were changing,

especially with the growth of industrialization, and the tsar's approach was not realistic in view of the new circumstances he faced.

Conclusion

The Second Industrial Revolution helped create a new material prosperity that led Europeans to believe they had ushered in a new "age of progress." A major feature of this age was the emergence of a mass society. The lower classes in particular benefited from the right to vote, a higher standard of living, and new schools that provided them with a modicum of education. New forms of mass transportation, combined with new work patterns, enabled large numbers of people to enjoy weekend excursions to amusement parks and seaside resorts and to participate in new mass leisure activities.

By 1871, the national state had become the focus of people's lives. Liberal and democratic reforms brought new possibilities for greater participation in the political process, although women were still largely excluded from political rights. After 1871, the national state also began to expand its functions beyond all previous limits. Fearful of the growth of socialism and trade unions, governments attempted to appease the working masses by adopting such social insurance measures as protection against accidents, illness, and old age. These social welfare measures were narrow in scope and limited in benefits, but they signaled a new direction for state action to benefit the mass of its citizens. The enactment of public health and housing measures, designed to curb the worst ills of urban living, were yet another indication of how state power could be used to benefit the people.

This extension of state functions took place in an atmosphere of increased national loyalty. After 1871, nation-states increasingly sought to solidify the social order and win the active loyalty and support of their citizens by deliberately cultivating national feelings. Yet this policy contained potentially great dangers. As we shall see in the next chapter, nations had discovered once again that imperialistic adventures and military successes could arouse nationalistic passions and smother domestic political unrest. But they also found that nationalistic feelings could also lead to intense international rivalries that made war almost inevitable.

NOTES

1. Quoted in David Landes, *The Unbound Prometheus: Technological Change and Industrial Development in Western Europe from 1750 to the Present* (Cambridge, 1969), p. 353.

2. Quoted in Barbara Franzoi, ". . . with the wolf always at the door. . . . Women's Work in Domestic Industry in Britain and Germany," in Marilyn J. Boxer and Jean H. Quataert, eds., *Connecting Spheres: Women in the Western World, 1500 to the Present* (New York, 1987), p. 151.

3. Quoted in W. L. Guttsman, *The German Social Democratic Party, 1875–1933* (London, 1981), p. 63.

4. Quoted in Leslie Derfler, *Socialism since Marx: A Century of the European Left* (New York, 1973), p. 58.

5. Karl Marx and Friedrich Engels, *The Communist Manifesto* (Harmondsworth, 1967), p. 102.

6. Quoted in Paul Avrich, *The Russian Anarchists* (Princeton, N.J., 1971), p. 67.

7. Quoted in Nicholas Bullock and James Read, *The Movement for Housing Reform in Germany and France, 1840–1914* (Cambridge, 1985), p. 42.

8. Quoted in Gary Cross, *A Social History of Leisure since 1600* (State College, Pa., 1990), pp. (in order of quotations) 116, 119.

9. Quoted in Sibylle Meyer, "The Tiresome Work of Conspicuous Leisure: On the Domestic Duties of the Wives of Civil Servants in the German Empire (1871–1918)," in Boxer and Quataert, *Connecting Spheres*, p. 161.

10. Quoted in Lenard R. Berlanstein, *The Working People of Paris, 1871–1914* (Baltimore, 1984), p. 141.

11. Quoted in Robert Gildea, *Barricades and Borders: Europe, 1800–1914* (Oxford, 1987), p. 249.

12. Quoted in Cross, *A Social History of Leisure since 1600*, p. 130.

13. Quoted in Shmuel Galai, *The Liberation Movement in Russia, 1900–1905* (Cambridge, 1973), p. 26.

SUGGESTIONS FOR FURTHER READING

In addition to the general works on the nineteenth century and individual European countries cited in Chapters 22 and 23, two more specialized works on the subject matter of this chapter are available in N. Stone, *Europe Transformed, 1878–1919* (London, 1983); and F. Gilbert, *The End of the European Era, 1890 to the Present*, 4th ed. (New York, 1991).

The subject of the Second Industrial Revolution is well covered in D. Landes, *The Unbound Prometheus*, cited in Chapter 21. For a fundamental survey of European industrialization, see A. S. Milward and S. B. Saul, *The Development of the Economies of Continental Europe, 1850–1914* (Cambridge, Mass., 1977). An examination of the business cycles of the period can be found in A. Lewis, *Growth and Fluctuations, 1870–1913* (London, 1978). For an introduction to the development of mass consumerism in Britain, see W. H. Fraser, *The Coming of the Mass Market, 1850–1914* (Hamden, Conn., 1981). The impact of the new technology on

European thought is imaginatively discussed in S. Kern, *The Culture of Time and Space, 1880–1918* (Cambridge, Mass., 1983).

For an introduction to international socialism, see J. Joll, *The Second International, 1889–1914*, 2d ed. (New York, 1975); and L. Derfler, *Socialism since Marx: A Century of the European Left* (New York, 1973). On the emergence of German social democracy, see W. L. Guttsman, *The German Social Democratic Party, 1875–1933* (London, 1981); and V. Lidtke, *The Outlawed Party: Social Democracy in Germany, 1878–1890* (Princeton, N.J., 1966). There is a good introduction to anarchism in G. Woodcock, *Anarchism: A History of Libertarian Ideas and Movements* (Cleveland, Ohio, 1962).

Demographic problems are examined in T. McKeown, *The Modern Rise of Population* (New York, 1976). On European emigration, see C. Erickson, *Emigration from Europe, 1815–1914* (Cambridge, 1976); and

L. P. Moch, *Moving Europeans: Migration in Western Europe since 1650* (Bloomington, Ind., 1993).

For a good introduction to housing reform on the Continent, see N. Bullock and J. Read, *The Movement for Housing Reform in Germany and France, 1840–1914* (Cambridge, 1985). Working-class housing in Paris during its reconstruction is the subject of A. L. Shapiro, *Housing the Poor of Paris, 1850–1902* (Madison, Wis., 1985). E. Gauldie, *Cruel Habitations* (London, 1974) is a good account of working-class housing in Britain. The reconstruction of Paris is discussed in D. Pinkney, *Napoleon III and the Rebuilding of Paris* (Princeton, N.J., 1958).

An interesting work on aristocratic life is G. D. Philips, *The Diehards: Aristocratic Society and Politics in Edwardian England* (Cambridge, 1979). The argument for the continuing importance of the aristocracy is presented in the provocative book by A. Mayer, *Persistence of the Old Regime: Europe to the Great War* (New York, 1981). On the working classes, see L. Berlanstein, *The Working People of Paris, 1871–1914* (Baltimore, 1984).

There are good overviews of women's experiences in the nineteenth century in B. S. Anderson and J. P. Zinsser, *A History of Their Own*, vol. 2 (New York, 1988); and M. J. Boxer and J. H. Quataert, eds., *Connecting Spheres: Women in the Western World, 1500 to the Present* (New York, 1987). The world of women's work is examined in L. A. Tilly and J. W. Scott, *Women, Work, and Family* (New York, 1978). Important studies of middle-class women include P. Branca, *Silent Sisterhood: Middle Class Women in the Victorian Home* (London, 1975); and B. G. Smith, *Ladies of the Leisure Class: The Bourgeoises of Northern France in the Nineteenth Century* (Princeton, N.J., 1981). Prostitution is discussed in J. R. Walkowitz, *Prostitution and Victorian Society: Women, Class, and the State* (Cambridge, 1980). On the family

and children, see M. Mitterauer and R. Sieder, *The European Family* (Chicago, 1982); and the controversial E. Shorter, *The Making of the Modern Family* (New York, 1975). The treatment of children is examined in G. Behlmer, *Child Abuse and Moral Reform in England, 1870–1908* (Stanford, 1982).

On various aspects of education, see M. J. Maynes, *Schooling in Western Europe: A Social History* (Albany, N.Y., 1985); and J. S. Hurt, *Elementary Schooling and the Working Classes, 1860–1918* (London, 1979). A concise and well-presented survey of leisure patterns is G. Cross, *A Social History of Leisure since 1600* (State College, Pa., 1990). On the expansion of reading material, see A. J. Lee, *The Origins of the Popular Press in Britain, 1855–1914* (London, 1978).

The domestic politics of the period can be examined in the general works on individual countries listed in the bibliographies for Chapters 22 and 23. There are also specialized works on aspects of each country's history. The Irish problem is covered in O. MacDonagh, *States of Mind: A Study of Anglo-Irish Conflict, 1780–1980* (London, 1983). For a detailed examination of French history from 1871 to 1914, see J. M. Mayeur and M. Reberioux, *The Third Republic from Its Origins to the Great War, 1871–1914* (Cambridge, 1984). On the Paris Commune, see R. Tombs, *The War against Paris, 1871* (Cambridge, 1981). On Italy, see C. Seton-Watson, *Italy from Liberalism to Fascism* (London, 1967). An important aspect of Spanish history is examined in S. G. Payne, *Politics and the Military in Modern Spain* (Stanford, 1967). On the nationalities problem in the Austro-Hungarian Empire, see R. Kann, *The Multinational Empire, Nationalism and National Reform in the Habsburg Monarchy, 1848–1918*, 2 vols. (New York, 1950). On aspects of Russian history, see H. Rogger, *Russia in the Age of Modernization and Revolution, 1881–1917* (London, 1983).

CHAPTER
25

An Age of
Modernity and
Anxiety,
1894–1914

Many Europeans after 1894 continued to believe they lived in an era of material and human progress. For some, however, progress entailed much struggle. Emmeline Pankhurst, who became the leader of the women's suffrage movement in Britain, said that her determination to fight for women's rights stemmed from a childhood memory: "My father bent over me, shielding the candle flame with his big hand and I heard him say, somewhat sadly, 'What a pity she wasn't born a lad.'" Eventually, Emmeline Pankhurst and her daughters marched and fought for women's right to vote. The struggle was often violent: "They came in bruised, hatless, faces scratched, eyes swollen, noses bleeding," one of the Pankhurst daughters recalled. Arrested and jailed in 1908, Pankhurst informed her judges: "If you had the power to send us to prison, not for six months, but for six years, or for our lives, the Government must not think they could stop this agitation. It would go on!" It did go on, and women in Britain did eventually receive the right to vote; to some, this was yet another confirmation of Europe's progress.

But the period after 1894 was not just a time of progress; it was also a time of great tension as imperialist adventures, international rivalries, and cultural uncertainties disturbed the apparent calm. After 1880, Europeans engaged in a great race for colonies around the world. This competition for lands abroad greatly intensified existing antagonisms among European states.

Ultimately, Europeans proved incapable of finding constructive ways to cope with their international rivalries. The development of two large alliance systems—the Triple Alliance and the Triple Entente—may have helped preserve peace for a time, but eventually the alliances made it easier for the European nations to be drawn into World War I. The alliances helped maintain a balance of power, but also led to the creation of large armies, enormous military establishments, and immense arsenals. The alliances also helped create tensions that were unleashed when Eu-

Freud, *The Interpretation of Dreams*

Einstein's special theory of relativity

Picasso, first Cubist painting

Stravinsky, *The Rite of Spring*

Dreyfus affair in France

Women's Social and Political Union in Britain

Social Democratic Party
as largest party in Germany

Revolution in Russia

"Open Door" Policy in China

Russo-Japanese War

Triple Entente: France, Britain, and Russia

First Balkan War

ropeans rushed into the catastrophic carnage of World War I.

The cultural life of Europe in the decades before 1914 reflected similar dynamic tensions. The advent of mass education produced more well-informed citizens, but also made it easier for governments to stir up the masses by nationalistic appeals through the new mass journalism. At the same time, despite the appearance of progress, European philosophers, writers, and artists were creating modern cultural expressions that questioned traditional ideas and values and increasingly provoked a crisis of confidence. Before 1914, many intellectuals had a sense of unease about the direction society was heading, accompanied by a feeling of imminent catastrophe. They proved remarkably prophetic.

Toward the Modern Consciousness: Intellectual and Cultural Developments

Before 1914, most Europeans continued to believe in the values and ideals that had been generated by the Scientific Revolution and the Enlightenment. Reason, science, and progress were still important words in the European vocabulary. The ability of human beings to improve themselves and achieve a better society seemed to be well demonstrated by a rising standard of living, urban improvements, and mass education. Such products of modern technology as electric lights, phonographs, and automobiles reinforced the popular prestige

of science and the belief in the ability of the human mind to comprehend the universe through the use of reason. Near the end of the nineteenth century, however, a dramatic transformation in the realm of ideas and culture challenged many of these assumptions. A new view of the physical universe, a flight to the irrational, alternative views of human nature, and radically innovative forms of literary and artistic expression shattered old beliefs and opened the way to a modern consciousness. Although the real impact of many of these ideas was not felt until after World War I, they served to provoke a sense of confusion and anxiety before 1914 that would become even more pronounced after the war.

Developments in the Sciences: The Emergence of a New Physics

Science was one of the chief pillars underlying the optimistic and rationalistic view of the world that many Westerners shared in the nineteenth century. Supposedly based on hard facts and cold reason, science offered a certainty of belief in the orderliness of nature that was comforting to many people for whom traditional religious beliefs no longer had much meaning. This faith in science's ability to explain the world was reflected in an introductory paragraph in the University of Chicago's catalog in 1893: "It seems probable that most of the grand underlying principles in the physical sciences have been firmly established and that further advances are to be sought chiefly in the rigorous application of these principles to all the phenomena which come under our notice." Many naively believed that the application of already known scientific laws would give humanity a complete understanding of the physical world and an accurate picture of reality. The new physics dramatically altered that perspective.

Throughout much of the nineteenth century, Westerners adhered to the mechanical conception of the universe postulated by the classical physics of Isaac Newton. In this perspective, the universe was viewed as a giant machine in which time, space, and matter were objective realities that existed independently of those observing them. Matter was thought to be composed of indivisible and solid material bodies called atoms.

These views were first seriously questioned at the end of the nineteenth century. Some scientists had discovered that certain elements such as radium and polonium spontaneously gave off rays or radiation that apparently came from within the atom itself. Atoms were not simply hard, material bodies but small worlds containing such subatomic particles as electrons and protons that behaved in seemingly random and inexplicable fashion. Inquiry into the disintegrative process within atoms became a central theme of the new physics.

Building upon this work, in 1900 a Berlin physicist, Max Planck (1858–1947), disclosed a discovery that he believed was "as important as that of Newton." Planck rejected the belief that a heated body radiates energy in a steady stream but maintained instead that energy is radiated discontinuously, in irregular packets that he called "quanta." The quantum theory raised fundamental questions about the subatomic realm of the atom. By 1900, the old view of atoms as the basic building blocks of the material world was being seriously questioned, and the world of Newtonian physics was in trouble.

Albert Einstein (1879–1955), a German-born patent officer working in Switzerland, pushed these new theories of thermodynamics into new terrain. In 1905, Einstein published a paper, entitled "The Electrodynamics of Moving Bodies," that contained his special theory of relativity. According to relativity theory, space and time are not absolute, but relative to the observer, and both are interwoven into what Einstein called a four-dimensional space-time continuum. Neither space nor time had an existence independent of human experience. As Einstein later explained simply to a journalist: "It was formerly believed that if all material things disappeared out of the universe, time and space would be left. According to the relativity theory, however, time and space disappear together with the things."[1] Moreover, matter and energy reflected the relativity of time and space. Einstein concluded that matter was nothing but another form of energy. His epochal formula $E = mc^2$ —that each particle of matter is equivalent to its mass times the square of the velocity

of light—was the key theory explaining the vast energies contained within the atom. It led to the atomic age.

Like many geniuses throughout the ages, Einstein soon learned that new ideas are not readily accepted by people accustomed to old patterns. His work threatened the long-accepted Newtonian celestial mechanics and was not well received initially. When Einstein applied for a position at the University of Bern in 1907, he was immediately rejected. Many scientists were also unable to comprehend Einstein's ideas. During a total eclipse of the sun in May 1919, however, scientists were able to demonstrate that light was deflected in the gravitational field of the sun, just as Einstein had predicted. This confirmed Einstein's general theory of relativity and opened the scientific and intellectual world to his ideas. The 1920s would become the "heroic age" of physics.

Flight to the Irrational

Intellectually, the decades before 1914 witnessed a combination of contradictory developments. Thanks to the influence of science, confidence in human reason and progress still remained a dominant thread. At the same time, however, a small group of intellectuals attacked the idea of optimistic progress, dethroned reason, and glorified the irrational. Although these thinkers and writers were a distinct minority, the destructiveness of World War I made their ideas even more appealing after 1918 when it seemed that they had been proved right.

Friedrich Nietzsche (1844–1900) was one of the intellectuals who glorified the irrational. According to Nietzsche, Western bourgeois society was decadent and incapable of any real cultural creativity, primarily because of its excessive emphasis on the rational faculty at the expense of emotions, passions, and instincts. Reason, claimed Nietzsche, actually played little role in human life because humans were at the mercy of irrational life forces.

Nietzsche believed that Christianity should shoulder much of the blame for Western civilization's enfeeblement. The "slave morality" of Christianity, he believed, had obliterated the human impulse for life and had crushed the human will:

> I call Christianity the one great curse, the one enormous and innermost perversion. . . . I call it the one immortal blemish of mankind. . . . Christianity has taken the side of everything weak, base, ill-constituted, it has made an ideal out of opposition to the preservative instincts of

strong life. . . . Christianity is called the religion of pity.—Pity stands in antithesis to the basic emotions which enhance the energy of the feeling of life: it has a depressive effect. One loses force when one pities.[2]

According to Nietzsche, Christianity had crushed spontaneous human instincts and inculcated weakness and humility.

How, then, could Western society be renewed? First, said Nietzsche, one must recognize that "God is dead." Europeans had killed God, he said, and it was no longer possible to believe in some kind of cosmic order. Eliminating God and hence Christian morality had liberated human beings and made it possible to create a higher kind of being Nietzsche called the superman: "I teach you the Superman. Man is something that is to be surpassed."[3] Superior intellectuals must free themselves from the ordinary thinking of the masses, "the slaves, or the populace, or the herd, or whatever name you care to give them." Beyond good and evil, the supermen would create their own values and lead the masses: "It is necessary for higher man to declare war upon the masses." Nietzsche rejected and condemned political democracy, social reform, and universal suffrage.

Another popular revolutionary against reason in the 1890s was Henri Bergson (1859–1941), a French Jewish philosopher whose lectures at the University of Paris made him one of the most important influences in French thought in the early twentieth century. Bergson accepted rational, scientific thought as a practical instrument for providing useful knowledge, but maintained that it was incapable of arriving at truth or ultimate reality. To him, reality was the "life force" that suffused all things; it could not be divided into analyzable parts. Reality was a whole that could only be grasped intuitively and experienced directly. When we analyze it, we have merely a description, no longer the reality we have experienced.

Georges Sorel (1847–1922), a French political theorist, combined Bergson's and Nietzsche's ideas on the limits of rational thinking with his own passionate interest in revolutionary socialism. Sorel understood the political potential of the nonrational and advocated violent action as the only sure way to achieve the aims of socialism. To destroy capitalist society, he recommended the use of the general strike, envisioning it as a mythic image that had the power to inspire workers to take violent, heroic action against the capitalist order. Sorel also came to believe that the new socialist society would have to be governed by a small elite ruling body because the masses were incapable of ruling themselves.

◆ **Friedrich Nietzsche.** Nietzsche was a German philosopher who claimed that irrational life forces, not reason, determined the lives of human beings. Nietzsche proclaimed the "death of God" and the arrival of the "Superman."

Sigmund Freud and the Emergence of Psychoanalysis

Although poets and mystics had revealed a world of unconscious and irrational behavior, many scientifically oriented intellectuals under the impact of Enlightenment thought continued to believe that human beings responded to conscious motives in a rational fashion. At the end of the nineteenth century and beginning of the twentieth, the Viennese doctor Sigmund Freud put forth a series of theories that undermined optimism about the rational nature of the human mind. Freud's thought, like the new physics and the irrationalism of Nietzsche, added to the uncertainties of the age. His major ideas were published in 1900 in *The Interpretation of Dreams*, which contained the basic foundation of what came to be known as psychoanalysis.

According to Freud, human behavior was strongly determined by the unconscious, by former experiences and inner drives of which people were largely oblivious. To explore the contents of the unconscious, Freud relied not only on hypnosis but also on dreams, but the latter were dressed in an elaborate code that had to be deciphered if the contents were to be properly understood.

But why did some experiences whose influence persisted in controlling an individual's life remain unconscious? According to Freud, the answer was repression

◆ **Sigmund Freud.** Freud was one of the intellectual giants of the nineteenth century. His belief that unconscious forces strongly determine human behavior formed the foundation for twentieth-century psychoanalysis.

(see the box on p. 851), a process by which unsettling experiences were blotted from conscious awareness but still continued to influence behavior because they had become part of the unconscious. To explain how repression worked, Freud elaborated an intricate theory of the inner life of human beings.

According to Freud, a human being's inner life was a battleground of three contending forces: the id, ego, and superego. The id was the center of unconscious drives and was ruled by what Freud termed the pleasure principle. As creatures of desire, human beings directed their energy toward pleasure and away from pain. The id contained all kinds of lustful drives and desires, crude appetites and impulses, loves and hates. The ego was the seat of reason and hence the coordinator of the inner life. It was governed by the reality principle. Although humans were dominated by the pleasure principle, a true pursuit of pleasure was not feasible. The reality principle meant that people rejected pleasure so that they might live together in society; reality thwarted the unlimited pursuit of pleasure. The superego was the locus of conscience and represented the inhibitions and moral values that society in general and parents in particular imposed upon people. The superego served to force the ego to curb the unsatisfactory drives of the id.

The human being was thus a battleground between id, ego, and superego. Ego and superego exerted restraining influences on the unconscious id and repressed or kept out of consciousness what they wanted to. The most important repressions, according to Freud, were sexual, and he went on to develop a theory of infantile sexual drives embodied in the Oedipus complex (Electra complex for females), or the infant's craving for exclusive possession of the parent of the opposite sex.

To Freud, the inner life of humans was not a pretty picture. Repression began in childhood, and psychoanalysis was accomplished through a dialogue between psychotherapist and patient in which the therapist probed deeply into memory in order to retrace the chain of repression all the way back to its childhood origins. By making the conscious mind aware of the unconscious and its repressed contents, the patient's psychic conflict was resolved.

Freud, Marx, and Darwin have often been linked together as the three intellectual giants of the nineteenth century. Although many of Freud's ideas have been shown to be wrong in many details, he is still regarded as an important figure because of the impact his theories have had. Many historians still accept Freud's judgment of himself: "I have the distinct feeling that I have touched on one of the great secrets of nature."

⇒ Freud and the Concept of Repression ⇐

Freud's psychoanalytical theories resulted from his attempt to understand the world of the unconscious. This excerpt is taken from a lecture given in 1909 in which Freud describes how he arrived at his theory of the role of repression. Although Freud valued science and reason, his theories of the unconscious produced a new image of the human being as governed less by reason than by irrational forces.

Sigmund Freud, *Five Lectures on Psychoanalysis*

I did not abandon it [his technique of encouraging patients to reveal forgotten experiences], however, before the observations I made during my use of it afforded me decisive evidence. I found confirmation of the fact hat the forgotten memories were not lost. They were in the patient's possession and were ready to emerge in association to what was still known by him; but there was some force that prevented them from becoming conscious and compelled them to remain unconscious. The existence of this force could be assumed with certainty, since one became aware of an effort corresponding to it if, in opposition to it, one tried to introduce the unconscious memories into the patient's consciousness. The force which was maintaining the pathological condition became apparent in the form of resistance on the part of the patient.

It was on this idea of resistance, then, that I based my view of the course of physical events in hysteria. In order to effect a recovery, it had proved necessary to remove these resistances. Starting out from the mechanism of cure, it now became possible to construct quite definite ideas of the origin of the illness. The same forces which, in the form of resistance, were now of-

fering opposition to the forgotten material's being made conscious, must formerly have brought about the forgetting and must have pushed the pathogenic experiences in question out of consciousness. I gave the name of "repression" to this hypothetical process, and I considered that it was proved by the undeniable existence of resistance.

The further question could then be raised as to what these forces were and what the determinants were of the repression in which we now recognized the pathogenic mechanism of hysteria. A comparative study of the pathogenic situations which we had come to know through the cathartic procedure made it possible to answer this question. All these experiences had involved the emergence of a wishful impulse which was in sharp contrast to the subject's other wishes and which proved incompatible with the ethical and aesthetic standards of his personality. There had been a short conflict, and the end of this internal struggle was that the idea which had appeared before consciousness as the vehicle of this irreconcilable wish fell a victim to repression, was pushed out of consciousness with all its attached memories, and was forgotten. Thus the incompatibility of the wish in question with the patient's ego was the motive for the repression; the subject's ethical and other standards were the repressing forces. An acceptance of the incompatible wishful impulse or a prolongation of the conflict would have produced a high degree of unpleasure; this unpleasure was avoided by means of repression, which was thus revealed as one of the devices serving to protect the mental personality.

The Impact of Darwin: Social Darwinism and Racism

In the second half of the nineteenth century, scientific theories were sometimes wrongly applied to achieve other ends. The application of Darwin's principle of organic evolution to the social order came to be known as Social Darwinism. The most popular exponent of Social Darwinism was the British philosopher Herbert Spencer (1820–1903). Using Darwin's terminology, Spencer argued that societies were organisms that evolved through time from a struggle with their envi-

ronment. Progress came from "the struggle for survival," as the "fit"—the strong—advanced while the weak declined. As Spencer expressed it in 1896 in his book *Social Statics*:

> Pervading all Nature we may see at work a stern discipline which is a little cruel that it may be very kind. . . . Meanwhile, the well-being of existing humanity and the unfolding of it into this ultimate perfection, are both secured by the same beneficial though severe discipline to which the animate creation at large is subject. It seems hard that an unskillfulness, which with all his efforts he

cannot overcome, should entail hunger upon the artisan. It seems hard that a laborer, incapacitated by sickness from competing with his stronger fellows, should have to bear the resulting privations. It seems hard that widows and orphans should be left to struggle for life or death. Nevertheless, when regarded not separately but in connection with the interests of universal humanity, these harsh fatalities are seen to be full of beneficence—the same beneficence which brings to early graves the children of diseased parents, and singles out the intemperate and the debilitated as the victims of an epidemic.[4]

The state, then, should not intervene in this natural process. Some prominent businessmen used Social Darwinism to explain their success in the competitive business world. The strong and fit, the able and energetic had risen to the top; the stupid and lazy had fallen by the wayside.

Darwin's ideas were also applied to human society in an even more radical way by rabid nationalists and racists. In their pursuit of national greatness, extreme nationalists argued that individual needs must be subordinated to those of the nation and often insisted that nations, too, were engaged in a "struggle for existence" in which only the fittest survived. The German general Friedrich von Bernhardi gave war a Darwinist interpretation in his book, *Germany and the Next War*, published in 1907. He argued that:

> War is a biological necessity of the first importance, a regulative element in the life of mankind which cannot be dispensed with, since without it an unhealthy development will follow, which excludes every advancement of the race, and therefore all real civilization. "War is the father of all things." The sages of antiquity long before Darwin recognized this.[5]

Numerous nationalist organizations preached the same doctrine as Bernhardi. The Nationalist Association of Italy, for example, founded in 1910, declared that "we must teach Italy the value of international struggle. But international struggle is war? Well, then, let there be war! And nationalism will arouse the will for a victorious war, . . . the only way to national redemption."[6]

Although certainly not new to Western society, racism, too, was dramatically revived and strengthened by new biological arguments. Darwinian concepts were used throughout the Western world to justify the new imperialism of the late nineteenth century (see The New Imperialism later in this chapter). Perhaps nowhere was the combination of extreme nationalism and racism more evident and more dangerous than in Germany where racist nationalism was expressed in volkish

thought. The concept of the *Volk* (nation, people, or race) had been an underlying idea in German history since the beginning of the nineteenth century. Volkish thought combined a belief in the superiority of German culture with the sense of a universal mission for the German people. One of the chief propagandists for German volkish ideology at the turn of the century was Houston Stewart Chamberlain (1855–1927), an Englishman who became a German citizen. His book, *The Foundations of the Nineteenth Century*, published in 1899, made a special impact on Germany. Modern-day Germans, according to Chamberlain, were the only pure successors of the Aryans who were portrayed as the true and original creators of Western culture. The Aryan race, under German leadership, must be prepared to fight for Western civilization and save it from the destructive assaults of such lower races as Jews, Negroes, and Orientals. Increasingly, Jews were singled out by German volkish nationalists as the racial enemy in biological terms and as parasites who wanted to destroy the Aryan race.

The Attack on Christianity and the Response of the Churches

The growth of scientific thinking as well as the forces of modernization presented new challenges to the Christian churches. Industrialization and urbanization had an especially adverse effect on religious institutions. The mass migration of people from the countryside to the city meant a change from the close-knit, traditional ties of the village in which the church had been a key force to new urban patterns of social life from which the churches were often excluded. The established Christian churches had a weak hold on workers. For one thing, new churches were rarely built in working-class neighborhoods. Although workers were not atheists, as is sometimes claimed, they tended to develop their own culture in which organized religion played little role.

The political movements of the late nineteenth century were also hostile to the established Christian churches. Beginning during the eighteenth-century Enlightenment and continuing well into the nineteenth century, European governments, especially in predominantly Catholic countries, had imposed controls over church courts, religious orders, and appointments of the clergy. But after the failure of the revolutions of 1848, governments were eager to use the churches' aid in reestablishing order and therefore relaxed these controls. In France, the murder of the archbishop of Paris by the Paris Commune of 1871 served as an impetus to return people temporarily to organized religion. As the British Catholic Cardinal Manning wrote to the British prime minister, "My belief is that society without Christianity is the Commune. What hope can you give me?"[7]

Eventually, however, the close union of state authorities with established churches produced a backlash in the form of anticlericalism, especially in the liberal nation-states of the late nineteenth century. As one example, in the 1880s the French republican government substituted civic training for religious instruction in order to undermine the Catholic church's control of education. In 1901, Catholic teaching orders were outlawed, and four years later, in 1905, church and state were completely separated.

Science became one of the chief threats to all the Christian churches and even to religion itself in the nineteenth century. Darwin's theory of evolution, accepted by ever-larger numbers of educated Europeans, seemed to contradict the doctrine of divine creation. By suppressing Darwin's books and forbidding the teaching of the evolutionary hypothesis, the churches often caused even more educated people to reject established religions.

The scientific spirit also encouraged a number of biblical scholars to apply critical principles to the Bible, leading to the so-called higher criticism. One of its leading exponents was Ernst Renan (1823–1892), a French Catholic scholar. In his *Life of Jesus,* Renan questioned the historical accuracy of the Bible and presented a radically different picture of Jesus Christ. He saw Christ not as the son of God, but as a human being whose value lay in the example he provided by his life and teaching. To Renan, Christ's belief in his own divinity was merely the result of hallucinations.

One response of the Christian churches to these attacks was the outright rejection of modern ideas and forces. Protestant fundamentalist sects were especially important in maintaining a literal interpretation of the Bible. The Catholic church under Pope Pius IX (1846–1878) also took a rigid stand against modern ideas. In 1864, Pope Pius issued a papal encyclical called the *Syllabus of Errors* in which he stated that it is "an error to believe that the Roman Pontiff can and ought to reconcile himself to, and agree with, progress, liberalism, and modern civilization." He condemned nationalism, socialism, religious toleration, lay-controlled education, and freedom of speech and press.

Rejection of the new was not the churches' only response, however. A religious movement called Modernism included an attempt by the churches to reinterpret Christianity in the light of new developments. The modernists viewed the Bible as a book of useful moral ideas, encouraged Christians to become involved in social reforms, and insisted that the churches must provide a greater sense of community. The Catholic church condemned Modernism in 1907 and had driven it underground by the beginning of World War I. In Protestant churches, modernists competed with fundamentalists and had more success.

Yet another response of the Christian churches to modern ideas was compromise, an approach especially evident in the Catholic church during the pontificate of Leo XIII (1878–1903). Pope Leo permitted the teaching of evolution as a hypothesis in Catholic schools and also responded to the challenges of modernization in the economic and social spheres. In his encyclical *De Rerum Novarum,* issued in 1891, he upheld the individual's right to private property but at the same time criticized "naked" capitalism for the poverty and degradation in which it had left the working classes. Much in socialism, he declared, was Christian in principle, but he condemned Marxian socialism for its materialistic and antireligious foundations. The pope recommended that Catholics form socialist parties and labor unions of their own to help the workers.

Other religious groups also made efforts to win support for Christianity among the working-class poor and to restore religious practice among the urban working classes. The mainstream churches played only a limited role, however, because their parish systems were not prepared to cope with the flood of urban immigrants. Sects of evangelical missionaries were more successful, especially the Salvation Army founded in London in 1865 by William Booth, the first "general" of the army. The Salvation Army established food centers, shelters where the homeless could sleep, and "rescue homes" for women, but all these had a larger purpose as Booth admitted: "it is primarily and mainly for the sake of saving the soul that I seek the salvation of the body."[8] The Salvation Army moved to Paris in the 1880s, but was not well received by French Protestants who considered its revivalist-style meetings vulgar.

The Culture of Modernity

The revolution in physics and psychology was paralleled by a revolution in literature and the arts. Before 1914, writers and artists were rebelling against the traditional literary and artistic styles that had dominated European cultural life since the Renaissance. The changes that they produced have since been called Modernism.

NATURALISM AND SYMBOLISM IN LITERATURE

Throughout much of the late nineteenth century, literature was dominated by Naturalism. Naturalists accepted the material world as real and felt that literature should be realistic. By addressing social problems, writers could contribute to an objective understanding of the world. Although Naturalism was a continuation of Realism, it lacked the underlying note of liberal optimism about people and society that had still been prevalent in the 1850s. The Naturalists were pessimistic about Europe's future and often portrayed characters caught in the grip of forces beyond their control.

The novels of the French writer, Émile Zola (1840–1902), provide a good example of Naturalism. Against a backdrop of the urban slums and coal fields of northern France, Zola showed how alcoholism and different environments affected people's lives. The materialistic science of his age had an important influence on Zola. He had read Darwin's *Origin of Species* and had been impressed by its emphasis on the struggle for survival and the importance of environment and heredity. These themes were central to his *Rougon-Macquart*, a twenty-volume series of novels on the "natural and social history of a family." Zola maintained that the artist must analyze life as a biologist would dissect a living organism. He said, "I have simply done on living bodies the work of analysis which surgeons perform on corpses."

The last half of the nineteenth century was a golden age for Russian literature. The nineteenth-century realistic novel reached its high point in the works of Leo Tolstoy (1828–1910) and Fyodor Dostoevsky (1821–1881). Tolstoy's greatest work was *War and Peace*, a lengthy novel played out against the historical background of Napoleon's invasion of Russia in 1812. It is realistic in its vivid descriptions of military life and character portrayal. Each person is delineated clearly and analyzed psychologically. Upon a great landscape, Tolstoy imposed a fatalistic view of history that ultimately proved irrelevant in the face of life's enduring values of human love and trust.

Fyodor Dostoevsky combined narrative skill and acute psychological and moral observation with profound insights into human nature. Dostoevsky maintained that the major problem of his age was a loss of spiritual belief. Western people were attempting to gain salvation through the construction of a materialistic paradise built only by human reason and human will. Dostoevsky feared that the failure to incorporate spirit would result in total tyranny. His own life experiences led him to believe that only through suffering and faith could the human soul be purified, views that are evident in his best-known works, *Crime and Punishment* and *The Brothers Karamazov*.

At the turn of the century, a new group of writers, known as the Symbolists, reacted against Realism. Primarily interested in writing poetry, the Symbolists believed that an objective knowledge of the world was impossible. The external world was not real but only a collection of symbols that reflected the true reality of the individual human mind. Art, they believed, should function for its own sake instead of serving, criticizing, or seeking to understand society. In the works of the Symbolist poets, W. B. Yeats and Rainer Maria Rilke, poetry ceased to be part of popular culture because only through a knowledge of the poet's personal language could one hope to understand what the poem was saying (see the box on p. 855).

MODERNISM IN THE ARTS

Since the Renaissance, artists had tried to represent reality as accurately as possible. By the late nineteenth century, however, artists were seeking new forms of expression. The preamble to modern painting can be found in Impressionism, a movement that originated in France in the 1870s when a group of artists rejected the studios and museums and went out into the countryside to paint nature directly. Camille Pissarro (1830–1903), one of Impressionism's founders, expressed what they sought:

> Precise drawing is dry and hampers the impression of the whole, it destroys all sensations. Do not define too closely the outlines of things; it is the brush stroke of the right value and color which should produce the drawing. . . . The eye should not be fixed on one point, but should take in everything, while observing the reflections which the colors produce on their surroundings. Work at the same time upon sky, water, branches, ground, keeping everything going on an equal basis and unceasingly rework until you have got it. . . . Don't proceed according to rules and principles, but paint what you observe and feel. Paint generously and unhesitatingly, for it is best not to lose the first impression.[9]

Impressionists like Pissarro sought to put into painting their impressions of the changing effects of light on objects in nature. Capturing the untold variety of ways in which light reflected off different kinds of surfaces proved especially challenging to them.

Pissarro's suggestions are visibly portrayed in the work of Claude Monet (1840–1926). He was especially en-

Symbolist Poetry: Art for Art's Sake

The Symbolist movement was an important foundation for Modernism. The Symbolists believed that the working of the mind was the proper study of literature. Arthur Rimbaud was one of Symbolism's leading practitioners in France. Although his verses seem to have little real meaning, they were not meant to describe the external world precisely, but to enchant the mind. Art was not meant for the masses, but only for "art's sake." Rimbaud wrote, "By the alchemy of the words, I noted the inexpressible. I fixed giddiness."

Arthur Rimbaud, The Drunken Boat

As I floated down impassable rivers,
I felt the boatmen no longer guiding me.
After them came redskins who with war cries
Nailed them naked to the painted poles.

I was oblivious to the crew,
I who bore Flemish wheat and English cotton.
When the racket was finished with my boatmen,
The waters let me drift my own free way.

In the tide's furious pounding,
I, the other winter, emptier than children's minds,
I sailed! And the unmoored peninsulas
Have not suffered more triumphant turmoils.

The tempest blessed my maritime watches.
Lighter than a cork I danced on the waves,
Those eternal rollers of victims,
Ten nights, without regretting the lantern-foolish eye!

Sweeter than the bite of sour apples to a child,
The green water seeped through my wooden hull,
Rinsed me of blue wine stains and vomit,
Broke apart grappling iron and rudder.

And then I bathed myself in the poetry
Of the star-sprayed milk-white sea,
Devouring the azure greens; where, pale
And ravished, a pensive drowned one sometimes floats;

Where, suddenly staining the blueness, frenzies
And slow rhythms in the blazing of day,
Stronger than alcohol, vaster than our lyres,
The russet bitterness of love ferments. . . .

I have dreamed of the green night bedazzled with snow,
A kiss climbing slowly to the eyes of the sea,
The flow of unforgettable sap,
And the yellow-blue waking of singing phosphorous!

Long months I have followed, like maddened cattle,
The surge assaulting the rocks
Without dreaming that the Virgin's luminous feet
Could force a muzzle on the panting ocean!

I have struck against the shares of incredible Floridas
Mixing panther-eyed flowers like human skins!
Rainbows stretched like bridle reins
Under the ocean's horizon, toward sea-green troops!

I have seen the fermenting of monstrous marshes,
Nets where a whole Leviathan rots in the reeds!
The waters collapsing in the middle of the calm,
And horizons plunging toward the abyss!

Glaciers, silver suns, waves of pearl, charcoal skies,
Hideous beaches at the bottom of brown gulfs
Where giant serpents devoured by vermin
Tumble from twisted trees with black perfumes!

I would have liked to show the children those dolphins
On the blue waves, those golden singing fish.
—The froth of flowers lulled my voyagings,
Ineffable winds gave me wings by the moment. . . .

chanted with water and painted many pictures in which he sought to capture the interplay of light, water, and atmosphere, especially evident in *Impression, Sunrise.* But the Impressionists did not just paint scenes from nature. Streets and cabarets, rivers, and busy boulevards—wherever people congregated for work and leisure—formed their subject matter.

By the 1880s, a new movement known as Post-Impressionism arose in France but soon spread to other European countries. Post-Impressionism retained the Impressionist emphasis upon light and color but revolutionized it even further by paying more attention to structure and form. Post-Impressionists sought to use both color and line to express inner feelings and produce a personal statement of reality rather than an imitation of objects. Impressionist paintings had retained a sense of realism, but the Post-Impressionists shifted from objective reality to subjective reality and, in so doing,

✦ **Claude Monet, *Impression, Sunrise*.** Impressionists rejected "rules and principles" and sought to paint what they observed and felt in order "not to lose the first impression." As is evident in *Impression, Sunrise*, Monet sought to capture his impression of the fleeting moments of sunrise through the simple interplay of light, water, and atmosphere.

began to withdraw from the artist's traditional task of depicting the external world. Post-Impressionists were the real forerunners of modern art.

Paul Cézanne (1839–1906) was one of the most important Post-Impressionists. Initially, he was influenced by the Impressionists but soon rejected their work. In his paintings, such as *Woman with Coffee Pot*, Cézanne sought to express visually the underlying structure and form of everything he painted. The geometric shapes (cylinders and triangles) of the human form are related to the geometric shapes (cylinders and rectangles) of the other objects in the picture. As Cézanne explained to one young painter: "You must see in nature the cylinder, the sphere, and the cone."

Another famous Post-Impressionist was the tortured and tragic figure, Vincent van Gogh (1853–1890). For van Gogh, art was a spiritual experience. He was especially interested in color and believed that it could act as its own form of language. Van Gogh maintained that artists should paint what they feel. In his *Starry Night*, he painted a sky alive with whirling stars that overwhelmed the buildings huddled in the village below.

By the beginning of the twentieth century, the belief that the task of art was to represent "reality" had lost much of its meaning. By that time, the new psychology and the new physics had made it evident that many people were not sure what constituted reality anyway. Then, too, the development of photography gave artists

another reason to reject visual realism. First invented in the 1830s, photography became popular and widespread after George Eastman produced the first Kodak camera for the mass market in 1888. What was the point of an artist doing what the camera did better? Unlike the camera, which could only mirror reality, artists could create reality. As in literature, so also in modern art, individual consciousness became the source of meaning. As one artist expressed it: "Each [artist] should follow where the pulse of his own heart leads. . . . Our pounding heart drives us down, deep down to the source of all. What springs from this source, whether it may be called dream, idea or phantasy—must be taken seriously."[10] Between 1905 and 1914, this search for individual expression produced a wide variety of schools of painting, all of which had their greatest impact after World War I.

✦ **Paul Cézanne, *Woman with Coffee Pot*.** Post-Impressionists sought above all to express their inner feelings and capture on canvas their own vision of reality. In *Woman with Coffee Pot*, Paul Cézanne tried to relate the geometric shapes of his central female figure to the geometric shapes of the coffee pot and the rectangles of the door panels.

◆ **Vincent van Gogh,** *The Starry Night,* **1889.** The Dutch painter Vincent van Gogh was a major figure among the Post-Impressionists. His originality and power of expression made a strong impact upon his artistic successors. In *The Starry Night,* van Gogh's subjective vision was given full play as the dynamic swirling forms of the heavens above overwhelmed the village below. The heavens seem alive with a mysterious spiritual force.

By 1905, one of the most important figures in modern art was just beginning his career. Pablo Picasso (1881–1973) was from Spain but settled in Paris in 1904. Picasso was extremely flexible and painted in a remarkable variety of styles. He was instrumental in the development of a new style called Cubism that used geometric designs as visual stimuli to recreate reality in the viewer's mind. Picasso's 1907 work *Les Demoiselles d'Avignon* has been called the first Cubist painting.

The modern artist's flight from "visual reality" reached a high point in 1910 with the beginning of abstract painting. A Russian who worked in Germany, Vasily Kandinsky (1866–1944), was one of the founders of Abstract Expressionism. As is evident in his *Painting with White Border,* Kandinsky sought to avoid representation altogether. He believed that art should speak directly to the soul. To do so, it must avoid any reference to visual reality and concentrate on color.

MODERNISM IN MUSIC

In the first half of the nineteenth century, the Romantics' attraction to exotic and primitive cultures had sparked a fascination with folk music, which became

◆ Pablo Picasso, *Les Demoiselles d'Avignon, 1907.*
  Pablo Picasso, a major pioneer and activist of modern art,
experimented with a remarkable variety of modern styles. His
Les Demoiselles d'Avignon was the first great example of Cubism,
which one art historian has called "the first style of this century
to break radically with the past." Geometric shapes replace
traditional forms, forcing the viewer to recreate reality in his or
her own mind.

increasingly important as musicians began to look for
ways to express their national identities. In the second
half of the century, new flames of nationalistic spirit
were fanned in both literary and musical circles. Nationalistic feelings were expressed in a variety of ways,
from the employment of national themes for operas to
the incorporation of folk songs and dances in new
compositions.

One example of this new nationalistic spirit may be
found in the Scandinavian composer Edvard Grieg
(1843–1907), who remained a dedicated supporter of
Norwegian nationalism throughout his life. Grieg's nationalism expressed itself in the lyric melodies found in
the folk music of his homeland. These simple melodies
were far better suited to smaller compositional forms, so
he tended not to write in the grand symphonic style.
Among his best-known works is the *Peer Gynt Suite*
(1876), incidental music to Henrik Ibsen's play. Grieg's
music paved the way for the creation of a national music
style in Norway.

The Impressionist movement in music followed its
artistic counterpart by some thirty years. Impressionist
music stressed elusive moods and haunting sensations
and is distinct in its delicate beauty and elegance of
sound. The composer most tangibly linked to the Impressionist movement was Claude Debussy (1862–
1918), whose musical compositions were often inspired
by the visual arts. The titles that Debussy often assigned
to his works, such as *Sketches, Images,* and *Prints,* are

◆ Vasily Kandinsky, *Composition
VIII, No. 2 (Painting with White
Border).* One of the founders of
Abstract Expressionism was the Russian
Vasily Kandinsky, who sought to
eliminate representation altogether by
focusing on color and avoiding any
resemblance to visual reality. In *Painting
with White Border,* Kandinsky used color
"to send light into the darkness of
men's hearts." He believed that color,
like music, could fulfill a spiritual goal
of appealing directly to the human
being.

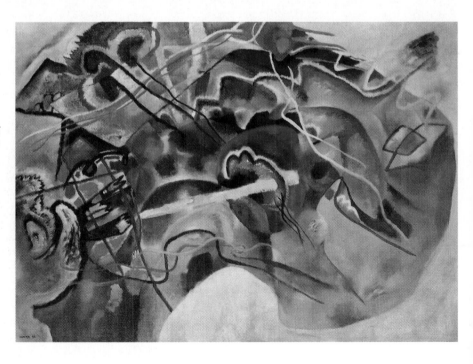

indicative of this close association between painters and musicians.

One of Debussy's most famous works, *Prelude to the Afternoon of a Faun* (1894), was actually inspired by a poem, "Afternoon of a Faun," composed by his friend, the Symbolist poet Stéphane Mallarmé. But Debussy did not tell a story in music, as was the goal of the Romantic tone poems. Rather, *Prelude to the Afternoon of a Faun* re-created in sound the overall feeling of the poem. Said Mallarmé upon listening to Debussy's piece, "I was not expecting anything like this. This music prolongs the emotion of my poem, and evokes the scene more vividly than color."[11]

Other composers adopted stylistic idioms that imitated presumably primitive forms in an attempt to express less refined, and therefore more genuine, feelings. A chief exponent of musical primitivism was Igor Stravinsky (1882–1971), one of the twentieth century's most important composers, both for his compositions and for his impact on other composers. He gained international fame as a ballet composer and together with the Ballet Russe, under the direction of Sergei Diaghilev (1872–1929), revolutionized the world of music with a series of ballets. The three most significant ballets Stravinsky composed for Diaghilev's company were *The Firebird* (1910), *Petrushka* (1911), and *The Rite of Spring* (1913). All three were based on Russian folk tales. *The Rite of Spring* proved to be a revolutionary piece in the development of music. At the premiere on May 29, 1913, the pulsating rhythms, sharp dissonances, and unusual dancing overwhelmed the Paris audience and caused a riot at the theater. Stravinsky's music was an important force in inaugurating the modern musical movement that explored new avenues of tonality.

Politics: New Directions and New Uncertainties

The uncertainties in European intellectual and cultural life were paralleled by growing anxieties in European political life. The seemingly steady progress in the growth of liberal principles and political democracy after 1871 was soon slowed or even halted altogether after 1894. The new mass politics had opened the door to changes that many nineteenth-century liberals found unacceptable, and liberals themselves were forced to move in new directions. The appearance of a new right-wing politics based on racism added an ugly note to the already existing anxieties. With their newfound voting rights, workers elected socialists who demanded

new reforms when they took their places in legislative bodies. Women, too, made new demands, insisting on the right to vote and using new tactics to gain it. In central and eastern Europe, tensions grew as authoritarian governments refused to meet the demands of reformers. And outside Europe, a new giant appeared in the Western world as the United States emerged as a great industrial power with immense potential.

The Movement for Women's Rights

In the 1830s, a number of women in the United States and Europe, who worked together in several reform movements, became frustrated by the apparent prejudices against females. They sought improvements for women by focusing on specific goals. Family and marriage laws were especially singled out since it was difficult for women to secure divorces and property laws gave husbands almost complete control over the property of their wives. These early efforts were not overly successful, however. For example, women did not gain the right to their own property until 1870 in Britain, 1900 in Germany, and 1907 in France.

Custody and property rights were only a beginning for the women's movement, however. Some middle- and upper-middle-class women gained access to higher edu-

◆ **The Arrest of Suffragists.** The nineteenth century witnessed the development of a strong movement for women's rights. For many feminists, the right to vote came to represent the key to other reforms that would benefit women. In Britain, suffragists attracted attention to their cause by unusual publicity stunts. This photograph shows the arrest of suffragists after a demonstration near Buckingham Palace, the London residence of the royal family.

cation while others sought entry into occupations dominated by men. The first to fall was teaching. As medical training was largely closed to women, they sought alternatives in the development of nursing. One nursing pioneer was Amalie Sieveking (1794–1859), who founded the Female Association for the Care of the Poor and Sick in Hamburg, Germany. As she explained: "To me, at least as important were the benefits which [work with the poor] seemed to promise for those of my sisters who would join me in such a work of charity. The higher interests of my sex were close to my heart."[12] Sieveking's work was followed by the more famous British nurse, Florence Nightingale (1820–1910), whose efforts during the Crimean War, along with those of Clara Barton (1821–1912) in the American Civil War, transformed nursing into a profession of trained, middle-class "women in white."

By the 1840s and 1850s, the movement for women's rights had entered the political arena with the call for equal political rights. Many feminists believed that the right to vote was the key to all other reforms to improve the position of women. This movement was most vibrant in Great Britain and the United States, both countries that had been influenced by the natural rights tradition of the Enlightenment. It was not as strong in Germany because of that country's authoritarian makeup nor in France where feminists were unable to organize mass rallies in support of women's rights.

The British women's movement was the most vocal and active in Europe, but divided over tactics. The liberal Millicent Fawcett (1847–1929) organized a moderate group who believed that women must demonstrate that they would use political power responsibly if they wanted Parliament to grant them the right to vote. Another group, however, favored a more radical approach. Emmeline Pankhurst (1858–1928) and her daughters, Christabel and Sylvia, founded the Women's Social and Political Union in 1903, which enrolled mostly middle- and upper-class women. Pankhurst's organization realized the value of the media and used unusual publicity stunts to call attention to its demands. Derisively labeled suffragettes by male politicians, they pelted government officials with eggs, chained themselves to lampposts, smashed the windows of department stores on fashionable shopping streets, burned railroad cars, and went on hunger strikes in jail. In 1913, Emily Davison accepted martyrdom for the cause when she threw herself in front of the king's horse at the Epsom Derby horse race. Suffragists had one fundamental aim, the right of women to full citizenship in the nation-state (see the box on p. 861).

Although demands for women's rights were heard throughout Europe and the United States before World War I, only in Finland, Norway, and some American states did women actually receive the right to vote before 1914. It would take the dramatic upheaval of World War I before male-dominated governments capitulated on this basic issue (see Chapter 26).

Jews within the European Nation-State

Near the end of the nineteenth century, a revival of racism combined with extreme nationalism to produce a new right-wing politics aimed primarily at the Jews. Of course, anti-Semitism was not new to European civilization. Since the Middle Ages, Jews had been portrayed as the murderers of Christ and subjected to mob violence; their rights had been restricted, and they had been physically separated from Christians in quarters known as ghettos.

In the nineteenth century, as a result of the ideals of the Enlightenment and the French Revolution, Jews were increasingly granted legal equality in many European countries. The French revolutionary decrees of 1790 and 1791 emancipated the Jews and admitted them to full citizenship. They were not completely accepted, however, and anti-Semitism remained a fact of French life. In 1805, Napoleon consolidated their position as citizens, but followed this in 1808 with an "Infamous Decree" that placed restrictions on Jewish moneylending and on the movement of Jews within France.

This ambivalence toward the Jews was apparent throughout Europe. In Prussia, for example, Jews were emancipated in 1812 but still restricted. They could not hold government offices or take advanced degrees in universities. After the revolutions of 1848, emancipation became a fact of life for Jews throughout western and central Europe. For many Jews, emancipation enabled them to leave the ghetto and become assimilated as hundreds of thousands of Jews entered what had been the closed worlds of parliaments and universities. In 1880, for example, Jews made up 10 percent of the population of the city of Vienna, Austria, but 39 percent of its medical students and 23 percent of its law students. "A Jew could leave his Jewishness" behind as the career of Benjamin Disraeli, who became prime minister of Great Britain, demonstrated. Many other Jews became eminently successful as bankers, lawyers, scientists, scholars, journalists, and stage performers.

These achievements represent only one side of the picture, however, as is evident from the Dreyfus affair in

Advice to Women: Be Independent

Although a majority of women probably followed the nineteenth-century middle-class ideal of women as keepers of the household and nurturers of husband and children, an increasing number of women fought for the rights of women. This selection is taken from Act III of Henrik Ibsen's A Doll's House (1879), in which the character Nora Helmer declares her independence from her husband's control.

Henrik Ibsen, A Doll's House

NORA: (*Pause*) Does anything strike you as we sit here?

HELMER: What should strike me?

NORA: We've been married eight years; does it not strike you that this is the first time we two, you and I, man and wife, have talked together seriously?

HELMER: Seriously? What do you mean, *seriously*?

NORA: For eight whole years, and more—ever since the day we first met—we have never exchanged one serious word about serious things. . . .

HELMER: Why, my dearest Nora, what have you to do with serious things?

NORA: There we have it! You have never understood me. I've had great injustice done to me, Torvald; first by father, then by you.

HELMER: What! Your father *and* me? We, who have loved you more than all the world!

NORA (*Shaking her head*): You have never loved me. You just found it amusing to think you were in love with me.

HELMER: Nora! What a thing to say!

NORA: Yes, it's true, Torvald. When I was living at home with father, he told me his opinions and mine were the same. If I had different opinions, I said nothing about them, because he would not have liked it. He used to call me his doll-child and played with me as I played with my dolls. Then I came to live in your house.

HELMER: What a way to speak of our marriage!

NORA (*Undisturbed*): I mean that I passed from father's hands into yours. You arranged everything to your taste and I got the same tastes as you; or pretended to—I don't know which—both, perhaps; sometimes one, sometimes the other. When I look back on it now, I seem to have been living here like a beggar, on hand-outs. I lived by performing tricks for you, Torvald. But that was how you wanted it. You and father have done me a great wrong. It is your fault that my life has come to naught.

HELMER: Why, Nora, how unreasonable and ungrateful! Haven't you been happy here?

NORA: No, never. I thought I was, but I never was.

HELMER: Not—not happy! . . .

NORA: I must stand quite alone if I am ever to know myself and my surroundings; so I cannot stay with you.

HELMER: Nora! Nora!

NORA: I am going at once. I daresay [my friend] Christina will take me in for tonight.

HELMER: You are mad! I shall not allow it! I forbid it!

NORA: It's no use your forbidding me anything now. I shall take with me only what belongs to me; from you I will accept nothing, either now or later.

HELMER: This is madness!

NORA: Tomorrow I shall go home—I mean to what was my home. It will be easier for me to find a job there.

HELMER: On, in your blind inexperience—

NORA: I must try to gain experience, Torvald.

HELMER: Forsake your home, you husband, your children! And you don't consider what the world will say.

NORA: I can't pay attention to that. I only know that I must do it.

HELMER: This is monstrous! Can you forsake your holiest duties?

NORA: What do you consider my holiest duties?

HELMER: Need I tell you that? Your duties to your husband and children.

NORA: I have other duties equally sacred.

HELMER: Impossible! What do you mean?

NORA: My duties toward myself.

HELMER: Before all else you are a wife and a mother.

NORA: That I no longer believe. Before all else I believe I am a human being just as much as you are—or at least that I should try to become one. I know that most people agree with you, Torvald, and that they say so in books. But I can no longer be satisfied with what most people say and what is in books. I must think things out for myself and try to get clear about them.

France. Alfred Dreyfus, a Jew, was a captain in the French general staff. Early in 1895, a secret military court found him guilty of selling army secrets and condemned him to life imprisonment on Devil's Island. During his trial, right-wing mobs yelled "Death to the Jews." Soon after the trial, however, evidence emerged that pointed to Dreyfus's innocence. Another officer, a Catholic aristocrat, was more obviously the traitor, but the army, a stronghold of aristocratic and Catholic officers, refused a new trial. Republican leaders insisted, however, after a wave of immense public outrage. Although the new trial failed to set aside the guilty verdict, the government pardoned Dreyfus in 1899, and in 1906, he was finally fully exonerated.

In Austrian politics, the Christian Socialists combined agitation for workers with a virulent anti-Semitism. They were most powerful in Vienna where they were led by Karl Lueger, mayor of Vienna from 1897 to 1910. Imperial Vienna at the turn of the century was a brilliant center of European culture, but it was also the home of an insidious German nationalism that blamed Jews for the corruption of German culture. It was in Vienna between 1907 and 1913 that Adolf Hitler later claimed to have found his worldview, one that was largely based on a violent German nationalism and a rabid anti-Semitism.

Germany, too, had its right-wing anti-Semitic parties, such as Adolf Stocker's Christian Social Workers. These parties used anti-Semitism to win the votes of traditional lower-middle-class groups who felt threatened by the new economic forces of the times. These German anti-Semitic parties were based on race. In medieval times Jews could convert to Christianity and escape from their religion. To modern racial anti-Semites, Jews were racially stained; this could not be altered by conversion. One could not be both German and Jew. Hermann Ahlwardt, an anti-Semitic member of the German Reichstag, made this clear in a speech to that body: "The Jew is no German. . . . A Jew who was born in Germany does not thereby become a German; he is still a Jew. Therefore it is imperative that we realize that Jewish racial characteristics differ so greatly from ours that a common life of Jews and Germans under the same laws is quite impossible because the Germans will perish."[13] After 1898, the political strength of the German anti-Semitic parties began to decline.

The worst treatment of Jews in the last two decades of the nineteenth century and the first decade of the twentieth occurred in eastern Europe where 72 percent of the entire world Jewish population lived. Anti-Semitism was a regular part of tsarist Russian life. Russian Jews were admitted to secondary schools and universities only under a quota system and were forced to live in certain regions of the country. Persecutions and pogroms were widespread. Between 1903 and 1906, pogroms took place in almost 700 Russian towns and villages, mostly in Ukraine. Hundreds of thousands of Jews decided to emigrate to escape the persecution. Between 1881 and 1899, an average of 23,000 Jews left Russia each year. Many of them went to the United States, although some (probably about 25,000) moved to Palestine, which soon became the focus for a Jewish nationalist movement called Zionism.

The emancipation of the nineteenth century had presented vast opportunities for some Jews, but dilemmas for others. What was the price of citizenship? Did emancipation mean full assimilation and did assimilation mean the disruption of traditional Jewish life? Many paid the price willingly, but others questioned its value and advocated a different answer, a return to Palestine. For many Jews, Palestine, the land of ancient Israel, had long been the land of their dreams. During the nineteenth century, as nationalist ideas spread and Italians, Poles, Irish, Greeks, and others sought national emancipation so too did the idea of national independence capture the imagination of some Jews. A key figure in the growth of political Zionism was Theodor Herzl (1860–1904). Herzl had received a law degree in Vienna where he became a journalist for a Viennese

◆ **Theodor Herzl.** A journalist for a Viennese newspaper, Herzl became an ardent advocate of political Zionism. In *The Jewish State,* he argued for the creation of a Jewish state in Palestine. He is seen here in Basel, Switzerland, where he was attending an international Zionist congress that he had helped to organize.

⋟ *The Voice of Zionism: Theodor Herzl and the Jewish State* ⋞

The Austrian Jewish journalist Theodor Herzl wrote The Jewish State *in the summer of 1895 in Paris while he was covering the Dreyfus case for his Vienna newspaper. During several weeks of feverish composition, he set out to analyze the fundamental causes of anti-Semitism and devise a solution to the "Jewish problem." In this selection, he discusses two of his major conclusions.*

Theodor Herzl, *The Jewish State*

I do not intend to arouse sympathetic emotions on our behalf. That would be a foolish, futile, and undignified proceeding. I shall content myself with putting the following questions to the Jews: Is it true that, in countries where we live in perceptible numbers, the position of Jewish lawyers, doctors, technicians, teachers, and employees of all descriptions becomes daily more intolerable? True, that the Jewish middle classes are seriously threatened? True, that the passions of the mob are incited against our wealthy people? True, that our poor endure greater sufferings than any other proletariat?

I think that this external pressure makes itself felt everywhere. In our economically upper classes it causes discomfort, in our middle classes continual and grave anxieties, in our lower classes absolute despair.

Everything tends, in fact, to one and the same conclusion, which is clearly enunciated in that classic Berlin phrase: "Juden 'raus!" (Out with the Jews!)

I shall now put the Jewish Question in the curtest possible form: Are we to "get out" now? And if so, to what place?

Or, may we yet remain? And if so, how long?

Let us first settle the point of staying where we are. Can we hope for better days, can we possess our souls in patience, can we wait in pious resignation till the princes and peoples of this earth are more mercifully disposed toward us? I say that we cannot hope for a change in the current of feeling. And why not? Were we as near to the hearts of princes as are their other subjects, even so they could not protect us. They would only feed popular hatred of Jews by showing us too much favor. By "too much," I really mean less than is claimed as a right by every ordinary citizen, or by every race. The nations in whose midst Jews live are all, either covertly or openly, Anti-Semitic. . . .

The whole plan is in its essence perfectly simple, as it must necessarily be if it is to come within the comprehension of all.

Let the sovereignty be granted us over a portion of the globe large enough to satisfy the rightful requirements of a nation; the rest we shall manage for ourselves.

The creation of a new State is neither ridiculous nor impossible. We have in our day witnessed the process in connection with nations which were not in the bulk of the middle class, but poorer, less educated, and consequently weaker than ourselves. The Governments of all countries scourged by Anti-Semitism will be keenly interested in assisting us to obtain the sovereignty we want. . . .

Palestine is our ever-memorable historic home. The very name of Palestine would attract our people with a force of marvellous potency. Supposing his Majesty the Sultan were to give us Palestine, we could in return undertake to regulate the whole finances of Turkey. We should there form a portion of the rampart of Europe against Asia, an outpost of civilization as opposed to barbarism. We should as a neutral State remain in contact with all Europe, which would have to guarantee our existence. The sanctuaries of Christendom would be safeguarded by assigning to them an extra-territorial status such as is well known to the law of nations. We should form a guard of honor about these sanctuaries, answering for the fulfillment of this duty with our existence. This guard of honor would be the great symbol of the solution of the Jewish Question after eighteen centuries of Jewish suffering.

---

newspaper. He was shocked into action on behalf of Jews when he covered the Dreyfus trial as a correspondent for his newspaper in Paris. In 1896, he published a book called *The Jewish State* (see the box above) in which he straightforwardly advocated that "The Jews who wish it will have their state." Financial support for the development of yishuvs or settlements in Palestine came from wealthy Jewish banking families, especially from Baron Edmond James de Rothschild, called "Father of the Yishuv" for his contributions. Rothschild and others like him wanted a refuge in Palestine for persecuted Jews, not a political Jewish state. Even settlements were difficult because Palestine was then part of the Ottoman Empire and Ottoman authorities were opposed to Jewish immigration. In 1891, one Jewish essayist pointed to the problems this would create:

We abroad are accustomed to believe that Erez Israel [the land of Israel] is almost totally desolate at present . . . but in reality it is not so. . . . Arabs, especially those in towns, see and understand our activities and aims in the country but keep quiet and pretend as if they did not know, . . . and they try to exploit us, too, and profit from the new guests while laughing at us in their hearts. But if the time comes and our people make such progress as to displace the people of the country . . . they will not lightly surrender the place.[14]

Despite the warnings, however, the First Zionist Congress, which met in Switzerland in 1897, proclaimed as its aim the creation of a "home in Palestine secured by public law" for the Jewish people. In 1900, 1,000 Jews migrated to Palestine. And although 3,000 Jews went annually to Palestine between 1904 and 1914, the Zionist dream remained just that on the eve of World War I.

The Transformation of Liberalism: Great Britain and Italy

In dealing with the problems created by the new mass politics, liberal governments often followed policies that undermined the basic tenets of liberalism. This was certainly true in Great Britain, where the demands of the working-class movement caused Liberals to move away from their ideals. Although workers were enjoying better wages and living standards, those improvements were relative to the miseries of the first half of the nineteenth century. Considerable suffering still remained. Neither Liberals nor Conservatives were moved to accommodate the working class with significant social reforms until they were forced to do so by the pressure of two new working-class organizations: trade unions and the Labour Party.

Trade unions began to advocate more radical change of the economic system, calling for "collective ownership and control over production, distribution and exchange." At the same time, a movement for laborers emerged among a group of intellectuals known as the Fabian Socialists who stressed the need for the workers to use their right to vote to capture the House of Commons and pass legislation that would benefit the laboring class. Neither the Fabian Socialists nor the British trade unions were Marxist oriented. They did not advocate class struggle and revolution but evolution toward a socialist state by democratic means. In 1900, representatives of the trade unions and Fabian Socialists coalesced to form the Labour Party. Initially, they were not too successful, but by 1906 they had managed to elect twenty-nine members to the House of Commons.

The Liberals, who gained control of the House of Commons in that year and held the government from 1906 to 1914, perceived that they would have to enact a program of social welfare or lose the support of the workers. The policy of reform was especially advanced by David Lloyd George (1863–1945), a brilliant young orator from Wales who had been deeply moved by the misery of Welsh coal miners. The Liberals abandoned the classical principles of laissez-faire and voted for a series of social reforms. The National Insurance Act of 1911 provided benefits for workers in case of sickness and unemployment, to be financed by compulsory contributions from workers, employers, and the state. Additional legislation provided a small pension for those over seventy and compensation for those injured in accidents while at work. To pay for the new program, Lloyd George increased the tax burden on the wealthy classes. Though both the benefits of the program and the tax increases were modest, they were the first hesitant steps toward the future British welfare state. Liberalism, which had been based on the principle that the government that governs least governs best, had been transformed.

Liberals had even greater problems in Italy. A certain amount of stability was achieved from 1903 to 1914 when the liberal leader Giovanni Giolitti served intermittently as prime minister. Giolitti was a master of using *trasformismo* or transformism, a system in which old political groups were transformed into new government coalitions by political and economic bribery. In the long run, however, Giolitti's devious methods, made Italian politics even more corrupt and unmanageable. When urban workers turned to violence to protest their living and working conditions, Giolitti tried to appease them with social welfare legislation and universal male suffrage in 1912. To strengthen his popularity, he also aroused nationalistic passions by conquering Libya. Despite his efforts, however, worker unrest continued, and in 1914 government troops had to be used to crush rioting workers.

Growing Tensions in Germany

The new imperial Germany begun by Bismarck in 1871 continued as an "authoritarian, conservative, military-bureaucratic power state" during the reign of Emperor William II (1888–1918). Unstable and aggressive, the emperor was inclined to tactless remarks, as when he told the soldiers of a Berlin regiment that they must be prepared to shoot their fathers and mothers if he ordered them to do so. A small group of about twenty powerful men joined William in setting government policy.

By 1914, Germany had become the strongest military and industrial power on the Continent. New social configurations had emerged as over 50 percent of German workers had jobs in industry while only 30 percent of the workforce was still in agriculture. Urban centers had mushroomed in number and size. The rapid changes in William's Germany helped to produce a society torn between modernization and traditionalism.

The growth of industrialization led to even greater expansion for the Social Democratic Party. Despite the enactment of new welfare legislation to favor the working classes, William II was no more successful than Bismarck in slowing the growth of the Social Democrats. By 1912, it had become the largest single party in the Reichstag. At the same time, the party increasingly became less revolutionary and more revisionist in its outlook. Nevertheless, its growth frightened the middle and upper classes who blamed labor for their own problems.

With the expansion of industry and cities came demands for more political participation and growing sentiment for reforms that would produce greater democratization. Conservative forces, especially the landowning nobility and representatives of heavy industry, two of the powerful ruling groups in Germany, tried to block it by supporting William II's activist foreign policy (see New Directions and New Crises later in this chapter). Expansionism, they believed, would divert people from further democratization.

The tensions in German society created by the conflict between modernization and traditionalism were also manifested in a new, radicalized, right-wing politics. A number of nationalist pressure groups arose to support nationalistic goals. Antisocialist and antiliberal, such groups as the Pan-German League stressed strong German nationalism and advocated imperialism as a tool to overcome social divisions and unite all classes. They were also anti-Semitic and denounced Jews as the destroyers of the national community. Traditional conservatives, frightened by the growth of the socialists, often made common cause with these radical right-wing groups, giving them respectability.

Industrialization and Revolution in Imperial Russia

Starting in the 1890s, Russia experienced a massive surge of state-sponsored industrialism under the guiding hand of Sergei Witte, the minister for finance from 1892 to 1903. Count Witte saw industrial growth as crucial to Russia's national strength. Believing that railroads were a very powerful weapon in economic development,

Witte pushed the government toward a program of massive railroad construction. By 1900, 35,000 miles of railroads, including large parts of the 5,000-mile trans-Siberian line between Moscow and Vladivostok on the Pacific Ocean, had been built. Witte also encouraged a system of protective tariffs to help Russian industry and persuaded Tsar Nicholas II (1894–1917) that foreign capital was essential for rapid industrial development. Witte's program made possible the rapid growth of a modern steel and coal industry in Ukraine, making Russia by 1900 the fourth largest producer of steel behind the United States, Germany, and Great Britain.

With industrialization came factories, an industrial working class, industrial suburbs around St. Petersburg and Moscow, and the pitiful working and living conditions that accompanied the beginnings of industrialization everywhere. Socialist thought and socialist parties developed, although repression in Russia soon forced them to go underground and become revolutionary. The Marxist Social Democratic Party, for example, held its first congress in Minsk in 1898, but the arrest of its

✦ **Nicholas II.** The last tsar of Russia hoped to preserve the traditional autocratic ways of his predecessors. In this photograph, Nicholas II and his wife Alexandra are shown returning from a church at Tsarskoe-Selo.

leaders caused the next one to be held in Brussels in 1903, attended by Russian émigrés. The Social Revolutionaries worked to overthrow the tsarist autocracy and establish peasant socialism. Having no other outlet for their opposition to the regime, they advocated political terrorism and attempted to assassinate government officials and members of the ruling dynasty. The growing opposition to the tsarist regime finally exploded into revolution in 1905.

THE REVOLUTION OF 1905

As happened elsewhere in Europe in the nineteenth century, defeat in war led to political upheaval at home. Russia's territorial expansion to the south and east, especially its designs on northern Korea, led to a confrontation with Japan. Japan made a surprise attack on the Russian Far Eastern fleet at Port Arthur on February 8, 1904. In turn, Russia sent its Baltic fleet halfway around the world to the Far East, only to be defeated by the new Japanese navy at Tsushima Strait off the coast of Japan. Much to the astonishment of many Europeans who could not believe that an Asian state was militarily superior to a great European power, the Russians admitted defeat and sued for peace in 1905.

In the midst of the war, the growing discontent of increased numbers of Russians rapidly led to upheaval. A middle class of business and professional people longed for liberal institutions and a liberal political system. Nationalities were dissatisfied with their domination by an ethnic Russian population that constituted only 45 percent of the empire's total population. Peas-

ants were still suffering from lack of land, and laborers felt oppressed by their working and living conditions in Russia's large cities. The breakdown of the transport system caused by the Russo-Japanese War led to food shortages in the major cities of Russia. As a result, on January 9, 1905, a massive procession of workers went to the Winter Palace in St. Petersburg to present a petition of grievances to the tsar (see the box on p. 867). Troops foolishly opened fire on the peaceful demonstration, killing hundreds and launching a revolution. This "Bloody Sunday" incited workers to call strikes and form unions while zemstvos demanded the formation of parliamentary government, ethnic groups revolted, and peasants burned the houses of landowners. After a general strike in October 1905, the government capitulated. Count Witte had advised the tsar to divide his opponents: "It is not on the extremists that the existence and integrity of the state depend. As long as the government has support in the broad strata of society, a peaceful solution to the crisis is still possible."[15] Nicholas II issued the October Manifesto, in which he granted civil liberties and agreed to create a Duma, or legislative assembly, elected directly by a broad franchise. This satisfied the middle-class moderates who now supported the government's repression of a workers' uprising in Moscow at the end of 1905.

But real constitutional monarchy proved short-lived. Under Peter Stolypin, who served as the tsar's chief adviser from late 1906 until his assassination in 1911, important agrarian reforms dissolved the village ownership of land and opened the door to private ownership by enterprising peasants. Nicholas II, however, was no friend of reform. Already by 1907, the tsar had curtailed the power of the Duma, and after Stolypin's murder he fell back on the army and bureaucracy to rule Russia. World War I would give revolutionary forces another chance to undo the tsarist regime, and this time they would not fail.

The Rise of the United States

Between 1860 and 1914, the United States made the shift from an agrarian to a mighty industrial nation. American heavy industry stood unchallenged in 1900. In that year, the Carnegie Steel Company alone produced more steel than Great Britain's entire steel industry. Industrialization also led to urbanization. While established cities, such as New York, Philadelphia, and Boston, grew even larger, other moderate-size cities, such as Pittsburgh, grew by leaps and bounds because of industrialization. Whereas 20 percent of Americans

Russian Workers Appeal to the Tsar

On January 9, 1905, a massive procession of workers led by an Orthodox priest loyal to the tsar, Father George Gapon, carried a petition to present to the tsar at his imperial palace in St. Petersburg. Although the tsar was not even there, government officials ordered troops to fire on the crowd. "Bloody Sunday," as it was called, precipitated the Revolution of 1905. This selection is an excerpt from the petition that was never presented.

George Gapon and Ivan Vasimov, Petition to the Tsar

Sovereign!

We, the workers and the inhabitants of various social strata of the city of St. Petersburg, our wives, children, and helpless old parents, have come to you, Sovereign, to seek justice and protection. We are impoverished; our employers oppress us, overburden us with work, insult us, consider us inhuman, and treat us as slaves who must suffer a bitter fate in silence. Though we have suffered, they push us deeper and deeper into a gulf of misery, disfranchisement, and ignorance. Despotism and arbitrariness strangle us and we are gasping for breath. Sovereign, we have no strength left. We have reached the limit of endurance. We have reached that terrible moment when death is preferable to the continuance of unbearable sufferings.

And so we left our work and informed our employers that we shall not resume work until they meet our demands. We do not demand much; we only want what is indispensable to life and without which life is nothing but hard labor and eternal suffering. Our first request was that our employers discuss our needs jointly with us. But they refused to do this; they even denied us the right to speak about our needs, saying that the law does not give us such a right. Also unlawful were our requests to reduce the working day to eight hours, to set wages jointly with us; to examine our disputes with lower echelons of factory administration; to increase the wages of unskilled workers and women to one ruble [about $1.00] per day; to abolish overtime work; to provide medical care without insult. . . .

Sovereign, there are thousands of us here; outwardly we resemble human beings, but in reality neither we nor the Russian people as a whole enjoy any human right, have any right to speak, to think, to assemble, to discuss our needs, or to take measures to improve our conditions. They have enslaved us and they did it under the protection of your officials, with their aid and with their cooperation. They imprison and send into exile any one of us who has the courage to speak on behalf of the interests of the working class and of the people. . . . All the workers and the peasants are at the mercy of bureaucratic administrators consisting of embezzlers of public funds and thieves who not only disregard the interests of the people but also scorn these interests. . . . The people are deprived of the opportunity to express their wishes and their demands and to participate in determining taxes and expenditures. The workers are deprived of the opportunity to organize themselves in unions to protect their interests.

Sovereign! Is all this compatible with God's laws, by the grace of which you reign? And is it possible to live under such laws? Wouldn't it be better for all of us if we, the toiling people of all Russia, died? . . . Sovereign, these are the problems that we face and these are the reasons that we have gathered before the walls of your palace. Here we seek our last salvation. Do not refuse to come to the aid of your people.

lived in cities in 1860, over 40 percent did in 1900. Four-fifths of the population growth in cities came from migration. Eight to ten million Americans moved from rural areas into the cities, and fourteen million foreigners came from abroad.

By 1900, the United States had become the world's richest nation and greatest industrial power. Yet serious questions remained about the quality of American life. In 1890, the richest 9 percent of Americans owned an incredible 71 percent of all the wealth. Labor unrest over unsafe working conditions, strict work discipline, and periodic cycles of devastating unemployment led workers to organize. By the turn of the century, one national organization, the American Federation of Labor, emerged as labor's dominant voice. Its lack of real power, however, is reflected in its membership figures. In 1900, it included only 8.4 percent of the American industrial labor force.

During the so-called Progressive Era after 1900, an age of reform swept through the United States. At the state level, reforming governors sought to achieve clean government by introducing elements of direct democracy, such as direct primaries for selecting nominees for public office. State governments also enacted economic and social legislation, such as laws that governed hours, wages, and working conditions, especially for women and children. The realization that state laws were ineffective in dealing with nationwide problems, however, led to a Progressive movement at the national level. The Meat Inspection Act and Pure Food and Drug Act provided for a limited degree of federal regulation of corrupt industrial practices. The presidency of Woodrow Wilson (1913–1921) witnessed the creation of a graduated federal income tax and the establishment of the Federal Reserve System, which permitted the federal government to play a role in important economic decisions formerly made by bankers. Like European nations, the United States was slowly adopting policies that extended the functions of the state.

The New Imperialism

Beginning in the 1880s, European states engaged in an intense scramble for overseas territory. This revival of imperialism, or the "new imperialism" as some have called it, led Europeans to carve up Asia and Africa. But why did Europeans begin their mad scramble for colonies after 1880? Although historians disagree, they have advanced a number of possible explanations for the rapid spread of imperialism.

Causes of the New Imperialism

The existence of competitive nation-states after 1870 was undoubtedly a major determinant in the growth of this new imperialism. As European affairs grew tense, heightened competition led European states to acquire colonies abroad that provided ports and coaling stations for their navies. Colonies were also a source of international prestige. Once the scramble for colonies began, failure to enter the race was perceived as a sign of weakness, totally unacceptable to an aspiring great power. Nationalistically oriented intellectuals reinforced these national aspirations when they argued that nations could not be great without colonies. The German historian Heinrich von Treitschke, for example, maintained that "all great nations in the fullness of their strength have desired to set their mark upon barbarian lands and those who fail to participate in this great rivalry will play a pitiable role in time to come."[16]

Treitschke's comments are a reminder that late nineteenth-century imperialism was closely tied to na-

tionalism, Social Darwinism, and racism. After the unification of Italy and Germany in 1871, nationalism entered a new stage of development. In the first half of the nineteenth century, nationalism had been closely identified with liberals who had pursued both individual rights and national unification and independence. Liberal nationalists maintained that unified, independent nation-states could best preserve individual rights. The new nationalism of the late nineteenth century, tied to conservatism, was loud and chauvinistic. As one exponent expressed it, "a true nationalist places his country above everything"; he believes in the "exclusive pursuit of national policies" and "the steady increase in national power—for a nation declines when it loses military might."

Then, too, imperialism was tied to Social Darwinism and racism. Social Darwinists believed that in the struggle between nations, the fit are victorious and survive. Superior races must dominate inferior races by military force to show how strong and virile they are. As the British professor of mathematics, Karl Pearson, arrogantly argued in 1900: "The path of progress is strewn with the wrecks of nations; traces are everywhere to be seen of the [slaughtered remains] of inferior races. . . . Yet these dead people are, in very truth, the stepping stones on which mankind has arisen to the higher intellectual and deeper emotional life of today."[17] Others were equally blunt. One Englishman wrote: "To the development of the White Man, the Black Man and the Yellow must ever remain inferior, and as the former raised itself higher and yet higher, so did these latter seem to shrink out of humanity and appear nearer and nearer to the brutes."[18]

Some Europeans took a more religious-humanitarian approach to imperialism when they argued that Europeans had a moral responsibility to civilize ignorant peoples. This notion of the "white man's burden" (see the box on p. 870) helped at least the more idealistic individuals to rationalize imperialism in their own minds. Nevertheless, the belief that the superiority of their civilization obligated them to impose modern cities and new medicines on supposedly primitive nonwhites was yet another form of racism.

Some historians have emphasized an economic motivation for imperialism. There was a great demand for natural resources and products not found in Western countries, such as rubber, oil, and tin. Instead of just trading for these products, European investors advocated direct control of the areas where the raw materials were found. The large surpluses of capital that bankers and industrialists were accumulating often encouraged them to seek higher rates of profit in underdeveloped areas. All of these factors combined to create an economic imperialism whereby European finance dominated the economic activity of a large part of the world. This economic imperialism, however, was not necessarily the same thing as colonial expansion. Businessmen invested where it was most profitable, not necessarily where their own countries had colonial empires. For example, less than 10 percent of French foreign investments before 1914 went to French colonies; most of the rest went to Latin American and European countries. It should also be remembered that much of the colonial territory that was acquired was mere wasteland from the point of view of industrialized Europe and cost more to administer than it produced economically. Only the search for national prestige could justify such losses.

Followers of Karl Marx were especially eager to argue that imperialism was economically motivated because they associated imperialism with the ultimate demise of the capitalist system. Marx had hinted at this argument, but it was one of his followers, the Russian Vladimir Lenin (see Chapter 26), who in *Imperialism, the Highest Stage of World Capitalism* developed the idea that capitalism leads to imperialism. According to Lenin, as the capitalist system concentrates more wealth in ever-fewer hands, the possibility for investment at home is exhausted, and capitalists are forced to invest abroad, establish colonies, and exploit small, weak nations. In his view, then, the only cure for imperialism was the destruction of capitalism.

The Creation of Empires

Whatever the reasons for the new imperialism, it had a dramatic effect on Africa and Asia as European powers competed for control of these two continents.

THE SCRAMBLE FOR AFRICA

Europeans controlled relatively little of the African continent before 1880. During the Napoleonic wars, the British had established themselves in south Africa by taking control of Capetown, originally founded by the Dutch. After the wars, the British encouraged settlers to come to what they called Cape Colony where they established a new administrative system with English as the official language. British policies disgusted the Boers or Afrikaners, as the descendants of the Dutch colonists were called, and led them in 1835 to migrate north on the Great Trek to the region between the Orange and Vaal Rivers (later known as the Orange Free State) and

north of the Vaal River (the Transvaal). Hostilities between the British and the Boers continued, however. In 1877, the British governor of Cape Colony seized the Transvaal, but a Boer revolt led the British government to recognize Transvaal as the independent South African Republic. These struggles between the British and the Boers did not prevent either white group from massacring and subjugating the Zulu and Xhosa peoples of south Africa.

In the 1880s, British policy in south Africa was largely determined by Cecil Rhodes (1853–1902). Rhodes founded both diamond and gold companies that monopolized production of these precious commodities and enabled him to gain control of a territory north of Transvaal that he named Rhodesia after himself. Rhodes was a great champion of British expansion. One of his goals was to create a series of British colonies "from the Cape to Cairo"—all linked by a railroad. His imperialist ambitions led to his downfall in 1896, however, when the British government forced him to resign as prime minister of Rhodesia after he conspired to overthrow the Boer government of the South African Republic without British approval. Although the British government had hoped to avoid war with the Boers, it could not stop extremists on both sides from precipitating a conflict. The Boer War dragged on from 1899 to 1902 when the Boers were overwhelmed by the larger British army. British policy toward the defeated Boers was remarkably conciliatory. Transvaal and the Orange Free State had representative governments by 1907, and in 1910, a Union of South Africa was created. Like Canada, Australia, and New Zealand, it became a fully self-governing dominion within the British Empire.

Before 1880, the only other European settlements in Africa had been made by the French and Portuguese. The Portuguese had held on to their settlements in Angola on the west coast and Mozambique on the east coast. The French had started the conquest of Algeria in Muslim North Africa in 1830, although it was not until 1879 that French civilian rule was established there. The next year, 1880, the European scramble for possession of Africa began in earnest. Before 1900, the French had added the huge area of French West Africa and Tunisia to their African empire. In 1912, they established a protectorate over much of Morocco; the rest was left to Spain.

The British took an active interest in Egypt after the Suez Canal was opened by the French in 1869. Believing that the canal was essential to their lifeline to India, the British sought to exercise as much control as possible over the canal area. Egypt was a well-

The White Man's Burden

One of the justifications for European imperialism was the notion that superior white peoples had the moral responsibility to raise ignorant native peoples to a higher level of civilization. The British poet Rudyard Kipling (1865–1936) captured this notion in his poem, The White Man's Burden.

Rudyard Kipling, *The White Man's Burden*

Take up the White Man's burden—
Send forth the best ye breed—
Go bind your sons to exile
To serve your captives' needs;
To wait in heavy harness,
On fluttered folk and wild—
Your new-caught sullen peoples,
Half-devil and half-child.

Take up the White Man's burden—
In patience to abide,
To veil the threat of terror
And check the show of pride;
By open speech and simple,
An hundred times made plain
To seek another's profit,
And work another's gain.

Take up the White Man's burden—
The savage wars of peace—
Fill full the mouth of Famine
And bid the sickness cease;
And when your goal is nearest
The end for others sought,
Watch sloth and heathen Folly
Bring all your hopes to nought.

Take up the White Man's burden—
No tawdry rule of kings,
But toil of serf and sweeper—
The tale of common things.
The ports ye shall not enter,
The roads ye shall not read,
Go mark them with your living,
And mark them with your dead.

Take up the White Man's burden—
And reap his old reward:
The blame of those ye better,
The hate of those ye guard—
The cry of hosts ye humour
(Ah, slowly;1) toward the light:—
'Why brought he us from bondage,
Our loved Egyptian night?'

Take up the White Man's burden—
Ye dare not stoop to less—
Nor call too loud on Freedom
To cloke your weariness;
By all ye cry or whisper,
By all you leave or do,
The silent, sullen peoples
Shall weigh your gods and you.

Take up the White Man's burden—
Have done with childish days—
The lightly proferred laurel,
The easy, ungrudged praise.
Comes now, to search your manhood
Through all the thankless years,
Cold, edged with dear-bought wisdom,
The judgment of your peers!

established state with an autonomous Muslim government, but that did not stop the British from landing an expeditionary force there in 1882. Although they asserted that their occupation was only temporary, they soon established a protectorate over Egypt. From Egypt, the British moved south into Sudan and seized it after narrowly averting a war with France. Not to be outdone, Italy joined in the imperialist scramble. Their humiliating defeat by the Ethiopians in 1896 only led the Italians to try again in 1911 when they invaded and seized Ottoman Tripoli, which they renamed Libya.

Central Africa was also added to the list of European colonies. Popular interest in the forbiddingly dense tropical jungles of central Africa was first aroused in the 1860s and 1870s by explorers, such as the Scottish missionary David Livingstone and the British-American journalist Henry M. Stanley. But the real driving force for the colonization of central Africa was King Leopold

⧫ The Black Man's Burden ⧫

The Western justification of imperialism that was based on a sense of moral responsibility, evident in Rudyard Kipling's poem, was often hypocritical. Edward Morel, a British journalist who spent time in the Congo, pointed out the destructive effects of Western imperialism on Africans in his book, The Black Man's Burden.

Edward Morel, *The Black Man's Burden*

It is [the Africans] who carry the "Black man's burden." They have not withered away before the white man's occupation. Indeed . . . Africa has ultimately absorbed within itself every Caucasian and, for that matter, every Semitic invader, too. In hewing out for himself a fixed abode in Africa, the white man has massacred the African in heaps. The African has survived, and it is well for the white settlers that he has. . . .

What the partial occupation of his soil by the white man has failed to do; what the mapping out of European political "spheres of influence" has failed to do; what the Maxim [machine gun] and the rifle, the slave gang, labour in the bowels of the earth and the lash, have failed to do; what imported measles, smallpox and syphilis have failed to do; whatever the overseas slave trade failed to do; the power of modern capitalistic exploitation, assisted by modern engines of destruction, may yet succeed in accomplishing.

For from the evils of the latter, scientifically applied and enforced, there is no escape for the African. Its destructive effects are not spasmodic: they are permanent. In its permanence resides its fatal consequences. It kills not the body merely, but the soul. It breaks the spirit. It attacks the African at every turn, from every point of vantage. It wrecks his polity, uproots him from the land, invades his family life, destroys his natural pursuits and occupations, claims his whole time, enslaves him in his own home. . . .

In Africa, especially in tropical Africa, which a capitalistic imperialism threatens and has, in part, already devastated, man is incapable of reacting against unnatural conditions. In those regions man is engaged in a perpetual struggle against disease and an exhausting climate, which tells heavily upon childbearing; and there is no scientific machinery for saving the weaker members of the community. The African of the tropics is capable of tremendous physical labours. But he cannot accommodate himself to the European system of monotonous, uninterrupted labour, with its long and regular hours, involving, moreover, as it frequently does, severance form natural surroundings and nostalgia, the condition of melancholy resulting from separation from home, a malady to which the African is specially prone. Climatic conditions forbid it. When the system is forced upon him, the tropical African droops and dies.

Nor is violent physical opposition to abuse and injustice henceforth possible for the African in any part of Africa. His chances of effective resistance have been steadily dwindling with the increasing perfectibility in the killing power of modern armament. . . .

Thus the African is really helpless against the material gods of the white man, as embodied in the trinity of imperialism, capitalistic exploitation, and militarism. . . .

To reduce all the varied and picturesque and stimulating episodes in savage life to a dull routine of endless toil for uncomprehended ends, to dislocate social ties and disrupt social ties and disrupt social institutions; to stifle nascent desires and crush mental development; to graft upon primitive passions the annihilating evils of scientific slavery, and the bestial imaginings of civilized man, unrestrained by convention or law; in fine, to kill the soul in a people—this is a crime which transcends physical murder.

II (1865–1909) of Belgium, who had rushed enthusiastically into the pursuit of empire in Africa: "To open to civilization," he said, "the only part of our globe where it has not yet penetrated, to pierce the darkness which envelops whole populations, is a crusade, if I may say so, a crusade worthy of this century of progress." Profit, however, was far more important to Leopold than progress; his treatment of the Africans was so brutal that even other Europeans condemned his actions. In 1876,

Leopold created the International Association for the Exploration and Civilization of Central Africa and engaged Henry Stanley to establish Belgian settlements in the Congo. Alarmed by Leopold's actions, the French also moved into the territory north of the Congo River.

Between 1884 and 1900, most of the rest of Africa was carved up by the European powers. Germany also entered the ranks of the imperialist powers at this time. Initially, Bismarck had downplayed the significance of colonies, but as domestic political pressures for a German empire intensified, Bismarck became a political convert to colonialism. As he expressed it, "All this colonial business is a sham, but we need it for the elections." The Germans established colonies in Southwest Africa, the Cameroons, Togoland, and East Africa.

By 1914, Britain, France, Germany, Belgium, Spain, and Portugal had divided Africa. Only Liberia, founded by emancipated American slaves, and Ethiopia remained free states. Despite the humanitarian rationalizations about the "white man's burden," Africa had been conquered by European states determined to create colonial empires (see the box on p. 871). Any peoples who dared to resist (with the exception of the Ethiopians, who defeated the Italians) were simply devastated by the superior military force of the Europeans. In 1898, Sudanese tribesmen attempted to defend their independence and stop a British expedition armed with the recently developed machine gun. In the ensuing Battle of Omdurman, the Sudanese were massacred. One observer noted: "It was not a battle but an execution. . . . The bodies were not in heaps—bodies hardly ever are; but they spread evenly over acres and acres. Some lay very composedly with their slippers placed under their

✖ **Map 25.1** Africa in 1914.

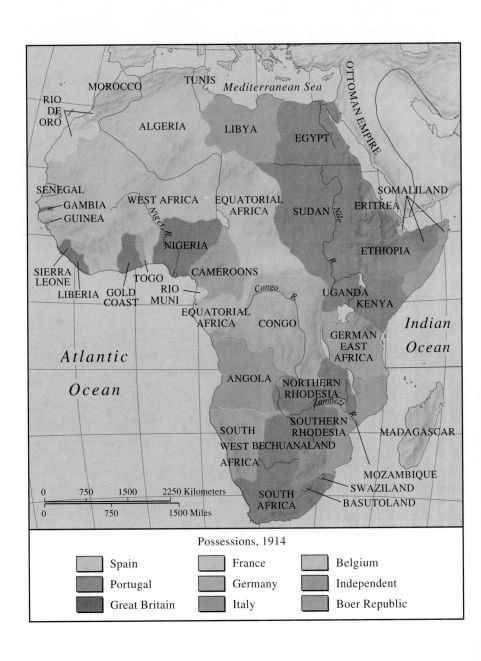

Possessions, 1914

Spain

Portugal

Great Britain

France

Germany

Italy

Belgium

Independent

Boer Republic

CHRONOLOGY

The New Imperialism: Africa

Great Trek of the Boers	1835
Opening of the Suez Canal	1869
Leopold of Belgium establishes settlements in the Congo	1876
British seizure of Transvaal	1877
French complete conquest of Algeria	1879
British expeditionary force in Egypt	1882
Ethiopians defeat the Italians	1896
Battle of Omdurman in the Sudan	1898
Boer War	1899–1902
Union of South Africa	1910
Italians seize Tripoli	1911
French protectorate over Morocco	1912

heads for a last pillow; some knelt, cut short in the middle of a last prayer. Others were torn to pieces."[19] The battle casualties at Omdurman tell the story of the one-sided conflicts between Europeans and Africans: 28 British deaths to 11,000 Sudanese. Military superiority was frequently accompanied by brutal treatment of blacks. Nor did Europeans hesitate to deceive the Africans to gain their way. One south African king, Lo Bengula, informed Queen Victoria about how he had been cheated:

> Some time ago a party of men came to my country, the principal one appearing to be a man called Rudd. They asked me for a place to dig for gold, and said they would give me certain things for the right to do so. I told them to bring what they could give and I would show them what I would give. A document was written and presented to me for signature. I asked what it contained, and was told that in it were my words and the words of those men. I put my hand to it. About three months afterwards I heard from other sources that I had given by that document the right to all the minerals of my country.[20]

ASIA IN AN AGE OF IMPERIALISM

Although Asia had been open to Western influence since the sixteenth century, not much of its immense territory had fallen under direct European control. The Dutch were established in the East Indies and the Spanish in the Philippines while the French and Portuguese had trading posts on the Indian coast. China,

Japan, Korea, and Southeast Asia had largely managed to exclude Westerners. The British and the Russians, however, had acquired the most Asian territory.

Britain's interest in the Far East dated back to the seventeenth century, but the British did not become actively involved there until the explorations of Australia by Captain James Cook between 1768 and 1771. By the 1780s, Britain had begun to use Australia as a penal colony to relieve overcrowded British prisons. The availability of land for grazing sheep and the discovery of gold led, however, to an influx of free settlers who slaughtered many of the indigenous inhabitants. In 1850, the British government granted the various Australian colonies virtually complete self-government, and fifty years later, on January 1, 1901, all the colonies were unified into a Commonwealth of Australia. Nearby New Zealand, which the British had declared a colony in 1840, was also granted dominion status in 1907.

A private trading company known as the British East India Company had been responsible for subjugating much of India. By the early nineteenth century, British control of the subcontinent had largely been consolidated. But Indian distrust of the British, fueled by British reforms that seemed to make a mockery of traditional religious customs, led to revolt. The Great Rebellion, directed by the sepoys or Indian troops of the East India Company's army, erupted in 1857. Within a year, however, Indian troops loyal to the British and fresh British troops had crushed the revolt. As a result of the uprising, the British Parliament transferred the company's powers directly to the government in London. In 1876, the title Empress of India was bestowed upon Queen Victoria; Indians were now her colonial subjects.

Russian expansion in Asia was a logical outgrowth of its traditional territorial aggrandizement. Russian explorers had penetrated the wilderness of Siberia in the seventeenth century and reached the Pacific coast in 1637. In the eighteenth century, Russians established a claim on Alaska, which was later sold to the United States in 1867. Gradually, Russian settlers moved into cold and forbidding Siberia. Altogether 7 million Russians settled in Siberia between 1800 and 1914; by 1914, 90 percent of the Siberian population were Slavs, not Asiatics.

In the nineteenth century, the Russians also moved south, attracted by warmer climates and the crumbling Ottoman Empire. By 1830, the Russians had established control over the entire northern coast of the Black Sea and then pressed on into central Asia, securing the trans-Caspian area by 1881 and Turkestan in 1885. These advances brought the Russians to the borders of

Persia and Afghanistan where the British also had interests because of their desire to protect their holdings in India. In 1907, the Russians and British agreed to make Afghanistan a buffer state between Russian Turkestan and British India and divide Persia into two spheres of influence. Halted by the British in their expansion to the south, the Russians moved east in Asia. The Russian occupation of Manchuria and their attempt to move into Korea brought war with the new imperialist power, Japan. After losing the Russo-Japanese War in 1905, the Russians agreed to a Japanese protectorate in Korea, and their Asian expansion was brought to a temporary halt.

Map 25.2 Asia in 1914.

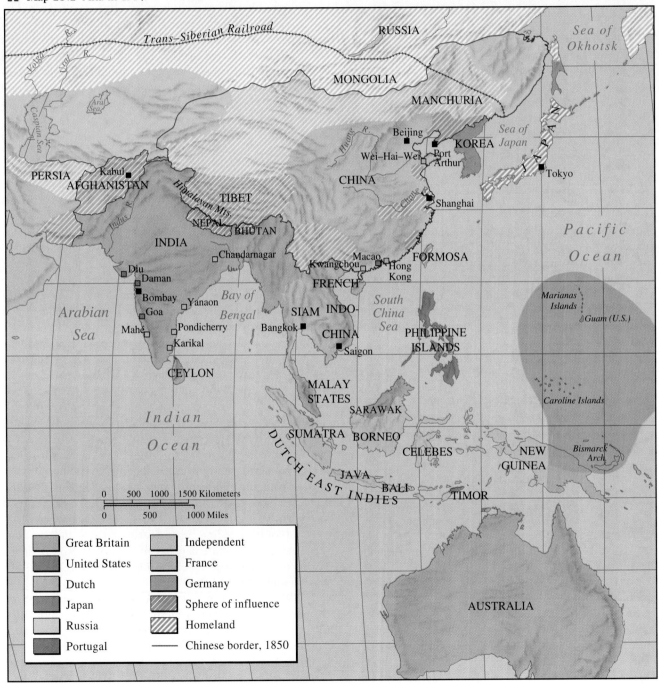

✦ **The British in India.** After their occupation of India, the British began to erect monumental buildings in stone that demonstrated their power and authority. This is evident in the opulent grandeur of the Victoria railway station in Bombay, which was meant to impress onlookers with the magnitude of the British rail network in India.

The thrust of imperialism after 1880 led Westerners to move into new areas of Asia hitherto largely free of Western influence. By the nineteenth century, the ruling Manchu dynasty of the Chinese empire was showing signs of decline. In 1842, the British had obtained (through war) the island of Hong Kong and trading rights in a number of Chinese cities. Other Western nations soon rushed in to gain similar trading privileges. Chinese attempts to resist this encroachment of foreigners led to military defeats and new demands. Only rivalry among the great powers themselves prevented the complete dismemberment of the Chinese empire. Instead, Britain, France, Germany, Russia, the United States, and Japan established spheres of influence and long-term leases of Chinese territory. In 1899, urged along by the American Secretary of State John Hay, they agreed to an "open door" policy in which one country would not restrict the commerce of the other countries in its sphere of influence.

Japan avoided Western intrusion until 1853–1854 when American naval forces under Commodore Matthew Perry forced the Japanese to grant the United States trading and diplomatic privileges. Japan, however, managed to avoid China's fate. Korea had also largely excluded Westerners. The fate of Korea was determined by the struggle first between China and Japan in 1894–1895 and later between Japan and Russia in 1904–1905. Japan's victories gave it a clear superiority, and in 1910 Japan formally annexed Korea.

In Southeast Asia, Britain established control over Burma and the Malay States while France played an active role in subjugating Indochina. The city of Saigon was occupied in 1858, and four years later Cochin China was taken. In the 1880s, the French extended "protection" over Cambodia, Annam, Tonkin, and Laos and organized them into a Union of French Indochina. Only Siam (Thailand) remained free as a buffer state because of British-French rivalry.

The Pacific islands were also the scene of great power competition and witnessed the entry of the United States onto the imperialist stage. The Samoan Islands became the first important American colony; the Hawaiian Islands were the next to fall. Soon after Americans had made Pearl Harbor into a naval station in 1887, American settlers gained control of the sugar industry on the islands. When Hawaiian natives tried to reassert their authority, the United States Marines were brought in to "protect" American lives. Hawaii was annexed by the United States in 1898 during the era of American nationalistic fervor generated by the Spanish-American War. The American defeat of Spain encouraged Americans to extend their empire by acquiring Cuba, Puerto Rico, Guam, and the Philippine Islands. Although the Filipinos hoped for independence, the Americans refused to grant it. As President William McKinley said, the United States had the duty "to educate the Filipinos and uplift and Christianize them," a remarkable statement in view of the fact that most of them had been Roman Catholics for centuries. It took three years and 60,000 troops to pacify the Philippines and establish American control. Not until 1946 did the Filipinos receive complete independence.

Asian Responses to Imperialism

When Europeans imposed their culture upon peoples they considered inferior, how did the conquered peoples respond? Initial attempts to expel the foreigners only led to devastating defeats at the hands of Westerners, whose industrial technology gave them modern weapons of war with which to crush the indigenous peoples. Accustomed to rule by small elites, most people simply accepted their new governors, making Western rule relatively easy. The conquered peoples subsequently adjusted to foreign rule in different ways. Traditionalists sought to maintain their cultural traditions while modernizers believed that adoption of Western ways would enable them to reform their societies and eventually challenge Western rule. Most people probably stood somewhere between these two extremes.

For advocates of change, Western ideas represented a two-edged sword, since they were a symbol of both oppression and liberation. Many Asian and African leaders resented Western attitudes of superiority and demanded that indigenous peoples be accorded basic human dignity, but at the same time they adopted the West's own ideologies for change. Liberalism, with its doctrine of civil rights and political self-determination, and nationalism, with its emphasis on the right of peoples to have their own nations, were used to foster independence movements wherever people suffered under foreign oppression. Three eventually powerful Asian nations—China, Japan, and India—present different approaches to the question of how Asian populations responded to foreign rule.

CHINA

The humiliation of China by the Western powers led to much antiforeign violence, but the Westerners only used this lawlessness as an excuse to extort further concessions from the Chinese. A major outburst of violence against foreigners occurred in the Boxer Rebellion in 1900–1901. Boxers was the popular name given to Chinese who belonged to a secret organization called the Society of Harmonious Fists, whose aim was to push the foreigners out of China. The Boxers murdered foreign missionaries, Chinese who had converted to Christianity, railroad workers, foreign businessmen, and even the German envoy to Beijing. Response to the killings was immediate and overwhelming. An allied army consisting of British, French, German, Russian, American, and Japanese troops attacked Beijing, restored order, and demanded more concessions from the Chinese government. The imperial government was so weakened that the forces of the revolutionary leader Sun Yat-sen (1866–1925), who adopted a program of "nationalism, democracy, and socialism," overthrew the Manchu dynasty in 1912. The new Republic of China remained weak and ineffective, and China's travails were far from over.

JAPAN

In the late 1850s and early 1860s, it looked as if Japan would follow China's fate and be carved up into spheres of influence by aggressive Western powers. A remarkably rapid transformation, however, produced a very different result. Before 1868, the shogun, a powerful hereditary military governor assisted by a warrior nobility known as the samurai, exercised real power in Japan. The emperor's functions had become primarily religious. After the shogun's concessions to the Western nations, antiforeign sentiment led to a samurai revolt in 1867 and the restoration of the emperor as the rightful head of the government. The new emperor was the astute, dynamic, young Mutsuhito (1867–1912), who called his reign the Meiji (Enlightened Government). The new leaders who controlled the emperor now inaugurated a remarkable transformation of Japan that has since been known as the Meiji Restoration.

Recognizing the obvious military and industrial superiority of the West, the new leaders decided to modernize Japan by absorbing and adopting Western methods. Thousands of young Japanese were sent abroad to receive Western educations, especially in the social and natural sciences. A German-style army and a British-style navy were established. The Japanese copied the industrial and financial methods of the United States and developed a modern commercial and industrial system. A highly centralized administrative system copied from the French replaced the old feudal system.

Initially, the Japanese adopted the French principles of social and legal equality, but by 1890 they had created a political system that was democratic in form but authoritarian in practice.

In imitating the West, Japan also developed a powerful military state. Universal military conscription was introduced in 1872, and a modern peacetime army of 240,000 was eventually established. The Japanese avidly pursued the Western imperialistic model. They defeated China in 1894–1895, annexed some Chinese territory, and established their own sphere of influence in China. After they had defeated the Russians in 1905, the Japanese made Korea a colony under harsh rule. The Japanese had proved that an Eastern power could play the "white man's" imperialistic game and provided a potent example to peoples in other regions of Asia and Africa.

INDIA

The British government had been in control of India since the mid-nineteenth century. After crushing the Great Rebellion in 1858, the British ruled India directly. Under Parliament's supervision, a small group of British civil servants directed the affairs of India's almost 300 million people.

The British brought order to a society that had been rent by civil wars for some time and created a relatively honest and efficient government. They also brought Western technology—railroads, banks, mines, industry, medical knowledge, and hospitals. The British introduced Western-style secondary schools and colleges where the Indian upper and middle classes and professional classes were educated so that they could serve as trained subordinates in the government and army.

But the Indian people paid a high price for the peace and stability brought by British rule. Due to population growth in the nineteenth century, extreme poverty was a way of life for most Indians; almost two-thirds of the population were malnourished in 1901. British industrialization brought little improvement for the masses. British manufactured goods destroyed local industries while Indian wealth was used to pay British officials and a large army. The system of education served only the elite, upper-class Indians, and it was only conducted in the rulers' English language while 90 percent of the population remained illiterate. Even for the Indians who benefited the most from their Western educations, British rule was degrading. The best jobs and the best housing were reserved for Britons. Despite their education, the Indians were never considered equals of the British whose racial attitudes were made quite clear by

CHRONOLOGY

The New Imperialism: Asia

Britain obtains Hong Kong and trading rights from Chinese government	1842
Australian colonies receive self-government	1850
Mission of Commodore Perry to Japan	1853–1854
Great Rebellion in India	1857–1858
French occupy Saigon	1858
Overthrow of the shogun in Japan	1867
Emperor Mutsuhito and the Meiji Restoration	1867–1912
Queen Victoria is made Empress of India	1876
Russians in central Asia (trans-Caspian area)	1881
Formation of Indian National Congress	1883
Russians in Turkestan	1885
Japanese defeat of China	1894–1895
Spanish-American War; United States annexes Philippines	1898
"Open Door" policy in China	1899
Boxer Rebellion in China	1900–1901
Commonwealth of Australia	1901
Commonwealth of New Zealand	1907
Russian-British agreement over Afghanistan and Persia	1907
Japan annexes Korea	1910
Overthrow of Manchu dynasty in China	1912

Lord Kitchener, one of Britain's foremost military commanders in India, when he said: "It is this consciousness of the inherent superiority of the European which has won for us India. However well educated and clever a native may be, and however brave he may prove himself, I believe that no rank we can bestow on him would cause him to be considered an equal of the British officer."[21] Such smug racial attitudes made it difficult for British rule, no matter how beneficent, ever to be ultimately accepted and led to the rise of an Indian nationalist movement. By 1883, when the Indian National Congress was formed, moderate, educated Indians were beginning to seek self-government. By 1919, in response to British violence and British insensitivity in trying to divide Bengal, Indians were demanding complete independence.

*I*nternational Rivalry and the Coming of War

Before 1914, Europeans had experienced almost fifty years of peace. There had been wars (including wars of conquest in the non-Western world), but none had involved the great powers. A series of crises had occurred, however, that might easily have led to general war. One reason they did not is that until 1890 Bismarck of Germany exercised a restraining influence on the Europeans.

The Bismarckian System

Bismarck knew that the emergence of a unified Germany in 1871 had upset the balance of power established at Vienna in 1815. By keeping the peace, he could best maintain the new status quo and preserve the new German state. Fearing the French desire for revenge over their loss of Alsace-Lorraine in the Franco-Prussian War, Bismarck made an alliance in 1873 with the traditionally conservative powers Austria-Hungary and Russia. The Three Emperors' League, as it was called, failed to work very well, however, primarily because of Russian-Austrian rivalry in eastern Europe, specifically, in the Balkans.

The problem in the Balkans was yet another chapter in the story of the disintegration of the Ottoman Empire. Subject peoples in the Balkans clamored for independence, while corruption and inefficiency weakened the Ottoman government. Only the interference of the great European powers, who were fearful of each other's designs on its territories, kept the Ottoman Empire alive. Complicating the situation was the rivalry between Russia and Austria, which both had designs on the Balkans. For Russia, the Balkans provided the shortest overland route to Istanbul and the Straits. Austria viewed the Balkans as fertile ground for Austrian expansion. Both Britain and France feared the extension of Russian power into the Mediterranean and Middle East. Although Germany had no real interests in the Balkans, Bismarck was fearful of the consequences of a war between Russia and Austria over the Balkans and served as a restraining influence on both powers. Events in the Balkans, however, precipitated a new crisis.

In 1876, the Balkan states of Serbia and Montenegro declared war on the Ottoman Empire. Both were defeated, but Russia, with Austrian approval, attacked and defeated the Ottomans. By the Treaty of San Stefano in 1878, a large Bulgarian state, extending from the Danube in the north to the Aegean Sea in the south, was created. As Bulgaria was viewed as a Russian satellite, this Russian success caused the other great powers to call for a congress of European powers to discuss a revision of the treaty.

The Congress of Berlin, which met in the summer of 1878, was dominated by Bismarck. The congress effectively demolished the Treaty of San Stefano, much to Russia's humiliation. The new Bulgarian state was considerably reduced while the rest of the territory was returned to Ottoman control. The three Balkan states of Serbia, Montenegro, and Romania, until then nominally under Ottoman control, were recognized as independent. The other Balkan territories of Bosnia and Herzegovina were placed under Austrian protection; Austria could occupy but not annex them. Although the Germans received no territory, they believed they had at least preserved the peace among the great powers.

After the Congress of Berlin, the European powers sought new alliances to safeguard their security. Angered by the Germans' actions at the Congress, the Russians had terminated the Three Emperors' League. Bismarck then made an alliance with Austria in 1879 that was joined by a third party—Italy—in 1882. The Triple Alliance of 1882 committed Germany, Austria, and Italy to support the existing political order while providing a defensive alliance against France or "two or more great powers not members of the alliance." At the same time, Bismarck sought to remain on friendly terms with the Russians and reestablished the Three Emperors' League in 1881 with Russia and Austria. When Austrian-Russian hostility over the Balkans caused the league to collapse once more in 1886, Bismarck made a separate Reinsurance Treaty with Russia the next year, hoping to prevent a French-Russian alliance that would threaten Germany with the possibility of a two-front war. The Bismarckian system of alliances, geared to preserving peace and the status quo, had worked, but in 1890 Emperor William II dismissed Bismarck and began to chart a new direction for Germany's foreign policy.

New Directions and New Crises

At the end of the nineteenth century and beginning of the twentieth, diplomatic activity was still largely the preserve of aristocrats who were guided by the eighteenth- and nineteenth-century concepts of balance of power, reason of state, and the concert of Europe. But the manipulation of national interests by the secret negotiations of aristocratic diplomats was increasingly threatened by mass interest in national affairs. The growth of nationalism and mass politics led to an increased emphasis on national competition. Politicians found that an appeal to nationalism carried great weight with the masses of people and could easily be reinforced by the new mass-circulation newspapers that fostered extreme patriotic feelings and encouraged the desire for national prestige. Driven by popular excitement, diplomats found themselves increasingly directed by events rather than by rational calculations, and they were forced to seek short-term successes regardless of the long-term consequences.

Bismarck's alliances had served to bring the European powers into an interlocking system in which no one state could be certain of much support if it chose to initiate a war of aggression. After 1890, a new European diplomacy unfolded in which Europe became divided into two opposing camps that became more and more inflexible and unwilling to compromise.

After Bismarck's dismissal, Emperor William II embarked upon an activist foreign policy dedicated to enhancing German power by finding, as he put it, Germany's rightful "place in the sun." One of his changes in Bismarck's foreign policy was to drop the Reinsurance Treaty with Russia, which he viewed as being at odds with Germany's alliance with Austria. Although William II tried to remain friendly with Russia, the ending of the alliance achieved what Bismarck had feared: it brought France and Russia together. Long isolated by Bismarck's policies, republican France leapt at the chance to draw closer to tsarist Russia, and in 1894 the two powers concluded a military alliance.

The attitude of the British now became crucial. Secure in their vast empire, the British had long pursued a policy of "splendid isolation" toward the Continent. The British were startled, however, when many Europeans condemned their activity in the Boer War (1899–1902) in south Africa. Fearful of an anti-British continental alliance, they saw the weakness of "splendid isolation" and sought an alliance with a continental power. Initially, neither France nor Russia seemed a logical choice. Britain's traditional enmity with France had only intensified because of their imperialistic rivalries in Africa and Asia. Likewise, British and Russian imperialistic interests had frequently collided.

Germany, therefore, seemed the most likely potential ally. Certainly, some people in both Britain and Germany believed that their common German heritage (Anglo-Saxons from Germany had settled in Britain in the Early Middle Ages) made them "natural allies." But Britain was not particularly popular in Germany, nor did the British especially like the Germans. Industrial and

CHRONOLOGY

European Diplomacy

Three Emperors' League	1873
Serbia and Montenegro attack the Ottoman Empire	1876
Treaty of San Stefano	1878
Congress of Berlin	1878
Defensive alliance: Germany and Austria	1879
Renewal of Three Emperors' League	1881
Triple Alliance: Germany, Austria, and Italy	1882
Collapse of Three Emperors' League	1886
Reinsurance Treaty: Germany and Russia	1887
Military alliance: Russia and France	1894
Entente Cordiale: France and Britain	1904
First Moroccan Crisis	1905–1906
Triple Entente: France, Britain, and Russia	1907
First Balkan War	1912
Second Balkan War	1913

commercial rivalry had created much ill feeling while William II's imperial posturing and grabbing for colonies made the British suspicious of Germany's ultimate aims (see the box on p. 880). Especially worrisome to the British was the Germans' construction of a large navy, including a number of battleships advocated by the persistent Admiral von Tirpitz, secretary of the German navy. The British now turned to their traditional enemy, France, and in 1904 concluded the Entente Cordiale by which the two settled all of their outstanding colonial disputes.

German response to the Entente was swift, creating what has been called the First Moroccan Crisis in 1905. The Germans chose to oppose French designs on Morocco in order to humiliate them and drive a wedge between the two new allies—Britain and France. Refusing to compromise, the Germans insisted upon an international conference to settle the problem. Germany's foolish saber rattling had the opposite effect of what had been intended and succeeded only in uniting Russia, France, Great Britain, and even the United States against Germany. The conference at Algeciras, Spain, in

The Emperor's "Big Mouth"

Emperor William II's world policy, which was aimed at finding Germany's "place in the sun," created considerable ill will and unrest among other European states, especially Britain. Moreover, the emperor had the unfortunate tendency to stir up trouble by his often tactless public remarks. In this 1908 interview, for example, William II intended to strengthen Germany's ties with Britain. His words had just the opposite effect and raised a storm of protest in both Britain and Germany.

Daily Telegraph Interview, October 28, 1908

As I have said, his Majesty honoured me with a long conversation, and spoke with impulsive and unusual frankness. "You English," he said, "are mad, mad, mad as March hares. What has come over you that you are so completely given over to suspicions quite unworthy of a great nation? What more can I do than I have done? I declared with all the emphasis at my command, in my speech at Guildhall, that my heart is set upon peace, and that it is one of my dearest wishes to live on the best of terms with England. Have I ever been false to my work? Falsehood and prevarication are alien to my nature. My actions ought to speak for themselves, but you listen not to them but to those who misinterpret and distort them. That is a personal insult which I feel and resent. To be forever misjudged, to have my repeated offers of friendship weighed and scrutinized with jealous, mistrustful eyes, taxes my patience severely. I have said time after time that I am a friend of England, and your Press—or, at least, a considerable section of it—bids the people of England to refuse my proffered hand, and insinuates that the other holds a dagger. How can I convince a nation against its will?"

"I repeat," continued his Majesty, "that I am a friend of England, but you make things difficult for me. My task is not of the easiest. The prevailing sentiment among large sections of the middle and lower classes of my own people is not friendly to England. I am, therefore, so to speak, in a minority in my own land, but it is a minority of the best elements as it is in England with respect to Germany. That is another reason why I resent your refusal to accept my pledged word that I am the friend of England. I strive without ceasing to improve relations, and you retort that I am your arch-enemy. You make it hard for me. Why is it? . . ."

"But, you will say, what of the German Navy? Surely, that is a menace to England! Against whom but England are my squadrons being prepared? If England is not in the minds of those Germans who are bent on creating a powerful fleet, why is Germany asked to consent to such new and heavy burdens of taxation? My answer is clear. Germany is a young and growing Empire. She has a world-wide commerce, which is rapidly expanding, and to which the legitimate ambition of patriotic Germans refuses to assign any bounds. Germany must have a powerful fleet to protect that commerce, and her manifold interests in even the most distant seas. She expects those interests to go on growing, and she must be able to champion them manfully in any quarter of the globe. Germany looks ahead. Her horizons stretch far away. She must be prepared for any eventualities in the Far East. Who can foresee what may take place in the Pacific in the days to come, days not so distant as some believe, but days, at any rate, for which all European Powers with Far Eastern interests ought steadily to prepare? Look at the accomplished rise of Japan; think of the possible national awakening of China; and then judge of the vast problems of the Pacific. Only those Powers which have great navies will be listened to with respect, when the future of the Pacific comes to be solved; and, if for that reason only, Germany must have a powerful fleet. It may even be that England herself will be glad that Germany has a fleet when they speak together on the same side in the great debates of the future."

January 1906 awarded control of Morocco to France. Germany came out of the conference with nothing.

The First Moroccan Crisis of 1905–1906 had important repercussions. France and Britain drew closer together as both began to view Germany as a real threat to European peace. German leaders, on the other hand, began to speak of sinister plots to encircle Germany and hinder its emergence as a world power. Russia, too, grew more and more suspicious of the Germans and signed an agreement in 1907 with Great Britain. By that year, Europe's division into two major blocs—the Triple Alliance of Germany, Austria-Hungary, and Italy and the Triple Entente, as the loose confederation of Russia, France, and Great Britain was called—grew increasingly rigid at the same time that the problems in the Balkans were heating up.

Three forces were now working against any peaceful resolution of the region's difficult problems. The forces of nationalism continued to grow as Slavic peoples gained their freedom from Ottoman overlordship and saw Austrian expansion as the new threat to their national aspirations. At the same time, Austrian and Russian rivalry in the Balkans only intensified. Finally, where Bismarck had labored to make Germany a mediator between Austria-Hungary and Russia, under Emperor William II, Germany became the chief advocate for maintaining the Ottoman Empire. No longer a mediator but a participant in Balkan affairs, Germany added a potentially dangerous element to the situation. Between 1908 and 1913, a new series of crises over the control of the remnants of the Ottoman Empire in the Balkans set the stage for World War I.

CRISES IN THE BALKANS, 1908–1913

The Bosnian Crisis of 1908–1909 initiated a chain of events that eventually went out of control. Since 1878, Bosnia and Herzegovina had been under the protection of Austria, but in 1908, Austria took the drastic step of annexing these two Slavic-speaking territories. Serbia

became outraged at this action because it dashed the Serbians' hopes of creating a large Serbian kingdom that would include most of the south Slavs. This was why the Austrians had annexed Bosnia and Herzegovina. To the Austrians, a large Serbia would be a threat to the unity of the Austro-Hungarian Empire with its large Slavic population. The Russians, as protectors of their fellow Slavs and with their own desire to increase their authority in the Balkans, supported the Serbs and opposed the Austrian action. Backed by the Russians, the Serbs prepared for war against Austria. At this point William II intervened and demanded that the Russians accept Austria's annexation of Bosnia and Herzegovina or face war with Germany. Weakened from their defeat in the Russo-Japanese War in 1904–1905, the Russians were afraid to risk war and backed down. Humiliated, the Russians vowed revenge.

European attention returned to the Balkans in 1912 when Serbia, Bulgaria, Montenegro, and Greece organized a Balkan League and defeated the Ottomans in the First Balkan War. When the victorious allies were unable to agree on how to divide the conquered Otto-

◆ **Ottoman Army in Retreat.** In 1912, a coalition of Serbia, Bulgaria, Montenegro, and Greece defeated the Ottomans and took possession of the Ottoman provinces of Macedonia and Albania. This picture shows the Ottoman army in retreat, pursued by Bulgarian forces.

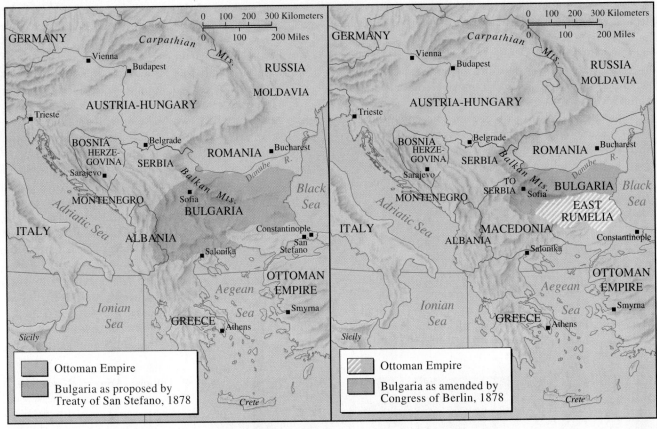

🌸 **Map 25.3a** The Balkans in 1878.

man provinces of Macedonia and Albania, a second Balkan War erupted in 1913. Greece, Serbia, Romania, and the Ottoman Empire attacked and defeated Bulgaria. As a result, Bulgaria obtained only a small part of Macedonia, and most of the rest was divided between Serbia and Greece. Yet Serbia's aspirations remained unfulfilled. The two Balkan wars left the inhabitants embittered and created more tensions among the great powers.

One of Serbia's major ambitions had been to acquire Albanian territory that would give it a port on the Adriatic. At the London Conference arranged by Austria at the end of the two Balkan wars, the Austrians had blocked Serbia's wishes by creating an independent Albania. The Germans, as Austrian allies, had supported this move. In their frustration, Serbian nationalists increasingly portrayed the Austrians as evil monsters who were keeping the Serbs from becoming a great nation. As Serbia's chief supporters, the Russians were also upset by the turn of events in the Balkans. A feeling had grown among Russian leaders that they could not

back down again in the event of a confrontation with Austria or Germany in the Balkans. One Russian military journal even stated early in 1914: "We are preparing for a war in the west. The whole nation must accustom itself to the idea that we arm ourselves for a war of annihilation against the Germans."

Austria-Hungary had achieved another of its aims, but it was still convinced that Serbia was a mortal threat to its empire and must at some point be crushed. Meanwhile, the French and Russian governments renewed their alliance and promised each other that they would not back down at the next crisis. Britain drew closer to France. By the beginning of 1914, two armed camps viewed each other with suspicion. An American in Europe observed, "The whole of Germany is charged with electricity. Everybody's nerves are tense. It only needs a spark to set the whole thing off." The German ambassador to France noted at the same time that "peace remains at the mercy of an accident." The European "age of progress" was about to come to an inglorious and bloody end.

Conclusion

What many Europeans liked to call their "age of progress" in the decades before 1914 was also an era of anxiety. Frenzied imperialist expansion had created vast European empires and spheres of influence around the globe. This feverish competition for colonies, however, had markedly increased the existing antagonisms among the European states. At the same time, the Western treatment of non-Western peoples as racial inferiors caused educated, non-Western elites in these colonies to initiate movements for national independence. Before these movements could be successful, however, the power that Europeans had achieved through their mass armies and technological superiority had to be weakened. The Europeans inadvertently accomplished this task for their colonial subjects by demolishing their own civilization on the battlegrounds of Europe in World War I and World War II.

The cultural revolutions before 1914 had also produced anxiety and a crisis of confidence in European civilization. A brilliant minority of intellectuals had created a modern consciousness that questioned most Europeans' optimistic faith in reason, the rational structure of nature, and the certainty of progress. The devastating experiences of World War I turned this culture of uncertainty into a way of life after 1918.

✖ **Map 25.3b** The Balkans in 1913.

NOTES

1. Quoted in Arthur E. E. McKenzie, *The Major Achievements of Science* (New York, 1960), 1:310.
2. Friedrich Nietzsche, *Twilight of the Idols and The Anti-Christ*, trans. R. J. Hollingdale (New York, 1972), pp. 117–18.
3. Friedrich Nietzsche, *Thus Spake Zarathustra*, in *The Philosophy of Nietzsche* (New York, 1954), p. 6.
4. Herbert Spencer, *Social Statics* (New York, 1896), pp. 146–50.
5. Friedrich von Bernhardi, *Germany and the Next War*, trans. Allen H. Powles (New York, 1914), pp. 18–19.
6. Quoted in Edward R. Tannenbaum, *1900: The Generation before the Great War* (Garden City, N.Y., 1976), p. 337.
7. Quoted in Owen Chadwick, *The Secularization of the European Mind in the Nineteenth Century* (Cambridge, 1975), p. 125.
8. William Booth, *In Darkest England and the Way Out* (London, 1890), p. 45.
9. Quoted in John Rewald, *The History of Impressionism* (New York, 1961), pp. 456–58.
10. Paul Klee, *On Modern Art*, trans. Paul Findlay (London, 1948), p. 51.
11. Quoted in Craig Wright, *Listening to Music* (St. Paul, Minn., 1992), p. 327.

12. Quoted in Catherine M. Prelinger, "Prelude to Consciousness: Amalie Sieveking and the Female Association for the Care of the Poor and the Sick," in John C. Fout, ed., *German Women in the Nineteenth Century: A Social History* (New York, 1984), p. 119.
13. Quoted in Paul Massing, *Rehearsal for Destruction: A Study of Political Anti-Semitism in Imperial Germany* (New York, 1949), p. 147.
14. Quoted in Abba Eban, *Heritage: Civilization and the Jews* (New York, 1984), p. 249.
15. Quoted in Geoffrey A. Hosking, *The Russian Constitutional Experiment, 1907–1914* (Cambridge, 1973), p. 5.
16. Quoted in G. H. Nadel and P. Curtis, eds., *Imperialism and Colonialism* (New York, 1964), p. 94.
17. Karl Pearson, *National Life from the Standpoint of Science* (London, 1905), p. 184.
18. Quoted in John Ellis, *The Social History of the Machine Gun* (New York, 1975), p. 80.
19. Quoted in ibid., p. 86.
20. Quoted in Louis L. Snyder, ed., *The Imperialism Reader* (Princeton, N.J., 1962), p. 220.
21. Quoted in K. M. Panikkar, *Asia and Western Dominance* (London, 1959), p. 116.

SUGGESTIONS FOR FURTHER READING

A well-regarded study of Freud is P. Gay, *Freud: A Life for Our Time* (New York, 1988). Also, see R. Clark, *Freud: The Man and the Cause* (New York, 1980). Nietzsche is examined in J. P. Stern, *The Mind of Nietzsche* (Oxford, 1980). On the impact of Nietzsche, see R. H. Thomas, *Nietzsche in German Politics and Society, 1890–1918* (Dover, N.H., 1983). On Bergson, see A. E. Pilkington, *Henri Bergson and His Influence* (Cambridge, 1976). The basic study on Sorel is J. J. Roth, *The Cult of Violence: Sorel and the Sorelians* (Berkeley, 1980). A useful study on the impact of Darwinian thought on religion is J. Moore, *The Post-Darwinian Controversies: A Study of the Protestant Struggle to Come to Terms with Darwin in Great Britain and America, 1870–1900* (Cambridge, 1979). Studies of the popular religion of the period include T. A. Kselman, *Miracles and Prophesies in Nineteenth-Century France* (New Brunswick, N.J., 1983); and J. Sperber, *Popular Catholicism in Nineteenth-Century Germany* (Princeton, N.J., 1984). Very valuable on modern art are J. Rewald, *The History of Impressionism*, 4th ed. (New York, 1973), and *Post-Impressionism*, 3d ed. (New York, 1962). See also D. M. Reynolds, *The Cambridge Introduction to the History of Art: The Nineteenth Century* (Cambridge, 1985). On literature, see R. Pascal, *From Naturalism to Expressionism: German Literature and Society, 1880–1918*

(New York, 1973). The intellectual climate of Vienna is examined in C. E. Schorske, *Fin de Siècle Vienna: Politics and Culture* (New York, 1980).

The rise of feminism is examined in J. Rendall, *The Origins of Modern Feminism: Women in Britain, France and the United States* (London, 1985). The subject of modern anti-Semitism is covered in J. Katz, *From Prejudice to Destruction* (Cambridge, Mass., 1980). For a more general overview of anti-Semitism, see A. Eban, *Heritage: Civilization and the Jews* (New York, 1984). European racism is analyzed in G. L. Mosse, *Toward the Final Solution* (New York, 1980); while German anti-Semitism as a political force is examined in P. J. Pulzer, *The Rise of Political Anti-Semitism in Germany and Austria* (New York, 1964). Anti-Semitism in France is the subject of S. Wilson, *Ideology and Experience: Anti-Semitism in France at the Time of the Dreyfus Affair* (Rutherford, N.J., 1982). The problems of Jews in Russia are examined in J. Frankel, *Prophecy and Politics: Socialism, Nationalism and the Russian Jews, 1862–1917* (Cambridge, 1981). For a recent biography of Theodor Herzl, see J. Kornberg, *Theodor Herzl: From Assimilation to Zionism* (Bloomington, Ind., 1993). The beginnings of the Labour Party are examined in H. Pelling, *The Origins of the Labour Party*, 2d ed. (Oxford, 1965). There is a good introduction to the political world of William II's Germany in J. C. G. Röhl, *Germany without Bismarck* (Berkeley, 1965). An important study on right-wing German politics is G. Eley, *Reshaping the German Right: Radical Nationalism and Political Change after Bismarck* (New Haven, Conn., 1980). The best, one-volume biography in English on Emperor William II is M. Balfour, *The Kaiser and His Times* (London, 1964). On Russia, see T. H. Von Laue, *Sergei Witte and the Industrialization of Russia* (New York, 1963); and A. Ascher, *The Revolution of 1905: Russia in Disarray*, 2 vols. (Stanford, 1988–1992).

For broad perspectives on imperialism, see the works by T. Smith, *The Pattern of Imperialism* (Cambridge, 1981); and P. Darby, *Three Faces of Imperialism: British and American Approaches to Asia and Africa, 1870–1970* (New Haven, Conn., 1987). Different aspects of imperialism are covered in R. Robinson and J. Gallagher, *Africa and the Victorians*, 2d ed. (New York, 1981); and W. Baumgart, *Imperialism: The Idea and Reality of British and French Colonial Expansion, 1880–1914* (London, 1982). British-Indian relations are examined in J. M. Brown, *Modern India: The Origins of an Asian Democracy* (New York, 1981).

Two fundamental works on the diplomatic history of the period are W. L. Langer, *European Alliances and Alignments*, 2d ed. (New York, 1966), and *The Diplomacy of Imperialism*, 2d ed. (New York, 1965). Also valuable are G. Kennan, *The Decline of Bismarck's European Order: Franco-Prussian Relations, 1875–1890* (Princeton, N.J., 1979); and the masterful study by P. Kennedy, *The Rise of Anglo-German Antagonism, 1860–1914* (London, 1982).

CHAPTER
26

The Beginning of the Twentieth-Century Crisis: War and Revolution

On July 1, 1916, British and French infantry forces attacked German defensive lines along a twenty-five-mile front near the Somme River in France. Each soldier carried almost seventy pounds of equipment, making it "impossible to move much quicker than a slow walk." German machine guns soon opened fire: "We were able to see our comrades move forward in an attempt to cross No-Man's Land, only to be mown down like meadow grass," recalled one British soldier. "I felt sick at the sight of this carnage and remember weeping." In one day more than 21,000 British soldiers died. After six months of fighting, the British had advanced five miles; one million British, French, and German soldiers had been killed or wounded.

World War I (1914–1918) was the defining event of the twentieth century. It devastated the prewar economic, social, and political order of Europe while its uncertain outcome served to prepare the way for an even more destructive war. Overwhelmed by the size of its battles, the extent of its casualties, and the effects of its impact on all facets of European life, contemporaries referred to it simply as the "Great War."

The Great War was all the more disturbing to Europeans because it came after a period that many believed to have been an age of progress. There had been international crises before 1914, but somehow Europeans had managed to avoid serious and prolonged military confrontations. When smaller European states had gone to war, as in the Balkans in 1912 and 1913, the great European powers had shown the ability to keep the conflict localized. Material prosperity and a fervid belief in scientific and technological progress had convinced many people that Europe stood on the verge of creating the utopia that humans had dreamed of for centuries. The historian Arnold Toynbee expressed what the pre–World War I era had meant to his generation:

Assassination of Archduke Francis Ferdinand		Battle of Verdun			
		United States enters the war		Surrender of Germany	
First Battle of the Marne		Easter Rebellion in Ireland			
		The Bolshevik Revolution		Civil War in Russia	
Ministry of Munitions in Britain		Complete mobilization for total war in Germany		Second Battle of the Marne • November Revolution in Germany	

[it was expected] that life throughout the World would become more rational, more humane, and more democratic and that, slowly, but surely, political democracy would produce greater social justice. We had also expected that the progress of science and technology would make mankind richer, and that this increasing wealth would gradually spread from a minority to a majority. We had expected that all this would happen peacefully. In fact we thought that mankind's course was set for an earthly paradise.[1]

After 1918, it was no longer possible to maintain naive illusions about the progress of Western civilization. As World War I was followed by the destructiveness of World War II and the mass murder machines of totalitarian regimes, it became all too apparent that instead of a utopia, European civilization had become a nightmare. The Great War resulted not only in great loss of life and property, but also in the annihilation of one of the basic intellectual precepts upon which Western civilization had been thought to have been founded—the belief in progress. A sense of hopelessness and despair soon replaced an almost blind faith in progress. World War I and the revolutions it spawned can properly be seen as the first stage in the crisis of the twentieth century.

The Road to World War I

On June 28, 1914, the heir to the Austrian throne, the Archduke Francis Ferdinand, was assassinated in the Bosnian city of Sarajevo. Although this event precipitated the confrontation between Austria and Serbia that led to World War I, war was not inevitable. Previous assassinations of European leaders usually had not led to war, and European statesmen had managed to localize such conflicts on a number of occasions. Although the decisions that European statesmen made during this crisis were crucial in leading to war, there were also long-range, underlying forces that were propelling Europeans toward armed conflict.

Nationalism and Internal Dissent

In the first half of the nineteenth century, liberals had maintained that the organization of European states along national lines would lead to a peaceful Europe based on a sense of international fraternity. They had been very wrong. The system of nation-states that had emerged in Europe in the last half of the nineteenth century led not to cooperation but to competition. Rivalries over colonial and commercial interests intensified during an era of frenzied imperialist expansion while the division of Europe's great powers into two loose alliances (Germany, Austria, and Italy and France, Great Britain, and Russia) only added to the tensions. The series of crises that tested these alliances in the 1900s and early 1910s had taught European states a dangerous lesson. Those governments that had exercised restraint in order to avoid war wound up being publicly humiliated, while those that went to the brink of war to maintain their national interests had often been praised for having preserved national honor. In either case, by 1914, the major European states had come to believe that their allies were important and that their security depended on supporting those allies, even when they took foolish risks.

Diplomacy based on brinkmanship was especially frightening in view of the nature of the European state system. Each nation-state regarded itself as sovereign, subject to no higher interest or authority. Each state was motivated by its own self-interest and success. As Emperor William II of Germany remarked, "In questions of honor and vital interests, you don't consult others." Such attitudes made war an ever-present possibility, particularly since most statesmen considered war an acceptable way to preserve the power of their national states.

The growth of nationalism in the nineteenth century had yet another serious consequence. Not all ethnic groups had achieved the goal of nationhood. Slavic minorities in the Balkans and the Austrian Empire, for example, still dreamed of creating their own national states. So did the Irish in the British Empire and the Poles in the Russian Empire.

National aspirations, however, were not the only source of internal strife at the beginning of the twentieth century. Socialist labor movements had grown more powerful and were increasingly inclined to use strikes, even violent ones, to achieve their goals. Some conservative leaders, alarmed at the increase in labor strife and class division, even feared that European nations were on the verge of revolution. Did these statesmen opt for war in 1914 because they believed that "prosecuting an active foreign policy," as one leader expressed it, would smother "internal troubles"? Some historians have argued that the desire to suppress internal disorder may have encouraged some leaders to take the plunge into war in 1914.

Militarism

The growth of large mass armies after 1900 not only heightened the existing tensions in Europe, but made it inevitable that if war did come it would be highly destructive. Conscription had been established as a regular practice in most Western countries before 1914 (the United States and Britain were major exceptions). European military machines had doubled in size be-

tween 1890 and 1914. With its 1.3 million men, the Russian army had grown to be the largest, but the French and Germans were not far behind with 900,000 each. The British, Italian, and Austrian armies numbered between 250,000 and 500,000 soldiers. Most European land armies were filled with peasants, since many young, urban working-class males were unable to pass the physical examinations required for military service.

Militarism, however, involved more than just large armies. As armies grew, so too did the influence of military leaders who drew up vast and complex plans for quickly mobilizing millions of men and enormous quantities of supplies in the event of war. Fearful that changes in these plans would cause chaos in the armed forces, military leaders insisted that their plans could not be altered. In the crises during the summer of 1914, the generals' lack of flexibility forced European political leaders to make decisions for military instead of political reasons.

The Outbreak of War: The Summer of 1914

Militarism, nationalism, and the desire to stifle internal dissent may all have played a role in the coming of World War I, but the decisions made by European leaders in the summer of 1914 directly precipitated the conflict. It was another crisis in the Balkans that forced this predicament upon European statesmen.

As we have seen, states in southeastern Europe had struggled to free themselves from Ottoman rule in the course of the nineteenth and early twentieth centuries. But the rivalry between Austria-Hungary and Russia for domination of these new states created serious tensions in the region. The crises between 1908 and 1913 had only intensified the antagonisms. By 1914, Serbia, supported by Russia, was determined to create a large, independent Slavic state in the Balkans, while Austria, which had its own Slavic minorities to contend with, was equally set on preventing that possibility. Many Europeans perceived the inherent dangers in this combination of Serbian ambition bolstered by Russian hatred of Austria and Austrian conviction that Serbia's success would mean the end of its empire. The British ambassador to Vienna wrote in 1913:

> Serbia will some day set Europe by the ears, and bring about a universal war on the Continent. . . . I cannot tell you how exasperated people are getting here at the continual worry which that little country causes to Austria under encouragement from Russia. . . . It will be

lucky if Europe succeeds in avoiding war as a result of the present crisis. The next time a Serbian crisis arises . . . , I feel sure that Austria-Hungary will refuse to admit of any Russian interference in the dispute and that she will proceed to settle her differences with her little neighbor by herself.[2]

It was against this backdrop of mutual distrust and hatred between Austria-Hungary and Russia, on the one hand, and Austria-Hungary and Serbia, on the other, that the events of the summer of 1914 were played out.

The assassination of the Austrian Archduke Francis Ferdinand and his wife Sophia on June 28, 1914, was carried out by a Bosnian activist who worked for the Black Hand, a Serbian terrorist organization dedicated to the creation of a pan-Slavic kingdom. Although the Austrian government did not know whether the Serbian government had been directly involved in the arch-duke's assassination, it saw an opportunity to "render Serbia impotent once and for all by a display of force," as the Austrian foreign minister put it. Fearful of Russian intervention on Serbia's behalf, Austrian leaders sought the backing of their German allies. Emperor William II and his chancellor, Theobald von Bethmann-Hollweg, responded with the infamous "blank check," their assurance that Austria-Hungary could rely on Germany's "full support," even if "matters went to the length of a war between Austria-Hungary and Russia."

CHRONOLOGY

The Road to World War I

	1914
Assassination of Archduke Francis Ferdinand	June 28
Austria's ultimatum to Serbia	July 23
Austria declares war on Serbia	July 28
Russia mobilizes	July 29
German ultimatum to Russia	July 31
Germany declares war on Russia	August 1
Germany declares war on France	August 3
German troops invade Belgium	August 4
Great Britain declares war on Germany	August 4

Much historical debate has focused on this "blank check" extended to the Austrians. Did the Germans realize that an Austrian-Serbian war could lead to a wider war? If so, did they actually want one? Historians are still seriously divided on the answers to these questions.

Strengthened by German support, Austrian leaders issued an ultimatum to Serbia on July 23. Austrian

◆ **Apprehension of an Assassin.** World War I was precipitated by the assassination of the Archduke Francis Ferdinand, heir to the Austrian throne, on June 28, 1914. His assassin was Gavrillo Princip, an eighteen-year-old Bosnian activist and student who favored the creation of a pan-Slavic kingdom at Austria's expense. As shown here, he was arrested soon after killing Francis Ferdinand and his wife.

leaders made their demands so extreme that Serbia had little choice but to reject some of them in order to preserve its sovereignty. Austria then declared war on Serbia on July 28. Although both Germany and Austria had hoped to keep the war limited to Serbia and Austria in order to ensure Austria's success in the Balkans, these hopes soon vanished.

Still smarting from its humiliation in the Bosnian crisis of 1908, Russia was determined to support Serbia's cause. On July 28, Tsar Nicholas II ordered partial mobilization of the Russian army against Austria. At this point, the rigidity of the military war plans played havoc with diplomatic and political decisions. The Russian General Staff informed the tsar that their mobilization plans were based on a war against both Germany and Austria simultaneously. They could not execute partial mobilization without creating chaos in the army. Consequently, the Russian government ordered full mobilization of the Russian army on July 29, knowing that the Germans would consider this an act of war against them (see the box on p. 891). Germany

responded to Russian mobilization with its own ultimatum that the Russians must halt their mobilization within twelve hours. When the Russians ignored it, Germany declared war on Russia on August 1.

At this stage of the conflict, German war plans determined whether or not France would become involved in the war. Under the guidance of General Alfred von Schlieffen, chief of staff from 1891 to 1905, the German General Staff had devised a military plan based on the assumption of a two-front war with France and Russia, since the two powers had formed a military alliance in 1894. The Schlieffen Plan called for a minimal troop deployment against Russia while most of the German army would make a rapid invasion of western France by way of neutral Belgium. After the planned quick defeat of the French, the German army expected to redeploy to the east against Russia. Under the Schlieffen Plan, Germany could not mobilize its troops solely against Russia and therefore declared war on France on August 3 after issuing an ultimatum to Belgium on August 2 demanding the right of German

Map 26.1 Europe in 1914.

"You Have to Bear the Responsibility for War or Peace"

After Austria declared war on Serbia on July 28, 1914, Russian support of Serbia and German support of Austria threatened to escalate the conflict in the Balkans into a wider war. As we can see in these last-minute telegrams between the Russians and Germans, neither side was able to accept the other's line of reasoning.

Communications between Berlin and St. Petersburg on the Eve of World War I

Emperor William II to Tsar Nicholas II, July 28, 10:45 P.M.

I have heard with the greatest anxiety of the impression which is caused by the action of Austria-Hungary against Servia [Serbia]. The inscrupulous agitation which has been going on for years in Servia, has led to the revolting crime of which Archduke Franz Ferdinand has become a victim. The spirit which made the Servians murder their own King and his consort still dominates that country. Doubtless You will agree with me that both of us, You as well as I, and all other sovereigns, have a common interest to insist that all those who are responsible for this horrible murder shall suffer their deserved punishment. . . .

Your most sincere and devoted friend and cousin

(*Signed*)   *Wilhelm*

Tsar Nicholas II to Emperor William II, July 29, 1:00 P.M.

I am glad that you are back in Germany. In this serious moment I ask You earnestly to help me. An ignominious war has been declared against a weak country and in Russia the indignation which I full share is tremendous. I fear that very soon I shall be unable to resist the pressure exercised upon me and that I shall be forced to take measures which will lead to war. To prevent a calamity as a European war would be, I urge You in the name of our old friendship to do all in Your power to restrain Your ally from going too far.

(*Signed*)   *Nicolas*

Emperor William II to Tsar Nicholas II, July 29, 6:30 P.M.

I have received Your telegram and I share Your desire for the conservation of peace. However: I cannot—as I told You in my first telegram—consider the action of Austria-Hungary as an "ignominious war." Austria-Hungary knows from experience that the promises of Servia as long as they are merely on paper are entirely unreliable. . . . I believe that a direct understanding is possible and desirable between Your Government and Vienna, an understanding which I—as I have already telegraphed You—my Government endeavors to aid with all possible effort. Naturally military measures by Russia, which might be construed as a menace by Austria-Hungary, would accelerate a calamity which both of us desire to avoid and would undermine my position as mediator which—upon Your appeal to my friendship and aid—I willingly accepted.

(*Signed*)   *Wilhelm*

Emperor William II to Tsar Nicholas II, July 30, 1:00 A.M.

My Ambassador has instructions to direct the attention of Your Government to the dangers and serious consequences of a mobilization. I have told You the same in my last telegram. Austria-Hungary has mobilized only against Servia, and only a part of her army. If Russia, as seems to be the case, according to Your advice and that of Your Government, mobilizes against Austria-Hungary, the part of the mediator with which You have entrusted me in such friendly manner and which I have accepted upon Your express desire, is threatened if not made impossible. The entire weight of decision now rests upon Your shoulders, You have to bear the responsibility for war or peace.

(*Signed*)   *Wilhelm*

German Chancellor to German Ambassador at St. Petersburg, July 31, URGENT

In spite of negotiations still pending and although we have up to this hour made no preparations for mobilization, Russia has mobilized her entire army and navy, hence also against us. On account of these Russian measures, we have been forced, for the safety of the country, to proclaim the threatening state of war, which does not yet imply mobilization. Mobilization, however, is bound to follow if Russia does not stop every measure of war against us and against Austria-Hungary within 12 hours, and notifies us definitely to this effect. Please to communicate this at once to M. Sasonof and wire hour of communication.

troops to pass through Belgian territory. On August 4, Great Britain declared war on Germany, officially over this violation of Belgian neutrality, but in fact over the British desire to maintain their world power. As one British diplomat argued, if Germany and Austria were to win the war, "what would be the position of a friendless England?" By August 4, all the great powers of Europe were at war. Through all the maneuvering of the last few days before the war, one fact stands out—all the great powers seemed willing to risk the Great War. They were not disappointed.

The War

Before 1914, many political leaders had become convinced that war involved so many political and economic risks that it was not worth fighting. Others had believed that "rational" diplomats could control any situation and prevent the outbreak of war. At the beginning of August 1914, both of these prewar illusions were shattered, but the new illusions that replaced them soon proved to be equally foolish.

◆ **The Excitement of War.** World War I was greeted with incredible enthusiasm. Each of the major belligerents was convinced of the rightness of its cause. Everywhere in Europe, jubilant civilians sent their troops off to war with joyous fervor. Their belief that the soldiers would be home by Christmas proved to be a pathetic illusion.

1914–1915: Illusions and Stalemate

Europeans went to war in 1914 with remarkable enthusiasm (see the box on p. 893). Government propaganda had been successful in stirring up national antagonisms before the war. Now in August of 1914, the urgent pleas of governments for defense against aggressors fell on receptive ears in every belligerent nation. Most people seemed genuinely convinced that their nation's cause was just. Even domestic differences were temporarily shelved in the midst of war fever. Socialists had long derided "imperialist war" as a blow against the common interests that united the working classes of all countries. Nationalism, however, proved more powerful than working-class solidarity in the summer of 1914 as socialist parties everywhere dropped plans for strikes and workers expressed their readiness to fight for their country. The German Social Democrats, for example, decided that it was imperative to "safeguard the culture and independence of our own country."

A new set of illusions fed the enthusiasm for war. Almost everyone in August 1914 believed that the war would be over in a few weeks. People were reminded that all European wars since 1815 had, in fact, ended in a matter of weeks, conveniently overlooking the American Civil War (1861–1865), which was the "real prototype" for World War I. The illusion of a short war was also bolstered by another illusion, the belief that in an age of modern industry war could not be conducted for more than a few months without destroying a nation's economy. Both the soldiers who exuberantly boarded the trains for the war front in August 1914 and the jubilant citizens who bombarded them with flowers when they departed believed that the warriors would be home by Christmas.

Then, too, war held a fatal attraction for many people. To some, war was an exhilarating release from humdrum bourgeois existence, from a "world grown old and cold and weary," as one poet wrote. To some, war meant a glorious adventure, as a young German student wrote to his parents: "My dear ones, be proud that you live in such a time and in such a nation and that you . . . have the privilege of sending those you love into so glorious a battle."[3] And finally some believed that the war would have a redemptive effect, that millions would abandon their petty preoccupations with material life, ridding the nation of selfishness and sparking a national rebirth based on self-sacrifice, heroism, and nobility. All of these illusions about war died painful deaths on the battlefields of World War I.

German hopes for a quick end to the war rested upon a military gamble. The Schlieffen Plan had called for

The Excitement of War

The incredible outpouring of patriotic enthusiasm that greeted the declaration of war at the beginning of August 1914 demonstrated the power that nationalistic feeling had attained at the beginning of the twentieth century. Many Europeans seemingly believed that the war had given them a higher purpose, a renewed dedication to the greatness of their nation. This selection is taken from the autobiography of Stefan Zweig, an Austrian writer who captured well the orgiastic celebration of war in Vienna in 1914.

Stefan Zweig, *The World of Yesterday*

The next morning I was in Austria. In every station placards had been put up announcing general mobilization. The trains were filled with fresh recruits, banners were flying, music sounded, and in Vienna I found the entire city in a tumult. . . . There were parades in the street, flags, ribbons, and music burst forth everywhere, young recruits were marching triumphantly, their faces lighting up at the cheering. . . .

And to be truthful, I must acknowledge that there was a majestic, rapturous, and even seductive something in this first outbreak of the people from which one could escape only with difficulty. And in spite of all my hatred and aversion for war, I should not like to have missed the memory of those days. As never before, thousands and hundreds of thousands felt what they should have felt in peace time, that they belonged together. A city of two million, a country of nearly fifty million, in that hour felt that they were participating in world history, in a moment which would never recur, and that each one was called upon to cast his infinitesimal self

into the glowing mass, there to be purified of all selfishness. All differences of class, rank, and language were flooded over at that moment by the rushing feeling of fraternity. Strangers spoke to one another in the streets, people who had avoided each other for years shook hands, everywhere one saw excited faces. Each individual experienced an exaltation of his ego, he was no longer the isolated person of former times, he had been incorporated into the mass, he was part of the people, and his person, his hitherto unnoticed person, had been given meaning. . . .

What did the great mass know of war in 1914, after nearly half a century of peace? They did not know war, they had hardly given it a thought. It had become legendary, and distance had made it seem romantic and heroic. They still saw it in the perspective of their school readers and of paintings in museums; brilliant cavalry attacks in glittering uniforms, the fatal shot always straight through the heart, the entire campaign a resounding march of victory—"We'll be home at Christmas," the recruits shouted laughingly to their mothers in August of 1914. . . . A rapid excursion into the romantic, a wild, manly adventure—that is how the war of 1914 was painted in the imagination of the simple man, and the younger people were honestly afraid that they might miss this most wonderful and exciting experience of their lives; that is why they hurried and thronged to the colors, and that is why they shouted and sang in the trains that carried them to the slaughter; wildly and feverishly the red wave of blood coursed through the veins of the entire nation.

the German army to make a vast encircling movement through Belgium into northern France that would sweep around Paris and encircle most of the French army. German troops crossed into Belgium on August 4 and by the first week of September had reached the Marne River, only twenty miles from Paris. The Germans seemed on the verge of success, but had underestimated the speed with which the British would be able to mobilize and put troops into battle in France. An unexpected counterattack by British and French forces under the French commander General Joseph Joffre stopped the Germans at the First Battle of the Marne (September 6–10). The German troops fell back, but the exhausted French army was unable to pursue its advantage. The war quickly turned into a stalemate as

neither the Germans nor the French could dislodge the other from the trenches they had begun to dig for shelter. Two lines of trenches soon extended from the English Channel to the frontiers of Switzerland. The Western Front had become bogged down in a trench warfare that kept both sides immobilized in virtually the same positions for four years.

In contrast to the West, the war in the East was marked by much more mobility, although the cost in lives was equally enormous. At the beginning of the war, the Russian army moved into eastern Germany but was decisively defeated at the Battles of Tannenberg on August 30 and the Masurian Lakes on September 15. These battles established the military reputations of the commanding general, Paul von Hindenburg, and his chief of staff, General Erich Ludendorff. The Russians were no longer a threat to German territory.

The Austrians, Germany's allies, fared less well initially. They had been defeated by the Russians in Galicia and thrown out of Serbia as well. To make matters worse, the Italians betrayed the Germans and Austrians and entered the war on the Allied side by attacking Austria in May 1915. By this time, the Germans had come to the aid of the Austrians. A German-Austrian army defeated and routed the Russian army in Galicia and pushed the Russians back three hundred miles into their own territory. Russian casualties stood at 2.5 million killed, captured, or wounded; the Russians had almost been knocked out of the war. Buoyed by their success, the Germans and Austrians, joined by the Bulgarians in September 1915, attacked and eliminated Serbia from the war.

1916–1917: The Great Slaughter

The successes in the East enabled the Germans to move back to the offensive in the West. The early trenches dug in 1914 had by now become elaborate systems of defense. Both lines of trenches were protected by barbed wire entanglements three to five feet high and thirty yards wide, concrete machine-gun nests, and mortar batteries, supported further back by heavy artillery. Troops lived in holes in the ground, separated from each other by a "no man's land."

The unexpected development of trench warfare baffled military leaders who had been trained to fight wars of movement and maneuver. But public outcries for action put them under heavy pressure. The only plan generals could devise was to attempt a breakthrough by throwing masses of men against enemy lines that had

Map 26.2 The Western Front, 1914–1918.

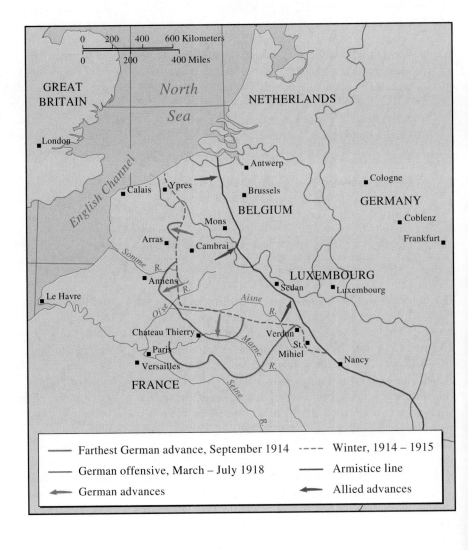

- —— Farthest German advance, September 1914
- ---- Winter, 1914–1915
- —— German offensive, March–July 1918
- —— Armistice line
- ← German advances
- ← Allied advances

first been battered by artillery barrages. Once the decisive breakthrough had been achieved, they thought, they could then return to the war of movement that they knew best. Periodically, the high command on either side would order an offensive that would begin with an artillery barrage to flatten the enemy's barbed wire and leave the enemy in a state of shock. After "softening up" the enemy in this fashion, a mass of soldiers would climb out of their trenches with fixed bayonets and try to work their way toward the enemy trenches. The attacks rarely worked, since the machine gun put hordes of men advancing unprotected across open fields at a severe disadvantage. In 1916 and 1917,

millions of young men were sacrificed in the search for the elusive breakthrough. In the German offensive at Verdun in 1916, the British campaign on the Somme in 1916, and the French attack in the Champagne in 1917, the senselessness of trench warfare became all too obvious. In ten months at Verdun, 700,000 men lost their lives over a few miles of terrain.

DAILY LIFE IN THE TRENCHES

Warfare in the trenches of the Western Front produced unimaginable horrors (see the box on p. 897). Many participants commented on the cloud of confusion that

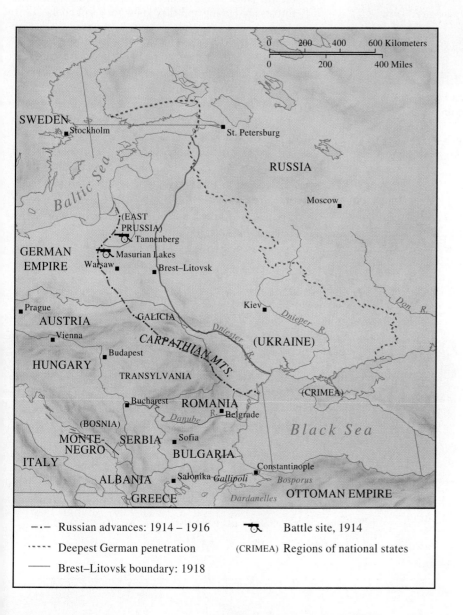

Map 26.3 The Eastern Front, 1914–1918.

- –·–   Russian advances: 1914 – 1916
- ·····   Deepest German penetration
- ——   Brest–Litovsk boundary: 1918
- Battle site, 1914
- (CRIMEA)   Regions of national states

◆ **The Horrors of War.** The slaughter of millions of men in the trenches of World War I created unimaginable horrors for the participants. For the sake of survival, many soldiers learned to harden themselves against the stench of decomposing bodies and the sight of bodies horribly dismembered by artillery barrages.

covered the battlefields. When attacking soldiers entered "no man's land," the noise, machine-gun fire, and exploding artillery shells often caused them to panic and lose their sense of direction; they went forward only because they were carried on by the momentum of the soldiers beside them. Rarely were battles as orderly as they were portrayed on military maps and in civilian newspapers.

Battlefields were hellish landscapes of barbed wire, shell holes, mud, and injured and dying men. The introduction of poison gas in 1915 produced new forms of injuries, as one British writer described:

> I wish those people who write so glibly about this being a holy war could see a case of mustard gas . . . could see the poor things burnt and blistered all over with great mustard-coloured suppurating blisters with blind eyes all sticky . . . and stuck together, and always fighting for breath, with voices a mere whisper, saying that their throats are closing and they know they will choke.[4]

Soldiers in the trenches also lived with the persistent presence of death. Since combat went on for months, they had to carry on in the midst of countless bodies of dead men or the remains of men dismembered by artillery barrages. Many soldiers remembered the stench of decomposing bodies and the swarms of rats that grew fat in the trenches.

Soldiers on the Western Front did not spend all of their time on the front line or in combat when they were on the front line. An infantryman spent one week out of every month in the front-line trenches, one week in the reserve lines, and the remaining two weeks somewhere behind the lines. Daily procedure in the trenches was predictable. Thirty minutes before sunrise,

◆ **The Destruction of Verdun.** In 1916, the German high command decided to take the offensive against the French fortifications at Verdun, which was 125 miles east of Paris. The ferocious Battle of Verdun cost 700,000 lives and resulted in an exchange of only a few miles of land. The city of Verdun was subjected to massive artillery shelling and, as this photograph shows, was severely damaged. The population of Verdun dropped from 15,000 to 3,000 in the course of the battle.

The Reality of War: Trench Warfare

The romantic illusions about the excitement and adventure of war that filled the minds of so many young men who marched off to battle (see the box on p. 893) quickly disintegrated after a short time in the trenches on the Western Front. This description of trench warfare is taken from the most famous novel that emerged from World War I, Erich Maria Remarque's All Quiet on the Western Front, *written in 1929. Remarque had fought in the trenches in France.*

Erich Maria Remarque, *All Quiet on the Western Front*

We wake up in the middle of the night. The earth booms. Heavy fire is falling on us. We crouch into corners. We distinguish shells of every calibre.

Each man lays hold of his things and looks again every minute to reassure himself that they are still there. The dug-out heaves, the night roars and flashes. We look at each other in the momentary flashes of light, and with pale faces and pressed lips shake our heads.

Every man is aware of the heavy shells tearing down the parapet, rooting up the embankment and demolishing the upper layers of concrete. . . . Already by morning a few of the recruits are green and vomiting. They are too inexperienced. . . .

The bombardment does not diminish. It is falling in the rear too. As far as one can see it spouts fountains of mud and iron. A wide belt is being raked.

The attack does not come, but the bombardment continues. Slowly we become mute. Hardly a man speaks. We cannot make ourselves understood.

Our trench is almost gone. At many places it is only eighteen inches high, it is broken by holes, and craters, and mountains of earth. A shell lands square in front of our post. At once it is dark. We are buried and must dig ourselves out. . . .

Towards morning, while it is still dark, there is some excitement. Through the entrance rushes in a swarm of fleeing rats that try to storm the walls. Torches light up the confusion. Everyone yells and curses and slaughters. The madness and despair of many hours unloads itself in this outburst. Faces are distorted, arms strike out, the beasts scream; we just stop in time to avoid attacking one another. . . .

Suddenly it howls and flashes terrifically, the dugout cracks in all its joints under a direct hit, fortunately only a light one that the concrete blocks are able to withstand. It rings metallically, the walls reel, rifles, helmets, earth, mud, and dust fly everywhere. Sulphur fumes pour in. . . . The recruit starts to rave again and two others follow suit. One jumps up and rushes out, we have trouble with the other two. I start after the one who escapes and wonder whether to shoot him in the leg—then it shrieks again, I fling myself down and when I stand up the wall of the trench is plastered with smoking splinters, lumps of flesh, and bits of uniform. I scramble back.

The first recruit seems actually to have gone insane. He butts his head against the wall like a goat. We must try tonight to take him to the rear. Meanwhile we bind him, but so that in case of attack he can be released.

Suddenly the nearer explosions cease. The shelling continues but it has lifted and falls behind us, our trench is free. We seize the hand-grenades, pitch them out in front of the dug-out and jump after them. The bombardment has stopped and a heavy barrage now falls behind us. The attack has come.

No one would believe that in this howling waste there could still be men; but steel helmets now appear on all sides out of the trench, and fifty yards from us a machine-gun is already in position and barking.

The wire-entanglements are torn to pieces. Yet they offer some obstacle. We see the storm-troops coming. Our artillery opens fire. Machine-guns rattle, rifles crack. The charge works its way across. Haie and Kropp begin with the hand-grenades. They throw as fast as they can, others pass them, the handles with the strings already pulled. Haie throws seventy-five yards, Kropp sixty, it has been measured, the distance is important. The enemy as they run cannot do much before they are within forty yards.

We recognize the distorted faces, the smooth helmets: they are French. They have already suffered heavily when they reach the remnants of the barbed-wire entanglements. A whole line has gone down before our machine-guns; then we have a lot of stoppages and they come nearer.

I see one of them, his face upturned, fall into a wire cradle. His body collapses, his hands remain suspended as though he were praying. Then his body drops clean away and only his hands with the stumps of his arms, shot off, now hang in the wire.

troops had to "stand to" or be combat ready to repel any attack. If no attack were forthcoming that day, the day's routine consisted of breakfast followed by inspection, sentry duty, restoration of the trenches, care of personal items, or whiling away the time as best they could. Soldiers often recalled the boredom of life in the dreary, lice-ridden, muddy or dusty trenches.

At many places along the opposing lines of trenches, a "live and let live" system evolved based on the realization that neither side was going to drive out the other anyway. The "live and let live" system resulted in such arrangements as not shelling the latrines or attacking during breakfast. Some parties even worked out agreements to make noise before lesser raids so that the opposing soldiers could retreat to their bunkers.

On both sides, troops produced their own humorous magazines to help pass the time and fulfill the need to laugh in the midst of their daily madness. The British trench magazine, the *B. E. F. Times*, devoted one of its issues to defining military terms. A typical definition "DUDS—These are of two kinds. A shell on impact failing to explode is called a dud. They are unhappily not as plentiful as the other kind, which often draws a big salary and explodes for no reason. These are plentiful away from the fighting areas."[5] Soldiers' songs also captured a mixture of the sentimental and the frivolous (see the box on p. 899).

◆ **Impact of the Machine Gun.** The development of trench warfare on the Western Front stymied military leaders who had expected to fight a war based on movement and maneuver. Their efforts to effect a breakthrough by sending masses of men against enemy lines was the height of folly in view of the machine gun. Masses of men advancing across open land made magnificent targets.

The Widening of the War

As another response to the stalemate on the Western Front, both sides sought to gain new allies who might provide a winning advantage. The Turkish or Ottoman Empire had already come into the war on Germany's side in August 1914. Russia, Great Britain, and France declared war on the Ottoman Empire in November. Although the forces of the British Empire attempted to open a Balkan front by landing forces at Gallipoli, southwest of Constantinople, in April 1915, the entry of Bulgaria into the war on the side of the Central Powers (as Germany, Austria-Hungary, and the Ottoman Empire were called) and a disastrous campaign at Gallipoli caused them to withdraw. The Italians, as we have seen, also entered the war on the Allied side after France and Britain promised to further their acquisition of Austrian territory. In the long run, however, Italian military incompetence forced the Allies to come to the assistance of Italy.

By 1917, the war that had begun in Europe was having an increasing impact on other parts of the world. In the Middle East, a British officer who came to be known as Lawrence of Arabia incited Arab princes to revolt against their Ottoman overlords. In 1918, British forces from Egypt destroyed the rest of the Ottoman Empire in the Middle East. For their Middle East campaigns, the British mobilized forces from India, Australia, and New Zealand. The Allies also took advantage of Germany's preoccupations in Europe and lack of naval strength to seize German colonies in the rest of the world.

ENTRY OF THE UNITED STATES

At first, the United States tried to remain neutral in the Great War, but found it more difficult to do so as the war dragged on. Although there was considerable sentiment for the British side in the conflict, the immediate cause of American involvement grew out of the naval conflict between Germany and Great Britain. Only once did the German and British naval forces engage in direct battle—at the Battle of Jutland on May 31, 1916, when the Germans won an inconclusive victory.

Britain used its superior naval power to maximum effect, however, by imposing a naval blockade on Germany. Germany retaliated with a counterblockade enforced by the use of unrestricted submarine warfare. At the beginning of 1915, the German government declared the area around the British Isles a war zone and threatened to torpedo any ship caught in it. Strong American protests over the German sinking of passenger liners, especially the British ship *Lusitania* on May 7,

The Songs of World War I

On the march, in bars, in trains, and even in the trenches, the soldiers of World War I spent time singing. The songs sung by soldiers of different nationalities varied considerably. A German favorite, The Watch on the Rhine, focused on heroism and patriotism. British war songs often partook of black humor, as in The Old Barbed Wire. An American favorite was the rousing Over There, written by the professional songwriter George M. Cohan.

From *The Watch on the Rhine*

There sounds a call like thunder's roar,
Like the crash of swords, like the surge of waves.
To the Rhine, the Rhine, the German Rhine!
Who will the stream's defender be?
    Dear Fatherland, rest quietly
    Sure stands and true the Watch,
    The Watch on the Rhine.

To heaven he gazes.
Spirits of heroes look down.
He vows with proud battle-desire:
O Rhine! You will stay as German as my breast!
    Dear Fatherland, etc.
Even if my heart breaks in death,
You will never be French.
As you are rich in water
Germany is rich in hero's blood.
    Dear Fatherland, etc.

So long as a drop of blood still glows,
So long a hand the dagger can draw,
So long an arm the rifle can hold—
Never will an enemy touch your shore.
    Dear Fatherland, etc.

From *The Old Barbed Wire*

If you want to find the old battalion,
I know where they are,
I know where they are.

If you want to find a battalion,
I know where they are,
They're hanging on the old barbed wire.
I've seen 'em, I've seen 'em,
Hanging on the old barbed wire,
I've seen 'em,
Hanging on the old barbed wire.

George M. Cohan, *Over There*

Over There
Over There
Send the word
Send the word
Over There
That the boys are coming
The drums rum-tuming everywhere.
Over There
Say a prayer
Send the word
Send the word
To Beware.
It will be over.
We're coming over
And we won't come back
Till it's over
Over There.

Johnnie get your gun
    get your gun
    get your gun
Back in town to run
Home to run
Home to run
Hear them calling you and me
Every son of liberty
Hurry right away
Don't delay go today
Make your Daddy glad
To have had such a lad
Tell your sweetheart not to pine
To be proud their boy's in line.

1915, when more than a hundred Americans lost their lives, forced the German government to modify its policy of unrestricted submarine warfare starting in September 1915 and to briefly suspend unrestricted submarine warfare a year later.

In January 1917, however, eager to break the deadlock in the war, the Germans decided on another military gamble by returning to unrestricted submarine warfare. German naval officers convinced Emperor William II that the use of unrestricted submarine warfare could starve the British into submission within five months. When the emperor expressed concern about the Americans, he was told not to worry. The Americans, the chief of the German Naval Staff said, were "disorganized and undisciplined." The British would starve before the Americans could act. And even if the Americans did intervene, Admiral Holtzendorff assured the emperor, "I give your Majesty my word as an officer, that not one American will land on the continent."

The return to unrestricted submarine warfare brought the United States into the war on April 6, 1917. Although American troops did not arrive in large numbers in Europe until 1918, the entry of the United States into the war in 1917 gave the Allied powers a psychological boost when they needed it. The year 1917 was not a good year for them. Allied offensives on the Western Front were disastrously defeated. The Italian armies were smashed in October, and in November 1917 the Bolshevik Revolution in Russia led to Russia's withdrawal from the war (see The Russian Revolution later in this chapter). The cause of the Central Powers looked favorable, although war weariness in the Ottoman Empire, Bulgaria, Austria-Hungary, and Germany was beginning to take its toll. The home front was rapidly becoming a cause for as much concern as the war front.

The Home Front: The Impact of Total War

The prolongation of World War I made it a total war that affected the lives of all citizens, however remote they might be from the battlefields. World War I transformed the governments, economies, and societies of the European belligerents in fundamental ways. The need to organize masses of men and matériel for years of combat (Germany alone had 5.5 million men in active units in 1916) led to increased centralization of government powers, economic regimentation, and manipulation of public opinion to keep the war effort going.

TOTAL WAR: POLITICAL CENTRALIZATION AND ECONOMIC REGIMENTATION

As we have seen, the outbreak of World War I was greeted with a rush of patriotism; even socialists joined enthusiastically into the fray. As the war dragged on, governments realized, however, that more than patriotism would be needed. Since the war was expected to be short, little thought had been given to economic problems and long-term wartime needs. Governments had to respond quickly, however, when the war machines failed

to achieve their knockout blows and made ever-greater demands for men and matériel.

The extension of government power was a logical outgrowth of these needs. Most European countries had already devised some system of mass conscription or military draft. It was now carried to unprecedented heights as countries mobilized tens of millions of young men for that elusive breakthrough to victory. Even countries that traditionally relied on volunteers (Great Britain had the largest volunteer army in modern history—one million men—in 1914 and 1915) were forced to resort to conscription, especially to ensure that skilled workers did not enlist but remained in factories that were crucial to the production of munitions. In 1916, despite widespread resistance to this extension of government power, compulsory military service was introduced in Great Britain.

Throughout Europe, wartime governments expanded their powers over their economies. Free-market capitalistic systems were temporarily shelved as governments experimented with price, wage, and rent controls, the rationing of food supplies and materials, the regulation of imports and exports, and the nationalization of transportation systems and industries. Some governments even moved toward compulsory labor employment. In effect, in order to mobilize the entire resources of their nations for the war effort, European nations had moved toward planned economies directed by government agencies. Under total war mobilization, the distinction between soldiers at war and civilians at home was narrowed. In the view of political leaders, all citizens constituted a national army dedicated to victory. As the American president Woodrow Wilson expressed it, the men and women "who remain to till the soil and man the factories are no less a part of the army than the men beneath the battle flags."

Not all European nations made the shift to total war equally well. Germany had the most success in developing a planned economy. At the beginning of the war, the government asked Walter Rathenau, head of the German General Electric Company, to use his business methods to organize a War Raw Materials Board that would allocate strategic raw materials to produce the goods that were most needed. Rathenau made it possible for the German war machine to be effectively supplied. The Germans were much less successful with the rationing of food, however. Even before the war, Germany had had to import about 20 percent of its food supply. The British blockade of Germany and a decline in farm labor made food shortages inevitable. Daily food rations in Germany were cut from 1,350 calories in 1916 to 1,000 by 1917, barely adequate for survival. As a result of a poor potato harvest in the winter of 1916–1917, turnips became the basic staple for the poor. An estimated 750,000 German civilians died of hunger during World War I.

The German war government was eventually consolidated under military authority. The two popular military heroes of the war, General Paul von Hindenburg, chief of the General Staff, and Erich Ludendorff, deputy chief of staff, came to control the government by 1916 and virtually became the military dictators of Germany. In 1916, Hindenburg and Ludendorff decreed a system of complete mobilization for total war. In the Auxiliary Service Law of December 2, 1916, they required all male noncombatants between the ages of seventeen and sixty to work only in jobs deemed crucial for the war effort.

Germany, of course, had already possessed a rather authoritarian political system before the war began. France and England did not, but even in those countries the power of the central government was dramatically increased. At first, Great Britain tried to fight the war by continuing its liberal tradition of limited government interference in the economy. The pressure of circumstances, however, forced the British government to take a more active role in economic matters. The need to

ensure an adequate production of munitions led to the creation in July 1915 of a Ministry of Munitions under the dynamic leader, David Lloyd George. The Ministry of Munitions took numerous steps to ensure that private industry would produce war matériel at limited profits. It developed a vast bureaucracy, which expanded from 20 to 65,000 clerks to oversee munitions plants. Beginning in 1915, it was given the power to take over plants manufacturing war goods that did not cooperate with the government. The British government also rationed food supplies and imposed rent controls.

The French were less successful than the British and Germans in establishing a strong war government during much of the war. For one thing, the French faced a difficult obstacle in organizing a total war economy. German occupation of northeastern France cost the nation 75 percent of its coal production and almost 80 percent of its steel-making capacity. Then, too, the relationship between civil and military authorities in France was extraordinarily strained. For the first three years of the war, military and civil authorities struggled over who would oversee the conduct of the war. Not until the end of 1917 did the French war government find a strong leader in Georges Clemenceau. Declaring that "war is too important to be left to generals,"

✦ **The Leaders of Germany.** Over the course of the war, the power of central governments was greatly enlarged in order to meet the demands of total war. In Germany, the two military heroes of the war, Paul von Hindenburg and Erich Ludendorf, became virtual military dictators by 1916. The two are shown here (Hindenburg on the left) with Emperor William II, whose power declined as the war dragged on.

✦ **British Recruiting Poster.** As the conflict persisted month after month, governments resorted to active propaganda campaigns to generate enthusiasm for the war. In this British recruiting poster, the government tried to pressure men into volunteering for military service. By 1916, the British were forced to adopt compulsory military service.

Clemenceau established clear civilian control of a total war government.

The three other major belligerents—Russia, Austria-Hungary, and Italy—had much less success than Great Britain, Germany, and France in mobilizing for total war. The autocratic empires of Russia and Austria-Hungary had backward economies that proved incapable of turning out the quantity of war matériel needed to fight a modern war. The Russians, for example, conscripted millions of men but could arm only one-fourth of them. Unarmed Russian soldiers were sent into battle anyway and advised to pick up rifles from their dead colleagues. With their numerous minorities, both the Russian and Austro-Hungarian Empires found it

difficult to achieve the kind of internal cohesion needed to fight a prolonged total war. Italy, too, lacked both the public enthusiasm and the industrial resources needed to wage a successful total war.

PUBLIC ORDER AND PUBLIC OPINION

As the Great War dragged on and both casualties and privations worsened, internal dissatisfaction replaced the patriotic enthusiasm that had marked the early stages of the war. By 1916, there were numerous signs that civilian morale was beginning to crack under the pressure of total war.

The first two years of the war witnessed only a few scattered strikes, but by 1916 strike activity had increased dramatically. In 1916, 50,000 German workers carried out a three-day work stoppage in Berlin to protest the arrest of a radical socialist leader. In both France and Britain, the number of strikes increased significantly. Even worse was the violence that erupted in Ireland when members of the Irish Republican Brotherhood and Citizens Army occupied government buildings in Dublin on Easter Sunday (April 24), 1916. British forces crushed the Easter Rebellion and then condemned its leaders to death.

Internal opposition to the war came from two major sources in 1916 and 1917, liberals and socialists. Liberals in both Germany and Britain sponsored peace resolutions calling for a negotiated peace without any territorial acquisitions. They were largely ignored. Socialists in Germany and Austria also called for negotiated settlements. By 1917, war morale had so deteriorated that more dramatic protests took place. Mutinies in the Italian and French armies were put down with difficulty. Czech leaders in the Austrian Empire openly called for an independent democratic Czech state. In April 1917, 200,000 workers in Berlin went out on strike for a week to protest the reduction of bread rations. Only the threat of military force and prison brought them back to their jobs. Despite the strains, all of the belligerent countries except Russia survived the stresses of 1917 and fought on.

War governments also fought back against the growing opposition to the war. Authoritarian regimes, such as those of Germany, Russia, and Austria-Hungary, had always relied on force to subdue their populations. Under the pressures of the war, however, even parliamentary regimes resorted to an expansion of police powers to stifle internal dissent. The British Parliament passed a Defence of the Realm Act (DORA) at the very beginning of the war that allowed the public authorities to arrest dissenters as traitors. The act was later extended to authorize public officials to censor newspapers by deleting objectionable material and even to suspend newspaper publication. In France, government authorities had initially been lenient about public opposition to the war. But by 1917, they began to fear that open opposition to the war might weaken the French will to fight. When Georges Clemenceau became premier near the end of 1917, the lenient French policies came to an end, and basic civil liberties were suppressed for the duration of the war. The editor of an antiwar newspaper was even executed on a charge of treason. Clemenceau also punished journalists who wrote negative war reports by having them drafted.

Wartime governments made active use of propaganda to arouse enthusiasm for the war. At the beginning, public officials needed to do little to achieve this goal. The British and French, for example, exaggerated German atrocities in Belgium and found that their citizens were only too willing to believe these accounts. But as the war progressed and morale sagged, governments were forced to devise new techniques to stimulate declining enthusiasm. In one British recruiting poster, for example, a small daughter asked her father, "Daddy, what did YOU do in the Great War?" while her younger brother played with toy soldiers and cannon.

THE SOCIAL IMPACT OF TOTAL WAR

Total war made a significant impact on European society, most visibly by bringing an end to unemployment. The withdrawal of millions of men from the labor market to fight, combined with the heightened demand for wartime products, led to jobs for everyone able to work.

The cause of labor also benefited from the war. The enthusiastic patriotism of workers was soon rewarded with a greater acceptance of trade unions. To ensure that labor problems would not disrupt production, war governments in Britain, France, and Germany not only sought union cooperation but also for the first time allowed trade unions to participate in making important government decisions on labor matters. In return, unions cooperated on wage limits and production schedules. Labor gained two benefits from this cooperation. It

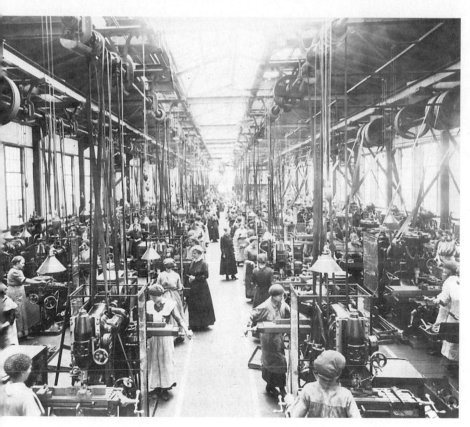

✦ **Women Workers in a German Munitions Factory.** World War I created new job opportunities for women. They were now employed in jobs that had earlier been considered beyond their capacity. As seen in this picture, this included factory work in heavy industry. These German women are performing a variety of tasks in a shell factory. Between 1913 and 1917, female metalworkers increased from 5 to 28 percent of the total labor force.

⇒ *Women in the Factories* ⇐

During World War I, women were called upon to assume new job responsibilities, including factory work. In this selection, Naomi Loughnan, a young, upper-middle-class woman, describes the experiences in a munitions plant that considerably broadened her perspective on life.

Naomi Loughnan, "Munition Work"

We little thought when we first put on our overalls and caps and enlisted in the Munition Army how much more inspiring our life was to be than we had dared to hope. Though we munition workers sacrifice our ease we gain a life worth living. Our long days are filled with interest, and with the zest of doing work for our country in the grand cause of Freedom. As we handle the weapons of war we are learning great lessons of life. In the busy, noisy workshops we come face to face with every kind of class, and each one of these classes has something to learn from the others. . . .

Engineering mankind is possessed of the unshakable opinion that no woman can have the mechanical sense. If one of us asks humbly why such and such an alteration is not made to prevent this or that drawback to a machine, she is told, with a superior smile, that a man has worked her machine before her for years, and that therefore if there were any improvement possible it would have been made. As long as we do exactly what we are told and do not attempt to use our brains, we give entire satisfaction, and are treated as nice, good children. Any swerving from the easy path prepared for us by our males arouses the most scathing contempt in their manly bosoms. . . . Women have, however, proved that their entry into the munition world has increased the output. Employers who forget things personal in their patriotic desire for large results are enthusiastic over the success of women in the shops. But their workmen have to be handled with the utmost tenderness and caution lest they should actually imagine it was being suggested that women could do their work equally well, given equal conditions of training—at least where muscle is not the driving force. . . .

The coming of the mixed classes of women into the factory is slowly but surely having an educative effect upon the men. "Language" is almost unconsciously becoming subdued. There are fiery exceptions who make our hair stand up on end under our close-fitting caps, but a sharp rebuke or a look of horror will often straighten out the most savage. . . . It is grievous to hear the girls also swearing and using disgusting language. Shoulder to shoulder with the children of the slums, the upper classes are having their eyes opened at last to the awful conditions among which their sisters have dwelt. Foul language, immorality, and many other evils are but the natural outcome of overcrowding and bitter poverty. . . . Sometimes disgust will overcome us, but we are learning with painful clarity that the fault is not theirs whose actions disgust us, but must be placed to the discredit of those other classes who have allowed the continued existence of conditions which generate the things from which we shrink appalled.

opened the way to the collective bargaining practices that became more widespread after World War I and increased the prestige of trade unions, enabling them to attract more members.

World War I also created new roles for women. With so many men off fighting at the front, women were called upon to take over jobs and responsibilities that had not been open to them before. These included certain clerical jobs that only small numbers of women had held earlier. In Britain, for example, the number of women who worked in banking rose from 9,500 to almost 64,000 in the course of the war, while the number of women in commerce rose from a half million to almost one million. Overall, 1,345,000 women in Britain obtained new jobs or replaced men during the war. Women were also now employed in jobs that had been considered beyond the "capacity of women." These included such occupations as chimney sweeps, truck drivers, farm laborers, and, above all, factory workers in heavy industry (see the box above). In France, 684,000 women worked in armaments plants for the first time; in Britain, the figure was 920,000. Thirty-eight percent of the workers in the Krupp Armaments works in Germany in 1918 were women.

Male resistance, however, often made it difficult for women to enter these new jobs, especially in heavy industry. One Englishwoman who worked in a munitions factory recalled her experience: "I could quite see it was hard on the men to have women coming into all their pet jobs and in some cases doing them a good deal better. I sympathized with the way they were torn between not wanting the women to undercut them, and yet hating them to earn as much."[6] While male workers expressed concern that the employment of females at lower wages would depress their own wages, women began to demand equal pay legislation. The French government passed a law in July 1915 that established a minimum wage for women homeworkers in textiles, an industry that had grown dramatically because of the need for military uniforms. Later in 1917, the government decreed that men and women should receive equal rates for piecework. Despite the noticeable increase in women's wages that resulted from government regulations, women's industrial wages still were not equal to men's wages by the end of the war.

Even worse, women had achieved little real security about their place in the workforce. Both men and women seemed to think that many of the new jobs for women were only temporary, an expectation quite evident in the British poem, "War Girls," written in 1916:

> There's the girl who clips your ticket for the train,
> And the girl who speeds the lift from floor to floor,
> There's the girl who does a milk-round in the rain,
> And the girl who calls for orders at your door.
> Strong, sensible, and fit,
> They're out to show their grit,
> And tackle jobs with energy and knack.
> No longer caged and penned up,
> They're going to keep their end up
> Till the khaki soldier boys come marching back.[7]

At the end of the war, governments moved quickly to remove women from the jobs they had encouraged them to take earlier. By 1919, there were 650,000 unemployed women in Britain while wages for women who were still employed were also lowered. The work benefits for women from World War I seemed to be short-lived.

Nevertheless, in some countries the role played by women in the wartime economies did have a positive impact on the women's movement for social and political emancipation. The most obvious gain was the right to vote that was given to women in Germany and Austria immediately after the war (in Britain already in January 1918). The Nineteenth Amendment to the Constitution gave women in the United States the right to vote in 1919. Contemporary media, however, tended to focus on the more noticeable, yet in some ways more superficial, social emancipation of upper- and middle-class women. In ever-larger numbers, these young

women took jobs, had their own apartments, and showed their new independence by smoking in public and wearing shorter dresses, cosmetics, and new hair styles.

In one sense, World War I had been a great social leveler. Death in battle did not distinguish between classes. Although all social classes suffered casualties in battle, two groups were especially hard-hit. Junior officers who led the charges across the "no man's land" that separated the lines of trenches experienced death rates that were three times higher than regular casualty rates. Many of these junior officers were members of the aristocracy (see the box on p. 906). The unskilled workers and peasants who made up the masses of soldiers mowed down by machine guns also suffered heavy casualties. The fortunate ones were the skilled laborers who gained exemptions from military service because they were needed at home to train workers in the war industries.

The burst of patriotic enthusiasm that marked the beginning of the war deceived many into believing that the war was creating a new sense of community that meant the end of the class conflict that had marked European society at the end of the nineteenth and beginning of the twentieth centuries. David Lloyd George, who became the British prime minister in 1916, wrote in September 1914 that "all classes, high and low, are shedding themselves of selfishness. . . . It is bringing a new outlook to all classes. . . . We can see for the first time the fundamental things that matter in life, and that have been obscured from our vision by the . . . growth of prosperity."[8] Lloyd George's optimistic opinion proved to be quite misguided, however. The Great War did not eliminate the class conflict that had characterized pre-1914 Europe, and this became increasingly apparent as the war progressed.

Certainly, the economic impact of the war was felt unevenly. One group of people who especially benefited were the owners of the large industries manufacturing the weapons of war. Despite public outrage, governments rarely limited the enormous profits made by the industrial barons. In fact, in the name of efficiency, wartime governments tended to favor large industries when scarce raw materials were allocated. Small firms considered less essential to the war effort even had to shut down because of a lack of resources.

Growing inflation also caused inequities. The combination of full employment and high demand for scarce consumer goods caused prices to climb. Many skilled workers were able to earn wages that enabled them to

The Reality of War: War and the Family

John Mott was a captain in the British army. He came from an aristocratic family with a strong military tradition. He married Muriel Backhouse in 1907, and they had three sons before he was called up for service in World War I. These excerpts are taken from four of Mott's letters to his wife and a letter informing her of her husband's death during the Gallipoli campaign. The human experience of World War I was made up of millions of stories like that of John Mott and his family.

One Family's War

1 July [1915]

My darling Childie,

I hope you got home safely. I have been promised that I shall know the ship we go on tomorrow. But it will be no good writing to Gibraltar as we should get there before the letter. Try Malta as that goes over land. If you get overdrawn go and see Cox. Goodbye Darling. Don't worry I shall come back alright. Your devoted husband John F. Mott

13 July

Mediterranean field force, Mudros

My darling Childie,

This island is very hot indeed but beastly windy. We have absolutely no news from the Front. Troops are pouring out now and I expect we shall be in it next week.

We have all gone through our little bout of diarrhea. I was not too bad and only had pains in my stomach otherwise I am very well indeed.

Everyone is standing the heat very well. The Brigadier has a tent but everybody else is out in the blazing sun.

31 July

My darling Childie,

I got more letters from you today dated 5th, 6th, 7th. I had no idea till I read the letter that they could do all that about writs. I would never have left things in such a muddle, I only hope you can get straight.

Yesterday I left here at 5:30 AM to go to the trenches with the Brigadier. We had an awful day, and I am not at all keen to go into that lot at all events. We sailed over in a trawler and had a long walk in the open under shrapnel fire. It was not very pleasant. Then we got to the communications trenches and had a mile and a half

of them to go up. When we got to the fire trenches the stink was awful. Arms and legs of Turks sticking out of the trench parapets and lying dead all round. In one place the bottom of the trench was made up by dead Turks, but this has been abandoned as the place was too poisonous.

Our battle ships have been shelling very heavily so there may be an attack on. I must write to my mother tonight. All my love and kisses for ever Your loving husband John F. Mott

6 August

My darling Childie,

We are off today just as we stand up, with four days rations. I can't say where we are going but we shall see spots. I shall not get a chance to write again for a bit as we shall be on the move. I expect you have got a map of the place by now and perhaps you will hear where we have gone.

Very good to get away. All my love and kisses for ever Your loving husband John F. Mott

Best love to all kids and baby

Pte A Thompson
6 Batt Y and L Red Cross Hospital

We landed on the 6th of Aug and took 2 hills and at daybreak on the 7th advanced across an open plain to the left of Salt Lake and got an awful shelling. We came to a small hill which was flat on top and it was about 2 hundred yards further on where the Capt was hit. They gave us it worse than ever when we got on there and I might have been happen 50 yds away when I saw the Capt and about 5 men fall badly hit. I could not say whether it was shrapnel or common shell but I think it was most probably shrapnel as they use that mostly. It was that thick that no one could get to the Capt at the time and I don't think he lived very long, well he could not the way they were hit and was afterwards buried when things had quietened down in the evening and a cross was put on his grave with an inscription and he got as good a burial as could be given out there. Well I think I have told you all I know about Capt Mott. I only wishe I could have given you better news, so I will close with Kind Regards

Yours Obediently,

Pte Thompson

keep up with the inflation, but this was not true for unskilled workers and for those in nonessential industries. Only in Great Britain did the wages of workers outstrip prices. Everywhere else in Europe, people experienced a loss of purchasing power.

Many middle-class people were especially hard-hit by inflation. They included both those who lived on fixed incomes, such as retired people on pensions, and professional people, such as clerks, lesser civil servants, teachers, small shopkeepers, and clergymen, whose incomes remained stable at a time when prices were rising. By the end of the war, many of these people were actually doing less well economically than skilled workers. Their discontent would find expression after the war.

War and Revolution

By 1917, total war was creating serious domestic turmoil in all of the European belligerent states. Most countries were able to prop up their regimes and convince their peoples to continue the war for another year, but others were coming close to collapse. In Austria, for example, a government minister warned that "if the monarchs of the Central Powers cannot make peace in the coming months, it will be made for them by their peoples." Russia, however, was the only belligerent that actually experienced the kind of complete collapse in 1917 that others were predicting might happen throughout Europe. Out of Russia's collapse came the Russian Revolution, whose impact would be widely felt in Europe for decades to come.

The Russian Revolution

After the Revolution of 1905 had failed to bring any substantial changes to Russia, Tsar Nicholas II fell back on the army and bureaucracy as the basic props for his autocratic regime. Perhaps Russia could have survived this way, as some have argued, but World War I magnified Russia's problems and severely challenged the tsarist government.

Russia was unprepared both militarily and technologically for the total war of World War I. Competent military leadership was lacking. Even worse, the tsar, alone of all European monarchs, insisted upon taking personal charge of the armed forces despite his obvious lack of ability and training for such an awesome burden. Russian industry was unable to produce the weapons needed for the army. Ill-led and ill-armed, Russian armies suffered incredible losses. Between 1914 and

1916, two million soldiers were killed while another four to six million were wounded or captured. By 1917, the Russian will to fight had vanished.

The tsarist government was totally inadequate for the tasks that it faced in 1914. The surge of patriotic enthusiasm that greeted the outbreak of war was soon dissipated by a government that distrusted its own people. When leading industrialists formed committees to improve factory production, a government suspicious of their motives undermined their efforts. Although the middle classes and liberal aristocrats still hoped for a constitutional monarchy, they were sullen over the tsar's revocation of the political concessions made during the Revolution of 1905. Peasant discontent flourished as conditions worsened. The concentration of Russian industry in a few large cities made workers' frustrations all the more evident and dangerous. Even conservative aristocrats were appalled by the incompetent and inefficient bureaucracy that controlled the political and military system. In the meantime, Tsar Nicholas II was increasingly insulated from events by his wife Alexandra.

This German-born princess was a stubborn, willful, and ignorant woman who had fallen under the influence of Rasputin, a Siberian peasant who belonged to a religious sect that indulged in sexual orgies. To the tsarina, Rasputin was a holy man for he alone seemed able to stop the bleeding of her hemophiliac son Alexis. Rasputin's influence made him an important power behind the throne, and he did not hesitate to interfere

◆ **Lenin Addresses a Crowd.** V. I. Lenin was the driving force behind the success of the Bolsheviks in seizing power in Russia and creating the Union of Soviet Socialist Republics. Here Lenin is seen addressing a rally in Moscow in 1917.

in government affairs. As the leadership at the top stumbled its way through a series of military and economic disasters, the middle class, aristocrats, peasants, soldiers, and workers grew more and more disenchanted with the tsarist regime. Even conservative aristocrats who supported the monarchy felt the need to do something to reverse the deteriorating situation. For a start, they assassinated Rasputin in December 1916. By then it was too late to save the monarchy, and its fall came quickly at the beginning of March 1917.

THE MARCH REVOLUTION

At the beginning of March, a series of strikes broke out in the capital city of Petrograd (formerly St. Petersburg). Here the actions of working-class women helped to change the course of Russian history. In February of 1917, the government had introduced bread rationing in the capital city after the price of bread had skyrocketed. Many of the women who stood in the lines waiting for bread were also factory workers who had put in twelve-hour days. The number of women working in Petrograd factories had doubled since 1914. The Russian government had become aware of the volatile situation in the capital from a police report:

> Mothers of families, exhausted by endless standing in line at stores, distraught over their half-starving and sick children, are today perhaps closer to revolution than [the liberal opposition leaders] and of course they are a great deal more dangerous because they are the combustible material for which only a single spark is needed to burst into flame.[9]

On March 8, a day celebrated since 1910 as International Women's Day, about ten thousand Petrograd women marched through the city demanding "Peace and Bread" and "Down with Autocracy." Soon the women were joined by other workers, and together they called for a general strike that succeeded in shutting down all the factories in the city on March 10. The tsarina wrote to Nicholas II at the battlefront that "This is a hooligan movement. If the weather were very cold they would all probably stay at home." Nicholas ordered the troops to disperse the crowds by shooting them if necessary. Initially, the troops did so, but soon significant numbers of the soldiers joined the demonstrators. The situation was out of the tsar's control. The Duma or legislative body, which the tsar had tried to dissolve, met anyway and on March 12 established a Provisional Government that urged the tsar to abdicate. He did so on March 15.

In just one week, the tsarist regime had fallen apart. It was not really overthrown since there had been no deliberate revolution. Even those who were conscious revolutionaries were caught by surprise at the rapidity of the monarchy's disintegration. Although no particular group had been responsible for the outburst, the moderate Constitutional Democrats were responsible for establishing the Provisional Government. They represented primarily a middle-class and liberal aristocratic minority. Their program consisted of a nineteenth-century liberal agenda: freedom of speech, religion, assembly, and civil liberties. Their determination to carry on the war to preserve Russia's honor was a major blunder since it satisfied neither the workers nor the peasants who above all wanted an end to the war.

The Provisional Government was also faced with another authority, the soviets, or councils of workers' and soldiers' deputies. The soviet of Petrograd had been formed in March 1917; at the same time soviets sprang up spontaneously in army units, factory towns, and rural areas. The soviets represented the more radical interests of the lower classes and were largely composed of socialists of various kinds. Most numerous were the Socialist Revolutionaries, who wished to establish peasant socialism by seizing the great landed estates and creating a rural democracy. Since the beginning of the twentieth century, the Socialist Revolutionaries had come to rely on the use of political terrorism to accomplish their goals. Since 1893, Russia had also had a Marxist Social Democratic Party, which had divided in 1903 into two factions known as the Mensheviks and Bolsheviks. The Mensheviks wanted the Social Democrats to be a mass electoral socialist party based on a Western model. Like the Social Democrats of Germany, they were willing to cooperate temporarily in a parliamentary democracy while working toward the ultimate achievement of the socialist state.

The Bolsheviks were a small faction of Russian Social Democrats who had come under the leadership of Vladimir Ulianov, known to the world as V. I. Lenin (1870–1924). Born in 1870 to a middle-class family, Lenin received a legal education and became a lawyer. In 1887, he turned into a dedicated enemy of tsarist Russia when his older brother was executed for planning to assassinate the tsar. Lenin's search for a revolutionary faith led him to Marxism, and in 1894 he moved to St. Petersburg where he organized an illegal group known as the Union for the Liberation of the Working Class.

Arrested for this activity, Lenin was shipped to Siberia. After his release, he chose to go into exile in Switzerland and eventually assumed the leadership of the Bolshevik wing of the Russian Social Democratic Party.

Under Lenin's direction, the Bolsheviks became a party dedicated to violent revolution. He believed that only a violent revolution could destroy the capitalist system and that a "vanguard" of activists must form a small party of well-disciplined professional revolutionaries to accomplish the task. Between 1900 and 1917, Lenin spent most of his time in Switzerland. When the Provisional Government was formed in March 1917, he believed that an opportunity for the Bolsheviks to seize power had come. In April 1917, with the connivance of the German High Command, who hoped to create disorder in Russia, Lenin, his wife, and a small group of his followers were shipped to Russia in a "sealed train" by way of Finland.

Lenin's arrival in Russia opened a new stage of the Russian Revolution. In his "April Theses," issued on April 20, Lenin presented a blueprint for revolutionary action based on his own version of Marxist theory. According to Lenin, it was not necessary for Russia to experience a bourgeois revolution before it could move toward socialism, as orthodox Marxists had argued. Instead, Russia could move directly into socialism. In the "April Theses," Lenin maintained that the soviets of soldiers, workers, and peasants were ready-made instruments of power. The Bolsheviks must work to gain control of these groups and then use them to overthrow the Provisional Government. At the same time, Bolshevik propaganda must seek mass support through promises geared to the needs of the people: an end to the war; the redistribution of all land to the peasants; the transfer of factories and industries from capitalists to committees of workers; and the relegation of government power from the Provisional Government to the soviets. Three simple slogans summed up the Bolshevik program: "Peace, Land, Bread," "Worker Control of Production," and "All Power to the Soviets."

In late spring and early summer, while the Bolsheviks set about winning over the masses to their program and gaining a majority in the Petrograd and Moscow soviets, the Provisional Government struggled to gain control of Russia against almost overwhelming obstacles. Although the Provisional Government promised that a constitutional convention called for the fall of 1917 would confiscate and redistribute royal and monastic lands, the offer was meaningless since many peasants had already starting seizing lands on their own in March. The

CHRONOLOGY

The Russian Revolution

	1916
Murder of Rasputin	December
	1917
March of women in Petrograd	March 8
General strike in Petrograd	March 10
Establishment of Provisional Government	March 12
Tsar abdicates	March 15
Formation of Petrograd soviet	March
Lenin arrives in Russia	April 3
Lenin's "April Theses"	April 20
Failed attempt to overthrow Provisional Government	July
Bolsheviks gain majority in Petrograd soviet	October
Bolsheviks overthrow Provisional Government	November 6–7
	1918
Lenin disbands the Constituent Assembly	January
Treaty of Brest-Litovsk	March 3
Civil war	1918–1921

military situation was also deteriorating. The Petrograd soviet had issued its Army Order No. 1 in March to all Russian military forces, encouraging them to remove their officers and replace them with committees composed of "the elected representatives of the lower ranks" of the army. Army Order No. 1 led to the collapse of all discipline and created military chaos. When the Provisional Government attempted to initiate a new military offensive in July, the army simply dissolved as masses of peasant soldiers turned their backs on their officers and returned home to join their families in seizing lands.

THE BOLSHEVIK REVOLUTION

In July 1917, Lenin and the Bolsheviks were falsely accused of inciting an attempt to overthrow the Provisional Government, and Lenin was forced to flee to Finland. But the days of the Provisional Government

Ten Days That Shook the World: Lenin and the Bolshevik Seizure of Power

John Reed was an American journalist who helped to found the American Communist Labor Party. Accused of sedition, he fled the United States and went to Russia. In Ten Days That Shook the World, Reed left an impassioned eyewitness account of the Russian Revolution. It is apparent from his comments that Reed considered Lenin the indispensable hero of the Bolshevik success.

John Reed, *Ten Days That Shook the World*

It was just 8:40 when a thundering wave of cheers announced the entrance of the presidium, with Lenin—great Lenin—among them. A short, stocky figure, with a big head set down in his shoulders, bald and bulging. Little eyes, a snubbish nose, wide, generous mouth, and heavy chin; clean-shaven now, but already beginning to bristle with the well-known beard of his past and future. Dressed in shabby clothes, his trousers much too long for him. Unimpressive, to be the idol of a mob, loved and revered as perhaps few leaders in history have been. A strange popular leader—a leader purely by virtue of intellect; colorless, humorless, uncompromising and detached; without picturesque idiosyncrasies—but with the power of explaining profound ideas in simple terms, of analyzing a concrete situation. And combined with shrewdness, the greatest intellectual audacity. . . .

Now Lenin, gripping the edge of the reading stand, letting his little winking eyes travel over the crowd as he stood there waiting, apparently oblivious to the long-rolling ovation, which lasted several minutes. When it finished, he said simply, "We shall now proceed to construct the Socialist order!" Again that overwhelming human roar.

"The first thing is the adoption of practical measures to realize peace. . . . We shall offer peace to the peoples of all the belligerent countries upon the basis of the Soviet terms—no annexations, no indemnities, and the right of self-determination of peoples. At the same time, according to our promise, we shall publish and repudiate the secret treaties. . . . The question of War and Peace is so clear that I think that I may, without preamble, read the project of a Proclamation to the Peoples of All the Belligerent Countries. . . ."

His great mouth, seeming to smile, opened wide as he spoke; his voice was hoarse—not unpleasantly so, but as if it had hardened that way after years and years of speaking—and went on monotonously, with the effect of being able to go forever. . . . For emphasis he bent forward slightly. No gestures. And before him, a thousand simple faces looking up in intent adoration.

[Reed then reproduces the full text of the Proclamation.]

When the grave thunder of applause had died away, Lenin spoke again: "We propose to the Congress to ratify this declaration. . . . This proposal of peace will meet with resistance on the part of the imperialist governments—we don't fool ourselves on that score. But we hope that revolution will soon break out in all the belligerent countries; that is why we address ourselves especially to the workers of France, England and Germany. . . ."

"The revolution of November 6th and 7th," he ended, "has opened the era of the Social Revolution. . . . The labor movement, in the name of peace and Socialism, shall win, and fulfill its destiny. . . ."

There was something quiet and powerful in all this, which stirred the souls of men. It was understandable why people believed when Lenin spoke.

were numbered. In July 1917, Alexander Kerensky, a Socialist Revolutionary, had become prime minister in the Provisional Government. In September, when General Lavr Kornilov attempted to march on Petrograd and seize power, Kerensky released Bolsheviks from prison and turned to the Petrograd soviet for help. Although General Kornilov's forces never reached Petrograd, Kerensky's action had strengthened the hands of the Petrograd soviet and had shown Lenin how weak the Provisional Government really was.

By the end of October, the Bolsheviks had achieved a slight majority in the Petrograd and Moscow soviets. The number of party members had also grown from 50,000 to 240,000. Reports of unrest abroad had convinced Lenin that "we are on the threshold of a world proletarian revolution," and he tried to persuade his fellow Bolsheviks that the time was ripe for the overthrow of the Provisional Government. Although he faced formidable opposition within the Bolshevik ranks, he managed to gain support for his policy. He was especially fortunate to have the close cooperation of Leon Trotsky (1877–1940), a former Menshevik turned fervid revolutionary. Lenin and Trotsky organized a Military Revolutionary Committee within the Petrograd soviet to plot the overthrow of the government. On the night of November 6–7, Bolshevik forces seized the Winter Palace, seat of the Provisional Government. The Provisional Government collapsed quickly with little bloodshed.

This coup d'etat had been timed to coincide with a meeting in Petrograd of the all-Russian Congress of Soviets representing local soviets from all over the country. Lenin nominally turned over the sovereignty of the Provisional Government to this Congress of Soviets. Real power, however, passed to a Council of People's Commissars, headed by Lenin (see the box on p. 910). One immediate problem faced by the Bolsheviks was the Constituent Assembly, which had been initiated by the Provisional Government and was scheduled to meet in January 1918. Elections to the assembly by universal male suffrage had resulted in a defeat for the Bolsheviks, who had only 225 delegates compared to the 420 garnered by the Socialist Revolutionaries. But no matter. Lenin simply broke the Constituent Assembly by force. "To hand over power," he said, "to the Constituent Assembly would again be compromising with malignant bourgeoisie." The Bolsheviks did not want majority rule, but rather the rule of the proletariat, exercised for them, of course, by the Bolsheviks.

But the Bolsheviks (soon renamed the Communists) still had a long way to go. Lenin, ever the opportunist, realized the importance of winning mass support as quickly as possible by fulfilling Bolshevik promises. In his first law, Lenin declared the land nationalized and turned it over to local rural soviets. In effect, this action merely ratified the peasants' seizure of the land and assured the Bolsheviks of peasant support, especially against any attempt by the old landlords to restore their power. Lenin also met the demands of urban workers by turning over control of the factories to committees of workers. To Lenin, however, this was merely a temporary expedient.

Lenin had also promised peace and that, he realized, was not an easy task because of the humiliating losses of Russian territory that it would entail. There was no real choice, however. On March 3, 1918, the new Communist government signed the Treaty of Brest-Litovsk with Germany and gave up eastern Poland, Ukraine, Finland, and the Baltic provinces. To his critics, Lenin argued that it made no difference since the spread of socialist revolution throughout Europe would make the treaty largely irrelevant. In any case, he had promised peace to the Russian people, but real peace did not come for the country soon lapsed into civil war.

CIVIL WAR

There was great opposition to the new Bolshevik or Communist regime, not only from groups loyal to the tsar but also from bourgeois and aristocratic liberals and anti-Leninist socialists, including Mensheviks and Socialist Revolutionaries. In addition, thousands of Allied troops were eventually sent to different parts of Russia in the hope of bringing Russia back into the war.

Between 1918 and 1921, the Bolshevik (or Red) Army was forced to fight on many fronts. The first serious threat to the Bolsheviks came from Siberia where a White (anti-Bolshevik) force under Admiral

◆ **"Agit-Prop" in the Civil War.** During the civil war in Russia, the Communists made effective use of agitational propaganda, or "agit-prop." Vibrant posters with brief slogans were used to educate the masses in the ideas of the Communists. The "agit-prop" poster shown here used the Red Army star to remind the people that Russia had become an armed camp.

Alexander Kolchak pushed westward and advanced almost to the Volga River before being stopped. Attacks also came from the Ukrainians in the southeast and from the Baltic regions. In mid-1919, White forces under General Anton Denikin, probably the most effective of the White generals, swept through Ukraine and advanced almost to Moscow. At one point in late 1919, three separate White armies seemed to be closing in on the Bolsheviks, but were eventually pushed back. By 1920, the major White forces had been defeated, and Ukraine retaken. The next year, the Communist regime regained control over the independent nationalist governments in the Caucasus: Georgia, Russian Armenia, and Azerbaijan.

How had Lenin and the Bolsheviks triumphed over what seemed at one time to be overwhelming forces? For

one thing, the Red Army became a well-disciplined and formidable fighting force, largely due to the organizational genius of Leon Trotsky. As commissar of war, Trotsky reinstated the draft and even recruited and gave commands to former tsarist army officers. Trotsky insisted on rigid discipline; soldiers who deserted or refused to obey orders were summarily executed. The Red Army also had the advantage of interior lines of defense and was able to move its troops rapidly from one battlefront to the other.

The disunity of the anti-Communist forces seriously weakened the efforts of the Whites. Political differences created distrust among the Whites and prevented them from cooperating effectively with each other. Some Whites, such as Admiral Kolchak, insisted on restoring the tsarist regime, while others understood that only a

Map 26.4 The Russian Revolution and Civil War.

more liberal and democratic program had any chance of success. Since the White forces were forced to operate on the exterior fringes of the Russian Empire, it was difficult enough to achieve military cooperation. Political differences made it virtually impossible.

The Whites' inability to agree on a common goal contrasted sharply with the Communists' single-minded sense of purpose. Inspired by their vision of a new socialist order, the Communists had the advantage of possessing the determination that comes from revolutionary fervor and revolutionary convictions.

The Communists also succeeded in translating their revolutionary faith into practical instruments of power. A policy of "war communism," for example, was used to ensure regular supplies for the Red Army. "War communism" included the nationalization of banks and most industries, the forcible requisition of grain from peasants, and the centralization of state administration under Bolshevik control. Another Bolshevik instrument was "revolutionary terror." Although the old tsarist secret police had been abolished, a new Red secret police—known as the Cheka—replaced it. The Red Terror instituted by the Cheka aimed at nothing less than the destruction of all those who opposed the new regime. "Class enemies"—the bourgeoisie—were especially singled out, at least according to a Cheka officer: "The first questions you should put to the accused person are: To what class does he belong, what is his origin, what was his education, and what is his profession? These should determine the fate of the accused." In practice, however, the Cheka promulgated terror against all classes, including the proletariat, if they opposed the new regime. The Red Terror added an element of fear to the Bolshevik regime.

Finally, the intervention of foreign armies enabled the Communists to appeal to the powerful force of Russian patriotism. Although the Allied powers had initially intervened in Russia to encourage the Russians to remain in the war, the end of the war on November 11, 1918, had made that purpose inconsequential. Nevertheless, Allied troops remained, and more were even sent as Allied countries did not hide their anti-Bolshevik feelings. At one point, over 100,000 foreign troops, mostly Japanese, British, American, and French, were stationed on Russian soil. These forces rarely engaged in pitched battles, however, nor did they pursue a common strategy, although they did give material assistance to anti-Bolshevik forces. This intervention by the Allies enabled the Communist government to appeal to patriotic Russians to fight the attempts of foreigners to control their country. Allied interference was never substantial enough to make a military difference in the civil war, but it did serve indirectly to help the Bolshevik cause.

By 1921, the Communists had succeeded in retaining control of Russia. In the course of the civil war, the Bolshevik regime had also transformed Russia into a bureaucratically centralized state dominated by a single party. It was also a state that was largely hostile to the Allied powers that had sought to assist the Bolsheviks' enemies in the civil war. To most historians, the Russian Revolution is unthinkable without the total war of World War I, for only the collapse of Russia made it possible for a radical minority like the Bolsheviks to seize the reins of power. In turn, the Russian Revolution had an impact on the course of World War I.

The Last Year of the War

For Germany, the withdrawal of the Russians from the war in March 1918 offered renewed hope for a favorable end to the war. The victory over Russia persuaded Ludendorff and most German leaders to make one final military gamble—a grand offensive in the west to break the military stalemate. The German attack was launched in March and lasted into July. The German forces succeeded in advancing forty miles to the Marne River, within thirty-five miles of Paris. But an Allied counterattack, led by the French General Ferdinand Foch and supported by the arrival of 140,000 fresh American troops, defeated the Germans at the Second Battle of the Marne on July 18. Ludendorff's gamble had failed. Having used up his reserves, Ludendorff knew that defeat was now inevitable. With the arrival of two million more American troops on the Continent, Allied forces began making a steady advance toward Germany.

On September 29, 1918, General Ludendorff informed German leaders that the war was lost. Unwilling to place the burden of defeat on the army, Ludendorff demanded that the government sue for peace at once. When German officials discovered that the Allies were unwilling to make peace with the autocratic imperial government, they instituted reforms to create a liberal government. But these constitutional reforms came too late for the exhausted and angry German people. On November 3, naval units in Kiel mutinied, and within days councils of workers and soldiers, German versions of the Russian soviets, were forming throughout northern Germany and taking over the supervision of civilian and military administrations. William II capitulated to

1914

Battle of Tannenberg	August 26–30
First Battle of the Marne	September 6–10
Battle of Masurian Lakes	September 15
Russia, Great Britain, and France declare war on Ottoman Empire	November

1915

Battle of Gallipoli begins	April 25
Italy declares war on Austria-Hungary	May 23
Entry of Bulgaria into the war	September

1916

Battle of Verdun	February 21– December 18
Battle of Jutland	May 31
The Somme offensive	July 1– November 19

1917

Germany returns to unrestricted submarine warfare	January
United States enters the war	April 6
The Champagne offensive	April 16–29

1918

Last German offensive	March 21– July 18
Second Battle of the Marne	July 18
Allied counteroffensive	July 18– November 10
Armistice between Allies and Germany	November 11

1919

Paris Peace Conference begins	January 18
Peace of Versailles	June 28

public pressure and left the country on November 9, while the Socialists under Friedrich Ebert announced the establishment of a republic. Two days later, on November 11, 1918, an armistice agreed to by the new German government went into effect. The war was over, but the revolutionary forces set in motion by the war were not yet exhausted.

Revolutionary Upheavals in Germany and Austria-Hungary

Like Russia, Germany and Austria-Hungary experienced political revolution as a result of military defeat. In November 1918, when Germany began to disintegrate in a convulsion of mutinies and mass demonstrations (known as the November Revolution), only the Social Democrats were numerous and well organized enough to pick up the pieces. But the German socialists had divided into two groups during the war. A majority of the Social Democrats still favored parliamentary democracy as a gradual approach to social democracy and the elimination of the capitalist system. A minority of German socialists, however, disgusted with the Social Democrats' support of the war, had formed an Independent Social Democratic Party in 1916. In 1918, the more radical members of the Independent Socialists favored an immediate social revolution carried out by the councils of soldiers, sailors, and workers. Led by Karl Liebknecht and Rosa Luxemburg, these radical, left-wing socialists formed the German Communist Party in December 1918. In effect, two parallel governments were established in Germany: the parliamentary republic proclaimed by the majority Social Democrats and the revolutionary socialist republic declared by the radicals.

Unlike Russia's Bolsheviks, Germany's radicals failed to achieve control of the government. By ending the war on November 11, the moderate socialists had removed a major source of dissatisfaction. When the radical socialists (now known as Communists) attempted to seize power in Berlin in January 1919, Friedrich Ebert and the moderate socialists called on the regular army and groups of antirevolutionary volunteers known as Free Corps to crush the rebels. The victorious forces brutally murdered Liebknecht and Luxemburg. A similar attempt at Communist revolution in the city of Munich in southern Germany was also crushed by the Free Corps and the regular army. The German republic had been saved, but only because the moderate socialists had relied on the traditional army—in effect, the same conservatives who had dominated the old imperial regime. Moreover, this "second revolution" of January 1919, bloodily crushed by the republican government, created a deep fear of communism among the German middle classes. All too soon, this fear would be cleverly manipulated by a politician named Adolf Hitler.

Austria-Hungary, too, experienced disintegration and revolution. In 1914, when it attacked Serbia, the imperial regime had tried to crush the nationalistic forces that it believed were destroying the empire. By 1918, those same nationalistic forces had brought the complete breakup of the Austro-Hungarian Empire. As war weariness took hold of the empire, ethnic minorities increasingly sought to achieve national independence. This desire was further encouraged by Allied war aims that included calls for the independence of the subject peoples. By the time the war ended, the Austro-Hungarian Empire had been replaced by the independent republics of Austria, Hungary, and Czechoslovakia and the large South Slav monarchical state called Yugoslavia. Other regions clamored to join Italy, Romania, and a reconstituted Poland. Rivalries among the nations that succeeded Austria-Hungary would weaken eastern Europe for the next eighty years. Ethnic pride and national statehood proved far more important to these states than class differences. Only in Hungary was there an attempt at social revolution when Béla Kun established a communist state. It was crushed after a brief five-month existence.

The Peace Settlement

In January 1919, the delegations of twenty-seven victorious Allied nations gathered in Paris to conclude a final settlement of the Great War. Some delegates believed that this conference would avoid the mistakes made at Vienna in 1815 (see Chapter 22) when aristocrats rearranged the map of Europe to meet the selfish desires of the great powers. Harold Nicolson, one of the British delegates, expressed what he believed this conference would achieve instead: "We were journeying to Paris not merely to liquidate the war, but to found a New Order in Europe. We were preparing not Peace only, but Eternal Peace. There was about us the halo of some divine mission. . . . For we were bent on doing great, permanent and noble things."[10]

National expectations, however, made Nicolson's quest for "eternal peace" a difficult one. Over the years, the reasons for fighting World War I had been transformed from selfish national interests to idealistic principles. At the end of 1917, after they had taken over the Russian government, Lenin and the Bolsheviks had publicly revealed the contents of secret wartime treaties found in the archives of the Russian foreign ministry. The documents made it clear that European nations had gone to war primarily to achieve territorial gains. But the American president Woodrow Wilson attempted at the beginning of 1918 to shift the discussion of war aims to a higher ground. Wilson outlined "Fourteen Points" to the American Congress that he believed justified the

enormous military struggle then being waged. Later, Wilson spelled out additional steps for a truly just and lasting peace. Wilson's proposals included "open covenants of peace, openly arrived at" instead of secret diplomacy; the reduction of national armaments to a "point consistent with domestic safety"; and the self-determination of people so that "all well-defined national aspirations shall be accorded the utmost satisfaction." Wilson characterized World War I as a people's war waged against "absolutism and militarism," two scourges of liberty that could only be eliminated by creating democratic governments and a "general association of nations" that would guarantee the "political independence and territorial integrity to great and small states alike" (see the box on p. 916). As the spokesman for a new world order based on democracy and international cooperation, Wilson was enthusiastically cheered by many Europeans when he arrived in Europe for the peace conference.

Wilson soon found, however, that other states at the Paris Peace Conference were guided by considerably more pragmatic motives. The secret treaties and agreements, for example, that had been made before the war could not be totally ignored, even if they did conflict with the principle of self-determination enunciated by Wilson.

National interests also complicated the deliberations of the Paris Peace Conference. David Lloyd George,

♦ **The Big Four at Paris.** Shown here are the Big Four at the Paris Peace Conference: Lloyd George of Britain, Orlando of Italy, Clemenceau of France, and Wilson of the United States. Although Italy was considered one of the Big Four powers, Britain, France, and the United States (the Big Three) made the major decisions at the peace conference.

Two Voices of Peacemaking: Woodrow Wilson and Georges Clemenceau

When the Allied powers met at Paris in January 1919, it soon became apparent that the victors had different opinions on the kind of peace they expected. The first excerpt is from a speech of Woodrow Wilson in which the American president presented his idealistic goals for a peace based on justice and reconciliation. The French wanted revenge and security. In the second selection, from Georges Clemenceau's Grandeur and Misery of Victory, *the French premier revealed his fundamental dislike and distrust of Germany.*

Woodrow Wilson, May 26, 1917

We are fighting for the liberty, the self-government, and the undictated development of all peoples, and every feature of the settlement that concludes this war must be conceived and executed for that purpose. Wrongs must first be righted and then adequate safeguards must be created to prevent their being committed again. . . .

No people must be forced under sovereignty under which it does not wish to live. No territory must change hands except for the purpose of securing those who inhabit it a fair chance of life and liberty. No indemnities must be insisted on except those that constitute payment for manifest wrongs done. No readjustments of power must be made except such as will tend to secure the future peace of the world and the future welfare and happiness of its peoples.

And then the free peoples of the world must draw together in some common covenant, some genuine and practical cooperation that will in effect combine their force to secure peace and justice in the dealings of nations with one another.

Georges Clemenceau, *Grandeur and Misery of Victory*

War and peace, with their strong contrasts, alternate against a common background. For the catastrophe of 1914 the Germans are responsible. Only a professional liar would deny this. . . .

I have sometimes penetrated into the sacred cave of the Germanic cult, which is, as every one knows, the *Bierhaus* [beer hall]. A great aisle of massive humanity where there accumulate, amid the fumes of tobacco and beer, the popular rumblings of a nationalism upheld by the sonorous brasses blaring to the heavens the supreme voice of Germany, *Deutschland über alles! Germany above everything!* Men, women, and children, all petrified in reverence before the divine stoneware pot, brows furrowed with irrepressible power, eyes lost in a dream of infinity, mouths twisted by the intensity of will-power, drink in long draughts the celestial hope of vague expectations. These only remain to be realized presently when the chief marked out by Destiny shall have given the word. There you have the ultimate framework of an old but childish race.

prime minister of Great Britain, had won a decisive electoral victory in December of 1918 on a platform of making the Germans pay for this dreadful war. Public opinion had been inflamed during the war by a government propaganda campaign that portrayed the Germans as beasts. With the war over, the influence of that propaganda continued to be felt as many British believed that only a total victory over Germany could ever compensate for the terrible losses of the war.

France's approach to peace was primarily determined by considerations of national security. Georges Clemenceau, the feisty premier of France who had led his country to victory, believed the French people had borne the brunt of German aggression. They deserved revenge and security against future German aggression (see the box above). The French knew that Germany's larger population (60 million to 40 million) posed a long-term threat to France. Clemenceau wanted a demilitarized Germany, vast German reparations to pay for the costs of the war, and a separate Rhineland as a buffer state between France and Germany, demands that Wilson viewed as vindictive and contrary to the principle of national self-determination.

Yet another consideration affected the negotiations at Paris, namely, the fear that Bolshevik revolution would spread from Russia to other European countries. This concern led the Allies to enlarge and strengthen such eastern European states as Poland, Czechoslovakia, and Romania at the expense of both Germany and Bolshevik Russia.

Although twenty-seven nations were represented at the Paris Peace Conference, the most important decisions were made by Woodrow Wilson, Georges Clemenceau, and David Lloyd George. Italy was considered one of the so-called Big Four powers, but played a much less important role than the other three countries. Germany, of course, was not invited to attend and Russia could not because of its civil war.

In view of the many conflicting demands at Versailles, it was inevitable that the Big Three would quarrel. Wilson was determined to create a League of Nations to prevent future wars. Clemenceau and Lloyd George were equally determined to punish Germany. In the end, only compromise made it possible to achieve a peace settlement. Wilson's wish that the creation of an international peacekeeping organization be the first order of business was granted, and already on January 25, 1919, the conference adopted the principle of a League of Nations. The details of its structure were left for later sessions, and Wilson willingly agreed to make compromises on territorial arrangements to guarantee the establishment of the league, believing that a functioning league could later rectify bad arrangements. Clemenceau also compromised to obtain some guarantees for French security. He renounced France's desire for a separate Rhineland and instead accepted a defensive alliance with Great Britain and the United States. Both states pledged to help France if it were attacked by Germany.

The final peace settlement of Paris consisted of five separate treaties with the defeated nations—Germany, Austria, Hungary, Bulgaria, and the Ottoman Empire. The Treaty of Versailles with Germany, signed on June 28, 1919, was by far the most important. The Germans considered it a harsh peace, conveniently overlooking that the Treaty of Brest-Litovsk, which they had imposed on Bolshevik Russia, was even more severe. The Germans were particularly unhappy with Article 231, the so-called War Guilt Clause, which declared Germany (and Austria) responsible for starting the war and ordered Germany to pay reparations for all the damage to which the Allied governments and their people were subjected as a result of the war "imposed upon them by the aggression of Germany and her allies." Reparations were a logical consequence of the wartime promises that Allied leaders had made to their people that the Germans would pay for the war effort. The treaty did not establish the amount to be paid, but left that to be determined later by a reparations commission (see Chapter 27).

The military and territorial provisions of the treaty also rankled the Germans, although they were by no means as harsh as the Germans claimed. Germany had to reduce its army to 100,000 men, cut back its navy,

and eliminate its air force. German territorial losses included the cession of Alsace and Lorraine to France and sections of Prussia to the new Polish state. German land west and as far as thirty miles east of the Rhine was established as a demilitarized zone and stripped of all armaments or fortifications to serve as a barrier to any future German military moves westward against France. Outraged by the "dictated peace," the new German government vowed to resist rather than accept the treaty, but it had no real alternative. Rejection meant a renewal of the war, and as the army pointed out, that was no longer possible.

The separate peace treaties made with the other Central Powers (Austria, Hungary, Bulgaria, and the Ottoman Empire) extensively redrew the map of eastern Europe. Many of these changes merely ratified what the war had already accomplished. The empires that had controlled eastern Europe for centuries had been destroyed or weakened, and a number of new states appeared on the map of Europe.

Both the German and Russian Empires lost considerable territory in eastern Europe while the Austro-Hungarian Empire disappeared altogether. New nation-states emerged from the lands of these three empires: Finland, Latvia, Estonia, Lithuania, Poland, Czechoslovakia, Austria, and Hungary. Territorial rearrangements were also made in the Balkans. Romania acquired additional lands from Russia, Hungary, and Bulgaria. Serbia formed the nucleus of a new South Slav state, called Yugoslavia, which combined Serbs, Croats, and Slovenes. Although the Paris Peace Conference was supposedly guided by the principle of self-determination, the mixtures of peoples in eastern Europe made it impossible to draw boundaries along neat ethnic lines. Compromises had to be made, sometimes to satisfy the national interest of the victors. France, for example, had lost Russia as its major ally on Germany's eastern border and wanted to strengthen and expand Poland, Czechoslovakia, Yugoslavia, and Romania as much as possible so that those states could serve as barriers against Germany and Communist Russia. As a result of compromises, virtually every eastern Europe state was left with a minorities problem that could lead to future conflicts. Germans in Poland, Hungarians, Poles, and Germans in Czechoslovakia, and the combination of Serbs, Croats, Slovenes, Macedonians, and Albanians in Yugoslavia all became sources of later conflict. Moreover, the new map of eastern Europe was based upon the temporary collapse of power in both Germany and Russia. Since neither country accepted the new eastern frontiers, it seemed only a matter of time before a resurgent Germany or Russia would make changes.

Yet another centuries-old empire—the Ottoman Empire—was dismembered by the peace settlement after the war. To gain Arab support against the Ottomans during the war, the Allies had promised to recognize the independence of Arab states in the Middle Eastern lands of the Ottoman Empire. But the imperialist habits of Europeans died hard. After the war, France took control of Lebanon and Syria while Britain received Iraq and Palestine. Officially, both acquisitions were called mandates. Since Woodrow Wilson had opposed the outright annexation of colonial territories by the Allies, the peace settlement had created a system of mandates whereby a nation officially administered a territory on behalf of the League of Nations. The system of mandates

Map 26.5 Europe in 1919.

could not hide the fact that the principle of national self-determination at the Paris Peace Conference was largely for Europeans.

The peace settlement negotiated at Paris soon came under attack, not only by the defeated Central Powers, but by others who felt that the peacemakers had been shortsighted. The famous British economist John Maynard Keynes, for example, condemned the preoccupation with frontiers at the expense of economic issues that left Europe "inefficient, unemployed, disorganized." Other people, however, thought the peace settlement was the best that could be achieved under the circumstances. Self-determination, they believed, had served reasonably well as a central organizing principle while the establishment of the League of Nations gave some hope that future conflicts could be resolved peacefully. And yet, within twenty years after the signing of the peace treaties, Europe was again engaged in deadly conflict. As some historians have suggested, perhaps lack of enforcement rather than the structure of the peace may have caused the failure of the peace of 1919.

Successful enforcement of the peace necessitated the active involvement of its principal architects, especially in assisting the new German state to develop a peaceful and democratic republic. The failure of the American Senate to ratify the Treaty of Versailles, however, meant that the United States never joined the League of Nations. In addition, the American Senate also rejected Wilson's defensive alliance with Great Britain and France. Already by the end of 1919, the United States was pursuing policies intended to limit its direct involvement in future European wars.

This retreat had dire consequences. American withdrawal from the defensive alliance with Britain and France led Britain to withdraw as well. By removing itself from European affairs, the United States forced France to stand alone facing its old enemy, leading the embittered nation to take strong actions against Germany that only intensified German resentment. By the end of 1919, it appeared that the peace of 1919 was already beginning to unravel.

Conclusion

World War I shattered the liberal and rational assumptions of late nineteenth- and early twentieth-century European society. The incredible destruction and the death of almost 10 million people undermined the whole idea of progress. New propaganda techniques had manipulated entire populations into sustaining their involvement in a meaningless slaughter.

World War I was a total war and involved a mobilization of resources and populations and increased government centralization of power over the lives of its citizens. Civil liberties, such as freedom of the press, speech, assembly, and movement, were circumscribed in the name of national security. Governments' need to plan the production and distribution of goods and to ration consumer goods restricted economic freedom. Although the late nineteenth and early twentieth centuries had witnessed the extension of government authority into such areas as mass education, social welfare legislation, and mass conscription, World War I made the practice of strong central authority a way of life.

Finally, World War I ended the age of European hegemony over world affairs. In 1917, the Russian Revolution laid the foundation for the creation of a new Soviet power, and the United States entered the war. The termination of the European age was not evident to all, however, for it was clouded by two developments— American isolationism and the withdrawal of the Soviets from world affairs while they nurtured the growth of their own socialist system. Although these developments were only temporary, they created a political vacuum in Europe that all too soon was filled by the revival of German power.

NOTES

1. Arnold Toynbee, *Surviving the Future* (New York, 1971), pp. 106–7.
2. Quoted in Joachim Remak, "1914—The Third Balkan War: Origins Reconsidered," *Journal of Modern History* 43 (1971): 364–65.
3. Quoted in Robert G. L. Waite, *Vanguard of Nazism* (New York, 1969), p. 22.
4. Quoted in J. M. Winter, *The Experience of World War I* (New York, 1989), p. 142.
5. Quoted in ibid., p. 137.

6. Quoted in Gail Braybon, *Women Workers in the First World War: The British Experience* (London, 1981), p. 79.
7. Quoted in Catherine W. Reilly, ed., *Scars upon My Heart: Women's Poetry and Verse of the First World War* (London, 1981), p. 90.
8. Quoted in Robert Paxton, *Europe in the Twentieth Century*, 2d ed. (New York, 1985), p. 110.

9. Quoted in William M. Mandel, *Soviet Women* (Garden City, N.Y., 1975), p. 43.
10. Harold Nicolson, *Peacemaking, 1919* (Boston and New York, 1933), pp. 31–32.

SUGGESTIONS FOR FURTHER READING

The historical literature on the causes of World War I is enormous. A good starting point is the work by J. Joll, *The Origins of the First World War* (London, 1984). Also useful is J. Remak, *The Origins of World War I, 1871–1914* (New York, 1967). The belief that Germany was primarily responsible for the war was argued vigorously by the German scholar F. Fischer, *Germany's Aims in the First World War* (New York, 1967); *World Power or Decline: The Controversy over Germany's Aims in World War I* (New York, 1974); and *War of Illusions: German Policies from 1911 to 1914* (New York, 1975). The role of each great power has been reassessed in a series of books on the causes of World War I. They include V. R. Berghahn, *Germany and the Approach of War in 1914* (London, 1973); Z. S. Steiner, *Britain and the Origins of the First World War* (New York, 1977); R. Bosworth, *Italy and the Approach of the First World War* (New York, 1983); J. F. Keiger, *France and the Origins of the First World War* (New York, 1984); and D. C. B. Lieven, *Russia and the Origins of the First World War* (New York, 1984). The domestic origins of the war are probed in A. Mayer, *The Persistence of the Old Regime* (New York, 1981).

There are two good recent accounts of World War I in M. Gilbert, *The First World War* (New York, 1994); and the lavishly illustrated book by J. M. Winter, *The Experience of World War I* (New York, 1989). For an account of the military operations of the war, see the classic work by B. H. Liddell Hart, *History of the First World War* (Boston, 1970). The nature of trench warfare is examined in T. Ashworth, *Trench Warfare, 1914–1918: The Live and Let-Live System* (London, 1980). The use of poison gas is examined in L. F. Haber, *The Poisonous Cloud: Chemical Warfare in the First World War* (Oxford, 1985). On the morale of soldiers in World War I, see J. Keegan, *The Face of Battle* (London, 1975). The war at sea is examined in R. Hough, *The Great War at Sea, 1914–18* (Oxford, 1983). In *The Great War and Modern Memory* (London, 1975), Paul Fussell attempted to show how British writers described their war experiences. Although scholars do not always agree with her conclusions, B. Tuchman's *The Guns of August* (New York, 1962) is a magnificently written account of the opening days of the war. For an interesting perspective on World War I and the beginnings of the modern world, see M. Eksteins, *Rites of Spring, The Great War and the Birth of the Modern Age* (Boston, 1989).

On the role of women in World War I, see G. Braybon, *Women Workers in the First World War: The British Experience* (London, 1981); and J. M. Winter and R. M. Wall, eds., *The Upheaval of War: Family, Work and Welfare in Europe, 1914–1918* (Cambridge, 1988). For a general survey of women in twentieth-century Europe, see B. Anderson and J. P. Zinsser, *A History of Their Own*, vol. 2 (New York, 1988).

A good introduction to the Russian Revolution can be found in S. Fitzpatrick, *The Russian Revolution, 1917–1932* (New York, 1982); and R. V. Daniels, *Red October* (New York, 1967). On Lenin, see R. W. Clark, *Lenin* (New York, 1988); and the valuable work by A. B. Ulam, *The Bolsheviks* (New York, 1965). The role of workers in the events of the Russian Revolution is examined in D. Koenker, *Moscow Workers and the 1917 Revolution* (Princeton, N.J., 1981). There is now a comprehensive study of the Russian civil war in W. B. Lincoln, *Red Victory: A History of the Russian Civil War* (New York, 1989). On the revolutions in Germany and Austria-Hungary, see F. L. Carsten, *Revolution in Central Europe* (Berkeley, 1972); and A. J. Ryder, *The German Revolution of 1918* (Cambridge, 1967).

The role of war aims in shaping the peace settlement is examined in V. H. Rothwell, *British War Aims and*

Peace Diplomacy, 1914–1918 (Oxford, 1971); and D. R. Stevenson, *French War Aims against Germany, 1914–1919* (New York, 1982).

World War I and the Russian Revolution are also well covered in two good general surveys of European history in the twentieth century, R. Paxton, *Europe in the Twentieth Century*, 2d ed. (New York, 1985); and A. Rudhart, *Twentieth Century Europe* (Englewood Cliffs, N.J., 1986).

The Futile Search for a New Stability: Europe between the Wars, 1919–1939

Only twenty years after the Treaty of Versailles, Europeans were again at war. And yet in the 1920s, many people assumed that Europe and the world were about to enter a new era of international peace, economic growth, and political democracy. In all of these areas, the optimistic hopes of the 1920s failed to be realized. After 1919, most people wanted peace but were unsure how to maintain it. The League of Nations, conceived as a new instrument to provide for collective security, failed to work well. New treaties that renounced the use of war looked good on paper but had no means of enforcement. Then, too, virtually everyone favored disarmament, but few could agree on how to achieve it.

At home, Europe was faced with severe economic problems after World War I. The European economy did not begin to recover from the war until 1922, and even then it was beset by financial problems left over from the war and, most devastating of all, the Great Depression that began at the end of 1929. The Great Depression brought untold misery to millions of people. Begging for food on the streets became widespread, especially when soup kitchens were unable to keep up with the demand. Larger and larger numbers of people were homeless and moved from place to place looking for work and shelter. In the United States, the homeless set up shantytowns they named "Hoovervilles" after the American president, Herbert Hoover. In their misery, some people saw but one solution; as one unemployed person expressed it: "Today, when I am experiencing this for the first time, I think that I should prefer to do away with myself, to take gas, to jump into the river, or leap from some high place. . . . would I really come to such a decision? I do not know. Animals die, plants wither, but men always go on living." Social unrest spread rapidly, and some unemployed staged hunger marches to get attention. In democratic countries, more and more people began to listen to and vote for radical voices calling for extreme measures.

Mussolini and Fascists come to power in Italy   Stalin gains control of Russia

Hitler and Nazis come to power in Germany   Popular Front in France

Locarno Pact   Spanish Civil War

Beginning of the Great Depression   Kristallnacht

Mass production of radios begins   Heisenberg's "uncertainty principle"

Hannah Höch, *Cut with the Kitchen Knife*   Dali, *The Persistence of Memory*

According to Woodrow Wilson, World War I had been fought to make the world safe for democracy, and for a while after 1919, political democracy seemed well established. But the hopes for democracy, too, soon faded as authoritarian regimes spread into Italy and Germany and across eastern Europe.

An Uncertain Peace: The Search for Security

The peace settlement at the end of World War I had tried to fulfill the nineteenth-century dream of nationalism by redrawing boundaries and creating new states. From its inception, however, this peace settlement had left nations unhappy. Conflicts over disputed border regions between Germany and Poland, Poland and Lithuania, Poland and Czechoslovakia, Austria and Hungary, and Italy and Yugoslavia poisoned mutual relations in eastern Europe for years. Many Germans viewed the Peace of Versailles as a dictated peace and vowed to seek its revision.

The American president Woodrow Wilson had recognized that the peace treaties contained unwise provisions that could serve as new causes for conflicts and had placed many of his hopes for the future in the League of Nations. The league, however, was not particularly effective in maintaining the peace. The failure of the United States to join the league and the subsequent American determination to be less involved in European affairs undermined the effectiveness of the league

from its beginning. Moreover, the league could only use economic sanctions to halt aggression. The French attempt to strengthen the league's effectiveness as an instrument of collective security by creating some kind of international army was rejected by nations that feared giving up any of their sovereignty to a larger international body.

The weakness of the League of Nations and the failure of both the United States and Great Britain to honor their promises to form defensive military alliances with France left France embittered and alone. Before World War I, France's alliance with Russia had served to threaten Germany with the possibility of a two-front war. But Communist Russia was now a hostile power. To compensate, France built a network of alliances in eastern Europe with Poland and the members of the so-called Little Entente (Czechoslovakia, Romania, Yugoslavia). Although these alliances looked good on paper as a way to contain Germany and maintain the new status quo, they overlooked the fundamental military weaknesses of those nations. Poland and the Little Entente states were no real substitutes for Russia.

The French Policy of Coercion, 1919–1924

France's search for security between 1919 and 1924 was founded primarily upon a strict enforcement of the Treaty of Versailles. This tough policy toward Germany began with the issue of reparations, or the payments that the Germans were supposed to make to compensate for the "damage done to the civilian population of the Allied and Associated Powers and to their property," as

♦ **The Effects of Inflation.** Germany experienced a number of serious economic problems after World War I. The inflationary pressures that had begun in Germany at the end of the war intensified during the French occupation of the Ruhr. By the early 1920s, the value of the German mark had fallen precipitously. This photograph shows a German housewife using the worthless currency to light a fire in her cooking stove.

the treaty asserted. In April 1921, the Allied Reparations Commission settled on a sum of 132 billion marks ($33 billion) for German reparations, payable in annual installments of 2.5 billion (gold) marks. Allied threats to occupy the Ruhr valley, Germany's chief industrial and mining center, led the new German republic to accept the reparations settlement and make its first payment in 1921. By the following year, however, faced with rising inflation, domestic turmoil, and lack of revenues due to low tax rates, the German government announced that it was unable to pay more. Outraged by what they considered to be Germany's violation of one aspect of the peace settlement, the French government sent troops to occupy the Ruhr valley. Since the Ger-

mans would not pay reparations, the French would collect reparations in kind by operating and using the Ruhr mines and factories.

Both Germany and France suffered from the French occupation of the Ruhr. The German government adopted a policy of passive resistance that was largely financed by printing more paper money, but this only intensified the inflationary pressures that had already appeared in Germany by the end of the war. The German mark soon became worthless. In 1914, 4.2 marks equaled one dollar; by November 1, 1923, the ratio had reached 130 billion to one; by the end of November, it had increased to an incredible 4.2 trillion. Economic disaster fueled political upheavals as Communists staged uprisings in October 1923, and Adolf Hitler's band of Nazis attempted to seize power in Munich in November (see Hitler and Nazi Germany later in this chapter). But the French were hardly victorious. The cost of the French occupation was not offset by the gains. Meanwhile, pressure from the United States and Great Britain against the French policy forced the French to agree to a new conference of experts to reassess the reparations problem. By the time the conference did its work in 1924, both France and Germany were opting to pursue a more conciliatory approach toward each other.

The Hopeful Years, 1924–1929

The formation of liberal-socialist governments in both Great Britain and France opened the door to conciliatory approaches to Germany and the reparations problem. At the same time, a new German government led by Gustav Stresemann (1878–1929) ended the policy of passive resistance and committed Germany to carry out most of the provisions of the Treaty of Versailles while seeking a new settlement of the reparations question.

In August 1924, an international commission produced a new plan for reparations. Named the Dawes Plan after the American banker who chaired the commission, it reduced reparations and stabilized Germany's payments on the basis of its ability to pay. The Dawes Plan also granted an initial $200 million loan for German recovery, which opened the door to heavy American investments in Europe that helped create a new era of European prosperity between 1924 and 1929.

A new era of European diplomacy accompanied the new economic stability. A spirit of international cooperation was fostered by the foreign ministers of Germany and France, Gustav Stresemann and Aristide Briand (1862–1932), who concluded the Treaty of Locarno in

1925. This guaranteed Germany's new western borders with France and Belgium. Although Germany's new eastern borders with Poland were conspicuously absent from the agreement, a clear indication that Germany did not accept those borders as permanent, the Locarno pact was viewed by many as the beginning of a new era of European peace. On the day after the pact was concluded, the headlines in the *New York Times* ran "France and Germany Ban War Forever," while the London *Times* declared, "Peace at Last."[1]

Germany's entry into the League of Nations in March 1926 soon reinforced the new spirit of conciliation engendered at Locarno. Two years later, similar optimistic attitudes prevailed in the Kellogg-Briand pact, drafted by the American secretary of state Frank B. Kellogg and the French foreign minister Aristide Briand. Sixty-three nations signed eventually agreed to the pact, in which they pledged "to renounce war as an instrument of national policy." Nothing was said, however, about what would be done if anyone violated the treaty.

The spirit of Locarno was based on little real substance. Germany lacked the military power to alter its western borders even if it wanted to. Pious promises to renounce war without mechanisms to enforce them were virtually worthless. And the issue of disarmament soon proved that even the spirit of Locarno could not induce nations to cut back on their weapons. The League of Nations Covenant had suggested the "reduction of national armaments to the lowest point consistent with national safety." Germany, of course, had been disarmed with the expectation that other states would do likewise. Numerous disarmament conferences, however, failed to achieve anything substantial as states proved unwilling to trust their security to anyone but their own military forces. When a World Disarmament Conference finally met in Geneva in 1932, the issue was already dead.

One other hopeful sign in the years between 1924 and 1929 was the new coexistence of the West with Soviet Russia. By the beginning of 1924, Soviet hopes for communist revolutions in Western states had largely dissipated. In turn, these states had realized by then that the Bolshevik regime could not be ousted. By 1924, Germany, Britain, France, and Italy, as well as several smaller European countries, had established full diplomatic relations with Soviet Russia. Nevertheless, Western powers remained highly suspicious of Soviet intentions, especially when the Soviet Union continued to support the propaganda activities of the Comintern, or Communist International, a worldwide organization of pro-Soviet Marxist parties originally formed in 1919 by Lenin to foster world revolution.

The Great Depression

After World War I, most European states hoped to return to the liberal ideal of a market economy based on private enterprise and largely free of state intervention. But the war had vastly strengthened business cartels and labor unions, making some government regulation of these powerful organizations appear necessary. At the same time, reparations and war debts had severely damaged the postwar international economy, making the prosperity that did occur between 1924 and 1929 at best a fragile one and the dream of returning to the liberal ideal of a self-regulating market economy merely an illusion. What destroyed the dream altogether was the Great Depression.

Two factors played a major role in the coming of the Great Depression: a downturn in domestic economies and an international financial crisis created by the collapse of the American stock market in 1929. Already in the mid-1920s, prices for agricultural goods were beginning to decline rapidly due to overproduction of basic commodities, such as wheat. In 1925, states in central and eastern Europe began to impose tariffs to close their markets to other countries' goods. An increase in the use of oil and hydroelectricity led to a slump in the coal industry even before 1929.

In addition to these domestic economic troubles, much of the European prosperity between 1924 and 1929 had been built upon American bank loans to Germany. Twenty-three billion marks had been invested in German municipal bonds and German industries since 1924. Already in 1928 and 1929, American investors had begun to pull money out of Germany in order to invest in the booming New York stock market. The crash of the American stock market in October 1929 led panicky American investors to withdraw even more of their funds from Germany and other European markets. The withdrawal of funds seriously weakened the banks of Germany and other central European states. The Credit-Anstalt, Vienna's most prestigious bank, collapsed on May 31, 1931. By that time, trade was slowing down, industrialists were cutting back production, and unemployment was increasing as the ripple effects of international bank failures had a devastating impact on domestic economies.

Economic depression was by no means a new phenomenon in European history. But the depth of the economic downturn after 1929 fully justifies the label Great Depression. During 1932, the worst year of the depression, one British worker in four was unemployed, while 6 million or 40 percent of the German labor force were out of work. Between 1929 and 1932, industrial production plummeted almost 50 percent in the United States and over 40 percent in Germany. The unemployed and homeless filled the streets of the cities throughout the advanced industrial countries (see the box on p. 927).

Governments seemed powerless to deal with the crisis. The classical liberal remedy for depression, a deflationary policy of balanced budgets, which involved cutting costs by lowering wages and raising tariffs to exclude other countries' goods from home markets, only served to worsen the economic crisis and create even greater mass discontent. This, in turn, led to serious political repercussions. Increased government activity in the economy was one reaction, even in countries like the United States that had a strong laissez-faire tradition. Another effect was a renewed interest in Marxist doctrines since Marx had predicted that capitalism would destroy itself through overproduction. Communism took on new popularity, especially with workers and intellectuals. Finally, the Great Depression increased the attractiveness of simplistic dictatorial solutions, especially from a new movement known as fascism. Everywhere in Europe, democracy seemed on the defensive in the 1930s. We can best understand the full impact of the depression on Europe by examining the domestic scene in the Western states between the two world wars.

The Democratic States

According to Woodrow Wilson, World War I had been fought to make the world safe for democracy. In 1919, there seemed to be some justification for his claim. Four major European states and a host of minor ones had functioning political democracies. In a number of states, universal male suffrage had even been replaced by universal suffrage as male politicians rewarded women for their contributions to World War I by granting them the right to vote (except in Italy, France, and Spain where women had to wait until the end of World War II). In the 1920s, Europe seemed to be returning to the political trends of the prewar era—the broadening of parliamentary regimes and the fostering of individual liberties. But it was not an easy process; four years of total war and four years of postwar turmoil made the "return to normalcy" a difficult and troublesome affair.

Great Britain

After World War I, Great Britain went through a period of painful readjustment and serious economic difficulties. During the war, Britain had lost many of its markets for industrial products, especially to the United States and Japan. The postwar decline of such staple industries as coal, steel, and textiles led to a rise in unemployment, which reached the 2 million mark in 1921. The Liberal

◆ **The Great Depression: Bread Lines in Paris.** The Great Depression devastated the European economy and had serious political repercussions. Because of its more balanced economy, France did not feel the effects of the depression as quickly as other European countries. By 1931, however, even France was experiencing lines of unemployed people at free-food centers.

The Great Depression: Unemployed and Homeless in Germany

In 1932, Germany had six million unemployed workers, many of them wandering aimlessly through the country, begging for food and seeking shelter in city lodging houses for the homeless. The Great Depression was an important factor in the rise to power of Adolf Hitler and the Nazis. This selection presents a description of unemployed homeless in 1932.

Heinrich Hauser, "With Germany's Unemployed"

An almost unbroken chain of homeless men extends the whole length of the great Hamburg-Berlin highway. ... All the highways in Germany over which I have traveled this year presented the same aspect. ...

Most of the hikers paid no attention to me. They walked separately or in small groups, with their eyes on the ground. And they had the queer, stumbling gait of barefooted people, for their shoes were slung over their shoulders. Some of them were guild members,—carpenters ... milkmen ... and bricklayers ... but they were in a minority. Far more numerous were those whom one could assign to no special profession or craft—unskilled young people, for the most part, who had been unable to find a place for themselves in any city or town in Germany, and who had never had a job and never expected to have one. There was something else that had never been seen before—whole families that had piled all their goods into baby carriages and wheelbarrows that they were pushing along as they plodded forward in dumb despair. It was a whole nation on the march.

I saw them—and this was the strongest impression that the year 1932 left with me—I saw them, gathered into groups of fifty or a hundred men, attacking fields of potatoes. I saw them digging up the potatoes and throwing them into sacks while the farmer who owned the field watched them in despair and the local policeman looked on gloomily from the distance. I saw them staggering toward the lights of the city as night fell, with their sacks on their backs. What did it remind me of? Of the War, of the worst periods of starvation in 1917 and 1918, but even then people paid for the potatoes. ...

I saw that the individual can know what is happening only by personal experience. I know what it is to be a tramp. I know what cold and hunger are. ... But there are two things that I have only recently experienced—begging and spending the night in a municipal lodging house.

I entered the huge Berlin municipal lodging house in a northern quarter of the city. ...

Distribution of spoons, distribution of enameled-ware bowls with the words "Property of the City of Berlin" written on their sides. Then the meal itself. A big kettle is carried. Men with yellow smocks have brought it in and men with yellow smocks ladle out the food. These men, too, are homeless and they have been expressly picked by the establishment and given free food and lodging and a little pocket money in exchange for their work about the house.

Where have I seen this kind of food distribution before? In a prison that I once helped to guard in the winter of 1919 during the German civil war. There was the same hunger then, the same trembling, anxious expectation of rations. Now the men are standing in a long row, dressed in their plain nightshirts that reach to the ground, and the noise of their shuffling feet is like the noise of big wild animals walking up and down the stone floor of their cages before feeding time. The men lean far over the kettle so that the warm steam from the food envelops them and they hold out their bowls as if begging and whisper to the attendant, "Give me a real helping. Give me a little more." A piece of bread is handed out with every bowl.

My next recollection is sitting at a table in another room on a crowded bench that is like a seat in a fourth-class railway carriage. Hundreds of hungry mouths make an enormous noise eating their food. The men sit bent over their food like animals who feel that someone is going to take it away from them. They hold their bowl with their left arm part way around it, so that nobody can take it away, and they also protect it with their other elbow and with their head and mouth, while they move the spoon as fast as they can between their mouth and the bowl.

---

government of David Lloyd George proved unable either to change this situation or to meet the demands of the working class for better housing and an improved standard of living.

By 1923, British politics experienced a major transformation when the Labour Party surged ahead of the Liberals as the second most powerful party in Britain after the Conservatives. In fact, after the elections of November 1923, a Labour-Liberal coalition enabled Ramsay MacDonald (1866–1937) to become the first Labour prime minister of Britain. Dependent on Liberal support, MacDonald rejected any extreme social or

The Struggles of a Democracy: Unemployment and Slums in Great Britain

During the 1920s and 1930s, Britain struggled with the problems of economic depression. Unemployment was widespread, especially after the onset of the Great Depression. Even after Britain began to recover in the late 1930s, many Britons still lived in wretched conditions. These selections reflect Britain's economic and social problems.

Men without Work: A Report Made to the Pilgrim Trust, 1938

A week's notice may end half a lifetime's service, with no prospects, if he is elderly, but the dole, followed by a still further reduction in his means of livelihood when the old age pension comes. We take as an example a shoe laster from Leicester, who had worked thirty-seven years with one firm. "When I heard the new manager going through and saying: "The whole of this side of this room, this room, and this room is to be stopped, I knew it would be uphill work to get something." He went on to describe to us how he had not been able to bring himself to tell his wife the bad news when he got home, how she had noticed that something was wrong, how confident she had been that he would get work elsewhere, but how he had known that the chances were heavily against him. For months and indeed often for years such men go on looking for work, and the same is true of many casual labourers. There were in the sample old men who have not a remote chance of working again but yet make it a practice to stand every morning at six o'clock at the works gates in the hope that perhaps they may catch the foreman's eye.

George Orwell, "A Woman in the Slums" from *The Road to Wigan Pier*, 1937

As we moved slowly through the outskirts of the town we passed row after row of little grey slum houses. . . . At the back of one of the houses a young woman was kneeling on the stones, poking a stick up the leaden waste-pipe which ran from the sink inside, and which I suppose was blocked. . . . She had a round pale face, the usual exhausted face of the slum girl who is twenty-five and looks forty, thanks to miscarriages and drudgery; and it wore, for the second in which I saw it, the most desolate, hopeless expression I have ever seen. It struck me then that we are mistaken when we say that "It isn't the same for them as it would be for us," and that people bred in the slums can imagine nothing but the slums. For what I saw in her face was not the ignorant suffering of an animal. She knew well enough what was happening to her—understood as well as I did how dreadful a destiny it was to be kneeling there in the bitter cold, on the slimy stones of a slum backyard, poking a stick up a foul drain-pipe.

economic experimentation. His government lasted only ten months, however, as the Conservative Party's charge that his administration was friendly toward communism proved to be a highly successful campaign tactic.

Under the direction of Stanley Baldwin (1867–1947) as prime minister, the Conservatives guided Britain during an era of renewed prosperity from 1925 to 1929. This prosperity, however, was relatively superficial. British exports in the 1920s never compensated for the overseas investments lost during the war, and even in these so-called prosperous years, unemployment remained at a startling 10 percent level. Coal miners were especially affected by the decline of the antiquated and inefficient British coal mines, which also suffered from a world glut of coal. Attempts by mine owners to lower coal miners' wages only led to a national strike (the General Strike of 1926) by miners and sympathetic trade unions. A compromise settled the strike, but many miners refused to accept the settlement and were eventually forced back to work at lower wages for longer hours.

In 1929, just as the Great Depression was beginning, a second Labour government came into power, but its failure to solve the nation's economic problems caused it to fall in 1931. A National Government (a coalition of all three parties) claimed credit for bringing Britain out of the worst stages of the depression, primarily by using the traditional policies of balanced budgets and protective tariffs. By 1936, unemployment had dropped to 1.6 million after reaching a depression high of 3 million in 1932 (see the box above).

British politicians largely ignored the new ideas of a Cambridge economist, John Maynard Keynes (1883–1946). In 1936, Keynes published his *General Theory of Employment, Interest, and Money*. Contrary to the traditional view that depressions should be left to work themselves out through the self-regulatory mechanisms of a free economy, Keynes argued that unemployment stemmed not from overproduction but from a decline in demand, and that demand could be increased by public works, financed, if necessary, through deficit spending to stimulate production. These policies, however, could only be accomplished by government intervention in the economy, and Britain's political leaders were unwilling to go that far in the 1930s.

France

After the defeat of Germany and the demobilization of the German army, France had become the strongest power on the European continent. Its biggest problem involved the reconstruction of the devastated areas of northern and eastern France. The conservative National Bloc government, led by Raymond Poincaré (1860–1934), sought to use German reparations for this purpose. Tying French economic stability to German reparations resulted in Poincaré's hard-line policy toward Germany and the Ruhr invasion. When Poincaré's conservative government was forced to raise taxes in 1924 to pay for the cost of the Ruhr fiasco, his National Bloc was voted out of power and replaced by the so-called Cartel of the Left.

The Cartel of the Left was a coalition government formed by two French parties of the left, the Radicals and Socialists. These two leftist parties shared beliefs in antimilitarism, anticlericalism, and the importance of education. But despite their name, the Radicals were a democratic party of small property owners while the Socialists were nominally committed to Marxist socialism. Although they cooperated to win elections, their differences on economic and financial issues made their efforts to solve France's financial problems between 1924 and 1926 largely futile. The failure of the Cartel of the Left led to the return of Raymond Poincaré, whose government from 1926 to 1929 stabilized the French economy during a period of relative prosperity.

France did not feel the effects of the depression as soon as other countries because of its more balanced economy. The French population was almost evenly divided between urban and agricultural pursuits while a slight majority of industrial plants were small enterprises employing five workers or less. Even large industrialists were more conservative and invested little in foreign goods. It was not until 1932 that France began to feel the full effects of the Great Depression, and economic instability soon had political repercussions. During a nineteen-month period in 1932 and 1933, six different

CHRONOLOGY

The Democratic States

Great Britain	
First Labour Party government	1923
Conservative government	1925–1929
General Strike	1926
Second Labour Party government	1929–1931
Beginnings of National Government coalition	1931
France	
Cartel of the Left	1924–1926
Poincaré's government	1926–1929
February riots	1934
Formation of the Popular Front	1936
The United States	
Election of Franklin D. Roosevelt	1932
Beginnings of the New Deal	1933
The Second New Deal	1935

cabinets were formed as France faced political chaos. During the same time, French Fascist groups, adhering to far-right policies similar to those of the Fascists in Italy and the Nazis in Germany (see Fascist Italy and Hitler and Nazi Germany later in this chapter), marched through French streets in a number of demonstrations. The February riots of 1934, caused by a number of French Fascist leagues, frightened many into believing that the Fascists intended to seize power. These fears began to drive the leftist parties together despite their other differences and led in 1936 to the formation of the Popular Front.

The first Popular Front government was formed in June 1936 and was a coalition of the Communists, Socialists, and Radicals. The Socialist leader, Léon Blum (1872–1950), served as prime minister. The Popular Front succeeded in initiating a program for workers that some have called the French New Deal. It established the right of collective bargaining, a forty-hour work week, two-week paid vacations, and minimum wages. The Popular Front's policies failed to solve the problems of the depression, however. In 1938, French industrial production was still below the levels of 1929. Although the Popular Front survived in name until 1938, it was for all intents and purposes dead before then. By 1938, the French were experiencing a serious decline of confidence in their political system that left them unprepared to deal with their aggressive Nazi enemy to the east.

The Scandinavian Example

The Scandinavian states were particularly successful in coping with the Great Depression. Socialist parties had grown steadily in the late nineteenth and early twentieth centuries and between the wars came to head the governments of Sweden, Denmark, Norway, and Finland. These Social Democratic governments encouraged the development of rural and industrial cooperative enterprises. Ninety percent of the Danish milk industry, for example, was organized on a cooperative basis by 1933. Privately owned and managed, Scandinavian cooperatives seemed to avoid the pitfalls of either communist or purely capitalist economic systems.

Social Democratic governments also greatly expanded social services. Not only did Scandinavian governments increase old age pensions and unemployment insurance, but they also provided such novel forms of assistance as subsidized housing, free prenatal care, maternity allowances, and annual paid vacations for workers. To achieve their social welfare states, the Scandinavian governments required high taxes and large bureaucracies, but these did not prevent both private and cooperative enterprises from prospering. Indeed, between 1900 and 1939, Sweden experienced a greater rise in real wages than any other European country.

The United States

After Germany, no Western nation was more affected by the Great Depression than the United States. Industrial production began to decline in the summer of 1929, but after the stock market crash in October, it plummeted. Between 1929 and the end of 1932, industrial production fell almost 50 percent. By 1933, there were 15 million unemployed. With no national unemployment payments or system of poor relief, state and local communities were overwhelmed by the needs of the dramatically increasing numbers of poor and homeless. When the administration of President Herbert Hoover seemed unable to halt the economic downswing, the Democrat Franklin Delano Roosevelt (1882–1945) won the 1932 presidential election by an electoral landslide.

During his first hundred days in office, the new president pushed for the rapid enactment of major new legislation to combat the worst effects of the depression. This policy of active government intervention in the economy came to be known as the New Deal. The first New Deal created a variety of new agencies designed to bring relief, recovery, and reform. To support the nation's banks, a Federal Deposit Insurance Corporation was established that insured the safety of bank deposits up to $5,000. The creation of a Securities and Exchange Commission was intended to provide closer supervision of the stock market. The Federal Emergency Relief Administration provided funds to help states and local communities meet the needs of the destitute and homeless. A Civilian Conservation Corps employed over two million people on reforestation projects. To deal with industrial problems, Roosevelt had Congress establish the National Recovery Administration (NRA), which was intended to provide an element of government planning in industrial output. The NRA was ineffective and accomplished little; in any case, the Supreme Court declared it unconstitutional in 1935.

By that time it was becoming apparent that the initial efforts of Roosevelt's administration had produced only a slow recovery at best. As his policies came under more and more criticism by people who advocated more radical change, Roosevelt inaugurated new efforts that collectively became known as the Second New Deal. These included a stepped-up program of public works, such as the Works Progress Administration (WPA) established in 1935. This government organization employed between 2 and 3 million people who worked at building bridges, roads, post offices, and airports. The Roosevelt administration was also responsible for social legislation that launched the American welfare state. In 1935, the Social Security Act created a system of old age pensions and unemployment insurance. Moreover, the National Labor Relations Act of 1935 encouraged the rapid growth of labor unions.

No doubt, the New Deal provided some social reform measures that perhaps averted the possibility of social revolution in the United States. It did not, however, solve the unemployment problems of the Great Depression. During the winter of 1937–1938, the economy experienced another downturn after the partial recovery between 1933 and 1937. In May 1937, American unemployment still stood at 7 million; by the following year, it had increased to 11 million. Only World War II and the subsequent growth of armaments industries brought American workers back to full employment.

The Retreat from Democracy: The Authoritarian and Totalitarian States

The apparent triumph of liberal democracy in 1919 proved extremely short-lived. By 1939, only two major states, France and Great Britain, and a host of minor ones, the Low Countries, the Scandinavian states, Switzerland, and Czechoslovakia, remained democratic. Italy and Germany had succumbed to the political movement called fascism while Soviet Russia under Stalin moved toward a repressive totalitarian state. A host of other European states, especially in eastern Europe, adopted authoritarian structures of various kinds. The crisis of European civilization, inaugurated in the total war of World War I, seemed only to be worsening with new assaults on individual liberties.

The dictatorial regimes between the wars assumed both old and new forms. Dictatorship was by no means a new phenomenon, but the modern totalitarian state was. The totalitarian regimes, whose best examples can be found in Stalinist Russia and Nazi Germany, extended the functions and power of the central state far beyond what they had been in the past. The immediate origins of totalitarianism can be found in the total warfare of World War I when governments, even in the democratic states, exercised controls over economic, political, and personal freedom in order to achieve victory.

The modern totalitarian state might have begun as an old-fashioned political dictatorship, but it soon moved beyond the ideal of passive obedience expected in a traditional dictatorship or authoritarian monarchy. The new "total states" expected the active loyalty and commitment of citizens to the regime's goals. They used modern mass propaganda techniques and high-speed modern communications to conquer the minds and hearts of their subjects. The total state aimed to control not only the economic, political, and social aspects of life, but the intellectual and cultural as well. But that control also had a purpose: the active involvement of the masses in the achievement of the regime's goals, whether they be war, a socialist state, or a thousand-year Reich.

The modern totalitarian state was to be led by a single leader and a single party. It ruthlessly rejected the liberal ideal of limited government power and constitutional guarantees of individual freedoms. Indeed, individual freedom was to be subordinated to the collective will of the masses, organized and determined for them by a leader or leaders. Modern technology also gave total states unprecedented police controls to enforce their wishes on their subjects.

Totalitarianism is an abstract term, and no state followed all its theoretical implications. The fascist states—Italy and Nazi Germany—as well as Stalin's Communist Russia have all been labeled totalitarian, although their regimes exhibited significant differences and met with varying degrees of success. Totalitarianism transcended traditional political labels. Fascism in Italy and Nazism in Germany grew out of extreme rightist preoccupations with nationalism and, in the case of Germany, with racism. Communism in Soviet Russia emerged out of Marxian socialism, a radical leftist program. Thus, totalitarianism could and did exist in what were perceived as extreme right-wing and left-wing regimes. This fact helped bring about a new concept of the political spectrum in which the extremes were no longer seen as opposites on a linear scale, but came to be viewed as being similar to each other in at least some respects.

Fascist Italy

In the early 1920s, in the wake of economic turmoil, political disorder, and the general insecurity and fear stemming from World War I, Benito Mussolini burst upon the Italian scene with a movement that he called the *Fascio di Combattimento* (League of Combat). It was the beginning of the first fascist movement in Europe.

THE BIRTH OF FASCISM

As a new European state after 1870, Italy faced a number of serious problems that were only magnified when it became a belligerent in World War I. The war's cost in lives and money was enormous. An estimated 700,000 Italian soldiers died, and the treasury reckoned the cost of war at 148 billion lire, twice the sum of all government expenditures between 1861 and 1913. Italy did gain some territory, namely, Trieste, and a new northern border that included the formerly Austrian South Tyrol area. Italy's demands for Fiume and Dalmatia on the Adriatic coast were rejected, however, which gave rise to the myth that Italy had been cheated of its just rewards by the other victors. The war created untold domestic confusion. Inflation undermined middle-class security. Demobilization of the troops created high unemployment and huge groups of dissatisfied veterans. The government, which continued to be characterized by parliamentary paralysis due to the politicians' reliance on tactical and often unprincipled maneuvering to maintain their grip on power, was unable to deal effectively with these problems.

Benito Mussolini (1883–1945) was an unruly and rebellious child who ultimately received a diploma as an elementary school teacher. After an unsuccessful stint as a teacher, Mussolini became a socialist and gradually became well known in Italian socialist circles. In 1912, he obtained the important position of editor of *Avanti* (*Forward*), the official socialist daily newspaper. After editorially switching his position from ardent neutrality, the socialist position, to intervention in World War I, he was expelled from the socialist party.

In 1919, Mussolini laid the foundations for a new political movement that came to be called fascism after the name of his group, the *Fascio di Combattimento*. Mussolini's small group received little attention and were themselves unclear about their beliefs. In elections held in November 1919, the Fascists won no delegates, and Mussolini reflected bitterly that fascism had "come to a dead end." But political stalemate in Italy's parliamentary system and strong nationalist sentiment saved Mussolini and the Fascists.

The new parliament elected in November quickly proved to be incapable of governing Italy. Three major parties, the socialists, liberals, and popolari (or Christian Democrats, a new Catholic party formed in January 1919), and numerous small ones were unable to form an effective governmental coalition. The socialists, who had now become the largest party, spoke theoretically of the need for revolution, which alarmed conservatives who quickly associated them with bolsheviks or communists. Thousands of industrial and agricultural strikes in 1919 and 1920 created a climate of class warfare and continual violence. Mussolini realized the advantages of capitalizing on the fear aroused by these conditions and shifted quickly from leftist to rightist politics. The rewards were immediate as Mussolini's Fascist movement began to gain support from middle-class industrialists fearful of working-class agitation and large landowners who objected to the agricultural strikes. Mussolini also perceived that Italians were angry over Italy's failure to receive more fruits of victory in the form of territorial acquisitions after World War I. He realized then that anticommunism, antistrike activity, and nationalist rhetoric combined with the use of brute force might help him obtain what he had been unable to achieve in free elections.

In 1920 and 1921, bands of armed Fascists called *squadristi* were formed and turned loose in attacks on socialist offices and newspapers. Strikes by trade unionists and socialist workers and peasant leagues were broken up by force. At the same time, Mussolini entered into a political alliance with the liberals under then Prime Minister Giovanni Giolitti. No doubt, Giolitti and the liberals believed that the Fascists could be used to crush socialism temporarily and then be dropped. In this game of mutual deceit, Mussolini soon proved to be the more skillful player. By allying with the government coalition, he gained respectability and a free hand for his *squadristi* violence. Mussolini's efforts were rewarded when the Fascists won thirty-five parliamentary seats, or 7 percent of the total, in the election of May 1921. Mussolini's Fascist movement had gained a new lease on life.

Crucial to Mussolini's plans was the use of violence. By 1921, the black-shirted Fascist squads numbered 200,000 and had become a regular feature of Italian life. World War I veterans and students were especially attracted to the *squadristi* and relished the opportunity to use unrestrained violence. Administering large doses of castor oil to unwilling victims became one of their favorite tactics.

Mussolini and the Fascists believed that these terrorist tactics would eventually achieve political victory. They deliberately created conditions of disorder knowing that fascism would flourish in such an environment. Fascists construed themselves as the party of order and drew the bulk of their support from the middle and upper classes; white-collar workers, professionals and civil servants, landowners, merchants and artisans, and students made up almost 60 percent of the membership of the Fascist Party. The middle-class fear of socialism, communist revolution, and disorder made the Fascists attractive.

With the further deterioration of the Italian political situation, Mussolini and the Fascists were emboldened to plan a march on Rome in order to seize power. In a speech in Naples to Fascist blackshirts on October 24, 1922, Mussolini exclaimed: ". . . either we are allowed to govern, or we will seize power by marching on Rome" to "take by the throat the miserable political class that governs us."[2] Bold words, but in truth the planned march on Rome was really a calculated bluff to frighten the government into giving them power. The bluff worked, and the government capitulated even before the march occurred. On October 29, 1922, King Victor Emmanuel III (1900–1946) made Mussolini prime minister of Italy. Twenty-four hours later, the Fascist blackshirts were allowed to march into Rome in order to create the "myth" that they had gained power by an armed insurrection after a civil war.

MUSSOLINI AND THE ITALIAN FASCIST STATE

Since the Fascists constituted but a small minority in parliament, the new prime minister was forced to move slowly. Mussolini also had to balance two conflicting interests. The rural Fascists were eager to assume complete power, but the traditional institutions, such as the industrialists, the landowners, the Catholic church, and the military, wanted a period of domestic tranquillity. In the summer of 1923, Mussolini began to prepare for a national election that would consolidate the power of his Fascist government and give him a more secure base from which to govern. In July 1923, parliament enacted the Acerbo Law, which stipulated that any party winning at least 25 percent of the votes in the next national election would automatically be allotted two-thirds of the seats in parliament. The national elections that were subsequently held on April 6, 1924, constituted an enormous victory for the Fascists. They won 65 percent of the votes and garnered 374 seats out of a total of 535 in parliament. Although the elections were conducted in an atmosphere of Fascist fraud, force, and intimidation, the size of the victory indicated the growing popularity of Mussolini and his Fascists.

With this victory, Mussolini moved faster to consolidate his power. A campaign of intimidation of opposition deputies reached its high point with the assassination of the socialist deputy Giacomo Matteotti in June of 1924. Mussolini was severely challenged for his assumed complicity in the murder of Matteotti. The public outcry even caused numerous Italian political leaders to predict in December 1924 that Mussolini would have to resign. At the beginning of 1925, yielding to extremists within his own Fascist Party who demanded decisive action and a "second wave" of Fascist change, Mussolini counterattacked. To save himself, Mussolini now pushed to establish a full dictatorship. This may have been his ultimate intention anyway, but the Matteotti crisis forced him to make his move at this time. In a speech to parliament on January 3, Mussolini accepted responsibility for all Fascist violence and vowed to establish a new order: "Italy wants peace, tranquility, calm in which to work; we will give it to her, by means of love if possible, by force if necessary."

By 1926, Mussolini had established the institutional framework for his Fascist dictatorship. Press laws gave the government the right to suspend any publications that fostered disrespect for the Catholic church, monarchy, or the state. The prime minister was made "Head of Government" with the power to legislate by decree. A police law empowered the police to arrest and confine

◆ **Mussolini—The Dynamic *Duce*.** Mussolini worked hard to portray himself as a dynamic and virile leader. He created numerous poses for photographers that were supposed to reinforce this image of himself. Here Mussolini is shown leading his officers on a jog in full uniform.

anybody for both nonpolitical and political crimes without due process of law. The government was given the power to dissolve political and cultural associations. In 1926, all anti-Fascist parties were outlawed. A secret police, known as the OVRA, was also established. By the end of 1926, Mussolini ruled Italy as *Il Duce*, the leader.

Mussolini conceived of the Fascist state as totalitarian: "Fascism is totalitarian, and the Fascist State, the synthesis and unity of all values, interprets, develops and gives strength to the whole life of the people"[3] (see the box on p. 934). Mussolini did try to create a totalitarian apparatus for police surveillance and for controlling mass communications, but this machinery was not all that effective. Police activities in Italy were never as repressive, efficient, or savage as those of Nazi Germany. Likewise, the Italian Fascists' attempt to exercise control over all forms of mass media, including newspapers, radio, and cinema, in order to use propaganda as an instrument to integrate the masses into the state failed to achieve its major goals. Most commonly, Fascist propaganda was disseminated through simple slogans, such as "Mussolini is always right," plastered on walls all over Italy.

Mussolini and the Fascists also attempted to mold Italians into a single-minded community by pursuing a Fascist educational policy and developing Fascist organizations. In 1939, Giuseppe Bottai, minister of educa-

The Voice of Italian Fascism

In 1932, an article on fascism appeared in the Italian Encyclopedia. Supposedly authored by Mussolini, it was largely written by the philosopher Giovanni Gentile. Mussolini had always argued that fascism was based only on the need for action, not on doctrines, but after its success he felt the need to summarize the basic political and social ideas of fascism. These excerpts are taken from Mussolini's article.

Benito Mussolini, *The Political and Social Doctrine of Fascism*

Above all, Fascism . . . believes neither in the possibility nor the utility of perpetual peace. It thus repudiates the doctrine of Pacifism—born of a renunciation of struggle and an act of cowardice in the face of sacrifice. War alone brings up to its highest tension all human energy and puts the stamp of nobility upon the peoples who have the courage to meet it. All other trials are substitutes, which never really put men into the position where they have to make the great decision—the alternative of life or death. Thus a doctrine which is founded upon this harmful postulate of peace is hostile to Fascism. . . . Thus the Fascist accepts life and loves it, knowing nothing of and despising suicide: he rather conceives of life as duty and struggle and conquest. . . .

Fascism is the complete opposite of Marxian socialism, the materialist conception of history; according to which the history of human civilization can be explained simply through the conflict of interests among the various social groups and by the change and development in the means and instruments of production. That the changes in the economic field have their importance no one can deny; but that these factors are sufficient to explain the history of humanity excluding all others is an absurd delusion. Fascism, now and always, believes in holiness and in heroism;

that is to say, in actions influenced by no economic motive, direct or indirect. . . .

After Socialism, Fascism combats the whole complex system of democratic ideology, and repudiates it, whether in its theoretical premises or in its practical application. Fascism denies that the majority, by the simple fact that it is a majority, can direct human society; it denies that numbers alone can govern by means of a periodical consultation, and it affirms the immutable, beneficial, and fruitful inequality of mankind, which can never be permanently leveled through the mere operation of a mechanical process such as universal suffrage.

The foundation of Fascism is the conception of the State, its character, its duty and its aim. Fascism conceives of the State as an absolute, in comparison with which all individuals or groups are relative, only to be conceived of in their relation to the State. . . . The Fascist state organizes the nation, but leaves a sufficient margin of liberty to the individual; the latter is deprived of all useless and possibly harmful freedom, but retains what is essential; the deciding power in the question cannot be the individual, but the State alone. . . .

For Fascism, the growth of empire, that is to say the expansion of the nation, is an essential manifestation of vitality, and its opposite a sign of decadence. Peoples which are rising, or rising again after a period of decadence, are always imperialist; any renunciation is a sign of decay and of death. Fascism is the doctrine best adapted to represent the tendencies and the aspirations of a people, like the people of Italy, who are rising again after many centuries of abasement and foreign servitude. But Empire demands discipline, the coordination of all forces and a deeply felt sense of duty and sacrifice.

---

tion, proposed a new School Charter whose basic aim was "the will to substitute, both in principle and practice, for the bourgeois schools a people's school, which will really be for everyone and which will really meet the needs of everyone, that is the needs of the State."[4] Bottai hoped to make the educational system an instrument to create the "new Fascist man," but his reforms were never implemented, primarily because the middle class resisted any alterations in the traditional paths of upward mobility.

Since the secondary schools maintained considerable freedom from Fascist control, the regime relied more and more on the activities of Fascist youth organizations, known as the Young Fascists, to indoctrinate the young people of the nation in Fascist ideals. By 1939, about 6.8 million children, teenagers, and young adults of both sexes, or 66 percent of the population between eight and eighteen, were enrolled in some kind of Fascist youth group. Activities for these groups included unpopular Saturday afternoon marching drills and calisthenics, seaside and mountain summer camps, and youth contests. An underlying motif for all of these activities was the Fascist insistence on militarization. Beginning in the 1930s, all male groups were given some kind of premilitary exercises to develop discipline and provide training for war. Results were mixed. Italian teenagers, who liked neither military training nor routine discipline of any kind, simply refused to attend Fascist youth meetings on a regular basis.

The Fascist organizations hoped to create a new Italian, who would be hard-working, physically fit, disciplined, intellectually sharp, and martially inclined; this ideal was symbolized by the phrase, "book and musket—the perfect Fascist." In practice, the Fascists largely reinforced traditional social attitudes in Italy, as is evident in their policies regarding women. The Fascists portrayed the family as the pillar of the state and women as the basic foundation of the family. "Woman into the home" became the Fascist slogan. Women were to be homemakers and baby producers, "their natural and fundamental mission in life," according to Mussolini, who viewed population growth as an indicator of national strength. To Mussolini, female emancipation was "unfascist." Employment outside the home was an impediment distracting women from conception. "It forms an independence and consequent physical and moral habits contrary to child bearing."[5] A practical consideration also underlay the Fascist attitude toward women. Working women would compete with males for jobs in the depression economy of the 1930s. Eliminating women from the market reduced male unemployment figures.

The Fascists translated their attitude toward women into law by a series of enactments in the 1930s that aimed at encouraging larger families by offering supplementary pay, loans, prizes, and subsidies for families with many offspring. Gold medals were given to mothers of many children. A national holiday of "the Mother and the Child" was held on December 24 with prizes awarded for fertility. Also in the 1930s, decrees were passed that set quotas on the employment of women, but they were not overly successful in accomplishing their goal.

Despite the instruments of repression, the use of propaganda, and the creation of numerous Fascist organizations, Mussolini never really achieved the degree of totalitarian control accomplished in Hitler's Germany or Stalin's Soviet Union. Mussolini and the Fascist Party never really destroyed the old power structure. Some institutions, including the armed forces and monarchy,

CHRONOLOGY

Fascist Italy

Creation of *Fascio di Combattimento*	1919
Squadristi violence	1920–1921
Fascists win thirty-five seats in Parliament	1921
Mussolini is made prime minister	1922 (October 29)
Acerbo Law	1923
Electoral victory for Fascists	1924
Establishment of Fascist dictatorship	1925–1926
Lateran Accords with Catholic church	1929
Fascist School Charter	1939

were never absorbed into the Fascist state and mostly managed to maintain their independence. Mussolini had boasted that he would help workers and peasants, but instead he generally allied himself with the interests of the industrialists and large landowners at the expense of the lower classes.

Even more indicative of Mussolini's compromise with the traditional institutions of Italy was his attempt to gain the support of the Catholic church. In the Lateran Accords of February 1929, Mussolini's regime recognized the sovereign independence of a small enclave of 109 acres within Rome, known as Vatican City, which had remained in the church's possession since unification in 1870; in return, the papacy recognized the Italian state. The Lateran Accords also guaranteed the church a large grant of money and recognized Catholicism as the "sole religion of the state." In return, the Catholic church urged Italians to support the Fascist regime.

In all areas of Italian life under Mussolini and the Fascists, there was a noticeable dichotomy between Fascist ideals and practice. The Italian Fascists promised much but actually delivered considerably less, and they were soon overshadowed by a much more powerful Fascist movement to the north. Adolf Hitler was a great admirer of Benito Mussolini, but the German pupil soon proved to be far more adept in the use of power than his Italian teacher.

Hitler and Nazi Germany

In 1923, a small, south German rightist party, known as the Nazis, led by an obscure Austrian rabble-rouser named Adolf Hitler, created a stir when it tried to seize power in southern Germany in conscious imitation of Mussolini's march on Rome in 1922. Although the attempt failed, Adolf Hitler and the Nazis achieved sudden national prominence. Within ten years, Hitler and the Nazis had taken over complete power.

WEIMAR GERMANY AND THE RISE OF THE NAZIS

After the Imperial Germany of William II had come to an end with Germany's defeat in World War I, a German democratic state known as the Weimar Republic had been established. From its beginnings, the Weimar Republic was plagued by a series of problems. The Republic had no truly outstanding political leaders. Even its more able leaders, such as Friedrich Ebert, who served as president, and Gustav Stresemann, the foreign minister and chancellor, died in the 1920s. When Ebert died in 1925, Paul von Hindenburg, the World War I military hero, was elected president. Hindenburg was a traditional military man, monarchist in sentiment, who at heart was not in favor of the Republic. The young Republic also suffered politically from attempted uprisings and attacks from both the left and the right.

Another of the Republic's problems was its inability to change the basic structure of Germany. The government never really controlled the army, which operated as a state within a state. This independence was true of other institutions as well. Hostile judges, teachers, and bureaucrats remained in office and used their positions to undermine democracy from within. At the same time, important groups of landed aristocrats and leaders of powerful business cartels refused to accept the overthrow of the imperial regime and remained hostile to the Weimar Republic.

The Weimar Republic also faced serious economic difficulties. Germany experienced runaway inflation in 1922 and 1923 with serious social effects. Widows, orphans, the retired elderly, army officers, teachers, civil servants, and others who lived on fixed incomes all watched their monthly stipends become worthless or their lifetime savings disappear. Their economic losses increasingly pushed the middle class to the rightist parties that were hostile to the Republic. To make matters worse, after a period of prosperity from 1924 to 1929, Germany faced the Great Depression. Unemployment increased to 3 million in March 1930 and 4.38

million by December of the same year. The depression paved the way for social discontent, fear, and extremist parties. The political, economic, and social problems of the Weimar Republic provided an environment in which Adolf Hitler and the Nazis were able to rise to power.

Born on April 20, 1889, Adolf Hitler was the son of an Austrian customs official. He was a total failure in secondary school and eventually made his way to Vienna to become an artist. Rejected by the Vienna Academy of Fine Arts and supported by an inheritance and orphan's pension, Hitler stayed on in Vienna to live the bohemian lifestyle of an artist. In his autobiography, *Mein Kampf,* Hitler characterized his years in Vienna from 1908 to 1913 as an important formative period in his life: "In this period there took shape within me a world picture and a philosophy which became the granite foundation of all my acts. In addition to what I then created, I have had to learn little, and I have had to alter nothing."[6]

Hitler experienced four major influences in Vienna. Georg von Schönerer, the leader of the Austrian Pan-German movement, was an extreme German nationalist who urged the union of all Germans in one national state. Karl Lueger was mayor of Vienna and leader of the anti-Semitic Christian Social Party. Hitler called him "the greatest German mayor of all time" and especially admired his demagogic methods and leadership of a mass party that was formed with the aid of emotional slogans. Much of Hitler's early anti-Semitism was imbibed from an ex-Catholic monk named Adolf Lanz who called himself Lanz von Liebenfels. Hitler was an avid reader of *Ostara,* a periodical published by Liebenfels in which he propagated his racial beliefs that the German Aryans were exalted beings destined to rule the earth. Liebenfels characterized the Jews and other allegedly inferior races as "animal-men" who must someday be eliminated by sterilization, deportation, forced labor, and even "direct liquidation." Finally, Hitler was also strongly influenced by Richard Wagner's operas, which he attended frequently in Vienna. Hitler absorbed Wagner's ideal of the true artist as a social outcast from the bourgeois world who is subject to his own rhythms. Wagner's music also spoke of a boundless will to power and a need to dominate.

In Vienna, then, Hitler established the basic ideas of an ideology from which he never deviated for the rest of his life. At the core of Hitler's ideas was racism, especially anti-Semitism (see the box on p. 937). His hatred of the Jews lasted to the very end of his life. Hitler had also become an extreme German nationalist

≽ *Adolf Hitler's Hatred of the Jews* ≼

A believer in Aryan racial supremacy, Adolf Hitler viewed the Jews as the archenemies of the Aryans. He believed that the first task of a true Aryan state would be the elimination of the Jewish threat. This is why Hitler's political career both began and ended with a warning against the Jews. In this excerpt from his autobiography, Mein Kampf, Hitler describes how he came to be an anti-Semite when he lived in Vienna in his early twenties.

Adolf Hitler, *Mein Kampf*

My views with regard to anti-Semitism thus succumbed to the passage of time, and this was my greatest transformation of all. . . .

Once, as I was strolling through the Inner City [of Vienna], I suddenly encountered an apparition in a black caftan and black hair locks. Is this a Jew? was my first thought.

For, to be sure, they had not looked like that in Linz. I observed the man furtively and cautiously, but the longer I stared at this foreign face, scrutinizing feature for feature, the more my first question assumed a new form:

Is this a German?

As always in such cases, I now began to try to relieve my doubts by books. For a few pennies I bought the first anti-Semitic pamphlets of my life. . . .

Yet I could no longer very well doubt that the objects of my study were not Germans of a special religion, but a people in themselves; for since I had begun to concern myself with this question and to take cognizance of the Jews, Vienna appeared to me in a different light than before. Wherever I went, I began to see Jews, and the more I saw, the more sharply they became distinguished in my eyes from the rest of humanity. . . .

In a short time I was made more thoughtful than ever by my slowly rising insight into the type of activity carried on by the Jews in certain fields.

Was there any form of filth or profligacy, particularly in cultural life, without at least one Jew involved in it? . . .

Sometimes I stood there thunderstruck.

I didn't know what to be more amazed at: the agility of their tongues or their virtuosity at lying.

Gradually I began to hate them.

who had learned from the mass politics of Vienna how political parties could effectively use propaganda and terror. Finally, in his Viennese years, Hitler also came to a firm belief in the need for struggle, which he saw as the "granite foundation of the world." Hitler emphasized a crude Social Darwinism (see Chapter 25); the world was a brutal place filled with constant struggle in which only the fit survived.

In 1913, Hitler moved to Munich, still without purpose and with no real future in sight. World War I saved him: "Overpowered by stormy enthusiasm, I fell down on my knees and thanked Heaven from an overflowing heart for granting me the good fortune of being permitted to live at this time."[7] As a dispatch runner on the Western Front, Hitler distinguished himself by his brave acts. At the end of the war, finding again that his life had no purpose or meaning, he returned to Munich and decided to enter politics and found, at last, his true profession.

As a Munich politician from 1919 to 1923, Hitler accomplished a great deal. He joined the obscure German Workers' Party, one of a number of right-wing extreme nationalist parties in Munich. By the summer of

1921, Hitler had assumed total control over the party, which he renamed the National Socialist German Workers' Party (NSDAP), or Nazi for short. His idea was that the party's name would distinguish the Nazis from the socialist parties while gaining support from both working-class and nationalist circles. Hitler worked assiduously to develop the party into a mass political movement with flags, party badges, uniforms, its own newspaper, and its own police force or party militia known as the SA, the *Sturmabteilung*, or Storm Troops. The SA was used to defend the party in meeting halls and to break up the meetings of other parties. It added an element of force and terror to the growing Nazi movement. Hitler's own oratorical skills were largely responsible for attracting an increasing number of followers. By 1923, the party had grown from its early hundreds into a membership of 55,000 with 15,000 SA members.

In its early years, the Nazi Party had been only one of many radical right-wing political groups in southern Germany. By 1923, it had become the strongest. When it appeared that the Weimar Republic was on the verge of collapse in the fall of 1923, the Nazis and other right-wing leaders in the south German state of Bavaria decided to march on Berlin to overthrow the Weimar government. When his fellow conspirators reneged, Hitler and the Nazis decided to act on their own by staging an armed uprising in Munich on November 8. The so-called Beer Hall Putsch was quickly crushed. Hitler was arrested, put on trial for treason, and sentenced to prison for five years, a lenient sentence indeed from sympathetic right-wing judges.

THE NAZI SEIZURE OF POWER

The Beer Hall Putsch proved to be a major turning point in Hitler's career. Rather than discouraging him, his trial and imprisonment reinforced his faith in himself and in his mission. He now saw clearly the need for a change in tactics. The Nazis could not overthrow the Weimar Republic by force, but would have to use constitutional means to gain power. This implied the formation of a mass political party that would actively compete for votes with the other political parties.

Hitler occupied himself in prison with the writing of *Mein Kampf* (*My Struggle*), an autobiographical account of his movement and its underlying ideology. Extreme German nationalism, virulent anti-Semitism, and vicious anti-communism are linked together by a Social Darwinian theory of struggle that stresses the right of superior nations to *Lebensraum* (living space) through expansion and the right of superior individuals to secure authoritarian leadership over the masses. The only originality in *Mein Kampf,* as historians have pointed out, is in Hitler's analysis of mass propaganda, mass psychology, and the mass organization of peoples. What is perhaps most remarkable about *Mein Kampf* is its elaboration of a series of ideas that directed Hitler's actions once he took power. That others refused to take Hitler and his ideas seriously was one of his greatest advantages.

When Hitler was released, the Nazi Party was in shambles, and he set about to reestablish his sole control over the party and organize it for the lawful takeover of power. Hitler's position on leadership in the party was quite clear. There was to be no discussion of ideas in the party, and the party was to follow the *Führerprinzip,* the leadership principle, which entailed nothing less than a single-minded party under one leader. As Hitler expressed it: "A good National Socialist is one who would let himself be killed for his Führer at any time."[8]

The late 1920s were a period of building and waiting. These were years of relative prosperity for Germany, and, as Hitler perceived, they were not conducive to the growth of extremist parties. He declared, however, that the prosperity would not last and that his time would come. In the meantime, Hitler worked to establish a highly structured party that could compete in elections and attract new recruits when another time of troubles arose. He reorganized the Nazi Party on a regional basis and expanded it to all parts of Germany. By 1929, the Nazi Party had a national party organization. It also grew from 27,000 members in 1925 to 178,000 by the end of 1929. Especially noticeable was the youthfulness of the regional, district, and branch leaders of the Nazi organization. Many were between the ages of twenty-five and thirty and were fiercely committed to Hitler because he gave them the kind of active politics they sought. Rather than democratic debate, they wanted brawls in beer halls, enthusiastic speeches, and comradeship in the building of a new Germany. One new, young Nazi member expressed his excitement about the party:

> For me this was the start of a completely new life. There was only one thing in the world for me and that was service in the movement. All my thoughts were centered on the movement. I could talk only politics. I was no longer aware of anything else. At the time I was a promising athlete; I was very keen on sport, and it was going to be my career. But I had to give this up too. My only interest was agitation and propaganda.[9]

Such youthful enthusiasm gave the Nazi movement an aura of a "young man's movement" and a sense of dynamism that the other parties could not match. In 1931, almost 40 percent of Nazi Party members were under thirty.

By 1929, the Nazi Party had also made a significant shift in strategy. Between 1925 and 1927, Hitler and the Nazis had pursued an urban strategy geared toward winning workers from the Socialists and Communists. But failure in the 1928 elections, when the Nazis gained only 2.6 percent of the vote and twelve seats in the Reichstag or German parliament, convinced Hitler of the need for a change. By 1929, the party began to pursue middle-class and lower-middle-class votes in small towns and rural areas, especially in northern, central, and eastern Germany. By the end of 1929, the Nazis had successfully made their shift to the new strategy. The end of 1929 was the beginning of the depression and the beginning of Hitler's real success.

Germany's economic difficulties made possible the Nazi rise to power. Unemployment rose dramatically, from 4.35 million in 1931 to 6 million by the winter of 1932. The economic and psychological impact of the Great Depression made the extremist parties more attractive. Already in the Reichstag elections of September 1930, the Nazis polled 18 percent of the vote and gained 107 seats in the Reichstag, making the Nazi Party one of the largest parties.

By 1930, Chancellor Heinrich Brüning (1885–1970) had found it impossible to form a working parliamentary majority in the Reichstag and relied on the use of emergency decrees by President Hindenburg to rule. In a real sense, then, parliamentary democracy was already dying in 1930, three years before Hitler destroyed it.

Hitler's quest for power from late 1930 to early 1933 depended on the political maneuvering around President Hindenburg. Nevertheless, the elections from 1930 through 1932 were indirectly responsible for the Nazi rise to power since they showed the importance of the Nazi Party. The party itself grew dramatically during this period, from 289,000 members in September 1930 to 800,000 by 1932. The SA also rose to 500,000 members.

The Nazis proved very effective in developing modern electioneering techniques. They crossed Germany in whirlwind campaigns by car, train, and airplane. His "Hitler Over Germany" campaign by airplane saw Hitler speaking in fifty cities in fifteen days. The Nazis were successful in presenting two fundamentally different approaches to the German voters. In their election campaigns, party members pitched their themes to the needs and fears of different social groups. In working-class districts, for example, the Nazis attacked international high finance, but in middle-class neighborhoods, they exploited fears of a Communist revolution and its threat to private property. At the same time that the Nazis made blatant appeals to class interests, they were denouncing conflicts of interest and maintaining that they stood above classes and parties. Hitler, in particular, claimed to stand above all differences and promised to create a new Germany free of class differences and party infighting. His appeal to national pride, national honor, and traditional militarism struck chords of emotion in his listeners.

Elections, however, proved to have their limits. In the elections of July 1932, the Nazis won 230 seats, making them the largest party in the Reichstag. But four months later, in November, they declined to 196 seats. It became apparent to many Nazis that they would not gain power simply by the ballot box. Hitler saw clearly, however, that the Reichstag after 1930 was not all that important, since the government ruled by decree with the support of President Hindenburg. Increasingly, the right-wing elites of Germany, the industrial magnates, landed aristocrats, military establishment, and higher

♦ **Hitler and the Blood Flag Ritual.** In developing his mass political movement, Adolf Hitler used ritualistic ceremonies as a means of binding party members to his own person. Hitler is shown here touching the "blood flag," which had supposedly been stained with the blood of Nazis killed during the Beer Hall Putsch, to an SS banner while the SS standard-bearer made a "blood oath" of allegiance: "I vow to remain true to my Führer, Adolf Hitler. I bind myself to carry out all orders conscientiously and without reluctance. Standards and flags shall be sacred to me."

bureaucrats, came to see Hitler as the man who had the mass support to establish a right-wing, authoritarian regime that would save Germany and their privileged positions from a Communist takeover. These people almost certainly thought that they could control Hitler and, like many others, may well have underestimated his abilities. Under pressure from these elites, President Hindenburg agreed to allow Hitler to become chancellor (on January 30, 1933) and to form a new government, but with supposed safeguards. There would be only three Nazis in the cabinet, and Franz von Papen (1878–1969), who had served as chancellor and done so much to win over Hindenburg to the arrangements, would serve as vice-chancellor. To those who reproached von Papen for giving power to Hitler, he responded: "What do you want? I have Hindenburg's trust. Within two months, we will have pushed Hitler so far into a corner that he will squeak."[10]

Within those two months, Hitler basically laid the foundations for the Nazis' complete control over Germany. One of Hitler's important cohorts, Hermann Göring (1893–1946), had been made minister of the interior and hence head of the police of the Prussian state, the largest of the federal states in Germany. He used his power to purge the police of non-Nazis and to establish an auxiliary police force composed of SA members. This action legitimized Nazi terror. On the day after a fire broke out in the Reichstag building (February 27), supposedly set by the Communists, but possibly by the Nazis themselves, Hitler was also able to convince President Hindenburg to issue a decree that gave the government emergency powers. It suspended all basic rights of citizens for the full duration of the emergency, thus enabling the Nazis to arrest and imprison anyone without redress. Although Hitler promised to return to the "normal order of things" when the Communist danger was past, in reality this decree provided the legal basis for the creation of a police state.

The crowning step of Hitler's "legal seizure" of power came after the Nazis had gained 288 Reichstag seats in the elections of March 5, 1933. Since they still did not possess an absolute majority, on March 23 the Nazis sought the passage of an Enabling Act, which would empower the government to dispense with constitutional forms for four years while it issued laws that would deal with the country's problems. Since the act was to be an amendment to the Weimar constitution, the Nazis needed and obtained a two-thirds vote to pass it. Only the Social Democrats had the courage to oppose Hitler. The Enabling Act provided the legal basis for Hitler's subsequent acts. He no longer needed either the Reichstag or President Hindenburg. In effect, Hitler became a dictator appointed by the parliamentary body itself.

With their new source of power, the Nazis acted quickly to enforce Gleichschaltung, or the coordination of all institutions under Nazi control. The civil service was purged of Jews and democratic elements, concentration camps were established for opponents of the new regime, the autonomy of the federal states was eliminated, trade unions were dissolved and swallowed up by a gigantic Labor Front, and all political parties except the Nazis were abolished. By the end of the summer of 1933, within seven months of being appointed chancellor, Hitler and the Nazis had established the foundations for a totalitarian state.

Why had this seizure of power been so quick and easy? The Nazis were not only ruthless in their use of force, but had also been ready to seize power. The depression had weakened what little faith the Germans had in their democratic state. But negative factors alone cannot explain the Nazi success. To many Germans, the Nazis offered a national awakening. "Germany Awake," one of the many Nazi slogans, had a powerful appeal to a people psychologically crushed by their defeat in World War I. The Nazis presented a strong image of a dynamic new Germany that was above parties and above classes.

By the end of 1933, there were only two sources of potential danger to Hitler's authority: the armed forces and the SA within his own party. The SA, under the leadership of Ernst Röhm, openly criticized Hitler and spoke of the need for a "second revolution" and the replacement of the regular army by the SA. Neither the army nor Hitler favored such a possibility. Hitler solved both problems simultaneously on June 30, 1934, by having Ernst Röhm and a number of other SA leaders killed in return for the army's support in allowing Hitler to succeed Hindenburg when the president died. When Hindenburg died on August 2, 1934, the office of Reich president was abolished, and Hitler became sole ruler of Germany. Public officials and soldiers were all required to take a personal oath of loyalty to Hitler as the "Führer of the German Reich and people." On August 19, 1934, Hitler held a plebiscite in which 85 percent of the German people indicated their approval of the new order. The Third Reich had begun.

THE NAZI STATE, 1933–1939

Having smashed the parliamentary state, Hitler now felt the real task was at hand: to develop the "total state." Hitler's aims had not been simply power for power's sake or a tyranny based on personal power. He had larger ideological goals. The development of an Aryan racial state that would dominate Europe and possibly the world for generations to come required a massive movement in which the German people would be actively involved, not passively cowed by force. Hitler stated:

> We must develop organizations in which an individual's entire life can take place. Then every activity and every need of every individual will be regulated by the collectivity represented by the party. There is no longer any arbitrary will, there are no longer any free realms in which the individual belongs to himself. . . . The time of personal happiness is over.[11]

The Nazis pursued the creation of this totalitarian state in a variety of ways.

Mass demonstrations and spectacles were employed to integrate the German nation into a collective fellowship and to mobilize it as an instrument for Hitler's policies (see the box on p. 942). These mass demonstrations, especially the Nuremberg party rallies that were held every September and the Harvest Festivals celebrated at the Bückeberg near Hamelin every fall, combined the symbolism of a religious service with the merriment of a popular amusement. They had great appeal and usually evoked mass enthusiasm and excitement. Even foreigners were frequently affected by the passions aroused by these mass demonstrations.

Some features of the state apparatus of Hitler's "total state" seem contradictory. One usually thinks of Nazi Germany as having an all-powerful government that maintained absolute control and order. In truth, Nazi Germany was the scene of almost constant personal and institutional conflict, which resulted in administrative chaos. In matters such as foreign policy, education, and economics, parallel government and party bureaucracies competed with each other over spheres of influence. Incessant struggle characterized relationships within the party, within the state, and between party and state. Why this "authoritarian anarchy," as one observer called it, existed is a source of much controversy. One group of historians has assumed that Hitler's aversion to making decisions resulted in the chaos that subverted his own authority and made him a "weak dictator." Another group believes that Hitler's style of leadership led to his regime's administrative chaos, but maintains that Hitler deliberately created this institutional confusion. By fostering rivalry within the party and between party and state, he would be the final decision maker and absolute ruler.

In the economic sphere, Hitler and the Nazis also established control, but industry was not nationalized as the left wing of the Nazi Party wanted. Hitler felt that it was irrelevant who owned the means of production so long as the owners recognized their master. Although the regime pursued the use of public works projects and "pump-priming" grants to private construction firms to foster employment and end the depression, there is little doubt that rearmament was a far more important contributor to solving the unemployment problem. Unemployment, which had stood at 6 million in 1932, dropped to 2.6 million in 1934 and less than 500,000 in 1937. The regime claimed full credit for solving Germa-

◆ **The Nazi Mass Spectacle.** Hitler and the Nazis made clever use of mass spectacles to rally the German people behind the Nazi regime. These mass demonstrations evoked intense enthusiasm, as is evident in this photograph of Hitler arriving at the Bückeberg near Hamelin for the Harvest Festival in 1937. Almost one million people were present for the celebration.

Propaganda and Mass Meetings in Nazi Germany

Propaganda and mass rallies were two of the chief instruments that Hitler used to prepare the German people for the tasks he set before them. In the first selection, taken from Mein Kampf, *Hitler explains the psychological importance of mass meetings in creating support for a political movement. In the second excerpt, taken from his speech to a crowd at Nuremberg, he describes the kind of mystical bond he hoped to create through his mass rallies.*

Adolf Hitler, *Mein Kampf*

The mass meeting is also necessary for the reason that in it the individual, who at first, while becoming a supporter of a young movement, feels lonely and easily succumbs to the fear of being alone, for the first time gets the picture of a larger community, which in most people has a strengthening, encouraging effect.... When from his little workshop or big factory, in which he feels very small, he steps for the first time into a mass meeting and has thousands and thousands of people of the same opinions around him, when, as a seeker, he is swept away by three or four thousand others into the mighty effect of suggestive intoxication and enthusiasm, when the visible success and agreement of thousands confirm to him the rightness of the new doctrine and for the first time arouse doubt in the truth of his previous conviction—then he himself has succumbed to the magic influence of what we designate as "mass suggestion." The will, the longing, and also the power of thousands are accumulated in every individual. The man who enters such a meeting doubting and wavering leaves it inwardly reinforced: he has become a link in the community.

Adolf Hitler, Speech at the Nuremberg Party Rally, 1936

Do we not feel once again in this hour the miracle that brought us together? Once you heard the voice of a man, and it struck deep into your hearts; it awakened you, and you followed this voice. Year after year you went after it, though him who had spoken you never even saw. You heard only a voice, and you followed it. When we meet each other here, the wonder of our coming together fills us all. Not everyone of you sees me, and I do not see everyone of you. But I feel you, and you feel me. It is the belief in our people that has made us small men great, that has made us poor men rich, that has made brave and courageous men out of us wavering, spiritless, timid folk; this belief made us see our road when we were astray; it joined us together into one whole! ... You come, that ... you may, once in a while, gain the feeling that now we are together; we are with him and he with us, and we are now Germany!

ny's economic woes, and this was an important factor in leading many Germans to accept the new regime, despite its excesses.

The German Labor Front under Robert Ley regulated the world of labor. The Labor Front was a single, state-controlled union. To control all laborers, it used the workbook. Every salaried worker had to have one in order to hold a job. Only by submitting to the policies of the Nazi-controlled Labor Front could a worker obtain and retain a workbook. The Labor Front also sponsored activities to keep the workers happy (see Mass Leisure later in this chapter).

For those who needed coercion, the Nazi total state had its instruments of terror and repression. Until 1934, the SA had been most visible in terrorizing the people, but after the June 30 purge, the SS took over that function in a much more systematic fashion. Originally created as Hitler's personal bodyguard, the SS, under the direction of Heinrich Himmler (1900–1945), came to control all of the regular and secret police forces. Himmler and the SS functioned on the basis of two principles: terror and ideology. Terror included the instruments of repression and murder: the secret police, criminal police, concentration camps, and later the execution squads and death camps for the extermination of the Jews (see Chapter 28). For Himmler, the SS was a crusading order whose primary goal was to further the Aryan master race. SS members, who constituted a carefully chosen elite, were thoroughly indoctrinated in racial ideology.

Other institutions, such as the Catholic and Protestant churches, primary and secondary schools, and universities, were also brought under the control of the Nazi totalitarian state. Nazi professional organizations and leagues were formed for civil servants, teachers, women, farmers, doctors, and lawyers. These groups were inspired by a sound principle perverted to other ends. Common flags, uniforms, meetings, and indoctrination gave individuals a sense of identity, a sense of belonging and human warmth, but one that was cultivated to produce inhuman brutality.

Since the early indoctrination of the nation's youth would create the foundation for a strong totalitarian state for the future, youth organizations, the *Hitler Jugend* (Hitler Youth) and its female counterpart, the *Bund deutscher Mädel* (League of German Maidens), were given special attention. The oath required of Hitler Youth members demonstrates the degree of dedication expected of youth in the Nazi state: "In the presence of this blood banner, which represents our Führer, I swear to devote all my energies and my strength to the savior of our country, Adolf Hitler. I am willing and ready to give up my life for him, so help me God."

The Nazi total state was intended to be an Aryan racial state. From its beginning, the Nazi Party reflected the strong anti-Semitic beliefs of Adolf Hitler. Once in power, it did not take long for the Nazis to translate anti-Semitic ideas into anti-Semitic policies. Already on April 1, 1933, the new Nazi government initiated a two-day boycott of Jewish businesses. A series of laws soon followed that excluded "non-Aryans" (defined as anyone "descended from non-Aryans, especially Jewish parents or grandparents") from the legal professions, civil service, judgeships, the medical profession, teaching positions, cultural and entertainment enterprises, and the press.

In 1935, the Nazis unleashed another stage of anti-Jewish activity when new racial laws were announced in September at the annual party rally in Nuremberg. These "Nuremberg laws" excluded German Jews from German citizenship and forbade marriages and extramarital relations between Jews and German citizens. The "Nuremberg laws" essentially separated Jews from the Germans politically, socially, and legally and were the natural extension of Hitler's stress upon the creation of a pure Aryan race.

Another, considerably more violent phase of anti-Jewish activity took place in 1938 and 1939; it was initiated on November 9–10, 1938, the infamous *Kristallnacht*, or night of shattered glass. The assassination of a third secretary in the German embassy in Paris became the occasion for a Nazi-led destructive rampage against the Jews in which synagogues were burned, 7,000 Jewish businesses were destroyed, and at least one hundred Jews were killed. Moreover, 30,000 Jewish males were rounded up and sent to concentration camps. *Kristallnacht* also led to further drastic steps. Jews were barred from all public buildings and prohibited from owning, managing,

◆ **Anti-Semitism in Nazi Germany.** At the core of Hitler's ideology was an intense anti-Semitism. Soon after seizing power, Hitler and the Nazis began to translate their anti-Semitic ideas into anti-Semitic policies. This photograph shows one example of Nazi action against the Jews. Two women clean up some of the debris the morning after *Kristallnacht*, the night of shattered glass.

Nazi Germany

Hitler as Munich politician	1919–1923
Beer Hall Putsch	1923
Election of Hindenburg as president	1925
Nazis win 107 seats in Reichstag	1930 (September)
Hitler is made chancellor	1933 (January 30)
Reichstag fire	1933 (February 27)
Enabling Act	1933 (March 23)
Purge of the SA	1934 (June 30)
Hindenburg dies; Hitler as sole ruler	1934 (August 2)
Nuremberg laws	1935
Kristallnacht	1938 (November 9–10)

or working in any retail store. Finally, under the direction of the SS, Jews were encouraged to "emigrate from Germany." After the outbreak of World War II, the policy of emigration was replaced by a more gruesome one.

The creation of the Nazi total state also had an impact on women. The Nazi attitude toward women was largely determined by ideological considerations. Women played a crucial role in the Aryan racial state as bearers of the children who would bring about the triumph of the Aryan race. To the Nazis, the differences between men and women were quite natural. Men were warriors and political leaders while women were destined to be wives and mothers. By maintaining this clear distinction, each could best serve to "maintain the whole community."

Nazi ideas determined employment opportunities for women. The Nazis hoped to drive women out of certain areas of the labor market. These included heavy industry or other jobs that might hinder women from bearing healthy children, as well as certain professions, including university teaching, medicine, and law, which were considered inappropriate for women, especially married women. The Nazis encouraged women to pursue professional occupations that had direct practical application, such as social work and nursing. In addition to restrictive legislation against females, the Nazi regime pursued its campaign against working women with such poster slogans as "Get ahold of pots and pans and broom and you'll sooner find a groom!" Nazi policy toward female workers remained inconsistent, however. Especially after the rearmament boom and increased conscription of males for military service produced a labor shortage, the government encouraged women to work, even in areas previously dominated by males.

Soviet Russia

Yet another example of totalitarianism was to be found in Soviet Russia. The civil war in Russia had come to an end by the beginning of 1921. It had taken an enormous toll of life, but the Red Terror and the victories of the Red Army had guaranteed the survival of the Communist regime. During the civil war, Lenin had pursued a policy of "war communism." Under this policy of expedience, the government had nationalized transportation and communication facilities as well as banks, mines, factories, and businesses that employed more than ten workers. The government had also assumed the right to requisition the produce of peasants. War communism worked during the civil war, but once the war was over, peasants began to sabotage the program by hoarding food. Added to this problem was drought, which caused a great famine between 1920 and 1922 that claimed as many as 5 million lives. Industrial collapse paralleled the agricultural disaster. By 1921, industrial output was only 20 percent of its 1913 levels. Russia was exhausted. As Leon Trotsky said, "the collapse of the productive forces surpassed anything of the kind that history had ever seen. The country, and the government with it, were at the very edge of the abyss."[12]

THE NEW ECONOMIC POLICY

In March 1921, Lenin pulled Russia back from the abyss by aborting war communism in favor of his New Economic Policy (NEP). Lenin's New Economic Policy was a modified version of the old capitalist system. Forced requisitioning of food from the peasants was halted as peasants were now allowed to sell their produce openly. Retail stores as well as small industries that employed fewer than twenty employees could now operate under private ownership, although heavy industry, banking, and mines remained in the hands of the government. Already by 1922, a revived market and good harvest had brought an end to famine; Soviet agriculture climbed to 75 percent of its prewar level. Industry, especially state-owned heavy industry, fared less well and continued to stagnate. Only coal production had reached prewar levels by 1926. Overall, the NEP had saved Communist Russia from complete economic disaster even though Lenin and other leading Communists intended it to be only a temporary, tactical retreat from the goals of communism.

Between 1922 and 1924, Lenin suffered a series of strokes that finally led to his death on January 21, 1924. Although Communist Party rule theoretically rested on a principle of collective leadership, in fact, Lenin had provided an example of one-man rule. His death inaugurated a struggle for power among the members of the Politburo, the institution that had become the leading organ of the party.

In 1924, the Politburo of seven members was severely divided over the future direction of Soviet Russia. The Left, led by Leon Trotsky, wanted to end the NEP and launch Russia on the path of rapid industrialization, primarily at the expense of the peasantry. This same group wanted to carry the revolution on, believing that the survival of the Russian Revolution ultimately depended on the spread of communism abroad. Another group in the Politburo, called the Right, rejected the cause of world revolution and wanted instead to concentrate on constructing a socialist state in Russia. Believing that too rapid industrialization would worsen the living standards of the Soviet peasantry, this group also favored a continuation of Lenin's NEP.

These ideological divisions were underscored by an intense personal rivalry between Leon Trotsky and Joseph Stalin. Trotsky had been a key figure in the success of the Bolshevik Revolution and the Red Army. In 1924, he held the post of commissar of war and was the leading spokesman for the Left in the Politburo. Joseph Stalin (1879–1953) had joined the Bolsheviks in 1903 and had come to Lenin's attention after staging a daring bank robbery to obtain funds for the Bolshevik cause. Stalin, who was neither a dynamic speaker nor a forceful writer, was content to hold the dull bureaucratic job of party general secretary while other Politburo members held party positions that enabled them to display their brilliant oratorical abilities. He was a good organizer (his fellow Bolsheviks called him "Comrade Card-Index"), and the other members of the Politburo soon found that the position of party secretary was really the most important in the party hierarchy. The general secretary appointed the regional, district, city, and town party secretaries. In 1922, for example, Stalin had made some 10,000 appointments, many of them trusted followers whose holding of key positions proved valuable in the struggle for power. Although Stalin at first refused to support either the Left or Right in the Politburo, he finally came to favor the goal of "socialism in one country" rather than world revolution.

Stalin used his post as party general secretary to gain complete control of the Communist Party. Trotsky was expelled from the party in 1927. Eventually, he made his way to Mexico where he was murdered in 1940, no doubt on Stalin's orders. By 1929, Stalin had succeeded in eliminating the Old Bolsheviks of the revolutionary era from the Politburo and establishing a dictatorship so powerful that the Russian tsars of old would have been envious.

THE STALIN ERA, 1929–1939

The Stalinist era marked the beginning of an economic, social, and political revolution that was more sweeping in its results than the revolutions of 1917. Stalin made a significant shift in economic policy in 1928 when he launched his first five-year plan. Its real goal was nothing less than the transformation of Russia from an agricultural country into an industrial state virtually overnight. Instead of consumer goods, the first five-year plan emphasized maximum production of capital goods and armaments and succeeded in quadrupling the production of heavy machinery and doubling oil production. Europe's largest electrical power station was also built during this period. Between 1928 and 1937, during the first two five-year plans, steel production increased from 4 to 18 million tons per year while hard coal output went from 36 to 128 million tons. The annual growth rate of the Soviet Union was between 14 and 20 percent a year, a phenomenal accomplishment. At the same time, new industrial cities, located near iron ore and coal deposits, sprang up overnight in the Urals and Siberia.

The social and political costs of industrialization were enormous. Little provision was made for absorbing the expanded labor force into the cities. While the industrial labor force increased by millions between 1932 and 1940, total investment in housing actually declined after 1929, with the result that millions of workers and their families lived in pitiful conditions. Real wages in industry also declined by 43 percent between 1928 and 1940 while strict laws limited workers' freedom of movement. To inspire and pacify the workers, government propa-

The Formation of Collective Farms

Accompanying the rapid industrialization of the Soviet Union was the collectivization of agriculture, a feat that involved nothing less than transforming Russia's 26 million family farms into 250,000 collective farms (kolkhozes). This selection provides a firsthand account of how the process worked.

Max Belov, *The History of a Collective Farm*

General collectivization in our village was brought about in the following manner: Two representatives of the [Communist] Party arrived in the village. All the inhabitants were summoned by the ringing of the church bell to a meeting at which the policy of general collectivization was announced. . . . The upshot was that although the meeting lasted two days, from the viewpoint of the Party representatives nothing was accomplished.

After this setback the Party representatives divided the village into two sections and worked each one separately. Two more officials were sent to reinforce the first two. A meeting of our section of the village was held in a stable which had previously belonged to a kulak. The meeting dragged on until dark. Suddenly someone threw a brick at the lamp, and in the dark the peasants began to beat the Party representatives who jumped out the window and escaped from the village barely alive. The following day seven people were arrested. The militia was called in and stayed in the village until the peasants, realizing their helplessness, calmed down. . . .

By the end of 1930 there were two kolkhozes in our village. Though at first these collectives embraced at most only 70 percent of the peasant households, in the months that followed they gradually absorbed more and more of them.

In these kolkhozes the great bulk of the land was held and worked communally, but each peasant household owned a house of some sort, a small plot of ground and perhaps some livestock. All the members of the kolkhoz were required to work on the kolkhoz a certain number of days each month; the rest of the time they were allowed to work on their own holdings. They derived their income partly from what they grew on their garden strips and partly from their work in the kolkhoz.

When the harvest was over, and after the farm had met its obligations to the state and to various special funds (for instance, seed, etc.) and had sold on the market whatever undesignated produce was left, the remaining produce and the farm's monetary income were divided among the kolkhoz members according to the number of "labor days" each one had contributed to the farm's work. . . . It was in 1930 that the kolkhoz members first received their portions out of the "communal kettle." After they had received their earnings, at the rate of 1 kilogram of grain and 55 kopecks per labor day, one of them remarked, "You will live, but you will be very, very thin."

In the spring of 1931 a tractor worked the fields of the kolkhoz for the first time. The tractor was "capable of plowing every kind of hard soil and virgin soil," as Party representatives told us at the meeting in celebration of its arrival. The peasants did not then know that these "steel horses" would carry away a good part of the harvest in return for their work. . . .

By late 1932 more than 80 percent of the peasant households . . . had been collectivized. . . . That year the peasants harvested a good crop and had hopes that the calculations would work out to their advantage and would help strengthen them economically. These hopes were in vain. The kolkhoz workers received only 200 grams of flour per labor day for the first half of the year; the remaining grain, including the seed fund, was taken by the government. The peasants were told that industrialization of the country, then in full swing, demanded grain and sacrifices from them.

ganda stressed the need for sacrifice to create the new socialist state. Soviet labor policy stressed high levels of achievement, typified by the Stakhanov cult. Alexei Stakhanov was a coal miner who mined 102 tons of coal in one shift, exceeding the norm by 1,300 percent. He was held up as an example to others.

Rapid industrialization was accompanied by an equally rapid collectivization of agriculture. Almost all of the Bolsheviks had been appalled by one result of Lenin's New Economic Policy, the growth of a class of well-to-do peasant proprietors known as kulaks who employed wage labor. Of the 26 million peasant households in 1929, 2 million were kulaks. It seemed an anomaly to have this capitalist group in the midst of a communist society. To rectify this, Stalin inaugurated a policy of collectivization of agriculture even before he initiated the first five-year plan. Its goal was to eliminate private farms and push people into collective farms (see the box on p. 946). One of its major aims was to stimulate industrial growth through profits from the rural economy.

Initially, Stalin planned to collectivize only the wealthier kulaks, but strong resistance from peasants who hoarded crops and killed livestock led him to step up the program. By 1930, 10 million peasant households had been collectivized; by 1934, Russia's 26 million family farms had been collectivized into 250,000 units. This was done at tremendous cost, since the hoarding of food and the slaughter of livestock produced widespread famine. Stalin himself is supposed to have told Winston Churchill during World War II that 10 million peasants died in the artificially created famines of 1932 and 1933. The only concession Stalin made to the peasants was to allow each household to have one tiny, privately owned garden plot.

Stalin's program of rapid industrialization entailed additional costs as well. To achieve his goals, Stalin strengthened the party bureaucracy under his control. Those who resisted were sent into forced labor camps in

Siberia. Stalin's desire for sole control of decision making also led to purges of the Old Bolsheviks. Between 1936 and 1938, the most prominent Old Bolsheviks were put on trial and condemned to death. During this same time, Stalin undertook a purge of army officers, diplomats, union officials, party members, intellectuals, and numerous ordinary citizens. Estimates are that 8 million Russians were arrested; millions were sent to Siberian forced labor camps, from which they never returned. The Stalinist blood bath made what some

♦ **Stalin Signs a Death Warrant.** Terror played an important role in the authoritarian system established by Joseph Stalin. In this photograph, Stalin is shown signing what is supposedly a death warrant in 1933. As the terror increased in the late 1930s, Stalin signed such lists everyday.

Western intellectuals had hailed as the "New Civilization" much less attractive by the late 1930s.

The Stalin era also reversed much of the permissive social legislation of the early 1920s. Advocating complete equality of rights for women, the Communists had made divorce and abortion easy to obtain while also encouraging women to work outside the home and liberate themselves sexually. After Stalin came to power, the family was praised as a miniature collective in which parents were responsible for inculcating values of duty, discipline, and hard work. Abortion was outlawed while divorced fathers who did not support their children were fined heavily. The new divorce law of June 1936 imposed fines for repeated divorces.

Authoritarianism in Eastern Europe

A number of other states in Europe were not totalitarian but did possess conservative authoritarian governments. These states adopted some of the trappings of totalitarian states, especially their wide police powers, but their greatest concern was not the creation of a mass movement aimed at the establishment of a new kind of society, but rather the defense of the existing social order. Consequently, the authoritarian states tended to limit the participation of the masses and were content with passive obedience rather than active involvement in the goals of the regime. A number of states in eastern Europe adopted this kind of authoritarian government.

Nowhere had the map of Europe been more drastically altered by World War I than in eastern Europe. The new states of Austria, Poland, Czechoslovakia, and Yugoslavia (known as the kingdom of the Serbs, Croats, and Slovenes until 1929) adopted parliamentary systems while the preexisting kingdoms of Romania and Bulgaria gained new parliamentary constitutions in 1920. Greece became a republic in 1924. Hungary's government was parliamentary in form, but controlled by its landed aristocrats. At the beginning of the 1920s, political democracy seemed well established, but almost everywhere in eastern Europe, parliamentary governments soon gave way to authoritarian regimes.

Several problems helped to create this situation. Eastern European states had little tradition of liberalism or parliamentary politics and no substantial middle class to support them. Then, too, these states were largely rural and agrarian in character. While many of the peasants were largely illiterate, much of the land was still dominated by large landowners who feared the growth of agrarian peasant parties with their schemes for land redistribution. Ethnic conflicts also threatened to tear these countries apart. Fearful of land reform, communist agrarian upheaval, and ethnic conflict, powerful landowners, the churches, and even some members of the small middle class looked to authoritarian governments to maintain the old system.

Already in the 1920s, some eastern European states began to move away from political democracy toward authoritarian structures. Poland established an authoritarian regime in 1926 when Marshal Joseph Pilsudski created a military dictatorship. King Alexander I (1921–1934) abolished the constitution and imposed a royal dictatorship on Yugoslavia in 1929. King Boris III (1918–1943) established an authoritarian regime in Bulgaria in 1923.

During the 1930s, all of the remaining parliamentary regimes (except Czechoslovakia) succumbed to authoritarianism. No doubt, the Great Depression was a crucial factor in this development. The collapse of farm prices worldwide in the late 1920s adversely affected a region so agrarian as eastern Europe. Eastern European states were increasingly attracted to the authoritarian examples of Fascist Italy and Nazi Germany.

Although Admiral Miklós Horthy had ruled Hungary as "regent" since 1919, the appointment of Julius Gömbös as prime minister in 1932 brought Hungary even closer to Italy and Germany. In Austria, the Christian Socialist chancellor Engelbert Dollfuss used the armed forces to crush the Social Democrats and create his own brand of authoritarian state, a Christian Corporate State. Romania witnessed the development of a strong fascist movement led by Corneliu Codreanu. Known as the Legion of the Archangel Michael, it possessed its own paramilitary squad called the Iron Guard. As Codreanu's fascist movement grew and became Romania's third largest political party, King Carol II (1930–1940) responded in 1938 by ending parliamentary rule, crushing the leadership of the legion, and imposing authoritarian rule. At the beginning of World War II, General Ian Antonescu seized power and established his own military dictatorship in Romania. In Greece, General John Metaxas imposed a dictatorship in 1936. The new Baltic republics of Lithuania, Latvia, and Estonia also succumbed to dictatorial governments after brief experiments with democracy.

Only Czechoslovakia, with its substantial middle class, liberal tradition, and strong industrial base, maintained its political democracy. Thomas Masaryk, an able and fair leader who served as president from 1918 to

1935, was able to maintain an uneasy but stable alliance of reformist socialists, agrarians, and Catholics.

Dictatorship in the Iberian Peninsula

Parliamentary regimes also failed to survive in both Spain and Portugal. Both countries were largely agrarian, illiterate, and dominated by powerful landlords and Catholic clergy.

Spain's parliamentary monarchy was unable to deal with the social tensions generated by the industrial boom and inflation that accompanied World War I. Supported by King Alfonso XIII (1886–1931), General Miguel Primo de Rivera led a successful military coup in September 1923 and created a personal dictatorship that lasted until 1930. But a faltering economy because of the Great Depression led to the collapse of Primo de Rivera's regime in January 1930 as well as to a widespread lack of support for the monarchy. King Alfonso XIII left Spain in 1931, and a new Spanish Republic was instituted, governed by a coalition of democrats and reformist socialists. Political turmoil ensued as control of the government passed from leftists to rightists until a Popular Front, an antifascist coalition composed of democrats, socialists, and the revolutionary left, took over in 1936. The Popular Front was unacceptable, however, to senior army officers. Led by General Francisco Franco (1892–1975), Spanish military forces revolted against the government and inaugurated a brutal and bloody civil war that lasted three years.

Foreign intervention complicated the Spanish Civil War. The Popular Front was assisted by trucks, planes, tanks, and military advisers from the Soviet Union and 40,000 volunteers from other countries, while Franco's forces were aided by arms, money, and men from the fascist regimes of Italy and Germany. Hitler used the Spanish Civil War as an opportunity to test the new weaponry of his revived air force. Gradually, Franco's forces wore down the Popular Front, and after the capture of Madrid on March 28, 1939, the Spanish Civil War finally came to an end.

General Francisco Franco soon established a dictatorship that lasted until his death in 1975. It was not a fascist government, although it was unlikely to oppose the Fascists in Italy or the Nazis in Germany. The fascist movement in Spain, known as the Falange and led by José Antonio Primo de Rivera, son of the former dictator, contributed little to Franco's success and played a minor role in the new regime. Franco's government,

which favored large landowners, businessmen, and the Catholic clergy, was yet another example of a traditional, conservative, authoritarian regime.

In 1910, the Portuguese had overthrown their monarchy and established a republic. Severe inflation after World War I, however, undermined support for the republic and helped to intensify political instability. In 1926, a group of army officers seized power, and by the early 1930s, the military junta's finance minister, Antonio Salazar (1889–1970), had become the strong man of the regime. Salazar controlled the Portuguese government for the next forty years.

The Expansion of Mass Culture and Mass Leisure

Technological innovations continued to have profound effects upon European society. Nowhere is this more evident than in mass culture and mass leisure. The mass

distribution of commercialized popular forms of entertainment had a profound effect on European society.

Radio and Movies

A series of technological inventions in the late nineteenth century had prepared the way for a revolution in
mass communications. Especially important was Marconi's discovery of "wireless" radio waves. But it was not
until June 16, 1920, that a radio broadcast (of a concert
by soprano Nellie Melba from London) for a mass
audience was attempted. Permanent broadcasting facilities were then constructed in the United States, Europe,
and Japan during 1921 and 1922, while mass production
of radios (receiving sets) also began. In 1926, when the
British Broadcasting Corporation (BBC) was made into
a public corporation, there were 2.2 million radios in
Great Britain. By the end of the 1930s, there were 9
million. Although broadcasting networks in the United
States were privately owned and financed by advertising,
those in Europe were usually controlled by the government.

The technical foundation for motion pictures had
already been developed in the 1890s when short moving
pictures were produced as novelties for music halls.
Shortly before World War I, full-length features, such as
the Italian film *Quo Vadis* and the American film *Birth of
a Nation*, became available and made it apparent that
cinema had created a new form of mass entertainment.
By 1939, about 40 percent of adults in the more
advanced industrial countries were attending a movie
once a week. That figure increased to 60 percent by the
end of World War II.

Mass forms of communication and entertainment
were, of course, not new. But the increased size of
audiences and the ability of radio and cinema, unlike
the printed word, to provide an immediate mass experience did add new dimensions to mass culture. Of course,
radio and movies could be used for political purposes.
Hitler had said, "without motor-cars, sound films, and
wireless, no victory of National Socialism." Radio
seemed to offer great opportunities for reaching the
masses, especially when it became apparent that the
emotional harangues of an Adolf Hitler had just as
much impact on people when heard on radio as in
person. The Nazi regime encouraged radio listening by
urging manufacturers to produce cheap radios that could
be bought on installment plans. The Nazis also erected
loudspeaker pillars in the streets to encourage communal
radio listening, especially to radio broadcasts of mass
meetings.

Film, too, had propaganda potential, a possibility not
lost on Joseph Goebbels (1897–1945), the propaganda
minister of Nazi Germany. Believing that film constituted one of the "most modern and scientific means of
influencing the masses," Goebbels created a special film
section in his Propaganda Ministry and encouraged the
production of both documentaries and popular feature
films that carried the Nazi message. *The Triumph of the
Will*, for example, was a documentary of the 1934
Nuremberg party rally that forcefully conveyed the
power of National Socialism to viewers. Both Fascist
Italy and Nazi Germany controlled and exploited the
content of newsreels.

Mass Leisure

Mass leisure activities had developed at the turn of the
century, but new work patterns after World War I
dramatically expanded the amount of free time available
to take advantage of them. By 1920, the eight-hour day
had become the norm for many office and factory
workers in northern and western Europe.

Professional sporting events for mass audiences became an especially important aspect of mass leisure.
Attendance at association football (soccer) games increased dramatically while the inauguration of the
World Cup contest in 1930 added to the nationalistic
rivalries that began to surround such mass sporting
events. Increased attendance also made the 1920s and
1930s a great era of stadium building. For the 1936
Olympics, the Germans built a stadium in Berlin that
seated 140,000 people. Strahav Stadium in Prague held
240,000 spectators for gymnastics and track meets. As
the popularity of mass spectator sports grew, so too did
the amount of money spent on betting.

Travel opportunities also added new dimensions to
mass leisure activities. The military use of aircraft during
World War I helped to improve planes and make
civilian air travel a reality. The first regular international
air mail service began in 1919, and regular passenger
service soon followed. Although air travel remained the
preserve of the wealthy or the adventurous, trains, buses,
and private cars made excursions to beaches or holiday
resorts more and more popular and affordable. Beaches,
such as the one at Brighton in Great Britain, were
increasingly mobbed by crowds of people from all social
classes.

Mass leisure provided totalitarian regimes with new
ways to control their populations. Mussolini's Italy created the *Dopolavoro* (Afterwork) as a vast national
recreation agency. The *Dopolavoro* was responsible for

establishing clubhouses with libraries, radios, and athletic facilities in virtually every town and village. In some places, they included auditoriums for plays and films and travel agencies that arranged tours, cruises, and resort vacations on the Adriatic at reduced rates. *Dopolavoro* groups introduced many Italians to various facets of mass culture and mass leisure with activities such as band concerts, movies, choral groups, roller skating, and ballroom dancing. Essentially, the *Dopolavoro* enabled the Italian government to provide, but also to supervise, recreational activities. By doing so, the state imposed new rules and regulations on previously spontaneous activities, thus breaking down old group solidarities and enabling these groups to be guided by the goals of the state.

The Nazi regime adopted a program similar to the *Dopolavoro* in its *Kraft durch Freude* (Strength through Joy). The purpose of the *Kraft durch Freude* was to coordinate the free time of the working class by offering a variety of leisure time activities, including concerts, operas, films, guided tours, and sporting events (see the box on p. 952). Especially popular were the inexpensive vacations, essentially the modern package tour. This could be a cruise to Scandinavia or the Mediterranean or, more likely for workers, a shorter trip to various sites in Germany. Only 130,000 workers took cruises in 1938, compared with the 7 million who took short trips.

More and more, mass culture and mass leisure had the effect of expanding the homogeneity of national populations, a process that had begun in the nineteenth century with the development of the national state. Local popular culture was increasingly replaced by national and even international culture as new forms of mass production and consumption brought similar styles of clothing and fashion to people throughout Europe.

Cultural and Intellectual Trends in the Interwar Years

The artistic and intellectual innovations of the pre–World War I period, which had shocked many Europeans, had been the preserve primarily of a small group of avant-garde artists and intellectuals. In the 1920s and 1930s, they became more widespread as artists and

♦ **New Patterns of Recreation: The Ford Model T.** Mass leisure activities expanded between the wars as new work patterns increased the free time available to members of the working class. For the middle classes, mass-produced automobiles, such as the American Ford Model T, made possible a new freedom of movement.

Mass Leisure: Strength through Joy

In November 1933, the German Labor Front established an organization called Kraft durch Freude (Strength through Joy), whose purpose was to organize the leisure time of workers in the interests of the Nazi regime. These excerpts are taken from the reports of the Social Democratic Party's contact men in Germany and give a fairly accurate account of the attitudes of the German workers toward the Kraft durch Freude (KdF) program.

The SOPADE [Social Democratic Party in Exile] Reports
Central Germany, *April 1939*

While Beauty of Labor [another Labor Front organization] makes no impressions whatsoever ... Strength through Joy is not without impact. However, workers' wages are only barely sufficient for essentials and nobody can afford a trip to Madeira, 150 Reichsmarks per person—300 RM with the wife. Even the shorter trips produce so many additional expenses that they often double the cost. But some people like them nonetheless. Anybody who has never made a trip in his life and sees the sea for the first time is much impressed. The effect is: "The Nazis have done some good things after all." The enthusiasm is, however, greater on the first trip. On the second, many are put off by the crowds.

Berlin, *February 1938*

Strength through Joy is very popular. The events appeal to the yearning of the little man who wants an opportunity to get out and about himself and to take part in the pleasures of the "top people." It is a clever appeal to the petty bourgeois inclinations of the unpolitical workers. For such a man it really means something to have been on a trip to Scandinavia, or even if he only went to the Black Forest or the Harz Mountains, he imagines that he has thereby climbed up a rung on the social ladder.

Bavaria, *April 1939*

On the group tours there is a sharp social differentiation. The "top people" only go on big trips where there will be a more select clientele. The big mass trips are for the proletariat. People now look for places where there are no KdF visitors. "Not visited by KdF" is now a particular asset for summer vacations. A landlord in a mountain village in Upper Bavaria wrote in his prospects: "Not visited by KdF tourists." The Labor Front, which was sent the prospectus by someone, took the landlord to court. He had to withdraw the prospectus and was not allowed to receive summer guests. Nevertheless, information about summer Pensions [boardinghouses] which are not used by KdF is becoming more and more widespread.

---

intellectuals continued to work out the implications of the ideas developed before 1914. But what made the prewar avant-garde culture acceptable in the 1920s and the 1930s? Perhaps the most important factor was the impact of World War I.

The optimistic liberal-rationalist clichés that many Europeans had taken for granted before 1914 seemed hopelessly outdated in 1918. Four years of devastating war left many Europeans with a profound sense of despair and disillusionment. World War I indicated to many people that something was dreadfully wrong with Western values. In his *Decline of the West*, the German writer Oswald Spengler (1880–1936) reflected the disillusionment when he emphasized the decadence of Western civilization and posited its collapse. To many people, the experiences of World War I seemed to confirm the prewar avant-garde belief that human beings were really violent and irrational animals who were incapable of creating a sane and rational world. The

Great Depression of the late 1920s and early 1930s, as well as the growth of fascist movements based on violence and the degradation of individual rights, only added to the uncertainties generated by World War I. The crisis of confidence in Western civilization indeed ran deep and was well captured in the words of the French poet Paul Valéry in the early 1920s:

> The storm has died away, and still we are restless, uneasy, as if the storm were about to break. Almost all the affairs of men remain in a terrible uncertainty. We think of what has disappeared, and we are almost destroyed by what has been destroyed; we do not know what will be born, and we fear the future. . . . Doubt and disorder are in us and with us. There is no thinking man, however shrewd or learned he may be, who can hope to dominate this anxiety, to escape from this impression of darkness.[13]

Political, economic, and social uncertainties were paralleled by intellectual uncertainties, which were quite evident in the cultural and intellectual achievements of the interwar years.

Nightmares and New Visions: Art and Music

Postwar artistic trends were largely a working out of the implications of prewar developments. Abstract Expressionism, for example, became ever more popular as many pioneering artists of the early twentieth century matured between the two world wars. In addition, prewar fascination with the absurd and the unconscious contents of the mind seemed even more appropriate after the nightmare landscapes of World War I battlefronts. This gave rise to both the Dada movement and Surrealism.

Dadaism attempted to enshrine the purposelessness of life (see the box on p. 954). Revolted by the insanity of life, the Dadaists tried to give it expression by creating anti-art. The 1918 Berlin Dada Manifesto maintained that "Dada is the international expression of our times, the great rebellion of artistic movements." In the hands of Hannah Höch (1889–1978), Dada became an instrument to comment on women's roles in the new mass culture. Höch was the only woman member of the Berlin Dada Club, which featured the use of photomontage. Her work was part of the first Dada show in Berlin in 1920. In *Dada Dance,* she seemed to criticize the "new woman" by making fun of the way women were inclined to follow new fashion styles. In other works, however, she created positive images of the modern woman and expressed a keen interest in new freedoms for women.

Perhaps more important as an artistic movement was Surrealism, which sought a reality beyond the material, sensible world and found it in the world of the unconscious through the portrayal of fantasies, dreams, or nightmares. Employing logic to portray the illogical, the Surrealists created disturbing and evocative images. The Spaniard Salvador Dali (1904–1989) became the high priest of Surrealism and in his mature phase became a master of representational Surrealism. In *The Persistence of Memory,* Dali portrayed recognizable objects that have nevertheless been divorced from their normal context. By placing these objects into unrecognizable relationships, Dali created a disturbing world in which the irrational had become tangible.

The move to functionalism in modern architecture also became more widespread in the 1920s and 1930s. First conceived near the end of the nineteenth century, functionalism meant that buildings, like the products of machines, should be "functional" or useful, fulfilling the

◆ **Hannah Höch, *Cut with the Kitchen Knife Dada through the Last Weimar Beer Belly Cultural Epoch of Germany.*** Hannah Höch, a prominent figure in the postwar Dada movement, used photomontage to create images that reflected on women's issues. In *Cut with the Kitchen Knife,* she combined pictures of Germany political leaders with sports stars, Dada artists, and scenes from urban life. One major theme emerged: the confrontation between the anti-Dada world of German political leaders and the Dada world of revolutionary ideals. Höch associated women with Dada and the new world.

purpose for which they were constructed. Art and engineering were to be unified, and all unnecessary ornamentation was to be stripped away.

The United States was a leader in these pioneering architectural designs. Unprecedented urban growth and the absence of restrictive architectural traditions allowed for new building methods, especially in the relatively "new city" of Chicago. The Chicago school of the 1890s, led by Louis H. Sullivan (1856–1924), used reinforced concrete, steel frames, and electric elevators

The Voice of Dadaism

The Dadaists attempted to give expression to what they saw as the meaninglessness and absurdity of life. In this excerpt, Tristan Tzara (1896–1945), a Romanian-French poet and one of the founders of Dadaism, expressed the Dadaist contempt for the Western tradition.

Tristan Tzara, "Lecture on Dada," 1922

I know that you have come here today to hear explanations. Well, don't expect to hear any explanations about Dada. You explain to me why you exist. You haven't the faintest idea. . . .

The acts of life have no beginning or end. Everything happens in a completely idiotic way. That is why everything is alike. Simplicity is called Dada. . . .

The beginnings of Dada were not the beginnings of an art, but of a disgust. Disgust with the magnificence of philosophers who for 3000 years have been explaining everything to us (what for?), disgust with the pretensions of these artists—God's-representatives-on-earth, . . . disgust with a false form of domination and restriction *en masse*, that accentuates rather than appeases man's instinct of domination, disgust with . . . the false prophets who are nothing but a front for the interests of money, pride, disease.

Dada is a state of mind. . . . Dada applies itself to everything, and yet it is nothing, it is the point where the yes and the no and all the opposites meet, not solemnly in the castles of human philosophies, but very simply at street corners, like dogs and grasshoppers.

Like everything in life, Dada is useless.

Dada is without pretension, as life should be.

---

to build skyscrapers virtually free of external ornamentation. One of Sullivan's most successful pupils was Frank Lloyd Wright (1869–1959), who became known for innovative designs in domestic architecture. Wright's private houses, build chiefly for wealthy patrons, featured geometric structures with long lines, overhanging roofs, and severe planes of brick and stone. The interiors were open spaced and included cathedral ceilings and built-in furniture and lighting fixtures. Wright pioneered the modern American house.

Especially important in the spread of functionalism was the Bauhaus school of art, architecture, and design,

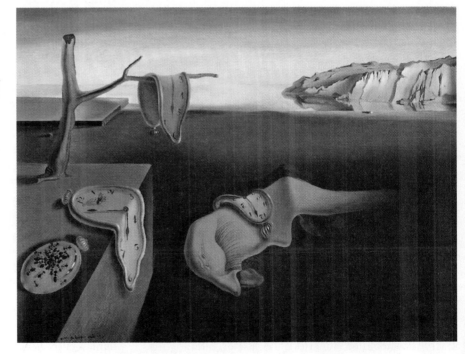

◆ **Salvador Dali, *The Persistence of Memory*, 1931.** Surrealism was another important artistic movement between the wars. Influenced by the theories of Freudian psychology, Surrealists sought to reveal the world of the unconscious, or the "greater reality" that they believed existed beyond the world of physical appearances. As is evident in this painting, Salvador Dali sought to portray the world of dreams by painting recognizable objects in unrecognizable relationships.

founded in 1919 at Weimar, Germany, by the Berlin architect Walter Gropius (1883–1969). The Bauhaus teaching staff consisted of architects, artists, and designers who worked together to blend the study of fine arts (painting and sculpture) with the applied arts (printing, weaving, and furniture making). Gropius urged his followers to foster a new union of arts and crafts to create the buildings and objects of the future. Gropius's own buildings were often unornamented steel boxes with walls of windows, reflecting his belief that the "sensibility of the artist must be combined with the knowledge of the technician to create new forms in architecture and design."

Important to the development of artistic expression between the wars was the search for a new popular audience. To attract a wider audience, artists and musicians began to involve themselves in the new mass culture. The German Kurt Weill, for example, had been a struggling composer of classical music before he turned to jazz rhythms and other popular musical idioms for the music for *The Threepenny Opera*. Some artists even regarded art as a means to transform society and located their studios in poor, working-class neighborhoods. Walter Gropius envisioned the Bauhaus as a means to "achieve the reunion of all forms and creative work" and thereby create a new civilization. Theater proved especially attractive as postwar artists sought to make an impact on popular audiences. The German director Erwin Piscator began his directing career by offering plays to workers on picket lines. Piscator hoped to reach workers by experimental drama with political messages. Like many other artists, however, he became frustrated by his failure to achieve a mass audience.

The postwar acceptance of modern art forms was by no means universal. Many traditionalists denounced what they considered the degeneracy and decadence in the arts. Nowhere was this more evident than in the totalitarian states of Nazi Germany and the Soviet Union.

In the 1920s, Weimar, Germany was one of the chief European centers for modern arts and sciences. Hitler and the Nazis rejected modern art as "degenerate" or "Jewish" art. In an address at the premiere of the Great German Art Exhibition in the newly opened House of German Art in July 1937, Hitler proclaimed:

> The people regarded this art [modern art] as the outcome of an impudent and unashamed arrogance or of a simply shocking lack of skill; it felt that . . . these achievements which might have been produced by untalented children

✦ **Walter Gropius, The Bauhaus.** Walter Gropius was one of Europe's pioneers in modern architecture. When the Bauhaus moved to Dessau in 1925, Gropius designed a building for its activities. His straightforward use of steel, reinforced concrete, and rows of windows reflects the move to functionalism in modern architecture.

of from eight to ten years old—could never be valued as an expression of our own times or of the German future.[14]

Hitler and the Nazis believed that they had laid the foundation for a new and genuine German art, which would glorify the strong, the healthy, and the heroic—all supposedly attributes of the Aryan race. The new German art was actually the old nineteenth-century genre art with its emphasis on realistic scenes of everyday life.

So, too, was the art produced by the school of "socialist realism" in the Soviet Union. After the bold experimentalism of the 1920s, the Stalinist era imposed a stifling uniformity on artistic creativity. Like German painting, Soviet painting was expected to focus on a nineteenth-century pictorial style aimed at realistic presentation. Both the new German art and "socialist realism" were intended to inculcate social values useful to the ruling regimes.

At the beginning of the twentieth century, a revolution in music parallel to the revolution in art had begun with the work of Igor Stravinsky (see Chapter 25). But Stravinsky still wrote music in a definite key. The Viennese composer Arnold Schönberg (1874–1951) began to experiment with a radically new style by creating musical pieces in which tonality is completely abandoned, a system that he called atonal music. Since the use of traditional forms was virtually impossible in atonal music, Schönberg created a new system of composition—twelve-tone composition—in which he used a scale composed of twelve notes independent of any tonal key.

Schönberg's atonal music, which grew out of a quarter century of experimentation, was closely akin to abstract painting. While the latter arranged colors and lines without reference to concrete images, so atonal music organized sounds without making recognizable harmonies. Resistance to modern music was even greater than to modern painting, and it did not begin to win favor until after World War II.

The Search for the Unconscious

The interest in the unconscious, evident in Surrealism, was also apparent in the new literary techniques that emerged in the 1920s. One of its most apparent manifestations was in the "stream of consciousness" technique in which the writer presented an interior monologue or a report of the innermost thoughts of each character. The most famous example of this genre was written by the Irish exile James Joyce (1882–1941). His *Ulysses,* published in 1922, told the story of one day in the life of ordinary people in Dublin by following the flow of their inner dialogue. Disconnected ramblings and veiled allusions pervade Joyce's work.

The German writer Hermann Hesse (1877–1962) dealt with the unconscious in a considerably different fashion. His novels reflected the influence of both Carl Jung's psychological theories (see the next section) and Eastern religions and focused among other things on the spiritual loneliness of modern human beings in a mechanized urban society. *Demian* was a psychoanalytic study of incest while *Steppenwolf* mirrored the psychological confusion of modern existence. Hesse's novels made a large impact on German youth in the 1920s. He won the Nobel Prize for literature in 1946.

The growing concern with the unconscious also led to greater popular interest in psychology. The full impact of Sigmund Freud's thought was not felt until after World War I. The 1920s witnessed a worldwide acceptance of his ideas. Freudian terms, such as unconscious, repression, id, ego, and Oedipus complex, entered the popular vocabulary. Popularization of Freud's ideas led to the widespread misconception that an uninhibited sex life was necessary for a healthy mental life. Despite such misconceptions, psychoanalysis did develop into a major profession, especially in the United States. But Freud's ideas did not go unchallenged, even by his own pupils. One of the most prominent challenges came from Carl Jung.

A disciple of Freud, Carl Jung (1856–1961) came to believe that Freud's theories were too narrow and based on Freud's own personal biases. Jung's study of dreams—his own and others—led him to diverge sharply from Freud. Whereas for Freud the unconscious was the seat of repressed desires or appetites, for Jung, it was an opening to deep spiritual needs and ever-greater vistas for humans. Two concepts were particularly important to his theories: the process of individuation and collective unconscious.

Jung believed that a person's dreams are linked together in some arrangement or pattern, which he called "the process of individuation." Only by examining one's dreams over a long period of time could a person see the pattern. He or she would then be able to understand the process of psychic growth or individuation as the mature personality emerges. The organizing center of the mind from which all this came was the "self," the whole psyche, rather than the ego. The general function of dreams, then, was to bring people back to the center, thereby restoring their psychological balance.

Jung viewed the unconscious as twofold: a "personal unconscious" and a "collective unconscious," which existed at a deeper level of the unconscious. The collective unconscious was the repository of memories that all human beings share and consisted of archetypes, mental forms or images that appear in dreams. The archetypes are not derived from the individual's experience, however, but from the biological, prehistoric, and unconscious development of mind. They are common to all people and have a special energy that creates myths, religions, and philosophies. To Jung, the archetypes proved that mind was only in part personal or individual because their origin was buried so far in the past that they seemed to have no human source. Their function was to bring the original mind of humans into a new, higher state of consciousness.

The "Heroic Age of Physics"

The prewar revolution in physics initiated by Max Planck and Albert Einstein continued in the interwar period. In fact, Ernest Rutherford (1871–1937), one of the physicists responsible for demonstrating that the atom could be split, dubbed the 1920s the "heroic age of physics." By the early 1940s, seven subatomic particles had been distinguished, and a sufficient understanding of the potential of the atom had been achieved to lay the foundations for the development of the atomic bomb.

The new picture of the universe that was unfolding continued to undermine the old scientific certainties of classical physics. Classical physics had rested on the fundamental belief that all phenomena could be predicted if they could be completely understood; thus, the weather could be accurately predicted if we only knew everything about the wind, sun, and water. In 1927, the German physicist Werner Heisenberg (1901–1976) upset this belief when he posited the "uncertainty principle." In essence, Heisenberg argued that no one could determine the path of an electron because the very act of observing the electron with light affected the electron's location. The "uncertainty principle" was more than an explanation for the path of an electron, however; it was a new worldview. Heisenberg shattered confidence in predictability and dared to propose that uncertainty was at the bottom of all physical laws.

Conclusion

The devastation wrought by World War I destroyed the liberal optimism of the prewar era. Yet many in the 1920s still hoped that the progress of Western civilization, so seemingly evident before 1914, could somehow be restored. These hopes proved largely unfounded as plans for economic reconstruction gave way to inflation and to an even more devastating Great Depression at the end of the 1920s. Likewise, confidence in political democracy was soon shattered by the rise of authoritarian governments that not only restricted individual freedoms but, in the cases of Italy, Germany, and the Soviet Union, sought even greater control over the lives of their subjects in order to manipulate and guide them to achieve the goals of their totalitarian regimes. For many people, despite the loss of personal freedom, these mass movements at least offered some sense of security in a world that seemed fraught with uncertainties.

But the seeming security of these mass movements gave rise to even greater uncertainties as Europeans, after a brief twenty-year interlude of peace, once again plunged into war, this time on a scale even more horrendous than that of World War I. The twentieth-century crisis, begun in 1914, seemed only to be worsening in 1939.

NOTES

1. Quoted in Robert Paxton, *Europe in the Twentieth Century*, 2d ed. (New York, 1985), p. 237.
2. Quoted in Denis Mack Smith, *Mussolini* (New York, 1982), p. 51.
3. Benito Mussolini, "The Doctrine of Fascism," in Adrian Lyttleton, ed., *Italian Fascisms from Pareto to Gentile* (London, 1973), p. 42.
4. Quoted in Edward Tannenbaum, *The Fascist Experience: Italian Society and Culture, 1922–1945* (New York, 1972), p. 170.
5. Quoted in Alexander De Grand, "Women under Italian Fascism," *Historical Journal* 19 (1976): 958–59.
6. Adolf Hitler, *Mein Kampf*, trans. Ralph Manheim (Boston, 1943), p. 22.
7. Ibid., p. 161.
8. Quoted in Joachim Fest, *Hitler*, trans. Richard and Clara Winston (New York, 1974), p. 241.
9. Quoted in Jeremy Noakes and Geoffrey Pridham, eds., *Nazism, 1919–1945* (Exeter, 1983), 1:50–51.
10. Quoted in Jackson Spielvogel, *Hitler and Nazi Germany: A History*, 3d ed. (Englewood Cliffs, N.J., 1996), p. 66.
11. Quoted in Fest, *Hitler*, p. 418.
12. Irving Howe, ed., *The Basic Writings of Trotsky* (London, 1963), p. 162.
13. Paul Valéry, *Variety*, trans. Malcolm Cowley (New York, 1927), pp. 27–28.
14. Norman H. Baynes, ed., *The Speeches of Adolf Hitler, 1922–1939* (Oxford, 1942), 1:591.

SUGGESTIONS FOR FURTHER READING

For a general introduction to the interwar period, see R. J. Sontag, *A Broken World, 1919–39* (New York, 1971); and the general survey by R. Paxton, *Europe in the Twentieth Century*, 2d ed. (New York, 1985). On European security issues after the Peace of Paris, see S. Marks, *The Illusion of Peace: Europe's International Relations, 1918–1933* (New York, 1976). The Locarno agreements have been well examined in J. Jacobson, *Locarno Diplomacy* (Princeton, N.J., 1972). The best study on the problem of reparations is now M. Trachtenberg, *Reparations in World Politics* (New York, 1980), which paints a positive view of French policies. The "return to normalcy" after the war is analyzed in C. S. Maier, *Recasting Bourgeois Europe: Stabilization in France, Germany, and Italy in the Decade after World War I* (Princeton, N.J., 1975). Also valuable is D. P. Silverman, *Reconstructing Europe after the Great War* (Cambridge, Mass., 1982). On the Great Depression, see C. P. Kindleberger, *The World in Depression, 1929–39*, rev. ed. (Berkeley, 1986).

The best biography of Mussolini is now D. Mack Smith, *Mussolini* (New York, 1982). Two brief, but excellent surveys of Fascist Italy are A. Cassels, *Fascist Italy*, 2d ed. (Arlington Heights, Ill., 1985); and A. De Grand, *Italian Fascism* (Lincoln, Neb., 1982). An excellent reference guide for all aspects of Fascist Italy is P. Cannistraro, ed., *Historical Dictionary of Fascist Italy* (Westport, Conn., 1982). On propaganda and other aspects of cultural life in Fascist Italy, see E. R. Tannenbaum, *The Fascist Experience: Italian Society and Culture, 1922–1945* (New York, 1972).

Two brief but sound surveys of Nazi Germany are J. Spielvogel, *Hitler and Nazi Germany: A History*, 3d ed. (Englewood Cliffs, N.J., 1996); and J. Bendersky, *A History of Nazi Germany* (Chicago, 1985). A more detailed examination can be found in K. Bracher, *The German Dictatorship: The Origins, Structure, and Effects of National Socialism* (New York, 1970). The best biographies of Hitler are A. Bullock, *Hitler: A Study in Tyranny* (New York, 1964); and J. Fest, *Hitler*, trans. R. and C. Winston (New York, 1974). A good regional study of the Nazi Party's rise to power is W. S. Allen's "classic" *The Nazi Seizure of Power: The Experience of a Single*

German Town, rev. ed. (New York, 1984). On the SA, see P. Merkl, *The Making of a Stormtrooper* (Princeton, N.J., 1980). On the Nazi administration of the state, see M. Broszat, *The Hitler State: The Foundations and Development of the Internal Structure of the Third Reich* (New York, 1981). A brief perspective on Germany's economic recovery can be found in R. J. Overy, *The Nazi Economic Recovery, 1932–1938* (London, 1982). Basic studies of the SS include R. Koehl, *The Black Corps: The Structure and Power Struggles of the Nazi SS* (Madison, Wis., 1983); and H. Krausnick and M. Broszat, *Anatomy of the SS State* (London, 1970). On women, see J. Stephenson, *Women in Nazi Society* (London, 1975); and C. Koonz, *Mothers in the Fatherland: Women, the Family, and Nazi Politics* (New York, 1987). The Hitler Youth is examined in H. W. Koch, *The Hitler Youth* (New York, 1976). The books on the Holocaust cited in Chapter 28 contain background information on Nazi anti-Jewish policies between 1933 and 1939. The importance of racial ideology in Nazi Germany is evident in R. Proctor, *Racial Hygiene: Medicine under the Nazis* (Cambridge, Mass., 1988).

For a general study of other fascist movements, see S. Payne, *A History of Fascism* (Madison, Wis. 1996). Starting points for the study of eastern Europe are J. Rothschild, *East Central Europe between the Two World Wars* (New York, 1974); and B. Jelavich, *History of the Balkans*, vol. 2: *The Twentieth Century* (New York, 1983). On Franco, see J. W. D. Trythall, *El Caudillo: A Political Biography* (New York, 1970). On the Spanish Civil War, see S. G. Payne, *The Spanish Revolution* (New York, 1970); and H. Thomas, *The Spanish Civil War*, rev. ed. (New York, 1977).

On Russia in the 1920s, see S. F. Cohen, *Bukharin and the Bolshevik Revolution: A Political Biography, 1888–1938* (New York, 1973). The collectivization of agriculture is examined in R. W. Davies, *The Socialist Offensive: The Collectivization of Soviet Agriculture, 1929–30* (Cambridge, Mass., 1980); Industrialization is covered in H. Kuromiya, *Stalin's Industrial Revolution: Politics and Workers, 1928–1932* (New York, 1988). Stalin's purges are examined in R. Conquest, *The Great Terror: Stalin's Purge of the Thirties*, rev. ed. (New York, 1973). For a biography of Stalin, see I. Deutscher, *Stalin*, 2d ed. (New York, 1967); and the more recent R. H. McNeal, *Stalin: Man and Ruler* (New York, 1988).

The use of cinema for propaganda purposes is well examined in D. Welch, *Propaganda and the German Cinema* (New York, 1985). The organization of leisure time in Fascist Italy is thoughtfully discussed in V. De Grazia, *The Culture of Consent: Mass Organization of Leisure in Fascist Italy* (New York, 1981). On the cultural and intellectual environment of Weimar Germany, see W. Laqueur, *Weimar: A Cultural History* (New York, 1974); and P. Gay, *Weimar Culture: The Outsider as Insider* (New York, 1968). For a study of Carl Jung, see G. Wehr, *Jung: A Biography* (New York, 1987).

CHAPTER
28

The Deepening of the European Crisis: World War II

On February 3, 1933, only four days after he had been appointed chancellor of Germany, Adolf Hitler met secretly with Germany's leading generals. He revealed to them his desire to remove the "cancer of democracy," create a new authoritarian leadership, and forge a new domestic unity. All Germans would need to realize that "only a struggle can save us and that everything else must be subordinated to this idea." Youth especially must be trained and their wills strengthened "to fight with all means." Since Germany's living space was too small for its people, above all, Hitler said, Germany must rearm and prepare for "the conquest of new living space in the east and its ruthless Germanization." Even before he had consolidated his power, Hitler had a clear vision of his goals, and their implementation meant another European war. World War II was clearly Hitler's war. Although other countries may have helped to make the war possible by not resisting Hitler's Germany earlier, it was Nazi Germany's actions that made World War II inevitable.

World War II was more than just Hitler's war, however. This chapter will focus on the European theater of war, but both European and American armies were also involved in fighting around the world. World War II consisted of two conflicts: one provoked by the ambitions of Germany in Europe, the other by the ambitions of Japan in Asia. By 1941, with the involvement of the United States in both wars, the two had merged into one global conflict.

Although World War I has been described as a total war, World War II was even more so and was fought on a scale unheard-of in history. Almost everyone in the warring countries was involved in one way or another: as soldiers; as workers in wartime industries; as ordinary citizens subject to invading armies, military occupation, or bombing raids; as refugees; or as victims of mass extermination. The world had never witnessed such widespread human-made death and destruction.

Hitler occupies demilitarized Rhineland

Occupation of the Sudetenland

Germany invades Poland

German surrender at Stalingrad

Munich Conference

Churchill becomes British prime minister

Teheran Conference   Surrender of Germany

Germany defeats France

Axis forces surrender in North Africa

Allied invasion of France •

Japan surrenders •

Prelude to War, 1933–1939

Only twenty years after the war to end war, Europe plunged back into the nightmare of total war. The efforts at collective security in the 1920s—the League of Nations, the attempts at disarmament, the pacts and treaties—all proved meaningless in view of the growth of Nazi Germany and its deliberate scrapping of the postwar settlement in the 1930s. Still weary from the last war, France and Great Britain refused to accept the possibility of another war. The Soviet Union, treated as an outcast by the Western powers, had turned in on itself, while the United States had withdrawn into its traditional isolationism. Finally, the small successor states to Austria-Hungary were too weak to oppose Germany. The power vacuum in the heart of Europe encouraged a revived and militarized Germany to ac-quire the living space that Hitler claimed Germany needed for its rightful place in the world.

The Role of Hitler

World War II in Europe had its beginnings in the ideas of Adolf Hitler, who believed that only the Aryans were capable of building a great civilization. But to Hitler, the Germans, in his view the leading group of Aryans, were threatened from the east by a large mass of inferior peoples, the Slavs, who had learned to use German weapons and technology. Germany needed more land to support a larger population and be a great power. Hitler was a firm believer in the doctrine of *Lebensraum* (living space), espoused by Karl Haushofer, a professor of geog-raphy at the University of Munich. The doctrine of *Lebensraum* maintained that a nation's power depended upon the amount and kind of land it occupied. Already in the 1920s, in the second volume of *Mein Kampf*, Hitler had indicated where a National Socialist regime would find this land: "And so we National Socialists . . . take up where we broke off six hundred years ago. We stop the endless German movement to the south and west, and turn our gaze toward the land in the east. . . . If we speak of soil in Europe today, we can primarily have in mind only Russia and her vassal border states."[1]

In Hitler's view, the Russian Revolution had created the conditions for Germany's acquisition of land to its east. Imperial Russia had only been strong because of its German leadership. The seizure of power by the Bolshe-viks (who, in Hitler's mind, were Jewish) had left Russia weak and vulnerable. Once it had been conquered, the land of Russia could be resettled by German peasants while the Slavic population could be used as slave labor to build the Aryan racial state that would dominate Europe for a thousand years. Hitler's conclusion was clear: Germany must prepare for its inevitable war with the Soviet Union. Hitler's ideas were by no means secret. He had spelled them out in *Mein Kampf*, a book readily available to anyone who wished to read it (see the box on p. 962).

Hitler and the Nazis were neither the first Europeans nor the first Germans to undertake European conquest and world power. Certainly, a number of elite circles in Germany before World War I had argued that Germany needed to annex lands to its south, east, and west if it wished to compete with the large states and remain a great power. The defeat in World War I destroyed this dream of world power, but the traditional conservative elites in the German military and the Foreign Office supported Hitler's foreign policy until 1937, largely

Hitler's Foreign Policy Goals

Adolf Hitler was a firm believer in the geopolitical doctrine of Lebensraum, which advocated that nations must find sufficient living space to be strong. This idea was evident in Mein Kampf, but it was explained in even more detail in a treatise that Hitler wrote in 1928. It was not published in his lifetime.

Hitler's Secret Book, 1928

I have already dealt with Germany's various foreign policy possibilities in this book. Nevertheless I shall once more briefly present the possible foreign policy goals so that they may yield a basis for the critical examination of the relations of these individual foreign policy aims to those of other European states.

(1) Germany can renounce setting a foreign policy goal altogether. This means that in reality she can decide for anything and need be committed to nothing at all. . . .[Hitler rejects this alternative.]

(2) Germany desires to effect the sustenance of the German people by peaceful economic means, as up to now. Accordingly even in the future she will participate most decisively in world industry, export and trade. . . . From a folkish standpoint setting this foreign policy aim is calamitous, and it is madness from the point of view of power politics.

(3) Germany establishes the restoration of the borders of the year 1914 as her foreign policy aim. This goal is insufficient from a national standpoint, unsatisfactory from a military point of view, impossible from a folkish standpoint with its eye on the future, and mad from the viewpoint of its consequences. . . .

(4) Germany decides to go over to [her future aim] a clear, far-seeing territorial policy. Thereby she abandons all attempts at world-industry and world-trade and instead concentrates all her strength in order, through the allotment of sufficient living space for the next hundred years to our people, also to prescribe a path of life. Since this territory can be only in the East, the obligation to be a naval power also recedes into the background. Germany tries anew to champion her interests through the formation of a decisive power on land.

This aim is equally in keeping with the highest national as well as folkish requirements. It likewise presupposes great military power means for its execution, but does not necessarily bring Germany into conflict with all European great powers. As surely as France here will remain Germany's enemy, just as little does the nature of such a political aim contain a reason for England, and especially for Italy, to maintain the enmity of the World War.

because it accorded with their own desires for German expansion. But, as they realized too late, Nazi policy went far beyond previous German goals. Hitler's desire to create an Aryan racial empire led to slave labor and even mass extermination on a scale that would have been incomprehensible to previous generations of Germans.

Although Hitler had defined his goals, he had no prearranged timetable for achieving them. During his rise to power, he had demonstrated the ability to be both ideologue and opportunist. After 1933, a combination of military and diplomatic situations, organizational chaos in the administration of Germany, and economic pressures, especially after 1936, caused Hitler periodically to take steps that seemed to contradict the foreign policy goals of *Mein Kampf*. But he always returned to his basic ideological plans for racial supremacy and empire. He was certain of one thing: only he had the ability to accomplish these goals, and his fears for his health pushed him to fulfill his mission as quickly as possible. His impatience would become a major cause of his own undoing.

The "Diplomatic Revolution," 1933–1936

Between 1933 and 1936, Hitler and Nazi Germany achieved a "diplomatic revolution" in Europe. When Hitler become chancellor of Germany on January 30, 1933, Germany's position in Europe seemed weak. The Versailles treaty had created a demilitarized zone on Germany's western border that would allow the French to move into the heavily industrialized parts of Germany in the event of war. To Germany's east, the smaller states, such as Poland and Czechoslovakia, had defensive treaties with France. The Versailles treaty had also limited Germany's army to 100,000 troops with no air and limited naval forces.

The Germans were not without advantages, however. Germany was the second most populous European state after the Soviet Union and still possessed a great industrial capacity. Hitler was also well aware that Great Britain and France, dismayed by the costs and losses of World War I, wanted to avoid another war. Hitler knew that France posed a threat to an unarmed Germany, but he believed that if he could keep the French from acting against Germany in his first years, he could remove the restrictions imposed on Germany by Versailles and restore its strength.

Hitler's ability to rearm Germany and fulfill his expansionist policies depended initially upon whether he could convince others that his intentions were peaceful. Posing as the man of peace in his public speeches, Hitler emphasized that Germany wished only to revise the unfair provisions of Versailles by peaceful means and achieve Germany's rightful place among the European states. During his first two years in office, Hitler pursued a prudent foreign policy without unnecessary risks. His dramatic action in October 1933, when he withdrew Germany from the Geneva Disarmament Conference and the League of Nations, was done primarily for domestic political reasons, to give the Germans the feeling that their country was no longer dominated by other European states.

By the beginning of 1935, Hitler had become convinced that Germany could break some of the provisions of the Treaty of Versailles without serious British and French opposition. Hitler had come to believe, based on their responses to his early actions, that both states wanted to maintain the international status quo, but without using force. Consequently, he decided to announce publicly what had been going on secretly for some time—Germany's military rearmament. On March 9, 1935, Hitler announced the creation of a new air force and, one week later, the introduction of a military draft that would expand Germany's army from 100,000 to 550,000 troops.

Hitler's unilateral repudiation of the disarmament clauses of the Versailles treaty brought a swift reaction as France, Great Britain, and Italy condemned Germany's action and warned against future aggressive steps. But nothing concrete was done. Even worse, Britain subsequently moved toward an open acceptance of Germany's right to rearm when it agreed to the Anglo-German Naval Pact on June 18, 1935. This treaty allowed Germany to build a navy that would be 35 percent of the size of the British navy, with equality in submarines. The British were starting a policy of appeasement, based on the belief that if European states satisfied the reasonable demands of dissatisfied powers, the latter would be content, and stability and peace would be achieved in Europe. British appeasement was grounded in large part upon Britain's desire to avoid another war, but it was also fostered by those British statesmen who believed that Nazi Germany offered a powerful bulwark against Soviet communism.

On March 7, 1936, buoyed by his conviction that the Western democracies had no intention of using force to maintain all aspects of the Treaty of Versailles, Hitler sent German troops into the demilitarized Rhineland. According to the Versailles treaty, the French had the right to use force against any violation of the demilitarized Rhineland. But France would not act without British support, and the British viewed the occupation of German territory by German troops as another reasonable action by a dissatisfied power. The London *Times* noted that the Germans were only "going into their own back garden." The French and British response only reinforced Hitler's growing conviction that they were weak nations unwilling to use force to defend the old order. At the same time, since the German generals had opposed his plan, Hitler became even more convinced of his own superior abilities. Many Germans expressed fresh enthusiasm for a leader who was restoring German honor.

Meanwhile, Hitler gained new allies. In October 1935, Benito Mussolini had committed Fascist Italy to imperial expansion by invading Ethiopia. Angered by French and British opposition to his invasion, Mussolini welcomed Hitler's support and began to draw closer to the German dictator he had once called a buffoon. The joint intervention of Germany and Italy on behalf of General Francisco Franco in the Spanish Civil War in 1936 also drew the two nations closer together. In October 1936, Mussolini and Hitler concluded an agreement that recognized their common political and economic interests, and one month later, Mussolini referred publicly to the new Rome-Berlin Axis. Also in November 1936, Germany and Japan (the rising military power in the Far East) concluded the Anti-Comintern Pact and agreed to maintain a common front against communism.

By the end of 1936, Hitler and Nazi Germany had achieved a "diplomatic revolution" in Europe. The Treaty of Versailles had been virtually scrapped and

Germany was once more a "World Power," as Hitler proclaimed. Hitler had demonstrated a great deal of diplomatic skill in taking advantage of Europeans' burning desire for peace. He had used the tactic of peaceful revision as skillfully as he had used the tactic of legality in his pursuit of power in Germany. By the end of 1936, Nazi power had increased enough that Hitler could initiate an even more daring foreign policy. As Hitler perceived, if the Western states were so afraid of war that they resisted its use when they were strong and Germany was weak, then they would be even more reluctant to do so now that Germany was strong. Although many Europeans still wanted to believe that Hitler desired peace, his moves had actually made war more possible.

The Path to War, 1937–1939

On November 5, 1937, at a secret conference with his military leaders in Berlin, Adolf Hitler revealed his

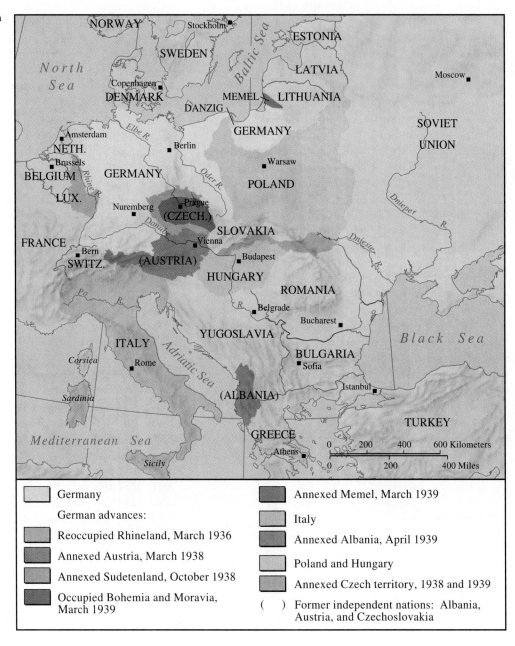

Map 28.1 Changes in Central Europe, 1936– Summer 1939.

Germany	Annexed Memel, March 1939
German advances:	Italy
Reoccupied Rhineland, March 1936	Annexed Albania, April 1939
Annexed Austria, March 1938	Poland and Hungary
Annexed Sudetenland, October 1938	Annexed Czech territory, 1938 and 1939
Occupied Bohemia and Moravia, March 1939	( ) Former independent nations: Albania, Austria, and Czechoslovakia

future aims. Germany's ultimate goal, he assured his audience, must be the conquest of living space in the east. Although this might mean war with France and Great Britain, Germany had no alternative if the basic needs of the German people were to be met. First, however, Germany must deal with Austria and Czechoslovakia and secure its eastern and southern flanks.

By the end of 1937, Hitler was convinced that neither the French nor the British would provide much opposition to his plans. Neville Chamberlain (1869–1940), who had become prime minister of Britain in May 1936, was a strong advocate of appeasement and believed that the survival of the British Empire depended upon an accommodation with Germany. Chamberlain had made it known to Hitler in November 1937 that he would not oppose changes in central Europe, provided that they were executed peacefully.

Hitler decided to move first on Austria. By threatening Austria with invasion, Hitler coerced the Austrian chancellor, Kurt von Schuschnigg (1897–1977), into putting Austrian Nazis in charge of the government. The new government promptly invited German troops to enter Austria and assist in maintaining law and order. One day later, on March 13, 1938, after his triumphal return to his native land, Hitler formally annexed Austria to Germany. Great Britain's ready acknowledgment of Hitler's action and France's inability to respond

due to a political crisis only increased the German dictator's contempt for Western weakness.

The annexation of Austria improved Germany's strategic position in central Europe and put Germany in position for Hitler's next objective—the destruction of Czechoslovakia. On May 30, 1938, Hitler had already told his generals that it was his "unalterable decision to smash Czechoslovakia by military action in the near future."[2] This goal might have seemed unrealistic since democratic Czechoslovakia was quite prepared to defend itself and was well supported by pacts with France and Soviet Russia. Nevertheless, Hitler believed that France and Britain would not use force to defend Czechoslovakia.

In the meantime, Hitler had stepped up his demands on the Czechs. Initially, the Germans had asked for autonomy for the Sudetenland, the mountainous northwestern border area of Czechoslovakia that was home to three million ethnic Germans. As Hitler knew, the Sudetenland also contained Czechoslovakia's most important frontier defenses and considerable industrial resources as well. But on September 15, 1938, Hitler demanded the cession of the Sudetenland to Germany and expressed his willingness to risk "world war" to achieve his objective. War was not necessary, however, as appeasement triumphed once again. On September 29, at the hastily arranged Munich Conference, the

◆ **Hitler Enters the Sudetenland.** The Sudetenland was an area of Czechoslovakia inhabited by 3.5 million Germans. The Munich Conference allowed the Germans to occupy the Sudetenland. This picture shows Hitler and his entourage arriving at Eger (now Cheb) in October 1938 to the cheers of an enthusiastic crowd.

The Munich Conference

At the Munich Conference, the leaders of France and Great Britain capitulated to Hitler's demands on Czechoslovakia. While the British prime minister, Neville Chamberlain, defended his actions at Munich as necessary for peace, another British statesman, Winston Churchill, characterized the settlement at Munich as "a disaster of the first magnitude."

Winston Churchill, Speech to the House of Commons, October 5, 1938

I will begin by saying what everybody would like to ignore or forget but which must nevertheless be stated, namely, that we have sustained a total and unmitigated defeat, and that France has suffered even more than we have. . . . The utmost my right honorable Friend the Prime Minister . . . has been able to gain for Czechoslovakia and in the matters which were in dispute has been that the German dictator, instead of snatching his victuals from the table, has been content to have them served to him course by course. . . . And I will say this, that I believe the Czechs, left to themselves and told they were going to get no help from the Western Powers, would have been able to make better terms than they have got. . . .

We are in the presence of a disaster of the first magnitude which has befallen Great Britain and France. Do not let us blind ourselves to that. . . .

And do not suppose that this is the end. This is only the beginning of the reckoning. This is only the first sip, the first foretaste of a bitter cup which will be proffered to us year by year unless by a supreme recovery of moral health and martial vigor, we arise again and take our stand for freedom as in the olden time.

Neville Chamberlain, Speech to the House of Commons, October 6, 1938

That is my answer to those who say that we should have told Germany weeks ago that, if her army crossed the border of Czechoslovakia, we should be at war with her. We had no treaty obligations and no legal obligations to Czechoslovakia. . . . When we were convinced, as we became convinced, that nothing any longer would keep the Sudetenland within the Czechoslovakian State, we urged the Czech Government as strongly as we could to agree to the cession of territory, and to agree promptly. . . . It was a hard decision for anyone who loved his country to take, but to accuse us of having by that advice betrayed the Czechoslovakian State is simply preposterous. What we did was to save her from annihilation and give her a chance of new life as a new State, which involves the loss of territory and fortifications, but may perhaps enable her to enjoy in the future and develop a national existence under a neutrality and security comparable to that which we see in Switzerland today. Therefore, I think the Government deserve the approval of this House for their conduct of affairs in this recent crisis which has saved Czechoslovakia from destruction and Europe from Armageddon.

British, French, Germans, and Italians (neither the Czechs nor the Russians were invited) reached an agreement that essentially met all of Hitler's demands. German troops were allowed to occupy the Sudetenland as the Czechs, abandoned by their Western allies, stood by helplessly. The Munich Conference was the high point of Western appeasement of Hitler. When Chamberlain returned to England from Munich, he boasted that the Munich agreement meant "peace for our time." Hitler had promised Chamberlain that he had made his last demand; all other European problems could be settled by negotiation. Like many German politicians, Chamberlain had believed Hitler's assurances (see the box above).

In fact, Munich confirmed Hitler's perception that the Western democracies were weak and would not fight. Increasingly, Hitler was convinced of his own infallibility, and he had by no means been satisfied at Munich. Already at the end of October 1938, Hitler told his generals to prepare for the final liquidation of the Czechoslovakian state. Using the internal disorder that he had deliberately fostered as a pretext, Hitler occupied the Czech lands (Bohemia and Moravia) while the Slovaks, with Hitler's encouragement, declared their independence of the Czechs and become a puppet state (Slovakia) of Nazi Germany. On the evening of March 15, 1939, Hitler triumphantly declared in Prague that he would be known as the greatest German of them all.

At last, the Western states reacted vigorously to Hitler's threat. After all, the Czechs were not Germans crying for reunion with Germany. Hitler's naked aggression made clear that his promises were utterly worthless.

When Hitler began to demand the return of Danzig (which had been made a free city by the Treaty of Versailles to serve as a seaport for Poland) to Germany, Britain recognized the danger and offered to protect Poland in the event of war. At the same time, both France and Britain realized that only the Soviet Union was powerful enough to help contain Nazi aggression and began political and military negotiations with Joseph Stalin and the Soviets. The West's distrust of Soviet communism, however, made an alliance unlikely.

Meanwhile, Hitler pressed on in the belief that the West would not really fight over Poland. He ordered his generals to prepare for the invasion of Poland on September 1, 1939. To preclude an alliance between the West and the Soviet Union, which would create the danger of a two-front war, Hitler, ever the opportunist, negotiated his own nonaggression pact with Stalin and shocked the world with its announcement on August 23, 1939. A secret protocol to the treaty created German and Soviet spheres of influence in eastern Europe: Finland, the Baltic states (Estonia, Latvia, and Lithuania), and eastern Poland would go to the Soviet Union while Germany would acquire western Poland. The treaty with the Soviet Union gave Hitler the freedom to attack Poland. He told his generals: "Now Poland is in the position in which I wanted her . . . I am only afraid that at the last moment some swine or other will yet submit to me a plan for mediation."[3] He need not have worried. On September 1, German forces invaded Poland; two days later, Britain and France declared war on Germany. Two weeks later, on September 17, Germany's newfound ally, the Soviet Union, sent its troops into eastern Poland. Europe was again at war.

The Course of World War II

Nine days before he attacked Poland, Hitler made clear to his generals what was expected of them: "When starting and waging a war it is not right that matters, but victory. Close your hearts to pity. Act brutally. Eighty million people must obtain what is their right . . . . The wholesale destruction of Poland is the military objective. Speed is the main thing. Pursuit until complete annihilation."[4] Hitler's remarks set the tone for what became the most destructive war in human history.

Victory and Stalemate

Using *Blitzkrieg*, or "lightning war," Hitler stunned Europe with the speed and efficiency of the German

attack. Armored columns or panzer divisions (a panzer division was a strike force of about three hundred tanks and accompanying forces and supplies) supported by airplanes broke quickly through Polish lines and encircled the overwhelmed Polish troops. Regular infantry units then moved in to hold the newly conquered territory. Within four weeks, Poland had surrendered. On September 28, 1939, Germany and the Soviet Union officially divided Poland between them.

Although Hitler's hopes of avoiding a war with the West were dashed when France and Britain declared war

✦ **Hitler Declares War.** Adolf Hitler believed that it was necessary for Germany to gain living space through conquest in the east. This policy meant war. Hitler's nonaggression pact with the Soviet Union on August 23, 1939, paved the way for his invasion of Poland on September 1. On that day, Hitler spoke to the German Reichstag and announced the outbreak of war.

on September 3, he was confident that he could control the situation. Expecting another war of attrition and economic blockade, Britain and France refused to go on the offensive. Between 1930 and 1935, France had built a series of concrete and steel fortifications armed with heavy artillery—known as the Maginot Line—along its border with Germany. Now France was quite happy to remain in its defensive shell. After a winter of waiting (called the "phony war"), Hitler resumed the war on April 9, 1940, with another *Blitzkrieg*, this time against Denmark and Norway. One month later, on May 10, the Germans launched their attack on the Netherlands,

Belgium, and France. The main assault through Luxembourg and the Ardennes forest was completely unexpected by the French and British forces. German panzer divisions broke through the weak French defensive positions there, outflanking the Maginot Line, and raced across northern France. The maneuver split the Allied armies and trapped French troops and the entire British army on the beaches of Dunkirk. A heroic rescue effort ensued with hundreds of ships and small boats ferrying troops from the French port to Britain. The British succeeded in evacuating an army of 330,000 Allied (mostly British) troops that would fight another day.

On June 5, the Germans launched another offensive into southern France. Five days later, Mussolini, believing that the war was over and eager to grab some of the spoils, declared war on France and invaded from the south. Dazed by the speed of the German offensive, the French were never able to mount an adequate resistance and surrendered on June 22. German armies occupied about three-fifths of France while the French hero of World War I, Marshal Henri Pétain (1856–1951), established an authoritarian regime (known as Vichy France) over the remainder. The Allies regarded the Pétain government as a Nazi puppet state, and a French government-in-exile took up residence in Britain. Germany was now in control of western and central Europe, but Britain still had not been defeated.

German victories in Denmark and Norway coincided with a change of government in Great Britain. On May 10, 1940, Winston Churchill (1874–1965), a longtime advocate for a hard-line policy toward Nazi Germany, replaced the apostle of appeasement, Neville Chamberlain. Churchill was confident that he could guide Britain to ultimate victory. "I thought I knew a great deal about it all," he later wrote, "and I was sure I should not fail." Churchill proved to be an inspiring leader who rallied the British people with stirring speeches. Hitler hoped that the British could be persuaded to make peace so that he could fulfill his long-awaited opportunity to gain living space in the east. Led by the stubbornly determined Churchill, the British refused, and Hitler was forced to prepare for an invasion of Britain, a prospect that he faced with little confidence.

As Hitler realized, an amphibious invasion of Britain would only be possible if Germany gained control of the air. At the beginning of August 1940, the *Luftwaffe* (the German air force) launched a major offensive against British air and naval bases, harbors, communication centers, and war industries. The British fought back doggedly, supported by an effective radar system that gave them early warning of German attacks. Moreover, the Ultra intelligence operation, which had broken German military codes, gave the British air force information about the specific targets of German air attacks. Nevertheless, the British air force suffered critical losses by the end of August and was probably saved by Hitler's change of strategy. In September, in retaliation for a British attack on Berlin, Hitler ordered a shift from military targets to massive bombing of cities to break British morale. The British rebuilt their air strength quickly and were soon inflicting major losses on *Luftwaffe* bombers. By the end of September, Germany had

lost the Battle of Britain, and the invasion of Britain had to be postponed.

At this point, Hitler pursued the possibility of a Mediterranean strategy, which would involve capturing Egypt and the Suez Canal and closing the Mediterranean to British ships, thereby shutting off Britain's supply of oil. Hitler's commitment to the Mediterranean was never wholehearted, however. His initial plan was to let the Italians, whose role was to secure the Balkan and Mediterranean flanks, defeat the British in North Africa, but this strategy failed when the British routed

Map 28.2 World War II in Europe and North Africa.

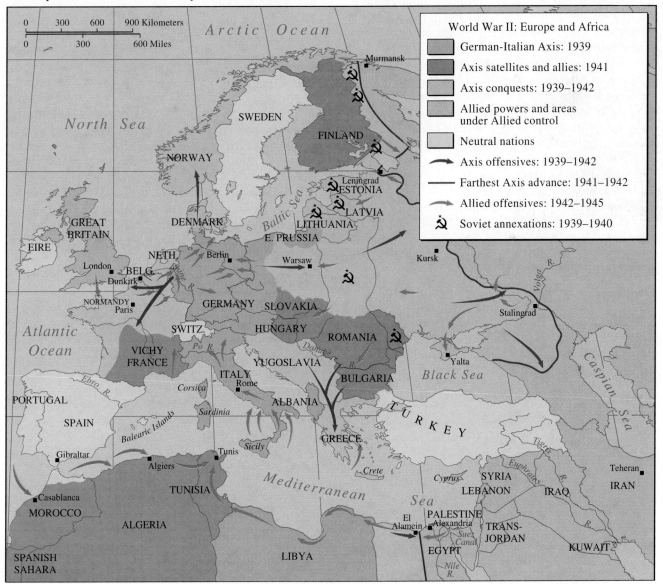

the Italian army. Although Hitler then sent German troops to the North African theater of war, his primary concern lay elsewhere: he had already reached the decision to fulfill his lifetime obsession with the acquisition of living space in the east.

Already at the end of July 1940, Hitler had told his army leaders to begin preparations for the invasion of the Soviet Union. Although he had no desire for a two-front war, Hitler became convinced that Britain was remaining in the war only because it expected Russian support. If Russia were smashed, Britain's last hope would be eliminated. Moreover, Hitler had convinced himself that the Soviet Union, with its Jewish-Bolshevik leadership and a pitiful army, could be defeated quickly and decisively. Although the invasion of the Soviet Union was scheduled for spring 1941, the attack was delayed because of problems in the Balkans. Hitler had already obtained the political cooperation of Hungary, Bulgaria, and Romania. Mussolini's disastrous invasion of Greece in October 1940 exposed Hitler's southern flank to British air bases in Greece. To secure his Balkan flank, German troops seized both Yugoslavia and Greece in April. Now reassured, Hitler turned to the east and invaded the Soviet Union on June 22, 1941, in the belief that the Russians could still be decisively defeated before winter set in.

The massive attack stretched out along an 1,800-mile front. German troops advanced rapidly, capturing two million Russian soldiers. By November, one German army group had swept through Ukraine, while a second was besieging Leningrad; a third approached within twenty-five miles of Moscow, the Russian capital. An early Russian winter and unexpected Russian resistance, however, brought a halt to the German advance. For the first time in the war, German armies had been stopped. Moreover, after the Japanese bombed Pearl Harbor on December 7, 1941, Stalin concluded that the Japanese would not strike at the Soviet Union and transferred troops from the Far East to the Moscow front. A counterattack in December 1941 by a Soviet army supposedly exhausted by Nazi victories brought an ominous ending to the year for the Germans. By that time, another of Hitler's decisions—the declaration of war on the United States—had probably made his defeat inevitable and turned another European conflict into a global war.

THE WAR IN ASIA

The war in Asia arose from the ambitions of Japan, whose rise to the status of world power had been swift. Japan had defeated China in 1895 and Russia in 1905 and had taken over many of Germany's eastern and Pacific colonies in World War I. By 1933, the Japanese empire included Korea, Formosa (now Taiwan), Manchuria, and the Marshall, Caroline, and Mariana Islands in the Pacific.

By the early 1930s, Japan was experiencing severe internal tensions. Its population had exploded from 30 million in 1870 to 80 million by 1937. Much of Japan's ability to feed its population and to pay for industrial raw materials depended upon the manufacture of heavy

✦ **German Panzer Troops in Russia.** At first, the German attack on Russia was enormously successful, leading one German general to remark in his diary, "It is probably no overstatement to say that the Russian campaign has been won in the space of two weeks." This picture shows German panzer troops jumping from their armored troop carriers to attack Red Army snipers who had taken refuge in a farmhouse.

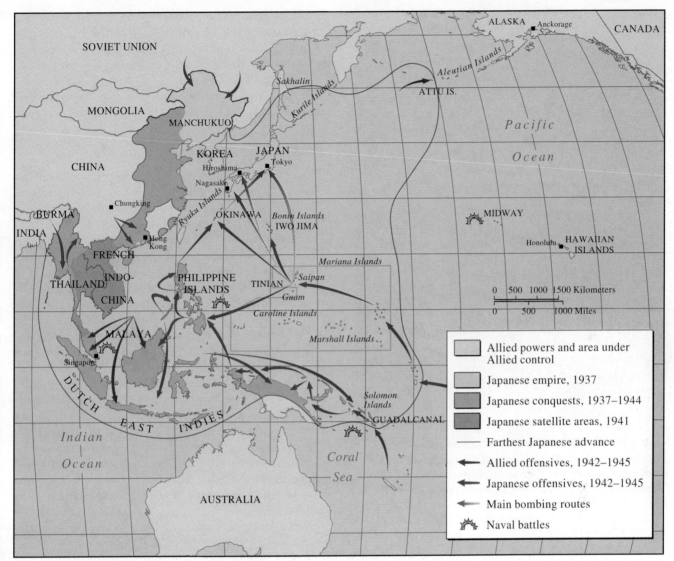

Map 28.3 World War II in Asia and the Pacific.

industrial goods (especially ships) and textiles. But in the 1930s, Western nations established tariff barriers to protect their own economies from the effects of the depression. Japan was devastated, both economically and politically.

Although political power had been concentrated in the hands of the emperor and his cabinet, Japan had also experienced a slow growth of political democracy with universal male suffrage in 1924 and the emergence of mass political parties. The economic crises of the 1930s stifled this democratic growth. Right-wing patriotic societies allied themselves with the army and navy to push a program of expansion at the expense of China and

Russia, while the navy hoped to make Japan self-sufficient in raw materials by conquering British Malaya and the Dutch East Indies. In 1935, Japan began to construct a modern naval fleet, and after 1936 the armed forces exercised much influence over the government.

The war in Asia began in July 1937 when Japanese troops invaded northern China. Moreover, Japanese naval expansion brought the Japanese into conflict with the European imperial powers—Britain (in India, Burma, Malaya), France (in Indochina), and the Netherlands (in Indonesia)—as well as with the other rising power in the Pacific, the United States. When the

◆ **The Air War.** Air power played a major role in the battles of World War II. Because his supply lines in North Africa were extended, the German general Erwin Rommel was forced to rely heavily on transport aircraft to keep his forces supplied. This photograph shows a group of German aircraft at an airfield in Libya during the summer of 1941. In the background are the three-engined Junkers Ju-52s used for transporting reinforcements and supplies. Two Messerschmidt fighter planes are in the foreground.

Japanese occupied Indochina in July 1941, the Americans responded by cutting off sales of vital scrap iron and oil to Japan. Japan's military leaders decided to preempt any further American response by attacking the American naval fleet at Pearl Harbor on December 7, 1941. The United States declared war on Japan the next day. Three days later, Hitler declared war on the United States, although he was by no means required to do so by his loose alliance with Japan. This action enabled President Roosevelt to overcome strong American isolationist sentiment and to bring the United States into the European conflict. Actually, the United States had made no pretense of neutrality from the beginning of World War II and had been supplying the Allies with military aid through its Lend-Lease program since March 11, 1941. The simultaneous involvement of the United States in both the European and Asian theaters made World War II a single, truly world war.

The Turning Point of the War, 1942–1943

The entry of the United States into the war created a coalition (the Grand Alliance) that ultimately defeated the Axis powers (Germany, Italy, Japan). Nevertheless, the three major Allies, Britain, the United States, and the Soviet Union, had to overcome mutual suspicions before they could operate as an effective alliance. Two factors aided that process. First, Hitler's declaration of war on the United States made it easier for the Americans to accept the British and Russian contention that the defeat of Germany should be the first priority of the United States. For that reason, the United States increased the quantity of trucks, planes, and other arms that it sent to the British and Soviets. Also important to the alliance was the tacit agreement of the three chief Allies to stress military operations while ignoring political differences and larger strategic issues concerning any postwar settlement. At the beginning of 1943, the Allies agreed to fight until the Axis powers surrendered unconditionally. Although this principle of unconditional surrender might have discouraged dissident Germans and Japanese from overthrowing their governments in order to arrange a negotiated peace, it also had the effect of cementing the Grand Alliance by making it nearly impossible for Hitler to divide his foes.

Defeat was far from Hitler's mind at the beginning of 1942, however. As Japanese forces advanced into Southeast Asia and the Pacific after crippling the American naval fleet at Pearl Harbor, Hitler and his European allies continued the war in Europe against Britain and the Soviet Union. Until the fall of 1942, it appeared that the Germans might still prevail on the battlefield. Reinforcements in North Africa enabled the Afrika Korps under General Erwin Rommel to break through the British defenses in Egypt and advance toward Alexandria. The Germans were also continuing their success in the Battle of the North Atlantic as their submarines continued to attack Allied ships carrying supplies to Great Britain. In the spring of 1942, a renewed German offensive in Russia led to the capture of the entire Crimea, causing Hitler to boast in August 1942:

As the next step, we are going to advance south of the Caucasus and then help the rebels in Iran and Iraq against the English. Another thrust will be directed along the Caspian Sea toward Afghanistan and India. Then the English will run out of oil. In two years we'll be on the borders of India. Twenty to thirty elite German divisions will do. Then the British Empire will collapse.[5]

But this would be Hitler's last optimistic outburst. By the fall of 1942, the war had turned against the Germans.

In North Africa, British forces had stopped Rommel's troops at El Alamein in the summer of 1942 and then forced them back across the desert. In November 1942, British and American forces invaded French North Africa and forced the German and Italian troops to surrender in May 1943. By that time, new detection devices had enabled the Allies to destroy increasing numbers of German submarines in the shipping war in the Atlantic. On the Eastern Front, the turning point of the war occurred at Stalingrad. After the capture of the Crimea, Hitler's generals wanted him to concentrate on the Caucasus and its oil fields, but Hitler decided that Stalingrad, a major industrial center on the Volga, should be taken first. Between November 1942 and February 1943, German troops were stopped, then encircled, and finally forced to surrender on February 2, 1943 (see the box on p. 974). The entire German Sixth Army of 300,000 men was lost. By February 1943, German forces in Russia were back to their positions of June 1942. By the spring of 1943, even Hitler knew that the Germans would not defeat the Soviet Union.

The tide of battle in the Far East also turned dramatically in 1942. In the Battle of the Coral Sea on May 7–8, 1942, American naval forces stopped the Japanese advance and temporarily relieved Australia of the threat of invasion. On June 4, at the Battle of Midway Island, American planes destroyed all four of the attacking Japanese aircraft carriers and established American naval superiority in the Pacific. After a series of bitter engagements in the waters near the Solomon Islands from August to November, Japanese fortunes began to fade.

The Last Years of the War

By the beginning of 1943, the tide of battle had turned against Germany, Italy, and Japan, but it would take a long time to achieve the goal of unconditional surrender of the three Axis powers. After the Axis forces had

CHRONOLOGY

The Course of World War II

Germany and the Soviet Union divide Poland	September 1939
Blitzkrieg against Denmark and Norway	April 1940
Blitzkrieg against Belgium, Netherlands, and France	May 1940
Churchill becomes British prime minister	May 10, 1940
France surrenders	June 22, 1940
Battle of Britain	Fall 1940
Nazi seizure of Yugoslavia and Greece	April 1941
Germany invades the Soviet Union	June 22, 1941
Japanese attack on Pearl Harbor	December 7, 1941
Battle of the Coral Sea	May 7–8, 1942
Battle of Midway Island	June 4, 1942
Allied invasion of North Africa	November 1942
German surrender at Stalingrad	February 2, 1943
Axis forces surrender in North Africa	May 1943
Battle of Kursk	July 5–12, 1943
Invasion of mainland Italy	September 1943
Allied invasion of France	June 6, 1944
Hitler commits suicide	April 30, 1945
Surrender of Germany	May 7, 1945
Atomic bomb dropped on Hiroshima	August 6, 1945
Japan surrenders	August 14, 1945

surrendered in Tunisia on May 13, 1943, the Allies crossed the Mediterranean and carried the war to Italy, an area that Winston Churchill had called the "soft underbelly" of Europe. After taking Sicily, Allied troops began the invasion of mainland Italy in September. In the meantime, after the ouster and arrest of Benito Mussolini, a new Italian government offered to surrender to Allied forces. But Mussolini was liberated by the

A German Soldier at Stalingrad

The Russian victory at Stalingrad was a major turning point in World War II. This excerpt comes from the diary of a German soldier who fought and died in the Battle of Stalingrad. His dreams of victory and a return home with medals were soon dashed by the realities of Russian resistance.

Diary of a German Soldier

Today, after we'd had a bath, the company commander told us that if our future operations are as successful, we'll soon reach the Volga, take Stalingrad and then the war will inevitably soon be over. Perhaps we'll be home by Christmas.

July 29. The company commander says the Russian troops are completely broken, and cannot hold out any longer. To reach the Volga and take Stalingrad is not so difficult for us. The Führer knows where the Russians' weak point is. Victory is not far away. . . .

August 10. The Führer's orders were read out to us. He expects victory of us. We are all convinced that they can't stop us.

August 12. This morning outstanding soldiers were presented with decorations. . . . Will I really go back to Elsa without a decoration? I believe that for Stalingrad the Führer will decorate even me. . . .

September 4. We are being sent northward along the front toward Stalingrad. We marched all night and by dawn had reached Voroponovo Station. We can already see the smoking town. It's a happy thought that the end of the war is getting nearer. That's what everyone is saying. . . .

September 8. Two days of non-stop fighting. The Russians are defending themselves with insane stubbornness. Our regiment has lost many men. . . .

September 16. Our battalion, plus tanks, is attacking the [grain storage] elevator, from which smoke is pour-ing—the grain in it is burning, the Russians seem to have set light to it themselves. Barbarism. The battalion is suffering heavy losses. . . .

October 10. The Russians are so close to us that our planes cannot bomb them. We are preparing for a decisive attack. The Führer has ordered the whole of Stalingrad to be taken as rapidly as possible. . . .

October 22. Our regiment has failed to break into the factory. We have lost many men; every time you move you have to jump over bodies. . . .

November 10. A letter from Elsa today. Everyone expects us home for Christmas. In Germany everyone believes we already hold Stalingrad. How wrong they are. If they could only see what Stalingrad has done to our army. . . .

November 21. The Russians have gone over to the offensive along the whole front. Fierce fighting is going on. So, there it is—the Volga, victory and soon home to our families! We shall obviously be seeing them next in the other world.

November 29. We are encircled. It was announced this morning that the Führer has said: "The army can trust me to do everything necessary to ensure supplies and rapidly break the encirclement."

December 3. We are on hunger rations and waiting for the rescue that the Führer promised. . . .

December 14. Everybody is racked with hunger. Frozen potatoes are the best meal, but to get them out of the ice-covered ground under fire from Russian bullets is not so easy. . . .

December 26. The horses have already been eaten. I would eat a cat; they say its meat is also tasty. The soldiers look like corpses or lunatics, looking for something to put in their mouths. They no longer take cover from Russian shells; they haven't the strength to walk, run away and hide. A curse on this war!

Germans in a daring raid and then set up as the head of a puppet German state in northern Italy while German troops moved in and occupied much of Italy. The new defensive lines established by the Germans in the hills south of Rome were so effective that the Allied advance up the Italian peninsula was a painstaking affair accompanied by heavy casualties. Rome did not fall to the Allies until June 4, 1944. By that time, the Italian war had assumed a secondary role anyway as the Allies opened their long-awaited "second front" in western Europe two days later.

Since the autumn of 1943, the Allies had been planning a cross-channel invasion of France from Britain. A series of Allied deceptions managed to trick the Germans into believing that the invasion would come on the flat plains of northern France. Instead, the Allies, under the direction of the American general, Dwight D. Eisenhower (1890–1969), landed five assault divisions on the Normandy beaches on June 6 in history's greatest naval invasion. An initially indecisive German response enabled the Allied forces to establish a beachhead. Within three months, they had landed two million men and a half-million vehicles that pushed inland and broke through German defensive lines.

After the breakout, Allied troops moved south and east and liberated Paris by the end of August. Supply problems as well as a last-minute, desperate (and unsuccessful) offensive by German troops in the Battle of the Bulge slowed the Allied advance. Nevertheless, by March 1945, Allied armies had crossed the Rhine River and advanced further into Germany. At the end of April, Allied forces in northern Germany moved toward the Elbe River where they finally linked up with the Russians.

The Russians had come a long way since the Battle of Stalingrad in 1943. In the summer of 1943, Hitler's generals had urged him to build an East Wall based on river barriers to halt the Russians. Instead, Hitler gambled on taking the offensive by making use of newly developed heavy tanks. German forces were soundly defeated by the Russians at the Battle of Kursk (July 5–12), the greatest tank battle of World War II. The Germans lost eighteen of their best panzer divisions. Soviet forces now began a relentless advance westward. The Soviets had reoccupied Ukraine by the end of 1943

and lifted the siege of Leningrad and moved into the Baltic states by the beginning of 1944. Advancing along a northern front, Soviet troops occupied Warsaw in January 1945 and entered Berlin in April. Meanwhile, Soviet troops swept along a southern front through Hungary, Romania, and Bulgaria.

In January 1945, Adolf Hitler had moved into a bunker fifty-five feet under Berlin to direct the final stages of the war. Hitler continued to arrange his armies on worn-out battle maps as if it still made a difference. In his final political testament, Hitler, consistent to the end in his rabid anti-Semitism, blamed the Jews for the war: "Above all I charge the leaders of the nation and those under them to scrupulous observance of the laws of race and to merciless opposition to the universal poisoner of all peoples, international Jewry."[6] Hitler committed suicide on April 30, two days after Mussolini had been shot by partisan Italian forces. On May 7, German commanders surrendered. The war in Europe was over.

The war in Asia continued. Beginning in 1943, American forces had gone on the offensive and advanced their way, slowly at times, across the Pacific. American forces took an increasing toll of enemy resources, especially at sea and in the air. When President Harry Truman (Roosevelt had died on April 12, 1945) and his advisers become convinced that American

◆ **Crossing the Rhine.** After landing at Normandy, Allied forces liberated France and prepared to move into Germany. Makeshift bridges enabled the Allies to cross the Rhine in some areas and advance deeper into Germany. Units of the 7th United States Army of General Patch are shown here crossing the Rhine at Worms on a pontoon bridge constructed by battalions of engineers alongside the ruins of the old bridge.

troops might suffer heavy casualties in the invasion of the Japanese homeland, they made the decision to drop the newly developed atomic bomb on Hiroshima and Nagasaki. The Japanese surrendered unconditionally on August 14. World War II, in which 17 million men died in battle and perhaps 18 million civilians perished as well (some estimate total losses at 50 million), was finally over.

The Nazi New Order

After the German victories in Europe between 1939 and 1941, Nazi propagandists painted glowing images of a new European order based on "equal chances" for all nations and an integrated economic community. This was not Hitler's conception of a European New Order. He saw the Europe he had conquered simply as subject to German domination. Only the Germans, he once said, "can really organize Europe."

The Nazi Empire

The Nazi empire stretched across continental Europe from the English Channel in the west to the outskirts of Moscow in the east. In no way was this empire organized systematically or governed efficiently. Some states—Spain, Portugal, Switzerland, Sweden, and Turkey—remained neutral and outside the empire. Germany's allies—Italy, Romania, Bulgaria, Hungary, and Finland—kept their independence, but found themselves increasingly restricted by the Germans as the war progressed. The remainder of Europe was largely organized in one of two ways. Some areas, such as western Poland, were directly annexed by Nazi Germany and made into German provinces. Most of occupied Europe was administered by German military or civilian officials, combined with varying degrees of indirect control from collaborationist regimes. Competing lines of authority by different offices in occupied Europe made German occupation inefficient.

Racial considerations played an important role in how conquered peoples were treated. German civil administrations were established in Norway, Denmark, and the Netherlands because the Nazis considered their peoples to be Aryan or racially akin to the Germans and hence worthy of more lenient treatment. "Inferior" Latin peoples, such as the occupied French, were given military administrations. By 1943, however, as Nazi losses continued to multiply, all the occupied territories of northern and western Europe were ruthlessly exploited for material goods and manpower for Germany's war needs.

Because the conquered lands in the east contained the living space for German expansion and were populated in Nazi eyes by racially inferior Slavic peoples, Nazi administration there was considerably more ruthless. Hitler's racial ideology and his plans for an Aryan racial empire were so important to him that he and the Nazis began to implement their racial program soon after the conquest of Poland. Heinrich Himmler, a strong believer in Nazi racial ideology and the leader of the SS, was put in charge of German resettlement plans in the east. Himmler's task was to evacuate the inferior Slavic peoples and replace them with Germans, a policy first applied to the new German provinces created from the lands of western Poland. One million Poles were uprooted and dumped in southern Poland. Hundreds of thousands of ethnic Germans (descendants of Germans who had migrated years earlier from Germany to various parts of southern and eastern Europe) were encouraged to colonize the designated areas in Poland. By 1942, two million ethnic Germans had been settled in Poland.

The invasion of the Soviet Union inflated Nazi visions of German colonization in the east. Hitler spoke to his intimate circle of a colossal project of social engineering after the war, in which Poles, Ukrainians, and Russians would become slave labor while German peasants settled on the abandoned lands and Germanized them (see the box on p. 977). Nazis involved in this kind of planning were well aware of the human costs. Himmler told a gathering of SS officers that although the destruction of 30 million Slavs was a prerequisite for German plans in the east, "Whether nations live in prosperity or starve to death interests me only insofar as we need them as slaves for our culture. Otherwise it is of no interest."[7]

Economically, the Nazi New Order meant the ruthless exploitation of conquered Europe's resources. In eastern Europe, economic exploitation was direct and severe. The Germans seized raw materials, machines, and food, leaving only enough to maintain local peoples at a bare subsistence level. Although the Germans adopted legal formalities in their economic exploitation of western Europe, military supplies and important raw materials were taken outright. As Nazi policies created drastic shortages of food, clothing, and shelter, many Europeans suffered severely.

Labor shortages in Germany led to a policy of ruthless mobilization of foreign labor for Germany. After the

Hitler's Plans for a New Order in the East

Hitler's nightly monologues to his postdinner guests, which were recorded by the Führer's private secretary, Martin Bormann, reveal much about the New Order he wished to create. On the evening of October 17, 1941, he expressed his views on what the Germans would do with their newly conquered territories in the east.

Hitler's Secret Conversations, October 17, 1941

In comparison with the beauties accumulated in Central Germany, the new territories in the East seem to us like a desert. . . . This Russian desert, we shall populate it. . . . We'll take away its character of an Asiatic steppe, we'll Europeanize it. With this object, we have undertaken the construction of roads that will lead to the southernmost point of the Crimea and to the Caucasus. These roads will be studded along their whole length with German towns, and around these towns our colonists will settle.

As for the two or three million men whom we need to accomplish this task, we'll find them quicker than we think. They'll come from Germany, Scandinavia, the Western countries and America. I shall no longer be here to see all that, but in twenty years the Ukraine will already be a home for twenty million inhabitants besides the natives. In three hundred years, the country will be one of the loveliest gardens in the world.

As for the natives, we'll have to screen them carefully. The Jew, that destroyer, we shall drive out. . . . We shan't settle in the Russian towns, and we'll let them fall to pieces without intervening. And, above all, no remorse on this subject! We're not going to play at children's nurses; we're absolutely without obligations as far as these people are concerned. To struggle against the hovels, chase away the fleas, provide German teachers, bring out newspapers—very little of that for us! We'll confine ourselves, perhaps, to setting up a radio transmitter, under our control. For the rest, let them know just enough to understand our highway signs, so that they won't get themselves run over by our vehicles. . . . There's only one duty: to Germanize this country by the immigration of Germans, and to look upon the natives as Redskins. If these people had defeated us, Heaven have mercy! But we don't hate them. That sentiment is unknown to us. We are guided only by reason. . . .

All those who have the feeling for Europe can join in our work.

In this business I shall go straight ahead, cold-bloodedly. What they may think about me, at this juncture, is to me a matter of complete indifference. I don't see why a German who eats a piece of bread should torment himself with the idea that the soil that produces this bread has been won by the sword.

invasion of Russia, the four million Russian prisoners of war captured by the Germans became a major source of heavy labor, but it was wasted by allowing three million of them to die from neglect. In 1942, a special office was created to recruit labor for German farms and industries. By the summer of 1944, seven million foreign workers were laboring in Germany and constituted 20 percent of Germany's labor force. At the same time, another seven million workers were supplying forced labor in their own countries on farms, in industries, and even in military camps. Forced labor often proved counterproductive, however, because it created economic chaos in occupied countries and disrupted industrial production that could have helped Germany. Even worse for the Germans, the brutal character of Germany's recruitment policies often led more and more people to resist the Nazi occupation forces.

Resistance Movements

German policies toward conquered peoples quickly led to the emergence of resistance movements throughout Europe, especially in the east, where brutality toward the native peoples produced a strong reaction. In Ukraine and the Baltic states, for example, the Germans were initially hailed as liberators from communist rule, but Hitler's policies of treating Slavic peoples as subhumans only drove those peoples to support and join guerrilla forces.

Resistance movements were formed throughout Europe. Active resisters committed acts of sabotage against German installations, assassinated German officials, spread anti-German newspapers, wrote anti-German sentiments on walls, and spied on German military positions for the Allies. Some anti-Nazi groups from occupied countries, such as the Free French movement under Charles de Gaulle, created governments-in-exile in London. In some countries, resistance groups even grew strong enough to take on the Germans in pitched battles. In Yugoslavia, for example, Josip Broz, known as Tito (1892–1980), led a band of guerrillas against German occupation forces. By 1944, his partisan army numbered 250,000.

After the invasion of Russia in 1941, Communists throughout Europe assumed leadership roles in underground resistance movements. This sometimes led to conflict with other local resistance groups who feared the postwar consequences of Communist power. Charles de Gaulle's Free French movement, for example, thwarted the attempt of French Communists to dominate the major French resistance groups.

Germany, too, had its resistance movements, although the increased control of the SS over everyday life made resistance both dangerous and ineffectual. The White Rose movement involved an attempt by a small group of students and one professor at the University of Munich to distribute pamphlets denouncing the Nazi regime as lawless, criminal, and godless. Its members were caught, arrested, and promptly executed. Likewise, Communist resistance groups were mostly crushed by the Gestapo.

Only one plot against Hitler and the Nazi regime came remotely close to success. It was the work primarily of a group of military officers and conservative politicians who were appalled at Hitler's warmongering and sickened by the wartime atrocities he had encouraged. One of their number, Colonel Count Claus von Stauffenberg (1907–1944), believed that only the elimination of Hitler would bring the overthrow of the Nazi regime. On July 20, 1944, a bomb planted by Stauffenberg in Hitler's East Prussian headquarters exploded, but failed to kill the dictator. The plot was then quickly uncovered and crushed. Five thousand people were executed, and Hitler remained in control of Germany.

The Holocaust

There was no more terrifying aspect of the Nazi New Order than the deliberate attempt to exterminate the Jewish people of Europe. Racial struggle was a key element in Hitler's ideology and meant to him a clearly defined conflict of opposites: the Aryans, creators of human cultural development, against the Jews, parasites who were trying to destroy the Aryans. At a meeting of the Nazi Party in 1922, Hitler proclaimed: "There can

be no compromise—there are only two possibilities: either victory of the Aryan or annihilation of the Aryan and the victory of the Jew."[8] Although Hitler later toned down his anti-Semitic message when his party sought mass electoral victories, anti-Semitism was a recurring theme in Nazism and resulted in a wave of legislative acts against the Jews between 1933 and 1939.

By the beginning of 1939, Nazi policy focused on promoting the "emigration" of German Jews from Germany. At the same time, Hitler had given ominous warnings about the future of European Jewry. When he addressed the German Reichstag on January 30, 1939, he stated:

> I have often been a prophet in life and was generally laughed at. During my struggle for power, the Jews primarily received with laughter my prophecies that I would someday assume the leadership of the state and thereby of the entire Volk and then, among many other things, achieve a solution of the Jewish problem.... Today I will be a prophet again: if international finance Jewry within Europe and abroad should succeed once more in plunging the peoples into a world war, then the consequence will be not the Bolshevization of the world and therewith a victory of Jewry, but on the contrary, the destruction of the Jewish race in Europe.[9]

At the time, emigration was still the favored policy. Once the war began in September 1939, the so-called Jewish problem took on new dimensions. For a while there was discussion of the Madagascar Plan, which aspired to the mass shipment of Jews to the African island of Madagascar. When war contingencies made this plan impractical, an even more drastic policy was conceived.

Heinrich Himmler and the SS organization closely shared Adolf Hitler's racial ideology. The SS was given responsibility for what the Nazis called their Final Solution to the Jewish problem, that is, the annihilation of the Jewish people. Reinhard Heydrich (1904–1942), head of the SS's Security Service, was given administrative responsibility for the Final Solution. After the defeat of Poland, Heydrich ordered the special strike forces (*Einsatzgruppen*) that he had created to round up all Polish Jews and concentrate them in ghettos established in a number of Polish cities.

In June 1941, the *Einsatzgruppen* were given new responsibilities as mobile killing units. These SS death squads followed the regular army's advance into Russia. Their job was to round up Jews in their villages and execute and bury them in mass graves, often giant pits dug by the victims themselves before they were shot.

The leader of one of these death squads described the mode of operation:

> The unit selected for this task would enter a village or city and order the prominent Jewish citizens to call together all Jews for the purpose of resettlement. They were requested to hand over their valuables to the leaders of the unit, and shortly before the execution to surrender their outer clothing. The men, women, and children were led to a place of execution which in most cases was located next to a more deeply excavated anti-tank ditch. Then they were shot, kneeling or standing, and the corpses thrown into the ditch.[10]

Such regular killing created morale problems among the SS executioners. During a visit to Minsk in the Soviet

♦ **The Holocaust: Activities of the *Einsatzgruppen*.** The activities of the mobile killing units known as the *Einsatzgruppen* were the first stage in the mass killings of the Holocaust. This picture shows the execution of a Jew by a member of one of these SS killing squads. Onlookers include members of the German Army, the German Labor Service, and even Hitler youth. When it became apparent that this method of killing was inefficient, it was replaced by the death camps.

Union, SS leader Himmler tried to build morale by pointing out that: "He would not like it if Germans did such a thing gladly. But their conscience was in no way impaired, for they were soldiers who had to carry out every order unconditionally. He alone had responsibility before God and Hitler for everything that was happening, . . . and he was acting from a deep understanding of the necessity for this operation."[11]

Although it has been estimated that as many as one million Jews were killed by the *Einsatzgruppen*, this approach to solving the Jewish problem was soon perceived as inadequate. Instead, the Nazis opted for the systematic annihilation of the European Jewish population in specially built death camps. The plan was basically simple. Jews from countries occupied by Germany (or sympathetic to Germany) would be rounded up, packed like cattle into freight trains, and shipped to Poland, where six extermination centers were built for this purpose. The largest and most infamous was Auschwitz-Birkenau. Technical assistance for the construction of the camps was provided by experts from the T-4 program, which had been responsible for the extermination of 80,000 alleged racially unfit, mental and physical defectives in Germany between 1938 and 1941. Based on their experiences, medical technicians chose Zyklon B (the commercial name for hydrogen cyanide) as the most effective gas for quickly killing large numbers of people in gas chambers designed to look like shower rooms to facilitate the cooperation of the victims. After gassing, the corpses would be burned in specially built crematoria.

To inform party and state officials of the general procedures for the Final Solution, a conference was held at Wannsee, outside Berlin, on January 20, 1942. Reinhard Heydrich outlined the steps that would now be taken to "solve the Jewish question." He explained how "in the course of the practical implementation of the final solution Europe is to be combed through from west to east" for Jews, who would then be brought "group by group, into so-called transit ghettos, to be transported from there farther to the east." The conference then worked out all of the bureaucratic details so that party and state officials would cooperate fully in the final elimination of the Jews.

By the spring of 1942, the death camps were in operation. Although initial priority was given to the elimination of the ghettos in Poland, by the summer of 1942, Jews were also being shipped from France, Belgium, and Holland. In 1943, there were shipments of Jews from the capital cities of Berlin, Vienna, and Prague and from Greece, southern France, Italy, and

◆ **The Holocaust: The Extermination Camp at Auschwitz.** After his initial successes in the east, Hitler set in motion the machinery for the physical annihilation of Europe's Jews. Shown here is a group of Hungarian Jewish women and children who have just arrived at Auschwitz, a major extermination camp. The picture was taken shortly before their extermination.

Denmark. Even as the Allies were making important advances in 1944, Jews were being shipped from Greece and Hungary. These shipments depended on the cooperation of Germany's Transport Ministry, and despite desperate military needs, the Final Solution had priority in using railroad cars for the transportation of Jews to death camps. Even the military argument that Jews

could be used to produce armaments was overridden by the demands of extermination.

A harrowing experience awaited the Jews when they arrived at one of the six death camps. Rudolf Höss, commandant at Auschwitz-Birkenau, described it:

> We had two SS doctors on duty at Auschwitz to examine the incoming transports of prisoners. The prisoners would be marched by one of the doctors who would make spot decisions as they walked by. Those who were fit for work were sent into the camp. Others were sent immediately to the extermination plants. Children of tender years were invariably exterminated since by reason of their youth they were unable to work. . . . at Auschwitz we endeavored to fool the victims into thinking that they were to go through a delousing process. Of course, frequently they realized our true intentions and we sometimes had riots and difficulties due to that fact.[12]

About 30 percent of the arrivals at Auschwitz were sent to a labor camp, while the remainder went to the gas chambers (see the box on p. 981). After they had been gassed, the bodies were burned in the crematoria. The victims' goods and even their bodies were used for economic gain. Female hair was cut off, collected, and turned into mattresses or cloth. Some inmates were also subjected to cruel and painful "medical" experiments. The Germans killed between five and six million Jews, over three million of them in the death camps. Virtually 90 percent of the Jewish populations of Poland, the

⚔ **Map 28.4** The Death Camps of the Holocaust.

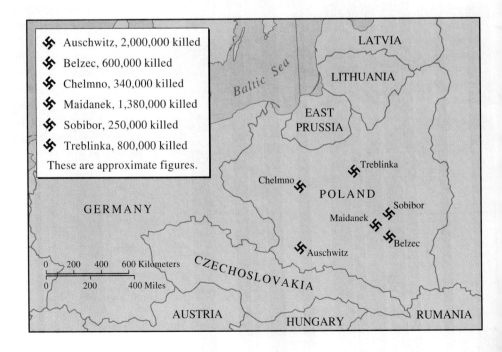

| ☠ Auschwitz, 2,000,000 killed |
| ☠ Belzec, 600,000 killed |
| ☠ Chelmno, 340,000 killed |
| ☠ Maidanek, 1,380,000 killed |
| ☠ Sobibor, 250,000 killed |
| ☠ Treblinka, 800,000 killed |
| These are approximate figures. |

The Holocaust: The Camp Commandant and the Camp Victims

The systematic annihilation of millions of men, women, and children in extermination camps makes the Holocaust one of the most horrifying events in history. The first document is taken from an account by Rudolf Höss, commandant of the extermination camp at Auschwitz-Birkenau. In the second document, a French doctor explains what happened to the victims at one of the crematoria described by Höss.

Commandant Höss Describes the Equipment

The two large crematoria, Nos. I and II, were built during the winter of 1942–43. . . . They each. . . could cremate c. 2,000 corpses within twenty-four hours. . . . Crematoria I and II both had underground undressing and gassing rooms which could be completely ventilated. The corpses were brought up to the ovens on the floor above by lift. The gas chambers could hold c. 3,000 people.

The firm of Topf had calculated that the two smaller crematoria, III and IV, would each be able to cremate 1,500 corpses within twenty-four hours. However, owing to the wartime shortage of materials, the builders were obliged to economize and so the undressing rooms and gassing rooms were built above ground and the ovens were of a less solid construction. But it soon became apparent that the flimsy construction of these two four-retort ovens was not up to the demands made on it. No. III ceased operating altogether after a short time and later was no longer used. No. IV had to be repeat-

edly shut down since after a short period in operation of 4–6 weeks, the ovens and chimneys had burnt out. The victims of the gassing were mainly burnt in pits behind crematorium IV.

The largest number of people gassed and cremated within twenty-four hours was somewhat over 9,000.

A French Doctor Describes the Victims

It is mid-day, when a long line of women, children, and old people enter the yard. The senior official in charge . . . climbs on a bench to tell them that they are going to have a bath and that afterward they will get a drink of hot coffee. They all undress in the yard. . . . The doors are opened and an indescribable jostling begins. The first people to enter the gas chamber begin to draw back. They sense the death which awaits them. The SS men put an end to this pushing and shoving with blows from their rifle butts beating the heads of the horrified women who are desperately hugging their children. The massive oak double doors are shut. For two endless minutes one can hear banging on the walls and screams which are no longer human. And then—not a sound. Five minutes later the doors are opened. The corpses, squashed together and distorted, fall out like a waterfall. . . . The bodies which are still warm pass through the hands of the hairdresser who cuts their hair and the dentist who pulls out their gold teeth. . . . One more transport has just been processed through No. IV crematorium.

Baltic countries, and Germany were exterminated. Overall, the Holocaust was responsible for the death of nearly two out of every three European Jews.

The Nazis were also responsible for the deliberate death by shooting, starvation, or overwork of at least another 9 to 10 million people. Because the Nazis also considered the Gypsies of Europe (like the Jews) a race containing alien blood, they were systematically rounded up for extermination. About 40 percent of Europe's one million Gypsies were killed in the death camps. The leading elements of the "subhuman" Slavic peoples—the clergy, intelligentsia, civil leaders, judges, and lawyers—were arrested and deliberately killed. Probably, an additional four million Poles, Ukrainians, and Belorussians lost their lives as slave laborers for Nazi

Germany while at least three to four million Soviet prisoners of war were killed in captivity. The Nazis also singled out homosexuals for persecution, and thousands lost their lives in concentration camps.

The Home Front

World War II was even more of a total war than World War I. Fighting was much more widespread and covered most of the world. Economic mobilization was more extensive; so too was the mobilization of women. The number of civilians killed was far higher; almost 20 million died as a result of bombing raids, mass extermination policies, and attacks by invading armies.

The Mobilization of Peoples: Four Examples

The home fronts of the major Western countries varied considerably, based on national circumstances. The British mobilized their resources more thoroughly than their allies or even Germany. By the summer of 1944, 55 percent of the British people were in the armed forces or civilian "war work." The British were especially determined to make use of women. Most women under forty years of age were called upon to do war work of some kind. By 1944, women held almost 50 percent of the civil service positions while the number of women in agriculture doubled as "Land Girls" performed agricultural labor usually undertaken by men.

The government encouraged a "Dig for Victory" campaign to increase food production. Fields normally reserved for athletic events were turned over to citizens to plant gardens in "Grow Your Own Food" campaigns. Even with 1.4 million new gardens in 1943, Britain still faced a shortage of food as German submarines continued to sink hundreds of British merchant vessels. Food rationing, with its weekly allotments of bacon, sugar, fats, and eggs, intensified during the war as the British became accustomed to a diet dominated by bread and potatoes. For many British people, hours after work were spent in such wartime activities as "Dig for Victory," the Civil Defence, or Home Guard. The latter had been founded in 1940 to fight off German invaders. Even elderly people were expected to help manufacture airplane parts in their homes.

During the war, the British placed much emphasis on a planned economy. In 1942, the government created a ministry for fuel and power to control the coal industry and a ministry for production to oversee supplies for the armed forces. Although controls and bureaucratic "red tape" became unpopular, especially with businessmen, most British citizens seemed to accept that total war required unusual governmental interference in people's lives. The British did make substantial gains in manufacturing war materials. Tank production quadrupled between 1940 and 1942 while the production of aircraft grew from 8,000 in 1939 to 26,000 in 1943 and 1944.

World War II had an enormous impact on the Soviet Union. Known to the Soviets as the Great Patriotic War, the German-Soviet war witnessed the greatest land battles in history as well as incredible ruthlessness. To Nazi Germany, it was a war of oppression and annihilation that called for merciless measures. Two out of every five persons killed in World War II were Soviet citizens.

The shift to a war footing necessitated only limited administrative change in the Soviet Union. As the central authority, the dictator Joseph Stalin simply created a system of "super-centralization," by which he directed military and political affairs. All civil and military organizations were subjected to the control of the Communist Party and Soviet police.

The initial defeats of the Soviet Union led to drastic emergency mobilization measures that affected the civilian population. Leningrad, for example, experienced 900 days of siege, during which its inhabitants became

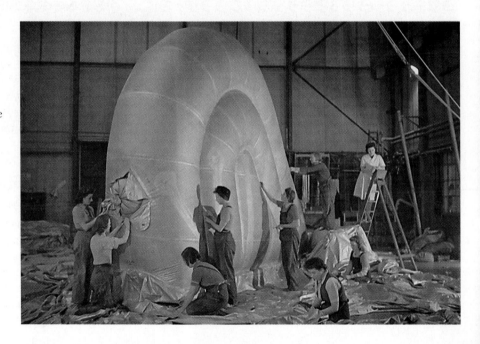

◆ **Women in the Factories.**
Although only the Soviet Union used women in combat positions, the number of women working in industry increased dramatically in most belligerent countries. British women, dressed in slacks for industrial work, are shown here building the barrage balloons that were used around British cities to defend them against air attacks.

so desperate for food that they ate dogs, cats, and mice. As the German army made its rapid advance into Soviet territory, the factories in the western part of the Soviet Union were dismantled and shipped to the interior—to the Urals, western Siberia, and the Volga region. Machines were placed on the bare ground, and walls went up around them as workers began their work. The Kharkov Tank Factory produced its first 25 T-34 tanks only ten weeks after the plant had been rebuilt.

This widespread military, industrial, and economic mobilization created yet another Industrial Revolution for the Soviet Union. Stalin labeled it a "battle of machines," and the Soviets won, producing 78,000 tanks and 98,000 artillery pieces. Fifty-five percent of Soviet national income went for war materials compared to 15 percent in 1940. As a result of the emphasis on military goods, Soviet citizens experienced incredible shortages of both food and housing. Civilian food consumption fell by 40 percent during the war while in the Volga area, the Urals, and Siberia, workers lived in dugouts or dilapidated barracks.

Soviet women played a major role in the war effort. Women and girls worked in industries, mines, and railroads. Women constituted between 26 and 35 percent of the laborers in mines and 48 percent in the oil industry. Overall, the number of women working in industry increased almost 60 percent. Soviet women were also expected to dig antitank ditches and work as air-raid wardens. In addition, the Soviet Union was the only country in World War II to use women as combatants. Soviet women functioned as snipers and also as aircrews in bomber squadrons. The female pilots who helped to defeat the Germans at Stalingrad were known as the "Night Witches."

Soviet peasants were asked to bear enormous burdens. Not only did the peasants furnish 60 percent of the military forces, at the same time, they were expected to feed the Red Army and the Soviet people under very trying conditions. The German occupation in the early months of the war resulted in the loss of 47 percent of the country's grain-producing regions. Although new land was opened in the Urals, Siberia, and Soviet Asia, a shortage of labor and equipment hindered the effort to expand agricultural production. Because farm tractors and trucks was requisitioned to carry guns for the military, women and children were literally harnessed to do the plowing while everywhere peasants worked long hours on collective farms for no pay. In 1943, the Soviet harvest was only 60 percent of its 1940 figure, a shortfall that meant extreme hardship for many people.

Total mobilization produced victory for the Soviet Union. Stalin and the Communist Party had quickly realized after the start of the German invasion that the Soviet people would not fight for communist ideology, but would do battle to preserve "Mother Russia." Government propaganda played on patriotic feelings. In a speech on the anniversary of the Bolshevik Revolution in November 1941, Stalin rallied the Soviet people by speaking of the country's past heroes, including the famous tsars of Imperial Russia.

The home front in the United States was quite different from those of its two chief wartime allies, largely because the United States faced no threat of war in its own territory. Although the economy and labor force were slow to mobilize, eventually the United States became the arsenal of the Allied powers, producing the military equipment they needed. The mobilization of the United States also had a great impact on American social and economic developments.

The American economy was never completely mobilized. In 1941, industries were hesitant to change over to full-time war operations because they feared too much production would inundate postwar markets and create another depression. Unemployment did not decrease significantly in the United States until mid-1943, a situation that affected the use of women in industrial jobs. Seventy-one percent of American women over eighteen years of age remained at home, in part due to male attitudes concerning women's traditional place in the home, but also because the services of women were not really necessary. During the high point of war production in the United States in November 1943, the nation was constructing six ships a day and $6 billion worth of other military equipment a month. Within a year many small factories were being shut down because of overproduction.

Even this partial mobilization of the American economy produced social problems. The construction of new factories created boomtowns where thousands came to work but then faced a shortage of houses, health facilities, and schools. The dramatic expansion of small towns into large cities often brought a breakdown in traditional social mores, especially evident in the growth of teenage prostitution. Economic mobilization also led to a widespread movement of people, which in turn created new social tensions. Sixteen million men and women were enrolled in the military, while another 16 million, mostly wives and sweethearts of the servicemen or workers looking for jobs, also relocated. Over one million blacks migrated from the rural South to the industrial cities of the North and West, looking for jobs in industry. The presence of blacks in areas where they had not lived before led to racial tensions and sometimes even racial riots. In Detroit in June 1943, white mobs roamed the streets attacking blacks. Many of the one million blacks who enlisted in the military, only to be segregated in their own battle units, were angered by the way they were treated. Some became militant and prepared to fight for their civil rights.

Japanese-Americans were treated even more shabbily. On the West Coast, 110,000 Japanese-Americans, 65 percent of whom had been born in the United States, were removed to camps encircled by barbed wire and required to take loyalty oaths. Although public officials claimed this policy was necessary for security reasons, no similar treatment of German-Americans or Italian-Americans ever took place. The racism inherent in this treatment of Japanese-Americans was evident when the California governor, Culbert Olson, said: "You know, when I look out at a group of Americans of German or Italian descent, I can tell whether they're loyal or not. I can tell how they think and even perhaps what they are thinking. But it is impossible for me to do this with inscrutable orientals, and particularly the Japanese."[13]

In August 1914, Germans had enthusiastically cheered their soldiers marching off to war. In September 1939, the streets were quiet. Many Germans were apathetic or, even worse for the Nazi regime, had a foreboding of disaster. Hitler was very aware of the importance of the home front. He believed that the collapse of the home front in World War I had caused Germany's defeat, and in his determination to avoid a repetition of that experience, he adopted economic policies that may indeed have cost Germany the war.

To maintain the morale of the home front during the first two years of the war, Hitler refused to convert production from consumer goods to armaments. *Blitzkrieg* allowed the Germans to win quick victories, after which they could plunder the food and raw materials of conquered countries in order to avoid diverting resources away from the civilian economy. After the German defeats on the Russian front and the American entry into the war, the economic situation changed. Early in 1942, Hitler finally ordered a massive increase in armaments production and the size of the army. Hitler's personal architect, Albert Speer, was made minister for armaments and munitions in 1942. By eliminating waste and rationalizing procedures, Speer was able to triple the production of armaments between 1942 and 1943 despite the intense Allied air raids. Speer's urgent plea for a total mobilization of resources for the war effort went unheeded, however. Hitler, fearful of civilian morale problems that would undermine the home front, refused any dramatic cuts in the production of consumer goods. A total mobilization of the economy was not implemented until 1944, when schools, theaters, and cafes were closed and Speer was finally permitted to use all remaining resources for the production of a few basic military items. By that time, it was in vain. Total war mobilization was too little and too late in July 1944 to save Germany from defeat.

The war produced a reversal in Nazi attitudes toward women. Nazi resistance to female employment declined as the war progressed and more and more men were called up for military service. Nazi magazines now proclaimed: "We see the woman as the eternal mother of our people, but also as the working and fighting comrade of the man."[14] But the number of women working in industry, agriculture, commerce, and domestic service increased only slightly. The total number of employed women in September 1944 was 14.9 million compared to 14.6 in May 1939. Many women, especially those of the middle class, resisted regular employment, particularly in factories. Even the introduction of labor conscription for women in January 1943 failed to achieve much as women found ingenious ways to avoid the regulations.

The Frontline Civilians: The Bombing of Cities

Bombing was used in World War II in a variety of ways: against nonhuman military targets; against enemy troops, and against civilian populations. The latter made World War II as devastating for civilians as for frontline soldiers (see the box on p. 985). A small number of bombing raids in the last year of World War I had given rise to the argument, expressed in 1930 by the Italian general Giulio Douhet, that the public outcry generated by the bombing of civilian populations would be an effective way to coerce governments into making peace. Consequently, European air forces began to develop long-range bombers in the 1930s.

The first sustained use of civilian bombing contradicted Douhet's theory. Beginning in early September 1940, the German *Luftwaffe* subjected London and many other British cities and towns to nightly air raids, making the Blitz (as the British called the German air raids) a national experience. Londoners took the first heavy blows and set the standard for the rest of the British population by refusing to panic. One British woman expressed well what many others apparently felt:

> It was a beautiful summer night, so warm it was incredible, and made more beautiful than ever by the red glow from the East, where the docks were burning. We stood and stared for a minute, and I tried to fix the scene in my

The Bombing of Civilians

The home front became a battle front when civilian populations became the targets of mass bombing raids. Many people believed that mass bombing could effectively weaken the morale of the people and shorten the war. Rarely did it achieve its goal. In these selections, British, German, and Japanese civilians relate their experiences during bombing raids.

London, 1940

Early last evening, the noise was terrible. My husband and Mr. P. were trying to play chess in the kitchen. I was playing draughts with Kenneth in the cupboard. . . . Presently I heard a stifled voice "Mummy! I don't know what's become of my glasses." "I should think they are tied up in my wool." My knitting had disappeared and wool seemed to be everywhere! We heard a whistle, a bang which shook the house, and an explosion. . . . Well, we straightened out, decided draughts and chess were no use under the circumstances, and waited for a lull so we could have a pot of tea.

Hamburg, 1943

As the many fires broke through the roofs of the burning buildings, a column of heated air rose more than two and a half miles·high and one and a half miles in diameter. . . . This column was turbulent, and it was fed from its base by in-rushing cooler ground-surface air. One and one and half miles from the fires this draught increased the wind velocity from eleven to thirty-three miles per hour. At the edge of the area the velocities must have been appreciably greater, as trees three feet in diameter were uprooted. In a short time the temperature reached ignition point for all combustibles, and the entire area was ablaze. In such fires complete burn-out occurred; that is, no trace of combustible material remained, and only after two days were the areas cool enough to approach.

Hiroshima, August 6, 1945

I heard the airplane; I looked up at the sky, it was a sunny day, the sky was blue. . . . Then I saw something drop—and pow!—a big explosion knocked me down. Then I was unconscious—I don't know for how long. Then I was conscious but I couldn't see anything. . . . Then I see people moving away and I just follow them. It is not light like it was before, it is more like evening. I look around; houses are all flat! . . . I follow the people to the river. I couldn't hear anything, my ears are blocked up. I am thinking a bomb has dropped! . . . I didn't know my hands were burned, nor my face. . . . My eyes were swollen and felt closed up.

mind, because one day this will be history, and I shall be one of those who actually saw it. I wasn't frightened any more.[15]

But London morale was helped by the fact that German raids were widely scattered over a very large city. Smaller communities were more directly affected by the devastation. On November 14, 1940, for example, the *Luftwaffe* destroyed hundreds of shops and a hundred acres of the city center of Coventry. The destruction of smaller cities did produce morale problems as wild rumors of heavy casualties spread quickly in these communities. Nevertheless, morale was soon restored. In any case, war production in these areas seems to have been little affected by the raids.

The British failed to learn from their own experience, however, and soon proceeded to bomb German cities. Churchill and his advisers believed that destroying German communities would break civilian morale and bring victory. Major bombing raids began in 1942 under the direction of Arthur Harris, the wartime leader of the British air force's Bomber Command, which was re-armed with four-engine heavy bombers capable of taking the war into the center of occupied Europe. On May 31, 1942, Cologne became the first German city to be subjected to an attack by a thousand bombers.

With the entry of the Americans into the war, the bombing strategy changed. American planes flew daytime missions aimed at the precision bombing of transportation facilities and war industries, while the British Bomber Command continued nighttime saturation bombing of all German cities with populations over 100,000. Bombing raids added an element of terror to circumstances already made difficult by growing shortages of food, clothing, and fuel. Germans especially feared the incendiary bombs that created firestorms that swept destructive paths through the cities. Four raids on Hamburg in August 1943 produced temperatures of

◆ **The Destruction of Clydebank.** The bombing of an enemy's cities brought the war home to civilian populations. This picture shows a street in Clydebank, near Glasgow in Scotland, the day after the city was bombed by the Germans in March 1941. Only seven of the city's 12,000 houses were left undamaged; 35,000 of the 47,000 inhabitants became homeless overnight. Clydebank was Scotland's only severe bombing experience.

1,800 degrees Fahrenheit, obliterated half the city's buildings, and killed 50,000 civilians. The ferocious bombing of Dresden from February 13 to 15, 1945, created a firestorm that may have killed as many as

100,000 inhabitants and refugees. Even some Allied leaders began to criticize what they saw as the unnecessary terror bombing of German cities. Urban dwellers became accustomed to living in air-raid shelters, usually cellars in businesses or houses. Occupants of shelters could be crushed to death if the shelters were hit directly or die by suffocation from the effects of high-explosive bombs. Not until 1943 did Nazi leaders begin to evacuate women and children to rural areas. This evacuation policy, however, created its own problems since people in country villages were often hostile to the urban newcomers.

Germany suffered enormously from the Allied bombing raids. Millions of buildings were destroyed, and possibly half a million civilians died from the raids. Nevertheless, it is highly unlikely that Allied bombing sapped the morale of the German people. Instead, Germans, whether pro-Nazi or anti-Nazi, fought on stubbornly, often driven simply by a desire to live. Nor did the bombing destroy Germany's industrial capacity. The Allied Strategic Bombing survey revealed that the production of war materials actually increased between 1942 and 1944. Even in 1944 and 1945, Allied raids cut German production of armaments by only 7 percent. Nevertheless, the widespread destruction of transportation systems and fuel supplies made it extremely difficult for the new materials to reach the German military. The

◆ **Hiroshima.** The most devastating destruction of civilians came near the end of World War II when the United States dropped atomic bombs on the Japanese cities of Hiroshima and Nagasaki. This panoramic view of Hiroshima after the bombing shows the incredible devastation produced by the atomic bomb.

destruction of German cities from the air did accomplish one major goal. There would be no stab-in-the-back myth after World War II as there had been after World War I. The loss of the war could not be blamed on the collapse of the home front. Many Germans understood that the home front had been a battlefront, and they had fought bravely on their front just as the soldiers had on theirs.

The bombing of civilians eventually reached a new level with the dropping of the first atomic bomb on Japan. Fearful of German attempts to create a super-bomb through the use of uranium, the American government pursued a dual strategy. While sabotaging German efforts, the United States and Britain recruited scientists, including many who had fled from Germany, to develop an atomic bomb. Working under the direction of J. Robert Oppenheimer at a secret laboratory in Los Alamos, New Mexico, Allied scientists built and tested the first atomic bomb by the summer of 1945. A new era in warfare was about to begin.

Japan was especially vulnerable to air raids because its air force had been virtually destroyed in the course of the war, and its crowded cities were built of flimsy materials. Attacks on Japanese cities by the new American B-29 Superfortresses, the biggest bombers of the war, had begun on November 24, 1944. By the summer of 1945, many of Japan's factories had been destroyed along with one-fourth of its dwellings. After the Japanese government decreed the mobilization of all people between the ages of thirteen and sixty into a People's Volunteer Corps, President Truman and his advisers feared that Japanese fanaticism might mean a million American casualties. This concern led them to drop the atomic bomb on Hiroshima (August 6) and Nagasaki (August 9). The destruction was incredible. Of 76,000 buildings near the hypocenter of the explosion in Hiroshima, 70,000 were flattened, while 140,000 of the city's 400,000 inhabitants died by the end of 1945. By the end of 1950, another 50,000 had perished from the effects of radiation.

The Aftermath of the War: The Emergence of the Cold War

The total victory of the Allies in World War II was not followed by a real peace, but by the beginnings of a new conflict known as the Cold War that dominated European and world politics until the end of the 1980s. The origins of the Cold War stemmed from the military, political, and ideological differences, especially between the Soviet Union and the United States, that became apparent at the Allied war conferences held in the last years of the war. Although Allied leaders were mostly preoccupied with how to end the war, they also were strongly motivated by differing, and often conflicting, visions of postwar Europe.

The Conferences at Teheran, Yalta, and Potsdam

Stalin, Roosevelt, and Churchill, the leaders of the Big Three of the Grand Alliance, met at Teheran (the capital of Iran) in November 1943 to decide the future course of the war. Their major tactical decision concerned the final assault on Germany. Churchill had wanted British and American forces to follow up their North African and Italian campaigns by an indirect attack on Germany through the Balkans. Although an extremely difficult route, this would give the Western Allies a better position in postwar central Europe. Stalin and Roosevelt, however, overruled Churchill and argued successfully for an American-British invasion of the Continent through France, which they scheduled for the spring of 1944. The acceptance of this plan had important consequences. It meant that Soviet and British-American forces would meet in defeated Germany along a north-south dividing line and that, most likely, Eastern Europe would be liberated by Soviet forces. The Allies also agreed to a partition of postwar Germany, but differences over questions like the frontiers of Poland were carefully set aside. Roosevelt was pleased with the accord with Stalin. Harry Hopkins, one of Roosevelt's advisers at the conference, remarked:

> We really believed in our hearts that this was the dawn of the new day. . . . We were absolutely certain that we had won the first great victory of the peace—and by "we," I mean *all* of us, the whole civilized human race. The Russians had proved that they could be reasonable and farseeing and there wasn't any doubt in the minds of the President or any of us that we could live with them and get along with them peacefully for as far into the future as any of us could imagine.[16]

Winston Churchill was more cautious about future relations with the Soviets. Although overruled at the Teheran Conference, in October of 1944, Churchill met with Stalin in Moscow and was able to pin him down to a more specific determination of postwar spheres of influence. The agreement between Churchill and Stalin, written on a scrap of paper, assigned the various Allies a certain percentage of political influence in a given area on the basis of past historical roles. The Soviet Union received 90 percent influence in Romania and 75 percent in Bulgaria, while Britain obtained 90 percent influence in Greece. Eastern European countries that had a strong tradition of Western ties, such as Yugoslavia and Hungary, were divided "fifty-fifty." Churchill perceived how callous this division of sovereign countries might seem from a distance. He remarked to Stalin, "Might it not be thought rather cynical if it seemed we had disposed of these issues, so fateful to millions of people, in such an offhand manner? Let us burn the paper." Stalin, not worried about what others might think, simply replied, "No, you keep it."[17]

By the time of the conference at Yalta in southern Russia in February 1945, the defeat of Germany was a foregone conclusion. The Western powers, which had earlier believed that the Soviets were in a weak position, were now faced with the reality of 11 million Red Army soldiers taking possession of Eastern and much of central Europe. Stalin was still operating under the notion of spheres of influence. He was deeply suspicious of the Western powers and desired a buffer to protect the Soviet Union from possible future Western aggression. At the same time, however, Stalin was eager to obtain economically important resources and strategic military positions. Roosevelt by this time was moving away from the notion of spheres of influence to the ideal of self-determination. He called for "the end of the system of unilateral action, exclusive alliances, and spheres of influence." The Grand Alliance approved a "Declaration on Liberated Europe." This was a pledge to assist liberated European nations in the creation of "democratic institutions of their own choice." Liberated countries were to hold free elections to determine their political systems.

At Yalta, Roosevelt sought Russian military help against Japan. The atomic bomb was not yet assured, and American military planners feared the possible loss of as many as one million men in amphibious assaults on the Japanese home islands. Roosevelt therefore agreed to Stalin's price for military assistance against Japan: possession of Sakhalin and the Kurile Islands as well as two warm water ports and railroad rights in Manchuria.

The creation of the United Nations was a major American concern at Yalta. Roosevelt hoped to ensure the participation of the Big Three powers in a postwar international organization before difficult issues divided them into hostile camps. After a number of compromises, both Churchill and Stalin accepted Roosevelt's plans for a United Nations organization and set the first meeting for San Francisco in April of 1945.

The issues of Germany and Eastern Europe were treated less decisively. The Big Three reaffirmed that Germany must surrender unconditionally and created four occupation zones. Churchill, over the objections of the Soviets and Americans, insisted that the French be given one occupation zone, carved out of the British and American zones. German reparations were set at $20 billion. A compromise was also worked out in regard to

✦ **The Victorious Allied Leaders at Yalta.** Even before World War II ended, the leaders of the Big Three of the Grand Alliance, Churchill, Roosevelt, and Stalin (shown from left to right), met in wartime conferences to plan the final assault on Germany and negotiate the outlines of the postwar settlement. At the Yalta meeting (February 5–11, 1945), the three leaders concentrated on postwar issues. The American president, who died two months later, was already a worn-out man at Yalta.

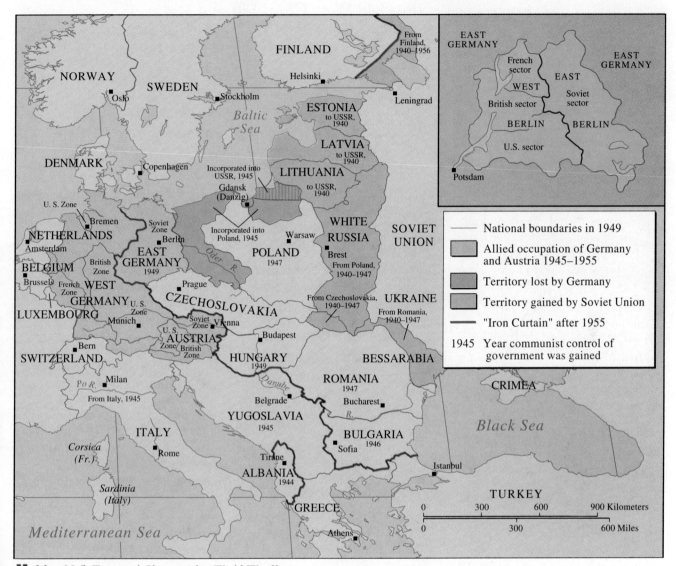

⚜ Map 28.5 Territorial Changes after World War II.

Poland. It was agreed that a provisional government would be established with members of both the Lublin Poles, who were Polish Communists living in exile in the Soviet Union, and the London Poles, who were non-Communists exiled in Britain. Stalin also agreed to free elections in the future to determine a new government. But the issue of free elections in Eastern Europe caused a serious rift between the Soviets and the Americans. The principle was that Eastern European governments would be freely elected, but they were also supposed to be pro-Soviet. As Churchill expressed it: "The Poles will have their future in their own hands, with the single limitation that they must honestly follow in harmony with their allies, a policy friendly to Russia."[18] This attempt to reconcile two irreconcilable goals was doomed to failure, as soon became evident at the next conference of the Big Three powers.

Even before the conference at Potsdam took place in July 1945, Western relations with the Soviets were deteriorating rapidly. The Grand Alliance had been one of necessity in which disagreements had been subordinated to the pragmatic concerns of the war. The Allied powers' only common aim was the defeat of Nazism. Once this aim had all but been accomplished, the many

⇒ *Emergence of the Cold War: Churchill and Stalin* ⇐

Less than a year after the end of World War II, the major Allies that had fought together to destroy Hitler's Germany had divided into two hostile camps. These excerpts, taken from Winston Churchill's speech to an American audience on March 5, 1946, and Joseph Stalin's reply to Churchill only nine days later, reveal the divisions in the Western world that marked the beginning of the Cold War.

Churchill's Speech at Fulton, Missouri, March 5, 1946

From Stettin in the Baltic to Trieste in the Adriatic, an iron curtain has descended across the continent. Behind that line lie all the capitals of the ancient states of central and eastern Europe. Warsaw, Berlin, Prague, Vienna, Budapest, Belgrade, Bucharest, and Sofia, all these famous cities and the populations around them lie in the Soviet sphere and all are subject, in one form or another, not only to Soviet influence but to a very high and increasing measure of control from Moscow. . . .

The Russian-dominated Polish Government has been encouraged to make enormous and wrongful inroads upon Germany, and mass expulsions of millions of Germans on a scale grievous and undreamed of are now taking place. The Communist parties, which were very small in all these eastern states of Europe, have been raised to preeminence and power far beyond their numbers and are seeking everywhere to obtain totalitarian control. Police governments are prevailing in nearly every case, and so far, except in Czechoslovakia, there is no true democracy. . . . Whatever conclusions may be drawn from these facts—and facts they are—this is certainly not the liberated Europe we fought to build up. Nor is it one which contains the essentials of permanent peace.

Stalin's Reply to Churchill, March 14, 1946

In substance, Mr. Churchill now stands in the position of a firebrand of war. And Mr. Churchill is not alone here. He has friends not only in England but also in the United States of America.

In this respect, one is reminded remarkably of Hitler and his friends. Hitler began to set war loose by announcing his racial theory, declaring that only people speaking the German language represent a fully valuable nation. Mr. Churchill begins to set war loose, also by a racial theory, maintaining that only nations speaking the English language are fully valuable nations, called upon to decide the destinies of the entire world.

The German racial theory brought Hitler and his friends to the conclusion that the Germans, as the only fully valuable nation, must rule over other nations. The English racial theory brings Mr. Churchill and his friends to the conclusion that nations speaking the English language, being the only fully valuable nations, should rule over the remaining nations of the world.

differences that troubled East-West relations came to the surface. Each side committed acts that the other viewed as unbecoming of "allies."

From the perspective of the Soviets, the United States' termination of Lend-Lease aid before the war was over and its failure to respond to the Soviet request for a $6 billion loan for reconstruction exposed the Western desire to keep the Soviet state weak. On the American side, the Soviet Union's failure to fulfill its Yalta pledge on the "Declaration on Liberated Europe" as applied to Eastern Europe set a dangerous precedent. This was evident in Romania as early as February 1945, when the Soviets engineered a coup and installed a new government under the Communist Petra Groza, called the "Little Stalin." One month later, the Soviets sabotaged the Polish settlement by arresting the London Poles and their sympathizers and placing the Soviet-backed Lublin Poles in power. To the Americans, the Soviets seemed to be asserting control of Eastern European countries under puppet Communist regimes.

The Potsdam Conference of July 1945 consequently began under a cloud of mistrust. Roosevelt had died on April 12 and had been succeeded by Harry Truman. During the conference, Truman received word that the atomic bomb had been successfully tested. Some historians have argued that this knowledge resulted in Truman's stiffened resolve against the Soviets. Whatever the reasons, there was a new coldness in the relations between the Soviets and Americans. At Potsdam, Truman demanded free elections throughout Eastern Europe. Stalin responded: "A freely elected government in any of these East European countries would be anti-Soviet, and that we cannot allow."[19] After a bitterly fought and devastating war, Stalin sought absolute military security. To him, it could only be gained by the presence of Communist states in Eastern Europe. Free elections might result in governments hostile to the Soviets. By the middle of 1945, only an invasion by Western forces could undo developments in Eastern Europe, and after the world's most destructive conflict had ended, few people favored such a policy.

The Soviets did not view their actions as dangerous expansionism but as legitimate security maneuvers. Was it not the West that had attacked the East? When Stalin sought help against the Nazis in the 1930s, had not the West turned a deaf ear? But there was little sympathy in the West for Soviet fears and even less trust in Stalin. When the American secretary of state James Byrnes proposed a twenty-five-year disarmament of Germany, the Soviet Union rejected it. In the West, many saw this as proof of Stalin's plans to expand in central Europe and create a Communist East German state. When Byrnes responded by announcing that American troops would be needed in Europe for an indefinite time and made moves that foreshadowed the creation of an independent West Germany, the Soviets saw this as a direct threat to Soviet security in Europe.

As the war slowly receded into the past, the reality of conflicting ideologies had reappeared. Many in the West interpreted Soviet policy as part of a worldwide Communist conspiracy. The Soviets, on the other hand, viewed Western, especially American, policy as nothing less than global capitalist expansionism or, in Leninist terms, as nothing less than economic imperialism. Vyacheslav Molotov, the Russian foreign minister, referred to the Americans as "insatiable imperialists" and "war-mongering groups of adventurers."[20] In March 1946, in a speech to an American audience, the former British prime minister, Winston Churchill, declared that "an iron curtain" had "descended across the continent," dividing Germany and Europe into two hostile camps. Stalin branded Churchill's speech a "call to war with the Soviet Union" (see the box on p. 990). Only months after the world's most devastating conflict had ended, the world seemed once again bitterly divided. Would the twentieth-century crisis of Western civilization never end?

Conclusion

Between 1933 and 1939, Europeans watched as Adolf Hitler rebuilt Germany into a great military power. For Hitler, military power was an absolute prerequisite for the creation of a German racial empire that would dominate Europe and the world for generations to come. If Hitler had been successful, the Nazi New Order, built upon authoritarianism, racial extermination, and the brutal oppression of peoples, would have meant a triumph of barbarism and the end of freedom and equality, which, however imperfectly realized, had become important ideals in Western civilization.

The Nazis lost, but only after tremendous sacrifices and costs. Much of European civilization lay in ruins, and the old Europe had disappeared forever. Europeans, who had been accustomed to dominating the world at the beginning of the twentieth century, now watched helplessly at mid-century as the two new superpowers created by the two world wars took control of their destinies. Even before the last battles had been fought, the United States and the Soviet Union had arrived at different visions of the postwar European world. No sooner had the war ended than their differences created a new and potentially even more devastating conflict known as the Cold War. Yet even though Europeans seemed merely pawns in the struggle between the two superpowers, they managed to stage a remarkable recovery of their own civilization.

NOTES

1. Adolf Hitler, *Mein Kampf*, trans. Ralph Manheim (Boston, 1971), p. 654.
2. *Documents on German Foreign Policy* (London, 1956), Series D, 2:358.
3. Ibid., 7:204.
4. Quoted in Norman Rich, *Hitler's War Aims* (New York, 1973), 1:129.
5. Albert Speer, *Spandau*, trans. Richard and Clara Winston (New York, 1976), p. 50.
6. *Nazi Conspiracy and Aggression* (Washington, D.C., 1946), 6:262.
7. International Military Tribunal, *Trial of the Major War Criminals* (Nuremberg, 1947–49), 22:480.
8. Adolf Hitler, *My New Order*, ed. Raoul de Roussy de Sales (New York, 1941), pp. 21–22.
9. Quoted in Lucy Dawidowicz, *The War against the Jews* (New York, 1975), p. 106.
10. *Nazi Conspiracy and Aggression*, 5:341–42.
11. Quoted in Raul Hilberg, *The Destruction of the European Jews*, rev. ed. (New York, 1985), 1:332–33.
12. *Nazi Conspiracy and Aggression*, 6:789.
13. Quoted in John Campbell, *The Experience of World War II* (New York, 1989), p. 170.
14. Quoted in Claudia Koonz, "Mothers in the Fatherland: Women in Nazi Germany," in Renate Bridenthal and Claudia Koonz, eds., *Becoming Visible: Women in European History* (Boston, 1977), p. 466.
15. Quoted in Campbell, *The Experience of World War II*, p. 177.
16. Quoted in Robert E. Sherwood, *Roosevelt and Hopkins: An Intimate History* (New York, 1948), p. 870.
17. Quoted in Walter Laqueur, *Europe since Hitler*, rev. ed. (New York, 1982), p. 102.
18. Quoted in Norman Graebner, *Cold War Diplomacy, 1945–1960* (Princeton, N.J., 1962), p. 117.
19. Quoted in ibid.
20. Quoted in Wilfried Loth, *The Division of the World, 1941–1955* (New York, 1988), p. 81.

SUGGESTIONS FOR FURTHER READING

The basic study of Germany's foreign policy from 1933 to 1939 can be found in G. Weinberg, *The Foreign Policy of Hitler's Germany: Diplomatic Revolution in Europe, 1933–36* (Chicago, 1970), and *The Foreign Policy of Hitler's Germany: Starting World War II, 1937–1939* (Chicago, 1980). For a detailed account of the immediate events leading to World War II, see D. C. Watt, *How War Came: The Immediate Origins of the Second World War, 1938–1939* (New York, 1989).

Hitler's war aims and the importance of ideology to those aims are examined in N. Rich, *Hitler's War Aims*, vol. 1, *Ideology, the Nazi State and the Course of Expansion* (New York, 1973), and vol. 2, *The Establishment of the New Order* (New York, 1974). General works on World War II include the comprehensive work by G. Weinberg, *A World at Arms: A Global History of World War II* (Cambridge, 1994); M. K. Dziewanowski, *War at Any Price: World War II in Europe, 1939–1945*, 2d ed.

(Englewood Cliffs, N.J., 1991); P. Calvocoressi and G. Wint, *Total War: Causes and Courses of the Second World War* (New York, 1979); J. Campbell, *The Experience of World War II* (New York, 1989); and G. Wright, *The Ordeal of Total War, 1939–1945* (New York, 1968). On Hitler as a military leader, see R. Lewin, *Hitler's Mistakes* (New York, 1986). The Eastern Front is covered in J. Erickson, *Stalin's War with Germany*, vol. 1, *The Road to Stalingrad*; vol. 2, *The Road to Berlin* (London, 1973, 1985); and O. Bartov, *The Eastern Front, 1941–45: German Troops and the Barbarisation of Warfare* (London, 1986). The second front in Europe is examined in C. D'Este, *Decision in Normandy* (London, 1983). See also S. E. Ambrose, *Eisenhower: The Soldier* (London, 1984). On the war at sea, see D. MacIntyre, *Battle of the Atlantic, 1939–1945* (London, 1970).

A standard work on the German New Order in Russia is A. Dallin, *German Rule in Russia, 1941–1945*, rev. ed. (London, 1981). On Poland, see J. T. Gross, *Polish Society under German Occupation* (Princeton, N.J., 1981). On foreign labor, see E. Homze, *Foreign Labor in Nazi Germany* (Princeton, N.J., 1967). Resistance movements in Europe are covered in M. R. D. Foot, *Resistance: An Analysis of European Resistance to Nazism* (London, 1976). A fundamental study on resistance in Germany is P. Hoffmann, *The History of the German Resistance, 1933–1945,* trans. R. Barry (Cambridge, Mass., 1977).

The best studies of the Holocaust include R. Hilberg, *The Destruction of the European Jews,* rev. ed., 3 vols. (New York, 1985); L. Dawidowicz, *The War against the Jews* (New York, 1975); L. Yahil, *The Holocaust* (Oxford, 1990); and M. Gilbert, *The Holocaust: The History of the Jews of Europe during the Second World War* (New York, 1985). There is a good overview of the scholarship on the Holocaust in M. Marrus, *The Holocaust in History* (New York, 1987). The role of Hitler in the Holocaust has been well examined in G. Fleming, *Hitler and the Final Solution* (Berkeley, 1984). On the extermination camps, see K. G. Feig, *Hitler's Death Camps: The Sanity of Madness* (New York, 1981). Other Nazi atrocities are examined in R. C. Lukas, *Forgotten Holocaust: The Poles under German Occupation, 1939–44* (Lexington, Ky., 1986); and B. Wytwycky, *The Other Holocaust* (Washington, D.C., 1980).

General studies on the impact of total war include J. Costello, *Love, Sex and War: Changing Values, 1939–1945* (London, 1985); A. Marwick, *War and Social Change in the Twentieth Century: A Comparative Study of Britain, France, Germany, Russia and the United States* (London, 1974); A. S. Milward, *War, Economy and Society, 1939–1945* (London, 1977); and M. R. Marrus, *The Unwanted: European Refugees in the Twentieth Century* (New York, 1985). On the home front in Germany, see E. R. Beck, *Under the Bombs: The German Home Front, 1942–1945* (Lexington, Ky., 1986); J. Stephenson, *The Nazi Organisation of Women* (London, 1981); and L. J. Rupp, *Mobilizing Women for War: German and American Propaganda, 1939–1945* (Princeton, N.J., 1978). On the home front in Britain, see A. Marwick, *The Home Front* (London, 1976). The Soviet Union during the war is examined in M. Harrison, *Soviet Planning in Peace and War, 1938–1945* (Cambridge, 1985). On the American home front, see G. Perrett, *Days of Sadness, Years of Triumph: The American People, 1939–1945* (New York, 1973).

On the destruction of Germany by bombing raids, see H. Rumpf, *The Bombing of Germany* (London, 1963). The German bombing of Britain is covered in T. Harrisson, *Living through the Blitz* (London, 1985). On Hiroshima, see A. Chisholm, *Faces of Hiroshima* (London, 1985).

On the emergence of the Cold War, see W. Loth, *The Division of the World, 1941–1955* (New York, 1988), and the more extensive list of references at the end of Chapter 29. On the wartime summit conferences, see H. Feis, *Churchill, Roosevelt, Stalin: The War They Waged and the Peace They Sought,* 2d ed. (Princeton, N.J., 1967). The impact of the atomic bomb on Truman's relationship to Stalin is discussed in M. Sherwin, *A World Destroyed: The Atomic Bomb and the Grand Alliance* (New York, 1975).

CHAPTER
29

Cold War and a
New Europe,
1945–1970

The end of World War II in Europe had been met with great joy. One visitor to Moscow reported: "I looked out of the window [at 2 A.M.], almost everywhere there were lights in the window—people were staying awake. Everyone embraced everyone else, someone sobbed aloud." But after the victory parades and celebrations, Europeans awoke to a devastating realization: their civilization was in ruins. Some wondered if Europe would ever regain its former prosperity and importance. Winston Churchill wrote: "What is Europe now? A rubble heap, a charnel house, a breeding ground of pestilence and hate." There was ample reason for his pessimism. Almost 40 million people (both soldiers and civilians) had been killed over the last six years. Massive air raids and artillery bombardments had reduced many of the great cities of Europe to heaps or rubble. The Polish capital of Warsaw had been almost completely obliterated. An American general described Berlin: "Wherever we looked we saw desolation. It was like a city of the dead. Suffering and shock were visible in every face. Dead bodies still remained in canals and lakes and were being dug out from under bomb debris." Millions of Europeans faced starvation as grain harvests were only half of what they had been in 1939. Millions were also homeless. In the parts of the Soviet Union that had been occupied by the Germans, almost 25 million people were without homes. The destruction of bridges, roads, and railroads had left transportation systems paralyzed. Untold millions of people had been uprooted by the war; now they became "displaced persons," trying to find food and then their way home. Eleven million prisoners of war had to be returned to their native countries while 15 million Germans and East Europeans were driven out of countries where they were no longer wanted. Yet, despite the chaos, Europe was soon on the road to a remarkable recovery. Already by 1950, Europe's industrial and agricultural output was 30 percent above prewar levels.

Emergence of welfare state in Britain

Formation of European Common Market

Marshall Plan

Student revolts

Creation of NATO

Formation of Warsaw Pact

Cuban Missile Crisis

Korean War

Vietnam War

Berlin blockade

Charles de Gaulle assumes power in France

Building of Berlin Wall •

Soviets crush "Prague Spring" in Czechoslovakia

World War II had cost Europe more than physical destruction, however. European supremacy in world affairs had also been destroyed. After 1945, the colonial empires of the European nations rapidly disintegrated while Europe's place in the world changed radically. As the Cold War conflict between the world's two superpowers—the United States and the Soviet Union—intensified, the European nations were divided into two armed camps dependent upon one or the other of these two major powers. The United States and the Soviet Union, whose rivalry raised the specter of nuclear war, seemed to hold the survival of Europe and the world in their hands.

The Development of the Cold War

Even before World War II had ended, the two major Allied powers—the United States and the Soviet Union—had begun to disagree on the nature of the postwar European world. Unity had been maintained during the war because of the urgent need to defeat the Axis powers, but once they were defeated, the differences between the Americans and Soviets again surged to the front. Stalin had never overcome his fear of capitalist superiority while Western leaders still had serious misgivings about communism.

The Confrontation of the Superpowers

There has been considerable historical debate about who was most responsible for the beginning of the Cold War. No doubt, both the United States and the Soviet Union took steps at the end of the war that were unwise or might have been avoided. Both nations, however, were working within a framework conditioned by the past. Ultimately, the rivalry between the two superpowers stemmed from their different historical perspectives and their irreconcilable political ambitions. Intense competition for political and military supremacy had long been a regular feature of Western civilization. The United States and the Soviet Union were the heirs of that European tradition of power politics, and it should not surprise us that two such different systems would seek to extend their way of life to the rest of the world. Because of its need to feel secure on its western border, the Soviet Union was not prepared to give up the advantages it had gained in Eastern Europe from Germany's defeat. But neither were American leaders willing to give up the power and prestige the United States had gained throughout the world. Suspicious of each other's motives, the United States and the Soviet Union soon raised their mutual fears to a level of intense competition. Between 1945 and 1949, a number of events entangled the two countries in continual conflict.

Eastern Europe was the first area of disagreement. The United States and Great Britain had championed self-determination and democratic freedom for the liberated nations of Eastern Europe. Stalin, however, fearful that the Eastern European nations would return to traditional anti-Soviet attitudes if they were permitted free elections, opposed the West's plans. Having liberated Eastern Europe from the Nazis, the Red Army proceeded to install pro-Soviet governing regimes in Poland, Romania, Bulgaria, and Hungary. These pro-

◆ **The Marshall Plan in Action.** Through the Marshall Plan, the United States provided assistance for the economic recovery of Europe. This photograph shows French farmers using American tractors as the Marshall Plan went into effect in 1947.

Soviet governments satisfied Stalin's desire for a buffer zone against the West, but the local populations and their sympathizers in the West saw the regimes as an expansion of Stalin's empire. Only another war could change this situation, and few people wanted another armed conflict.

A civil war in Greece created another arena for confrontation between the superpowers. In 1946, the Communist People's Liberation Army and the anti-Communist forces supported by the British were fighting each other for control of Greece. But continued postwar economic problems caused the British to withdraw from the active role they had been playing in both Greece and Turkey. President Harry S Truman of the United States, alarmed by British weakness and the possibility of Soviet expansion into the eastern Mediterranean, responded with the Truman Doctrine (see the box on p. 997). According to the president, "It must be the policy of the United States to support free peoples who are resisting attempted subjugation by armed minorities or by outside pressures." This statement was made to the American Congress in March 1947 when Truman requested $400 million in economic and military aid for Greece and Turkey. The Truman Doctrine said in essence that the United States would provide money to countries that claimed they were threatened by Communist expansion. If the Soviets were not stopped in Greece, the Truman argument ran, then the United States would have to face the spread of communism throughout the free world. As Dean Acheson, the American secretary of state explained, "Like apples in a barrel infected by disease, the corruption of Greece would infect Iran and all the East . . . likewise Africa . . . Italy . . . France. . . . Not since Rome and Carthage had there been such a polarization of power on this earth."[1]

The proclamation of the Truman Doctrine was soon followed in June 1947 by the European Recovery Program, better known as the Marshall Plan. Intended to rebuild prosperity and stability, this program included $13 billion for the economic recovery of war-torn Europe. Underlying it was the belief that Communist aggression fed off economic turmoil. General George C. Marshall had noted in his commencement speech at Harvard: "Our policy is not directed against any country or doctrine but against hunger, poverty, desperation and chaos."[2] From the Soviet perspective, the Marshall Plan was nothing less than capitalist imperialism, a thinly veiled attempt to buy the support of the smaller European countries, which in return would be expected to submit to economic exploitation by the United States. A Soviet spokesman described the United States as the "main force in the imperialist camp," whose ultimate goal was "the strengthening of imperialism, preparation for a new imperialist war, a struggle against socialism and democracy, and the support of reactionary and anti-democratic, profascist regimes and movements." The Marshall Plan did not intend to shut out either the Soviet Union or its Eastern European satellite states, but they refused to participate. According to the Soviet view, the Marshall Plan aimed at the "construction of a bloc of states bound by obligations to the USA, and to guarantee the American loans in return for the relinquishing by the European states of their economic and later also their political independence."[3] The Soviets, however, were in no position to compete financially with the United States and could do little to counter the Marshall Plan.

By 1947, the split in Europe between East and West had become a fact of life. At the end of World War II, the United States had favored a quick end to its commitments in Europe. But American fears of Soviet aims caused the United States to play an increasingly important role in European affairs. In an important article in *Foreign Affairs* in July 1947, George Kennan, a well-known American diplomat with much knowledge of Soviet affairs, advocated a policy of containment against further aggressive Soviet moves. Kennan favored the "adroit and vigilant application of counter-force at a series of constantly shifting geographical and political points, corresponding to the shifts and manoeuvres of

⇒ *The Truman Doctrine* ⇐

By 1947, the battlelines had been clearly drawn in the Cold War. This selection is taken form a speech by President Harry S Truman to the American Congress in which he justified his request for aid to Greece and Turkey. Truman expressed the urgent need to contain the expansion of communism.

President Harry S Truman Addresses Congress, March 12, 1947

The peoples of a number of countries of the world have recently had totalitarian regimes forced upon them against their will. The Government of the United States has made frequent protests against coercion and intimidation, in violation of the Yalta agreement, in Poland, Romania, and Bulgaria. I must also state that in a number of other countries there have been similar developments.

At the present moment in world history nearly every nation must choose between alternative ways of life. The choice is too often not a free one.

One way of life is based upon the will of the majority, and is distinguished by free institutions, representative government, free elections, guaranties of individual liberty, freedom of speech and religion, and freedom from political oppression.

The second way of life is based upon the will of a minority forcibly imposed upon the majority. It relies upon terror and oppression, a controlled press and radio, fixed elections, and the suppression of personal freedoms.

I believe that it must be the policy of the United States to support free peoples who are resisting attempted subjugation by armed minorities or by outside pressures.

I believe that we must assist free people to work out their own destinies in their own way.

I believe that our help should be primarily through economic and financial aid which is essential to economic stability and orderly political processes. . . . I therefore ask the Congress for assistance to Greece and Turkey in the amount of $400,000,000.

Soviet policy." After the Soviet blockade of Berlin in 1948, containment of the Soviet Union became formal American policy.

The fate of Germany also became a source of heated contention between East and West. Besides denazification and the partitioning of Germany (and Berlin) into four occupied zones, the Allied powers had agreed on little else with regard to the conquered nation. Even denazification proceeded differently in the various zones of occupation. The Americans and British proceeded methodically—the British had tried two million cases by 1948—while the Soviets (and French) went after major Nazi criminals and allowed lesser officials to go free. The Soviets, hardest hit by the war, took reparations from Germany in the form of booty. The technology-starved Soviets dismantled and removed to Russia 380 factories from the western zones of Berlin before transferring their control to the Western powers. By the summer of 1946, 200 chemical, paper, and textile factories in the Soviets' East German zone had likewise been shipped to the Soviet Union. At the same time, the German Communist Party was reestablished under the control of Walter Ulbricht (1893–1973) and was soon in charge of the political reconstruction of the Soviet zone in eastern Germany.

Although the foreign ministers of the four occupying powers (the United States, Soviet Union, Britain, and France) kept meeting in an attempt to arrive at a final peace treaty with Germany, they moved further and further apart. At the same time, the British, French, and Americans gradually began to merge their zones economically and, by February 1948, were making plans for the unification of these three Western sections of Germany and the formal creation of a West German federal government. The Soviets responded with a blockade of West Berlin that allowed neither trucks nor trains to enter the three Western zones of Berlin. The Russians hoped to secure economic control of all Berlin and force the Western powers to halt the creation of a separate West German state.

The Western powers were faced with a dilemma. Direct military confrontation seemed dangerous, and no one wished to risk World War III. Therefore, an attempt to break through the blockade with tanks and trucks was ruled out. The solution was the Berlin Air Lift. At its peak, 13,000 tons of supplies were flown to Berlin daily. The Soviets, also not wanting war, did not interfere and finally lifted the blockade in May 1949. The blockade of Berlin had severely increased tensions between the United States and the Soviet Union and brought the

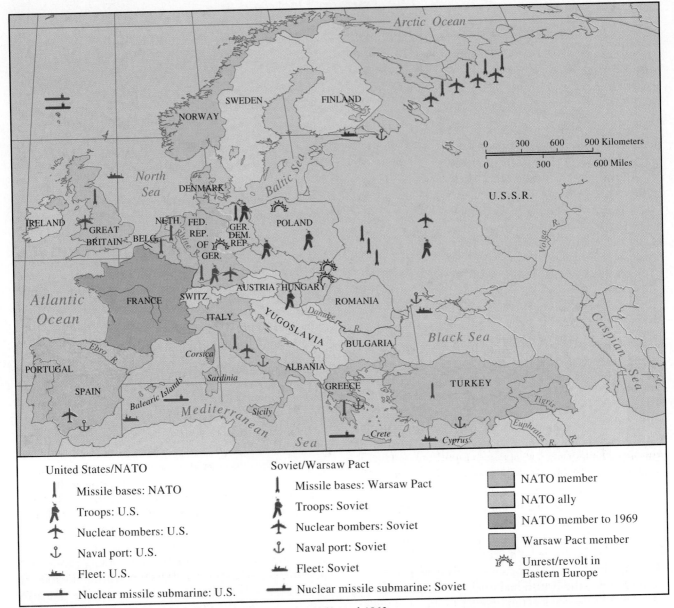

United States/NATO

↑ Missile bases: NATO

🧍 Troops: U.S.

✈ Nuclear bombers: U.S.

⚓ Naval port: U.S.

🚢 Fleet: U.S.

▬ Nuclear missile submarine: U.S.

Soviet/Warsaw Pact

↑ Missile bases: Warsaw Pact

🧍 Troops: Soviet

✈ Nuclear bombers: Soviet

⚓ Naval port: Soviet

🚢 Fleet: Soviet

▬ Nuclear missile submarine: Soviet

NATO member

NATO ally

NATO member to 1969

Warsaw Pact member

💥 Unrest/revolt in Eastern Europe

Map 29.1 The New European Alliance Systems in the 1950s and 1960s.

separation of Germany into two states. The West German Federal Republic was formally created in September 1949, and a month later, a separate German Democratic Republic was established in East Germany. Berlin remained a divided city and the source of much contention between East and West.

In that same year, the Cold War spread from Europe to the rest of the world. The victory of the Chinese Communists in 1949 in the Chinese civil war created a new Communist regime and only intensified American fears about the spread of communism. The Soviet Union also detonated its first atomic bomb in 1949, and all too soon both powers were involved in an escalating arms race that resulted in the construction of ever more destructive nuclear weapons. Soon the search for security took the form of mutual deterrence or the belief that an arsenal of nuclear weapons prevented war by assuring that even if one nation launched its nuclear weapons in a preemptive first strike, the other nation would still be able to respond and devastate the attacker. Therefore, the assumption was that neither side would risk using the massive arsenals that had been assembled.

The search for security in the new world of the Cold War also led to the creation of military alliances. The North Atlantic Treaty Organization (NATO) was formed in April 1949 when Belgium, Luxembourg, the Netherlands, France, Britain, Italy, Denmark, Norway, Portugal, and Iceland signed a treaty with the United States and Canada. All the powers agreed to provide mutual assistance if any one of them was attacked. A few years later West Germany, Greece, and Turkey joined NATO.

The Eastern European states soon followed suit. In 1949, they had already formed the Council for Mutual Economic Assistance (COMECON) for economic cooperation. Then in 1955, Albania, Bulgaria, Czechoslovakia, East Germany, Hungary, Poland, Romania, and the Soviet Union organized a formal military alliance in the Warsaw Pact. Once again, Europe was tragically divided into hostile alliance systems.

A system of military alliances spread to the rest of the world after the United States became involved in the Korean War in 1950. Korea had been liberated from the Japanese in 1945, but was soon divided into two parts. The land north of the thirty-eighth parallel became the Democratic People's Republic (North Korea) and was supported by the Soviet Union. The Republic of Korea (South Korea) received aid from the United States. On June 25, 1950, with the apparent approval of Joseph Stalin, North Korean troops invaded South Korea. The Americans, seeing this as yet another example of Communist aggression and expansion, gained the support of the United Nations and intervened by sending American troops to turn back the invasion. By September, United Nations forces (mostly Americans and South Koreans) under the command of General Douglas MacArthur marched northward across the thirty-eighth parallel with the aim of unifying Korea under a single non-Communist government. But Mao Zedong (1893–1976), the leader of Communist China, then sent Chinese forces into the fray and forced MacArthur's troops to retreat back to South Korea. Believing that the Chinese were simply the puppets of Moscow, American policymakers created an image of communism as a monolithic force directed by the Soviet Union. When two more years of fighting failed to produce a conclusive victory, an armistice was finally signed in 1953. The thirty-eighth parallel remained the boundary line between North and South Korea. To many Americans, the policy of containing communism had succeeded in Asia, just as it had earlier in Europe, despite the cost of losing more than fifty thousand men in the war.

◆ **The Berlin Air Lift.** The Berlin Air Lift enabled the United States to fly 13,000 tons of supplies daily to Berlin and thus break the Soviet land blockade of the city. In this photograph, children in West Berlin are watching another American plane arrive with supplies for the city.

The Korean experience seemed to confirm American fears of Communist expansion and reinforced American determination to contain Soviet power. In the mid-1950s, the administration of President Dwight D. Eisenhower (1890–1969) adopted a policy of massive retaliation, which advocated the full use of American nuclear bombs to counteract even a Soviet ground attack in Europe. Moreover, American military alliances were extended around the world. As President Eisenhower explained, "The freedom we cherish and defend in Europe and in the Americas is no different from the freedom that is imperiled in Asia." The Central Treaty Organization (CENTO) of Turkey, Iraq, Iran, Pakistan, Britain, and the United States was intended to prevent the Soviet Union from expanding at the expense of its southern neighbors. To stem Soviet aggression in the Far East, the United States, Britain, France, Pakistan, Thai-

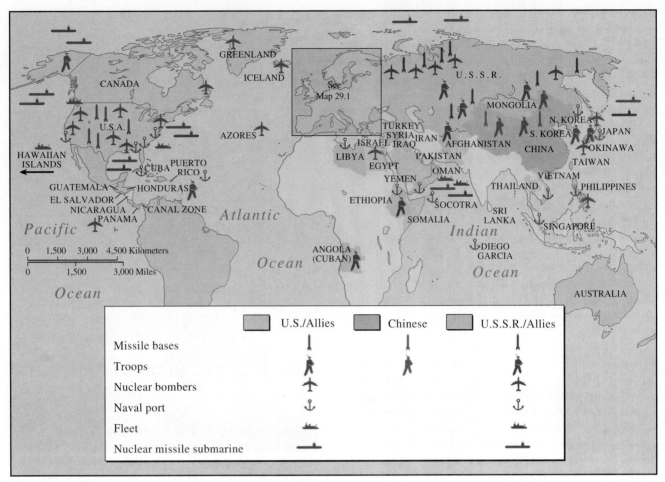

✖ **Map 29.2** The Global Cold War in the 1950s and 1960s.

land, the Philippines, Australia, and New Zealand formed the Southeast Asia Treaty Organization (SEATO). By the mid-1950s, the United States found itself allied militarily with forty-two states around the world.

Despite the continued escalation of the Cold War, hopes for a new era of peaceful coexistence also appeared. Certainly, the death of Stalin in 1953 caused some people in the West to think that the new Soviet leadership might be more flexible in its policies. But this optimism seemed premature. A summit conference at Geneva in 1955 between President Eisenhower and Nikolai Bulganin, then leader of the Soviet government, produced no real benefits. A year later, all talk of rapprochement between East and West temporarily ceased when the Soviet Union used its armed forces to crush Hungary's attempt to assert its independence from Soviet control.

A crisis over Berlin also added to the tension in the late 1950s. In August 1957, the Soviet Union had launched its first Intercontinental Ballistic Missile (ICBM) and, shortly after, *Sputnik I*, the first space satellite. Fueled by partisan political debate, fears of a missile gap between the United States and the Soviet Union seized the American public. Nikita Khrushchev (1894–1971), the new leader of the Soviet Union, attempted to take advantage of the American frenzy over missiles to solve the problem of West Berlin. West Berlin had remained a "Western island" of prosperity in the midst of the relatively poverty-stricken East Germany. Many East Germans also managed to escape East Germany by fleeing through West Berlin.

In November 1958, Khrushchev announced that, unless the West removed its forces from West Berlin within six months, he would turn over control of the access routes to Berlin to the East Germans. Unwilling to accept an ultimatum that would have abandoned West Berlin to the Communists, Eisenhower and the West stood firm, and Khrushchev eventually backed down. In 1961, the East German government built a wall separating West Berlin from East Berlin, and the Berlin issue faded.

It was revived when John F. Kennedy (1917–1963) became the American president. During a summit meeting in Vienna in June 1961, Khrushchev threatened Kennedy with another six-month ultimatum over West Berlin. Kennedy left Vienna convinced of the need to deal firmly with the Soviet Union, and Khrushchev was forced once again to lift his six-month ultimatum. However, determined to achieve some foreign policy success, the Soviet leader soon embarked on an even more dangerous adventure in Cuba.

The Cuban Missile Crisis and the Move toward Détente

The Cold War confrontation between the United States and the Soviet Union reached frightening levels during the Cuban Missile Crisis. In 1959, a left-wing revolutionary named Fidel Castro (b. 1927) had overthrown the Cuban dictator Fulgencio Batista and established a Soviet-supported totalitarian regime. In 1961, an American-supported attempt (the "Bay of Pigs" incident) to overthrow Castro's regime ended in utter failure. The next year, in 1962, the Soviet Union decided to place nuclear missiles in Cuba. The United States was not prepared to allow nuclear weapons to be within such close striking distance of the American mainland, even though it had placed nuclear weapons in Turkey within easy range of the Soviet Union. Khrushchev was quick to point out that "your rockets are in Turkey. You are worried by Cuba . . . because it is 90 miles from the American coast. But Turkey is next to us."[4] When American intelligence discovered that a Soviet fleet carrying missiles was heading to Cuba, President Kennedy decided to blockade Cuba and prevent the fleet from reaching its destination. This approach to the problem had the benefit of delaying confrontation and giving each side time to find a peaceful solution (see the box on p. 1002). Khrushchev agreed to turn back the fleet if Kennedy pledged not to invade Cuba. In a conciliatory letter to Kennedy, Khrushchev wrote, "We and you ought not to pull on the ends of the rope in which you have tied the knot of war, because the more the two of us pull, the tighter that knot will be tied. And a moment may come when that

knot will be tied too tight that even he who tied it will not have the strength to untie it. . . . Let us not only relax the forces pulling on the ends of the rope, let us take measures to untie that knot. We are ready for this."[5]

The Cuban Missile Crisis brought the world frighteningly close to nuclear war. Indeed, in 1992 a high-ranking Soviet officer revealed that short-range rockets armed with nuclear devices would have been used against American troops if the United States had invaded Cuba, an option that President Kennedy fortunately had rejected. The intense feeling that the world might have been annihilated in a few days had a profound influence on both sides. A hotline communications system between Moscow and Washington was installed in 1963 to expedite rapid communications between the two superpowers in a time of crisis. In the same year, the two powers agreed to ban nuclear tests in the atmosphere, a step that at least served to lessen the tensions between the two nations.

By that time, the United States had also been drawn into a new confrontation that had an important impact on the Cold War—the Vietnam War. After Vietnamese forces had defeated their French colonial masters in 1954, Vietnam had been divided. A strongly nationalis-

The Cuban Missile Crisis: Khrushchev's Perspective

The Cuban Missile Crisis was one of the sobering experiences of the Cold War. It led the two superpowers to seek new ways to lessen the tensions between them. This version of the events is taken from the memoirs of Nikita Khrushchev.

Khrushchev Remembers

I will explain what the Caribbean crisis of October 1962, was all about. . . . At the time that Fidel Castro led his revolution to victory and entered Havana with his troops, we had no idea what political course his regime would follow. . . . All the while the Americans had been watching Castro closely. At first they thought that the capitalist underpinnings of the Cuban economy would remain intact. So by the time Castro announced that he was going to put Cuba on the road toward Socialism, the Americans had already missed their chance to do any thing about it by simply exerting their influence: there were no longer any forces left which could be organized to fight on America's behalf in Cuba. That left only one alternative—invasion! . . .

After Castro's crushing victory over the counter-revolutionaries we intensified our military aid to Cuba . . . We were sure that the Americans would never reconcile themselves to the existence of Castro's Cuba. They feared, as much as we hoped, that a Socialist Cuba might become a magnet that would attract other Latin American countries to Socialism. . . . It was clear to me that we might very well lose Cuba if we didn't take some decisive steps in her defense. . . . We had to think up some way of confronting America with more than words. We had to establish a tangible and effective deterrent to American interference in the Caribbean. But what exactly? The logical answer was missiles. We knew that American missiles were aimed against us in Turkey and Italy, to say nothing of West Germany. . . . My thinking went like this: if we installed the missiles secretly and then if the United States discovered the missiles were there after they were already poised and ready to strike, the Americans would think twice before trying to liquidate our installations by military means. . . . I want to make one thing absolutely clear: when we put our ballistic missiles in Cuba we had no desire to start a war. On the contrary, our principal aim was only to deter America from starting a war. . . .

President Kennedy issued an ultimatum, demanding that we remove our missiles and bombers from Cuba. . . . We sent the Americans a note saying that we agreed to remove our missiles and bombers on the condition that the President give us his assurance that there would be no invasion of Cuba by the forces of the United States or anybody else. Finally Kennedy gave in and agreed to make a statement giving us such an assurance. . . . It had been, to say the least, an interesting and challenging situation. The two most powerful nations of the world had been squared off against each other, each with its finger on the button. You'd have thought that war was inevitable. But both sides showed that if the desire to avoid war is strong enough, even the most pressing dispute can be solved by compromise. And a compromise over Cuba was indeed found. The episode ended in a triumph of common sense. . . . It was a great victory for us, though, that we had been able to extract from Kennedy a promise that neither America nor any of her allies would invade Cuba. . . . The Caribbean crisis was a triumph of Soviet foreign policy and a personal triumph in my own career as a statesman and as a member of the collective leadership. We achieved, I would say, a spectacular success without having to fire a single shot!

---

tic regime in the north under Ho Chi Minh (1890–1969) received Soviet aid, while American sponsors worked to establish a pro-Western regime in South Vietnam. President Kennedy maintained Eisenhower's policy of providing military and financial aid to the regime of Ngo Dinh Diem, the autocratic ruler of South Vietnam. But the Kennedy administration grew increasingly disenchanted with the Diem regime, which was corrupt and seemed incapable of gaining any strong support from the people. From the American point of view, this lack of support simply undermined the ability of the South Vietnamese government to deal with the Vietcong, the South Vietnamese Communist guerrillas who were being supported by the North Vietnamese. In November 1963, the American government supported a military coup that overthrew the Diem regime. However, the new military government seemed even less able to govern the country.

In 1964, under President Lyndon Johnson (1908–1973), increasing numbers of American troops were sent to Vietnam to defeat the Vietcong and keep the Communist regime of the north from uniting the entire country under its control. Although nationalism played a powerful role in this conflict, American policymakers saw it in terms of a domino theory concerning the spread of communism. If the Communists succeeded in Vietnam, so the argument went, all the other countries in the Far East freeing themselves from colonial domination would fall (like dominoes) to communism.

Despite their massive superiority in equipment and firepower, American forces failed to prevail over the persistence of the North Vietnamese and especially the Vietcong. These guerrilla forces were extremely effective against American troops. Natives of Vietnam, they were able to live off the land, disappear among the people, and attack when least expected. Many South Vietnamese villagers were so opposed to their own government that they sheltered and supported the Vietcong.

The growing number of American troops sent to Vietnam soon produced a persistent antiwar movement in the United States, especially among college students of draft age. The mounting destruction and increasing brutalization of the war, brought into American homes every evening on television, also turned American public opinion against the war. Finally, in 1973 President Richard Nixon (1913-1994) reached an agreement with North Vietnam that allowed the United States to withdraw its forces. Within two years, Vietnam had been forcibly reunited by Communist armies from the North.

Despite the success of the North Vietnamese Communists, the domino theory proved unfounded. A noisy rupture between Communist China and the Soviet Union put an end to the idea of a monolithic communism directed by Moscow. Under President Nixon, American relations with China were resumed. New nations in Southeast Asia also managed to avoid Communist governments. Above all, Vietnam helped to show the limitations of American power. By the end of the Vietnam War, a new era in American-Soviet relations—known as détente—had begun to emerge.

Recovery and Renewal in Europe

At the height of Nazi success in 1942, a new era of barbarism seemed to challenge the very existence of European civilization. But Europeans made a remarkable recovery, and within a few years after the defeat of Germany and Italy, economic revival brought a renewed growth to European society, although major differences remained between Western and Eastern Europe. Moreover, many Europeans, who had feared that European states would suffer tremendously from the loss of their colonies, found that they could even adjust to decolonization.

The End of European Colonies

Not only did World War II leave Europe in ruins, but it also cost Europe its supremacy in world affairs. World

◆ **John F. Kennedy and the Cuban Missile Crisis.** During the Cuban Missile Crisis, the United States and the Soviet Union came frighteningly close to a direct nuclear confrontation. This photograph shows President John F. Kennedy meeting with his cabinet and advisers during the Cuban crisis in October 1962. At Kennedy's left is Robert McNamara, the secretary of defense, and to his right is Dean Rusk, the secretary of state.

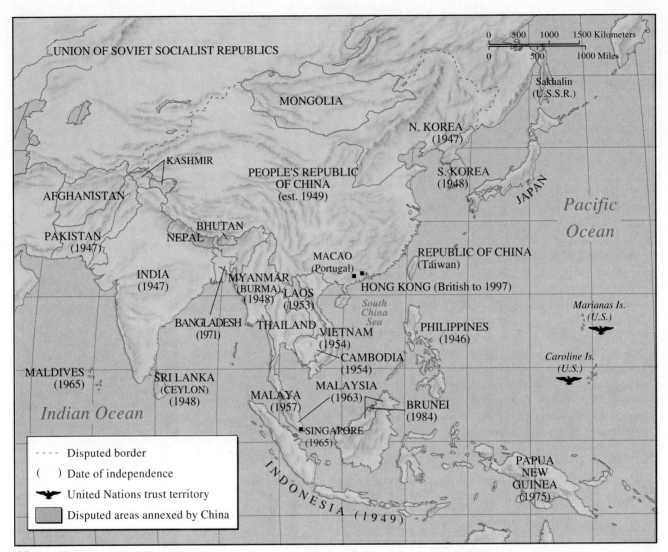

🎴 **Map 29.3** Asia after World War II.

War I had initiated nationalistic movements against colonial rule, and World War II greatly accelerated this process. The Japanese had already humiliated the Western states by overrunning their colonial empires during the war. In addition, colonial soldiers who had fought on behalf of the Allies were well aware that Allied war aims included the principle of self-determination for the peoples of the world. Equally important to the process of decolonization after the war, the power of the European states had been destroyed by the exhaustive struggles of World War II. The greatest colonial empire builder, Great Britain, no longer had the energy or wealth to maintain its colonial empire after the war and quickly

sought to let its colonies go. Given the combination of circumstances, a rush of decolonization swept through the world. Between 1947 and 1962, virtually every colony achieved independence and attained statehood. Although some colonial powers willingly relinquished their control, others, especially the French, had to be driven out by national wars of liberation (see the box on p. 1005). Decolonization was a difficult and even bitter process, but it created a new world as the non-Western states ended the long-held ascendancy of the Western nations.

In Asia, the United States initiated the process of decolonization in 1946 when it granted independence

≈ Frantz Fanon and the Wretched of the Earth ≈

Born in French Martinique, Frantz Fanon (1925–1961) studied psychiatry in France. His work as head of a psychiatric hospital in Algeria led him to favor violence as a necessary instrument to overthrow Western imperialism, which to Fanon was itself rooted in violence. The Wretched of the Earth, published in 1961, provided an argument for national liberation movements in the Third World. In the last part of the book, Fanon discussed the problem of mental disorders that arose from Algeria's war of national liberation.

The Wretched of the Earth
Colonial War and Mental Disorders, Series B

We have here brought together certain cases or groups of cases in which the event giving rise to the illness is in the first place the atmosphere of total war which reigns in Algeria.

Case No. 1: The murder by two young Algerians, thirteen and fourteen years old respectively, of their European playmate.

We had been asked to give expert medical advice in a legal matter. Two young Algerians thirteen and fourteen years old, pupils in a secondary school, were accused of having killed one of their European schoolmates. They admitted having done it. The crime was reconstructed, and photos were added to the record. Here one of the children could be seen holding the victim while the other struck at him with a knife. The little defendants did not go back on their declarations. We had long conversations with them. We here reproduce the most characteristic of their remarks:

The boy fourteen years old:

This young defendant was in marked contrast to his school fellow. He was already almost a man, and an adult in his muscular control, his appearance, and the content of his replies. He did not deny having killed

either. Why had he killed? He did not reply to the question but asked me had I ever seen a European in prison. Had there ever been a European arrested and sent to prison after the murder of an Algerian? I replied that in fact I had never seen any Europeans in prison.

"And yet there are Algerians killed every day, aren't there?"

"Yes."

"So why are only Algerians found in the prisons? Can you explain that to me?"

"No. But tell me why you killed this boy who was your friend."

"I'll tell you why. You've heard tell of the Rivet business?" [Rivet was a village near Algiers where in 1956 the French militia dragged forty men from their own beds and afterward murdered them.]

"Yes."

"Two of my family were killed then. At home, they said that the French had sworn to kill us all, one after the other. And did they arrest a single Frenchman for all those Algerians who were killed?"

"I don't know."

"Well, nobody at all was arrested. I wanted to take to the mountains, but I was too young. So [my friend] and I said we'd kill a European."

"Why?"

"In your opinion, what should we have done?"

"I don't know. But you are a child and what is happening concerns grown-up people."

"But they kill children too.'"

"That is no reason for killing your friend."

"Well, kill him I did. Now you can do what you like."

"Had your friend done anything to harm you?"

"Not a thing."

"Well?"

"Well, there you are."

---

to the Philippines. Britain soon followed suit with its oldest and largest nonwhite possession—India. The conflict between India's Hindu and Muslim populations was solved by forming two states, a mostly Hindu India and a predominantly Muslim Pakistan in 1947. In 1948, Britain granted independence to Ceylon (modern Sri Lanka) and Burma (modern Myanmar). When the Dutch failed to reestablish control over the Dutch East Indies, Indonesia emerged as an independent nation in 1949. The French effort to remain in Indochina led to a bloody struggle with the Vietminh, Vietnamese nationalist guerrillas, led by Ho Chi Minh, the Communist and nationalist leader of the Vietnamese. After their defeat in 1954, the French granted independence to Laos and Cambodia, while Vietnam was temporarily divided in anticipation of elections in 1956 that would decide its fate. But the elections were never held, and the division of Vietnam by Communist and pro-Western regimes eventually led to the Vietnam War.

In the midst of the decolonization of Asia, the Nationalist Chinese under Chiang Kai-Shek (1887–1975) and the Communists under Mao Zedong were fighting a bloody civil war. Mao's victory in 1949 led to the creation of a powerful Communist state in Asia.

In the Middle East and North Africa, Arab nationlism was a powerful factor in ending colonial empires. Some Arab states had already become independent before the end of World War II. Now they were joined by other free Arab states, but not without considerable bloodshed and complications. When the British left Palestine in 1947, the United Nations voted to create both an Arab state and a Jewish state. When the Arabs attempted to destroy the new Israeli state, Israel's victories secured its existence. But the problem of the Palestinian refugees, supported by existing Arab states, created an Arab-Israeli conflict that has lasted to this day.

In North Africa, the French, who were simply not strong enough to maintain control of their far-flung colonial empire, granted full independence to Morocco and Tunisia in 1956. Since Algeria was home to two million French settlers, however, France chose to retain its dominion there. But a group of Algerian nationalists organized the National Liberation Front (FLN) and in 1954 initiated a guerrilla war to liberate their homeland. The French people became so divided over this war that the French leader, Charles de Gaulle, accepted the inevitable and granted Algerian independence in 1962.

Decolonization in Africa south of the Sahara took place less turbulently. Ghana proclaimed its independence in 1957, and by 1960, almost all French and British possessions in Africa had gained their freedom. In 1960, the Belgians freed the Congo (modern Zaire). The Portuguese held on stubbornly but were also driven out of Africa by 1975. Nevertheless, the continuing European economic presence in sub-Saharan Africa led radicals to accuse Europeans of "neocolonial" attitudes.

Although expectations ran high in the new states, they soon found themselves beset with problems of extreme poverty and antagonistic tribal groups that felt little loyalty to the new nations. These states come to be known collectively as the "Third World" (the "First World consisted of the advanced industrial countries—Japan and the states of Western Europe and North

Map 29.4 The Middle East after World War II.

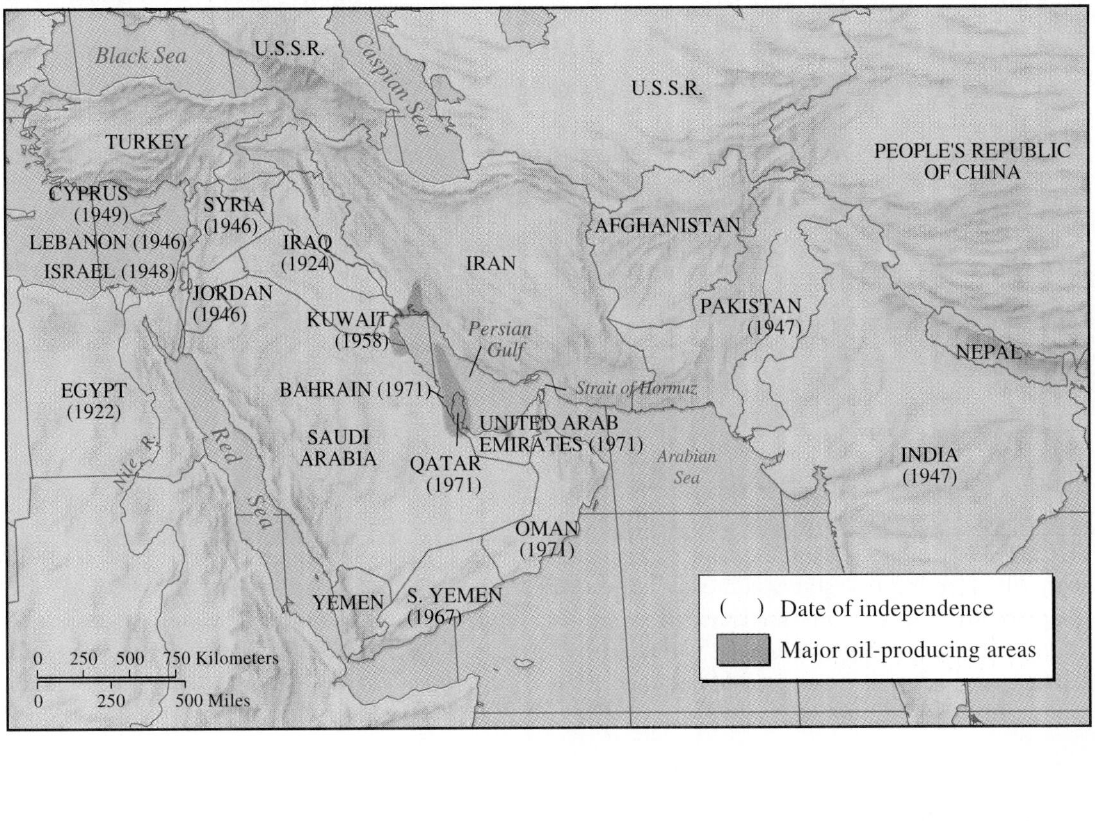

America; the "Second World" comprised the Soviet Union and its satellites). Their status as "backward" nations led many Third World countries to modernize by pursuing Western technology and industrialization. In many instances, this has basically meant that these peoples have had to adjust to the continuing imposition of Western institutions and values upon their societies.

The Soviet Union: From Stalin to Khrushchev

World War II devastated the Soviet Union. To create a new industrial base, Stalin returned to the method that he had used in the 1930s—the acquisition of develop-

ment capital from Soviet labor. Working hard for little pay, poor housing, and precious few consumer goods, Soviet laborers were expected to produce goods for export with little in return for themselves. The incoming capital from abroad could then be used to purchase machinery and Western technology. The loss of millions of men in the war meant that much of this tremendous workload fell upon Soviet women. Almost 40 percent of heavy manual labor was performed by women.

Economic recovery in the Soviet Union was nothing less than spectacular. By 1947, Russian industrial production had attained prewar levels; three years later, it had surpassed them by 40 percent. New power plants,

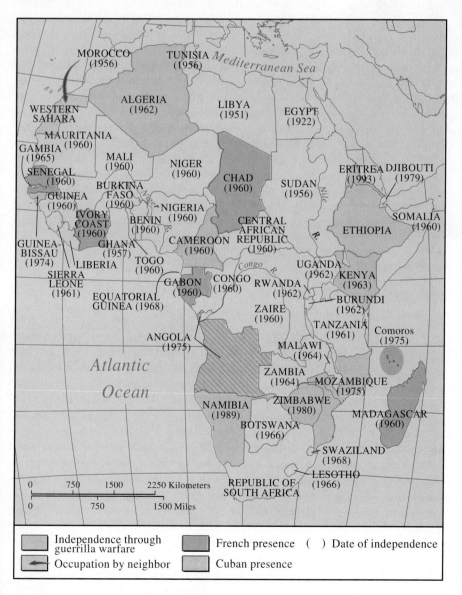

Map 29.5 Africa after World War II.

◆ **Algerian Independence.** Although the French wanted to retain control of their Algerian colony, a bloody war of liberation finally led to Algeria's freedom. This photograph shows a group of Algerians celebrating the announcement of independence on July 3, 1962.

canals, and giant factories were built, while new industries and oil fields were established in Siberia and Soviet Central Asia. Stalin's newly announced five-year plan of 1946 reached its goals in less than five years.

Although Stalin's economic policy was successful in promoting growth in heavy industry, primarily for the benefit of the military, consumer goods were scarce. While the development of thermonuclear weapons in 1953, MIG fighters from 1950 to 1953, and the first space satellite (*Sputnik*) in 1957 elevated the Soviet state's reputation as a world power abroad, domestically the Russian people were shortchanged. Heavy industry grew at a rate three times that of personal consumption. Moreover, the housing shortage was acute. A British military attaché in Moscow reported that "all houses, practically without exception, show lights from every window after dark. This seems to indicate that every room is both a living room by day and a bedroom by night. There is no place in overcrowded Moscow for the luxury of eating and sleeping in separate rooms."[6]

To sustain the war effort against the Germans, Stalin had fostered superpatriotism among all Soviets, but found that contact with Western ways during the war had shaken many people's belief in the superiority of the Soviet system. Returning Russian soldiers brought back stories of the prosperity of the West, and the obvious disparity between the Western and Soviet systems led to a "crisis of faith" for many young Communists. Partly for this reason, Stalin imprisoned many soldiers, who were simply shipped from German concentration camps to Soviet concentration camps. In Stalin's view, Western influence was a threat to Communist ideals.

When World War II ended in 1945, Stalin had been in power for more than fifteen years. During that time, he had removed all opposition to his rule and remained the undisputed master of the Soviet Union. Other leading members of the Communist Party were completely obedient to his will. Increasingly distrustful of competitors, Stalin exercised sole authority and pitted his subordinates against one another.

Stalin's morbid suspicions fueled the constantly increasing repression that was a characteristic of his regime. In 1946, the government decreed that all literary and scientific works must conform to the political needs of the state. Along with this anti-intellectual campaign came political terror. A new series of purges seemed imminent in 1953 when a number of Jewish doctors were implicated in a spurious plot to kill high-level party officials. Only Stalin's death on March 5, 1953, prevented more bloodletting.

A new collective leadership succeeded Stalin until Nikita Khrushchev emerged as the chief Soviet policymaker. Khrushchev had been responsible for ending the system of forced-labor camps, a regular feature of Stalinist Russia. At the Twentieth Congress of the Communist Party in 1956, Khrushchev condemned Stalin for his "administrative violence, mass repression, and terror" (see the box on p. 1009).

Once in power, Khrushchev took steps to undo some of the worst features of Stalin's repressive regime. A certain degree of intellectual freedom was now permitted; as Khrushchev said, "readers should be given the chance to make their own judgments" regarding the acceptability of controversial literature, and "police measures shouldn't be used."[7] In 1962, he allowed the publication of Alexander Solzhenitsyn's *A Day in the Life of Ivan Denisovich,* a grim portrayal of the horrors of Russia's forced-labor camps. Most importantly, Khrush-

Khrushchev Denounces Stalin

Three years after the death of Stalin, the new Soviet premier, Nikita Khrushchev, addressed the Twentieth Congress of the Communist Party and denounced the former Soviet dictator for his crimes. This denunciation was the beginning of a policy of destalinization.

Nikita Khrushchev Addresses the Twentieth Party Congress, February 1956

Comrades, . . . quite a lot has been said about the cult of the individual and about its harmful consequences. . . . The cult of the person of Stalin . . . became at a certain specific stage the source of a whole series of exceedingly serious and grave perversions of Party principles, of Party democracy, of revolutionary legality.

Stalin absolutely did not tolerate collegiality in leadership and in work and . . . practiced brutal violence, not only toward everything which opposed him, but also toward that which seemed to his capricious and despotic character, contrary to his concepts.

Stalin abandoned the method of ideological struggle for that of administrative violence, mass repressions and terror. . . . Arbitrary behavior by one person encouraged and permitted arbitrariness in others. Mass arrests and deportations of many thousands of people, execution without trial and without normal investigation created conditions of insecurity, fear and even desperation.

Stalin showed in a whole series of cases his intolerance, his brutality and his abuse of power. . . . He often chose the path of repression and annihilation, not only against actual enemies, but also against individuals who had not committed any crimes against the Party and the Soviet government. . . .

Many Party, Soviet and economic activists who were branded in 1937—8 as "enemies" were actually never enemies, spies, wreckers and so on, but were always honest communists; they were only so stigmatized, and often, no longer able to bear barbaric tortures, they charged themselves (at the order of the investigative judges-falsifiers) with all kinds of grave and unlikely crimes.

This was the result of the abuse of power by Stalin, who began to use mass terror against the Party cadres. . . . Stalin put the Party and the NKVD [the secret police] up to the use of mass terror when the exploiting classes had been liquidated in our country and when there were no serious reasons for the use of extraordinary mass terror. The terror was directed . . . against the honest workers of the Party and the Soviet state. . . .

Stalin was a very distrustful man, sickly suspicious. . . . Everywhere and in everything he saw "enemies," "two-facers" and "spies." Possessing unlimited power, he indulged in great wilfulness and choked a person morally and physically. A situation was created where one could not express one's own will. When Stalin said that one or another would be arrested, it was necessary to accept on faith that he was an "enemy of the people." What proofs were offered? The confession of the arrested. . . . How is it possible that a person confesses to crimes that he had not committed? Only in one way—because of application of physical methods of pressuring him, tortures, bringing him to a state of unconsciousness, deprivation of his judgment, taking away of his human dignity.

chev extended the process of destalinization by reducing the powers of the secret police, freeing a number of political prisoners, and closing some of the Siberian prison camps. Nevertheless, when Khrushchev's revelations about Stalin at the Twentieth Congress created turmoil in Communist ranks everywhere and encouraged a spirit of rebellion in Soviet satellite countries in Eastern Europe, there was a reaction. Soviet troops crushed an uprising in Hungary in 1956 (see the next section), and Khrushchev and the Soviet leaders, fearful of further undermining the basic foundations of the regime, downplayed their campaign of destalinization.

Economically, Khrushchev tried to place more emphasis on light industry and consumer goods. Likewise, he encouraged the decentralization of agriculture by allowing more local decision making with less interference from Moscow. Khrushchev's attempts to increase agricultural output by growing corn and cultivating vast lands east of the Ural Mountains proved less successful and damaged his reputation within the party. These failures, combined with increased military spending, hurt the Soviet economy. The industrial growth rate, which had soared in the early 1950s, now declined dramatically from 13 percent in 1953 to 7.5 percent in 1964.

Khrushchev's personality also did not endear him to the higher Soviet officials who frowned at his tendency to crack jokes and play the clown. Nor were the higher

◆ **Khrushchev's Visit to Yugoslavia.** The leadership of Nikita Khrushchev appeared for a while to open the door to more flexible Soviet policies. In 1955, he visited Yugoslavia in an attempt to improve relations with a Communist state that had deviated from Soviet policies. Khrushchev is shown here making a conciliatory speech with Marshall Tito, the leader of Yugoslavia, looking on.

members of the party bureaucracy pleased when Khrushchev tried to curb their privileges. Foreign policy failures caused additional damage to Khrushchev's reputation among his colleagues. His rash plan to place missiles in Cuba was the final straw. While he was away on vacation in 1964, a special meeting of the Soviet Politburo voted him out of office (because of "deteriorating health") and forced him into retirement. Although a group of leaders succeeded him, real power came into the hands of Leonid Brezhnev (1906–1982), the "trusted" supporter of Khrushchev who had engineered his downfall.

Eastern Europe: Behind the Iron Curtain

At the end of World War II, Soviet military forces had occupied all of Eastern Europe and the Balkans (except Greece, Albania, and Yugoslavia). All of the occupied states came to be part of the Soviet sphere of influence and, after 1945, experienced similar political developments. Coalitions of all political parties (except fascist or right-wing parties) were formed to run the government, but within a year or two, the Communist parties in these coalitions had assumed the lion's share of power. The next step was the creation of one-party Communist governments. The timetables in these takeovers varied from country to country, but between 1945 and 1947, Communist governments became firmly entrenched in East Germany, Bulgaria, Romania, Poland, and Hungary. In Czechoslovakia which had a strong tradition of democratic institutions, the Communists did not achieve their goals until 1948. In the elections of 1946, the Communist Party of Czechoslovakia had become the largest party. But it was not all-powerful and shared control of the government with the non-Communist parties. When it appeared that the latter might win new elections early in 1948, the Communists seized control of the government on February 25. All other parties were dissolved, and Klement Gottwald, the leader of the Communists, became the new president of Czechoslovakia.

Albania and Yugoslavia were notable exceptions to this progression of Soviet dominance in Eastern Europe. Both had had strong Communist resistance movements during the war, and in both countries, the Communist Party simply took over power when the war ended. In

Albania, local Communists established a rigidly Stalinist regime, but one that grew increasingly independent of the Soviet Union.

In Yugoslavia, Josip Broz, known as Tito (1892–1980), leader of the Communist resistance movement, seemed to be a loyal Stalinist. After the war, however, he moved toward the establishment of an independent Communist state in Yugoslavia. Stalin hoped to take control of Yugoslavia, just as he had done in other Eastern European countries, but Tito refused to capitulate to Stalin's demands and gained the support of the people by portraying the struggle as one of Yugoslav national freedom. In 1958, the Yugoslav party congress asserted that Yugoslav Communists did not see themselves as deviating from communism, only Stalinism. They considered their way closer to the Marxist-Leninist ideal. This included a more decentralized economic and political system in which workers could manage themselves and local communes could exercise some political power.

Between 1948 and Stalin's death in 1953, the Eastern European satellite states followed a policy of Stalinization. They instituted Soviet-type five-year plans with emphasis on heavy industry rather than consumer goods. They began to collectivize agriculture. They eliminated all non-Communist parties and established the institutions of repression—secret police and military forces. But communism—a foreign product—had not developed deep roots among the peoples of Eastern Europe. Moreover, Soviet economic exploitation of Eastern Europe made living conditions harsh for most people. The Soviets demanded reparations from their defeated wartime enemies Bulgaria, Romania, and Hungary—often in the form of confiscated plants and factories removed to the Soviet Union—and forced all of the Eastern European states to trade with the Soviet Union to the latter's advantage.

After Stalin's death, many Eastern European states began to pursue a new, more nationalistically oriented course, while the new Soviet leaders, including Khrushchev, interfered less in the internal affairs of their satellites. But in the late 1950s and 1960s, the Soviet Union also made it clear, particularly in Poland, Hungary, and Czechoslovakia, that it would not allow its Eastern European satellites to become independent of Soviet control.

In 1956, after the circulation of Khrushchev's denunciation of Stalin, protests—especially by workers—erupted in Poland. In response, the Polish Communist Party adopted a series of reforms in October 1956 and elected Wladyslaw Gomulka (1905–1982) as first secretary. Gomulka declared that Poland had the right to

follow its own socialist path. Fearful of Soviet armed response, however, the Poles compromised. Poland pledged to remain loyal to the Warsaw Pact, while the Soviets agreed to allow Poland to follow its own path to socialism. The Catholic church, an extremely important institution to many Poles, was also permitted to administer its own affairs.

The developments in Poland in 1956 inspired national Communists in Hungary to seek the same kinds of reforms and independence. Intense debates eventually resulted in the ouster of the ruling Stalinist and the selection of Imry Nagy (1896–1958) as the new Hungarian leader. Internal dissent, however, was not simply directed against the Soviets, but against communism in general, which was viewed as a creation of the Soviets, not the Hungarians. The Stalinist secret police had also bred much terror and hatred. This dissatisfaction, combined with economic difficulties, created a situation ripe for revolt. In order to quell the rising rebellion, Nagy declared Hungary a free nation on November 1, 1956. He promised free elections, and the mood of the country made it clear that this could mean the end of Communist rule in Hungary. But Khrushchev was in no position at home to allow a member of the Communist flock to leave. Just three days after Nagy's declaration, the Red Army attacked the capital city of Budapest (see the box on p. 1012). The Soviets reestablished control over the country while János Kádár (1912–1989), a reform-minded cabinet minister, replaced Nagy and worked with the Soviets to squash the revolt. By collaborating with the Soviet invaders, Kádár saved many of Nagy's economic reforms.

The developments in Poland and Hungary in 1956 did not generate similar revolts in Czechoslovakia. The

Soviet Repression in Eastern Europe: Hungary, 1956

Developments in Poland in 1956 inspired the Communist leaders of Hungary to begin to remove their country from Soviet control. But there were limits to Khrushchev's tolerance, and he sent Soviet troops to crush Hungary's movement for independence. The first selection is a statement by the Soviet government justifying the use of Soviet troops, while the second is a brief and tragic final statement from Imry Nagy, the Hungarian leader.

Statement of the Soviet Government,
October 30, 1956

The Soviet Government regards it as indispensable to make a statement in connection with the events in Hungary.

The course of the events has shown that the working people of Hungary, who have achieved great progress on the basis of their people's democratic order, correctly raise the question of the necessity of eliminating serious shortcomings in the field of economic building, the further raising of the material well-being of the population, and the struggle against bureaucratic excesses in the state apparatus.

However, this just and progressive movement of the working people was soon joined by forces of black reaction and counterrevolution, which are trying to take advantage of the discontent of part of the working people to undermine the foundations of the people's democratic order in Hungary and to restore the old landlord and capitalist order.

The Soviet Government and all the Soviet people deeply regret that the development of events in Hungary has led to bloodshed. On the request of the Hungarian People's Government the Soviet Government consented to the entry into Budapest of the Soviet Army units to assist the Hungarian People's Army and the Hungarian authorities to establish order in the town.

The Last Message of Imry Nagy,
November 4, 1956

This fight is the fight for freedom by the Hungarian people against the Russian intervention, and it is possible that I shall only be able to stay at my post for one or two hours. The whole world will see how the Russian armed forces, contrary to all treaties and conventions, are crushing the resistance of the Hungarian people. They will also see how they are kidnapping the Prime Minister of a country which is a Member of the United Nations, taking him from the capital, and therefore it cannot be doubted at all that this is the most brutal form of intervention. I should like in these last moments to ask the leaders of the revolution, if they can, to leave the country. I ask that all that I have said in my broadcast, and what we have agreed on with the revolutionary leaders during meetings in Parliament, should be put in a memorandum, and the leaders should turn to all the peoples of the world for help and explain that today it is Hungary and tomorrow, or the day after tomorrow, it will be the turn of other countries because the imperialism of Moscow does not know borders, and is only trying to play for time.

"Little Stalin," Antonin Novotny (1904–1975), placed in power in 1952 by Stalin himself, remained firmly in control. By the late 1960s, however, Novotny had alienated many members of his own party and was particularly resented by Czechoslovakia's writers, such as the playwright Vaclav Havel (b. 1936). A writers' rebellion late in 1967, in fact, led to Novotny's resignation. In January 1968, Alexander Dubcek (1921–1992) was elected first secretary of the Communist Party and soon introduced a number of reforms, including freedom of speech and press, freedom to travel abroad, and a relaxation of secret police activities. Dubcek hoped to create "communism with a human face." A period of euphoria erupted that came to be known as the "Prague Spring."

It proved to be short-lived. This euphoria had led many to call for more far-reaching reforms, including neutrality and withdrawal from the Soviet bloc. To forestall the spreading of this "spring" fever, the Red Army invaded Czechoslovakia in August of 1968 and crushed the reform movement. Gustav Husák (b. 1913), a committed nonreformist, replaced Dubcek, crushed his reforms, and maintained the old order until the end of 1987.

Western Europe: The Revival of Democracy and the Economy

All the countries of Western Europe faced similar kinds of problems at the end of World War II. They needed to rebuild their economies, recreate their democratic institutions, and face the growth of Communist parties.

The important role that Communists had played in the resistance movements against the Nazis gained them a new respectability and strength once the war was over. Communist parties did well in elections in Italy and France in 1946 and 1947 and even showed strength in some countries, such as Belgium and the Netherlands, where they had not been much of a political factor before the war. But Communist success was short-lived. After the hardening of the divisions in the Cold War, their advocacy of Soviet policies hurt the Communist parties at home, and their support began to dwindle. The Communist Party in Belgium, for example, received 14 percent of the vote in 1946, but only 4 percent in the 1960s. Only in France and Italy, where social inequities remained their focus, did Communist parties still garner significant support—about 25 percent of the vote.

As part of their electoral strategy, Communist parties had often joined forces with other left-wing parties, such as the Social Democrats. The Socialist parties had also fared well immediately after the war as the desire to overthrow the old order led to the abandonment of conservative parties. But support for the Socialists soon waned. In France, for example, Socialists won 23 percent of the vote in 1945, but 18 percent in 1946 and only 12.6 percent in 1962. The Cold War also hurt the cause of socialism. Socialist parties had originally been formed in the late nineteenth century as Marxist parties, and their identification with Communist parties in postwar coalitions cost them dearly. In the late 1950s, many Socialist parties on the Continent perceived the need to eliminate their old doctrinal emphasis on class struggle and began to call for social justice and liberty. While they advocated economic and social planning, they no longer demanded the elimination of the capitalist system.

By 1950, moderate political parties had made a remarkable comeback in Western Europe. Especially important was the rise of Christian Democratic parties. The new Christian Democrats were not connected to the prewar church-based parties that had been advocates of church interests and had crusaded against both liberal and socialist causes. The new Christian Democrats were sincerely interested in democracy and in significant economic reforms. They were especially strong in Italy

✦ **Soviet Invasion of Czechoslovakia, 1968.** The attempt of Alexander Dubcek, the new first secretary of the Communist Party, to liberalize Communist rule in Czechoslovakia failed when Soviet troops invaded and crushed the reform movement. This photograph shows a confrontation between Soviet tanks and Czechs in Prague. The tanks won.

and Germany and played a particularly important role in achieving Europe's economic restoration.

Western European countries recovered relatively rapidly from the devastation of World War II. No doubt, the Marshall Plan played a significant role in this process. Between 1947 and 1950, European countries received $9.4 billion to be used for new equipment and raw materials. By 1950, industrial output in Europe was 30 percent above prewar levels. Between 1947 and 1950, steel production alone expanded by 70 percent. And this economic recovery continued well into the 1950s and 1960s. The decades of the 1950s and 1960s were periods of dramatic economic growth and prosperity in Western Europe. Indeed, Western Europe experienced virtually full employment during these decades.

FRANCE: THE DOMINATION OF DE GAULLE

The history of France for nearly a quarter century after the war was dominated by one man—Charles de Gaulle (1890–1970)—who possessed an unshakable faith that he had a historical mission to reestablish the greatness of the French nation. During the war, de Gaulle had assumed leadership of some resistance groups and played an important role in ensuring the establishment of a French provisional government after the war. The creation of the Fourth Republic, with a return to a parlia-

◆ **Charles de Gaulle.** As president, Charles de Gaulle sought to revive the greatness of the French nation. He is shown here dressed in his military uniform participating in a formal state ceremony.

mentary system based on parties that de Gaulle considered weak, led him to withdraw from politics. Eventually, he formed the "French Popular Movement," a decidedly rightist organization. It blamed the parties for France's political mess and called for an even stronger presidency, a goal that de Gaulle finally achieved in 1958.

The fragile political stability of the Fourth Republic had been badly shaken by the Algerian crisis. The French army had suffered defeat in Indochina in 1954 and was determined to resist Algerian demands for independence. But a strong antiwar movement among French intellectuals and church leaders led to bitter divisions within France. The army's unwillingness to accept anything but complete victory in Algeria led some French army officers to instigate a revolt against their own government and open the door to the possibility of civil war in France. The panic-stricken leaders of the Fourth Republic offered to let de Gaulle take over the government and revise the constitution.

In 1958, de Gaulle immediately drafted a new constitution for the Fifth Republic that greatly enhanced the power of the president, who now had the right to choose the prime minister, dissolve parliament, and supervise both defense and foreign policy. DeGaulle had always believed in strong leadership, and the new Fifth Republic was by no means a democratic system. As the new president, de Gaulle sought to return France to the position of a great power (see the box on p. 1015). He believed that playing a pivotal role in the Cold War might enhance France's stature. For that reason, he pulled France out of the NATO high command. He increased French prestige among the Third World countries by consenting to Algerian independence despite strenuous opposition from the army. With an eye toward achieving the status of a world power, de Gaulle invested heavily in the nuclear arms race. France exploded its first nuclear bomb in 1960. Despite his successes, de Gaulle did not really achieve his ambitious goals of world power. Although his successors maintained that France was the "third nuclear power" after the United States and the Soviet Union, in truth France was too small for such global ambitions.

Although the cost of the nuclear program increased the defense budget, de Gaulle did not neglect the French economy. Economic decision making was centralized, a reflection of the overall centralization undertaken by the Gaullist government. Between 1958 and 1968, the French gross national product experienced an annual increase of 5.5 percent, faster than that of the United States. By the end of de Gaulle's era, France was a major industrial producer and exporter, particularly in such areas as automobiles and armaments. Nevertheless, problems remained. France failed to build the hospitals, houses, and schools that it needed. Moreover, the expansion of traditional industries, such as coal, steel, and railroads, which had all been nationalized (put under government ownership), led to large government deficits. The cost of living increased faster than in the rest of Europe. Consumer prices were 45 percent higher in 1968 than they had been ten years earlier.

Increased dissatisfaction with the inability of de Gaulle's government to deal with these problems soon led to more violent action. In May 1968, a series of student protests, followed by a general strike by the labor unions, shook the government. Although de Gaulle managed to restore order, the events of May 1968 had seriously undermined the French people's respect for their aloof and imperious president. Tired and discouraged, de Gaulle resigned from office in April 1969 and died within a year.

⚛ *De Gaulle Calls for French Autonomy* ⚛

In the 1960s, the French president Charles de Gaulle sought to maintain France's independence from both the Soviet Union and the United States. In this 1966 speech, de Gaulle denounced those who were trying to subordinate France to international organizations.

A Speech of Charles de Gaulle, 1966

It is true that, among our contemporaries, there are many minds . . . who have envisaged that our country renounce its independence under the cover of one or another international group. Having thus handed over to foreign bodies the responsibility for our destiny, our leaders would. . . have nothing more to do than "plead France's case."

Thus some—exulting in the dream of the international—wanted to see our country itself, as they placed themselves, under the obedience of Moscow. Thus others—invoking either the supranational myth, or the danger from the East, or the advantage that the Atlantic West could derive from unifying its economy, or even the imposing utility of world arbitration—maintained that France should allow her policy to be dissolved in a tailor-made Europe, her defense in NATO, her monetary concepts in the Washington Fund, her personality in the United Nations.

Certainly, it is a good thing that such institutions exist, and it is only in our interest to belong to them; but if we had listened to their extreme apostles, these organs in which, as everyone knows, the political protection, military protection, economic power and multiform aid of the United States predominate—these organs would have been for us only a cover for our submission to American hegemony. Thus, France would disappear swept away by illusion.

WEST GERMANY: A NEW NATION?

Already by the end of 1945, the Western powers (the United States, Britain, and France) occupying Germany had allowed the reemergence of political parties in their zones. Three major parties came forth: the Social Democrats (SPD), the Christian Democrats (CDU), and the Free Democrats (FDP). Over the next three years, the occupation forces gradually allowed the political parties to play greater roles in their zones.

As a result of the pressures of the Cold War, the unification of the three Western zones into the West German Federal Republic became a reality in 1949. Konrad Adenauer (1876–1967), the leader of the Christian Democratic Union (CDU) who served as chancellor from 1949 to 1963, became the "founding hero" of the Federal Republic. Adenauer sought respect for Germany by cooperating with the United States and the other Western European nations. He was especially desirous of reconciliation with France—Germany's long-time enemy. The beginning of the Korean War in June of 1950 had unexpected repercussions for West Germany. The fear that South Korea might fall to the Communist forces of the north led many Germans and Westerners to worry about the security of West Germany and led to calls for the rearmament of West Germany. Although many people, concerned about a revival of German militarism, condemned this proposal, Cold War tensions were decisive. West Germany rearmed in 1955 and became a member of NATO.

Adenauer's chancellorship is largely associated with the resurrection of the West German economy, often referred to as the "economic miracle." It was largely guided by the minister of finance, Ludwig Erhard. Although West Germany had only 75 percent of the population and 52 percent of the territory of prewar Germany, by 1955 the West German gross national product exceeded that of prewar Germany. Real wages doubled between 1950 and 1965 even though work hours were cut by 20 percent. Unemployment fell from 8 percent in 1950 to 0.4 percent in 1965. In order to maintain its economic expansion, West Germany even imported hundreds of thousands of guest workers, primarily from Italy, Spain, Greece, Turkey, and Yugoslavia.

Throughout its postwar existence, West Germany was troubled by its Nazi past. The surviving major Nazi leaders had been tried and condemned as war criminals at the Nuremberg war crimes trials in 1945 and 1946. As part of the denazification of Germany, the victorious Allies continued war crimes trials of lesser officials, but these diminished as the Cold War produced a shift in attitudes. By 1950, German courts had begun to take over the war crimes trials, and the German legal machine persisted in prosecuting cases. Beginning in 1953, the West German government also began to make payments to Israel and to Holocaust survivors and their relatives in order to make some restitution for the crimes of the Nazi era. The German president Richard von Weizsäcker was especially eloquent in reminding Germans of their responsibility "for the unspeakable sorrow that occurred in the name of Germany."

Adenauer resigned in 1963, after fourteen years of firmly guiding West Germany through its postwar recovery. Basically conservative, Adenauer had wanted no grand experimentation at home or abroad; he was content to give Germany time to regain its equilibrium. Ludwig Erhard succeeded Adenauer and largely continued his policies. But an economic downturn in the mid-1960s opened the door to the rise of the Social Democrats, and in 1969, they became the leading party.

GREAT BRITAIN: THE WELFARE STATE

The end of World War II left Britain with massive economic problems. In elections held immediately after the war, the Labour Party overwhelmingly defeated Churchill's Conservative Party. The Labour Party had promised far-reaching reforms, particularly in the area of social welfare, and in a country with a tremendous shortage of consumer goods and housing, its platform was quite appealing. The new Labour government proceeded to enact the reforms that created a modern welfare state. Clement Attlee (1883–1967), the new prime minister, was a pragmatic reformer and certainly not the leftist revolutionary that Churchill had warned against in the election campaign.

The establishment of the British welfare state began with the nationalization of the Bank of England, the coal and steel industries, public transportation, and public utilities, such as electricity and gas. In the area of social welfare, the new government enacted the National Insurance Act and the National Health Service Act in 1946. The insurance act established a comprehensive social security program and nationalized medical insurance, thereby enabling the state to subsidize the unemployed, the sick, and the aged. The health act created a system of socialized medicine that required doctors and dentists to work with state hospitals, although private practices could be maintained. This measure was especially costly for the state, but within a few years 90 percent of the medical profession were participating. The British welfare state became the norm for most European states after the war.

The cost of building a welfare state at home forced the British to reduce expenses abroad. This meant the dismantling of the British Empire and the reduction of military aid to such countries as Greece and Turkey. Not a belief in the morality of self-determination, but economic necessity brought an end to the British Empire.

Continuing economic problems, however, brought the Conservatives back into power from 1951 to 1964. Although they favored private enterprise, the Conservatives accepted the welfare state and even extended it when they undertook an ambitious construction program to improve British housing. Although the British economy had recovered from the war, it had done so at a slower rate than other European countries. Moreover, the slow rate of recovery masked a long-term economic decline caused by a variety of factors. The demands of British trade unions for wages that rose faster than productivity were certainly a problem in the late 1950s and 1960s. The unwillingness of the British to invest in modern industrial machinery and to adopt new methods also did not help. Underlying the immediate problems, however, was a deeper issue. As a result of World War II, Britain had lost much of its prewar revenues from abroad but was left with a burden of debt from its many international commitments.

At the same time, with the rise of the United States and the Soviet Union, Britain's ability to play the role of a world power declined substantially—as was evident in the Suez Crisis. On July 26, 1956, Colonel Gamal Abdel Nasser, the leader of Egypt, nationalized the Suez Canal, an act strongly condemned by the British as a threat to their vital interests. On October 29, British, French, and Israeli forces attacked Egypt. Strong American opposition forced the British to accept a United Nations cease-fire resolution and withdraw their troops. The Suez debacle made it clear that Britain was no longer a world power.

ITALY: THE WEAKNESS OF COALITION GOVERNMENT

After the war, Italy faced a period of heavy reconstruction. No other Western country, except Germany, had sustained more physical destruction. The monarchy was abolished when 54 percent of Italian voters rejected the royal house, and in June 1946, Italy became a democratic republic.

In the first postwar parliamentary elections held in April 1948, the Christian Democrats, still allied with the Catholic church, emerged as the leading political party. Alcide de Gasperi (1881–1954) served as prime minister from 1948 to 1953, an unusually long span of time for an Italian government. Like prefascist governments, postwar Italian coalitions, largely dominated by the Christian Democrats, were famous for their instability and short lives. Although the Italian Communist Party was one of Italy's three largest parties, it was largely excluded from all of these government coalitions, although it managed to gain power in a number of provinces and municipalities in the 1960s. The Christian Democrats were able to maintain control by keeping the support of the upper and middle classes and the southern peasantry.

Italy, too, experienced an "economic miracle" after the war, although it was far less publicized than Germany's. In 1945, Italy's industrial production was only 20 percent of prewar levels while agricultural output was about 50 percent. The Marshall Plan helped to stabilize the postwar Italian economy. Especially during the late 1950s and early 1960s, Italy made rapid strides in economic growth. The production of electrical appliances, cars, and office machinery made the most significant leap. As in other Western welfare states, the Italian economy combined private enterprise with government management, particularly of heavy industry. In 1965, for example, the government controlled 60 percent of Italy's steel production. The major economic problem continued to be the backwardness of southern Italy, a region that possessed 36 percent of the total population and only 25 percent of the national income. In the 1960s, millions of Italians from the south migrated to the more prosperous north.

Western Europe: The Move toward Unity

As we have seen, the divisions created by the Cold War led the nations of Western Europe to form the North Atlantic Treaty Organization in 1949. But military unity was not the only kind of unity fostered in Europe after 1945. The destructiveness of two world wars caused many thoughtful Europeans to consider the need for some form of European unity. National feeling was still too powerful, however, for European nations to give up their political sovereignty. Consequently, the desire for unity was forced to focus primarily on the economic arena, not the political.

The Marshall Plan had called for European economic cooperation. To provide a framework for this American aid, European nations created the Organization for European Economic Cooperation (OEEC), which served primarily to encourage European trade. By 1950, Europeans had perceived the need for further cooperative efforts beyond the limited goals of the OEEC.

In 1951, France, West Germany, the Benelux countries (Belgium, Netherlands, and Luxembourg), and

CHRONOLOGY

Western Europe

Welfare state emerges in Great Britain	1946
Italy becomes a democratic republic	1946
Alcide de Gasperi becomes prime minister of Italy	1948
Konrad Adenauer becomes chancellor of West Germany	1949
Formation of European Coal and Steel Community	1951
West Germany joins NATO	1955
Suez Crisis	1956
Formation of EURATOM	1957
Formation of European Economic Community (Common Market)	1957
Charles de Gaulle assumes power in France	1958
Erhard becomes chancellor of Germany	1963
Student protests in France	1968

Italy formed the European Coal and Steel Community (ECSC). Its purpose was to create a common market for coal and steel products among the six nations by eliminating tariffs and other trade barriers. The success of the ECSC encouraged its members to proceed further, and in 1957 they created the European Atomic Energy Community (EURATOM) to further European research on the peaceful uses of nuclear energy.

In the same year, these six nations signed the Rome Treaty, which created the European Economic Community (EEC), also known as the Common Market. The EEC eliminated customs barriers for the six member nations and created a large free-trade area protected from the rest of the world by a common external tariff. By promoting free trade, the EEC also encouraged cooperation and standardization in many aspects of the six nations' economies. All the member nations benefited economically. By the decade of the 1960s, the EEC nations had become an important trading bloc. With a total population of 165 million, the EEC became the world's largest exporter and purchaser of raw materials. Only the United States surpassed the EEC in steel production.

The Emergence of a New Society

During the postwar era, Western society witnessed remarkably rapid change. Such products of new technologies as computers, television, jet planes, contraceptive devices, and new surgical techniques all dramatically and quickly altered the pace and nature of human life. The rapid changes in postwar society, fueled by scientific advances and rapid economic growth, led many to view it as a new society. Called a technocratic society by some and the consumer society by others, postwar Western society was characterized by a changing social structure and new movements for change.

The Structure of European Society

The structure of European society was altered after 1945. Especially noticeable were the changes in the middle class. Such traditional middle-class groups as businesspeople and professionals in law, medicine, and the universities were greatly augmented by a new group of managers and technicians, as large companies and government agencies employed increasing numbers of white-collar supervisory and administrative personnel. Whether in Eastern or Western Europe, the new managers and experts were very much alike. Everywhere their positions depended upon specialized knowledge

Map 29.6 The Economic Division of Europe during the Cold War.

acquired from some form of higher education. Everywhere they focused on the effective administration of their organizations. Since their positions usually depended upon their skills, they took steps to ensure that their own children would be educated.

Changes also occurred among the traditional lower classes. Especially noticeable was the dramatic shift of people from rural to urban areas. The number of people in agriculture declined dramatically; by the 1950s, the number of peasants throughout most of Europe had dropped by 50 percent. Nor did the size of the industrial labor force expand. In West Germany, industrial workers made up 48 percent of the labor force throughout the 1950s and 1960s. Thereafter, the number of industrial workers began to dwindle as the number of white-collar service employees increased. At the same time, a substantial increase in their real wages enabled the working classes to aspire to the consumption patterns of the middle class, leading to what some observers have called the "consumer society." Buying on the installment plan, which was introduced in the 1930s, became widespread in the 1950s and gave workers a chance to imitate the middle class by buying such products as televisions, washing machines, refrigerators, vacuum cleaners, and stereos. But the most visible symbol of mass consumerism was the automobile. Before World War II, cars were reserved mostly for the European upper classes. In 1948, there were 5 million cars in all of Europe, but by 1957, the number had tripled. By the 1960s, there were almost 45 million cars.

Rising incomes, combined with shorter working hours, created an even greater market for mass leisure activities. Between 1900 and 1960, the work week was reduced from sixty hours to a little more than forty hours, and the number of paid holidays increased. In the 1960s, German and Italian workers received between thirty-two and thirty-five paid holidays a year. All aspects of popular culture—music, sports, media—became commercialized and offered opportunities for leisure activities including concerts, sporting events, and television viewing.

Another visible symbol of mass leisure was the growth of mass tourism. Before World War II, mostly the upper and middle classes traveled for pleasure. After the war, the combination of more vacation time, increased prosperity, and the flexibility provided by package tours with their lower rates and low-budget rooms enabled millions to expand their travel possibilities. By the mid-1960s, one hundred million tourists were crossing European boundaries each year. Domestic travel was even more widespread. In Sweden, three out of four people spent a holiday outside their home towns.

✦ **Welfare State: Free Milk at School.** The creation of the welfare state was a prominent social development in postwar Europe. The desire to improve the health of children led to welfare programs that provided free food for young people. Pictured here are boys at Manchester Grammar School in England during a milk break.

Creation of the Welfare State

One of the most noticeable social developments in postwar Europe was the creation of the welfare state. In one sense, the welfare state represents another extension of the power of the state over the lives of its citizens, a process that had increased dramatically as a result of two world wars. Yet the goal of the welfare state was to make it possible for people to live better and more meaningful lives. Advocates of the welfare state believed that eliminating poverty and homelessness, providing medical services for all, ensuring dignity for older people, and extending educational opportunities for all who wanted them would free people to achieve happiness by satisfying their material needs.

Social welfare schemes were, of course, not new to Europe. Beginning in the late nineteenth century, some states had provided for the welfare of the working class by instituting old age pensions, medical insurance, and unemployment compensation. But these efforts were piecemeal and were by no means based on a general belief that society had a responsibility to care for all of its citizens.

The new postwar social legislation greatly extended earlier benefits and created new ones as well. Of course, social welfare benefits differed considerably from country to country in quantity and quality as well as in how they were paid for and managed. Nevertheless, there were some common trends.

In many countries, already existing benefits for sickness, accidents, unemployment, and old age were simply extended to cover more people and provide larger payments. Men were generally eligible for old age pensions at age 65 and women at 60, although in France and Italy the ages were 60 and 55. Old age benefits were not always generous. In both France and Britain, for example, a person was entitled to receive $40 per month, but only after forty years of work.

Affordable health care for all people was another goal of the welfare state, although the methods of achieving this goal varied. In Britain, Italy, and Germany, for example, medical care was free to all people with some kind of insurance, while in France, the Scandinavian countries, Belgium, and Switzerland, people had to contribute toward the cost of their medical care. The amount ranged from 10 to 25 percent of the total cost.

Two other features of welfare states were family allowances and new educational policies. Family allowances were instituted in some countries to provide a minimum level of material care for children. Most family allowance programs provided a fixed amount per child. In 1964, for example, France granted $60 per month per child, Italy $24, and Britain only $10. Welfare states also sought to remove class barriers to opportunity by expanding the number of universities and providing scholarship aid to allow everyone to attend these institutions of higher learning. Overall, European states moved toward free tuition or modest fees for university attendance. These policies did not always achieve their goals, however. In the early 1960s, most students in Western European universities still came from privileged backgrounds. In Britain, 25 percent of university students came from working-class backgrounds; in France, the figure was only 17.6 percent.

The welfare state dramatically increased the amount of money states expended on social services. In 1967, such spending constituted 17 percent of the gross national product of the major European countries; by the 1980s, it absorbed 40 to 50 percent. To some critics, these figures proved that the welfare state had produced a new generation of citizens overly dependent on the state. But most people favored the benefits, and most leaders were well aware that it was political suicide to advocate curtailing or seriously lowering those benefits.

The Permissive Society

The "permissive society" was yet another term used by critics to describe the new society of postwar Europe. World War I had seen the first significant crack in the

◆ **The "Love-in."** In the 1960s, a number of outdoor public festivals for young people combined music, drugs, and sex. Flamboyant dress, facial painting, free-form dancing, and drugs were vital ingredients in creating an atmosphere dedicated to "love and peace." Shown here is a "love-in" that was held on the grounds of an English country estate in the Summer of Love, 1967.

rigid code of manners and morals of the nineteenth century. Subsequently, the 1920s had witnessed experimentation with drugs, the appearance of hard-core pornography, and a new sexual freedom (police in Berlin, for example, issued cards that permitted female and male homosexual prostitutes to practice their trade). But these indications of a new attitude appeared mostly in major cities and touched only small numbers of people. After World War II, changes in manners and morals were far more extensive and far more noticeable.

Sweden took the lead in the propagation of the so-called sexual revolution of the 1960s, but the rest of Europe and the United States soon followed. Sex education in the schools and the decriminalization of homosexuality were but two aspects of Sweden's liberal legislation. The introduction of the birth control pill, which became widely available by the mid-1960s, gave people more freedom in sexual behavior. Meanwhile, sexually explicit movies, plays, and books broke new ground in the treatment of once-hidden subjects. Cities like Amsterdam, which allowed open prostitution and the public sale of hard-core pornography, attracted thousands of curious tourists.

The new standards were evident in the breakdown of the traditional family. Divorce rates increased dramatically, especially in the 1960s, while premarital and extramarital sexual experiences also rose substantially. A survey in the Netherlands in 1968 revealed that 78 percent of men and 86 percent of women had participated in extramarital sex.

The decade of the 1960s also saw the emergence of a drug culture. Marijuana was widely used among college and university students as the recreational drug of choice. For young people more interested in mind expansion into higher levels of consciousness, Timothy Leary, who had done psychedelic research at Harvard on the effects of LSD (lysergic acid diethylamide), became the high priest of hallucinogenic experiences.

New attitudes toward sex and the use of drugs were only two manifestations of a growing youth movement in the 1960s that questioned authority and fostered rebellion against the older generation. Spurred on by the Vietnam War and a growing political consciousness, the youth rebellion became a youth protest movement by the second half of the 1960s (see the box on p. 1022).

Education and Student Revolt

Before World War II, higher education had largely remained the preserve of Europe's wealthier classes. Even in 1950, for example, only 3 or 4 percent of West European young people were enrolled in a university. In addition, European higher education remained largely centered on the liberal arts, pure science, and preparation for the professions of law and medicine.

Much of this changed after World War II. European states began to foster greater equality of opportunity in higher education by reducing or eliminating fees, and universities experienced an influx of students from the middle and lower classes. Enrollments grew dramatically; in France, 4.5 percent of young people attended a university in 1950. By 1965, the figure had increased to 14.5 percent. Enrollments in European universities more than tripled between 1940 and 1960.

But there were problems. Classrooms with too many students, professors who paid little attention to their students, and administrators who acted in an authoritarian fashion led to student resentment. In addition, despite changes in the curriculum, students often felt that the universities were not providing an education relevant to the realities of the modern age. This discontent led to an outburst of student revolts in the late 1960s (see the box on p. 1024). In part, these protests were an extension of the spontaneous disruptions in American universities in the mid-1960s, which were often sparked by student opposition to the Vietnam War. Perhaps the most famous student revolt occurred in France in 1968. It erupted at the University of Nanterre outside Paris but soon spread to the Sorbonne, the main campus of the University of Paris. French students demanded a greater voice in the administration of the university, took over buildings, and then expanded the scale of their protests by inviting workers to support them. Half of France's workforce went on strike in May 1968. After the Gaullist government instituted a hefty wage hike, the workers returned to work and the police repressed the remaining student protesters.

The French revolt spurred student protests elsewhere in Europe, although none of them succeeded in becoming mass movements. In West Berlin, university students led a protest against Axel Springer, leader of Germany's largest newspaper establishment. Many German students were motivated by a desire to destroy what they considered to be the corrupt old order and were especially influenced by the ideas of the German-American social philosopher, Herbert Marcuse. In *One-Dimensional Man*, published in 1964, Marcuse argued that capitalism had undermined the dissatisfaction of the oppressed masses by encouraging the consumption of material things. He proposed that a small cadre of unindoctrinated students could liberate the masses from the control of the capitalist ruling class. But the German students' attempt at revolutionary violence backfired as angry Berliners supported police repression of the students.

≽ "The Times They Are a-Changin' ": The Music of Youthful Protest ≼

In the l960s, the lyrics of rock music reflected the rebellious mood of many young people. Bob Dylan (b. 1941), a well-known recording artist, expressed the feelings of the younger generation. His song, "The Times They Are a-Changin'," released in 1964, has been called an "anthem for the protest movement."

Bob Dylan, *The Times They Are a-Changin'*

Come gather round people
Wherever you roam
And admit that the waters
Around you have grown
And accept it that soon
You'll be drenched to the bone
If your time to you
Is worth savin'
Then you better start swimmin'
Or you'll sink like a stone
For the times they are a'changin'

Come writers and critics
Who prophesize with your pen
And keep your eyes wide
The chance won't come again
And don't speak too soon
For the wheel's still in spin
And there's no tellin' who
That it's namin'
For the loser now
Will be later to win
For the times they are a'changin'

Come senators, congressmen
please heed the call
Don't stand in the doorway

Don't block up the hall
For he that gets hurt
Will be he who has stalled
There's a battle outside
And it is ragin'
It'll soon shake your windows
And rattle your walls
For the times they are a'changin'

Come mothers and fathers
Throughout the land
And don't criticize
What you can't understand
Your sons and your daughters
Are beyond your command
Your old road
Is rapidly agin'
Please get out of the new one
If you can't lend your hand
For the times they are a'changin'

The line it is drawn
The curse it is cast
The slow one now
Will later be fast
As the present now
Will later be past
The order is
Rapidly fadin'
And the first one now
Will later be last
For the times they are a'changin'

The student protest movement reached its high point in 1968, although scattered incidents lasted into the early 1970s. There were several reasons for the student radicalism. Some students were genuinely motivated by the desire to reform the university. Others were protesting the Vietnam War, which they viewed as a product of Western imperialism. They also attacked other aspects of Western society, such as its materialism, and ex-pressed concern about becoming cogs in the large and impersonal bureaucratic jungles of the modern world. For many students, the calls for democratic decision making within the universities were a reflection of their deeper concerns about the direction of Western society. Although student revolts fizzled out in the 1970s, the larger issues they raised have been increasingly revived in the 1990s.

◆ **Student Revolt in Paris, 1968.** The discontent of university students exploded in the late 1960s in a series of student revolts. Perhaps best known was the movement in Paris in 1968. This photograph shows the barricades erected on a Parisian street on the morning of May 11 during the height of the revolt.

Conclusion

At the end of World War II, a new conflict erupted in the Western world as the two new superpowers, the United States and the Soviet Union, competed for political domination. Europeans, whether they wanted to or not, were forced to become supporters of one side or the other. But this ideological division also spread to the rest of the world as the United States fought in Korea and Vietnam to prevent the spread of communism, while the Soviet Union used its armies to prop up pro-Soviet regimes in Eastern Europe.

In addition to the Cold War conflict, the postwar era was characterized by decolonization and the creation of a new Europe. After World War II, the colonial empires of the European states were largely dissolved, and the liberated territories of Africa, Asia, and the Middle East emerged as sovereign states. By the late 1980s, the approximately 160 sovereign states of the world would become an emerging global community.

Western Europe also became a new community in the 1950s and the 1960s. Although Western Europeans staged a remarkable economic recovery, the Cuban Missile Crisis made it clear that their future still depended on the conflict between the two superpowers. At the same time, the student protests of the late 1960s caused many to rethink some of their basic assumptions. And yet, looking back, the student upheavals were not a "turning point in the history of postwar Europe," as some people thought at the time. In the 1970s and 1980s, student rebels would become middle-class professionals, and the vision of a revolutionary politics would remain mostly a memory.

1968: The Year of Student Revolts

The outburst of student upheavals in the late 1960s reached its high point in 1968. These two very different selections illustrate some of the issues that prompted university students to occupy campus buildings and demand reforms.

A Student Manifesto in Search of a Real and Human Educational Alternative (University of British Columbia), June 1968

Today we as students are witnessing a deepening crisis within our society. We are intensely aware, in a way perhaps not possible for the older generation, that humanity stands on the edge of a new era. Because we are young, we have insights into the present and visions of the future that our parents do not have. Tasks of an immense gravity wait solution in our generation. We have inherited these tasks from our parents. We do not blame them so much for that . . . but we do blame them for being unwilling to admit that there are problems or for saying that it is we who have visited these problems on ourselves because of our perversity, ungratefulness and unwillingness to listen to "reason."

Much of the burden of solving the problems of the new era rests on the university. We have been taught to look to it for leadership. While we know that part of the reason for the university is to render direct services to the community, we are alarmed at its servility to industry and government as to what and how it teaches. We are scandalized that the university fails to realize its role in renewing and vivifying those intellectual and moral energies necessary to create a new society—one in which a sense of personal dignity and human community can be preserved.

Student Inscriptions on the Walls of Paris, May and June 1968

The dream is the reality.

May 1968. World revolution is the order of the day.

I decree a state of permanent happiness.

To be free in 1968 is to take part.

Take the trip every day of your life.

Make love, not war.

No exams.

The mind travels farther than the heart but it doesn't go as far.

Run, comrade, the old are behind you!

Don't make a revolution in the image of your confused and hide-bound university.

Exam = servility, social promotion, hierarchic society.

Love each other.

SEX. It's good, said Mao, but not too often.

Alcohol kills. Take LSD.

Are you consumers or participants?

Professors, you are as old as your culture; your modernism is only the modernization of the police.

Live in the present.

Revolution, I love you.

Long live direct democracy!

NOTES

1. Quoted in Joseph M. Jones, *The Fifteen Weeks (February 21–June 5, 1947)*, 2d ed. (New York, 1964), pp. 140–41.

2. Quoted in Walter Laqueur, *Europe in Our Time*, (New York, 1992), p. 111.

3. Quoted in Wilfried Loth, *The Division of the World, 1941–1955* (New York, 1988), pp. 160–61.

4. Quoted in Peter Lane, *Europe since 1945: An Introduction* (Totowa, N.J., 1985), p. 248.

5. Quoted in Robert F. Kennedy, *Thirteen Days: A Memoir of the Cuban Missile Crisis* (New York, 1969), pp. 89–90.

6. R. Hilton, *Military Attaché in Moscow* (London, 1949), p. 41.

7. Nikita Khrushchev, *Khrushchev Remembers*, trans. Strobe Talbott (Boston, 1970), p. 77.

SUGGESTIONS FOR FURTHER READING

Three introductory surveys on postwar Europe are P. Lane, *Europe since 1945: An Introduction* (Totowa, N.J., 1985); J. R. Wegs, *Europe since 1945: A Concise History*, 2d ed. (New York, 1984); and W. Laqueur, *Europe in Our Time* (New York, 1992). A convenient reference guide is J. Krieger, ed., *The Oxford Companion to Politics of the World* (Oxford, 1993). There is a detailed literature on the Cold War. Two general accounts are J. W. Langdon, *A Hard and Bitter Peace: A Global History of the Cold War* (Englewood Cliffs, N.J., 1995); and B. A. Weisberger, *Cold War, Cold Peace: The United States and Russia since 1945* (New York, 1984). There is a brief survey of the early Cold War in M. Dockrill, *The Cold War 1945–1963* (Atlantic Highlands, N.J., 1988). The following works maintain that the Soviet Union was chiefly responsible for the Cold War: H. Feis, *From Trust to Terror: The Onset of the Cold War, 1945–1950* (New York, 1970); and A. Ulam, *The Rivals: America and Russia since World War II* (New York, 1971). Revisionist studies on the Cold War have emphasized the responsibility of the United States for the Cold War, especially its global aspects. These works include J. and G. Kolko, *The Limits of Power: The World and United States Foreign Policy, 1945–1954* (New York, 1972); W. LaFeber, *America, Russia and the Cold War, 1945–1966*, 2d ed. (New York, 1972); and M. Sherwin, *A World Destroyed: The Atomic Bomb and the Grand Alliance* (New York, 1975). For a critique of the revisionist studies, see R. L. Maddox, *The New Left and the Origins of the Cold War* (Princeton, N.J., 1973). For important studies of Soviet foreign policy, see A. B. Ulam, *Expansion and Coexistence: Soviet Foreign Policy 1917–1973*, 2d ed. (New York, 1974), and *Dangerous Relations: The Soviet Union in World Politics, 1970–1982* (New York, 1983). The effects of the Cold War on Germany are examined in J. H. Backer, *The Decision to Divide Germany: American Foreign Policy in Transition* (Durham, N.C., 1978). For a good introduction to the arms race, see E. M. Bottome, *The Balance of Terror: A Guide to the Arms Race*, rev. ed. (Boston, 1986). On the Cuban Missile Crisis, see R. A. Chayes, *The Cuban Missile Crisis* (New York, 1974).

On decolonization after World War II, see R. F. Holland, *European Decolonization, 1918–1981: An Introductory Survey* (London, 1985); A. Mazrui and M. Tidy, *Nationalism and New States in Africa* (London, 1984); and D. K. Shipler, *Arab and Jew: Wounded Spirits in a Promised Land* (New York, 1986). On the problems of the Third World, see P. Harrison, *Inside the Third World*, 2d ed. (New York, 1984).

For a general view of Soviet society, see D. K. Shipler, *Russia: Broken Idols, Solemn Dreams* (New York, 1983). On the Khrushchev years, see C. A. Linden, *Khrushchev and the Soviet Leadership* (Baltimore, 1990). For a general study of the Soviet satellites in Eastern Europe, see A. Brown and J. Gary, *Culture and Political Changes in Communist States* (London, 1977). On the Soviet Union's actions against Czechoslovakia in 1968, see J. Valenta, *Intervention in Czechoslovakia in 1968* (Baltimore, 1979). The unique path of Yugoslavia is examined in L. J. Cohen and P. Warwick, *Political Cohesion in a Fragile Mosaic: The Yugoslav Experience* (Boulder, Colo., 1983). On Romania, see L. S. Graham, *Rumania: A Developing Socialist State* (Boulder, Colo., 1978). On Hungary, see B. Kovrig, *The Hungarian People's Republic* (Baltimore, 1970). On East Germany, see C. B. Scharf, *Politics and Change in East Germany* (Boulder, Colo., 1984).

The rebuilding of postwar Europe is examined in A. S. Milward, *The Reconstruction of Western Europe, 1945–51* (Berkeley, 1984). For a general survey, see F. Tipton and R. Aldrich, *An Economic and Social History of Europe from 1939 to the Present* (Baltimore, 1987). On the building of common institutions in Western Europe, see J. Pinder, *European Community: The Building of a Union*, 2d ed. (New York, 1995). For a survey of West Germany, see M. Balfour, *West Germany: A Contemporary History* (London, 1983). France under de Gaulle is examined in P. Williams and M. Harrison, *Politics and Society in de Gaulle's Republic* (New York, 1971). On Britain, see K. O. Morgan, *The People's Peace: British History 1945–1990* (Oxford, 1992). On Italy, see P. Ginsbourg, *A History of Contemporary Italy: Society and Politics, 1943–1988* (New York, 1990).

For a survey of contemporary Western society, see A. Sampson, *The New Europeans* (New York, 1968). The student revolts of the late 1960s are put into a broader context in L. S. Feuer, *The Conflict of Generations* (New York, 1969). On the welfare state, see A. de Swann, *In Care of the State: Health Care, Education, and Welfare in Europe and the United States in the Modern Era* (New York, 1988).

CHAPTER
30

The Contemporary Western World (since 1970)

Between 1945 and 1970, Europe not only recovered from the devastating effects of World War II, but also experienced an economic recovery that seemed nothing less than miraculous to many people. Some historians have even labeled the years from 1950 to 1973 "the golden age of the European economy." Economic growth and virtually full employment continued so long that the first postwar recession in 1973 came as a shock to Western Europe.

By that time, too, after more than two decades of the Cold War, Europeans had become accustomed to a new division of Europe between West and East. A prosperous Western Europe allied to the United States stood opposed to a still-struggling Eastern Europe that remained largely subject to the Soviet Union. The division of Germany symbolized the new order that seemed so well established. And yet, within two decades, a revolutionary upheaval in the Soviet Union and Eastern Europe brought an end to the Cold War and destroyed the long-standing division of postwar Europe. Even the Soviet Union ceased to exist as a single nation. On August 19, 1991, a group of Soviet leaders opposed to reform arrested Mikhail Gorbachev, the president of the Soviet Union, and tried to seize control of the government. Hundreds of thousands of Russians, led by Boris Yeltsin, poured into the streets of Moscow and Leningrad to resist the attempted coup. Some army units, sent out to enforce the wishes of the rebels, defected to Yeltsin's side, and within days, the rebels were forced to surrender. This failed attempt to seize power had unexpected results as Russia and a host of other Soviet states declared their independence. By the end of 1991, the Soviet Union—one of the largest empires in world history—had come to an end, and a new era of cooperation between the successor states in the old Soviet Union and the nations of the West had begun.

In the midst of the transformation from Cold War to post–Cold War, other changes also shaped a new Western world. New artistic and intellectual currents, the growth of science and technology, a religious re-

Era of Brezhnev

Emergence of Solidarity in Poland •

• Gorbachev comes to power in Soviet Union

Revolutions in Eastern Europe •

Dissolution of the Soviet Union •

ommon Market expands (European Community)

Margaret Thatcher becomes prime minister of Britain

Reunification of Germany   European Union

Active terrorist groups •

John Paul II becomes pope•

Organization of Green Party in Germany

Anselm Kiefer, *Departure from Egypt*

---

vival, new threats from terrorists, the realization of environmental problems, the surge of a women's liberation movement—all of these spoke of a vibrant, ever-changing, and yet challenging new world.

From Cold War to Post–Cold War: Toward a New World Order?

By the 1970s, American-Soviet relations had entered a new phase known as détente, which was marked by a reduction of tensions between the two superpowers. In the late 1970s, however, the apparent collapse of détente initiated a new period of East-West confrontation. But after the accession of Mikhail Gorbachev in 1985, the Soviet Union began to make changes in its foreign policy, and the Cold War came rapidly to an end.

An appropriate symbol of détente was the Antiballistic Missiles (ABM) Treaty in 1972. Despite some lessening of tensions after the Cuban Missile Crisis, both the Soviet Union and the United States had continued to expand their nuclear arsenals. In the 1960s, both nations sought to extend the destructive power of their missiles by arming them with multiple warheads. By 1970, Americans had developed the capacity to arm their intercontinental ballistic missiles (ICBMs) with "multiple independently targeted re-entry vehicles" (MIRVs) that enabled one missile to hit ten different targets. The Soviet Union soon followed suit. Between 1968 and 1972, both sides had also developed antiballistic missiles (ABMs), whose purpose was to hit and destroy incoming missiles. In the 1972 ABM Treaty, the

two nations agreed to limit their antiballistic missile systems.

In 1975, the Helsinki Agreements provided yet another example of reduced tensions between the superpowers. Signed by the United States, Canada, and all European nations, these accords recognized all borders in central and eastern Europe that had been established since the end of World War II, thereby acknowledging the Soviet sphere of influence in Eastern Europe. The Helsinki Agreements also committed the signatory powers to recognize and protect the human rights of their citizens.

This protection of human rights became one of the major foreign policy goals of the next American president, Jimmy Carter (b. 1924). Although hopes ran high for the continuation of détente, the Soviet invasion of Afghanistan in 1979, undertaken to restore a pro-Soviet regime, hardened relations between the United States and the Soviet Union. President Carter canceled American participation in the 1980 Olympic Games held in Moscow and placed an embargo on the shipment of American grain to the Soviet Union.

The early administration of President Ronald Reagan (b. 1911) witnessed a return to the harsh rhetoric, if not all of the harsh practices, of the Cold War. Calling the Soviet Union an "evil empire," Reagan began a military buildup that stimulated a renewed arms race. In 1982, the Reagan administration introduced the nuclear-tipped cruise missile, whose ability to fly at low altitudes made it difficult to detect. President Reagan also became an ardent proponent of the Strategic Defense Initiative (SDI), nicknamed "Star Wars." Its purpose was to create a space shield that could destroy incoming missiles. By

♦ **Reagan and Gorbachev.** The willingness of Mikhail Gorbachev and Ronald Reagan to dampen the arms race was a significant factor in ending the Cold War confrontation between the United States and the Soviet Union. Reagan and Gorbachev are shown here standing before St. Basil's Cathedral during Reagan's visit to Moscow in 1988.

providing military support to the Afghan insurgents, the Reagan administration helped to maintain a Vietnam-like war in Afghanistan that the Soviet Union could not win. Like the Vietnam War, the war in Afghanistan demonstrated that the power of a superpower was actually limited in the face of strong nationalist, guerrilla-type opposition.

The End of the Cold War

The accession of Mikhail Gorbachev to power in the Soviet Union (see The Gorbachev Era later in this

chapter) in 1985 eventually brought a dramatic end to the Cold War. Gorbachev was willing to rethink many of the fundamental assumptions underlying Soviet foreign policy, and his "New Thinking," as it was called, opened the door to a series of stunning changes. For one, Gorbachev initiated a plan for arms limitation that led in 1987 to an agreement with the United States to eliminate intermediate-range nuclear weapons (the INF Treaty). Both sides had incentives to dampen the expensive arms race. Gorbachev hoped to make extensive economic and internal reforms while the United States had serious deficit problems. During the Reagan years, the United States had moved from being a creditor nation to being the world's biggest debtor nation. By 1990, both countries were becoming aware that their large military budgets made it difficult for them to solve their serious social problems.

The years 1989 and 1990 were a crucial period in the ending of the Cold War. The postwar settlements that had become the norm in central and eastern Europe came unstuck as a mostly peaceful revolutionary upheaval swept through Eastern Europe. Gorbachev's policy of allowing greater autonomy for the Communist regimes of Eastern Europe meant that the Soviet Union would no longer militarily support Communist governments that were faced with internal revolt. The unwillingness of the Soviet regime to use force to maintain the status quo, as it had in Hungary in 1956 and in Czechoslovakia in 1968, opened the door to the overthrow of the Communist regimes (see Eastern Europe: The Collapse of the Communist Order later in this chapter). On October 3, 1990, the reunification of Germany destroyed one of the most prominent symbols of the Cold War era.

The Gulf War provided the first major opportunity for testing the new relationship between the United States and the Soviet Union in the post–Cold War era. In early August 1990, Iraqi military forces suddenly moved across the border and occupied the small neighboring country of Kuwait in the northeastern corner of the Arabian peninsula at the head of the Persian Gulf. The immediate pretext was Iraq's claim that Kuwait was pumping oil from fields inside Iraqi territory, but the deeper reason was the former's contention that Kuwait was legally a part of Iraq. The Iraqi invasion of Kuwait sparked an international outcry and the creation of an international force led by the United States that liberated Kuwait and destroyed a substantial part of Iraq's armed forces in the early months of 1991.

The Gulf War was the first important military conflict in the post–Cold War period. Although Mikhail Gorbachev made some attempt to persuade Iraq to withdraw its forces from Kuwait before the war began, overall the Soviets played a minor role in the crisis and supported the American action. By the end of 1991, the Soviet Union had disintegrated, making any renewal of global rivalry between two competing superpowers impossible. Although the United States emerged as the world's leading military power by 1992, its role in the creation of the "New World Order" that President George Bush advocated at the time of the Gulf War was not clear. After some hesitation, President Bill Clinton (b. 1946) began to reassert American power in the world. He sent American troops to Haiti in September 1994 to restore that country's fragile democratic system. In December 1995, the United States took the lead in bringing a negotiated end to the war in Bosnia. As part of the agreement signed by the warring parties, 20,000 American troops were sent to the region as part of a NATO military presence intended to enforce the peace.

*T*oward a New European Order

Between 1945 and 1970, economic recovery had brought renewed growth to Europe. Nevertheless, the political divisions between Western and Eastern Europe remained; so, too, did the disparity in levels of prosperity. But in the late 1980s and early 1990s, the Soviet Union and its Eastern European satellite states underwent a revolutionary upheaval that dramatically altered the European scene and left many Europeans with both new hopes and new fears.

The Revolutionary Era in the Soviet Union

Between 1964 and 1982, revolutionary change in the Soviet Union appeared highly unlikely. The man in charge—Leonid Brezhnev (1906–1982)—had as his slogan "no experimentation." Brezhnev had entered the ranks of the party leadership under Stalin and, after the overthrow of Khrushchev in 1964, had become head of both party and state. He was always optimistic, yet reluctant to reform. Overall, the Brezhnev years were relatively calm, although the Brezhnev doctrine—the right of the Soviet Union to intervene if socialism was threatened in another "socialist state" —became an article of faith and led to the use of Soviet troops in Czechoslovakia in 1968.

Brezhnev benefited from the more relaxed atmosphere associated with détente. The Soviets had reached a rough parity with the United States in nuclear arms and enjoyed a sense of external security that seemed to allow for a relaxation of authoritarian rule. The regime permitted more access to Western styles of music, dress, and art, although dissenters were still punished. Andrei Sakharov, for example, who had played an important role in the development of the Soviet hydrogen bomb, was placed under house arrest for his defense of human rights.

In his economic policies, Brezhnev continued to emphasize heavy industry. Overall industrial growth declined, although the Soviet production of iron, steel, coal, and cement surpassed that of the United States. Two problems bedeviled the Soviet economy. The government's insistence on vigorous central planning led to a huge, complex bureaucracy that discouraged efficiency and reduced productivity. Moreover, the Soviet system, based on guaranteed employment and a lack of incentives, bred apathy, complacency, absenteeism, and drunkenness.

Agricultural problems added to Soviet economic woes. Collective farmers lacked incentives. Many preferred working their own small private plots to laboring in the collective work brigades. To make matters worse, bad harvests in the mid-1970s, caused by a series of droughts, heavy rains, and early frosts, forced the Soviet government to buy grain from the West, particularly the United States. To their chagrin, the Soviets were increasingly dependent on capitalist countries.

By the 1970s, the Soviet Union had developed a ruling system that depended on patronage as a major avenue of advancement. Those who aspired to rise in the party and the state bureaucracy needed the support of successful party leaders. At the same time, party and state leaders—as well as leaders of the army and the secret police (KGB)—received awards and numerous material privileges. Brezhnev was unwilling to tamper with the party leadership and state bureaucracy despite the inefficiency and corruption that the system encouraged. Increasingly, the lack of vigorous leadership in the Soviet Union was becoming all too apparent and difficult to rectify.

By 1980, the Soviet Union was seriously ailing. A declining economy, a rise in infant mortality rates, a dramatic surge in alcoholism, and a deterioration in working conditions all gave impetus to a decline in morale and a growing perception that the system was floundering. Within the party, a small group of reformers emerged who understood the real condition of the Soviet Union. One member of this group was Yuri Andropov (1914–1985), head of the KGB and successor to Brezhnev after the latter's death in November

1982. But Andropov was already old and in poor health when he came to power, and he was unable to make any substantive changes. His most significant move may have been his support for a young reformer—Mikhail Gorbachev—who was climbing the rungs of the party ladder. Finally, after a brief interlude under Konstantin Chernenko (1911–1985)—another old and ailing member of the Soviet leadership—a new era began when party leaders chose Gorbachev to succeed Chernenko in March 1985.

THE GORBACHEV ERA

Born into a peasant family in 1931, Mikhail Gorbachev combined farm work with school and received the Order of the Red Banner for his agricultural efforts. This award and his good school record enabled him to study law at the University of Moscow. After receiving his law degree in 1955, he returned to his native southern Russia, where he eventually became first secretary of the Communist Party in the city of Stavropol (he had joined the Communist Party in 1952) and then first secretary of the regional party committee. In 1978, Gorbachev was made a member of the party's Central Committee in Moscow. Two years later, he became a full member of the ruling Politburo and secretary of the Central Committee. In March 1985, party leaders elected him general secretary of the party, and he became the new leader of the Soviet Union.

Map 30.1 The New Europe.

➤ Gorbachev and Perestroika ⬅

After assuming the leadership of the Soviet Union in 1985, Mikhail Gorbachev worked to liberalize and restructure the country. His policies opened the door to rapid changes in Eastern Europe and in Soviet-American relations at the end of the 1980s. In his book Perestroika, *Gorbachev explained some of his "New Thinking."*

Mikhail Gorbachev, *Perestroika*

The fundamental principle of the new political outlook is very simple: *nuclear war cannot be a means of achieving political, economic, ideological or any other goals.* This conclusion is truly revolutionary, for it means discarding the traditional notions of war and peace. It is the political function of war that has always been a justification for war, a "rational" explanation. Nuclear war is senseless; it is irrational. There would be neither winners nor losers in a global nuclear conflict: world Civilization would inevitably perish. . . .

But military technology has developed to such an extent that even a non-nuclear war would now be comparable with a nuclear war in its destructive effect. That is why it is logical to include in our category of nuclear wars this "variant" of an armed clash between major powers as well.

Thereby, an altogether different situation has emerged. A way of thinking and a way of acting, based on the use of force in world politics, have formed over centuries, even millennia. It seems they have taken root as something unshakable. Today, they have lost all reasonable grounds . . . . For the first time in history, basing international politics on moral and ethical norms that are common to all humankind, as well as humanizing interstate relations, has become a vital requirement. . . .

There is a great thirst for mutual understanding and mutual communication in the world. It is felt among politicians, it is gaining momentum among the intelligentsia, representatives of culture, and the public at large. And if the Russian work "perestroika" has easily entered the international lexicon, this due to more than just interest in what is going on in the Soviet Union. Now the whole world needs restructuring, i.e., progressive development, a fundamental change.

People feel this and understand this. They have to find their bearings, to understand the problems besetting mankind, to realize how they should live in the future. The restructuring is a must for a world overflowing with nuclear weapons; for a world ridden with serious economic and ecological problems; for a world laden with poverty, backwardness and disease; for a human race now facing the urgent need of ensuring its own survival.

We are all students, and our teacher is life and time. I believe that more and more people will come to realize that through RESTRUCTURING in the broad sense of the word, the integrity of the world will be enhanced. Having earned good marks from our main teacher—life—we shall enter the twenty-first century well prepared and sure that there will be further progress.

Educated during the reform years of Khrushchev, Gorbachev seemed intent on taking earlier reforms to their logical conclusions. By the 1980s, Soviet economic problems were obvious. Rigid, centralized planning led to mismanagement and stifled innovation. Although the Soviets still excelled in space exploration, they fell behind the West in high technology, especially in the development and production of computers for private and public use. Most noticeable to the Soviet people was the actual decline in the standard of living. In February 1986, at the Twenty-Seventh Congress of the Communist Party, Gorbachev made clear the need for changes in Soviet society: "The practical actions of the Party and state agencies lag behind the demands of the times and of life itself. . . . Problems grow faster than they are solved. Sluggishness, ossification in the forms, and methods of management decrease the dynamism of work. . . . Stagnation begins to show up in the life of society."[1] Thus, from the start, Gorbachev preached the need for radical reforms.

The cornerstone of Gorbachev's radical reforms was *perestroika* or "restructuring" (see the box above). At first this meant only a reordering of economic policy as Gorbachev called for the beginning of a market economy with limited free enterprise and some private property. His initial economic reforms proved difficult to implement, however. Radicals demanded decisive measures; conservatives feared that rapid changes would be too painful. In his attempt to compromise, Gorbachev often pursued partial liberalization, which satisfied neither faction and also failed to work, producing only more discontent.

Gorbachev soon perceived that in the Soviet system, the economic sphere was intimately tied to the social and political spheres. Attempts to reform the economy without political or social reform would be doomed to failure. One of the most important instruments of *perestroika* was *glasnost* or "openness." Soviet citizens and officials were encouraged to discuss openly the strengths and weaknesses of the Soviet Union. This policy could be seen in *Pravda,* the official newspaper of the Communist Party, which gave increased coverage to such disasters as the nuclear accident at Chernobyl in 1986 and collisions of ships in the Black Sea. Soon the paper was including reports of official corruption, sloppy factory work, and protests against government policy. The arts also benefited from the new policy as previously banned works were now published, and motion pictures began to show negative aspects of Soviet life. Music based on Western styles, such as jazz and rock, began to be performed openly.

Political reforms were equally revolutionary. In June 1987, the principle of two-candidate elections was introduced; previously, voters had been presented with only one candidate. Most dissidents, including Andrei Sakharov, who had spent years in internal exile, were released. At the Communist Party conference in 1988, Gorbachev called for the creation of a new Soviet parliament, the Congress of People's Deputies, whose members were to be chosen in competitive elections. It convened in 1989, the first such meeting in Russia since 1918. Because of its size, the Congress chose a Supreme Soviet of 450 members to deal with day-to-day activities. The revolutionary nature of Gorbachev's political reforms was evident in Sakharov's rise from dissident to an elected member of the Congress of People's Deputies. As a leader of the dissident deputies, Sakharov called for the end to the Communist monopoly of power and, on the day he died, December 11, 1989, urged the creation of a new non-Communist party. Early in 1990, Gorbachev legalized the formation of other political parties and struck Article 6, which had guaranteed the "leading role" of the Communist Party, from the Soviet constitution. At the same time, Gorbachev attempted to consolidate his power by creating a new state presidency. The new position was a consequence of the separation of the state from the Communist Party. Hitherto, the position of first secretary of the party had been the most important post in the Soviet Union, but as the Communist Party became less closely associated with the state, the powers of this office diminished correspondingly. In March 1990, Gorbachev became the Soviet Union's first president.

One of Gorbachev's most serious problems stemmed from the character of the Soviet Union. The Union of Soviet Socialist Republics was a truly multiethnic country, containing 92 nationalities and 112 recognized languages. Previously, the iron hand of the Communist Party, centered in Moscow, had kept a lid on the centuries-old ethnic tensions that had periodically erupted. As Gorbachev released this iron grip, tensions resurfaced, a by-product of *glasnost* that Gorbachev had not anticipated. Ethnic groups took advantage of the new openness to protest what they perceived to be ethnically motivated slights. As violence erupted, the Soviet army, in disrepair since Afghanistan, had difficulty controlling the situation.

The period 1988 to 1990 also witnessed the appearance of nationalist movements throughout the republics of the Soviet Union. Many were motivated by ethnic concerns, with calls for sovereignty of the republics and independence from the Russian-based rule centered in Moscow. These movements first sprang up in Georgia in late 1988 and then in Latvia, Estonia, Moldavia, Uzbekistan, Azerbaijan, and, most dramatically, Lithuania. In December of 1989, the Communist Party of Lithuania declared itself independent of the Communist Party of the Soviet Union, and three months later, on March 11, 1990, the Lithuanian Supreme Council proclaimed Lithuania an independent state. Four days later, the Soviet Congress of People's Deputies declared the Lithuanian proclamation null and void and stated that proper procedures must be established and followed before secession would be acceptable.

THE END OF THE SOVIET UNION

During 1990 and 1991, Gorbachev struggled to deal with Lithuania and the other problems unleashed by his reforms. On the one hand, he tried to appease conservatives who complained about the growing disorder within the Soviet Union. On the other hand, he tried to accommodate the liberals, especially those in the Soviet republics, who increasingly favored a new kind of decentralized Soviet federation. In particular, Gorbachev labored to cooperate more closely with Boris Yeltsin, who had been elected president of the Russian Republic in June 1991.

By 1991, the conservative leaders of the traditional Soviet institutions—the army, government, KGB, and military industries—had grown increasingly worried about the impending dissolution of the Soviet Union and its impact on their own fortunes. On August 19, 1991, a group of these discontented rightists arrested

Gorbachev and attempted to seize power. Gorbachev's unwillingness to work with the conspirators and the brave resistance in Moscow of Yeltsin and thousands of Russians who had grown accustomed to their new liberties caused the coup to disintegrate rapidly. The actions of these right-wing plotters, however, served to accelerate the very process they had hoped to stop—namely, the disintegration of the Soviet Union.

Despite desperate pleas by Gorbachev, the Soviet republics soon moved for complete independence. Ukraine voted for independence on December 1, 1991, and, a week later, the leaders of Russia, Ukraine, and Belarus announced that the Soviet Union had "ceased to exist" and would be replaced by a Commonwealth of Independent States. Gorbachev resigned on December 25, 1991, and turned over his responsibilities as commander-in-chief to Boris Yeltsin, the president of Russia. By the end of 1991, one of the largest empires in world history had come to an end, and a new era had begun in its lands.

Within Russia, a new power struggle soon ensued. Yeltsin was committed to introducing a free market economy as quickly as possible, but the transition was not easy. Economic hardships and social disarray, made worse by a dramatic rise in the activities of organized crime mobs, led increasing numbers of Russians to support both former Communists and hard-line nation-alists who criticized Russia's loss of prestige in world affairs. His brutal use of force against the Chechens, who wanted to secede from Russia and create their own independent republic, also undermined support for Yeltsin. When he announced that he would run again for the presidency, most political observers gave him little chance to win. A vigorous political campaign, however, led to his re-election on July 3, 1996.

Eastern Europe: The Collapse of the Communist Order

Stalin's postwar order had imposed Communist regimes throughout Eastern Europe. The process of sovietization seemed so complete that few people believed that the new order could be undone. But discontent with their Soviet-style regimes always simmered beneath the surface of these satellite states, and after Mikhail Gorbachev made it clear that his government would not intervene militarily, the Communist regimes fell quickly in the revolutions of 1989.

Under Wladyslaw Gomulka, Poland had achieved a certain stability in the 1960s, but economic problems led to his replacement in 1971 by Edward Gierek, who attempted to solve Poland's economic problems by borrowing heavily from the West. But in 1980, when he announced huge increases in food prices in an effort to

◆ **Yeltsin Resists a Right-Wing Coup.** In August 1991, the attempt of right-wing plotters to overthrow Mikhail Gorbachev and seize power in the Soviet Union was thwarted by the efforts of Boris Yeltsin, president of the Russian Republic, and his supporters. Yeltsin is shown here atop a tank in front of the Russian parliament building in Moscow, urging the Russian people to resist the conspirators.

CHRONOLOGY

◆◆◆◆◆◆◆◆◆◆◆◆◆◆◆◆◆◆◆◆

The Soviet Bloc and Its Demise

Rule of Enver Hoxha in Albania	1944–1985
Era of Brezhnev	1964–1982
Rule of Ceausescu in Romania	1965–1989
Honecker succeeds Ulbricht in East Germany	1971
Emergence of Solidarity in Poland	1980
Rule of Andropov and Chernenko	1982–1985
Gorbachev comes to power in the Soviet Union	1985
	1989
Zhivkov loses power in Bulgaria	November 10
Collapse of Communist government in Czechoslovakia	December
East German government collapses	December
Execution of Ceausescu in Romania	December 25
	1990
Lithuania declares independence	March 11
East German elections—victory of Christian Democrats	March 18
Hungarian elections	March 25
Union of currencies—West and East Germany	July 1
Reunification of Germany	October 3
Walesa becomes president of Poland	December
	1991
Yeltsin becomes president of Russia	June
Slovenia and Croatia declare independence	June
Right-wing coup in the Soviet Union	August 19
Dissolution of the Soviet Union	December
	1992
Havel resigns as president of Czechoslovakia	July
	1993
Czechoslovakia splits into Czech Republic and Slovakia	January 1
Havel becomes president of Czech Republic	February 2
	1995
Aleksander Kwasniewski becomes Polish president	November
Dayton accords—end of war in Bosnia	December
	1996
Russian presidential elections	June–July

pay off part of the Western debt, workers' protests erupted once again. Unlike the protests of 1956, however, this time the revolutionary demands of the workers led directly to the rise of the independent labor movement called Solidarity. Led by Lech Walesa (b. 1943), Solidarity represented 10 million of Poland's 35 million people. Almost instantaneously, Solidarity became a tremendous force for change and a threat to the government's monopoly of power. With the support of the workers, many intellectuals, and the Catholic church, Solidarity was able to win a series of concessions. The Polish government seemed powerless to stop the flow of concessions until December 1981, when it arrested Walesa and other Solidarity leaders, outlawed the union, and imposed military rule under General Wojciech Jaruzelski (b. 1923).

But martial rule did not solve Poland's serious economic problems, and in 1988, new demonstrations led the Polish regime to agree to free parliamentary elections—the first free elections in Eastern Europe in forty years. Bowing to the inevitable, Jaruzelski's regime allowed the newly elected Solidarity coalition to form a new government, thus ending forty-five years of Communist rule in Poland. In December 1990, Lech Walesa was chosen as the new Polish president. But Poland's new path was not an easy one. Rapid free market reforms led to severe unemployment and popular discontent, and in November 1995, Aleksander Kwasniewski, a former Communist, defeated Walesa and became the new Polish president.

In Hungary, too, the process of liberation from Communist rule had begun before 1989. Remaining in power for over thirty years, the government of János Kádár enacted the most far-reaching economic reforms in Eastern Europe. In the early 1980s, Kádár legalized small private enterprises, such as retail stores, restaurants, and artisan shops. His economic reforms were termed "Communism with a capitalist facelift." Under his leadership, Hungary moved slowly away from its strict adherence to Soviet dominance and even established fairly friendly relations with the West.

As the 1980s progressed, however, the economy sagged, and Kádár fell from power in 1988. By 1989, the Hungarian Communist government was aware of the growing dissatisfaction and began to undertake reforms. But they came too late as new political parties called for Hungary to become a democratic republic. In elections in March 1990, the Communists came in fourth, winning only 8.5 percent of the vote, a clear repudiation of communism. The Democratic Forum, a right-of-center, highly patriotic party, won the election and formed a new coalition government that committed Hungary to democratic government and the institution of a free market economy.

Communist regimes in Poland and Hungary had attempted to make some political and economic reforms in the 1970s and 1980s, but this was not the case in Czechoslovakia. After Soviet troops had crushed the reform movement in 1968, hard-line Czech Communists under Gustav Husák purged the party and instituted a policy of massive repression to maintain their power. Only writers and other intellectuals provided any real opposition to the government, but they did not have any success until the later 1980s. Government attempts to suppress mass demonstrations in Prague and other Czechoslovakian cities in 1988 and 1989 only led to more and larger demonstrations. By November 1989, crowds as large as 500,000, which included many students, were forming in Prague. A new opposition group, the Civic Forum, emerged and was officially recognized on November 17. In December 1989, as demonstrations continued, the Communist government, lacking any real support, collapsed. President Husák resigned and at the end of December was replaced by Vaclav Havel, a dissident playwright who had played an important role in bringing the Communist government down. In January 1990, Havel declared amnesty for some 30,000 political prisoners. He also set out on a goodwill tour to various Western countries in which he proved to be an eloquent spokesman for Czech democracy and a new order in Europe (see the box on p. 1036).

Within Czechoslovakia, the shift to non-Communist rule was complicated by old problems, especially ethnic issues. Czechs and Slovaks disagreed over the makeup of the new state, but were able to agree to a peaceful division of the country. On January 1, 1993, Czechoslovakia split into the Czech Republic and Slovakia. Vaclav Havel was elected the first president of the new Czech Republic.

Czechoslovakia's revolutionary path was considerably less violent than Romania's. By 1948, with Soviet assistance, a Communist People's Democratic Front had assumed complete power in Romania. In 1965, leadership of the Communist government passed into the hands of Nicolae Ceausescu (1918–1989), who with his wife Elena established a rigid and dictatorial regime. Ceausescu ruled Romania with an iron grip, using a secret police force—the Securitate—as his personal weapon against any dissent. Nevertheless, opposition to his regime grew as Ceausescu rejected the reforms in Eastern Europe promoted by Gorbachev. Ceausescu's regime had for years stood aloof from the Soviet Union, especially in foreign policy. In addition, Ceausescu's extreme measures to reduce Romania's external debt led to economic difficulties. Although he was successful in reducing foreign debt, the sharp drop in living standards that resulted from those hardship measures angered many. Despite food shortages and the rationing of bread, flour, and sugar, Ceausescu insisted that the country should continue exporting such goods. Ceausescu's plan for rapid urbanization, especially a program that called for the bulldozing of entire villages, further incited the populace.

A small incident became the spark that ignited heretofore suppressed flames of discontent. The ruthless crushing of a demonstration in Timisoara in December 1989 led to other mass demonstrations. After the dictator was booed at a mass rally on December 21, the army

◆ **A Romanian Revolutionary.** The revolt against Communist rule in Eastern Europe in 1989 came last to Romania. It was also more violent as the government at first tried to stem the revolt by massacring demonstrators. This picture shows a young Romanian rebel waving the national flag with the Communist emblem cut out of the center.

➤ *Vaclav Havel: The Call for a New Politics* ➤

In attempting to deal with the world's problems, some European leaders have pointed to the need for a new perspective, especially a moral one, if people are to live in a sane world. These two excerpts are taken from speeches by Vaclav Havel, who was elected the new president of Czechoslovakia at the end of 1989. The first is from his inaugural address as president of Czechoslovakia on January 1, 1990; the second is from a speech given to the American Congress.

Vaclav Havel, Address to the People of Czechoslovakia, January 1, 1990

But all this is still not the main problem [the environmental devastation of the country by its Communist leaders]. The worst thing is that we live in a contaminated moral environment. We fell morally ill because we became used to saying something different from what we thought. We learned not to believe in anything, to ignore each other, to care only about ourselves. Concepts such as love, friendship, compassion, humility, or forgiveness lost their depth and dimensions, and for many of us they represented only psychological peculiarities, or they resembled gone-astray greetings from ancients, a little ridiculous in the era of computers and spaceships. Only a few of us were able to cry out loud that the powers that be should not be all-powerful, and that special farms, which produce ecologically pure and top-quality food just for them should send their produce to schools, children's homes and hospitals if our agriculture was unable to offer them to all. The previous regime—armed with its arrogant and intolerant ideology—reduced man to a force of production and nature to a tool of production. In this it attacked both their very substance and their mutual relationship. It reduced gifted and autonomous people, skillfully working in their own country, to nuts and bolts of some monstrously huge, noisy, and stinking machine, whose real meaning is not clear to anyone.

Vaclav Havel, Speech to Congress, February 21, 1990

For this reason, the salvation of this human world lies nowhere else than in the human heart, in the human power to reflect, in human meekness and in human responsibility.

Without a global revolution in the sphere of human consciousness, nothing will change for the better in the sphere of our being as humans, and the catastrophe toward which this world is headed—be it ecological, social, demographic or a general breakdown of civilization— will be unavoidable. . . .

We are still a long way from that "family of man." In fact, we seem to be receding from the ideal rather than growing closer to it. Interests of all kinds— personal, selfish, state, nation, group, and if you like, company interests—still considerably outweigh genuinely common and global interests. We are still under the sway of the destructive and vain belief that man is the pinnacle of creation and not just a part of it and that therefore everything is permitted. . . .

In other words, we still don't know how to put morality ahead of politics, science and economics. We are still incapable of understanding that the only genuine backbone of all our actions, if they are to be moral, is responsibility.

Responsibility to something higher than my family, my country, my company, my success— responsibility to the order of being where all our actions are indelibly recorded and where and only where they will be properly judged.

The interpreter or mediator between us and this higher authority is what is traditionally referred to as human conscience.

refused to support any more repression. Ceausescu and his wife were captured on December 22 and tried and executed on Christmas Day, 1989. Leadership now passed into the hands of a hastily formed National Salvation Front, which won elections in the spring of 1990. Questions remained, however, about the new government's commitment to democracy.

In Bulgaria, too, Soviet cooperation after the war enabled the local Communist Party to assume control of the country. In 1954, Todor Zhivkov (b. 1911) became the leader of the Bulgarian Communist party and hence leader of the nation. Not until the late 1980s did a number of small opposition groups begin to emerge. In October of 1989, antigovernment demonstrations were held in the capital city of Sofia, and a month later, Zhivkov was unexpectedly relieved of his post as general secretary of the Communist Party, a position he had held for thirty-five years. Elections in November 1991 brought about a new government coalition, led by the United Democratic Front. Nevertheless, the Socialist Party (the former Communists) remained a potent force in Bulgarian politics.

Albania was Eastern Europe's smallest and poorest country. Isolated from its neighbors, Albania maintained its hard-line Stalinist political system well into the 1980s. The oppressive regime of Enver Hoxha (1908– 1985) ruled the country from 1944 to 1985, when Hoxha's handpicked successor, Ramiz Alia (b. 1925), assumed power. Throughout this period, Albania remained a closed society; it had little contact with the rest of the world, which in turn knew little about it. Nevertheless, the revolutionary upheaval of 1989 also reached Albania. Antigovernment demonstrations broke out in the Albanian capital of Tirana in 1990, forcing Alia's government to promise reforms. New political parties were legalized, and Albania's first free election was held in March 1991. Political and social unrest as well as economic decline have continued to trouble the new Republic of Albania.

The Reunification of Germany

Until 1989, the existence of West Germany and East Germany remained the most powerful symbol of a divided postwar Europe. In the early 1950s, the ruling Communist government in East Germany, led by Walter Ulbricht, had consolidated its position and become a faithful Soviet satellite. Industry was nationalized and agriculture collectivized. After a worker's revolt in 1953 was crushed by Soviet tanks, a steady flight of East Germans to West Germany ensued, primarily through the city of Berlin. This exodus of mostly skilled laborers created economic problems and led the East German government in 1961 to build the infamous Berlin Wall separating West from East Berlin, as well as equally fearsome barriers along the entire border with West Germany.

After building the wall, East Germany succeeded in developing the strongest economy among the Soviet Union's Eastern European satellites. In 1971, Walter Ulbricht was succeeded by Erich Honecker (b. 1912), a party hard-liner who made use of the *Stasi*, the secret police, to rule with an iron fist for the next eighteen years.

In 1988, however, popular unrest, partly fueled by the continual economic slump of the 1980s (which affected most of Eastern Europe) as well as the ongoing oppressiveness of Honecker's regime, caused another mass exodus of East German refugees. Violent repression as well as Honecker's refusal to institute reforms only led to a larger exodus and mass demonstrations against the regime in the summer and fall of 1989. By the beginning of November 1989, the Communist government had fallen into complete disarray. Capitulating to popular pressure on November 9, it opened the entire border with the West. Hundreds of thousands of Germans swarmed across the border, mostly to visit and return. The Berlin Wall, long the symbol of the Cold War, became the site of massive celebrations as thousands of people used sledgehammers to tear down the wall. By December, new political parties had emerged, and on March 18, 1990, in East Germany's first free elections

◆ **And the Wall Came Tumbling Down.** The Berlin Wall, long a symbol of Europe's Cold War divisions, became the site of massive celebrations after the East German government opened its border with the West. The activities included spontaneous acts of demolition as Germans used sledgehammers and crowbars to tear down parts of the wall.

ever, the Christian Democrats won almost 50 percent of the vote.

The Christian Democrats supported rapid monetary unification followed shortly by political unification with West Germany. On July 1, 1990, the economies of West and East Germany were united with the West German deutsche mark becoming the official currency of the two countries. Political reunification was achieved on October 3, 1990. What had seemed almost impossible at the beginning of 1989 had become a reality by the end of 1990—the country of East Germany had ceased to exist.

The Disintegration of Yugoslavia

From its beginning in 1919, Yugoslavia had been an artificial creation. After World War II, the dictatorial Tito had managed to hold the six republics and two autonomous provinces that constituted Yugoslavia together. After his death in 1980, no strong leader emerged, and his responsibilities passed to a collective state presidency and the League of Communists of Yugoslavia. At the end of the 1980s, Yugoslavia was caught up in the reform movements sweeping through Eastern Europe. On January 20, 1990, the League of Communists called for the creation of a pluralistic political system with freedom of speech, other civil liberties, and free elections. But divisions between Slovenes who wanted a loose federation and Serbians who

wanted to retain the centralized system caused the collapse of the party congress, and hence the Communist Party. New parties quickly emerged.

The Yugoslav political scene was complicated by the development of separatist movements that brought the disintegration of Yugoslavia in the 1990s. When new non-Communist parties won elections in 1990 in the republics of Slovenia, Croatia, Bosnia-Herzegovina, and the Former Yugoslav Republic of Macedonia, they began to lobby for a new federal structure of Yugoslavia that would fulfill their separatist desires. Slobodan Milošević, who had become the leader of the Serbian Communist Party in 1987 and had managed to stay in power by emphasizing his Serbian nationalism, rejected these efforts. He maintained that these republics could only be independent if new border arrangements were made to accommodate the Serb minorities in those republics who did not want to live outside the boundaries of a Greater Serbian state. Serbs constituted 11.6 percent of Croatia's population and 32 percent of Bosnia-Herzegovina's population in 1981.

After negotiations among the six republics failed, Slovenia and Croatia declared their independence in June 1991. Milošević's government sent the Yugoslavian army, which it controlled, into Slovenia, but without much success. In September 1991, it began a full assault against Croatia. Increasingly, the Yugoslavian army was becoming the Serbian army, while Serbian irregular

◆ **The War in Bosnia.** By mid-1993, irregular Serb forces had overrun much of Bosnia-Herzegovina amid scenes of untold suffering. This photograph shows two brothers in Sarajevo, the Bosnian capital, holding each other and weeping during the funeral of a third brother.

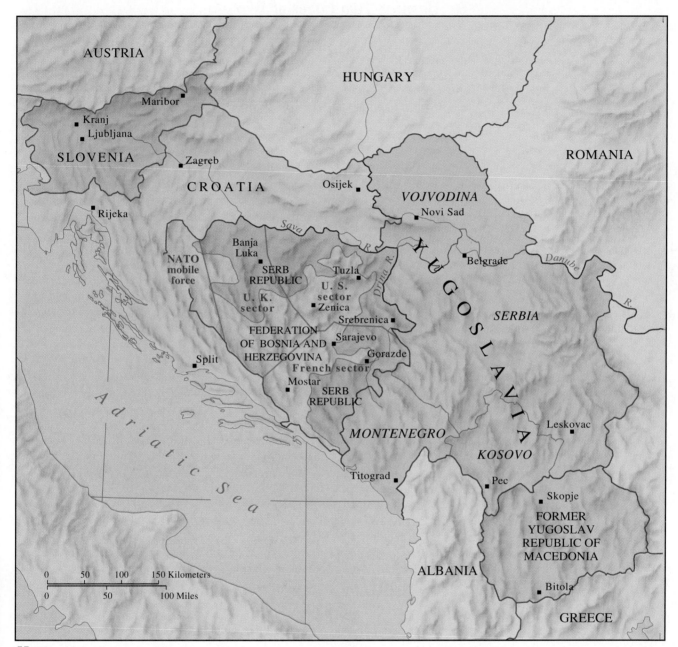

Map 30.2 The Lands of Former Yugoslavia.

forces played a growing role in military operations. Before a cease-fire was arranged, the Serbian forces had captured one-third of Croatia's territory in brutal and destructive fighting.

The recognition of Slovenia, Croatia, and Bosnia-Herzegovina by many European states and the United States early in 1992 did not stop the Serbs from turning their guns on Bosnia-Herzegovina. By mid-1993, Serbian forces had acquired 70 percent of Bosnian territory (see the box on p. 1040). The Serbian policy of "ethnic cleansing"—killing or forcibly removing Bosnian Muslims from their lands—revived memories of Nazi atrocities in World War II. Nevertheless, despite worldwide outrage, European governments failed to take a decisive and forceful stand against these Serbian activities. By 1995, 250,000 Bosnians (mostly civilians) had been killed while 2 million others were left homeless, often driven from their homes by "ethnic cleansing."

❧ *Bosnia: Two Faces of War* ❧

In April 1993, Serbian forces surrounded the Muslim town of Srebrenica in eastern Bosnia. After ferocious shelling by the Serbs, the town appeared ready to surrender. On April 17, 1993, newspapers in Sarajevo (the capital of Bosnia-Herzegovina) and Belgrade (the capital of Serbia) gave their readers very different versions of what was happening in Srebrenica.

Olsobodjenje (Sarajevo)

Tomorrow, a Canadian battalion serving with the United Nations Protection Force should enter Srebrenica as a result of negotiations between Lieut. Gen. Lars-Eric Wahlgren, commander of the U.N. force, and the war criminal Karadzic [Radovan Karadzic, leader of the Bosnia Serbs]. A Golgotha continues for the citizens of Srebrenica. . . . Zlatko Lagumdzija, the Deputy Prime Minister of Bosnia and Herzegovina, has told the world that Mladic's army [General Ratko Mladic, commander of the Bosnian Serb forces], that is Milŏsevic's army [President Slobodan Milŏsević' of Serbia], has to be stopped, that the only thing that the aggressor army understands is force, and that the only way it can be stopped is by confronting it with a greater force. . . . The aggressor forces continued their offensive at Srebrenica throughout the day yesterday with undiminished intensity, and the people of the town continued to give a heroic account of themselves in resisting the attempt by the more numerous and better-armed attackers to penetrate the town's outskirts. Besides their push across the front lines, the Chetniks [Serbian forces] continued to use their heavy artillery to shell the center of Srebrenica, massacring civilians. During the morning hours alone, the Chetnik artillery killed six people and injured 15, including several children. In Tuzla . . . local and foreign reporters were presented with a transcript of an intercepted radio-telephone conversation between war criminal Mladic and the Chetnik commanders in the area . . . . in which he ordered them to press the attacks so as to enter Srebrenica before he began his negotiations on a cease-fire.

Politika (Belgrade)

In spite of the fact that the Muslim armed forces are facing a total military defeat, they again launched attacks this morning from various directions from the territory of Srebrenica. According to Tanjug [Yugoslav news agency] reporting from this region, the Muslim units are using all their artillery and firing equipment. The Serbian sources say that Serbian defenders had tens of dead and wounded following attacks by Muslim forces which lasted for days. The army of the Republika Srpska [the name Serb nationalists gave to their self-proclaimed government in Bosnia] was forced to respond strongly in a counterattack and it has reached strategically important peaks around Srebrenica. The Serbian lines are only about one kilometer by air from Srebrenica. Using the fact that the Serbian side is not undertaking any action against Srebrenica itself, the Muslim extremists continued to attack. During the morning the most severe attacks of the Muslims were launched on Ratkovic, Zeleni Jadar, Podravanje and Milici. According to Tanjug, the Serbian sources are reporting that Muslim soldiers have started surrendering arms yesterday. There were such individual cases in the region of Skelani, Bratunac, Derventa and Podravanje. The Muslim extremists are in a hopeless situation from the military point of view. They are still reluctant to surrender because they were the ones to destroy 56 Serbian villages near Srebrenica, Bratunac and Skelani and on several occasions have killed in a most brutal way more than 1,300 Serbs, mostly women, children and aged people.

The Bosnian Serbs seemed well in control of Bosnia until 1995 when a sudden turn of events occurred. New offensives by mostly Muslim Bosnian government army forces and by the Croatian army regained considerable territory that had been lost to Serbian forces. Air strikes by NATO bombers, strongly advocated by President Bill Clinton, were launched in retaliation for Serb attacks on civilians and weakened the Serb military positions. All sides were now encouraged by the United States to end the war and met in Dayton, Ohio, in November 1995 for negotiations. A formal peace treaty, based on the Dayton accords, was signed in Paris on December 14. The agreement split Bosnia into a loose union of a Serb republic (with 49 percent of the land) and a Muslim-Croat federation (with 51 percent of the land). NATO agreed to send a force of 60,000 troops (20,000 American troops made up the largest single contingent) that would monitor the frontier between the new political entities. It remained to be seen whether the agreement would bring a lasting peace to war-torn Bosnia.

After the Fall

The fall of Communist governments in Eastern Europe during the revolutions of 1989 brought a wave of euphoria to Europe. The new structures meant an end to a postwar European order that had been imposed on unwilling peoples by the victorious forces of the Soviet Union. In 1989 and 1990, new governments throughout Eastern Europe worked diligently to scrap the remnants of the old system and introduce the democratic procedures and market systems that they believed would revitalize their scarred lands. But this process proved to be neither simple nor easy, and the mood of euphoria had largely faded by 1992.

Most Eastern European countries had little or virtually no experience with democratic systems. Moreover, most people had had little or no chance under Communist rule to participate in public life in general and in democratic debate in particular. Then, too, ethnic divisions, which had troubled these areas before World War II and had been forcibly submerged under Communist rule, reemerged with a vengeance, making political unity almost impossible. While Czechoslovakia resolved its differences peacefully, Yugoslavia descended into the kind of brutal warfare that had not been seen in Europe since World War II. In the lands of the former Soviet Union, ethnic and nationalist problems threatened to tear some of the new states apart.

The rapid conversion to market economies also proved painful. The adoption of "shock-therapy" austerity measures produced much suffering and uncertainty. Unemployment climbed to over 15 percent in the former East Germany and 13 percent in Poland in 1992. Wages remained low while prices skyrocketed. Russia experienced a 2,000 percent inflation rate in 1992. At the same time, in many countries former Communists were able to retain important positions of power or become the new owners of private property. Resentment against former Communists created yet another source of social instability. For both political and economic reasons, the new non-Communist states of Eastern Europe faced dangerous and uncertain futures. Nevertheless, by 1996, some of these states, such as Poland and the Czech Republic, were making a successful transition to both free markets and democracy.

Western Europe: The Winds of Change

After two decades of incredible economic growth, Europe experienced severe economic recessions in the mid-1970s and early 1980s (specifically, 1973–1974 and 1979–1983). Both inflation and unemployment rose dramatically. No doubt, the substantial increase in the price of oil that followed the Arab-Israeli conflict in 1973 was a major cause for the first downturn. But other factors were present as well. A worldwide recession had led to a decline in demand for European goods, while in Europe itself the reconstruction of many European cities after their devastation in World War II had largely been completed. The economies of the Western European states recovered in the course of the 1980s, although problems remained. Unemployment was still high, even after almost a decade of growth. France had a 10.6 unemployment rate in 1993; it reached 11.7 percent by the end of 1995. Nevertheless, despite their economic woes, Western Europeans were full participants in the technological growth of the age and seemed quite capable of standing up to American and Japanese economic competition.

Europeans also moved toward further integration of their economies after 1970. The European Economic Community expanded in 1973 when Great Britain, Ireland, and Denmark joined what its members now began to call the European Community (EC). By 1986, three additional members—Spain, Portugal, and Greece—had been added. The economic integration of the members of the European Community led to cooperative efforts in international and political affairs as well. The foreign ministers of the twelve members consulted frequently and provided a common front for negotiations on important issues.

Nevertheless, the European Community was still primarily an economic union, not a political one. By 1992, the European Community comprised 344 million people and constituted the world's largest single trading entity, transacting almost one-fourth of the world's commerce. In the 1980s and 1990s, the European Community moved toward even greater economic integration. The Treaty on European Union (also called the Maastricht Treaty after the city in the Netherlands where the agreement was reached) represented an attempt to create a true economic and monetary union of all European Community members. The treaty did not go into effect until all members agreed. Finally, on January 1, 1994, the European Community became the European Union. One of its first goals was to introduce a common currency, called the "euro," by 2002.

Politically, Western Europe had also become accustomed to democracy. Even Spain and Portugal, which had maintained their prewar dictatorial regimes until the mid-1970s, established democratic systems in the late 1970s. Western European Communist parties also declined drastically. During the mid-1970s, a new variety of Communism called Eurocommunism briefly emerged as Communist parties tried to work within the democratic system as mass movements committed to better government. But by the 1980s, internal political developments in Western Europe and events within the Communist world itself had combined to undermine the Eurocommunist experiment.

FROM WEST GERMANY TO GERMANY

After the Adenauer era, German voters moved politically from the center-right politics of the Christian Democrats to center-left politics, and in 1969, the Social Democrats became the leading party. By forming a ruling coalition with the small Free Democratic Party (FPD), the Social Democrats remained in power until 1982. The first Social Democratic chancellor was Willy Brandt (1913–1992). Brandt was especially successful with his "opening toward the east" (known as *Ostpolitik*), for which he received the Nobel Peace Prize in 1972. In the same year, Brandt made a Basic Treaty with East Germany that called for "good neighborly" relations, which soon led to greater cultural, personal, and economic contacts between West and East Germany. Despite this success, the discovery of an East German spy among Brandt's advisers caused his resignation in 1974.

His successor, Helmut Schmidt (b. 1918), was more of a technocrat than a reform-minded socialist and concentrated primarily on the economic problems largely brought about by high oil prices between 1973 and 1975. Schmidt was successful in eliminating a deficit of 10 billion marks in three years. In 1982, when the coalition of Schmidt's Social Democrats with the Free Democrats fell apart over the reduction of social welfare expenditures, the Free Democrats joined with the Christian Democratic Union of Helmut Kohl (b. 1930) to form a new government.

Helmut Kohl was a clever politician who benefited greatly from an economic boom in the mid-1980s. Gradually, however, discontent with the Christian Democrats increased, and, by 1988, their political prospects seemed diminished. But unexpectedly, the 1989 revolution in East Germany led to the reunification of the two Germanies, leaving the new Germany with its 79 million people the leading power in Europe. Reunification, accomplished during Kohl's administration, brought rich political dividends to the Christian Demo-

crats. In the first all-German federal election, Kohl's Christian Democrats won 44 percent of the vote, while their coalition partners—the Free Democrats—received 11 percent.

But the excitement over reunification soon dissipated as new problems arose. All too soon, the realization set in that the revitalization of eastern Germany would take far more money than was originally thought, and Kohl's government was soon forced to face the politically undesirable task of raising taxes substantially. Moreover, the virtual collapse of the economy in eastern Germany led to extremely high levels of unemployment and severe discontent. One of the responses was an attack on foreigners. For years foreigners seeking asylum and illegal immigrants had found haven in Germany because of its extremely liberal immigration laws. In 1992, more than 440,000 immigrants came to Germany seeking asylum; 123,000 came from former Yugoslavia alone. Attacks against foreigners by right-wing extremists—expecially young neo-Nazis—became an all-too-frequent part of German life.

GREAT BRITAIN: THATCHER AND THATCHERISM

Between 1964 and 1979, Conservatives and Labour alternated in power in Britain. Both parties had to deal with bitter conflict between Catholics and Protestants in Northern Ireland. Violence increased as the Irish Republican Army (IRA) staged a series of dramatic terrorist acts in response to the suspension of Northern Ireland's parliament in 1972 and the establishment of direct rule by London. The problems in Northern Ireland have not yet been solved. Nor was either party able to deal with Britain's ailing economy. Failure to modernize made British industry less and less competitive. Moreover, Britain was hampered by frequent labor strikes, many of them caused by conflicts between rival labor unions.

In 1979, after Britain's economic problems had seemed to worsen during five years under a Labour government, the Conservatives returned to power under Margaret Thatcher (b. 1925). She became the first woman to serve as prime minister in British history. Thatcher pledged to lower taxes, reduce government bureaucracy, limit social welfare, restrict union power, and end inflation. The "Iron Lady," as she was called, did break the power of the labor unions. While she did not eliminate the basic components of the social welfare system, she did use austerity measures to control inflation. "Thatcherism," as her economic policy was termed, improved the British economic situation but at a price. The south of England, for example, prospered, but the old industrial areas of the Midlands and north declined and were beset by high unemployment, poverty, and even violence. Cutbacks in education seriously undermined the quality of British education, long regarded as one of the world's finest.

In the area of foreign policy, Thatcher, like Ronald Reagan in the United States, took a hard-line approach against communism. She oversaw a large military buildup aimed at replacing older technology and reestablishing Britain as a world policeman. In 1982, when Argentina attempted to take control of the Falkland Islands (one of Britain's few remaining colonial outposts) 300 miles off its coast, the British successfully rebuked the Argentines, although at great economic cost and the loss of 255 lives. The Falklands War, however, did generate much popular patriotic support for Thatcher.

Margaret Thatcher dominated British politics in the 1980s. The Labour Party, beset by divisions between its moderate and radical wings, offered little effective opposition. Only in 1990 did Labour's fortunes seem to revive when Thatcher's government attempted to replace local property taxes with a flat-rate tax payable by every adult to his or her local authority. Though Thatcher maintained that this would make local government more responsive to its electors, many argued that this was nothing more than a poll tax that would enable the rich to pay the same rate as the poor. In 1990, after antitax riots broke out, Thatcher's once remarkable popularity fell to all-time lows. At the end of November, a revolt within her own party caused Thatcher to resign as prime minister. She was replaced by John Major, whose Conservative Party won a narrow victory in the general elections held in April 1992. His government, however, has failed to capture the imagination of most Britons.

UNCERTAINTIES IN FRANCE

The worsening of France's economic situation in the 1970s brought a shift to the left politically. By 1981, the Socialists had become the dominant party in the National Assembly, and the Socialist leader, François Mitterrand (1916-1995), was elected president. His first concern was with France's economic difficulties. In 1982, Mitterrand froze prices and wages in the hope of reducing the huge budget deficit and high inflation. He also passed a number of liberal measures to aid workers:

✦ **Margaret Thatcher.** Great Britain's first woman prime minister, Margaret Thatcher was a strong leader who dominated British politics in the 1980s. This picture of Thatcher was taken at the Chelsea Flower Show in May 1990. Six months later, a revolt within her own party caused her to resign as prime minister.

an increased minimum wage, expanded social benefits, a mandatory fifth week of paid vacation for salaried workers, a thirty-nine-hour workweek, and higher taxes for the rich. Mitterrand's administrative reforms included both centralization (nationalization of banks and industry) and decentralization (granting local governments greater powers). Their victory had convinced the Socialists that they could enact some of their more radical reforms. Consequently, the government nationalized the steel industry, major banks, the space and electronics industries, and important insurance firms.

The Socialist policies largely failed to work, however, and within three years, a decline in support for the Socialists caused the Mitterrand government to pursue what it called "modernization," basically a return of some of the economy to private enterprise and a narrowing of bureaucratic powers. Some economic improvement in the late 1980s enabled Mitterrand to win a second seven-year term in the 1988 presidential elections. But France's economic decline continued. In 1993, French unemployment stood at 10.6 percent, and, in the elections in March of that year, the Socialists won only 28 percent of the vote while a coalition of conservative parties gained 80 percent of the seats in the National Assembly. The move to the right in France was strengthened when the conservative mayor of Paris, Jacques Chirac, was elected president in May 1995.

CONFUSION IN ITALY

In the 1970s and 1980s, Italy continued to practice the politics of coalitions that had characterized much of its history. Italy witnessed the installation of its fiftieth postwar government in 1991, and its new prime minister, Giulio Andreotti, had already served six times in that office. Italian governments continued to consist of coalitions mostly led by the Christian Democrats.

In the 1980s, even the Communists had been included briefly in the government. The Italian Communists had become advocates of Eurocommunism, basically an attempt to broaden communism's support by dropping its Marxist ideology. Although its vote declined in the 1980s, even in 1987, the Communist Party still garnered 26 percent of the vote. The Communists also won a number of local elections and took charge of municipal governments in several cities, including Rome and Naples for a brief time.

In the 1970s, Italy suffered from a severe economic recession. The Italian economy, which depended on imported oil as its chief source of energy, was especially vulnerable to the steep increase in oil prices in 1973. Parallel to the economic problems was a host of political and social problems: student unrest, mass strikes, and terrorist attacks. In 1978, a former prime minister, Aldo Moro, was kidnapped and killed by the Red Brigades, a terrorist organization. Then, too, there was the all-pervasive and corrupting influence of the Mafia, which had always been an important factor in southern Italy, but spread to northern Italy as well in the 1980s.

Italy survived the crises of the 1970s and in the decade of the 1980s began to experience remarkable economic growth. But severe problems remained. Corruption continued to trouble Italian politics. In 1993, hundreds of politicians and business leaders were under investigation for their involvement in a widespread scheme to use political bribes to secure public contracts. Public disgust with political corruption became so intense that in April 1996 Italian voters took the unusual step of giving control of the government to a center-left coalition that included the Communists.

New Directions and New Problems in Western Society

Dramatic social developments have accompanied political and economic changes since the 1960s. New opportunities for women emerged, and a women's liberation movement sought to bring new meaning to the principle of equality with men. New problems for Western society also arose with the advent of terrorism, a reaction against foreign workers and immigrants, and a growing awareness of environmental dangers.

New (and Old) Patterns: Women since the 1960s

After World War II, the trend toward earlier marriage continued. In Sweden, the average age of first marriage dropped from twenty-six in the 1940s to twenty-three in 1970. Although birthrates rose immediately after World War II, they have mostly declined since the war as both contraceptive devices and abortion have become widely available. It is estimated that mothers need to average 2.1 children in order to ensure a natural replacement of a country's population. In many European countries, the population stopped growing in the 1960s, and the trend has continued since then. By 1992, fertility rates were down drastically; among the twelve nations of the

European Community, the average number of children per mother was 1.58. No doubt, the trend toward early marriage and smaller families contributed to the changes in the character of women's employment in both Europe and the United States as women experienced considerably more years when they were not involved in rearing children.

The most important development was the increased number of married women in the workforce. At the beginning of the twentieth century, even working-class wives tended to stay at home if they could afford to do so. In the postwar period, this was no longer the case. In the United States, for example, in 1900, married women made up about 15 percent of the female labor force; by 1970, their number had increased to 62 percent. The percentage of married women in the female labor force in Sweden increased from 47 to 66 percent between 1963 and 1975. Figures for the Soviet Union and its satellites were even higher. In 1970, 92.5 percent of all women in the Soviet Union held jobs compared to around 50 percent in France and West Germany. The industrial development of the Soviet Union relied on female labor.

But the increased number of women in the workforce has not changed some old patterns. Working-class women in particular still earn salaries lower than those of men for equal work. Women still tend to enter traditionally female jobs. As one Swedish woman guidance counselor remarked in 1975: "Every girl now thinks in terms of a job. This is progress. They want children, but they don't pin their hopes on marriage. They don't intend to be housewives for some future husband. But there has been no change in their vocational choices."[2] A 1980 study of twenty-five European nations revealed that women still made up over 80 percent of the typists, nurses, tailors, and dressmakers in their countries. Many European women also still faced the double burden of earning income on the one hand and raising a family and maintaining the household on the other. Such inequalities led increasing numbers of women to rebel.

THE FEMINIST MOVEMENT: THE SEARCH FOR LIBERATION

The participation of women in World War I and II helped them achieve one of the major aims of the nineteenth-century feminist movement—the right to vote. Already after World War I, many governments acknowledged the contributions of women to the war effort by granting them the right to vote. Sweden, Great Britain, Germany, Poland, Hungary, Austria, and

◆ **Women's Liberation Movement.** In the late 1960s, as women began once again to assert their rights, a revived women's liberation movement emerged. Feminists in the movement maintained that women themselves must alter the conditions of their lives. During this women's liberation rally, some women climbed the statue of Admiral Farragut in Washington, D.C., to exhibit their signs.

Czechoslovakia did so in 1918, followed by the United States in 1920. Women in France and Italy did not obtain the right to vote until 1945. After World War II, European women tended to fall back into the traditional roles expected of them, and little was heard of feminist concerns. But by the late 1960s, women began to assert their rights again and speak as feminists. Along with the student upheavals of the late 1960s came renewed interest in feminism, or the women's liberation movement as it was now called. Increasingly, women protested that the acquisition of political and legal equality had not brought true equality with men:

> We are economically oppressed: in jobs we do full work for half pay, in the home we do unpaid work full time. We are commercially exploited by advertisement, television

and the press; legally we often have only the status of children. We are brought up to feel inadequate, educated to narrower horizons than men. This is our specific oppression as women. It is as women that we are, therefore, organizing.[3]

These were the words of a British Women's Liberation Workshop in 1969.

Of great importance to the emergence of the postwar women's liberation movement was the work of Simone de Beauvoir (1908–1986). Born into a Catholic middle-class family and educated at the Sorbonne in Paris, she supported herself as a teacher and later as a novelist and writer. She maintained a lifelong relationship (but not marriage) with Jean-Paul Sartre. Her involvement in the existentialist movement—the leading intellectual movement of its time—led to her involvement in political causes. De Beauvoir believed that she lived a "liberated" life for a twentieth-century European woman, but for all her freedom, she still came to perceive that as a woman she faced limits that men did not. In 1949, she published her highly influential work, *The Second Sex,* in which she argued that as a result of male-dominated societies, women had been defined by their differences from men and consequently received second-class status: "What peculiarly signalizes the situation of woman is that she—a free and autonomous being like all human creatures—nevertheless finds herself living in a world where men compel her to assume the status of the Other."[4] De Beauvoir took an active role in the French women's movement of the 1970s, and her book was a major influence on both the American and European women's movements (see the box on p. 1047).

Feminists in the women's liberation movement came to believe that women themselves must transform the fundamental conditions of their lives. They did so in a variety of ways. First, in the 1960s and 1970s, they formed numerous "consciousness-raising" groups to further awareness of women's issues. Women also sought and gained a measure of control over their own bodies by seeking to overturn the illegality of both contraception and abortion. In the 1960s and 1970s, hundreds of thousands of European women worked to repeal the laws that outlawed contraception and abortion and began to meet with success. A French law in 1968 permitted the sale of contraceptive devices. In 1979, another French law legalized abortion. Even in Catholic countries, where the church remained strongly opposed to abortion, legislation allowing contraception and abortion was passed in the 1970s and 1980s.

As more women became activists, they also became involved in new issues. In the 1980s and 1990s, women faculty in universities concentrated on developing new cultural attitudes through the new academic field of "women's studies." Other women began to try to affect the political and natural environment by allying with the antinuclear and ecological movements. As one German writer who was concerned with environmental issues said, it is women "who must give birth to children, willingly or unwillingly, in this polluted world of ours."

The Growth of Terrorism

Acts of terror by those opposed to governments became a frightening aspect of modern Western society. During the late 1970s and early 1980s in particular, concern about terrorism was often at the top of foreign policy agendas in the United States and many European countries. Small bands of terrorists used assassination, indiscriminate killing of civilians, especially by bombing, the taking of hostages, and the hijacking of airplanes to draw attention to their demands or to destabilize governments in the hope of achieving their political goals. Terrorist acts garnered considerable media attention. When Palestinian terrorists kidnapped and killed eleven Israeli athletes at the Munich Olympic games in 1972, hundreds of millions of people watched the drama unfold on television. Indeed, some observers believe that media exposure has been an important catalyst for some terrorist groups.

Motivations for terrorist acts varied considerably. Left- and right-wing terrorist groups flourished in the late 1970s and early 1980s. Left-wing groups, such as the Baader-Meinhof gang (also known as the Red Army Faction) in Germany and the Red Brigades in Italy, consisted chiefly of affluent middle-class young people who denounced the injustices of capitalism and supported acts of revolutionary terrorism in order to bring down the system. Right-wing terrorist groups, such as the New Order in Italy and the Charles Martel Club in France, used bombings to foment disorder and bring about authoritarian regimes. These groups received little of no public support, and authorities were able to crush them fairly quickly.

But terrorist acts also stemmed from militant nationalists who wished to create separatist states. Because they received considerable support from local populations sympathetic to their cause, these terrorist groups could maintain their activities over a long period of time. Most prominent was the Irish Republican Army (IRA), which resorted to vicious attacks against the

The Voice of the Women's Liberation Movement

Simone de Beauvoir was an important figure in the emergence of the postwar women's liberation movement. This excerpt is taken from her influential book, The Second Sex, *in which she argued that women have been forced into a position subordinate to men.*

Simone de Beauvoir, *The Second Sex*

Now, woman has always been man's dependent, if not his slave; the two sexes have never shared the world in equality. And even today woman is heavily handicapped, though her situation is beginning to change. Almost nowhere is her legal status the same as man's and frequently it is much to her disadvantage. Even when her rights are legally recognized in the abstract, long-standing custom prevents their full expression in the mores. In the economic sphere men and women can almost be said to make up two castes; other things being equal, the former hold the better jobs, get higher wages, and have more opportunity for success than their new competitors. In industry and politics men have a great many more positions and they monopolize the most important posts. In addition to all this they enjoy a traditional prestige that the education of children tends in every way to support, for the present enshrines the past—and in the past all history has been made by men. At the present time, when women are beginning to take part in the affairs of the world, it is still a world that belongs to men—they have no doubt of it at all and women have scarcely any. To decline to be the Other, to refuse to be a party to a deal—this would be for women to renounce all the advantages conferred upon them by their alliance with the superior caste. Man-the-sovereign will provide woman-the-liege with material protection and will undertake the moral justification of her existence; thus she can evade at once both economic risk and the metaphysical risk of a liberty in which ends and aims must be contrived without assistance. Indeed, along with the ethical urge of each individual to affirm his subjective existence, there is also the temptation to forgo liberty and become a thing. This is an inauspicious road, for he who takes it—passive, lost, ruined—becomes henceforth the creature of another's will, frustrated in his transcendence and deprived of every value. But it is an easy road; on it one avoids the strain involved in undertaking an authentic existence. When man makes of woman the *Other* he may, then, expect her to manifest deep-seated tendencies toward complicity. Thus woman may fail to lay claim to the status of subject because she lacks definite resources, because she feels the necessary bond that ties her to man regardless of reciprocity, and because she is often very well pleased with her role as the *Other*.

Now, what peculiarly signalizes the situation of woman is that she—a free and autonomous being like all human creatures—nevertheless finds herself living in a world where men compel her to assume the status of the Other.

ruling government and innocent civilians in Northern Ireland. Over a period of twenty years, IRA terrorists were responsible for the death of two thousand people in Northern Ireland; three-fourths of the victims were civilians.

Although left- and right-wing terrorist activities declined in Europe in the 1980s, international terrorism remained rather commonplace. Angered over the loss of their territory to Israel by 1967, some militant Palestinians responded with a policy of terrorist attacks against Israel's supporters. Palestinian terrorists operated throughout European countries, attacking both Europeans and American tourists; vacationers at airports in Rome and Vienna were massacred by Palestinian terrorists in 1985. State-sponsored terrorism was often an integral part of international terrorism. Militant governments, especially in Iran, Libya, and Syria, assisted terrorist organizations that made attacks on Europeans and Americans. On December 21, 1988, Pan American flight 103 from Frankfurt to New York exploded over Lockerbie, Scotland, killing all 259 passengers and crew members. A massive investigation finally revealed that the bomb responsible for the explosion had been planted by two Libyan terrorists who were connected to terrorist groups based in both Iran and Syria.

Governments fought back by creating special antiterrorist units that became extremely effective in responding to terrorist acts. In 1977, for example, the German special antiterrorist unit, known as GSG, rescued 91 hostages from a Lufthansa airplane that had been hijacked to Mogadishu in Somalia. Counterterrorism, or a calculated policy of direct retaliation against terrorists,

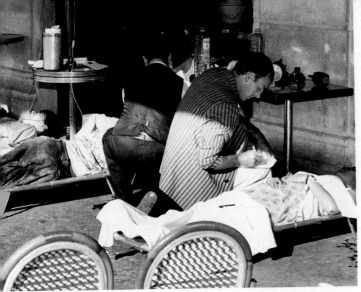

◆ **Terrorism in Europe.** Terrorist acts became a regular feature of European life beginning in the 1970s. This photograph shows some of the victims of a bomb set off in a subway during rush hour in Paris in July 1995. Fifty people were injured by the explosion.

also made states that sponsored terrorism more cautious. In 1986, the Reagan administration responded to the terrorist bombing of a West German disco club popular with American soldiers by an air attack on Libya, long suspected as a major sponsor of terrorist organizations. Some observers attribute the overall decline in terrorist attacks in the late 1980s to the American action. In the 1990s, however, acts of terrorism have continued to be a disturbing element in Western life.

Guest Workers and Immigrants

As the economies of the Western European countries revived in the 1950s and 1960s, a severe labor shortage forced them to rely on foreign workers. Scores of Turks and eastern and southern Europeans came to Germany, North Africans to France, and people from the Caribbean, India, and Pakistan to Great Britain. Overall, there were probably 15 million guest workers in Europe in the 1980s. They constituted 17 percent of the labor force in Switzerland and 10 percent in Germany.

Although these workers were necessary for economic reasons, socially and politically their presence created problems for their host countries. Many foreign workers complained that they received lower wages and inferior social benefits. Moreover, their concentration in certain cities and even certain sections of those cities often created tensions with the local native populations. Foreign workers, many of them nonwhites, constituted almost one-fifth of the population in the German cities of Frankfurt, Munich, and Stuttgart. Having become settled in their new countries, many were unwilling to leave, even after the end of the postwar boom in the early 1970s led to mass unemployment. Moreover, as guest workers settled permanently in their host countries, additional family members migrated to join them. Although they had little success in getting guest workers already there to leave, some European countries passed legislation or took other measures to restrict new immigration. In 1991, thousands of Albanians fled their homeland after its Communist government began to fall apart, but when they arrived in Italy, the Italian authorities forcibly evicted them and sent them back to Albania.

In the 1980s, the problem of foreign workers was intensified by an influx of other refugees, especially to West Germany, which had liberal immigration laws that permitted people seeking asylum for political persecution to enter the country. During the 1970s and 1980s, West Germany absorbed over a million refugees from Eastern Europe and East Germany. In 1986 alone, two hundred thousand political refugees from Pakistan, Bangladesh, and Sri Lanka entered the country.

This great influx of foreigners, many of them nonwhite, strained not only the social services of European countries, but the patience of many native residents who opposed making their countries ethnically diverse. Antiforeign sentiment, especially in a time of growing unemployment, increased and was encouraged by new right-wing political parties that catered to people's complaints. Thus, the National Front in France, organized by Jean-Marie Le Pen, and the Republican Party in Germany, led by Franz Schönhuber, a former SS officer, advocated restricting all new immigration and limiting the assimilation of settled immigrants. Although these parties have had only limited success in elections so far, even that modest accomplishment has encouraged traditional conservative and even moderately conservative parties to adopt more nationalistic policies. Even more frightening, however, have been the organized campaigns of violence, especially against African and Asian immigrants, by radical, right-wing groups (see the box on p. 1049).

The Environment and the Green Movements

Beginning in the 1970s, environmentalism became an important item on the European political agenda. By that time, serious ecological problems had become all too apparent. Air pollution, produced by nitrogen oxide

Violence against Foreigners in Germany

As the number of foreign guest workers and immigrants increased in Europe, violent attacks against them also escalated. Especially in the former East Germany, where unemployment rose dramatically after reunification, gangs of neo-Nazi youth have perpetrated violent attacks on foreigners. This document is taken from a German press account of an attack on guest workers from Vietnam and Mozambique who had originally been recruited by the East German government.

Knud Pries, "East Germans Have Yet to Learn Tolerance"

The police headquarters in Dresden, the capital of Saxony, announced that "a political situation" had developed in the town of Hoyerswerda. Political leaders and the police needed to examine the problem and corresponding measures should be taken: "In the near future the residents of the asylum hostel will be moved."

The people of Hoyerswerda prefer to be more direct, referring to the problem of *Neger* (niggers) and *Fidschis* (a term for Asian foreigners). The loudmouths of the neo-fascist gangs make the message clear: "Niggers Go Home!"

It looks as if some Germans have had enough of bureaucratic officialese. What is more, they will soon make sure that no more foreign voices are heard in Hoyerswerda.

The municipality in northern Saxony has a population of just under 70,000, including 70 people from Mozambique and Vietnam who live in a hostel for foreigners and about 240 asylum-seekers in a hostel at the other end of town.

The "political situation" was triggered by an attack by a neo-Nazi gang on Vietnamese traders selling their goods on the market square on 17 September. After being dispersed by the police the Faschos carried out their first attack on the hostel for foreigners.

The attacks then turned into a regular evening "hunt" by a growing group of right-wing radicals, some of them minors, who presented their idea of a clean Germany by roaming the streets armed with truncheons, stones, steel balls, bottles and Molotov cocktails. Seventeen people were injured, some seriously.

After the police stepped in on a larger scale the extremists moved across the town to the asylum hostel. To begin with, only the gang itself and onlookers were outside the building, but on the evening of 22 September members of the "Human Rights League" and about 100 members of "autonomous" groups turned up to help the foreigners who had sought refuge in the already heavily damaged block of flats.

A large police contingent, reinforced by men from Dresden and the Border Guard, prevented the situation from becoming even more critical. Two people were seriously injured. The mob was disbanded with the help of dogs, tear gas and water-cannons.

Thirty-two people were arrested, and blank cartridge guns, knives, slings and clubs were seized. On 23 September, a police spokesman announced that the situation was under control. It seems doubtful whether things will stay this way, since the pogroms have become an evening ritual. Politicians and officials are racking their brains about how to grapple with the current crisis and the basic problem. One thing is clear: without a massive intervention by the police the problem cannot even be contained. But what then?

Saxony's Interior Minister, Rudolf Krause, initially recommended that the hostels concerned should be "fenced in," but then admitted that this was "not the final solution." Providing the Defence Ministry approves, the "provisional solution" will be to move the foreigners to a barracks in Kamenz.

Even if this operation is completed without violence it would represent a shameful success for the right-wing radicals. Although the Africans and Asians still living in Hoyerswerda will have to leave at the end of November anyway once the employment contracts drawn up in the former [East Germany] expire, they are unwilling to endure the terror that long. "Even if we're going anyway—they want all foreigners to go now," says the 29-year-old Martinho from Mozambique.

His impression is that the gangs of thugs are doing something for which others are grateful: "The neighbors are glad when the skinheads arrive."

Interior Minister Krause feels that the abuse of asylum laws, the social problems in East Germany and an historically rooted deficit explain this situation: "The problem is that we were unable in the past to practice the tolerance needed to accept alien cultures."

and sulfur dioxide emissions from road vehicles, power plants, and industrial factories, was causing respiratory illnesses and having corrosive effects on buildings and monuments. Many rivers, lakes, and seas had become so polluted that they posed serious health risks. Dying forests and disappearing wildlife alarmed more and more people. The opening of Eastern Europe after the revolutions of 1989 brought to the world's attention the incredible environmental destruction of that region caused by unfettered industrial pollution. Communist governments had obviously operated under the assumption that production quotas were much more significant than protection of the environment.

Environmental concerns forced the major political parties in Europe to advocate new regulations for the protection of the environment. The Soviet nuclear power disaster at Chernobyl in 1986 made Europeans even more aware of potential environmental hazards, and 1987 was touted as the "year of the environment." Many European states also established government ministries to oversee environmental issues.

Growing ecological awareness also gave rise to the Green movements and Green parties that emerged throughout Europe in the 1970s. The origins of these movements were by no means uniform. Some came from the antinuclear movement; others arose out of such causes as women's liberation and concerns for foreign workers. Most started at the local level and then gradually expanded to include activities at the national level, where they became formally organized as political parties. Most visible was the Green Party in Germany, which was officially organized in 1979 and, by 1987, had elected forty-two delegates to the West German parliament. Green parties also competed successfully in Sweden, Austria, and Switzerland.

Despite their repressive policies, Communist countries in Eastern Europe also witnessed the formation of ecologically conscious groups. In the 1980s, environmental groups emerged in East Germany and Czechoslovakia, two especially environmentally devastated countries, as well as in Poland and Hungary. The Czech dissident group, Charter 77, emphasized environmental damage as one of the chief crimes of its Communist government.

Although the Green movements and parties have played an important role in making people aware of ecological problems, they have by no means replaced the traditional political parties, as some political analysts in the mid-1980s forecast. For one thing, the coalitions that made up the Greens found it difficult to agree on all issues and tended to splinter into different cliques. Then, too, many of the founders of these movements, who often expressed a willingness to work with the traditional political parties, were ousted from leadership positions by fundamentalists unwilling to compromise their principles in any way. Finally, traditional political parties have co-opted the environmental issues of the Greens. By the early 1990s, more and more European governments were beginning to sponsor projects to safeguard the environment and clean up the worst sources of pollution.

The World of Western Culture

Intellectually and culturally, the Western world during the last half of the twentieth century has been marked by much diversity. Although many trends represent a continuation of prewar modern developments, new directions in the last two decades have led some to speak of a postmodern cultural world.

Recent Trends in Art, Music, and Literature

Modern art continued to prevail at exhibitions and museums. For the most part, the United States dominated the art world, much as it did the world of popular culture (see Popular Culture and the Americanization of the World later in this chapter). American art, often vibrantly colored and filled with activity, reflected the energy and exuberance of postwar America. After 1945, New York City became the artistic center of the Western world. The Guggenheim Museum, the Museum of Modern Art, and the Whitney Museum of American art, together with New York's numerous art galleries, promoted modern art and helped determine artistic tastes not only in New York and the United States, but throughout much of the world.

Abstractionism, especially Abstract Expressionism, emerged as the artistic mainstream (see Chapters 25 and 27). American exuberance in Abstract Expressionism is evident in the enormous canvases of Jackson Pollock (1912–1956). In such works as *Lavender Mist* (1950), paint seems to explode, assaulting the viewer with emotion and movement. Pollock's swirling forms and seemingly chaotic patterns broke all conventions of form and structure. His drip paintings, with their total abstraction, were extremely influential with other artists, although the public was initially quite hostile to his work. Pollock also introduced the technique of painting with the canvas laid on the floor. He said: "On the floor I am more at ease. I feel nearer, more a part of the painting, since this way I can walk around in, work from four sides and be literally *in* the painting. When I am *in* the painting I am not aware of what I am doing. There is pure harmony."

The early 1960s saw the emergence of Pop Art, which took images of popular culture and transformed them into works of fine art. Andy Warhol (1930–1987), who began as an advertising illustrator, was the most famous of the pop artists. Warhol adapted images from commercial art, such as the Campbell soup cans, and photographs of such celebrities as Marilyn Monroe. Derived from mass culture, these works were mass produced and deliberately "of the moment," expressing the fleeting whims of popular culture.

In the 1980s, styles emerged that some have referred to as Postmodern. Although as yet ill-defined, Postmodernism tends to move away from the futurism or "cutting edge" qualities of Modernism. Instead it favors "utilizing tradition," whether that includes more styles of painting or elevating traditional craftsmanship to the level of fine art. Weavers, potters, glassmakers, metalsmiths, and furniture makers have gained respect as artists.

Another response to Modernism can be seen in a return to realism in the arts. Some extreme realists paint or sculpt with such minute attention to realistic detail that their paintings appear to be photographs and their sculptures living human beings. Their subjects are often ordinary individuals, stuck in ordinary lives. These works are often pessimistic and cynical.

Abstract Expressionism, however, continues to proliferate. Anselm Kiefer, born in Germany in 1945, combines aspects of Abstract Expressionism, collage, and German Expressionism to create works that are stark and haunting. His *Departure from Egypt* (1984) is a meditation on Jewish history and its descent into the horrors of Nazism. Kiefer hoped that a portrayal of Germany's atrocities could free Germans from their past and bring some good out of evil. His international stature reflects a movement away from American dominance in the fine arts, a trend that gained momentum in the 1980s.

Like modern art, modern music has focused on variety and radical experimentation. Also, like modern art, modern classical music witnessed a continuation of prewar developments. Some composers, the neoclassicists, remained closely tied to nineteenth-century Romantic music, although they occasionally incorporated some twentieth-century developments, such as atonality

✦ **Jackson Pollock Does a Painting.** One of the best-known practitioners of Abstract Expressionism, which remained at the center of the artistic mainstream after World War II, was the American Jackson Pollock, who achieved his ideal of total abstraction in his drip paintings. He is shown here at work in his Long Island studio. Pollock found it easier to cover his large canvases with exploding patterns of color when he put them on the floor.

and dissonance. Their style was strongly reminiscent of Stravinsky (see Chapter 25).

The major musical trend since the war, however, has been serialism. Inspired mostly by the twelve-tone music of Schönberg (see Chapter 27), serialism is a compositional procedure where an order of succession is set for specific values: pitch (for tones of the tempered scale); loudness (for dynamic levels); and units of time (for rhythm). By predetermining the order of succession, the

✦ **Anselm Kiefer, *Departure for Egypt*.** Although Western artists experimented with a variety of modern and even postmodern styles in the 1970s and 1980s, Abstract Expressionism continued to be popular. The German artist Anselm Kiefer used the tradition of Abstract Expressionism to create haunting images that reflect the horrors of Germany's Nazi past.

composer restricts his or her intuitive freedom as the work to some extent creates itself. However, the mechanism the composer initially establishes could generate unanticipated musical events, thereby creating new and exciting compositions. Serialist composition diminishes the role of intuition and emotion in favor of intellect and mathematical precision. The first recognized serialist was the Frenchman Olivier Messiaen (b. 1908). Significantly, Messiaen was influenced in part by Indian and Greek music, plain chant, folk music, and birdsongs. Most critics have respected serialism, although the public has been largely indifferent, if not hostile, to it.

An offshoot of serialism that has won popular support, but not the same critical favor, is minimalism. Like serialism, this style uses repeated patterns and series and steady pulsation with gradual changes occurring over time. But whereas serialism is often atonal, minimalism is usually tonal and more harmonic. Perhaps the most successful minimalist composer is Philip Glass (b. 1937), who demonstrated in *Einstein on the Beach* that minimalist music could be adapted to full-scale opera. Like other modern American composers, Glass found no contradiction in moving between the worlds of classical music and popular music. His *Koyaanisqatsi* was used as background music to a documentary film on the disintegrative forces in Western society.

The most significant new trend in postwar literature has been called the "Theater of the Absurd." This new convention in drama began in France in the 1950s,

although its most famous proponent was the Irishman Samuel Beckett (1906–1990), who lived in France. In Beckett's *Waiting for Godot* (1952), it is readily apparent that the action on stage is not realistic. Two men wait incessantly for the appearance of someone, with whom they may or may not have an appointment. No background information on the two men is provided. During the course of the play, nothing seems to be happening. The audience is never told if the action in front of them is real or unreal. Unlike traditional theater, suspense is maintained not by having the audience wonder, "what is going to happen next?" but by having them ask simply, "what is happening now?"

The Theater of the Absurd reflected its time. The postwar period was a time of disillusionment with fixed ideological beliefs in politics or religion. A sense of the world's meaninglessness underscored the desolate world view of absurdist drama and literature. This can be seen in Günter Grass's *Tin Drum*, published in 1959, which reflected postwar Germany's preoccupation with the seeming incomprehensibility of Nazi Germany.

The Theater of the Absurd also questioned the ability of language to reflect reality accurately. Beckett's play *Act without Words* contains no dialogue. In another play, Beckett used a beam of light and a buzzing sound as "words" of the discourse. The Czech playwright, Vaclav Havel, in his *Memorandum* (1966), examined the language and mechanics of bureaucracy. The plot revolved around the introduction of an artificial language that is imposed on people in the hope of fostering more efficient communication. Because no one can understand the new language, communication breaks down and, therefore, so do human relationships. The artificial language is finally eliminated, only to be replaced by an equally incomprehensible language imposed from above. The overt critique of Communist bureaucracy and the absurdity of imposing artificial systems in the hope of re-creating society along ideological lines did little for Havel's position in Communist Czechoslovakia.

The Philosophical Dilemma: Existentialism

The sense of meaninglessness that inspired the Theater of the Absurd also underscored the philosophy of existentialism. It was largely born of the desperation caused by two world wars and the breakdown of traditional values. Existentialism reflected the anxieties of the twentieth century and became especially well known after World War II through the works of two Frenchmen, Jean-Paul Sartre (1905–1980) and Albert Camus (1913–1960).

The Voice of Existentialism

Jean-Paul Sartre, a famous French intellectual of the early postwar years, became identified with the existentialist movement. He himself had been a student of German philosophy and was especially affected by the ideas of Martin Heidegger, whose Being and Time *is considered an influential existentialist work. This selection is taken from* Existentialism, *written by Sartre in 1946 to provide a general description of existentialism. In this passage, he discusses atheistic existentialism.*

Jean-Paul Sartre, *Existentialism*

Dostoievsky said, "If God didn't exist, everything would be possible." That is the very starting point of existentialism. Indeed, everything is permissible if God does not exist, and as a result man is forlorn, because neither within him nor without does he find anything to cling to. He can't start making excuses for himself.

If existence really does precede essence, there is no explaining things away by reference to a fixed and given human nature. In other words, there is no determinism, man is free, man is freedom. On the other hand, if God does not exist, we find no values or commands to turn to which legitimize our conduct. So, in the bright realm of values, we have no excuse behind us, nor justification before us. We are alone with no excuses.

That is the idea I shall try to convey when I say that man is condemned to be free. Condemned, because he did not create himself, yet, in other respects is free; because, once thrown into the world, he is responsible for everything he does. The existentialist does not believe in the power of passion. He will never agree that a sweeping passion is a ravaging torrent which fatally leads a man to certain acts and is therefore an excuse. He thinks that man is responsible for his passion.

The existentialist does not think that man is going to help himself by finding in the world some omen by which to orient himself. Because he thinks that man will interpret the omen to suit himself. Therefore, he thinks that man, with no support and no aid, is condemned every moment to invent man. . . .

There can be no other truth to take off from than this: *I think; therefore, I exist.* There we have the absolute truth of consciousness becoming aware of itself. Every theory which takes man out of the moment in which he becomes aware of himself is, at its very beginning, a theory which confounds truth, for outside the Cartesian *cogito,* all views are only probable, and a doctrine of probability which is not bound to a truth dissolves into thin air. In order to describe the probable, you must have a firm hold on the true. Therefore, before there can be any truth whatsoever, there must be an absolute truth; and this one is simple and easily arrived at; it's on everyone's doorstep; it's a matter of grasping it directly.

Secondly, this theory is the only one which gives man dignity, the only one which does not reduce him to an object. The effect of all materialism is to treat all men, including the one philosophizing, as objects, that is, as an ensemble of determined reactions in no way distinguished from the ensemble of qualities and phenomena which constitute a table or a chair or a stone. We definitely wish to establish the human realm as an ensemble of values distinct from the material realm. . . .

Moreover, to say that we invent values means nothing else but this: life has no meaning a priori. Before you come alive, life is nothing; it's up to you to give it a meaning, and value is nothing else but the meaning that you choose. In that way, you see, there is a possibility of creating a human community.

The beginning point of the existentialism of Sartre and Camus was the absence of God in the universe (see the box above). While the death of God was tragic, it meant that humans had no preordained destiny and were utterly alone in the universe with no future and no hope. As Camus expressed it:

A world that can be explained even with bad reasons is a familiar world. But, on the other hand, in a universe suddenly divested of illusions and lights, man feels an alien, a stranger. His exile is without remedy since he is deprived of the memory of a lost home or the hope of a promised land. This divorce between man and his life, the actor and his setting, is properly the feeling of absurdity.[5]

According to Camus, then, the world was absurd and without meaning; humans, too, are without meaning and purpose. Reduced to despair and depression, humans have but one ground of hope—themselves.

While the world might be absurd, Camus argued, it could not be absurd unless people judged it to be so.

◆ Sartre and de Beauvoir. Jean-Paul Sartre and Simone de Beauvoir were two of the leading intellectuals in twentieth-century Europe. Sartre and de Beauvoir had a lifelong relationship that lasted until his death in 1980. Both were actively involved in the existentialist movement. De Beauvoir also played a crucial role in the emergence of the postwar women's liberation movement.

People are unique in the world, and their kind of being is quite different from that of all others. In the words of Sartre, human "existence precedes essence." Humans are beings who first exist and then afterward define themselves. They determine what they will be. According to Sartre: "Man is nothing else but what he makes of himself. Such is the first principle of existentialism." People then must take full responsibility for what they are. They create their values and give their lives meaning. And this can only be done by their involvement in life. Only through a person's acts can one determine his or her values. According to Sartre: "I may say that I like so-and-so well enough to sacrifice a certain amount of money for him, but I may say so only if I've done it."

Existentialism, therefore, involved an ethics of action, of involvement in life. But people could not define themselves without their involvement with others. Thus, existentialism's ethical message was just as important as its philosophy of being. Essentially, the message of existentialism was one of authenticity. Individuals true to themselves refused to be depersonalized by their society. As one author noted, "Existentialism is the struggle to discover the human person in a depersonalized age."

The Revival of Religion

Existentialism was one response to the despair generated by the apparent collapse of civilized values in the twentieth century. The revival of religion has been another. Ever since the Enlightenment of the eighteenth century, Christianity and religion had been on the defensive. But a number of religious thinkers and leaders attempted to bring new life to Christianity in the twentieth century. Despite the attempts of the Communist world to build an atheistic society and the West to build a secular society, religion continued to play an important role in the lives of many people.

One expression of this religious revival was the attempt by such theologians as the Protestant Karl Barth (1886–1968) and the Catholic Karl Rahner (1904–1984) to infuse traditional Christian teachings with new life. In his numerous writings, Barth attempted to reinterpret the religious insights of the Reformation era for the modern world. To Barth, the sinful and hence imperfect nature of human beings meant that humans could know religious truth not through reason, but only through the grace of God. Karl Rahner attempted to revitalize traditional Catholic theology by incorporating aspects of modern thought. He was careful, however, to emphasize the continuity between ancient and modern interpretations of Catholic doctrine.

In the Catholic church, attempts at religious renewal also came from two charismatic popes—John XXIII and John Paul II. Pope John XXIII (1881–1963) reigned as pope for only a short time (1958–1963), but sparked a dramatic revival of Catholicism when he summoned the twenty-first ecumenical council of the Catholic church. Known as Vatican Council II, it liberalized a number of Catholic practices. New avenues of communication with other Christian faiths were also opened for the first time since the Reformation.

John Paul II (b. 1920), who had been the archbishop of Cracow in Poland before his elevation to the papacy

Pope John Paul II: An Appeal for Peace

P ope John Paul II became the spiritual leader of the Catholic church in 1978. He has made numerous trips to all parts of the globe, advocating a variety of spiritual and social issues. He has made a point of speaking directly to as many lay groups as possible, often focusing on one of his chief themes—the desire for peace.

Pope John Paul II, Speeches

Today peace has become, throughout the world, a preoccupation not only for those responsible for the destiny of nations but even more so for broad sections of the population and innumerable individuals who generously and tenaciously dedicate themselves to creating an outlook of peace and to establishing genuine peace between peoples and nations. This is comforting. But there is no hiding the fact that in spite of the efforts of all men and women of good will, there are still serious threats to peace in the world. Some of these threats take the form of divisions within various nations; others stem from deep-rooted and acute tensions between opposing nations and blocs within the world community. In reality, the confrontations that we witness today are distinguished from those of past history by certain new characteristics. In the first place they are worldwide: even a local conflict is often an expression of tensions originating elsewhere in the world. In the same way, it often happens that a conflict has profound effects far from where it broke out. Another characteristic is totality: present day tensions mobilize all the forces of the nations involved; moreover, selfish monopoliza-

tion and even hostility are to be found today as much in the way economic life is run and in the technological application of science as in the way that the mass media or military resources are utilized . . . .

Elsewhere, fear of a precarious peace, military and political imperatives, and economic and commercial interests lead to the establishment of arms stockpiles or to the sale of weapons capable of appalling destruction. The arms race, then, prevails over the great tasks of peace, which ought to unite peoples in new solidarity; it fosters sporadic but murderous conflicts and builds up the gravest threats. It is true that at first sight the cause of peace seems to be handicapped to a crippling extent.

But we must reach peace. Peace, as I said earlier, is threatened when uncertainty, doubt, and suspicion reign, and violence makes good use of this. Do we really want peace? Then we must dig deep within ourselves, and going beyond the divisions we find within us and between us, we must find the areas in which we can strengthen our conviction that human beings' basic driving forces and the recognition of their real nature carry them toward openness to others, mutual respect, community, and peace. The course of this laborious search for the objective and universal truth about humanity, and the result of the search, will develop men and women of peace and dialogue, people who draw both strength and humility from a truth that they realize they must serve and not make use of for partisan interests.

in 1978, was the first non-Italian to be elected pope since the sixteenth century. Although he alienated a number of people by reasserting traditional Catholic teaching on such issues as birth control, women in the priesthood, and clerical celibacy, John Paul's numerous travels around the world helped strengthen the Catholic church throughout the non-Western world. A strong believer in social justice, John Paul II has been a powerful figure in reminding Europeans of their spiritual heritage and the need to temper the pursuit of materialism with spiritual concerns. He has also condemned nuclear weapons and constantly reminded leaders and laity of their obligations to prevent war (see the box above).

The New World of Science and Technology

Since the Scientific Revolution of the seventeenth century and the Industrial Revolution of the nineteenth century, science and technology have played increasingly important roles in Western civilization. Many of the scientific and technological achievements since World War II have revolutionized people's lives. When American astronauts walked on the moon, millions watched the event on their televisions in the privacy of their living rooms.

Before World War II, theoretical science and technology were largely separated. Pure science was the domain of university professors who were quite far

✦ **On the Moon.** The first landing on the moon in 1969 was one of the great technological achievements of the twentieth century. This picture shows astronaut James Irwin shortly after he erected the American flag during a moonwalk in 1971. The lunar module and lunar rover are also visible in the picture.

removed from the practical technological concerns of technicians and engineers. But during World War II, university scientists were recruited to work for their governments and develop new weapons and practical instruments of war. British physicists played a crucial role in the development of an improved radar system in 1940 that helped to defeat the German air force in the Battle of Britain. German scientists converted coal to gasoline to keep the German war machine moving and created self-propelled rockets as well as jet airplanes to keep Hitler's hopes alive for a miraculous turnaround in the war. The computer, too, was a wartime creation. The British mathematician Alan Turing designed a primitive computer to assist British intelligence in breaking the secret codes of German ciphering machines. The most famous product of wartime scientific research was the atomic bomb, created by a team of American and European scientists under the guidance of the physicist J. Robert Oppenheimer. Obviously, most wartime devices were created for destructive purposes, but merely to mention computers and jet airplanes demonstrates that they could easily be adapted for peacetime uses.

The sponsorship of research by governments and the military during World War II created a new scientific model. Science had become very complex, and only large organizations with teams of scientists, huge labora-

tories, and complex equipment could undertake such large-scale projects. Such facilities were so expensive, however, that they could only be provided by governments and large corporations. Because of its postwar prosperity, the United States was able to lead in the development of the new science. Almost 75 percent of all scientific research funds in the United States came from the government in 1965. Unwilling to lag behind, especially in military developments, the Soviet Union was also forced to provide large outlays for scientific and technological research. In fact, the defense establishments of the United States and the Soviet Union generated much of postwar scientific research. One-fourth of the trained scientists and engineers after 1945 were utilized in the creation of new weapons systems. Universities found their research agendas increasingly determined by government funding for military-related projects. In his farewell address to the American people in 1961, President Dwight Eisenhower coined the phrase "military-industrial complex" and warned of the danger inherent in the new mutual relationship between industrial corporations and the military services: "In the councils of government, we must guard against the acquisition of unwarranted influence, whether sought or unsought, by the military-industrial complex. The potential for the disastrous rise of misplaced power exists and will persist."

There was no more stunning example of how the new scientific establishment operated than the space race of the 1960s. The announcement by the Soviets in 1957 that they had sent the first space satellite—*Sputnik I*—into orbit around the earth caused the United States to launch a gigantic project to place a manned spacecraft on the moon within a decade. Massive government funds financed the scientific research and technological advances that attained this goal in 1969.

The postwar alliance of science and technology led to an accelerated rate of change that became a fact of life in Western society. One product of this alliance—the computer—may yet prove to be the most revolutionary of all the technological inventions of the twentieth century. Early computers, which required thousands of vacuum tubes to function, were large and took up considerable room space. The development of the transistor and then the silicon chip produced a revolutionary new approach to computers. In 1971, the invention of the microprocessor, a machine that combines the equivalent of thousands of transistors on a single, tiny silicon chip, opened the road for the development of the personal computer.

⋟ *Small Is Beautiful: The Limits of Modern Technology* ⋞

Although science and technology have produced an amazing array of achievements in the postwar world, some voices have been raised in criticism of their sometimes destructive aspects. In 1975, in his book Small Is Beautiful, *the British economist E. F. Schumacher examined the effects modern industrial technology has had on the earth's resources.*

E. F. Schumacher, *Small Is Beautiful*

Is it not evident that our current methods of production are already eating into the very substance of industrial man? To many people this is not at all evident. Now that we have solved the problem of production, they say, have we ever had it so good? Are we not better fed, better clothed, and better housed than ever before—and better educated? Of course we are: most, but by no means all, of us: in the rich countries. But this is not what I mean by "substance." The substance of man cannot be measured by Gross National Product. Perhaps it cannot be measured at all, except for certain symptoms of loss. However, this is not the place to go into the statistics of these symptoms, such as crime, drug addiction, vandalism, mental breakdown, rebellion, and so forth. Statistics never prove anything.

I started by saying that one of the most fateful errors of our age is the belief that the problem of production has been solved. This illusion, I suggested, is mainly due to our inability to recognize that the modern industrial system, with all its intellectual sophistication, consumes the very basis on which it has been erected. To use the language of the economist, it lives on irreplaceable capital which it cheerfully treats as income. I specified three categories of such capital: fossil fuels, the tolerance margins of nature, and the human substance. Even if some readers should refuse to accept all three parts of my argument, I suggest that any one of them suffices to make my case.

And what is my case? Simply that our most important task is to get off our present collision course. And who is there to tackle such a task? I think every one of us. . . . To talk about the future is useful only if it leads to action *now*. And what can we do *now*, while we are still in the position of "never having had it so good"? To say the least . . . we must thoroughly understand the problem and begin to see the possibility of evolving a new life-style, with new methods of production and new patterns of consumption: a life-style designed for permanence. To give only three preliminary examples: in agriculture and horticulture, we can interest ourselves in the perfection of production methods which are biologically sound, build up soil fertility, and produce health, beauty and permanence. Productivity will then look after itself. In industry, we can interest ourselves in the evolution of small-scale technology, relatively nonviolent technology, "technology with a human face," so that people have a chance to enjoy themselves while they are working, instead of working solely for their pay packet and hoping, usually forlornly, for enjoyment solely during their leisure time.

The computer is a new kind of machine whose chief function is to store and produce information, now considered an essential element of our fast-paced civilization. By the 1990s, the personal computer had become a regular fixture in businesses, schools, and homes. It not only makes a whole host of tasks much easier, but it has also become an important tool in virtually every area of modern life. Indeed, other tools and machines now depend for their functioning on computers. Many of the minute-by-minute decisions involved in flying an airplane, for example, are made by a computer.

Despite the marvels that were produced by the alliance of science and technology, some people came to question the underlying assumption of this alliance—that scientific knowledge gave human beings the ability to manipulate the environment for their benefit. They maintained that some technological advances had far-reaching side effects damaging to the environment. The chemical fertilizers, for example, that were touted for producing larger crops wreaked havoc with the ecological balance of streams, rivers, and woodlands. *Small Is Beautiful*, written by the British economist E. F. Schumacher (1911–1977), was a fundamental critique of the dangers of the new science and technology (see the box above). The widespread proliferation of fouled beaches and dying forests and lakes made environmentalism one of the important issues of the 1990s.

After World War II, a number of physicists continued to explore the implications of Einstein's revolution in physics and raised fundamental questions about the nature of reality. To some physicists, quantum and relativity theory described the universe as a complicated web of relations in which there were no isolated building blocks. Thus, the universe was not a "collection of physical objects," but a complicated web of relations between "various parts of a unified whole." Moreover, this web of relations that is the universe also included the human observer. Human beings could not be objective observers of objects detached from themselves because the very act of observation made them participants in the process itself. These speculations implied that the old Newtonian conception of the universe as a machine was an outdated tool for understanding the nature of the universe.

The Explosion of Popular Culture

Since World War II, popular culture has played an increasingly important role in helping Western people define themselves. At one level popular culture is but the history of the ever-changing whims of mass taste, but on another level "it is a history of how modern society has created images of itself and expressed its fantasies, its fears, its ambitions."[6]

The history of popular culture is also the history of the economic system that supports it, for this system manufactures, distributes, and sells the images that people consume as popular culture. As popular culture and its economic support system become increasingly intertwined, industries of leisure emerge. As one historian of popular culture has argued, "industrial societies turn the provision of leisure into a commercial activity, in which their citizens are sold entertainment, recreation, pleasure, and appearance as commodities that differ from the goods at the drugstore only in the way they are used."[7] Modern popular culture therefore is an integral part of the mass consumer society in which it has emerged, making it quite different from the folk culture of preceding centuries. Folk culture is something people make whereas popular culture is something people buy.

POPULAR CULTURE AND THE AMERICANIZATION OF THE WORLD

The United States has been the most influential force in shaping popular culture in the West and, to a lesser degree, the entire world. Through movies, music, advertising, and television, the United States has spread its particular form of consumerism and the American

Dream to millions around the world. Already in 1923 the New York *Morning Post* noted that "the film is to America what the flag was once to Britain. By its means Uncle Sam may hope some day . . . to Americanize the world."[8] In movies, television, and popular music, the impact of American popular culture on the Western world is apparent.

Motion pictures were the primary vehicle for the diffusion of American popular culture in the years immediately following the war and continued to dominate both European and American markets in the next decades (40 percent of Hollywood's income in the 1960s came from the European market). Nevertheless, the existence of a profitable art-house circuit in America and Europe enabled European filmmakers to make films whose themes and avant-garde methods were quite different from those of Hollywood. Italy and Sweden, for example, developed a tradition of "national cinema" that reflected "specific cultural traits in a mode in which they could be successfully exported." The 1957 film *The Seventh Seal*, by the Swedish director Ingmar Bergman, was a good example of the successful European art film. Bergman's films caused him to be viewed as "an artist of comparable stature to a novelist or playwright." So too were François Truffaut in France and Federico Fellini in Italy; such directors gloried in experimenting with subject matter and technique and produced films dealing with more complex and daring themes than Hollywood would attempt.

Although developed in the 1930s, television did not become readily available until the late 1940s. By 1954, there were 32 million sets in the United States as television became the centerpiece of middle-class life. It has been said that television was perfect for the suburban home, the "nuclear family's bunker," as it was "a piece of furniture that did something."

In the 1960s, as television spread around the world, American networks unloaded their products on Europe and the Third World at extraordinarily low prices. For instance, the British Broadcasting Corporation (BBC) could buy American programs for one-tenth the cost per viewer of producing its own. Only the establishment of quota systems prevented American television from completely inundating these countries. Nevertheless, American shows have remained popular in Europe.

Unlike the United States, television and radio in Europe have largely been controlled by the state. The BBC model strongly influenced German broadcasting after the war. In France, de Gaulle saw state control of television as an important counterbalance to the opposition French press. The 1980s, however, saw an increasing trend toward commercial television in Western Europe. In the Communist countries of Eastern Europe and the Soviet Union, state control was even more pervasive, but as communism lost its grip in Eastern Europe in the revolutions of 1989, calls for freedom of speech and press were extended to mass media. In 1990, independent television and radio productions were allowed in the Soviet Union for the first time.

The United States has dominated popular music since the end of World War II. Jazz, blues, rhythm and blues, rap, and rock and roll have been by far the most popular music forms in the Western world—and much of the non-Western world—during this time. All of them originated in the United States, and all are rooted in African-American musical innovations. These forms later spread to the rest of the world, inspiring local artists who then transformed the music in their own way. Often these transformed models then returned to the United States to inspire American artists. This was certainly the case with rock and roll. Through the 1950s, American figures such as Chuck Berry, Little Richard, and Elvis Presley inspired the Beatles and other British performers, who then led an "invasion" of the United States in the 1960s, creating a sensation and in part sparking new rockers in America. Rock music itself developed in the 1950s. In 1952, white disc jockeys began playing rhythm and blues and traditional blues music performed by African-Americans to young white audiences. The music was popular with this audience, and record companies began recording watered-down white cover versions of this music. It was not until such individuals as Elvis Presley mixed white "folkabilly"

with rhythm and blues that rock and roll became popular with the larger white audience.

The period from 1967 to 1973 was probably the true golden age of rock. During this brief period, much experimentation in rock music took place, as it did in society in general. Straightfoward rock and roll competed with a new hybrid blues rock, created in part by British performers such as the Rolling Stones, who were in turn inspired by African-American blues artists. Many musicians also experimented with non-Western musical sounds, such as Indian sitars. Some of the popular music of the 1960s also focused on social issues. It was against the Vietnam War and materialism and promoted "peace and love" as alternatives to the prevailing "establishment" culture.

The same migration of a musical form from the United States to Britain and back to the United States occurred when the early punk movement in New York spread to Britain in the mid-1970s after failing to make an immediate impact in the United States. The more influential British punk movement of 1976–1979 was also fueled by an economic crisis that had resulted in large numbers of unemployed and undereducated young people. However, punk was not simply a proletarian movement. Many of its supporters, performers, and promoters were British art school graduates who applied avant-garde experimentation to the movement. Punk rockers rejected most social conventions and preached anarchy and rebellion. They often wore tattered clothes and clothespins in their cheeks, symbolizing their rejection of a materialistic and degenerate culture. Musically, punk was extremely primitive in structure and perfor-

✦ **The Beatles in Concert.** Although rock and roll originated in the United States, it also inspired musical groups in Europe. This was certainly true of Britain's Beatles, who created a sensation among young people when they came to the United States in the 1960s. Here the Beatles are shown during a performance on *The Ed Sullivan Show.*

mance, with noise and distortion elevated to art. Pure punk was short-lived, partly because its intense energy quickly burned out (as did many of its performers) and partly because, as ex-punk Mick Hucknall said, "the biggest mistake of the punks was that they rejected music." Offshoots of punk proliferated through the 1980s, however, and continue to influence the rock and roll scene.

THE GROWTH OF MASS SPORTS

In the postwar years, sports have become a major product of both popular culture and the leisure industry. The development of satellite television and various electronic breakthroughs helped make sports a global phenomenon. Olympic Games could now be broadcast across the globe from anywhere in the world. Sports became a cheap form of entertainment for the consumer as fans did not have to leave their homes to enjoy athletic competitions. In fact, some sports organizations initially resisted television fearing that it would hurt ticket sales. Soon, however, the tremendous revenues possible from television contracts overcame this hesitation. As sports television revenue escalated, many sports came to receive the bulk of their yearly revenue from television contracts. The Olympics, for example, are now funded primarily by American television. These contracts are paid for by advertising sponsors, mostly for products to be consumed along with the sport: beer, soda, and snack foods.

Sports have become big politics as well as big business. The politicization of sports has been one of the most significant trends in sports during the second half of the twentieth century. Football (soccer) remains the dominant world sport and more than ever has become a vehicle for nationalist sentiment and expression. The World Cup is the most watched event on television. Although the sport can be a positive outlet for national and local pride, all too often it has been marred by violence as nationalistic energies have overcome rational behavior. Events in Britain in particular have been marred by fan violence as extreme hooligans have rioted at matches.

The most telling example of the potent mix of politics and sport continues to be the Olympic Games. When the Soviets entered Olympic competition in 1952, the Olympics began to take on Cold War implications and became known as the "war without weapons." The Soviets saw the Olympics as a way to stimulate nationalist spirit, as well as to promote the Communist system as the best path for social progress.

The Soviets led the Olympics in terms of total medals won between 1956 and 1988. The nature of the Olympics, with their daily medal count by nation and elaborate ceremonies and rituals such as the playing of the national anthem of the winning athletes and the parade of nations, virtually ensured the politicization of the games originally intended to foster international cooperation through friendly competition.

The political nature of the games found expression in other ways as well. In 1956, six nations withdrew from the games to protest the Soviet crushing of the Hungarian uprising. In 1972, twenty-seven African nations threatened to pull out of the Munich Olympics because of apartheid in South Africa. Also at the Munich Games, the Palestinian terrorist group Black September seized eleven Israeli athletes as hostages, all of whom died in a confrontation at an airport. The United States led a boycott of the 1980 Moscow Games to protest the Soviet invasion of Afghanistan, and the Soviets responded by boycotting the Los Angeles Games in 1984.

POPULAR CULTURE: TOWARD A NEW GLOBALISM

Media critic and theorist Marshall McLuhan predicted in the 1960s that advances in mass communications technology, such as satellites and electronics, would eventually lead to a shrinking of the world, a lessening of cultural distinctions, and a breaking down of cultural barriers, all of which would in time transform the world into a single "global village." McLuhan was quite optimistic about these developments, and his ideas became quite popular at the time. Many critics have since argued that McLuhan was too utopian about the benefits of technological progress and maintain that the mass media that these technological breakthroughs created are still controlled by a small number of multinational corporations that "colonize the rest of the world, sometimes benignly, sometimes not." They argue that this has allowed Western popular culture to disrupt the traditional cultures of less developed countries and inculcate new patterns of behavior as well as new desires and new dissatisfactions.

Cultural contacts, however, often move in two directions. While the world has been "Americanized" to a great extent, formerly unfamiliar ways of life and styles of music have also come into the world of the West. This has expanded the horizons of Westerners and led to the creation of new cultural hybrids in music, philosophy, and religion. This emergence of a global culture has been part of the new globalism at the end of the twentieth century.

Toward a Global Civilization?

Increasingly, more and more people are becoming aware of the political and economic interdependence of the world's nations as well as the global nature of our contemporary problems. On the threshold of the twenty-first century, human beings are coming to understand that destructive forces generated in one part of the world soon affect the entire world. Nuclear proliferation makes nuclear war an ever-present possibility; nuclear war would mean radioactive fallout for the entire planet. Smokestack pollution in one nation can produce acid rain in another. Oil spills and dumping of wastes in the ocean have an impact on the shores of many nations. The consumption of drugs in the world's wealthy nations affects the stability of both wealthy and less developed nations. As food, water, energy, and natural resources crises proliferate, one nation's solutions often become other nations' problems. The new globalism includes the recognition that the challenges that seem to threaten human existence at the end of the twentieth century are global. As a Soviet physicist and an American engineer jointly concluded in 1988: "The emergence of global problems and the recognition of their importance is perhaps the greatest accomplishment of contemporary thought."[9]

As the heirs of Western civilization have become aware that the problems humans face are global—not only national—they have responded to this challenge in different ways. One approach has been to develop grass-roots social movements, including environmental, women's and men's liberation, human potential, appropriate-technology, and nonviolence movements. "Think globally, act locally" is frequently the slogan of these grass-roots groups. Related to the emergence of these social movements is the growth of nongovernmental organizations (NGOs). According to one analyst, NGOs are an important instrument in the cultivation of global perspectives: "Since NGOs by definition are identified with interests that transcend national boundaries, we expect all NGOs to define problems in global terms, to take account of human interests and needs as they are found in all parts of the planet."[10] NGOs are often represented at the United Nations and include professional, business, and cooperative organizations; foundations; religious, peace, and disarmament groups; youth and women's organizations; environmental and human rights groups; and research institutes. The number of international NGOs increased from 176 in 1910 to 18,000 in 1988.

◆ **The Earth.** For many people in the West as in the rest of the world, the view of Earth from outer space fostered an important image of global unity. The American astronaut Russell Schweickart wrote: "From where you see it, the thing is a whole, and it is so beautiful." In a similar reaction, Yuri Gagarin, a Soviet cosmonaut, remarked: "What strikes me, is not only the beauty of the continents . . . but their closeness to one another . . . their essential unity."

And yet, hopes for global approaches to global problems have also been hindered by political, ethnic, and religious disputes. Pollution of the Rhine River by factories along its banks provokes angry disputes among European nations, while the United States and Canada have argued about the effects of acid rain on Canadian forests. The collapse of the Soviet Union and its satellite system between 1989 and 1991 seemed to provide an enormous boost to the potential for international cooperation on global issues. In fact, the collapse of the Soviet empire has had almost the opposite effect, as the disintegration of the Soviet Union has led to the emergence of squabbling new nations and an atmosphere of conflict and tension throughout much of Eastern Europe. The bloody conflict in the lands of the former Yugoslavia clearly indicates the dangers inherent in the rise of nationalist sentiment among various ethnic and religious groups in Eastern Europe.

Thus, even as the world becomes more global in culture and interdependent in its mutual relations, centrifugal forces are still at work attempting to redefine the political, cultural, and ethnic ways in which the world is divided. Such efforts are often disruptive and can sometimes work against measures to enhance our human destiny.

Many lessons can be learned from the history of Western civilization, but one of them is especially clear.

Lack of involvement in the affairs of one's society can lead to a sense of powerlessness. In an age that is often crisis-laden and chaotic, an understanding of our Western heritage and its lessons can be instrumental in helping us create new models for the future. For we are all creators of history and upon us depends the future of Western and indeed world civilization.

NOTES

1. Mikhail Gorbachev, "Report to the 27th Party Congress," February 25, 1986, in *Current Soviet Policies* 9 (1986): 10.
2. Quoted in Hilda Scott, *Sweden's 'Right to be Human'—Sex-Role Equality: The Goal and the Reality* (London, 1982), p. 125.
3. Quoted in Marsha Rowe et al., *Spare Rib Reader* (Harmondsworth, 1982), p. 574.
4. Simone de Beauvoir, *The Second Sex*, trans. H. M. Parshley (New York, 1961), p. xxviii.
5. Quoted in Henry Grosshans, *The Search for Modern Europe* (Boston, 1970), p. 421.
6. Richard Maltby, ed., *Passing Parade: A History of Popular Culture in the Twentieth Century* (Oxford, 1989), p. 8.
7. Ibid.
8. Quoted in ibid., p. 11.
9. Sergei Kapitza and Martin Hellman, "A Message to the Scientific Community," in Anatoly Gromyko and Martin Hellman, eds., *Breakthrough—Emerging New Thinking: Soviet and Western Scholars Issue a Challenge to Build a World beyond War* (New York, 1988), p. xii.
10. Elise Boulding, *Women in the Twentieth Century World* (New York, 1977), pp. 186–87.

SUGGESTIONS FOR FURTHER READINGS

For general surveys of contemporary European history, see the references in Chapter 29. General studies on the Cold War are also listed in Chapter 29. There is a detailed analysis of American-Soviet relations in the 1970s and 1980s in R. Garthoff, *Détente and Confrontation: American-Soviet Relations from Nixon to Reagan* (Washington, D.C., 1985). On the end of the Cold War, see B. Denitch, *The End of the Cold War* (Minneapolis, Minn., 1990); W. G. Hyland, *The Cold War Is Over* (New York, 1990); and W. Laqueur, *Soviet Union 2000: Reform or Revolution?* (New York, 1990).

Recent problems in the Soviet Union are analyzed in M. Lewin, *The Gorbachev Phenomenon* (Berkeley, Calif., 1988); G. Hosking, *The Awakening of the Soviet Union* (London, 1990); and S. White, *Gorbachev and After* (Cambridge, 1991). For general studies of the Soviet satellites in Eastern Europe, see S. Fischer-Galati, *Eastern Europe in the 1980s* (London, 1981); and the references in Chapter 29. Additional studies on the recent history of these countries include T. G. Ash, *The Polish Revolution: Solidarity* (New York, 1984); B. Kovrig, *Communism in Hungary from Kun to Kadar* (Stanford, Calif., 1979); T. G. Ash, *The Magic Lantern: The Revolution of '89 Witnessed in Warsaw, Budapest, Berlin and Prague* (New York, 1990); M. Shafir, *Romania: Politics, Economics and Society* (London, 1985); and S. Ramet, *Nationalism and Federalism in Yugoslavia* (Bloomington, Ind., 1992).

For general works on Western Europe and individual countries, see the references in Chapter 29. On the recent history of these countries, see P. Riddell, *The Thatcher Decade* (Oxford, 1989); P. Jenkins, *Mrs. Thatcher's Revolution* (London, 1989); P. A. Hall, *Governing the Economy: The Politics of State Intervention in Britain and France* (New York, 1986); G. Ross, S. Hoffmann, and S. Malzacher, *The Mitterrand Experiment* (New York, 1987); R. J. Dalton, *Politics in West Germany* (Glenview, Ill., 1989); and K. Jarausch, *The Rush to German Unity* (New York, 1994).

The changing role of women is examined in A. Cherlin, *Marriage, Divorce, Remarriage* (Cambridge, Mass., 1981). On the women's liberation movement, see D. Bouchier, *The Feminist Challenge: The Movement for Women's Liberation in Britain and the United States* (New York, 1983). More general works that include much information on the contemporary period are B. S. Anderson and J. P. Zinsser, *A History of Their Own*, vol. 2 (New York, 1988); and B. G. Smith, *Changing Lives: Women in European History since 1700* (Lexington, Mass., 1989). On terrorism, see the works by W. Laqueur, *Terrorism*, 2d ed. (New York and London, 1988); and R. Rubenstein, *Alchemists of Revolution: Terrorism in the Modern World* (London, 1987). The problems of guest workers and immigrants are examined in J. Miller, *Foreign Workers in Western Europe* (London, 1981); and S. Castles, *Here for Good: Western Europe's New Ethnic Minorities* (London, 1984). On the development of the Green parties, see F. Müller-Rommel, ed., *New Politics in Western Europe: The Rise and Success of Green Parties and Alternative Lists* (Boulder, Colo., 1989).

For a general view of postwar thought, see R. N. Stromberg, *European Intellectual History since 1789*, 5th ed. (Englewood Cliffs, N.J. 1990). On contemporary art, see R. Lambert, *Cambridge Introduction to the History of Art: The Twentieth Century* (Cambridge, 1981); and the general work by B. Cole and A. Gealt, *Art of the Western World* (New York, 1989). A physicist's view of science is contained in J. Ziman, *The Force of Knowledge: The Scientific Dimension of Society* (Cambridge, 1976). A physicist's view of a new conception of reality is D. Bohm, *Wholeness and the Implicate Order* (Boston, 1980). The space race is examined in W. A. McDougall, *The Heavens and the Earth: A Political History of the Space Age* (New York, 1984). A classic work on existentialism is W. Barrett, *Irrational Man* (Garden City, N.Y., 1962). There is an excellent survey of twentieth-century popular culture in R. Maltby, ed., *Passing Parade: A History of Popular Culture in the Twentieth Century* (Oxford, 1989). On film and the media, see L. May, *Screening Out the Past: The Birth of Mass Culture and the Motion Picture Industry* (New York, 1980); and F. Wheen, *Television* (London, 1985). On popular music, see P. Eberly, *Music in the Air* (New York, 1982). Sport is examined in A. Guttmann, *From Ritual to Record: The Nature of Modern Sports* (New York, 1978); and R. Mandell, *Sport: A Cultural History* (New York, 1984). On the "global village" idea, see M. McLuhan, *Understanding Media: The Extensions of Man* (London, 1964).

Index

Photo credits continued

CHAPTER 21

706 © Ann Ronan at Image Select; **711** Reproduced by permission of the Trustees of the Science Museum (neg. 607/56); **712** (Top) Mansell Collection, London; (Bottom) © Ann Ronan at Image Select; **713** (Bottom) Thomas V. Robins, *Opening of the Royal Albert Bridge, Saltash, 2 May 1859,* Elton Collection/Ironbridge Gorge Museum Trust; (Top) Reproduced from the Collections of the Library of Congress; **715** Bridgeman Art Library/Art Resource, NY; **723** © Ann Ronan at Image Select; **724** Gustave Dore, *Over London by Rail,* from *London, A Pilgrimage;* Billy Rose Theatre Collection, The New York Public Library at Lincoln Center; Astor, Lenox and Tilden Foundations; **727** Bettmann/Hulton; **731** Bridgeman/Art Resource, NY

CHAPTER 22

736 Lecomte, *Battle in the rue de Rohan,* 1830, (Detail) Giraudon/Art Resource, NY; **738** Austrian Information Service; **743** Bordeaux Musee des Beaux-Arts; **748** © British Museum, London, reproduced by Courtesy of the Trustees of the British Museum; **752** E.T. Archive, London; **754** Lecomte, *Battle in the rue de Rohan,* 1830, Giraudon/Art Resource, NY; **760** Historisches Museum der Stadt Wien; **764** The Mansell Collection, London; **768** © David H. Endersbee/TSW; **771** Caspar David Friedrich, *Man and Woman Gazing at the Moon,* Nationalgalerie SMPK Berlin, Photo: Jorg P. Anders, © Bildarchiv Preussischer Kulturbesitz, Berlin; **772** J. M. W. Turner, *Rain, Steam, and Speed—The Great Western Railway,* Reproduced by courtesy of the Trustees, The National Gallery, London; **773** Eugene Delacroix, *Women of Algiers,* Musee du Louvre, © Photo R.M.N.

CHAPTER 23

776 *Proclamation of the German Empire at Versailles, 1871,* (Detail) Anton von Werner, Photo © Bildarchiv Preussischer Kulturbesitz, Berlin; **779** Flandrin, *Napoleon III,* Musee National des Chateau de Versailles, © Photo R.M.N.; **783** Stock Montage, Chicago; **789** *Proclamation of the German Empire at Versailles, 1871,* Anton von Werner, Photo © Bildarchiv Preussischer Kulturbesitz, Berlin; **793** © Ullstein Bilderdienst, Berlin; **795** Bettman/Hulton; **798** *Opening of the Suez Canal,* Photo © Bildarchiv Preussischer Kulturbesitz, Berlin; **799** The Granger Collection, New York; **806** Thomas Eakins, *The Gross Clinic,* Jefferson Medical College of Thomas Jefferson University, Philadelphia, PA; **807** Gustave Courbet, *The Stonebreakers,* Gemaldegalerie Neue Meister, Staatliche Kunstsammlungen Dresden; Photo by Reinhold, Leipzig-Molkau; **809** Jean Francois Millet, *The Sower,* Gift of Quincy Adams Shaw through Quincy Adams Shaw, Jr. and Mrs. Marion Shaw Haughton; Courtesy, Museum of Fine Arts, Boston

CHAPTER 24

812 William Powell Frith, *Many Happy Returns of the Day,* (Detail) Harrogate Museums and Art Gallery/Bridgeman Art Library, London; **814** The Fotomas Index; **818** Musee de la Poste, Paris, photo J.L. Charmet; **820** Verein fur Geschichte der Arbeiterbewegung, Vienna; **826** Tate Gallery/Art Resource, NY; **830** Bettmann/Hulton; **832** William Powell Frith, *Many Happy Returns of the Day,* Harrogate Museums and Art Gallery/Bridgeman Art Library, London; **835** Courtesy, Vassar College Library; **836**

The Mansell Collection, London; **838** The Mansell Collection, London; **841** The Bettmann Archive

CHAPTER 25

846 Bettmann/Hulton; **849** The Bettman Archive; **850** Bild-Archiv der Osterreichischen Nationalbibliothek, Vienna; **856** (Top) Scala/Art Resource, NY; (Bottom) Paul Cezanne, *Femme a la cafetiere,* Paris, Musee d'Orsay, © Photo R.M.N.; **857** Vincent van Gogh, *The Starry Night,* (1889), Oil on canvas, 29 × 36 1/4", Collection, The Museum of Modern Art, New York; Acquired through the Lillie P. Bliss Bequest; **858** (Top) Pablo Picasso, *Les Demoiselles d'Avignon,* Paris (Begun May reworked July 1907), Oil on canvas, 8' × 7'8", Collection, The Museum of Modern Art, New York; Acquired through the Lillie P. Bliss Bequest; (Bottom) Vasily Kandinsky, *Painting with White Border,* May 1913; The Solomon R. Guggenheim Museum, New York; Photograph by David Heald, © The Solomon R. Guggerheim Foundation, New York (FN37.245); **859** Bettmann/Hulton; **862** Courtesy of Central Zionist Archives, Jerusalem; **866** David King Collection, London; **875** By permission of the British Library, London, Oriental and India Office Collections, WD.2443; **881** E.T. Archive, London

CHAPTER 26

886 Bilderdienst Suddeutscher Verlag, Munich; **889** The Bettmann Archive; **892** Librairie Larousse, Paris; **896** (Top) © Roger-Viollet, Paris; (Bottom) Librairie Larousse, Paris; **898** Bilderdienst Suddeutscher Verlag, Munich; **901** The Bettmann Archive; **902** E.T. Archive, London; **903** © Ullstein Bilderdienst; **907** Brown Brothers; **911** © David King Collection, London; **915** Bettmann/Hulton

CHAPTER 27

922 Hugo Jaeger, Life Magazine, © Time Warner, Inc.; **924** UPI/Bettman; **926** © Roger-Viollet; **933** © Popperfoto; **939** Hugo Jaeger, Life Magazine, © Time Warner, Inc.; **941** Hugo Jaeger, Life Magazine, © Time Warner, Inc.; **943** Paulman, 10 November, 1938, Photo © Bildarchiv Preussischer Kulturbesitz, Berlin; **947** David King Collection, London; **951** Courtesy of the Ford Motor Company; **953** Erich Lessing/Art Resource, NY, © Copyright ARS, NY, Stiftung Kulturbesitz, Berlin, Germany; **954** Salvador Dali, *The Persistence of Memory,* 1931, Oil on canvas, 9 1/2 × 13", Collection, The Museum of Modern Art, New York, Given Anonymously; **955** Gian Berto Vanni/Art Resource, NY

CHAPTER 28

960 © The Hulton Getty Picture Collection, Limited; **965** Hugo Jaeger, Life Magazine, © Time Warner, Inc.; **968** National Archives (#306-NT-1222E); **970** © The Hulton Getty Picture Collection, Limited; **972** © Topham/The Image Works; **975** National Archives (#111-C-273); **979** YIVO Institute for Jewish Research, courtesy of the USHMM Photo Archives; **980** Courtesy of Yad Vashem; **982** Popperfoto; **986** (Top) The Herald & Evening Times Picture Library, © Caledonian Newspapers Ltd.; (Bottom) J. R. Eyerman, Life Magazine, © Time Warner, Inc.; **988** E.T. Archive

CHAPTER 29

994 Popperfoto; **996** The Bettmann Archive; **999** UPI/Corbis-Bettmann; **1003** The Bettmann Archive; **1008** © Marc Riboud/Magnum Photos; **1010** © Camera Press (Jugo) London;

Document credits continued

Department of History and Archaeology, University of Exeter. Reprinted by permission of Pantheon Books, A Division of Random House, Inc.

The Voice of Dadaism   954
From "Lecture on Dada" by Tristan Tsara in *The Dada Painters and Poets*, edited by Robert Motherwell. Copyright © 1922. Reprinted with permission of Wittenborn Art Books, Inc.

Chapter 28

Hitler's Foreign Policy Goals   962
From the book *Hitler's Secret Book* by Adolf Hitler, translated by Salvator Attanasio. Copyright © 1961 by Grove Press. Used with permission of Grove/Atlantic Inc.

The Munich Conference   966
From *Parliamentary Debates, House of Commons* (London: His Majesty's Stationery Office, 1938), vol. 339, pp. 361–369; from Neville Chamberlain, *In Search of Peace* (New York: Putnam, 1939), pp. 213–215, 217.

A German Soldier at Stalingrad   974
From Vasili Chuikov, *The Battle for Stalingrad* (Grafton Books).

Hitler's Plans for a New Order in the East   977
From *Hitler's Secret Conversations*, Hugh Trevor Roper, copyright © 1953 by New American Library. Published by Octagon Books, A Div. of Hippocrene Books, Inc. Used with permission.

The Holocaust: The Camp Commandant and the Camp Victims   981
From *Nazism: A History in Documents & Eyewitness Accounts*, Vol. II by J. Noakes and G. Pridham. Copyright © 1988 by Department of History and Archaeology, University of Exeter. Reprinted by permission of Pantheon Books, A Division of Random House, Inc.

The Bombing of Civilians   985
From John Campbell, ed., *The Experience of World War II* (New York: Oxford University Press, 1989), p. 177; from Hans Rumpf, *The Bombing of Germany* (New York: Holt, Rinehart, and Winston, 1963), p. 94; from John Campbell, ed., *The Experience of World War II* (New York: Oxford University Press, 1989), p. 180.

Emergence of the Cold War: Churchill and Stalin   990
From *The Congressional Record*, 79th Congress, 2d Session, A (Washington, D.C.: U.S. Government Printing Office), pp. 1145–1147; From "Stalin's Reply to Churchill," *The New York Times*, March 14, 1946, p. 4.

Chapter 29

The Truman Doctrine   997
Reprinted from the *Congressional Record*, 80th Congress, 1st Session (Washington, D.C.: U.S. Government Printing Office), Vol. 93, p. 1981.

The Cuban Missile Crisis: Khrushchev's Perspective   1002
From *Khrushchev Remembers* by Nikita Khruschchev, translated and edited by Strobe Talbot. Copyright © 1970 by Little, Brown and Company (Inc.) By permission of Little, Brown and Company.

Frantz Fanon and the Wretched of the Earth   1005
From the book *The Wretched of the Earth* by Frantz Fanon, Copyright © 1963 by Presence Africaine, copyright renewed 1991 by Presence. Used with the permission of Grove/Atlantic Inc.

Khrushchev Denounces Stalin   1009
Reprinted from the *Congressional Record*, 84th Congress, 2d Session (Washington, D.C.: U.S. Government Printing Office), Vol. 102, Part 7, pp. 9389–9402.

Soviet Repression in Eastern Europe: Hungary, 1956   1012
Selections reprinted from the *Department of State Bulletin*, Nov. 12, 1956, pp. 746–747.

De Gaulle Calls for French Autonomy   1015
Reprinted from Ronald G. Monticone, *Charles de Gaulle* (Boston: Twayne Publishers, 1975), pp. 67–68.

"The Times They Are a-Changin' ": The Music of Youthful Protest   1022
Bob Dylan, *The Times They Are a–Changin'*, Lyrics, 1962—1985 (New York: Alfred A. Knopf, 1992), p. 91.

1968: The Year of Student Revolts   1024
Reprinted from Gerald F. McGuigan, *Student Protest*, © 1968 by Methuen & Co., publisher; from *The Western Tradition from the Renaissance to the Present* by Eugen Weber. Copyright © 1972 (Lexington, Mass: D.C. Heath and Company), pp. 1003–1006.

Chapter 30

Gorbachev and Perestroika   1031
Excerpt from *Perestroika* by Mikhail Gorbachev. Copyright © 1987 by Mikhail Gorbachev. Reprinted by permission of HarperCollins Publishers Inc.

Vaclav Havel: The Call for a New Politics   1036
From Vaclav Havel, *The Washington Post*, February 22, 1990, page A28d. Copyright © The Washington Post. Reprinted with permission.

Bosnia: Two Faces of War   1040
From "Does the World Still Recognize a Holocaust?" by John Darnton. In *New York Times*, April 25, 1993. Copyright © 1946, 93 by The New York Times Co. Reprinted by Permission.

The Voice of the Women's Liberation Movement   1047
From *The Second Sex* by Simone De Beauvoir, trans. H M Parshley. Copyright 1952 and renewed 1980 by Alfred A. Knopf, Inc. Reprinted by permission of the publisher.

Violence against Foreigners in Germany   1049

Published in English in *The German Tribune*, October 6, 1991, pp. 3-5; reprinted in Merry Wiesner, Julius R. H. William Wheeler, eds., *Discovering the Western Past: A Look at the Evidence*, 2nd ed. (Boston: Houghton Mifflin Company, 1993), pp. 446—47.

The Voice of Existentialism   1053

From *Existentialism* by Jean-Paul Sarte. Copyright by The Philosophical Library. Used with permission.

Pope John Paul II: An Appeal for Peace   1055

From *John Paul II and the Laity*, Leonard Doohan, (The Jesuit Educational Center for Human Development; published by Le Jacq Publishing, Inc. 1984), pp. 48—50.

Small Is Beautiful: The Limits of Modern Technology   1057

Excerpt from *Small Is Beautiful* by E. F. Schumacher. Copyright © 1973 by E. F. Schumacher. Reprinted by permission of HarperCollins Publishers Inc.